Systems Performance

Systems Performance

Enterprise and the Cloud

Brendan Gregg

PRENTICE
HALL

Upper Saddle River, NJ • Boston • Indianapolis • San Francisco
New York • Toronto • Montreal • London • Munich • Paris • Madrid
Capetown • Sydney • Tokyo • Singapore • Mexico City

The publisher offers excellent discounts on this book when ordered in quantity for bulk purchases or special sales, which may include electronic versions and/or custom covers and content particular to your business, training goals, marketing focus, and branding interests. For more information, please contact:

U.S. Corporate and Government Sales
(800) 382-3419
corpsales@pearsontechgroup.com

For sales outside the United States, please contact:

International Sales
international@pearson.com

Visit us on the Web: informit.com/ph

Library of Congress Cataloging-in-Publication Data

Gregg, Brendan.
   Systems performance : enterprise and the cloud / Brendan Gregg.
      pages cm
   Includes bibliographical references and index.
   ISBN-13: 978-0-13-339009-4 (alkaline paper)
   ISBN-10: 0-13-339009-8 (alkaline paper)
  1. Operating systems (Computers)—Evaluation. 2. Application software—Evaluation. 3. Business Enterprises—Data processing. 4. Cloud computing. I. Title.
   QA76.77.G74 2014
   004.67'82—dc23

                                      2013031887

ISBN-13: 978-0-13-339009-4
ISBN-10:   0-13-339009-8
4 16

Contents

Preface

> There are known knowns; there are things we know we know.
> We also know there are known unknowns; that is to say we
> know there are some things we do not know.
> But there are also unknown unknowns—
> there are things we do not know we don't know.
> —U.S. Secretary of Defense Donald Rumsfeld, February 12, 2002

While the above statement was met with chuckles from those attending the press briefing, it summarizes an important principle that is as relevant in complex technical systems as it is in geopolitics: performance issues can originate from anywhere, including areas of the system that you know nothing about and are therefore not checking (the unknown-unknowns). This book may reveal many of these areas, while providing methodologies and tools for their analysis.

About This Book

Welcome to *Systems Performance: Enterprise and the Cloud*! This book is about the performance of operating systems and of applications from operating system context, and it is written for both enterprise and cloud computing environments. My aim is to help you get the most out of your systems.

When working with application software that is under constant development, you may be tempted to think of operating system performance—where the kernel has been developed and tuned for decades—as a solved problem. It isn't! The operating system is a complex body of software, managing a variety of ever-changing physical devices with new and different application workloads. The kernels are also in constant development, with features being added to improve the performance of particular workloads, and newly encountered bottlenecks being removed as systems continue to scale. Analyzing and working to improve the performance of the operating system is an ongoing task that should lead to continual performance improvements. Application performance can also be analyzed in the operating system context; I'll cover that here as well.

Operating System Coverage

The main focus of this book is the study of systems performance, with tools, examples, and tunable parameters from Linux- and Solaris-based operating systems used as examples. Unless noted, the specific distribution of an operating system is not important in the examples used. For Linux-based systems, the examples are from a variety of bare-metal systems and virtualized cloud tenants, running either Ubuntu, Fedora, or CentOS. For Solaris-based systems, the examples are also either bare-metal or virtualized and are from either Joyent SmartOS or OmniTI OmniOS. SmartOS and OmniOS use the open-source illumos kernel: the active fork of the OpenSolaris kernel, which itself was based on the development version of what became Oracle Solaris 11.

Covering two different operating systems provides an additional perspective for each audience, offering a deeper understanding of their characteristics, especially where each OS has taken a different design path. This helps the reader to understand performance more comprehensively, without being limited to a single OS, and to think about operating systems more objectively.

Historically, more performance work has been done for Solaris-based systems, making them the better choice for some examples. The situation for Linux has been greatly improving. When *System Performance Tuning* [Musumeci 02] was written, over a decade ago, it also addressed both Linux and Solaris but was heavily oriented toward the latter. The author noted reasons for this:

> Solaris machines tend to be more focused on performance. I suspect this is because Sun systems are more expensive than their Linux counterparts, on average. As a result, people tend to be a lot more picky about performance, so more work has been done in that area on Solaris. If your Linux box doesn't perform well enough, you can just buy another one and split up the workload—it's cheap. If your several-million-dollar Ultra Enterprise 10000 doesn't perform well and your company is losing nontrivial sums of money every minute because of it, you call Sun Service and start demanding answers.

This helps explain Sun's historical performance focus: Solaris profits were tied to hardware sales, and real money was frequently on the line for performance improvements. Sun needed—and could afford to hire—over 100 full-time performance engineers (including, at times, myself and Musumeci). Together with Sun's kernel engineering teams, many developments were made in the field of systems performance.

Linux has come a long way in terms of performance work and observability, especially now that it is being used in large-scale cloud computing environments. Many performance features for Linux, included in this book, have been developed only within the past five years.

Other Content

Example screen shots from performance tools are included, not just for the data shown, but also to illustrate the types of data available. The tools often present the data in intuitive ways, many in the style of earlier Unix tools, producing output that is familiar and often self-explanatory. This means that screen shots can be a powerful way to convey the purpose of these tools, some requiring little additional description. (If a tool does require laborious explanation, that may be a failure of design!)

The history of technologies can provide useful insight to deepen your understanding, and it has been mentioned in places. It is also useful to learn a bit about the key people in this industry (it's a small world): you're likely to come across them or their work in performance and other contexts. A "who's who" list has been provided in Appendix G.

What Isn't Covered

This book focuses on performance. To perform all the example tasks given will require, at times, some system administration activities, including the installation or compilation of software (which is not covered here). Specifically on Linux, you will need to install the sysstat package, as many of its tools are used in this text.

The content also summarizes operating system internals, which are covered in more detail in separate dedicated texts. Advanced performance analysis topics are summarized so that you are aware of their existence and can then study them from additional sources if and when needed.

How This Book Is Structured

The book includes the following:

- **Chapter 1, Introduction,** is an introduction to systems performance analysis, summarizing key concepts and providing examples of performance activities.
- **Chapter 2, Methodology,** provides the background for performance analysis and tuning, including terminology, concepts, models, methodologies for observation and experimentation, capacity planning, analysis, and statistics.
- **Chapter 3, Operating Systems,** summarizes kernel internals for the performance analyst. This is necessary background for interpreting and understanding what the operating system is doing.
- **Chapter 4**, **Observability Tools,** introduces the types of system observability tools available, and the interfaces and frameworks upon which they are built.
- **Chapter 5, Applications,** discusses application performance topics and observing them from the operating system.
- **Chapter 6, CPUs,** covers processors, cores, hardware threads, CPU caches, CPU interconnects, and kernel scheduling.
- **Chapter 7, Memory,** is about virtual memory, paging, swapping, memory architectures, busses, address spaces, and allocators.
- **Chapter 8, File Systems,** is about file system I/O performance, including the different caches involved.
- **Chapter 9, Disks,** covers storage devices, disk I/O workloads, storage controllers, RAID, and the kernel I/O subsystem.
- **Chapter 10, Network,** is about network protocols, sockets, interfaces, and physical connections.
- **Chapter 11, Cloud Computing,** introduces operating-system- and hardware-based virtualization methods in common use for cloud computing and their performance overhead, isolation, and observability characteristics.
- **Chapter 12, Benchmarking,** shows how to benchmark accurately, and how to interpret others' benchmark results. This is a surprisingly tricky topic, and this chapter shows how you can avoid common mistakes and try to make sense of it.
- **Chapter 13, Case Study,** contains a systems performance case study, showing how a real cloud customer issue was analyzed from beginning to end.

Chapters 1 to 4 provide essential background. After reading them, you can reference the remainder of the book as needed.

Chapter 13 is written differently, using a storytelling approach to paint a bigger picture of a performance engineer's work. If you're new to performance analysis, you might want to read this first, for context, and then return to it again when you've read the other chapters.

As a Future Reference

This book has been written to provide value for many years, by focusing on background and methodologies for the systems performance analyst.

To support this, many chapters have been separated into two parts. The first part consists of terms, concepts, and methodologies (often with those headings), which should stay relevant many years from now. The second provides examples of how the first part is implemented: architecture, analysis tools, and tunables, which, while they will become out-of-date, will still be useful in the context of examples.

Tracing Examples

We frequently need to explore the operating system in depth, which can be performed by kernel tracing tools. There are many of these at various stages of development, for example, ftrace, perf, DTrace, SystemTap, LTTng, and ktap. One of them has been chosen for most of the tracing examples here and is demonstrated on both Linux- and Solaris-based systems: DTrace. It provides the features needed for these examples, and there is also a large amount of external material about it, including scripts that can be referenced as use cases of advanced tracing.

You may need or wish to use different tracing tools, which is fine. The DTrace examples are examples of tracing and show the questions that you can ask of the system. It is often these questions, and the methodologies that pose them, that are the most difficult to know.

Intended Audience

The intended audience for this book is primarily systems administrators and operators of enterprise and cloud computing environments. It is also a reference for developers, database administrators, and web server administrators who need to understand operating system and application performance.

As the lead performance engineer at a cloud computing provider, I frequently work with support staff and customers who are under enormous time pressure to solve multiple performance issues. For many, performance is not their primary job, and they need to know just enough to solve the issues at hand. This has encouraged me to keep this book as short as possible, knowing that your time to study it may be very limited. But not too short: there is much to cover to ensure that you are prepared.

Another intended audience is students: this book is also suitable as a supporting text for a systems performance course. During the writing of this book (and for many years before it began), I developed and taught such classes myself, which included simulated performance issues for the students to solve (without providing the answers beforehand!). This has helped me to see which types of material work best in leading students to solve performance problems, and that has guided my choice of content for this book.

Whether you are a student or not, the chapter exercises give you an opportunity to review and apply the material. These include (by suggestion from reviewers) some optional advanced exercises, which you are not expected to solve (they may be impossible; they should be thought-provoking at least).

In terms of company size, this book should contain enough detail to satisfy small to large environments, including those with dozens of dedicated performance staff. For many smaller companies, the book may serve as a reference when needed, with only some portions of it used day to day.

Typographic Conventions

The following typographical conventions are used throughout this book:

`netif_receive_skb()`	function name
`iostat(1)`	man page
Documentation/ . . .	Linux docs
CONFIG_ . . .	Linux configuration option
kernel/ . . .	Linux kernel source code
fs/	Linux kernel source code, file systems
usr/src/uts/ . . .	Solaris-based kernel source code
#	superuser (root) shell prompt
$	user (non-root) shell prompt
^C	a command was interrupted (Ctrl-C)
[. . .]	truncation
mpstat 1	typed command or highlighting

Supplemental Material and References

The following selected texts (the full list is in the Bibliography) can be referenced for further background on operating systems and performance analysis:

[Jain 91]   Jain, R. *The Art of Computer Systems Performance Analysis: Techniques for Experimental Design, Measurement, Simulation, and Modeling*. Wiley, 1991.

[Vahalia 96]   Vahalia, U. *UNIX Internals: The New Frontiers*. Prentice Hall, 1996.

[Cockcroft 98]   Cockcroft, A., and R. Pettit. *Sun Performance and Tuning: Java and the Internet*. Prentice Hall, 1998.

[Musumeci 02]   Musumeci, G. D., and M. Loukidas. *System Performance Tuning, 2nd Edition*. O'Reilly, 2002.

[Bovet 05]   Bovet, D., and M. Cesati. *Understanding the Linux Kernel, 3rd Edition*. O'Reilly, 2005.

[McDougall 06a]   McDougall, R., and J. Mauro. *Solaris Internals: Solaris 10 and OpenSolaris Kernel Architecture*. Prentice Hall, 2006.

[McDougall 06b]   McDougall, R., J. Mauro, and B. Gregg. *Solaris Performance and Tools: DTrace and MDB Techniques for Solaris 10 and OpenSolaris*. Prentice Hall, 2006.

[Gove 07]   Gove, D. *Solaris Application Programming*. Prentice Hall, 2007.

[Love 10]   Love, R. *Linux Kernel Development, 3rd Edition*. Addison-Wesley, 2010.

[Gregg 11]   Gregg, B., and J. Mauro. *DTrace: Dynamic Tracing in Oracle Solaris, Mac OS X and FreeBSD*. Prentice Hall, 2011.

Acknowledgments

Deirdré Straughan has, once again, provided amazing help, sharing my interest in technical education deeply enough to survive another book. She has been involved from concept to manuscript, at first helping me plan what this book would be, then spending countless hours editing and discussing every draft page, identifying many parts I hadn't explained properly. At this point I've worked with her on over 2,000 pages of technical content (plus blog posts!), and I'm lucky to have had such outstanding help.

Barbara Wood performed the copy edit and worked through the text in great detail and in great time, making numerous final improvements to its quality, readability, and consistency. With the length and complexity, this is a difficult text to work on, and I'm very glad for Barbara's help and hard work.

I'm very grateful for everyone who provided feedback on some or all of the book. This is a deeply technical book with many new topics and has required serious effort to review the material—frequently requiring kernel source code from different kernels to be double-checked and understood.

Darryl Gove provided outstanding feedback, both at a deeply technical level and for the high-level presentation and organization of material. He is an author himself, and I look forward to any of his future books, knowing how driven he is to provide the best possible material to our readers.

I'm very grateful to Richard Lowe and Robert Mustacchi, who both worked through the entire book and found topics I had missed or needed to explain better. Richard's understanding of different kernel internals is astonishing, and also a little terrifying. Robert also helped considerably with the Cloud Computing chapter, bringing to bear his expertise from working on the KVM port to illumos.

Thanks for the feedback from Jim Mauro and Dominic Kay: I've worked with them on books before, and they have great minds for comprehending difficult technical content and then explaining it to readers.

Jerry Jelinek and Max Bruning, both of whom have kernel engineering expertise, also provided detailed feedback on multiple chapters.

Adam Leventhal provided expert feedback for the File Systems and Disks chapters, notably helping me to understand the current nuances of flash memory—an area where he has longstanding expertise, having invented innovative new uses of flash memory while at Sun.

David Pacheco provided excellent feedback on the Applications chapter, and Dan McDonald on the Network chapter. I'm lucky to have them bring their expertise to areas they know so well.

Carlos Cardenas worked through the entire book and provided some unique feedback that I was seeking regarding statistical analysis.

I'm grateful to Bryan Cantrill, Keith Wesolowski, Paul Eggleton, Marsell Kukuljevic-Pearce, and Adrian Cockcroft, for their feedback and contributions. Adrian's comments encouraged me to reshuffle the chapter order, helping the reader better relate to the material covered.

I'm grateful to authors before me, whose names are listed in the Bibliography, who have forged paths into systems performance and documented their findings. I've also captured expertise I've learned from performance experts I've worked with over the years, including Bryan Cantrill, Roch Bourbonnais, Jim Mauro, Richard McDougall, and many others, from whom I've learned much.

Thanks to Bryan Cantrill for supporting this project, and to Jason Hoffman for his enthusiasm.

Thanks to Claire, Mitchell, and other family and friends for making the sacrifices to support me in a project like this.

And a special thanks to Greg Doench, senior editor at Pearson, for his help, patience, and advice on the project.

I've enjoyed working on this book, though it has at times been daunting. It would have been much easier for me to write it over a decade ago, when I knew less about the complexities and subtle nuances of systems performance. Since then, I've worked as a software engineer, a kernel engineer, and a performance engineer, and in enterprise, storage, and cloud computing. I've debugged performance issues everywhere in the stack, from applications to metal. This experience, and knowing how much has not yet been documented, has both discouraged and encouraged me to write about it. This is the book I thought needed to be written, and it's a relief to have it done.

About the Author

Brendan Gregg is the lead performance engineer at Joyent, where he analyzes performance and scalability for small to large cloud computing environments, at any level of the software stack. He is the primary author of *DTrace* (Prentice Hall, 2011), and coauthor of *Solaris Performance and Tools* (Prentice Hall, 2007), as well as numerous articles about systems performance. He was previously a performance lead and kernel engineer at Sun Microsystems, and also a performance consultant and trainer. He developed the DTraceToolkit and the ZFS L2ARC, and many of his DTrace scripts are shipped by default in Mac OS X and Oracle Solaris 11. His recent work has included performance visualizations.

1

Introduction

Performance is an exciting, varied, and challenging discipline. This chapter introduces you to the field of performance, specifically systems performance, describing roles, activities, perspectives, and challenges. It also introduces latency, an essential performance metric, and some newer developments in computing: dynamic tracing and cloud computing. Examples of performance activities are also included, to provide context.

1.1 Systems Performance

Systems performance is the study of the entire system, including all physical components and the full software stack. Anything in the data path, software or hardware, is included, as it can affect performance. For distributed systems, this means multiple servers and applications. If you don't have a diagram of your environment showing the data path, find one or draw it yourself; it will help you understand the relationships between components and help ensure that you don't overlook whole areas.

Figure 1.1 shows a generic system software stack on a single server, including the operating system (OS) kernel, with example database and application tiers. The term *entire stack* is sometimes used to describe only the application environment, including databases, applications, and web servers. When speaking of systems performance, however, we use *entire stack* to mean everything, including system libraries and the kernel.

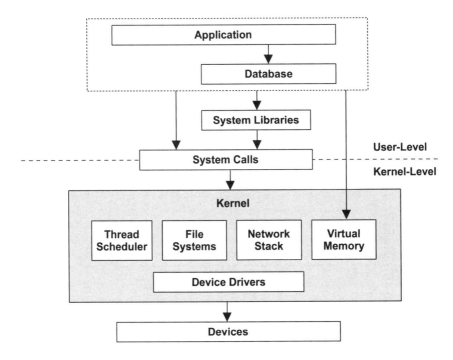

Figure 1.1 Generic system software stack

This stack is discussed in Chapter 3, Operating Systems, and investigated in more detail in later chapters. The following sections describe systems performance and performance in general.

1.2 Roles

Systems performance as an activity can be done by a variety of roles, including system administrators, support staff, application developers, database administrators, and web administrators. For many of these, performance is a part-time activity, and there may be a tendency to explore performance only within the role's area of responsibility (the network team checks the network, the database team checks the database, and so on). However, for some performance issues, finding the root cause requires a cooperative effort from these teams.

Some companies employ *performance engineers*, whose primary activity is systems performance. They can work with multiple teams and perform a holistic study of the environment, an approach that may be vital in resolving complex performance issues. They can also identify opportunities to develop better tooling and metrics for system-wide analysis and capacity planning across the environment.

There are also specialty application-specific occupations in the field of performance, for example, for Java performance and MySQL performance. These often begin with a limited check of system performance before moving to application-specific tools.

1.3 Activities

The field of performance includes the following activities, listed in an ideal order of execution:

1. Setting performance objectives and performance modeling
2. Performance characterization of prototype software or hardware
3. Performance analysis of development code, pre-integration
4. Performing non-regression testing of software builds, pre- or post-release
5. Benchmarking/benchmarketing for software releases
6. Proof-of-concept testing in the target environment
7. Configuration optimization for production deployment
8. Monitoring of running production software
9. Performance analysis of issues

Steps 1 to 5 are part of traditional software product development. The product is then launched, followed by either proof-of-concept testing in the customer environment, or deployment and configuration. If an issue is encountered in the customer environment (steps 6 to 9), it means that the issue was not detected or fixed during the development stages.

Performance engineering should ideally begin before hardware is chosen or software is written. This can be the first step, involving setting objectives and creating a performance model. Often, products are developed without this step, deferring performance engineering work to later on when a problem arises. With each step of the development process, however, it can become progressively harder to fix performance issues, due to architectural decisions made earlier.

The term *capacity planning* can refer to a number of the preceding activities. During design, it includes studying the resource footprint of development software, to see how well the design can meet the target needs. After deployment, it includes monitoring resource usage, to predict problems before they occur.

Methodologies and tools to help perform these activities are covered in this book.

Environments and activities vary from company to company and product to product, and in many cases not all nine steps are performed. Your job may also focus on only some or just one of these activities.

1.4 Perspectives

Apart from a focus on different activities, performance roles can be viewed from different perspectives. Two perspectives for performance analysis are labeled on Figure 1.2: *workload analysis* and *resource analysis*, which approach the software stack from different directions.

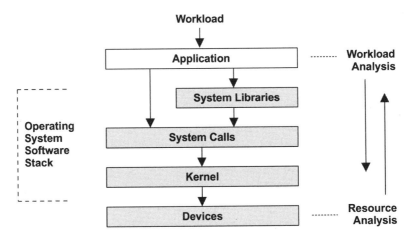

Figure 1.2 Analysis perspectives

The resource analysis perspective is commonly employed by system administrators, who are responsible for the system resources. Application developers, who are responsible for the delivered performance of the workload, commonly focus on the workload analysis perspective. Each perspective has its own strengths, discussed in detail in Chapter 2, Methodology. For challenging issues, it may help to try analysis from both perspectives.

1.5 Performance Is Challenging

Systems performance engineering is a challenging field for a number of reasons, including the fact that it is subjective, it is complex, and it often involves multiple issues.

1.5.1 Performance Is Subjective

Technology disciplines tend to be *objective*, so much so that people in the industry are known for seeing in black and white. This can be true of software troubleshooting, where a bug is either present or absent and is either fixed or not fixed. Such bugs often manifest as error messages that can be easily interpreted and understood to mean the presence of an error.

Performance, on the other hand, is often *subjective*. With performance issues, it can be unclear whether there is an issue to begin with, and if so, when it has been fixed. What may be considered "bad" performance for one user, and therefore an issue, may be considered "good" performance for another.

Consider the following information:

The average disk I/O response time is 1 ms.

Is this "good" or "bad"? While response time, or latency, is one of the best metrics available, interpreting latency information is difficult. To some degree, whether a given metric is "good" or "bad" may depend on the performance expectations of the application developers and end users.

Subjectivity can be made objective by defining clear goals, such as having a target average response time, or requiring a percentage of requests to fall within a certain latency range. Other ways to deal with this subjectivity are introduced in Chapter 2, Methodology, including latency analysis for expressing issues as a ratio of their operation latency.

1.5.2 Systems Are Complex

In addition to subjectivity, performance can be a challenging discipline due to the complexity of systems and the lack of a clear starting point for analysis. Sometimes we begin with a guess, such as blaming the network, and the performance analyst must figure out if this is even the right direction.

Performance issues may also originate from complex interactions between subsystems that perform well when analyzed in isolation. This can occur due to a *cascading failure*, when one failed component causes performance issues in others. To understand the resulting issue, you must untangle the relationships between components and understand how they contribute.

Bottlenecks can also be complex and related in unexpected ways; fixing one may simply move the bottleneck elsewhere in the system, with overall performance not improving as much as hoped.

Apart from the complexity of the system, performance issues may be caused by a complex characteristic of the production workload. In these cases, they may never be reproducible in a lab environment, or only intermittently so.

Solving complex performance issues often requires a holistic approach. The whole system—both its internals and its external interactions—may need to be investigated. This requires a wide range of skills, not typically found in one person, and can make performance engineering a varied and intellectually challenging line of work.

Different methodologies can be used to guide us through these complexities, as introduced in Chapter 2; Chapters 6 to 10 include specific methodologies for the system resources: CPUs, Memory, File Systems, Disks, and Network.

1.5.3 There Can Be Multiple Performance Issues

Finding *a* performance issue is usually not the problem; in complex software there are often many. To illustrate this, try finding the bug database for your operating system or applications and search for the word *performance*. You might be surprised! Typically, there will be a number of performance issues that are known but not yet fixed, even in mature software that is considered to have high performance. This poses yet another difficulty when analyzing performance: the real task isn't finding an issue, it's identifying the issue or issues that matter *the most*.

To do this, the performance analyst must *quantify* the magnitude of issues. Some performance issues may not apply to your workload or may apply only to a very small degree. Ideally, you will not just quantify the issues but also estimate the speedup if each is fixed. This information can be valuable when management looks for justification for spending engineering or operations resources.

A metric well suited to performance quantification, when available, is *latency*.

1.6 Latency

Latency is a measure of time spent waiting. Used broadly, it can mean the time for any operation to complete, such as an application request, a database query, a file system operation, and so forth. For example, latency can express the time for a website to load completely, from link click to screen paint. This is an important metric for both the customer and the website provider: high latency can cause frustration, and customers may take their business elsewhere.

As a metric, latency can allow maximum speedup to be estimated. For example, Figure 1.3 depicts a database query that takes 100 ms (which is the latency), during which it spends 80 ms blocked waiting for disk reads. The maximum performance improvement by eliminating disk reads (e.g., by caching) can be calculated: up to five times (5x). This is the estimated *speedup*, and the calculation has also quantified the performance issue: disk reads are causing the query to run up to 5x more slowly.

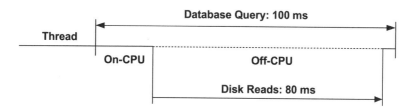

Figure 1.3 Disk I/O latency example

Such a calculation is not possible with other metrics. I/O operations per second (IOPS), for example, depend on the type of I/O and are often not directly comparable. If a change were to reduce the IOPS rate by 80%, it's difficult to know what the performance impact would be. There might be 5x fewer IOPS, but what if each of these I/O increased in size (bytes) by 10x?

In the context of networking, latency can refer to the time for a connection to be established, but not the data transfer time. Throughout this book, terminology is clarified at the beginning of each chapter so that such context differences are clear.

While latency is a useful metric, it hasn't always been available when and where needed. Some system areas provide average latency only; some provide no latency metrics at all. With the advent of dynamic tracing, latency can be measured from arbitrary points of interest and can provide data showing the full distribution of latency.

1.7 Dynamic Tracing

Dynamic tracing allows all software to be instrumented, live and in production. It is a technique of taking in-memory CPU instructions and dynamically building instrumentation upon them. This allows custom performance statistics to be created from any running software, providing observability far beyond what the baked-in statistics provide. Issues that were previously impossible to solve due to a lack of observability can now be solved. Issues that were previously possible to solve, but prohibitively difficult, are now often easier.

Dynamic tracing is so different from traditional observation that it can be difficult, at first, to grasp its role. Consider an operating system kernel: analyzing kernel internals can be like venturing into a dark room, with candles (system statistics) placed where the kernel engineers thought they were needed. Dynamic tracing is like a flashlight that you can point anywhere.

It was first made available as a production-ready tool with DTrace, which provides many other features, including its own programming language, D. DTrace was developed by Sun Microsystems and released for the Solaris 10 operating system in 2005. It was also the first component of Solaris to be made available as open source, from which it has been ported to Mac OS X and FreeBSD, and it is currently being ported to Linux.

Prior to DTrace, system tracing was commonly performed using *static probes*: a small set of instrumentation points placed in the kernel and other software. Their visibility was limited, and their usage was often time-consuming, requiring a cycle of configuration, tracing, dumping data, and then analysis.

DTrace provides both static and *dynamic* tracing of user- and kernel-level software and can provide data in real time. The following simple example traces process execution during an ssh login. Tracing is system-wide (not associated with a particular process ID):

```
# dtrace -n 'exec-success { printf("%d %s", timestamp, curpsinfo->pr_psargs); }'
dtrace: description 'exec-success ' matched 1 probe
CPU     ID                FUNCTION:NAME
  2    1425    exec_common:exec-success 732006240859060 sh -c /usr/bin/locale -a
  2    1425    exec_common:exec-success 732006246584043 /usr/bin/locale -a
  5    1425    exec_common:exec-success 732006197695333 sh -c /usr/bin/locale -a
  5    1425    exec_common:exec-success 732006202832470 /usr/bin/locale -a
  0    1425    exec_common:exec-success 732007379191163 uname -r
  0    1425    exec_common:exec-success 732007449358980 sed -ne /^# START exclude/,/^#
FINISH exclude/p /etc/bash/bash_completion
  1    1425    exec_common:exec-success 732007353365711 -bash
  1    1425    exec_common:exec-success 732007358427035 /usr/sbin/quota
  2    1425    exec_common:exec-success 732007368823865 /bin/mail -E
 12    1425    exec_common:exec-success 732007374821450 uname -s
 15    1425    exec_common:exec-success 732007365906770 /bin/cat -s /etc/motd
```

In this example, DTrace was instructed to print timestamps (nanoseconds) with process names and arguments. Much more sophisticated scripts can be written in the D language, allowing us to create and calculate custom measures of latency.

DTrace and dynamic tracing are explained in Chapter 4, Observability Tools. There are many examples of DTrace one-liners and scripts in later chapters, on both Linux- and Solaris-based systems. For more advanced usage, there is a separate book on DTrace [Gregg 11].

1.8 Cloud Computing

The most recent development affecting systems performance is the rise of cloud computing and the virtualization technologies upon which the cloud is commonly built.

Cloud computing has enabled rapid scaling by using an architecture that can balance an application across a growing number of small systems. This approach has also decreased the need for rigorous capacity planning, as more capacity can be added from the cloud at short notice. In some cases it has also increased the desire for performance analysis: using fewer resources can mean fewer systems. Since cloud usage is typically charged by the hour, a performance win resulting in fewer systems can mean immediate cost savings. Compare this scenario to an enterprise customer, who may be locked into a fixed support contract for years and may not be able to realize cost savings until the contract has ended.

New difficulties caused by cloud computing and virtualization include the management of performance effects from other tenants (sometimes called *performance isolation*) and physical system observability from each tenant. For example, unless managed properly by the system, disk I/O performance may be poor due to contention with a neighbor. In some environments, the true usage of the physical disks may not be observable by each tenant, making identification of this issue difficult.

These topics are covered in Chapter 11, Cloud Computing.

1.9 Case Studies

If you are new to systems performance, case studies showing when and why various activities are performed can help you relate them to your current environment. Two hypothetical examples are summarized here; one is a performance issue involving disk I/O, and one is performance testing of a software change.

These case studies describe activities that are explained in other chapters of this book. The approaches described here are also intended to show not the right way or the only way, but rather *a* way that these performance activities can be conducted, for your critical consideration.

1.9.1 Slow Disks

Scott is a system administrator at a medium-size company. The database team has filed a support ticket complaining of "slow disks" on one of their database servers.

Scott's first task is to learn more about the issue, gathering details to form a problem statement. The ticket claims that the disks are slow, but it doesn't explain if this is causing a database issue or not. Scott responds by asking these questions:

- Is there currently a database performance issue? How is it measured?
- How long has this issue been present?
- Has anything changed with the database recently?
- Why were the disks suspected?

The database team replies: "We have a log for queries slower than 1,000 ms. These usually don't happen, but during the past week they have been growing to dozens per hour. AcmeMon showed that the disks were busy."

This confirms that there is a real database issue, but it also shows that the disk hypothesis is likely a guess. Scott wants to check the disks, but he also wants to check other resources quickly in case that guess was wrong.

AcmeMon is the company's basic server monitoring system, providing historical performance graphs based on operating system tools: `mpstat(1)`, `iostat(1)`, and others. Scott logs in to AcmeMon to see for himself.

Scott begins with a methodology called the USE method to quickly check for resource bottlenecks. As the database team reported, utilization for the disks is high, around 80%, while for the other resources (CPU, network) utilization is much lower. The historical data shows that disk utilization has been steadily increasing during the past week, while CPU utilization has been steady. AcmeMon doesn't provide saturation or error statistics for the disks, so to complete the USE method Scott must log in to the server and run some commands.

He checks disk error counters from /proc; they are zero. He runs `iostat` with an interval of one second and watches utilization and saturation metrics over time. AcmeMon reported 80% utilization but uses a one-minute interval. At one-second granularity, Scott can see that disk utilization fluctuates, often hitting 100% and causing levels of saturation and increased disk I/O latency.

To further confirm that this is blocking the database—and isn't asynchronous with respect to the database queries—he uses a dynamic tracing-based script to capture timestamps and database stack traces whenever the database was descheduled by the kernel. This shows that the database is often blocking during a file system read, during a query, and for many milliseconds. This is enough evidence for Scott.

The next question is why. The disk performance statistics appear to be consistent with high load. Scott performs workload characterization to understand this further, using `iostat(1)` to measure IOPS, throughput, average disk I/O latency, and the read/write ratio. From these, he also calculates the average I/O size and estimates the access pattern: random or sequential. For more details, Scott can use disk I/O level tracing; however, he is satisfied that this already points to a case of high disk load, and not a problem with the disks.

Scott adds more details to the ticket, stating what he checked and including screen shots of the commands used to study the disks. His summary so far is that the disks are under high load, which increases I/O latency and is slowing the queries. However, the disks appear to be acting normally for the load. He asks if there is a simple explanation: Did the database load increase?

The database team responds that it did not, and that the rate of queries (which isn't reported by AcmeMon) has been steady. This sounds consistent with an earlier finding, that CPU utilization was also steady.

Scott thinks about what else could cause higher disk I/O load without a noticeable increase in CPU and has a quick talk with his colleagues about it. One of them suggests file system fragmentation, which is expected when the file system approaches 100% capacity. Scott finds that it is only at 30%.

Scott knows he can perform drill-down analysis to understand the exact causes of disk I/O, but this can be time-consuming. He tries to think of other easy explanations that he can check quickly first, based on his knowledge of the kernel I/O stack. He remembers that this disk I/O is largely caused by file system cache (page cache) misses.

Scott checks the file system cache hit rate and finds it is currently at 91%. This sounds high (good), but he has no historical data to compare it to. He logs in to other database servers that serve similar workloads and finds their cache hit rate to be over 97%. He also finds that the file system cache size is much larger on the other servers.

Turning his attention to the file system cache size and server memory usage, he finds something that had been overlooked: a development project has a prototype application that is consuming a growing amount of memory, even though it isn't under production load yet. This memory is taken from what is available for the file system cache, reducing its hit rate, therefore increasing disk I/O, and hurting the production database server.

Scott contacts the application development team and asks them to shut down the application and move it to a different server, referring to the database issue. After they do this, Scott watches disk utilization creep downward in AcmeMon, as the file system cache recovers to its original size. The slow queries return to zero, and he closes the ticket as resolved.

1.9.2 Software Change

Pamela is a performance and scalability engineer at a small company and works on all performance-related activities. The application developers have developed a new core feature and are unsure whether its introduction could hurt performance. Pamela decides to perform non-regression testing of the new application version, before it is deployed in production. (Non-regression testing is an activity for confirming that a software or hardware change does *not* regress performance, hence, *non*-regression testing.)

Pamela acquires an idle server for the purpose of testing and searches for a client workload simulator. The application team had written one a while ago, although it has various limitations and known bugs. She decides to try it but wants to confirm that it adequately resembles the current production workload.

She configures the server to match the current deployment configuration and runs the client workload simulator from a different system to the target. The client workload can be characterized by studying an access log, and there is already a company tool to do this, which she uses. She also runs the tool on a production server log for different times of day and compares workloads. It appears that the client simulator applies an average production workload but doesn't account for variance. She notes this and continues her analysis.

Pamela knows a number of approaches to use at this point. She picks the easiest: increasing load from the client simulator until a limit is reached. The client simulator can be configured to execute a target number of client requests per second, with a default of 1,000 that she had used earlier. She decides to increase load starting at 100 and adding increments of 100 until a limit is reached, each level being tested for one minute. She writes a shell script to perform the test, which collects results in a file for plotting by other tools.

With the load running, she performs active benchmarking to determine what the limiting factors are. The server resources and server threads seem largely idle. The client simulator shows that the completed requests level off at around 700 per second.

She switches to the new software version and repeats the test. This also reaches the 700 mark and levels off. She also analyzes the server to look for limiting factors but again cannot see any.

She plots the results, showing completed request rate versus load, to visually identify the scalability profile. Both appear to reach an abrupt ceiling.

While it appears that the software versions have similar performance characteristics, Pamela is disappointed that she wasn't able to identify the limiting factor causing the scalability ceiling. She knows she checked only server resources, and the limiter could instead be an application logic issue. It could also be elsewhere: the network or the client simulator.

Pamela wonders if a different approach may be needed, such as running a fixed rate of operations and then characterizing resource usage (CPU, disk I/O, network I/O), so that it can be expressed in terms of a single client request. She runs the simulator at a rate of 700 per second for the current and new software and measures resource consumption. The current software drove the 32 CPUs to an average of 20% utilization for the given load. The new software drove the same CPUs to 30% utilization, for the same load. It would appear that this is indeed a regression, one that consumes more CPU resources.

Curious to understand the 700 limit, Pamela launches a higher load and then investigates all components in the data path, including the network, the client system, and the client workload generator. She also performs drill-down analysis of the server and client software. She documents what she has checked, including screen shots, for reference.

To investigate the client software she performs thread state analysis and finds that it is single-threaded. That one thread is spending 100% of its time executing on-CPU. This convinces her that this is the limiter of the test.

As an experiment, she launches the client software in parallel on different client systems. In this way, she drives the server to 100% CPU utilization for both the current and new software. The current version reaches 3,500 requests/s, and the new version 2,300 requests/s, consistent with earlier findings of resource consumption.

Pamela informs the application developers that there is a regression with the new software version, and she begins to profile its CPU usage to understand why: what code paths are contributing. She notes that an average production workload was tested, and that varied workloads were not. She also files a bug to note that the client workload generator is single-threaded, which can become a bottleneck.

1.9.3 More Reading

A more detailed case study is provided as Chapter 13, Case Study, which documents how I resolved a particular cloud performance issue. The next chapter introduces the methodologies used for performance analysis, and remaining chapters cover the necessary background and specifics.

Methodology

It is a capital mistake to theorize before one has data. Insensibly one begins to twist facts to suit theories, instead of theories to suit facts.

Sherlock Holmes in "A Scandal in Bohemia" by Sir Arthur Conan Doyle

When faced with an underperforming and complicated system environment, the first challenge can be knowing where to begin your analysis, what data to collect, and how to analyze it. As I said in Chapter 1, performance issues can arise from anywhere, including software, hardware, and any component along the data path.

Methodologies can help the performance analyst approach complex systems by showing where to start and what steps to take to locate and analyze performance issues. For beginners, methodologies show where to begin and provide enumerated steps for how to proceed. For casual users or experts, they can serve as checklists to ensure that details are not missed. They include methods to quantify and confirm the findings, identifying the performance issues that matter the most.

This chapter has three parts:

- **Background** introduces terminology, basic models, key performance concepts, and perspectives.
- **Methodology** discusses performance analysis methodologies, both observational and experimental; modeling; and capacity planning.
- **Metrics** introduces performance statistics, monitoring, and visualizations.

Many of the methodologies introduced here are explored in more detail in later chapters, including the methodology sections in Chapters 5 through 10.

2.1 Terminology

The following are key terms for systems performance. Later chapters provide additional terms and describe some of these in different contexts.

- **IOPS:** Input/output operations per second is a measure of the rate of data transfer operations. For disk I/O, IOPS refers to reads and writes per second.
- **Throughput:** the rate of work performed. Especially in communications, the term is used to refer to the *data rate* (bytes per second or bits per second). In some contexts (e.g., databases), throughput can refer to the *operation rate* (operations per second or transactions per second).
- **Response time:** the time for an operation to complete. This includes any time spent waiting and time spent being serviced (*service time*), including the time to transfer the result.
- **Latency:** Latency is a measure of time an operation spends waiting to be serviced. In some contexts, it can refer to the entire time for an operation, equivalent to response time. See Section 2.3, Concepts, for examples.
- **Utilization:** For resources that service requests, utilization is a measure of how busy a resource is, based on how much time in a given interval it was actively performing work. For resources that provide storage, utilization may refer to the capacity that is consumed (e.g., memory utilization).
- **Saturation:** the degree to which a resource has queued work it cannot service.
- **Bottleneck:** In system performance, a bottleneck is a resource that limits the performance of the system. Identifying and removing systemic bottlenecks is a key activity of systems performance.
- **Workload:** The input to the system or the load applied is the workload. For a database, the workload consists of the database queries and commands sent by the clients.
- **Cache:** a fast storage area that can duplicate or buffer a limited amount of data, to avoid communicating directly with a slower tier of storage, thereby improving performance. For economic reasons, a cache is smaller than the slower tier.

The Glossary includes basic terminology for reference if needed.

2.2 Models

The following simple models illustrate some basic principles of systems performance.

2.2.1 System under Test

The performance of a system under test (SUT) is shown in Figure 2.1.

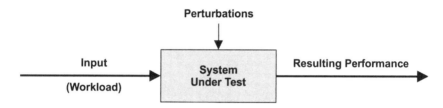

Figure 2.1 System under test

It is important to be aware that perturbations (interference) can affect results, including those caused by scheduled system activity, other users of the system, and other workloads. The origin of the perturbations may not be clear, and careful study of system performance may be required to determine it. This can be particularly difficult in some cloud environments, where other activity (by guest tenants) on the physical host system is not observable from within a guest SUT.

Another difficulty with modern environments is that they may be composed of several networked components needed to service the input workload, including load balancers, web servers, database servers, application servers, and storage systems. The mere act of mapping the environment may help to reveal previously overlooked sources of perturbations. The environment may also be modeled as a network of queueing systems, for analytical study.

2.2.2 Queueing System

Some components and resources can be modeled as a queueing system. Figure 2.2 shows a simple queueing system.

The field of queueing theory, introduced in Section 2.6, Modeling, studies queueing systems and networks of queueing systems.

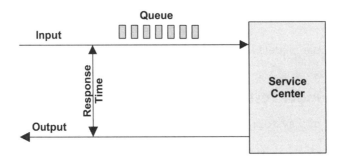

Figure 2.2 Simple queueing model

2.3 Concepts

The following are important concepts of systems performance and are assumed knowledge for the rest of this chapter and this book. The topics are described in a generic manner, before implementation-specific details are introduced in the architecture and analysis sections of later chapters.

2.3.1 Latency

For some environments, latency is the sole focus of performance. For others, it is the top one or two key areas of analysis, along with throughput.

As an example of latency, Figure 2.3 shows a network transfer, such as an HTTP GET request, with the time split into latency and data transfer components.

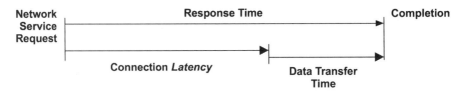

Figure 2.3 Network connection latency

The latency is the time spent waiting before an operation is performed. In this example, the operation is a network service request to transfer data. Before this operation can take place, the system must wait for a network connection to be established, which is latency for this operation. The *response time* spans this latency and the operation time.

Because latency can be measured from different locations, it is often expressed with the target of the measurement. For example, the load time for a website may be composed of three different times measured from different locations: *DNS latency*, *TCP connection latency*, and then *TCP data transfer time*. DNS latency refers to the entire DNS operation. TCP connection latency refers to the initialization only (TCP handshake).

At a higher level, all of these, including the TCP data transfer time, may be treated as latency of something else. For example, the time from when the user clicks a website link to when the resulting page is fully loaded may be termed *latency*, which includes the time for the browser to render the web page.

As latency is a time-based metric, various calculations are possible. Performance issues can be quantified using latency and then ranked because they are expressed using the same units (time). Predicted speedup can also be calculated, by considering when latency can be reduced or removed. Neither of these can be accurately performed using an IOPS metric, for example.

For reference, time orders of magnitude and their abbreviations are listed in Table 2.1.

Table 2.1 Units of Time

Unit	Abbreviation	Fraction of 1 s
Minute	m	60
Second	s	1
Millisecond	ms	0.001 or 1/1000 or 1×10^{-3}
Microsecond	μs	0.000001 or 1/1000000 or 1×10^{-6}
Nanosecond	ns	0.000000001 or 1/1000000000 or 1×10^{-9}
Picosecond	ps	0.000000000001 or 1/1000000000000 or 1×10^{-12}

When possible, other metric types can be converted to latency or time so that they can be compared. If you had to choose between 100 network I/O or 50 disk I/O, how would you know which would perform better? This would be a complicated choice, involving many factors: network hops, rate of network drops and retransmits, I/O size, random or sequential I/O, disk types, and so on. But if you compare 100 ms of total network I/O and 50 ms of total disk I/O, the difference is clear.

2.3.2 Time Scales

While time can be compared numerically, it also helps to have an instinct about time, and expectations for latency from different sources. System components operate over vastly different time scales (orders of magnitude), to the extent that it can be difficult to grasp just how big those differences are. In Table 2.2, example latencies are pro-vided, starting with CPU register access for a 3.3 GHz processor. To demonstrate the differences in time scales we're working with, the table shows an average time that each operation might take, scaled to an imaginary system in which register access—0.3 ns (about one-third of one-billionth of a second) in real life—takes one full second.

Table 2.2 Example Time Scale of System Latencies

Event	Latency	Scaled
1 CPU cycle	0.3 ns	1 s
Level 1 cache access	0.9 ns	3 s
Level 2 cache access	2.8 ns	9 s
Level 3 cache access	12.9 ns	43 s
Main memory access (DRAM, from CPU)	120 ns	6 min
Solid-state disk I/O (flash memory)	50–150 µs	2–6 days
Rotational disk I/O	1–10 ms	1–12 months
Internet: San Francisco to New York	40 ms	4 years
Internet: San Francisco to United Kingdom	81 ms	8 years
Internet: San Francisco to Australia	183 ms	19 years
TCP packet retransmit	1–3 s	105–317 years
OS virtualization system reboot	4 s	423 years
SCSI command time-out	30 s	3 millennia
Hardware (HW) virtualization system reboot	40 s	4 millennia
Physical system reboot	5 m	32 millennia

As you can see, the time scale for CPU cycles is tiny. The time it takes light to travel 0.5 m, perhaps the distance from your eyes to this page, is about 1.7 ns. During the same time, a modern CPU may have executed five CPU cycles and pro-cessed several instructions.

For more about CPU cycles and latency, see Chapter 6, CPUs, and for disk I/O latency, Chapter 9, Disks. The Internet latencies included are from Chapter 10, Network, which has more examples.

2.3.3 Trade-offs

You should be aware of some common performance trade-offs. The good/fast/cheap "pick two" trade-off is shown in Figure 2.4, alongside the terminology adjusted for IT projects.

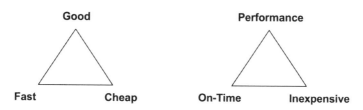

Figure 2.4 Trade-offs: pick two

Many IT projects have picked on-time and inexpensive, leaving performance to be fixed later down the road. This choice can become problematic when the earlier decisions inhibit improving performance, such as choosing and populating a suboptimal storage architecture, or using a programming language or operating system that lacks comprehensive performance analysis tools.

A common trade-off in performance tuning is that between CPU and memory, as memory can be used to cache results, reducing CPU usage. On modern systems with an abundance of CPU, the trade may work the other way: CPU may be spent to compress data to reduce memory usage.

Tunable parameters often come with trade-offs. Here are a couple of examples:

- **File system record size** (or block size): Small record sizes, close to the application I/O size, will perform better for random I/O workloads and make more efficient use of the file system cache while the application is running. Large record sizes will improve streaming workloads, including file system backups.

- **Network buffer size:** Small buffer sizes will reduce the memory overhead per connection, helping the system scale. Large sizes will improve network throughput.

Look for such trade-offs when making changes to the system.

2.3.4 Tuning Efforts

Performance tuning is most effective when done closest to where the work is performed. For workloads driven by applications, this means within the application itself. Table 2.3 shows an example software stack, with tuning possibilities.

By tuning at the application level, it may be possible to eliminate or reduce database queries and improve performance by a large factor (e.g., 20x). Tuning down to the storage device level may eliminate or improve storage I/O, but a tax

Table 2.3 Example Targets of Tuning

Layer	Tuning Targets
Application	database queries performed
Database	database table layout, indexes, buffering
System calls	memory-mapped or read/write, sync or async I/O flags
File system	record size, cache size, file system tunables
Storage	RAID level, number and type of disks, storage tunables

has already been paid executing higher-level OS stack code, so this may improve resulting application performance by only percentages (e.g., 20%).

There is another reason for finding large performance wins at the application level. Many of today's environments target rapid deployment for features and functionality. Thus, application development and testing tend to focus on correctness, leaving little or no time for performance measurement or optimization before production deployment. These activities are conducted later, when performance becomes a problem.

While the application can be the most effective level to tune, it isn't necessarily the most effective level from which to base observation. Slow queries may be best understood from their time spent on-CPU, or from the file system and disk I/O that they perform. These are observable from operating system tools.

In many environments (especially cloud computing), the application level is under constant development, pushing software changes into production weekly or daily. Large performance wins, including fixes for regressions, are frequently found as the application code changes. In these environments, tuning for the operating system and observability from the operating system can be easy to overlook. Remember that operating system performance analysis can also identify application-level issues, not just OS-level issues, in some cases more easily than from the application alone.

2.3.5 Level of Appropriateness

Different organizations and environments have different requirements for performance. You may have joined an organization where it is the norm to analyze much deeper than you've seen before, or even knew was possible. Or you may find that what you consider basic analysis is considered advanced and has never before been performed (good news: low-hanging fruit!).

This doesn't necessarily mean that some organizations are doing it right and some wrong. It depends on the return on investment (ROI) for performance expertise. Organizations with large data centers or cloud environments may need a team of performance engineers who analyze everything, including kernel internals and CPU performance counters, and frequently use dynamic tracing. They may also formally model performance and develop accurate predictions for future growth. Small start-ups may have time only for superficial checks, trusting third-party monitoring solutions to check their performance and provide alerts.

The most extreme environments include stock exchanges and high-frequency traders, where performance and latency are critical and can justify intense effort and expense. As an example of this, a new transatlantic cable is currently planned between the New York and London exchanges at the cost of $300 million, to reduce transmission latency by 6 ms [1].

2.3.6 Point-in-Time Recommendations

The performance characteristics of environments change over time, due to the addition of more users, newer hardware, and updated software or firmware. An environment currently limited by a 1 Gbit/s network infrastructure may start to feel the pinch in disk or CPU performance after an upgrade to 10 Gbits/s.

Performance recommendations, especially the values of tunable parameters, are valid only at a specific *point in time*. What may have been the best advice from a performance expert one week may become invalid a week later after a software or hardware upgrade, or after adding more users.

Tunable parameter values found by searching on the Internet can provide quick wins—in *some* cases. They can also cripple performance if they are not appropriate for your system or workload, were appropriate once but are not now, or are appropriate only as a temporary work-around for a software bug, which is fixed properly in a later software upgrade. It's akin to raiding someone else's medicine cabinet and taking drugs that may not be appropriate for you, or may have expired, or were supposed to be taken only for a short duration.

It can be useful to browse such recommendations just to see which tunable parameters exist and have needed changing in the past. The task then becomes to see whether these should be tuned for your system and workload, and to what. But you may still miss an important parameter if others have not needed to tune that one before, or have tuned it but haven't shared their experience anywhere.

2.3.7 Load versus Architecture

An application can perform badly due to an issue with the software configuration and hardware on which it is running: its architecture. However, an application can also perform badly simply due to too much load applied, resulting in queueing and long latencies. Load and architecture are pictured in Figure 2.5.

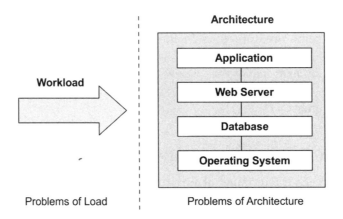

Figure 2.5 Load versus architecture

If analysis of the architecture shows queueing of work but no problems with how the work is performed, the issue may be one of too much load applied. In a cloud computing environment, this is the point where more nodes can be introduced to handle the work.

For example, an issue of architecture may be a single-threaded application that is busy on-CPU, with requests queueing while other CPUs are available and idle. In this case, performance is limited by the application's single-threaded architecture.

An issue of load may be a multithreaded application that is busy on all available CPUs, with requests still queueing. In this case, performance is limited by the available CPU capacity, or put differently, by more load than the CPUs can handle.

2.3.8 Scalability

The performance of the system under increasing load is its *scalability*. Figure 2.6 shows a typical throughput profile as a system's load increases.

For some period, linear scalability is observed. A point is then reached, marked with a dotted line, where contention for a resource begins to affect performance. This point can be described as a *knee point*, as it is the boundary between two pro-

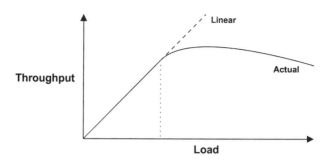

Figure 2.6 Throughput versus load

files. Beyond this point, the throughput profile departs from linear scalability, as contention for the resource increases. Eventually the overheads for increased contention and coherency cause less work to be completed and throughput to decrease.

This point may occur when a component reaches 100% utilization: the *saturation point*. It may also occur when a component approaches 100% utilization, and queueing begins to be frequent and significant.

An example system that may exhibit this profile is an application that performs heavy compute, with more load added as threads. As the CPUs approach 100% utilization, performance begins to degrade as CPU scheduler latency increases. After peak performance, at 100% utilization, throughput begins to decrease as more threads are added, causing more context switches, which consume CPU resources and cause less actual work to be completed.

The same curve can be seen if you replace "load" on the x axis with a resource such as CPU cores. For more on this topic, see Section 2.6, Modeling.

The degradation of performance for nonlinear scalability, in terms of average response time or latency, is graphed in Figure 2.7 [Cockcroft 95].

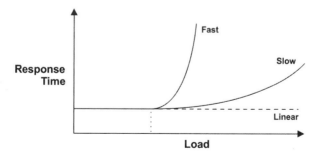

Figure 2.7 Performance degradation

Higher response time is, of course, bad. The "fast" degradation profile may occur for memory load, when the system begins to page (or swap) to supplement main memory. The "slow" degradation profile may occur for CPU load.

Another "fast" profile example is disk I/O. As load (and the resulting disk utilization) increases, I/O becomes more likely to queue behind other I/O. An idle rotational disk may serve I/O with a response time of about 1 ms, but when load increases, this can approach 10 ms. This is modeled in Section 2.6.5 under M/D/1 and 60% Utilization.

Linear scalability of response time could occur if the application begins to return errors when resources are unavailable, instead of queueing work. For example, a web server may return 503 "Service Unavailable" instead of adding requests to a queue, so that those requests that are served can be performed with a consistent response time.

2.3.9 Known-Unknowns

Introduced in the Preface, the notion of *known-knowns*, *known-unknowns*, and *unknown-unknowns* is important for the field of performance. The breakdown is as follows, with examples for systems performance analysis:

- **Known-knowns:** These are things you know. You know you should be checking a performance metric, and you know its current value. For example, you know you should be checking CPU utilization, and you also know that the value is 10% on average.

- **Known-unknowns:** These are things you know that you do not know. You know you can check a metric or the existence of a subsystem, but you haven't yet observed it. For example, you know you could be checking what is making the CPUs busy by the use of profiling but have yet to do so.

- **Unknown-unknowns:** These are things you do not know you do not know. For example, you may not know that device interrupts can become heavy CPU consumers, so you are not checking them.

Performance is a field where "the more you know, the more you don't know." It's the same principle: the more you learn about systems, the more unknown-unknowns you become aware of, which are then known-unknowns that you can check on.

2.3.10 Metrics

Performance metrics are statistics generated by the system, applications, or additional tools that measure activity of interest. They are studied for performance analysis and monitoring, either numerically at the command line or graphically using visualizations.

Common types of systems performance metrics include

- **IOPS:** I/O operations per second
- **Throughput:** either operations or volume per second
- **Utilization**
- **Latency**

The usage of throughput depends on its context. Database throughput is usually a measure of queries or requests (operations) per second. Network throughput is a measure of bits or bytes (volume) per second.

IOPS is a throughput measurement, but one for I/O operations only (reads and writes). Again, context matters, and definitions can vary.

Overhead

Performance metrics are not free; at some point, CPU cycles must be spent to gather and store them. This causes overhead, which can negatively affect the performance of the target of measurement. This is called the *observer effect*. (It is often confused with Heisenberg's Uncertainty Principle, which describes the limit of precision at which pairs of physical properties, such as position and momentum, may be known.)

Issues

The temptation is to assume that the software vendor has provided metrics that are well chosen, are bug-free, and provide complete visibility. In reality, metrics can be confusing, complicated, unreliable, inaccurate, and even plain wrong (due to bugs). Sometimes a metric was correct on one software version but did not get updated to reflect the addition of new code and code paths.

For more about problems with metrics, see Section 4.6, Observing Observability, in Chapter 4, Observability Tools.

2.3.11 Utilization

The term *utilization* is often used for operating systems to describe device usage, such as for the CPU and disk devices. Utilization can be time-based or capacity-based.

Time-Based

Time-based utilization is formally defined in queueing theory. For example [Gunther 97]:

> the average amount of time the server or resource was busy

along with the ratio

$$U = B/T$$

where U = utilization, B = total time the system was busy during T, the observation period.

This is also the "utilization" most readily available from operating system performance tools. The disk monitoring tool `iostat(1)` calls this metric `%b` for *percent busy*, a term that better conveys the underlying metric: B/T.

This utilization metric tells us how busy a component is: when a component approaches 100% utilization, performance can seriously degrade when there is contention for the resource. Other metrics can be checked to confirm and to see if the component has therefore become a system bottleneck.

Some components can service multiple operations in parallel. For them, performance may not degrade much at 100% utilization, as they can accept more work. To understand this, consider a building elevator. It may be considered utilized when it is moving between floors, and not utilized when it is idle waiting. However, the elevator may be able to accept more passengers even when it is busy 100% of the time responding to calls—that is, it is at 100% utilization.

A disk that is 100% busy may also be able to accept and process more work, for example, by buffering writes in the on-disk cache to be completed later. Storage arrays frequently run at 100% utilization because *some* disk is busy 100% of the time, but the array has plenty of idle disks and can accept much more work.

Capacity-Based

The other definition of utilization is used by IT professionals in the context of capacity planning [Wong 97]:

> A system or component (such as a disk drive) is able to deliver a certain amount of throughput. At any level of performance, the system or component is working at some proportion of its capacity. That proportion is called the utilization.

This defines utilization in terms of capacity instead of time. It implies that a disk at 100% utilization *cannot* accept any more work. With the time-based definition, 100% utilization only means it is busy 100% of the time.

100% busy does not mean 100% capacity.

For the elevator example, 100% capacity may mean the elevator is at its maximum payload capacity and cannot accept more passengers.

In an ideal world, we would be able to measure both types of utilization for a device, so that, for example, you would know when a disk is 100% busy and performance begins to degrade due to contention, and also when it is at 100% capacity and cannot accept more work. Unfortunately, this usually isn't possible. For a disk, it would require knowledge of what the disk's on-board controller was doing, and a prediction of capacity. Disks do not currently provide this information.

In this book, *utilization* usually refers to the time-based version. The capacity version is used for some volume-based metrics, such as memory usage.

Non-Idle Time

The problem of defining utilization came up during the development of a cloud monitoring project at my company. The lead engineer, Dave Pacheco, asked me to define utilization. I did (as above). Unsatisfied with the possibility of confusion, he came up with a different term to make it self-evident: *non-idle time*.

While this is more accurate, it is not yet in common usage (which refers to this metric as *percent busy*, as described earlier).

2.3.12 Saturation

The degree to which more work is requested of a resource than it can process is *saturation*. Saturation begins to occur at 100% utilization (capacity-based), as extra work cannot be processed and begins to queue. This is pictured in Figure 2.8.

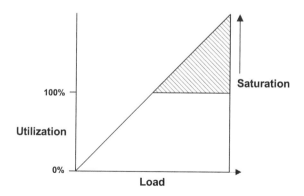

Figure 2.8 Utilization versus saturation

The figure pictures saturation increasing linearly beyond the 100% capacity-based utilization mark as load continues to increase. Any degree of saturation is a performance issue, as time is spent waiting (latency). For time-based utilization (percent busy), queueing and therefore saturation may not begin at the 100% utilization mark, depending on the degree to which the resource can operate on work in parallel.

2.3.13 Profiling

Profiling builds a picture of a target that can be studied and understood. In the field of computing performance, profiling is typically performed by *sampling* the state of the system at timed intervals, and then studying the set of samples.

Unlike the previous metrics covered, including IOPS and throughput, the use of sampling provides a *coarse* view of the target's activity, depending on the rate of sampling.

As an example of profiling, CPU usage can be understood in reasonable detail by sampling the CPU program counter or stack backtrace at frequent intervals to gather statistics on the code paths that are consuming CPU resources. This topic is covered in Chapter 6, CPUs.

2.3.14 Caching

Caching is frequently used to improve performance. A cache stores results from a slower storage tier in a faster storage tier for reference. An example is caching disk blocks in main memory (RAM).

Multiple tiers of caches may be used. CPUs commonly employ multiple hardware caches for main memory (Levels 1, 2, and 3), beginning with a very fast but small cache (Level 1) and increasing in both storage size and access latency. This is an economic trade-off between density and latency; levels and sizes are chosen for the best performance for the on-chip space available.

There are many other caches present in a system, many of them implemented in software using main memory for storage. See Section 3.2.11, Caching, in Chapter 3, Operating Systems, for a list of caching layers.

One metric for understanding cache performance is each cache's *hit ratio*—the number of times the needed data was found in the cache (hits) versus the number of times it was not (misses):

hit ratio = hits/total accesses (hits + misses)

The higher, the better, as a higher ratio reflects more data successfully accessed from faster media. Figure 2.9 shows the expected performance improvement for increasing cache hit ratios.

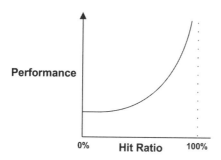

Figure 2.9 Cache hit ratio and performance

The performance difference between 98% and 99% is much greater than that between 10% and 11%. This is a nonlinear profile because of the difference in speed between cache hits and misses—the two storage tiers at play. The greater the difference, the steeper the slope becomes.

Another metric for understanding cache performance is the *cache miss rate*, in terms of misses per second. This is proportional (linear) to the performance penalty of each miss and can be easier to interpret.

For example, workloads A and B perform the same task using different algorithms and use a main memory cache to avoid reading from disk. Workload A has a cache hit ratio of 90%, and workload B a cache hit ratio of 80%. This information alone suggests workload A performs better. What if workload A had a miss rate of 200/s and workload B, 20/s? In those terms, workload B performs 10x *fewer* disk reads, which may complete the task much sooner than A. To be certain, the total runtime for each workload can be calculated as

runtime = (hit rate x hit latency) + (miss rate x miss latency)

This calculation uses the average hit and miss latencies and assumes the work is serialized.

Algorithms

Cache management algorithms and policies determine what to store in the limited space available for a cache.

Most recently used (MRU) refers to a cache *retention policy*, which decides what to favor keeping in the cache: the objects that have been used most recently. *Least recently used* (LRU) can refer to an equivalent cache *eviction policy*, deciding what objects to remove from the cache when more space is needed. There are also *most frequently used* (MFU) and *least frequently used* (LFU) policies.

You may encounter *not frequently used* (NFU), which may be an inexpensive but less thorough version of LRU.

Hot, Cold, and Warm Caches

These words are commonly used to describe the state of the cache:

- **Cold:** A *cold cache* is empty, or populated with unwanted data. The hit ratio for a cold cache is zero (or near zero as it begins to warm up).
- **Hot:** A *hot cache* is populated with commonly requested data and has a high hit ratio, for example, over 99%.
- **Warm:** A *warm cache* is one that is populated with useful data but doesn't have a high enough hit ratio to be considered hot.
- **Warmth:** Cache warmth describes how hot or cold a cache is. An activity that improves cache warmth is one that aims to improve the cache hit ratio.

When caches are first initialized, they begin cold and then warm up over time. When the cache is large or the next-level storage is slow (or both), the cache can take a long time to become populated and warm.

For example, I worked on a storage appliance that had 128 Gbytes of DRAM as a file system cache, 600 Gbytes of flash memory as a second-level cache, and rotational disks for storage. With a random read workload, the disks delivered around 2,000 reads/s. With an 8 Kbyte I/O size, this meant that the caches could warm up at a rate of only 16 Mbytes/s (2,000 x 8 Kbytes). When both caches began cold, it took over 2 hours for the DRAM cache to warm up, and over 10 hours for the flash memory cache.

2.4 Perspectives

There are two common perspectives for performance analysis, each with different audiences, metrics, and approaches. They are *workload analysis* and *resource analysis*. They can be thought of as either top-down or bottom-up analysis of the operating system software stack, as shown in Figure 2.10.

Section 2.5, Methodology, provides specific strategies to apply for each. These perspectives are introduced here in more detail.

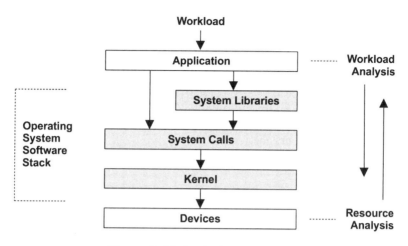

Figure 2.10 Analysis perspectives

2.4.1 Resource Analysis

Resource analysis begins with analysis of the system resources: CPUs, memory, disks, network interfaces, busses, and interconnects. It is most likely performed by system administrators—those responsible for the physical environment resources. Activities include

- **Performance issue investigations:** to see if a particular type of resource is responsible
- **Capacity planning:** for information to help size new systems, and to see when existing system resources may become exhausted

This perspective focuses on utilization, to identify when resources are at or approaching their limit. Some resource types, such as CPUs, have utilization metrics readily available. Utilization for other resources can be estimated based on available metrics, for example, estimating network interface utilization by comparing the send and receive megabits per second (throughput) with the known maximum bandwidth.

Metrics best suited for resource analysis include

- IOPS
- Throughput
- Utilization
- Saturation

These measure what the resource is being asked to do, and how utilized or saturated it is for a given load. Other types of metrics, including latency, are also of use to see how well the resource is responding for the given workload.

Resource analysis is a common approach to performance analysis, in part because of the widely available documentation on the topic. Such documentation focuses on the operating system "stat" tools: `vmstat(1)`, `iostat(1)`, `mpstat(1)`. It's important when you read such documentation to understand that this is a perspective, but not the only perspective.

2.4.2 Workload Analysis

Workload analysis (see Figure 2.11) examines the performance of the applications: the workload applied and how the application is responding. It is most commonly used by application developers and support staff—those responsible for the application software and configuration.

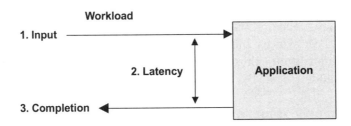

Figure 2.11 Workload analysis

The targets for workload analysis are

- **Requests:** the workload applied
- **Latency:** the response time of the application
- **Completion:** looking for errors

Studying workload requests typically involves checking and summarizing their attributes: the process of *workload characterization* (described in more detail in Section 2.5, Methodology). For databases, these attributes may include the client host, database name, tables, and query string. This data may help identify unnecessary work, or unbalanced work. While the work may be performing well (low latency), examining these attributes may identify ways to reduce or eliminate the work applied. (The fastest query is the one you don't do at all.)

Latency (response time) is the most important metric for expressing application performance. For a MySQL database, it's query latency; for Apache, it's HTTP request latency; and so on. In these contexts, the term *latency* is used to mean the same as response time (refer back to Section 2.3.1, Latency, for more about context).

The tasks of workload analysis include identifying and confirming issues—for example, by looking for latency beyond an acceptable threshold—then finding the source of the latency (drill-down analysis) and confirming that the latency is improved after applying a fix. Note that the starting point is the application. To investigate latency usually involves drilling down deeper into the application, libraries, and the operating system (kernel).

System issues may be identified by studying characteristics related to the completion of an event, including its error status. While a request may complete quickly, it may do so with an error status that causes the request to be retried, accumulating latency.

Metrics best suited for workload analysis include

- Throughput (transactions per second)
- Latency

These measure the rate of requests and the resulting performance.

2.5 Methodology

This section describes numerous methodologies and procedures for system performance analysis and tuning and introduces some that are new, particularly the USE method. Some *anti-methodologies* have also been included.

To help summarize their role, these methodologies have been categorized as different types, such as observational analysis and experimental analysis, as shown in Table 2.4.

Table 2.4 Generic System Performance Methodologies

Methodology	Type
Streetlight anti-method	observational analysis
Random change anti-method	experimental analysis
Blame-someone-else anti-method	hypothetical analysis
Ad hoc checklist method	observational and experimental analysis
Problem statement	information gathering

continues

Table 2.4 Generic System Performance Methodologies (*Continued*)

Methodology	Type
Scientific method	observational analysis
Diagnosis cycle	analysis life cycle
Tools method	observational analysis
USE method	observational analysis
Workload characterization	observational analysis, capacity planning
Drill-down analysis	observational analysis
Latency analysis	observational analysis
Method R	observational analysis
Event tracing	observational analysis
Baseline statistics	observational analysis
Performance monitoring	observational analysis, capacity planning
Queueing theory	statistical analysis, capacity planning
Static performance tuning	observational analysis, capacity planning
Cache tuning	observational analysis, tuning
Micro-benchmarking	experimental analysis
Capacity planning	capacity planning, tuning

Performance monitoring, queueing theory, and capacity planning are covered later in this chapter. Later chapters also recast some of these methodologies in different contexts and provide some additional methodologies specific to particular areas of performance analysis.

The following sections begin with commonly used but weaker methodologies for comparison, including the anti-methodologies. For the analysis of performance issues, the first methodology you should attempt is the problem statement method, before moving on to others.

2.5.1 Streetlight Anti-Method

This method is actually the *absence* of a deliberate methodology. The user analyzes performance by choosing observability tools that are familiar, found on the Internet, or just at random to see if anything obvious shows up. This approach is hit or miss and can overlook many types of issues.

Tuning performance may be attempted in a similar trial-and-error fashion, setting whatever tunable parameters are known and familiar to different values to see if that helps.

Even when this method reveals an issue, it can be slow as tools or tunings unrelated to the issue are found and tried, just because they're familiar. This methodology is therefore named after an observational bias called the *streetlight effect*, illustrated by this parable:

> One night a police officer sees a drunk searching the ground beneath a streetlight and asks what he is looking for. The drunk says he has lost his keys. The police officer can't find them either and asks: "Are you sure you lost them here, under the streetlight?" The drunk replies: "No, but this is where the light is best."

The performance equivalent would be looking at top(1), not because it makes sense, but because the user doesn't know how to read other tools.

An issue that this methodology does find may be *an* issue but not *the* issue. Other methodologies quantify findings, so that false positives can be ruled out more quickly.

2.5.2 Random Change Anti-Method

This is an experimental anti-methodology. The user randomly guesses where the problem may be and then changes things until it goes away. To determine whether performance has improved or not as a result of each change, a metric is studied, such as application runtime, operation time, latency, operation rate (operations per second), or throughput (bytes per second). The approach is as follows:

1. Pick a random item to change (e.g., a tunable parameter).
2. Change it in one direction.
3. Measure performance.
4. Change it in the other direction.
5. Measure performance.
6. Were the results in step 3 or step 5 better than the baseline? If so, keep the change and go back to step 1.

While this process may eventually unearth tuning that works for the tested workload, it is very time-consuming and can also leave behind tuning that doesn't make sense in the long term. For example, an application change may improve performance because it works around a database or operating system bug—a bug that is then later fixed. But the application will still have that tuning that no longer makes sense, and that no one understood properly in the first place.

Another risk is where a change that isn't properly understood causes a worse problem during peak production load and a need to back out the change during this time.

2.5.3 Blame-Someone-Else Anti-Method

This anti-methodology follows these steps:

1. Find a system or environment component for which you are not responsible.
2. Hypothesize that the issue is with that component.
3. Redirect the issue to the team responsible for that component.
4. When proven wrong, go back to step 1.

> Maybe it's the network. Can you check with the network team if they have had dropped packets or something?

Instead of investigating performance issues, the user of this methodology makes them someone else's problem, which can be wasteful of other teams' resources when it turns out not to be their problem after all. This anti-methodology can be identified by a lack of data leading to the hypothesis.

To avoid becoming a victim of blame-someone-else, ask the accuser for screen shots showing which tools were run and how the output was interpreted. You can take these screen shots and interpretations to someone else for a second opinion.

2.5.4 Ad Hoc Checklist Method

Stepping through a canned checklist is a common methodology used by support professionals when asked to check and tune a system, often in a short time frame. A typical scenario involves the deployment of a new server or application in production, and a support professional spending half a day checking for common issues now that the system is under real load. These checklists are ad hoc and are built from recent experience and issues for that system type.

Here is an example checklist entry:

> Run `iostat −x 1` and check the `await` column. If this is consistently over 10 (ms) during load, then the disks are either slow or overloaded.

A checklist may be composed of a dozen or so such checks.

While these checklists can provide the most value in the shortest time frame, they are point-in-time recommendations (see Section 2.3, Concepts) and need to be frequently refreshed to stay current. They also tend to focus on issues for which there are known fixes that can be easily documented, such as the setting of tunable parameters, but not custom fixes to the source code or environment.

If you are managing a team of support professionals, an ad hoc checklist can be an effective way to ensure that everyone knows how to check for the worst of the issues, and that all the obvious culprits have been checked. A checklist can be written to be clear and prescriptive, showing how to identify each issue and what the fix is. But of course, this list must be constantly updated.

2.5.5 Problem Statement

Defining the problem statement is a routine task for support staff when first responding to issues. It's done by asking the customer the following questions:

1. What makes you think there is a performance problem?
2. Has this system ever performed well?
3. What changed recently? Software? Hardware? Load?
4. Can the problem be expressed in terms of latency or runtime?
5. Does the problem affect other people or applications (or is it just you)?
6. What is the environment? What software and hardware are used? Versions? Configuration?

Just asking and answering these questions often points to an immediate cause and solution. The problem statement has therefore been included here as its own methodology and should be the first approach you use when tackling a new issue.

2.5.6 Scientific Method

The scientific method studies the unknown by making hypotheses and then testing them. It can be summarized in the following steps:

1. Question
2. Hypothesis
3. Prediction
4. Test
5. Analysis

The question is the performance problem statement. From this you can hypothesize what the cause of poor performance may be. Then you construct a test, which may be observational or experimental, that tests a prediction based on the hypothesis. You finish with analysis of the test data collected.

For example, you may find that application performance is degraded after migrating to a system with less main memory, and you hypothesize that the cause of poor performance is a smaller file system cache. You might use an *observational test* to measure the cache miss rate on both systems, predicting that cache misses will be higher on the smaller system. An *experimental test* would be to increase the cache size (adding RAM), predicting that performance will improve. Another, perhaps easier, experimental test is to artificially reduce the cache size (using tunable parameters), predicting that performance will be worse.

The following are some more examples.

Example (Observational)

1. Question: What is causing slow database queries?
2. Hypothesis: Noisy neighbors (other cloud computing tenants) are performing disk I/O, contending with database disk I/O (via the file system).
3. Prediction: If file system I/O latency is measured during a query, it will show that the file system is responsible for the slow queries.
4. Test: Tracing of database file system latency as a ratio of query latency shows that less than 5% of the time is spent waiting for the file system.
5. Analysis: The file system and disks are not responsible for slow queries.

Although the issue is still unsolved, some large components of the environment have been ruled out. The person conducting this investigation can return to step 2 and develop a new hypothesis.

Example (Experimental)

1. Question: Why do HTTP requests take longer from host A to host C than from host B to host C?
2. Hypothesis: Host A and host B are in different data centers.
3. Prediction: Moving host A to the same data center as host B will fix the problem.
4. Test: Move host A and measure performance.
5. Analysis: Performance has been fixed—consistent with the hypothesis.

If the problem wasn't fixed, reverse the experimental change (move host A back, in this case) before beginning a new hypothesis!

Example (Experimental)

1. Question: Why did file system performance degrade as the file system cache grew in size?

2. Hypothesis: A larger cache stores more records, and more compute is required to manage a larger cache than a smaller one.

3. Prediction: Making the record size progressively smaller, and therefore causing more records to be used to store the same amount of data, will make performance progressively *worse*.

4. Test: Test the same workload with progressively smaller record sizes.

5. Analysis: Results are graphed and are consistent with the prediction. Drilldown analysis is now performed on the cache management routines.

This is an example of a negative test—deliberately hurting performance to learn more about the target system.

2.5.7 Diagnosis Cycle

Similar to the scientific method is the *diagnosis cycle*:

hypothesis → instrumentation → data → hypothesis

Like the scientific method, this method also deliberately tests a hypothesis through the collection of data. The cycle emphasizes that the data can lead quickly to a new hypothesis, which is tested and refined, and so on. This is similar to a doctor making a series of small tests to diagnose a patient and refining the hypothesis based on the result of each test.

Both of these approaches have a good balance of theory and data. Try to move from hypothesis to data quickly, so that bad theories can be identified early and discarded, and better ones developed.

2.5.8 Tools Method

A tools-oriented approach is as follows:

1. List available performance tools (optionally, install or purchase more).

2. For each tool, list useful metrics it provides.

3. For each metric, list possible rules for interpretation.

The result of this is a prescriptive checklist showing which tool to run, which metrics to read, and how to interpret them. While this can be fairly effective, it relies exclusively on available (or known) tools, which can provide an incomplete view of the system, similar to the streetlight anti-method. Worse, the user is unaware that he or she has an incomplete view—and may remain unaware. Issues that require custom tooling (e.g., dynamic tracing) may never be identified and solved.

In practice, the tools method does identify certain resource bottlenecks, errors, and other types of problems, though often not efficiently.

When a large number of tools and metrics are available, it can be time-consuming to iterate through them. The situation gets worse when multiple tools appear to have the same functionality, and you spend additional time trying to understand the pros and cons of each. In some cases, such as file system micro-benchmark tools, there are over a dozen tools to choose from, when you may need only one.[1]

2.5.9 The USE Method

The utilization, saturation, and errors (USE) method should be used early in a performance investigation, to identify systemic bottlenecks [Gregg 13]. It can be summarized this way:

> For every resource, check utilization, saturation, and errors.

These terms are defined as follows:

- **Resource:** all physical server functional components (CPUs, busses, . . .). Some software resources can also be examined, provided the metrics make sense.
- **Utilization:** for a set time interval, the percentage of time that the resource was busy servicing work. While busy, the resource may still be able to accept more work; the degree to which it cannot do so is identified by saturation.
- **Saturation:** the degree to which the resource has extra work that it can't service, often waiting on a queue.
- **Errors:** the count of error events.

For some resource types, including main memory, utilization is the *capacity* of the resource that is used. This is different from the time-based definition and was explained earlier in Section 2.3.11, Utilization. Once a capacity resource reaches 100% utilization, more work cannot be accepted, and the resource either queues the work (saturation) or returns errors, which are also identified using the USE method.

---

1. As an aside, an argument I've encountered to support multiple overlapping tools is that "competition is good." My counterargument is that developing those tools divides resources, which can accomplish more in combination, and that it also wastes end users' time as they try to pick through them.

Errors should be investigated because they can degrade performance and may not be immediately noticed when the failure mode is recoverable. This includes operations that fail and are retried, and devices that fail in a pool of redundant devices.

In contrast with the tools method, the USE method involves iterating over system resources instead of tools. This helps you create a complete list of questions to ask, and only then do you search for tools to answer them. Even when tools cannot be found to answer questions, the knowledge that these questions are unanswered can be extremely useful for the performance analyst: they are now "known-unknowns."

The USE method also directs analysis to a limited number of key metrics, so that all system resources are checked as quickly as possible. After this, if no issues have been found, other methodologies can be used.

Procedure

The USE method is pictured as the flowchart in Figure 2.12. Errors are placed first before utilization and saturation are checked. Errors are usually quick and easy to interpret, and it can be time-efficient to rule them out before investigating the other metrics.

This method identifies problems that are likely to be system bottlenecks. Unfortunately, a system may be suffering from more than one performance problem, so the first thing you find may be *a* problem but not *the* problem. Each discovery can be investigated using further methodologies, before returning to the USE method as needed to iterate over more resources.

Expressing Metrics

The USE method metrics are usually expressed as follows:

- **Utilization:** as a percent over a time interval (e.g., "One CPU is running at 90% utilization")
- **Saturation:** as a wait-queue length (e.g., "The CPUs have an average run-queue length of four")
- **Errors:** number of errors reported (e.g., "This network interface has had 50 late collisions")

Though it may seem counterintuitive, a short burst of high utilization can cause saturation and performance issues, even though the overall utilization is *low* over a long interval. Some monitoring tools report utilization over 5-minute averages. CPU utilization, for example, can vary dramatically from second to second, so a 5-minute average may disguise short periods of 100% utilization and, therefore, saturation.

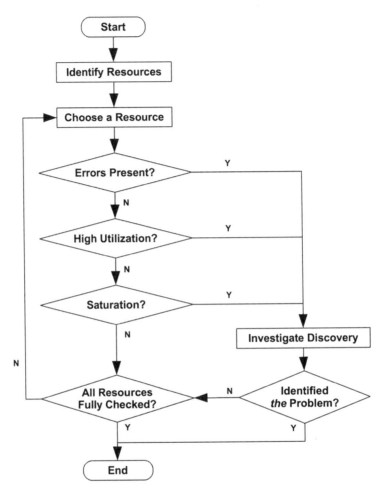

Figure 2.12 The USE method flow

Consider a toll plaza on a highway. Utilization can be defined as how many toll-booths were busy servicing a car. Utilization at 100% means you can't find an empty booth and must queue behind someone (saturation). If I told you the booths were at 40% utilization across the entire day, could you tell me whether any cars had queued at any time during that day? They probably did during rush hour, when utilization was at 100%, but that isn't visible in the daily average.

Resource List

The first step in the USE method is to create a list of resources. Try to be as complete as possible. Here is a generic list of server hardware resources, along with specific examples:

- **CPUs:** sockets, cores, hardware threads (virtual CPUs)
- **Main memory:** DRAM
- **Network interfaces:** Ethernet ports
- **Storage devices**: disks
- **Controllers:** storage, network
- **Interconnects:** CPU, memory, I/O

Each component typically acts as a single resource type. For example, main memory is a *capacity* resource, and network interfaces are an I/O resource (which can mean either IOPS or throughput). Some components can behave as multiple resource types: for example, a storage device is both an I/O resource and a capacity resource. Consider all types that can lead to performance bottlenecks. Also note that I/O resources can be further studied as *queueing systems*, which queue and then service these requests.

Some physical components, such as hardware caches (e.g., CPU caches), can be left out of your checklist. The USE method is most effective for resources that suffer performance degradation under high utilization or saturation, leading to bottlenecks, while caches *improve* performance under high utilization. These can be checked using other methodologies. If you are unsure whether to include a resource, include it, then see how well the metrics work in practice.

Functional Block Diagram

Another way to iterate over resources is to find or draw a functional block diagram for the system, such as the one shown in Figure 2.13. Such a diagram also shows relationships, which can be very useful when looking for bottlenecks in the flow of data.

CPU, memory, and I/O interconnects and busses are often overlooked. Fortunately, they are not common system bottlenecks, as they are typically designed to provide an excess of throughput. Unfortunately, if they are, the problem can be difficult to solve. Maybe you can upgrade the main board, or reduce load; for example, "zero copy" projects lighten memory bus load.

For investigating interconnects, see CPU Performance Counters in Section 6.4.1, Hardware, of Chapter 6, CPUs.

Metrics

Once you have your list of resources, consider the metric types: utilization, saturation, and errors. Table 2.5 shows some example resources and metric types, along with possible metrics (generic OS).

These metrics can be either averages per interval or counts.

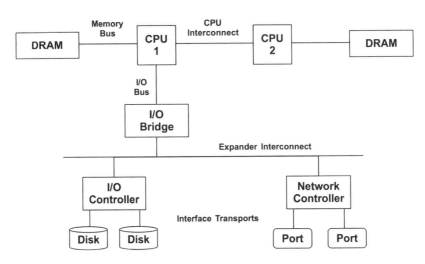

Figure 2.13 Example two-processor functional block diagram

Table 2.5 Example USE Method Metrics

Resource	Type	Metric
CPU	utilization	CPU utilization (either per CPU or a system-wide average)
CPU	saturation	dispatcher-queue length (aka run-queue length)
Memory	utilization	available free memory (system-wide)
Memory	saturation	anonymous paging or thread swapping (page scanning is another indicator), or out-of-memory events
Network interface	utilization	receive throughput/max bandwidth, transmit throughput/max bandwidth
Storage device I/O	utilization	device busy percent
Storage device I/O	saturation	wait-queue length
Storage device I/O	errors	device errors ("soft," "hard")

Repeat for all combinations, and include instructions for fetching each metric. Take note of metrics that are not currently available; these are the known-unknowns. You'll end up with a list of about 30 metrics, some of which are difficult to measure, and some of which can't be measured at all. Fortunately, the most common issues are usually found with the easier metrics (e.g., CPU saturation, memory capacity saturation, network interface utilization, disk utilization), so these can be checked first.

Some examples of harder combinations are provided in Table 2.6.

Table 2.6 Example USE Method Advanced Metrics

Resource	Type	Metric
CPU	errors	for example, correctable CPU cache error-correcting code (ECC) events or faulted CPUs (if the OS + HW supports that)
Memory	errors	for example, failed `malloc()`s (although this is usually due to virtual memory exhaustion, not physical)
Network	saturation	saturation-related network interface or OS errors, e.g., Linux "overruns" or Solaris "nocanputs"
Storage controller	utilization	depends on the controller; it may have a maximum IOPS or throughput that can be checked against current activity
CPU interconnect	utilization	per-port throughput/maximum bandwidth (CPU performance counters)
Memory interconnect	saturation	memory stall cycles, high cycles per instruction (CPU performance counters)
I/O interconnect	utilization	bus throughput/maximum bandwidth (performance counters may exist on your HW, e.g., Intel "uncore" events)

Some of these may not be available from standard operating system tools and may require the use of dynamic tracing or the CPU performance counter facility.

Appendix A is an example USE method checklist for Linux systems, iterating over all combinations for hardware resources with the Linux observability toolset. Appendix B provides the same for Solaris-based systems. Both appendixes also include some software resources.

Software Resources

Some software resources can be similarly examined. This usually applies to smaller components of software, not entire applications, for example:

- **Mutex locks:** Utilization may be defined as the time the lock was held, saturation by those threads queued waiting on the lock.

- **Thread pools:** Utilization may be defined as the time threads were busy processing work, saturation by the number of requests waiting to be serviced by the thread pool.

- **Process/thread capacity:** The system may have a limited number of processes or threads, whose current usage may be defined as utilization; waiting on allocation may be saturation; and errors are when the allocation failed (e.g., "cannot fork").

- **File descriptor capacity:** similar to process/thread capacity, but for file descriptors.

If the metrics work well in your case, use them; otherwise, alternative methodologies such as latency analysis can be applied.

Suggested Interpretations

Here are some general suggestions for interpreting the metric types:

- **Utilization:** Utilization at 100% is usually a sign of a bottleneck (check saturation and its effect to confirm). Utilization beyond 60% can be a problem for a couple of reasons: depending on the interval, it can hide short bursts of 100% utilization. Also, some resources such as hard disks (but not CPUs) usually cannot be interrupted during an operation, even for higher-priority work. As utilization increases, queueing delays become more frequent and noticeable. See Section 2.6.5, Queueing Theory, for more about 60% utilization.

- **Saturation:** Any degree of saturation can be a problem (nonzero). It may be measured as the length of a wait queue, or as time spent waiting on the queue.

- **Errors:** Nonzero error counters are worth investigating, especially if they are increasing while performance is poor.

It's easy to interpret the negative cases: low utilization, no saturation, no errors. This is more useful than it sounds—narrowing down the scope of an investigation can help you focus quickly on the problem area, having identified that it is likely *not* a resource problem. This is the process of elimination.

Cloud Computing

In a cloud computing environment, software resource controls may be in place to limit or throttle tenants who are sharing one system. At Joyent we primarily use OS virtualization (SmartOS Zones), which imposes memory limits, CPU limits, and storage I/O throttling. Each of these resource limits can be examined with the USE method, similarly to examining the physical resources.

For example, "memory capacity utilization" can be the tenant's memory usage versus its memory cap. "Memory capacity saturation" can be seen by anonymous paging activity, even though the traditional page scanner may be idle.

2.5.10 Workload Characterization

Workload characterization is a simple and effective method for identifying a class of issues: those due to the load applied. It focuses on the *input* to the system, rather than the resulting performance. Your system may have no architectural or configuration issues present, but it is under more load than it can reasonably handle.

Workloads can be characterized by answering the following questions:

- **Who** is causing the load? Process ID, user ID, remote IP address?
- **Why** is the load being called? Code path, stack trace?
- **What** are the load characteristics? IOPS, throughput, direction (read/write), type? Include variance (standard deviation) where appropriate.
- **How** is the load changing over time? Is there a daily pattern?

It can be useful to check all of these, even when you have strong expectations about what the answers will be, because you may be surprised.

Consider this scenario: You have a performance issue with a database, whose clients are a pool of web servers. Should you check the IP addresses of who is using the database? You already expect them to be the web servers, as per the configuration. You check anyway and discover that the entire Internet appears to be throwing load at the databases, destroying their performance. You are actually under a denial-of-service (DoS) attack!

The best performance wins are the result of *eliminating unnecessary work*. Sometimes unnecessary work is caused by applications malfunctioning, for example, a thread stuck in a loop creating unnecessary CPU work. It can also be caused by bad configurations—for example, system-wide backups that run during the day—or even a DoS attack as described previously. Characterizing the workload can identify these issues, and with maintenance or reconfiguration they may be eliminated.

If the identified workload cannot be eliminated, another approach may be to use system resource controls to throttle it. For example, a system backup task may be interfering with a production database by consuming CPU resources to compress the backup, and then network resources to transfer it. This CPU and network usage may be throttled using resource controls (if the system supports them), so that the backup still occurs (more slowly) without hurting the database.

Apart from identifying issues, workload characterization can also be input for the design of simulation benchmarks. If the workload measurement is an average, ideally you will also collect details of the distribution and variation. This can be important for simulating the variety of workloads expected, rather than testing only an average workload. See Section 2.8, Statistics, for more about averages and variation (standard deviation), and Chapter 12, Benchmarking.

Analysis of the workload also helps separate problems of load from problems of architecture, by identifying the former. Load versus architecture was introduced in Section 2.3, Concepts.

The specific tools and metrics for performing workload characterization depend on the target. Some applications record detailed logs of client activity, which can be the source for statistical analysis. They may also already provide daily or monthly reports of client usage, which can be mined for details.

2.5.11 Drill-Down Analysis

Drill-down analysis starts with examining an issue at a high level, then narrowing the focus based on the previous findings, discarding areas that seem uninteresting, and digging deeper into those areas that are. The process can involve digging down through deeper layers of the software stack, to hardware if necessary, to find the root cause of the issue.

A drill-down analysis methodology for system performance is provided in *Solaris Performance and Tools* [McDougall 06b] and has three stages:

1. **Monitoring:** This is used for continually recording high-level statistics over time, and identifying or alerting if a problem may be present.

2. **Identification:** Given a suspected problem, this narrows the investigation to particular resources or areas of interest, identifying possible bottlenecks.

3. **Analysis:** Further examination of particular system areas is done to attempt to root-cause and quantify the issue.

Monitoring may be performed company-wide and the results of all servers or cloud instances aggregated. A traditional means to do this is the Simple Network Monitoring Protocol (SNMP), which can be used to monitor any network-attached device that supports it. The resulting data may reveal long-term patterns that may be missed when using command-line tools over short durations. Many monitoring solutions provide alerts if a problem is suspected, prompting analysis to move to the next stage.

Identification is performed interactively on the server, using standard observability tools to check system components: CPUs, disks, memory, and so on. It is usually done via a command-line session using tools such as vmstat(1), iostat(1), and mpstat(1). Some newer tools allow real-time interactive performance analysis via a GUI (for example, Oracle ZFS Storage Appliance Analytics).

Analysis tools include those based on tracing or profiling, for deeper inspection of suspect areas. Such deeper analysis may involve the creation of custom tools and inspection of source code (if available). Here is where most of the drilling takes place, peeling away layers of the software stack as necessary to find the root cause. Tools for performing this include `strace(1)`, `truss(1)`, perf, and DTrace.

Five Whys

An additional methodology you can use during the analysis stage is the *Five Whys* technique: ask yourself "why?" then answer the question, and repeat up to five times in total (or more). Here is an example procedure:

1. A database has begun to perform poorly for many queries. Why?
2. It is delayed by disk I/O due to memory paging. Why?
3. Database memory usage has grown too large. Why?
4. The allocator is consuming more memory than it should. Why?
5. The allocator has a memory fragmentation issue.

This is a real-world example that very unexpectedly led to a fix in a system memory allocation library. It was the persistent questioning and drilling down to the core issue that led to the fix.

2.5.12 Latency Analysis

Latency analysis examines the time taken to complete an operation, then breaks it into smaller components, continuing to subdivide the components with the highest latency so that the root cause can be identified and quantified. Similarly to drill-down analysis, latency analysis may drill down through layers of the software stack to find the origin of latency issues.

Analysis can begin with the workload applied, examining how that workload was processed in the application, then drilling down into the operating system libraries, system calls, the kernel, and device drivers.

For example, analysis of MySQL query latency could involve answering the following questions (example answers are given here):

1. Is there a query latency issue? (yes)
2. Is the query time largely spent on-CPU or waiting off-CPU? (off-CPU)
3. What is the off-CPU time spent waiting for? (file system I/O)
4. Is the file system I/O time due to disk I/O or lock contention? (disk I/O)
5. Is the disk I/O time likely due to random seeks or data transfer time? (transfer time)

For this example, each step of the process posed a question that divided the latency into two parts, and then proceeded to analyze the larger part: a binary search of latency, if you will. The process is pictured in Figure 2.14.

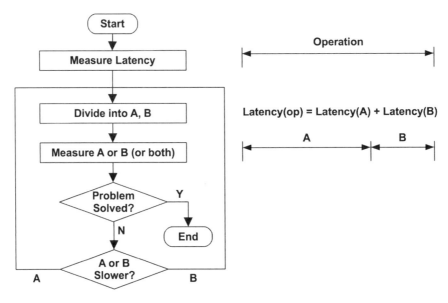

Figure 2.14 Latency analysis procedure

As the slower of A or B is identified, it is then further split into A or B, analyzed, and so on.

Latency analysis of database queries is the target of method R.

2.5.13 Method R

Method R is a performance analysis methodology developed for Oracle databases that focuses on finding the origin of latency, based on Oracle trace events [Millsap 03]. It is described as "a response time-based performance improvement method that yields maximum economic value to your business" and focuses on identifying and quantifying where time is spent during queries. While this is used for the study of databases, its approach could be applied to any system and is worth mentioning here as an avenue of possible study.

2.5.14 Event Tracing

Systems operate by processing discrete events. These include CPU instructions, disk I/O and other disk commands, network packets, system calls, library calls, application transactions, database queries, and so on. Performance analysis usually studies summaries of these events, such as operations per second, bytes per second, or average latency. Sometimes important detail is lost in the summary, and the events are best understood when inspected individually.

Network troubleshooting often requires packet-by-packet inspection, with tools such as tcpdump(1). This example summarizes packets as single lines of text:

```
# tcpdump -ni eth4 -ttt
tcpdump: verbose output suppressed, use -v or -vv for full protocol decode
listening on eth4, link-type EN10MB (Ethernet), capture size 65535 bytes
00:00:00.000000 IP 10.2.203.2.22 > 10.2.0.2.33986: Flags [P.], seq
1182098726:1182098918, ack 4234203806, win 132, options [nop,nop,TS val 1751498743
ecr 1751639660], length 192
00:00:00.000392 IP 10.2.0.2.33986 > 10.2.203.2.22: Flags [.], ack 192, win 501,
options [nop,nop,TS val 1751639684 ecr 1751498743], length 0
00:00:00.009561 IP 10.2.203.2.22 > 10.2.0.2.33986: Flags [P.], seq 192:560, ack 1,
win 132, options [nop,nop,TS val 1751498744 ecr 1751639684], length 368
00:00:00.000351 IP 10.2.0.2.33986 > 10.2.203.2.22: Flags [.], ack 560, win 501,
options [nop,nop,TS val 1751639685 ecr 1751498744], length 0
00:00:00.010489 IP 10.2.203.2.22 > 10.2.0.2.33986: Flags [P.], seq 560:896, ack 1,
win 132, options [nop,nop,TS val 1751498745 ecr 1751639685], length 336
00:00:00.000369 IP 10.2.0.2.33986 > 10.2.203.2.22: Flags [.], ack 896, win 501,
options [nop,nop,TS val 1751639686 ecr 1751498745], length 0
```

Varying amounts of information can be printed by tcpdump(1) as needed (see Chapter 10, Network).

Storage device I/O at the block device layer can be traced using iosnoop(1M) (DTrace-based; see Chapter 9, Disks):

```
# ./iosnoop -Dots
STIME(us)     TIME(us)      DELTA DTIME UID   PID D   BLOCK    SIZE  COMM ...
722594048435 722594048553  117   130   0     485 W 95742054  8192  zpool-...
722594048879 722594048983  104   109   0     485 W 95742106  8192  zpool-...
722594049335 722594049552  217   229   0     485 W 95742154  8192  zpool-...
722594049900 722594050029  128   137   0     485 W 95742178  8192  zpool-...
722594050336 722594050457  121   127   0     485 W 95742202  8192  zpool-...
722594050760 722594050864  103   110   0     485 W 95742226  8192  zpool-...
722594051190 722594051262  72    80    0     485 W 95742250  8192  zpool-...
722594051613 722594051678  65    72    0     485 W 95742318  8192  zpool-...
722594051977 722594052067  90    97    0     485 W 95742342  8192  zpool-...
722594052417 722594052515  98    105   0     485 W 95742366  8192  zpool-...
722594052840 722594052902  62    68    0     485 W 95742422  8192  zpool-...
722594053220 722594053290  69    77    0     485 W 95742446  8192  zpool-...
```

Multiple timestamps are printed here, including the start time (STIME), end time (TIME), delta time between request and completion (DELTA), and estimated time to service this I/O (DTIME).

The system call layer is another common location for tracing, with tools including strace(1) on Linux and truss(1) on Solaris-based systems (see Chapter 5, Applications). These tools also have options to print timestamps.

When performing event tracing, look for the following information:

- **Input:** all attributes of an event request: type, direction, size, and so on
- **Times:** start time, end time, latency (difference)
- **Result:** error status, result of event (size)

Sometimes performance issues can be understood by examining attributes of the event, for either the request or the result. Event timestamps are particularly useful for analyzing latency and can often be included by using event tracing tools. The preceding tcpdump(1) output included delta timestamps, measuring the time between packets, using -ttt.

The study of prior events provides more information. A particularly bad latency event, known as a *latency outlier*, may be caused by previous events rather than the event itself. For example, the event at the tail of a queue may have high latency but is caused by the previous queued events, not its own properties. This case can be identified from the traced events.

2.5.15 Baseline Statistics

Comparing current performance metrics with past values is often enlightening. Changes in load or resource usage can be identified, and problems traced back to when they first began. Some observability tools (those based on kernel counters) can show the summary-since-boot, for comparison with current activity. This is coarse, but better than nothing. Another approach is the collection of *baseline statistics*.

This can involve executing a wide range of system observability tools and logging the output for future reference. Unlike the summary-since-boot, which can hide variation, the baseline can include per-second statistics so that variation can be seen.

A baseline may be collected before and after system or application changes, so that performance changes can be analyzed. It may also be collected irregularly and included with site documentation, so that administrators have a reference for what is "normal." To perform this task at regular intervals each day is an activity that is served by *performance monitoring* (see Section 2.9, Monitoring).

2.5.16 Static Performance Tuning

Static performance tuning focuses on issues of the configured architecture. Other methodologies focus on the performance of the applied load: the *dynamic performance* [Elling 00]. Static performance analysis can be performed when the system is at rest and no load is applied.

For static performance analysis and tuning, step through all the components of the system and check the following:

- Does the component make sense?
- Does the configuration make sense for the intended workload?
- Was the component autoconfigured in the best state for the intended workload?
- Has the component experienced an error and is it in a degraded state?

Here are some examples of issues that may be found using static performance tuning:

- Network interface negotiation: selecting 100 Mbits/s instead of 1 Gbit/s
- Failed disk in a RAID pool
- Older version of the operating system, applications, or firmware used
- Mismatched file system record size compared to workload I/O size
- Server accidentally configured as a router
- Server configured to use resources, such as authentication, from a remote data center instead of locally

Fortunately, these types of issues are easy to check for. The hard part is remembering to do it!

2.5.17 Cache Tuning

Applications and operating systems may employ multiple caches for improving I/O performance, from the application down to the disks. See Section 3.2.11, Caching, in Chapter 3, Operating Systems, for a full list. Here is a general strategy for tuning each cache level:

1. Aim to cache as high in the stack as possible, closer to where the work is performed, reducing the operational overhead of cache hits.

2. Check that the cache is enabled and working.

3. Check the cache hit/miss ratios and miss rate.

4. If the cache size is dynamic, check its current size.

5. Tune the cache for the workload. This task depends on available cache tunable parameters.

6. Tune the workload for the cache. Doing this includes reducing unnecessary consumers of the cache, which frees up more space for the target workload.

Look out for double caching—for example, two different caches that consume main memory and cache the same data twice.

Also consider the overall performance gain of each level of cache tuning. Tuning the CPU Level 1 cache may save nanoseconds, as cache misses may then be served by Level 2. But improving CPU Level 3 cache may avoid much slower DRAM accesses and result in a greater overall performance gain. (These CPU caches are described in Chapter 6, CPUs.)

2.5.18 Micro-Benchmarking

Micro-benchmarking tests the performance of simple and artificial workloads. It may be performed to support the scientific method, putting hypotheses and predictions to the test, or it may be part of a capacity planning exercise.

This differs from *industry benchmarking*, which typically aims to test a real-world and natural workload. Such benchmarking is performed by running workload simulations and can become complex to conduct and understand.

Micro-benchmarking is less complicated to conduct and understand, as fewer factors are in play. It can be performed by a *micro-benchmark tool* that applies the workload and measures the performance. Or a *load generator* tool can be used that just applies the workload, leaving measurements of performance to the standard system tools. Either approach is fine, but it can be safest to use a micro-benchmark tool *and* to double-check performance using standard system tools.

Some example targets of micro-benchmarks, including a second dimension for the tests, are

- **Syscall time:** for `fork()`, `exec()`, `open()`, `read()`, `close()`
- **File system reads:** from a cached file, varying the read size from 1 byte to 1 Mbyte
- **Network throughput:** transferring data between TCP endpoints, for varying socket buffer sizes

Micro-benchmarking typically conducts the target operation as quickly as possible and measures the time for a large number of these operations to complete. The average time can then be calculated (average time = runtime/operation count).

Later chapters include specific micro-benchmarking methodologies, listing the targets and attributes to test. The topic of benchmarking is covered in more detail in Chapter 12, Benchmarking.

2.6 Modeling

Analytical modeling of a system can be used for various purposes, in particular *scalability analysis*: studying how performance scales as load or resources scale. Resources may be hardware, such as CPU cores, or software, such as processes or threads.

Analytical modeling can be considered as the third type of performance evaluation activity, along with observability of a production system ("measurement") and experimental testing ("simulation") [Jain 91]. Performance is best understood when at least two of these activities are performed: analytical modeling and simulation, or simulation and measurement.

If the analysis is for an existing system, you can begin with measurement: characterizing the load and resulting performance. Experimental analysis, by testing a workload simulation, can be used if the system does not yet have production load, or to test workloads beyond what is seen in production. Analytical modeling can be used to predict performance and can be based on the results of measurement or simulation.

Scalability analysis may reveal that performance stops scaling linearly at a particular point, called the *knee point*, due to a resource constraint. Finding whether these points exist, and where, can direct an investigation to performance issues that inhibit scalability, so that they can be fixed before they are encountered in production.

See Section 2.5.10, Workload Characterization, and Section 2.5.18, Micro-Benchmarking, for more on those steps.

2.6.1 Enterprise versus Cloud

While modeling allows us to simulate large-scale enterprise systems without the expense of owning one, the performance of large-scale environments is often complex and difficult to model accurately.

With cloud computing, environments of any scale can be rented for short durations—the length of a benchmark test. Instead of creating a mathematical model from which to predict performance, the workload can be characterized, simulated, and then tested on clouds of different scales. Some of the findings, such as knee points, may be the same but will now be based on measured data rather than theoretical models, and by testing a real environment you may discover limiters that were not included in your model.

2.6.2 Visual Identification

When enough results can be collected experimentally, plotting them as delivered performance versus a scaling parameter may reveal a pattern.

Figure 2.15 shows throughput of an application as the number of threads is scaled. There appears to be a knee point around eight threads, where the slope changes. This can now be investigated, such as by looking at the application and system configuration for any setting around the value of eight.

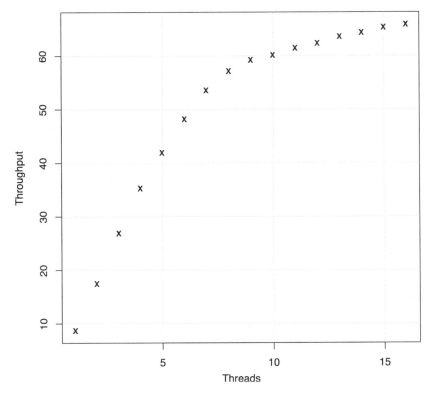

Figure 2.15 Scalability test results

In this case, the system was an eight-core system, each core having two hardware threads. To further confirm that this is related to the CPU core count, the CPU effects at fewer than and more than eight threads can be investigated and compared (e.g., CPIs; see Chapter 6, CPUs). Or, this may be investigated experimentally by repeating the scaling test on a system with a different core count and confirming that the knee point moves as expected.

There are a number of scalability profiles to look for which may be identified visually, without using a formal model. These are shown in Figure 2.16.

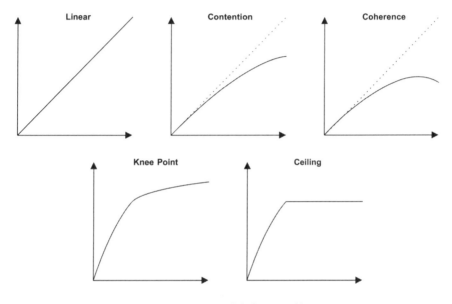

Figure 2.16 Scalability profiles

For each of these, the x axis is the scalability dimension, and the y axis is the resulting performance (throughput, transactions per second, etc.). The patterns are

- **Linear scalability:** Performance increases proportionally as the resource is scaled. This may not continue forever and may instead be the early stages of another scalability pattern.
- **Contention:** Some components of the architecture are shared and can be used only serially, and contention for these shared resources begins to reduce the effectiveness of scaling.
- **Coherence:** The tax to maintain data coherency including propagation of changes begins to outweigh the benefits of scaling.

- **Knee point:** A factor is encountered at a scalability point that changes the scalability profile.
- **Scalability ceiling:** A hard limit is reached. This may be a device bottleneck, such as a bus or interconnect reaching maximum throughput, or a software-imposed limit (system resource control).

While visual identification can be easy and effective, you can learn more about system scalability by using a mathematical model. The model may deviate from the data in an unexpected way, which can be useful to investigate: either there is a problem with the model, and hence with your understanding of the system, or the problem is in the real scalability of the system. The next sections introduce Amdahl's Law of Scalability, the Universal Scalability Law, and queueing theory.

2.6.3 Amdahl's Law of Scalability

Named after computer architect Gene Amdahl [Amdahl 67], this law models system scalability, accounting for serial components of workloads that do not scale in parallel. It can be used to study the scaling of CPUs, threads, workloads, and more.

Amdahl's Law of Scalability was pictured in the earlier scalability profiles as contention, which describes contention for the serial resource or workload component. It can be defined as [Gunther 97]

$$C(N) = N/1 + \alpha(N - 1)$$

The relative capacity is $C(N)$, and N is the scaling dimension, such as the CPU count or user load. The α parameter (where $0 <= \alpha <= 1$) represents the degree of seriality and is how this deviates from linear scalability.

Amdahl's Law of Scalability can be applied by taking the following steps:

1. Collect data for a range of N, either by observation of an existing system or experimentally using micro-benchmarking or load generators.
2. Perform regression analysis to determine the Amdahl parameter (α); this may be done using statistical software, such as gnuplot or R.
3. Present the results for analysis. The collected data points can be plotted along with the model function to predict scaling and reveal differences between the data and the model. This may also be done using gnuplot or R.

The following is example gnuplot code for Amdahl's Law of Scalability regression analysis, to provide a sense of how this step can be performed:

```
inputN = 10                    # rows to include as model input
alpha = 0.1                    # starting point (seed)
amdahl(N) = N1 * N/(1 + alpha * (N - 1))
# regression analysis (non-linear least squares fitting)
fit amdahl(x) filename every ::1::inputN using 1:2 via alpha
```

A similar amount of code is required to process this in R, involving the `nls()` function for nonlinear least squares fitting to calculate the coefficients, which are then used during plotting. See the Performance Scalability Models toolkit in the references at the end of the chapter for the full code in both gnuplot and R [2].

An example Amdahl's Law of Scalability function is shown in the next section.

2.6.4 Universal Scalability Law

The Universal Scalability Law (USL), previously called *super-serial model* [Gunther 97], was developed by Dr. Neil Gunther to include a parameter for coherency delay. This was pictured earlier as the coherence scalability profile, which includes the effects of contention.

USL can be defined as

$$C(N) = N/1 + \alpha(N - 1) + \beta N(N - 1)$$

$C(N)$, N, and α are as with Amdahl's Law of Scalability. β is the coherence parameter. When $\beta == 0$, this becomes Amdahl's Law of Scalability.

Examples of both USL and Amdahl's Law of Scalability analysis are graphed in Figure 2.17.

The input dataset has a high degree of variance, making it difficult to visually determine the scalability profile. The first ten data points, drawn as circles, were provided to the models. An additional ten data points are also plotted, drawn as crosses, which check the model prediction against reality.

For more on USL analysis, see [Gunther 97] and [Gunther 07].

2.6.5 Queueing Theory

Queueing theory is the mathematical study of systems with queues, providing ways to analyze their queue length, wait time (latency), and utilization (time-based). Many components in computing, both software and hardware, can be modeled as *queueing systems*. The modeling of multiple queueing systems is called *queueing networks*.

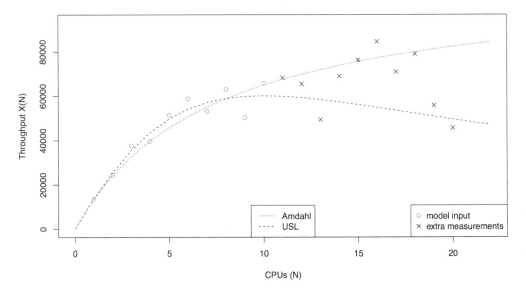

Figure 2.17 Scalability models

This section summarizes the role of queueing theory and provides an example, to help you understand its role. It is a large field of study that is covered in detail in other texts ([Jain 91], [Gunther 97]), should the need arise.

Queueing theory builds upon various areas of mathematics and statistics, including probability distributions, stochastic processes, Erlang's C formula (Agner Krarup Erlang invented queueing theory), and Little's Law. Little's Law can be expressed as

$$L = \lambda W$$

which determines the average number of requests in a system, L, as the average arrival rate, λ, multiplied by average service time, W.

Queueing systems can be used to answer a variety of questions, including the following:

- What will the mean response time be if the load doubles?
- What will be the effect on mean response time after adding an additional processor?
- Can the system provide a 90th percentile response time of under 100 ms when the load doubles?

Apart from response time, other factors, including utilization, queue lengths, and number of resident jobs, can be studied.

A simple queueing system model is shown in Figure 2.18.

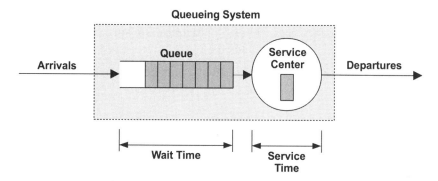

Figure 2.18 Queueing model

This has a single service center that processes jobs from the queue. Queueing systems can have multiple service centers that process work in parallel. In queueing theory, the service centers are often called *servers*.

Queueing systems can be categorized by three factors:

- **Arrival process:** This describes the inter-arrival time for requests to the queueing system, which may be random, fixed-time, or a process such as Poisson (which uses an exponential distribution for arrival time).

- **Service time distribution:** This describes the service times for the service center. They may be fixed (deterministic), exponential, or of another distribution type.

- **Number of service centers:** one or many.

These factors can be written in Kendall's notation.

Kendall's Notation

This notation assigns codes for each attribute. It has the form

A/S/m

These are the arrival process (*A*), service time distribution (*S*), and number of service centers (*m*). There is also an extended form of Kendall's notation that includes more factors: number of buffers in the system, population size, and service discipline.

Examples of commonly studied queueing systems are

- **M/M/1:** Markovian arrivals (exponentially distributed arrival times), Markovian service times (exponential distribution), one service center
- **M/M/c:** same as M/M/1, but multiserver
- **M/G/1:** Markovian arrivals, general distribution of service times (any), one service center
- **M/D/1:** Markovian arrivals, deterministic service times (fixed), one service center

M/G/1 is commonly applied to study the performance of rotational hard disks.

M/D/1 and 60% Utilization

As a simple example of queueing theory, consider a disk that responds to a workload deterministically (this is a simplification). The model is M/D/1.

The question posed is: How does the disk's response time vary as its utilization increases?

Queueing theory allows the response time for M/D/1 to be calculated:

$$r = s(2 - \rho)/2(1 - \rho)$$

where the response time, r, is defined in terms of the service time, s, and the utilization, ρ.

For a service time of 1 ms, and utilizations from 0 to 100%, this relationship has been graphed in Figure 2.19.

Beyond 60% utilization, the average response time doubles. By 80%, it has tripled. As disk I/O latency is often the bounding resource for an application, increasing the average latency by double or higher can have a significant negative effect on application performance. This is why disk utilization can become a problem well before it reaches 100%, as it is a queueing system where requests (typically) cannot be interrupted and must wait their turn. This is different from CPUs, for example, where higher-priority work can preempt.

This graph can visually answer an earlier question—What will the mean response time be if the load doubles?—when utilization is relative to load.

This model is simple, and in some ways it shows the best case. Variations in service time can drive the mean response time higher (e.g., using M/G/1 or M/M/1). There is also a distribution of response times, not pictured in Figure 2.19, such that the 90th and 99th percentiles degrade much faster beyond 60% utilization.

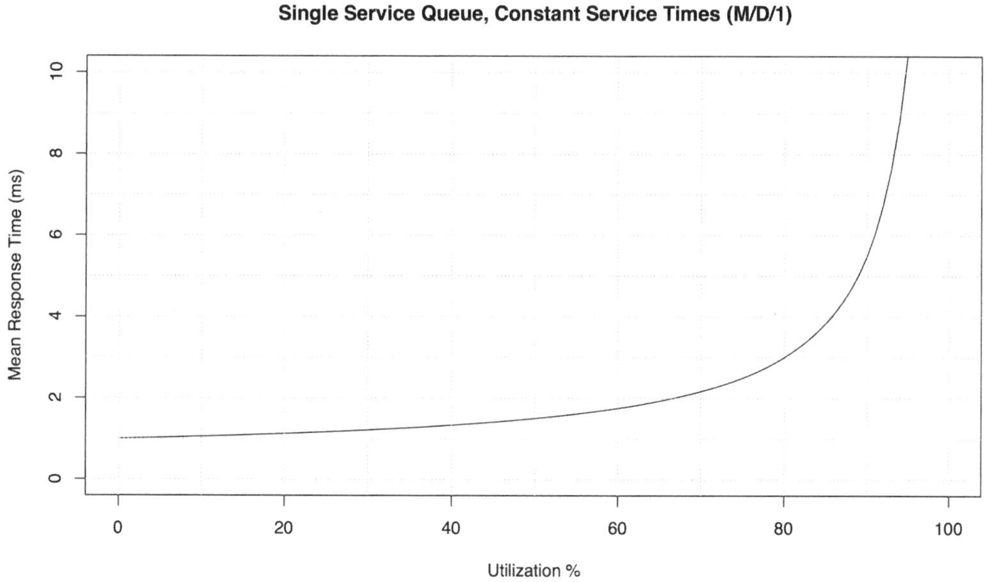

Single Service Queue, Constant Service Times (M/D/1)

Figure 2.19 M/D/1 mean response time versus utilization

As with the earlier gnuplot example for Amdahl's Law of Scalability, it may be illustrative to show some actual code, for a sense of what may be involved. This time the R statistics software was used [3]:

```
svc_ms <- 1                 # average disk I/O service time, ms
util_min <- 0               # range to plot
util_max <- 100             # "
ms_min <- 0                 # "
ms_max <- 10                # "
# Plot mean response time vs utilization (M/D/1)
plot(x <- c(util_min:util_max), svc_ms * (2 - x/100) / (2 * (1 - x/100)),
    type="l", lty=1, lwd=1,
    xlim=c(util_min, util_max), ylim=c(ms_min, ms_max),
    xlab="Utilization %", ylab="Mean Response Time (ms)")
```

The earlier M/D/1 equation has been passed to the `plot()` function. Much of this code specifies limits to the graph, line properties, and axis labels.

2.7 Capacity Planning

Capacity planning examines how well the system will handle load, and how it will scale as load scales. It can be performed in a number of ways, including studying resource limits and factor analysis, which are described here, and modeling, as introduced previously. This section also includes solutions for scaling, including load balancers and sharding. For more on this topic, see *The Art of Capacity Planning* [Allspaw 08].

For capacity planning of a particular application, it helps to have a quantified performance objective to plan for. Determining this is discussed early on in Chapter 5, Applications.

2.7.1 Resource Limits

This approach is a search for the resource that will become the bottleneck under load. The steps are:

1. Measure the rate of server requests, and monitor this rate over time.
2. Measure hardware and software resource usage. Monitor this rate over time.
3. Express server requests in terms of resources used.
4. Extrapolate server requests to known (or experimentally determined) limits for each resource.

Begin by identifying the role of the server and the type of requests it serves. For example, a web server serves HTTP requests, a Network File System (NFS) server serves NFS protocol requests (operations), and a database server serves query requests (or command requests, for which queries are a subset).

The next step is to determine the system resource consumption per request. For an existing system, the current rate of requests along with resource utilization can be measured. Extrapolation can then be used to see which resource will hit 100% utilization first, and what the rate of requests will be.

For a future system, micro-benchmarking or load generation tools can be used to simulate the intended requests in a test environment, while measuring resource utilization. Given sufficient client load, you may be able to find the limit experimentally.

The resources to monitor include

- **Hardware:** CPU utilization, memory usage, disk IOPS, disk throughput, disk capacity (volume used), network throughput
- **Software:** virtual memory usage, processes/tasks/threads, file descriptors

Let's say you're looking at an existing system currently performing 1,000 requests/s. The busiest resources are the 16 CPUs, which are averaging 40% utilization; you predict that they will become the bottleneck for this workload once they become 100% utilized. The question becomes: What will the requests-per-second rate be at that point?

CPU% per request = total CPU%/requests = 16 x 40%/1,000 = 0.64% CPU per request

max requests/s = 100% x 16 CPUs/CPU% per request = 1,600 / 0.64 = 2,500 requests/s

The prediction is 2,500 requests/s, at which point the CPUs will be 100% busy. This is a rough best-case estimate of capacity, as some other limiting factor may be encountered before the requests reach that rate.

This exercise used only one data point: application throughput (requests per second) of 1,000 versus device utilization of 40%. If monitoring over time is enabled, multiple data points at different throughput and utilization rates can be included, to improve the accuracy of the estimation. Figure 2.20 illustrates a visual method for processing these and extrapolating the maximum application throughput.

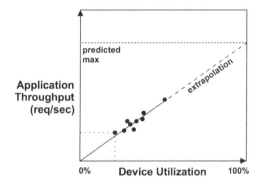

Figure 2.20 Resource limit analysis

Is 2,500 requests/s enough? Answering this question requires understanding what the peak workload will be, which shows up in daily access patterns. For an existing system that you have monitored over time, you may already have an idea of what the peak will look like.

Consider a web server that is processing 100,000 website hits per day. This may sound like many, but it is averaging only about 1 request/s—not much. However, it may be that most of the 100,000 website hits occur in the seconds after new content is posted, so the peak is significant.

2.7.2 Factor Analysis

When purchasing and deploying new systems, there are often many factors that can be changed to achieve the desired performance. These may include varying the number of disks and CPUs, the amount of RAM, the use of flash devices, RAID configurations, file system settings, and so forth. The task is usually to achieve the performance required for the minimum cost.

Testing all combinations would determine which has the best price/performance ratio; however, this can quickly get out of hand: eight binary factors would require 256 tests.

A solution is to test a limited set of combinations. Here is an approach based on knowing the maximum system configuration:

1. Test performance with all factors configured to maximum.

2. Change factors one by one, testing performance (it should drop for each).

3. Attribute a percentage performance drop to each factor, based on measurements, along with the cost savings.

4. Starting with maximum performance (and cost), choose factors to save cost, while maintaining the required requests per second based on their combined performance drop.

5. Retest the calculated configuration for confirmation of delivered performance.

For an eight-factor system, this approach may require only ten tests.

As an example, consider capacity planning for a new storage system, with a requirement of 1 Gbyte/s read throughput and a 200 Gbyte working set size. The maximum configuration achieves 2 Gbytes/s and includes four processors, 256 Gbytes of DRAM, 2 x dual-port 10 GbE network cards, jumbo frames, and no compression or encryption enabled (which is costly to activate). Switching to two processors reduces performance by 30%, one network card by 25%, non-jumbo by 35%, encryption by 10%, compression by 40%, and less DRAM by 90% as the workload is no longer expected to fully cache. Given these performance drops and their known savings, the best price/performance system that meets the requirements can now be calculated; it might be a two-processor system with one network card, which meets the throughput needed: $2 \times (1 - 0.30) \times (1 - 0.25) = 1.04$ Gbytes/s estimated. It would then be wise to test this configuration, in case these components perform differently from their expected performance when used together.

2.7.3 Scaling Solutions

Meeting higher performance demands has often meant larger systems, a strategy called *vertical scaling*. Spreading load across numerous systems, usually fronted by systems called *load balancers* that make them all appear as one, is called *horizontal scaling*.

Cloud computing takes horizontal scaling further, by building upon smaller virtualized systems rather than entire systems. This provides finer granularity when purchasing compute to process the required load and allows scaling in small, efficient increments. Since no initial large purchase is required, as with enterprise mainframes (including a support contract commitment), there is less need for rigorous capacity planning in the early stages of a project.

A common scaling strategy for databases on the cloud is *sharding*, where data is split into logical components, each managed by its own database (or redundant group of databases). For example, a customer database may be split into parts by dividing the customer names into alphabetical ranges.

Scalability design depends very much on the workloads you need to handle and the applications you wish to use. For more on this topic, see *Scalable Internet Architectures* [Schlossnagle 06].

2.8 Statistics

It's important to have a good understanding of how to use statistics and what their limitations are. This section discusses quantifying performance issues using statistics (metrics) and statistical types including averages, standard deviations, and percentiles.

2.8.1 Quantifying Performance

Quantifying issues and the potential performance improvement for fixing them allows them to be compared and prioritized. This task may be performed using observation or experiments.

Observation-Based

To quantify performance issues using observation:

1. Choose a reliable metric.
2. Estimate the performance gain from resolving the issue.

For example:

- Observed: Application request takes 10 ms.
- Observed: Of that, 9 ms is disk I/O.
- Suggestion: Configure the application to cache I/O in memory, with expected DRAM latency around ~10 µs.
- Estimated gain: 10 ms → 1.01 ms (10 ms - 9 ms + 10 µs) =~ 9x gain.

As introduced in Section 2.3, Concepts, latency (time) is well suited for this, as it can be directly compared between components, which makes calculations like this possible.

When using latency, ensure that it is measured as a synchronous component of the application request. Some events occur asynchronously, such as background disk I/O (write flush to disk), and do not directly affect application performance.

Experimentation-Based

To quantify performance issues experimentally:

1. Apply the fix.
2. Quantify before versus after using a reliable metric.

For example:

- Observed: Application transaction latency averages 10 ms.
- Experiment: Increase the application thread count to allow more concurrency instead of queueing.
- Observed: Application transaction latency averages 2 ms.
- Gain: 10 ms → 2 ms = 5x.

This approach may not be appropriate if the fix is expensive to attempt in the production environment!

2.8.2 Averages

An average represents a dataset by a single value: an index of central tendency. The most common type of average used is an *arithmetic mean* (or *mean* for short), which is a sum of values divided by the count of values. Other types include the geometric mean and harmonic mean.

Geometric Mean

The *geometric mean* is the *n*th root (where *n* is the count of values) of multiplied values. This is described in [Jain 91], which includes an example of using it for network performance analysis: if the performance improvement of each layer of the kernel network stack is measured individually, what is the average performance improvement? Since the layers work together on the same packet, performance improvements have a "multiplicative" effect, which can be best summarized by the geometric mean.

Harmonic Mean

The *harmonic mean* is the count of values divided by the sum of their reciprocals. It can be more appropriate for taking the average of rates, for example, calculating the average transfer rate for 800 Mbytes of data, when the first 100 Mbytes will be sent at 50 Mbytes/s and the remaining 700 Mbytes at a throttled rate of 10 Mbytes/s. The answer, using the harmonic mean, is 800/(100/50 + 700/10) = 11.1 Mbytes/s.

Averages over Time

With performance, many metrics we study are averages over time. A CPU is never "at 50% utilization"; it has been utilized during 50% of some interval, which could be a second, minute, or hour. It is important to check for intervals whenever considering averages.

For example, I had an issue where a customer had performance problems caused by CPU saturation (scheduler latency) even though their monitoring tools showed CPU utilization was never higher than 80%. The monitoring tool was reporting *5-minute averages*, which masked periods in which CPU utilization hit 100% for seconds at a time.

Decayed Average

A *decayed average* is sometimes used in systems performance. Examples include the system "load averages" reported by uptime(1) and per-process CPU utilization on Solaris-based systems.

A decayed average is still measured over a time interval, but recent time is weighted more heavily than time further past. This reduces (dampens) short-term fluctuations in the average.

See Load Averages in Section 6.6, Analysis, of Chapter 6, CPUs, for more on this.

2.8.3 Standard Deviations, Percentiles, Median

Standard deviations and percentiles (e.g., 99th percentile) are statistical techniques to provide information on the *distribution* of data. The standard deviation is a measure of *variance*, with larger values indicating greater variance from the average (mean). The 99th percentile shows the point in the distribution that includes 99% of the values. Figure 2.21 pictures these for a *normal distribution*, along with the minimum and maximum.

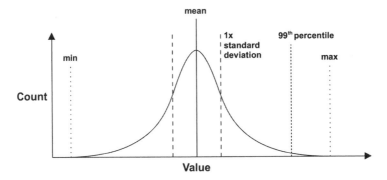

Figure 2.21 Statistical values

Percentiles such as 99th, 90th, 95th, and 99.9th are used in performance monitoring of request latency to quantify the slowest in the population. These may also be specified in service-level agreements (SLAs) as a way to measure that performance is acceptable for most users.

The 50th percentile, called the *median*, can be examined to show where the bulk of the data is.

2.8.4 Coefficient of Variation

Since standard deviation is relative to the mean, variance can be understood only when considering both standard deviation and mean. A standard deviation of 50 alone tells us little. That plus a mean of 200 tells us a lot.

There is a way to express variation as a single metric: the ratio of the standard deviation to the mean, which is called the *coefficient of variation* (CoV or CV). For this example, the CV is 25%. Lower CVs mean less variance.

2.8.5 Multimodal Distributions

There is a problem with means, standard deviations, and percentiles, which may be obvious from the previous chart: they are intended for *normal*-like or unimodal distributions. System performance is often *bimodal*, returning low latencies for a fast code path and high latencies for a slow one, or low latencies for cache hits and high latencies for cache misses. There may also be more than two modes.

Figure 2.22 shows the distribution of disk I/O latency for a mixed workload of reads and writes, which includes random and sequential I/O.

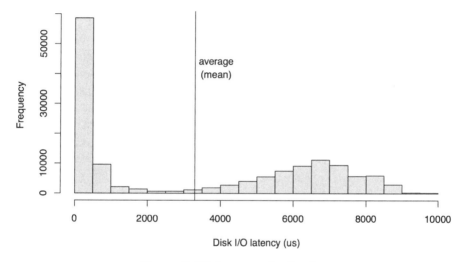

Figure 2.22 Latency distribution

This is presented as a histogram, which shows two modes. The mode on the left shows latencies of less than 1 ms, which is for on-disk cache hits. The right, with a peak around 7 ms, is for on-disk cache misses: random reads. The average (mean) I/O latency is 3.3 ms, which is plotted as a vertical line. This average is not the index of central tendency (as described earlier); in fact, it is almost the opposite. As a metric, the average for this distribution is seriously misleading.

> Then there was the man who drowned crossing a
> stream with an average depth of six inches.
>
> W. I. E. Gates

Every time you see an average used as a performance metric, especially an average latency, ask: What is the distribution? Section 2.10, Visualizations, provides another example and shows how effective different visualizations and metrics are at showing this distribution.

2.8.6 Outliers

Another statistical problem is the presence of *outliers*: a very small number of extremely high or low values that don't appear to fit the expected distribution (single- or multimode).

Disk I/O latency outliers are an example—very occasional disk I/O that can take over 1,000 ms, when the majority of disk I/O is between 0 and 10 ms. Latency outliers like these can cause serious performance problems, but their presence can be difficult to identify from most metric types, other than as a maximum.

For a normal distribution, the presence of outliers is likely to shift the mean by a little, but not the median (which may be useful to consider). The standard deviation and 99th percentile have a better chance of identifying outliers, but this is still dependent on their frequency.

To better understand multimodal distributions, outliers, and other complex yet common behaviors, inspect the full distribution, such as by using a histogram. See Section 2.10, Visualizations, for more ways to do this.

2.9 Monitoring

System performance monitoring records performance statistics over time (a *time series*), so that the past can be compared to the present and time-based usage patterns can be identified. This is useful for capacity planning, quantifying growth, and showing peak usage. Historic values can also provide context for understanding the current value of performance metrics, by showing what the "normal" range and average have been in the past.

2.9.1 Time-Based Patterns

Examples of time-based patterns are shown in Figures 2.23, 2.24, and 2.25, which plot file system reads from a cloud computing server over different time intervals.

These graphs show a daily pattern that begins to ramp up around 8:00 a.m., dips a little in the afternoon, then decays during the night. The longer-scale charts show that activity is lower on the weekend days. A couple of short spikes are also visible in the 30-day chart.

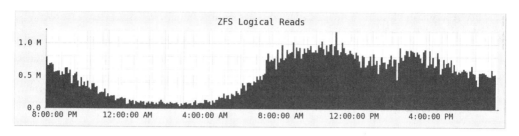

Figure 2.23 Monitoring activity: one day

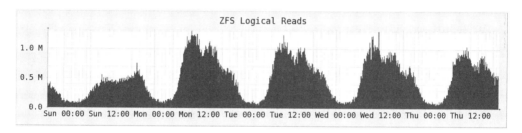

Figure 2.24 Monitoring activity: five days

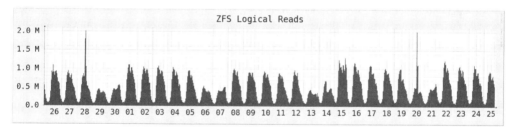

Figure 2.25 Monitoring activity: 30 days

Various cycles of behavior including those shown in the figures can commonly be seen in historic data, including

- **Hourly:** Activity may occur every hour from the application environment, such as monitoring and reporting tasks. It's also common for these to execute with a 5- or 10-minute cycle.

- **Daily:** There may be a daily pattern of usage that coincides with work hours (9:00 a.m. to 5:00 p.m.), which may be stretched if the server is for multiple time zones. For Internet servers, the pattern may follow when worldwide users are active. Other daily activity may include nightly log rotation and backups.

- **Weekly:** As well as a daily pattern, there may be a weekly pattern present based on workdays and weekends.
- **Quarterly:** Financial reports are done on a quarterly schedule.

Irregular increases in load may be present from other activities, such as releasing new content on a website.

2.9.2 Monitoring Products

There are many third-party products for system performance monitoring. Typical features include archiving data and presenting it as browser-based interactive graphs, and providing configurable alerts.

Some of these operate by running *agents* on the system to gather their statistics. These agents either execute operating system observability tools (such as `sar(1)`) and process the output (which is considered inefficient and can even contribute to performance issues!), or link directly to operating system libraries and interfaces to read statistics directly.

There are also monitoring solutions that use SNMP. They usually avoid the need to run custom agents on the system, provided it has SNMP support.

As systems become more distributed and the usage of cloud computing grows, you will more often need to monitor numerous systems, perhaps hundreds or thousands. This is where a centralized monitoring product can be especially useful, allowing an entire environment to be monitored from one interface.

Some companies prefer to develop their own monitoring solutions, to better suit their custom environment and needs.

2.9.3 Summary-since-Boot

If monitoring has not been performed, check whether at least *summary-since-boot* values are available from the operating system, which can be used to compare with the current values.

2.10 Visualizations

Visualizations allow more data to be examined than can be seen in a text display. They also enable pattern recognition and pattern matching. This can be an effective way to identify correlations between different metric sources, which may be difficult to accomplish programmatically, but easy to do visually.

2.10.1 Line Chart

A line chart (also called *line graph*) is a well-known, basic visualization. It is commonly used for examining performance metrics over time, showing the passage of time on the *x* axis.

Figure 2.26 is an example, showing the average (mean) disk I/O latency for a 20 s period. This was measured on a production cloud server running a MySQL database, where disk I/O latency was suspected to be causing slow queries.

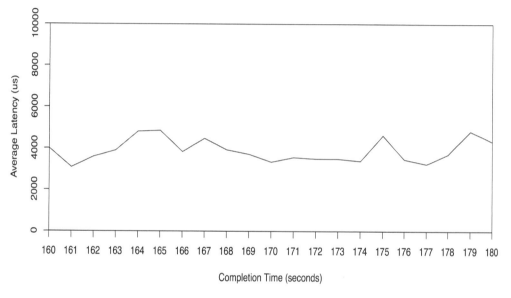

Figure 2.26 Line chart of average latency

This line chart shows fairly consistent average read latency of around 4 ms, which is higher than expected for these disks.

Multiple lines can be plotted, showing related data on the same set of axes. With this example, a separate line may be plotted for each disk, showing whether they exhibit similar performance.

Statistical values can also be plotted, providing more information on the distribution of data. Figure 2.27 shows the same range of disk I/O events, with lines added for the per-second median, standard deviation, and percentiles. Note that the *y* axis now has a much greater range than the previous line chart (8x).

This shows why the average is higher than expected: the distribution includes higher-latency I/O. Specifically, 1% of the I/O is over 20 ms, as shown by the 99th percentile. The median also shows where I/O latency was expected, around 1 ms.

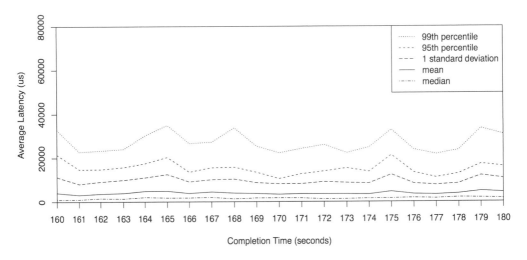

Figure 2.27 Median, mean, standard deviation, percentiles

2.10.2 Scatter Plots

Figure 2.28 shows disk I/O events for the same stretch of time as a scatter plot, which enables all data to be seen. Each disk I/O is drawn as a point, with its completion time on the x axis and latency on the y axis.

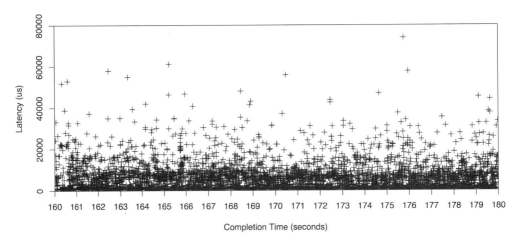

Figure 2.28 Scatter plot

Now the source of the higher-than-expected average latency can be understood fully: there are many disk I/O with latencies of 10 ms, 20 ms, even over 50 ms. The scatter plot has shown all the data, revealing the presence of these outliers.

Many of the I/O were sub-millisecond, shown close to the x axis. This is where the resolution of scatter plots begins to become a problem, as the points overlap and become difficult to distinguish. This gets worse with more data: imagine plotting events from an entire cloud, involving millions of data points, on one scatter plot. Another problem is the volume of data that must be collected and processed: x and y coordinates for every I/O.

2.10.3 Heat Maps

Heat maps can solve the scatter plot scalability problem by quantizing x and y ranges into groups called *buckets*. These are displayed as large pixels, colored based on the number of events in that x and y range. This quantizing also solves the scatter plot visual density limit, allowing heat maps to show data from a single system or thousands of systems in the same way. They can be used for the analysis of latency, utilization, and other metrics [Gregg 10a].

The same dataset as plotted earlier is shown in Figure 2.29 as a heat map.

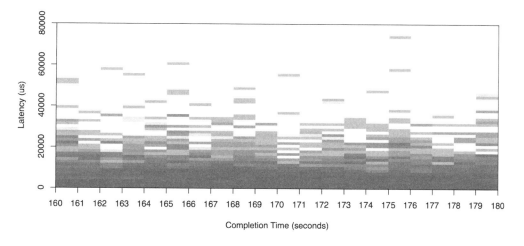

Figure 2.29 Heat map

High-latency outliers can be identified as blocks that are high in the heat map, usually of light colors as they span few I/O (often a single I/O). Patterns in the bulk of the data begin to emerge, which may be impossible to see with a scatter plot.

The full range of seconds for this disk I/O trace (not shown earlier) is shown in the Figure 2.30 heat map.

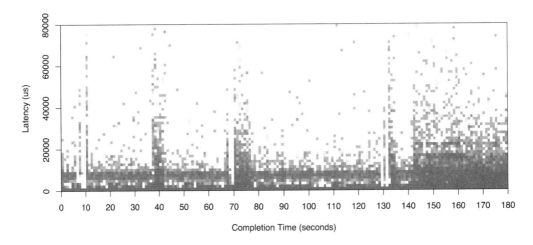

Figure 2.30 Heat map: full range

Despite spanning nine times the range, the visualization is still very readable. A bimodal distribution can be seen for much of the range, with some I/O returning with near-zero latency (likely a disk cache hit), and others with a little less than 1 ms (likely a disk cache miss).

A problem with heat maps is that they are not yet as well known as line charts, so users must gain some understanding to use them effectively.

There are various other examples of heat maps later in this book.

2.10.4 Surface Plot

This is a representation of three dimensions, rendered as a three-dimensional surface. It works best when the third-dimension value does not frequently change dramatically from one point to the next, producing a surface resembling rolling hills. A surface plot is often rendered as a *wireframe model*.

Figure 2.31 shows a wireframe surface plot of per-CPU utilization. It contains 60 s of per-second values from many servers (this is cropped from an image that spanned a data center of over 300 physical servers and 5,312 CPUs) [4].

Each server is represented by plotting its 16 CPUs as rows on the surface, the 60 per-second utilization measurements as columns, and then setting the height of the surface to the utilization value. Color is also set to reflect the utilization value. Both hue and saturation could be used, if desired, to add fourth and fifth dimensions of

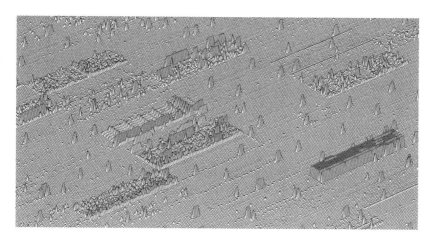

Figure 2.31 Wireframe surface plot: data center CPU utilization

data to the visualization. (If the resolution is sufficient, a pattern could be used to indicate a sixth dimension.)

These 16 x 60 server rectangles are then mapped across the surface as a checkerboard. Even without markings, some server rectangles can be clearly seen in the image. One that appears as an elevated plateau on the right shows that its CPUs are almost always at 100%.

The use of grid lines highlights subtle changes in elevation. Some faint lines are visible, which indicate a single CPU constantly running at low utilization (a few percent).

2.10.5 Visualization Tools

Unix performance analysis has historically focused on the use of text-based tools, due in part to limited graphical support. Such tools can be executed quickly over a login session and report data in real time. Visualizations have been more time-consuming to access and often require a trace-and-report cycle. When working urgent performance issues, the speed at which you can access metrics can be critical.

Modern visualization tools provide real-time views of system performance, accessible from the browser and mobile devices. There are many products that do this, including many that can monitor your entire cloud, such as Joyent's Cloud Analytics, a DTrace-based cloud-wide analysis tool that produces real-time visualizations including latency heat maps.

2.11 Exercises

1. Answer the following questions about key performance terminology:
   - What are IOPS?
   - What is utilization and saturation?
   - What is latency?
   - What is micro-benchmarking?

2. Choose five methodologies to use for your (or a hypothetical) environment. Select the order in which they can be conducted, and explain the reason for choosing each.

3. Summarize the problems when using average latency as a sole performance metric. Can these problems be solved by including the 99th percentile?

2.12 References

[Amdahl 67]	Amdahl, G. "Validity of the Single Processor Approach to Achieving Large Scale Computing Capabilities." AFIPS, 1967.
[Jain 91]	Jain, R. *The Art of Computer System Performance Analysis: Techniques for Experimental Design, Measurement, Simulation and Modeling.* Wiley, 1991.
[Cockcroft 95]	Cockcroft, A. *Sun Performance and Tuning.* Prentice Hall, 1995.
[Gunther 97]	Gunther, N. *The Practical Performance Analyst.* McGraw-Hill, 1997.
[Wong 97]	Wong, B. *Configuration and Capacity Planning for Solaris Servers.* Prentice Hall, 1997.
[Elling 00]	Elling, R. *Static Performance Tuning.* Sun Blueprints, 2000.
[Millsap 03]	Millsap, C., and J. Holt. *Optimizing Oracle Performance.* O'Reilly, 2003.
[McDougall 06b]	McDougall, R., J. Mauro, and B. Gregg. *Solaris Performance and Tools: DTrace and MDB Techniques for Solaris 10 and OpenSolaris.* Prentice Hall, 2006.

[Schlossnagle 06]   Schlossnagle, T. *Scalable Internet Architectures*. Sams Publishing, 2006.

[Gunther 07]   Gunther, N. *Guerrilla Capacity Planning*. Springer, 2007.

[Allspaw 08]   Allspaw, J. *The Art of Capacity Planning*. O'Reilly, 2008.

[Gregg 10a]   Gregg, B. "Performance Visualizations." USENIX LISA invited talk, 2010.

[Gregg 13]   Gregg, B. "Thinking Methodically about Performance," *Communications of the ACM*, February 2013.

[1]   www.telegraph.co.uk/technology/news/8753784/The-300m-cable-that-will-save-traders-milliseconds.html

[2]   https://github.com/brendangregg/PerfModels

[3]   www.r-project.org

[4]   http://dtrace.org/blogs/brendan/2011/12/18/visualizing-device-utilization

3

Operating Systems

An understanding of the operating system and its kernel is essential for systems performance analysis. You will frequently need to develop and then test hypotheses about system behavior, such as how system calls are being performed, how CPUs are scheduling threads, how limited memory could be affecting performance, or how a file system processes I/O. These behaviors will require you to apply your knowledge of the operating system and the kernel.

This chapter provides an overview of operating systems and the kernel and is assumed knowledge for the rest of the book. If you missed operating systems class, you can treat this as a crash course. Keep an eye out for any gaps in your knowledge, as there will be an exam at the end (I'm kidding; it's just a quiz). For more on kernel internals, see the references at the end of this chapter and the Bibliography.

This chapter has two parts:

- **Background** introduces terminology and operating system fundamentals.
- **Kernels** summarizes Linux and Solaris-based kernels.

Areas related to performance, including CPU scheduling, memory, disks, file systems, networking, and many specific performance tools, are covered in more detail in the chapters that follow.

3.1 Terminology

For reference, here is the core operating system terminology used in this book:

- **Operating system:** This refers to the software and files that are installed on a system so that it can boot and execute programs. It includes the kernel, administration tools, and system libraries.
- **Kernel:** The kernel is the program that manages the system, including devices (hardware), memory, and CPU scheduling. It runs in a privileged CPU mode that allows direct access to hardware, called *kernel mode*.
- **Process:** an OS abstraction and environment for executing a program. The program normally runs in *user mode*, with access to kernel mode (e.g., for performing device I/O) via system calls or traps.
- **Thread:** an executable context that can be scheduled to run on a CPU. The kernel has multiple threads, and a process contains one or more.
- **Task:** a Linux runnable entity, which can refer to a process (with a single thread), a thread from a multithreaded process, or kernel threads.
- **Kernel-space:** the memory address space for the kernel.
- **User-space:** the memory address space for processes.
- **User-land:** user-level programs and libraries (/usr/bin, /usr/lib, . . .).
- **Context switch:** a kernel routine that switches a CPU to operate in a different address space (context).
- **System call (syscall):** a well-defined protocol for user programs to request the kernel to perform privileged operations, including device I/O.
- **Processor:** Not to be confused with *process*, a processor is a physical chip containing one or more CPUs.
- **Trap:** a signal sent to the kernel, requesting a system routine (privileged action). Trap types include system calls, processor exceptions, and interrupts.
- **Interrupt:** a signal sent by physical devices to the kernel, usually to request servicing of I/O. An interrupt is a type of trap.

The Glossary includes more terminology for reference if needed for this chapter, including *address space*, *buffer*, *CPU*, *file descriptor*, *POSIX*, and *registers*.

3.2 Background

The following sections describe operating system concepts and generic kernel internals. Specific kernel differences are covered after these sections.

3.2.1 Kernel

The kernel manages CPU scheduling, memory, file systems, network protocols, and system devices (disks, network interfaces, etc.). It provides access to devices and kernel services built upon them via system calls. It is pictured in Figure 3.1.

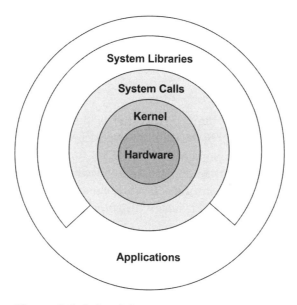

Figure 3.1 Role of the operating system kernel

Also shown are system libraries, which are often used to provide a richer and easier programming interface than the system calls alone. Applications include all running user-level software, including databases, web servers, administration tools, and operating system shells.

System libraries are pictured here as a broken ring, to show that applications can call system calls directly (if permitted by the operating system). Traditionally, this diagram is drawn with complete rings, which reflect decreasing levels of privilege starting with the kernel at the center (a model that originated in Multics [Graham 68], the predecessor of Unix).

Kernel Execution

The kernel is a large program, typically hundreds of thousands of lines of code. It primarily executes on demand, when a user-level program makes a system call, or a device sends an interrupt. Some kernel threads operate asynchronously for housekeeping, which may include the kernel clock routine and memory management tasks, but these try to be lightweight and consume very little CPU resources.

Workloads that perform frequent I/O, such as web servers, frequently execute in kernel context. Workloads that are compute-intensive are left alone as much as possible by the kernel, so they can run uninterrupted on-CPU. It may be tempting to think that the kernel cannot affect the performance of these workloads, but there are many cases where it does. The most obvious is CPU contention, when other threads are competing for CPU resources and the kernel scheduler needs to decide which will run and which will wait. The kernel also chooses which CPU a thread will run on and can choose CPUs with warmer hardware caches or better memory locality for the process, to significantly improve performance.

Clock

A core component of the original Unix kernel is the clock() routine, executed from a timer interrupt. It has historically been executed at 60, 100, or 1,000 times per second,[1] and each execution is called a *tick*. Its functions have included updating the system time, expiring timers and time slices for thread scheduling, maintaining CPU statistics, and executing *callouts* (scheduled kernel routines).

There have been performance issues with the clock, improved in later kernels, including

- **Tick latency:** For 100 Hz clocks, up to 10 ms of additional latency may be encountered for a timer as it waits to be processed on the next tick. This has been fixed using high-resolution real-time interrupts, so that execution occurs immediately without waiting.
- **Tick overhead:** Modern processors have dynamic power features, which can power down parts during idle periods. The clock routine interrupts this process, which for idle systems can consume power needlessly. Linux has implemented *dynamic ticks*, so that when the system is idle, the timer routine (clock) does not fire.

Modern kernels have moved much functionality out of the clock routine to on-demand interrupts, in an effort to create a *tickless kernel*. This includes Linux, where the clock routine—which is the *system timer interrupt*—performs little work

---

1. Other rates include 250 for Linux 2.6.13, 256 for Ultrix, and 1,024 for OSF/1 [RFC 1589].

other than updating the system clock and jiffies counter (*jiffies* is a Linux unit of time, similar to *ticks*).

Kernel Mode

The kernel is the only program running in a special CPU mode called *kernel mode*, allowing full access to devices and the execution of privileged instructions. The kernel arbitrates device access to support multitasking, preventing processes and users from accessing each other's data unless explicitly allowed.

User programs (processes) run in user mode, where they request privileged operations from the kernel via system calls, such as for I/O. To perform a system call, execution will *context-switch* from user to kernel mode, and then execute with the higher privilege level. This is shown in Figure 3.2.

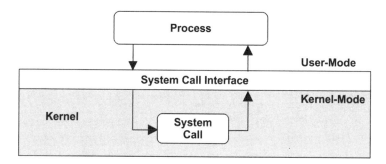

Figure 3.2 System call execution modes

Each mode has its own software execution context, including a stack and registers. The execution of privileged instructions in user mode causes *exceptions*, which are then properly handled by the kernel.

The context switch between these modes takes time (CPU cycles), which adds a small amount of overhead for each I/O. Some services, such as NFS, have been implemented as kernel-mode software (instead of a user-mode daemon), so that they can perform I/O from and to devices without needing to context-switch to user mode.

Context switches can also occur directly between different processes, such as for CPU scheduling.

3.2.2 Stacks

A stack contains the execution ancestry for a thread in terms of functions and registers. Stacks are used by CPUs for efficient processing of function execution in native software.

When a function is called, the current set of CPU registers (which store the state of the CPU) is saved to the stack, and a new stack frame is added to the top for the current execution of the thread. Functions end execution by calling a "return" CPU instruction, which removes the current stack and returns execution to the previous one, restoring its state.

Stack inspection is an invaluable tool for debugging and performance analysis. Stacks show the call path to current execution, which often answers *why* something is executing.

How to Read a Stack

The following example kernel stack (from Linux) shows the path taken for TCP transmission, as printed by a debugging tool:

```
kernel`tcp_sendmsg+0x1
kernel`inet_sendmsg+0x64
kernel`sock_aio_write+0x13a
kernel`do_sync_write+0xd2
kernel`security_file_permission+0x2c
kernel`rw_verify_area+0x61
kernel`vfs_write+0x16d
kernel`sys_write+0x4a
kernel`sys_rt_sigprocmask+0x84
kernel`system_call_fastpath+0x16
```

The top of the stack is usually shown as the first line. In this example it includes tcp_sendmsg—the name of the function currently executing. To the left and right of the function name are details typically included by debuggers: the kernel module location (`kernel) and the instruction offset (0x1, which refers to the address of the instruction within the function).

The function that called tcp_sendmsg() (its parent) can be seen below it: inet_sendmsg(). And its parent is below it: sock_aio_write(). By reading down the stack, the full ancestry can be seen: function, parent, grandparent, and so on. Or, by reading bottom-up, you can follow the path of execution to the current function: how we got here.

Since stacks expose the internal path taken through source code, there is typically no documentation for these functions other than the code itself. For this example stack, this is the Linux kernel source code. An exception to this is where functions are part of an API and have public documentation.

User and Kernel Stacks

While executing a system call, a process thread has two stacks: a user-level stack and a kernel-level stack. Their scope is pictured in Figure 3.3.

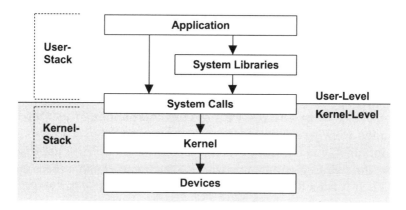

Figure 3.3 User and kernel stacks

The user-level stack of the blocked thread does not change for the duration of a system call, as the thread is using a separate kernel-level stack while executing in kernel context. (An exception to this may be signal handlers, which may borrow a user-level stack depending on their configuration.)

3.2.3 Interrupts and Interrupt Threads

Apart from responding to system calls, the kernel also responds to service requests from devices. These are called *interrupts*, as they interrupt current execution. These are pictured in Figure 3.4.

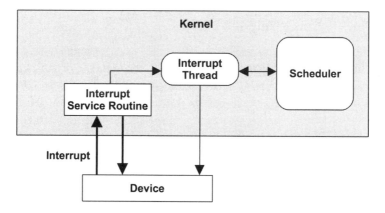

Figure 3.4 Interrupt processing

An *interrupt service routine* is registered to process the device interrupt. Such routines are designed to operate as quickly as possible, to reduce the effects of interrupting active threads. If an interrupt needs to perform more than a little work, especially if it may block on locks, it can be processed by an interrupt thread that can be scheduled by the kernel.

How this is implemented depends on the kernel version. On Linux, device drivers can be modeled as two halves, with the top half handling the interrupt quickly, and scheduling work to a bottom half to be processed later [Corbet 05]. Handling the interrupt quickly is important as the top half runs in *interrupt-disabled* mode to postpone the delivery of new interrupts, which can cause latency problems for other threads if it runs for too long. The bottom half can be either *tasklets* or *work queues*; the latter are threads that can be scheduled by the kernel and can sleep when necessary. Solaris-based systems promote interrupts to interrupt threads if more work needs to be performed [McDougall 06a].

The time from an interrupt arrival to when it is serviced is the *interrupt latency*, which is dependent on the implementation. This is a subject of study for real-time or low-latency systems.

3.2.4 Interrupt Priority Level

The interrupt priority level (IPL) represents the priority of the currently active interrupt service routine. It is read from the processor during the delivery of an interrupt signal, and the interrupt succeeds only if its level exceeds the currently executing interrupt (if any); otherwise the interrupt is queued for later delivery. This prevents higher-priority work from being interrupted by lower-priority work.

An example IPL range is shown in Figure 3.5, which for this kernel services IPLs 1 through 10 as interrupt threads.

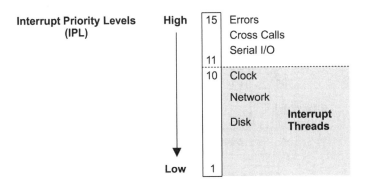

Figure 3.5 Example interrupt priority level range

Serial I/O has a high interrupt because its hardware buffer is usually small and needs quick servicing to avoid overflows.

3.2.5 Processes

A process is an environment for executing a user-level program. It consists of a memory address space, file descriptors, thread stacks, and registers. In some ways, a process is like a virtual early computer, where only one program is executing, with its own registers and stacks.

Processes are multitasked by the kernel, which typically supports the execution of thousands of processes on a single system. They are individually identified by their *process ID* (PID), which is a unique numeric identifier.

A process contains one or more *threads*, which operate in the process address space and share the same file descriptors (state describing open files). A thread is an executable context consisting of a stack, registers, and program counter. Multiple threads allow a single process to execute in parallel across multiple CPUs.

Process Creation

Processes are normally created using the fork() system call. This creates a duplicate of the process, with its own process ID. The exec() system call can then be called to begin execution of a different program.

Figure 3.6 shows an example process creation for the shell (sh) executing the ls command.

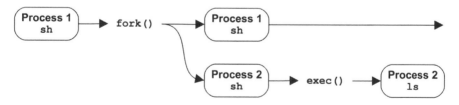

Figure 3.6 Process creation

The fork() syscall may use a copy-on-write (COW) strategy to improve perfor- mance. This adds references to the previous address space rather than copying all of the contents. Once either process modifies the multiply-referenced memory, a separate copy is then made for the modifications. This strategy either defers or eliminates the need to copy memory, reducing memory and CPU usage.

Process Life Cycle

The life cycle of a process is shown in Figure 3.7. This is a simplified diagram; for modern multithreaded operating systems it is the threads that are scheduled and run, and there are some additional implementation details regarding how these map to process states (for reference, see proc.h in your kernel source code).

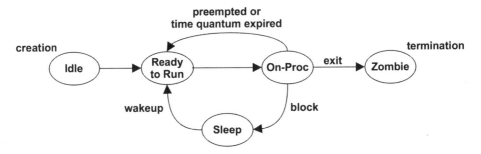

Figure 3.7 Process life cycle

The on-proc state is for running on a processor (CPU). The ready-to-run state is when the process is runnable but is waiting on a CPU run queue for its turn on a CPU. I/O will block, putting the process in the sleep state until the I/O completes and the process is woken up. The zombie state occurs during process termination, when the process waits until its process status has been read by the parent process, or until it is removed by the kernel.

Process Environment

The process environment is shown in Figure 3.8; it consists of data in the address space of the process and metadata (context) in the kernel.

The kernel context consists of various process properties and statistics: its process ID (PID), the owner's user ID (UID), and various times. These are commonly examined via the ps(1) command. It also has a set of file descriptors, which refer to open files and which are (usually) shared between threads.

This example pictures two threads, each containing some metadata, including a priority in kernel context and its stack in the user address space. The diagram is not drawn to scale; the kernel context is very small compared to the process address space.

The user address space contains memory segments of the process: executable, libraries, and heap. For more details, see Chapter 7, Memory.

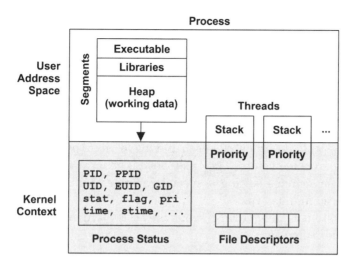

Figure 3.8 Process environment

3.2.6 System Calls

System calls request the kernel to perform privileged system routines. The number of system calls available is in the hundreds, but some effort is made to keep that number as small as possible, to keep the kernel simple (Unix philosophy; [Thompson 78]). More sophisticated interfaces can be built upon them in user-land as system libraries, where they are easier to develop and maintain.

Key system calls to remember are listed in Table 3.1.

Table 3.1 Key System Calls

System Call	Description
read()	read bytes
write()	write bytes
open()	open a file
close()	close a file
fork()	create a new process
exec()	execute a new program
connect()	connect to a network host
accept()	accept a network connection
stat()	fetch file statistics

continues

Table 3.1 Key System Calls (*Continued*)

System Call	Description
ioctl()	set I/O properties, or other miscellaneous functions
mmap()	map a file to the memory address space
brk()	extend the heap pointer

System calls are well documented, each having a man page that is usually shipped with the operating system. They also have a generally simple and consistent interface, which includes setting a special variable, errno, to indicate if an error was encountered and its type.

Many of these system calls have an obvious purpose. Here are a few whose common usage may be less obvious:

- ioctl(): This is commonly used to request miscellaneous actions from the kernel, especially for system administration tools, where another (more obvious) system call isn't suitable. See the example that follows.

- mmap(): This is commonly used to map executables and libraries to the process address space, and for memory-mapped files. It is sometimes used to allocate the working memory of a process, instead of the brk()-based malloc(), to reduce the syscall rate and improve performance (which doesn't always work due to the trade-off involved: memory-mapping management).

- brk(): This is used to extend the heap pointer, which defines the size of the working memory of the process. It is typically performed by a system memory allocation library, when a malloc() (memory allocate) call cannot be satisfied from the existing space in the heap. See Chapter 7, Memory.

If a system call is unfamiliar, you can learn more in its man page (these are in section 2: syscalls).

The ioctl() syscall may be the most difficult to learn, due to its ambiguous nature. As an example of its usage, the Linux perf(1) tool (introduced in Chapter 6, CPUs) performs privileged actions to coordinate performance instrumentation. Instead of system calls being added for each action, a single system call is added: perf_event_open(), which returns a file descriptor for use with ioctl(). This ioctl() can then be called using different arguments to perform the different desired actions. For example, ioctl(fd, PERF_EVENT_IOC_ENABLE) enables instrumentation. The arguments, in this example PERF_EVENT_IOC_ENABLE, can be more easily added and changed by the developer.

3.2.7 Virtual Memory

Virtual memory is an abstraction of main memory, providing processes and the kernel with their own, almost infinite, private view of main memory. It supports multitasking, allowing processes and the kernel to operate on their own private address spaces without worrying about contention. It also supports oversubscription of main memory, allowing the operating system to transparently map virtual memory between main memory and secondary storage (disks) as needed.

The role of virtual memory is shown in Figure 3.9. Primary memory is main memory (RAM), and secondary memory is the storage devices (disks).

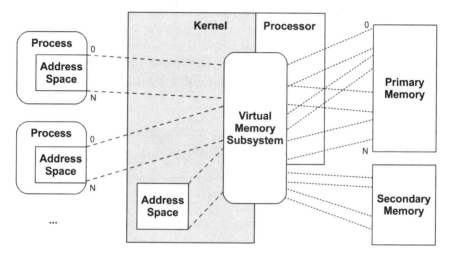

Figure 3.9 Virtual memory address spaces

Virtual memory is made possible by support in both the processor and operating system. It is not real memory, and most operating systems map virtual memory to real memory only on demand, when the memory is first populated (written).

See Chapter 7, Memory, for more about virtual memory.

3.2.8 Memory Management

While virtual memory allows main memory to be extended using secondary storage, the kernel strives to keep the most active data in main memory. There are two kernel routines for this:

- **Swapping** moves entire processes between main memory and secondary storage.
- **Paging** moves small units of memory called pages (e.g., 4 Kbytes).

Swapping is the original Unix method and can cause severe performance loss. Paging is more efficient and was added to BSD with the introduction of paged virtual memory. In both cases, least recently used (or not recently used) memory is moved to secondary storage and moved back to main memory only when needed again.

In Linux, the term *swapping* is used to refer to *paging*. The Linux kernel does not support the (older) Unix-style swapping of entire threads and processes.

For more on paging and swapping, see Chapter 7, Memory.

3.2.9 Schedulers

Unix and its derivatives are time-sharing systems, allowing multiple processes to run at the same time by dividing execution time among them. The scheduling of processes on processors and individual CPUs is performed by the *scheduler*, a key component of the operating system kernel. The role of the scheduler is pictured in Figure 3.10, which shows that the scheduler operates on threads (in Linux, *tasks*), mapping them to CPUs.

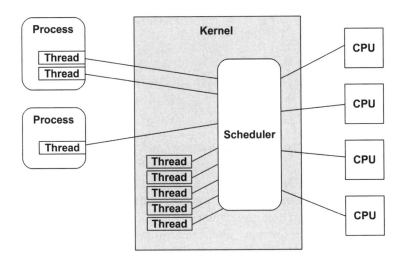

Figure 3.10 Kernel scheduler

The basic intent is to divide CPU time among the active processes and threads, and to maintain a notion of *priority* so that more important work can execute sooner. The scheduler keeps track of all threads in the ready-to-run state, traditionally on per-priority queues called *run queues* [Bach 86]. Modern kernels may implement these queues per CPU and may also use other data structures, apart from queues, to track the threads. When more threads want to run than there are available CPUs, the lower-priority threads wait their turn. Most kernel threads run with a higher priority than user-level processes.

Process priority can be modified dynamically by the scheduler to improve the performance of certain workloads. Workloads can be categorized as either

- **CPU-bound:** applications that perform heavy compute, for example, scientific and mathematical analysis, which is expected to have long runtimes (seconds, minutes, hours). These become limited by CPU resources.
- **I/O-bound:** applications that perform I/O, with little compute, for example, web servers, file servers, and interactive shells, where low-latency responses are desirable. When their load increases, they are limited by I/O to storage or network resources.

The scheduler can identify CPU-bound workloads and decrease their priority, allowing I/O-bound workloads—where low-latency responses are more desirable—to run sooner. This can be achieved by calculating the ratio of recent compute time (time executing on-CPU) to real time (elapsed time) and decreasing the priority of processes with a high (compute) ratio [Thompson 78]. This mechanism gives preference to shorter-running processes, which are usually those performing I/O, including human interactive processes.

Modern kernels support multiple *scheduling classes*, which apply different algorithms for managing priority and runnable threads. These may include the *real-time scheduling class*, which uses a priority higher than all noncritical work, including kernel threads. Along with preemption support (described later), the real-time scheduling class provides low-latency scheduling for real-time systems.

See Chapter 6, CPUs, for more about the kernel scheduler and other scheduling classes.

3.2.10 File Systems

File systems are an organization of data as files and directories. They have a file-based interface for accessing them, which is usually based on the POSIX standard. Kernels can support multiple file system types and instances. Providing a file system is one of the most important roles of the operating system, once described as *the* most important role [Ritchie 74].

The operating system provides a global file namespace, organized as a top-down tree topology starting with the root level ("/"). File systems join the tree by *mounting*, attaching their own tree to a directory (the *mount point*). This allows the end user to navigate the file namespace transparently, regardless of the underlying file system type.

A typical operating system may be organized as shown in Figure 3.11.

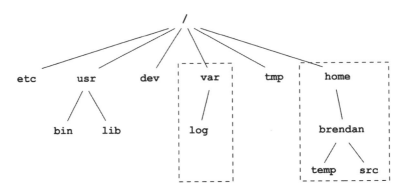

Figure 3.11 Operating system file hierarchy

The top-level directories include etc for system configuration files, usr for system-supplied user-level programs and libraries, dev for device files, var for varying files including system logs, tmp for temporary files, and home for user home directories. In the example pictured, var and home may reside on their own file system instances and separate storage devices; however, they can be accessed like any other component of the tree.

Most file system types use storage devices (disks) to store their contents. Some file system types are dynamically created by the kernel, such as /proc or /dev.

VFS

The virtual file system (VFS) is a kernel interface to abstract file system types, originally developed by Sun Microsystems so that the Unix file system (UFS) and NFS could more easily coexist. Its role is pictured in Figure 3.12.

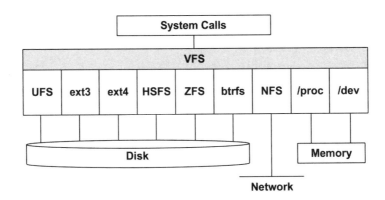

Figure 3.12 Virtual file system

The VFS interface makes it easier to add new file system types to the kernel. It also supports providing the global file namespace, pictured earlier, so that user programs and applications can access various file system types transparently.

I/O Stack

For storage-device-based file systems, the path from user-level software to the storage device is called the *I/O stack*. This is a subset of the entire software stack shown earlier. A generic I/O stack is shown in Figure 3.13.

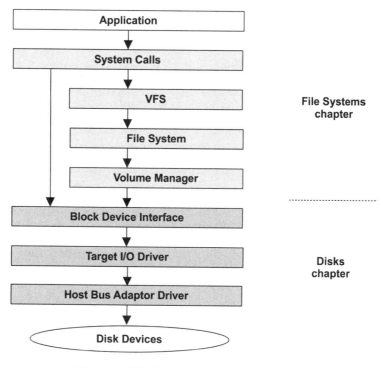

Figure 3.13 Generic I/O stack

File systems and their performance are covered in detail in Chapter 8, File Systems, and the storage devices they are built upon are covered in Chapter 9, Disks.

3.2.11 Caching

Since disk I/O has historically had high latency, many layers of the software stack attempt to avoid it by caching reads and buffering writes. Caches may include those shown in Table 3.2 (in the order in which they are checked).

Table 3.2 Example Cache Layers for Disk I/O

	Cache	Example
1	application cache	—
2	web server cache	Apache cache
3	caching server	memcached
4	database cache	MySQL buffer cache
5	directory cache	DNLC
6	file metadata cache	inode cache
7	operating system buffer cache	segvn
8	file system primary cache	ZFS ARC
9	file system secondary cache	ZFS L2ARC
10	device cache	ZFS vdev
11	block cache	buffer cache
12	disk controller cache	RAID card cache
13	storage array cache	—
14	on-disk cache	—

For example, the buffer cache is an area of main memory that stores recently used disk blocks. Disk reads may be served immediately from the cache if the requested block is present, avoiding the high latency of disk I/O.

The types of caches present will vary based on the system and environment.

3.2.12 Networking

Modern kernels provide a stack of built-in network protocols, allowing the system to communicate on the network and take part in distributed system environments. The stack is referred to as the *TCP/IP stack*, after the commonly used TCP and IP protocols. User-level applications access the network through programmable endpoints called *sockets*.

The physical device that connects to the network is the *network interface* and is usually provided on a *network interface card* (NIC). A common duty of the system administrator is to associate an IP address with a network interface, so that it can communicate with the network.

Network protocols do not change often, but enhancements and options do, such as newer TCP options and TCP congestion control algorithms, which require kernel support. Another change is support for different network interface cards, which require new device drivers for the kernel.

For more on networking and network performance, see Chapter 10, Networking.

3.2.13 Device Drivers

A kernel must communicate with a wide variety of physical devices. Such communication is achieved using *device drivers*: kernel software for device management and I/O. Device drivers are often provided by the vendors who develop the hardware devices. Some kernels support *pluggable* device drivers, which can be loaded and unloaded without requiring a system restart.

Device drivers can provide *character* and/or *block* interfaces to their devices. Character devices, also called *raw devices*, provide unbuffered sequential access of any I/O size down to a single character, depending on the device. Such devices include keyboards and serial ports (and in original Unix, paper tape and line printer devices).

Block devices perform I/O in units of blocks, which have historically been 512 bytes each. These can be accessed randomly based on their block offset, which begins at 0 at the start of the block device. In original Unix, the block device interface also provided caching of block device buffers to improve performance, in an area of main memory called the *buffer cache*.

3.2.14 Multiprocessor

Multiprocessor support allows the operating system to use multiple CPU instances to execute work in parallel. It is usually implemented as symmetric multiprocessing (SMP), where all CPUs are treated equally. This was technically difficult to accomplish, posing problems for accessing and sharing memory and CPUs among threads running in parallel. See Chapter 6, CPUs, for details, including scheduling and thread synchronization, and Chapter 7, Memory, for details on memory access and architectures.

CPU Cross Calls

For a multiprocessor system, there are times when CPUs need to coordinate, such as for cache coherency of memory translation entries (informing other CPUs that an entry, if cached, is now stale). A CPU can request other CPUs, or all CPUs, to immediately perform such work using a CPU *cross call*. Cross calls are processor interrupts that are designed to be executed quickly, to minimize interruption of other threads.

Cross calls can also be used by preemption.

3.2.15 Preemption

Kernel preemption support allows high-priority user-level threads to interrupt the kernel and execute. This enables *real-time* systems—those that have strict response time requirements. A kernel that supports preemption is said to be *fully preemptable*, although practically it will still have some small critical code paths that cannot be interrupted.

An approach supported by Linux is *voluntary kernel preemption*, where logical stopping points in the kernel code can check and perform preemption. This avoids some of the complexity of supporting a fully preemptive kernel and provides low-latency preemption for common workloads.

3.2.16 Resource Management

The operating system may provide various configurable controls for fine-tuning access to system resources, such as CPUs, memory, disk, and the network. These are *resource controls* and can be used on systems that run different applications or tenants (cloud computing) to manage performance. Such controls may impose fixed limits per process (or groups of processes) for resource usage, or a more flexible approach—allowing spare usage to be shared among them.

Early versions of Unix and BSD have had basic per-process resource controls, including CPU priorities with nice(1), and some resource limits with ulimit(1).

Solaris-based systems have provided advanced resource controls since Solaris 9 (2002) and are documented in the resources_controls(5) man page.

For Linux, control groups (cgroups) have been developed and integrated in 2.6.24 (2008), since which various additional controls have been added. These are documented in the kernel source under Documentation/cgroups.

Specific resource controls are mentioned in later chapters as appropriate. An example use case is described in Chapter 11, Cloud Computing, for managing the performance of OS-virtualized tenants.

3.2.17 Observability

The operating system consists of the kernel, libraries, and programs. These programs include tools to observe system activity and analyze performance, typically installed in /usr/bin and /usr/sbin. Third-party tools may also be installed on the system to provide additional observability.

Observability tools, and the operating system components upon which they are built, are introduced in the next chapter.

3.3 Kernels

This section introduces Solaris-based and Linux kernels (in chronological order), their history and features, and discusses differences with a focus on performance. Unix origins are also discussed for background.

Some obvious differences between modern kernels include the file systems they support (see Chapter 8, File Systems) and the observability frameworks they provide (see Chapter 4, Observability Tools). There are also differences with their system call (syscall) interfaces, network stack architecture, real-time support, and CPU, disk, and network I/O scheduling.

Table 3.3 shows recent kernel versions, with syscall counts based on the number of entries in section 2 of the OS man pages. This is a crude comparison, but enough to see some differences.

Table 3.3 Kernel Versions with Documented Syscall Counts

Kernel Version	Syscalls
Linux 2.6.32-21-server	408
Linux 2.6.32-220.el6.x86_64	427
Linux 3.2.6-3.fc16.x86_64	431
SunOS 5.9	221
SunOS 5.10	218
SunOS 5.11	142

These are just the syscalls with documentation; more are usually provided by the kernel for private use by operating system software. Apart from differences between kernels, there is a pattern over time: Linux has been adding system calls. Solaris has been removing them.

> UNIX had twenty system calls at the very first, and today Linux—which is a direct descendant—has over a thousand . . . I just worry about the complexity and the size of things that grow.
>
> Ken Thompson, ACM Turing Centenary Celebration, 2012

Both kernels are actually growing in complexity and exposing this to user-land in different ways, either by adding new system calls or through other kernel interfaces.

3.3.1 Unix

Unix was developed by Ken Thompson, Dennis Ritchie, and others at AT&T Bell
Labs during 1969 and the years that followed. Its exact origin was described in
The UNIX Time-Sharing System [Ritchie 74]:

> The first version was written when one of us (Thompson), dissatisfied with the avail-
> able computer facilities, discovered a little-used PDP-7 and set out to create a more
> hospitable environment.

The developers of UNIX had previously worked on the Multiplexed Information
and Computer Services (Multics) operating system. UNIX was developed as a
lightweight multitasked operating system and kernel, originally named UNiplexed
Information and Computing Service (UNICS), as a pun on Multics. From *UNIX
Implementation* [Thompson 78]:

> The kernel is the only UNIX code that cannot be substituted by a user to his own lik-
> ing. For this reason, the kernel should make as few real decisions as possible. This
> does not mean to allow the user a million options to do the same thing. Rather, it
> means to allow only one way to do one thing, but have that way be the least-common
> divisor of all the options that might have been provided.

While the kernel was small, it did provide some features for high performance.
Processes had scheduler priorities, reducing run-queue latency for higher-priority
work. Disk I/O was performed in large (512-byte) blocks for efficiency and cached
in an in-memory per-device buffer cache. Idle processes could be swapped out to
storage, allowing busier processes to run in main memory. And the system was, of
course, multitasking—allowing multiple processes to run in parallel, improving job
throughput.

To support networking, multiple file systems, paging, and other features we now
consider standard, the kernel had to grow. And with multiple derivatives, including BSD, SunOS (Solaris), and later Linux, kernel performance became competitive, which drove the addition of more features and code.

3.3.2 Solaris-Based

The Solaris kernel is not just Unix-derived but even has some surviving code from
the original Unix kernel. Solaris began as SunOS, created by Sun Microsystems in
1982. Based on BSD, SunOS was kept small and compact so that it performed well
on Sun workstations. By the late 1980s, Sun had developed new operating system
features that were contributed, along with features from BSD and Xenix, to

AT&T's Unix System V Release 4 (SVR4). As SVR4 became the new Unix standard, Sun created a new kernel and operating system based on it: SunOS 5. Sun marketing called this Solaris 2.0 and back-named prior SunOS as Solaris 1.0. The engineers, however, kept the SunOS name in the kernel.

Sun kernel developments, especially those related to performance, include the following:

- **NFS:** The NFS protocol allows files to be shared over a network and used transparently as part of the global file system tree (mounted). NFS is in popular use today as versions 3 and 4, each of which has introduced many performance improvements.

- **VFS:** The virtual file system (VFS) is an abstraction and interface that allows multiple file systems to easily coexist. Sun initially created it so that NFS and UFS could coexist. VFS is covered in Chapter 8, File Systems.

- **Page cache:** This caches virtual memory pages and has been the primary file system cache for most operating systems since its introduction (the ZFS ARC is an exception). It was introduced in SunOS 4 during a virtual memory rewrite, which also supported shared pages. See Chapter 8, File Systems, for more on the page cache.

- **Memory-mapped files:** can be used to reduce the overhead of file I/O and were introduced by the SunOS virtual memory rewrite for SVR4.

- **RPC:** the remote procedure call interface.

- **NIS:** Network Information Services is a simple flat-topology framework for sharing information over a network, including the passwd and hosts files. It was commonly used for many years but is now giving way to LDAP.

- **CacheFS:** The caching file system, introduced in Solaris 2.4 (1994), was used to improve performance when accessing slow NFS servers. Since then, the performance of NFS servers has improved to the point where CacheFS is no longer commonly used or considered.

- **Fully preemptable kernel:** An early Sun differentiator was its fully preemptable kernel, ensuring low latency for high-priority work, including real-time work.

- **Scheduler classes:** Multiple scheduler classes are provided for tuning the performance of different classes of workloads. These include time-sharing (TS), interactive (IA), real-time (RT), system (SYS), fixed (FX), and fair-share scheduler (FSS). See Chapter 6, CPUs.

- **Multiprocessor support:** In the early 1990s, Sun invested heavily in multi-processor operating system support, developing kernel support for both asymmetric and symmetric multiprocessing (ASMP and SMP) [Mauro 01].

- **Slab allocator:** Replacing the SVR4 buddy allocator, the kernel slab allocator provided better performance via per-CPU caches of preallocated buffers that could be quickly reused. This allocator type, and its derivatives, has become the standard for operating systems.

- **Crash analysis:** Sun developed a mature kernel crash dump analysis framework that is enabled by default for all systems and includes the modular debugger (mdb(1)) for crash dump, kernel, and application analysis.

- **M:N thread scheduling:** This implemented an additional object between threads and processes for the purpose of efficient thread scheduling. This object was called a *lightweight process* (LWP), which could have its own user-level scheduling behavior that differed from the kernel scheduler. Sun's implementation was later found to have issues and not worth the complexity [Cantrill 96]. It was removed in Solaris 9, but the terminology (LWP) and some data structures are left over in some parts of Solaris.

- **STREAMS network stack:** Sun built its TCP/IP network stack on the AT&T STREAMS interface, which provided communications between user-space and kernel-space. It eventually did not scale with faster networks, and by Solaris 10 much of the STREAMS plumbing had been removed.

- **64-bit support:** The Solaris 7 kernel (1998) provided support for 64-bit processors.

- **Lock statistics:** Lock performance statistics were introduced in Solaris 7.

- **MPSS:** Multiple page size support allows the OS to use different-size memory pages provided by the processor, including large (or huge) pages, improving efficiency of memory operations.

- **MPO:** Memory Placement Optimization was added to Solaris 9 to improve how memory was allocated with respect to processor architecture (locality), which can significantly improve memory access performance.

- **Resource controls:** a facility for limiting various resource usage by processes or groups of processes called *projects* (later used by Zones).

- **FireEngine:** a set of high-performance TCP/IP stack enhancements for Solaris 10, including *vertical perimeters* to improve CPU and memory locality of packet processing, and *IP fanout* for spreading load across CPUs.

- **DTrace:** a static and dynamic tracing framework and tool, providing virtually unlimited observability of the entire software stack, in real time and in production. It was released for Solaris 10 in 2005 and was the first widely successful implementation of dynamic tracing. It has been ported to other operating systems, including Mac OS X and FreeBSD, and is currently being ported to Linux. DTrace is covered in Chapter 4, Observability Tools.

- **Zones:** an OS-based virtualization technology that allows instances of operating systems to be created that share the same host kernel. It was released for Solaris 10, but the concept was first accomplished by FreeBSD jails in 1998. Compared to other virtualization technologies, these are lightweight and provide high performance. See Chapter 11, Cloud Computing.

- **Crossbow:** an architecture for providing high-performing virtualized network interfaces and network bandwidth resource controls. This feature has been crucial for building high-performing and reliable clouds.

- **ZFS:** The ZFS file system provided enterprise-level features and was released with Solaris 10 update 1 and also as open source. It is now available for other operating systems and is the basis for many filer appliances. See Chapter 8, File Systems.

Many of these features have been ported or reimplemented for Linux, and some are still in development.

Under pressure from Linux, Sun open-sourced Solaris in 2005 as the OpenSolaris project. It remained open until Oracle purchased Sun in 2010 and stopped releasing source code updates. The last released version of OpenSolaris, which mirrored the development version of Solaris 11, became the basis of the open-source illumos kernel. Today there are several operating systems based on the illumos kernel, including Joyent's SmartOS, which is used for many of the Solaris-based examples in this book.

3.3.3 Linux-Based

Linux was created in 1991 by Linus Torvalds as a free operating system for Intel personal computers. He announced the project in a Usenet post:

> I'm doing a (free) operating system (just a hobby, won't be big and professional like gnu) for 386(486) AT clones. This has been brewing since April, and is starting to get ready. I'd like any feedback on things people like/dislike in minix, as my OS resembles it somewhat (same physical layout of the file-system (due to practical reasons) among other things).

This refers to the MINIX operating system, which was being developed as a free and small (mini) version of Unix for small computers. BSD was also aiming to provide a free Unix version although at the time had legal troubles.

The Linux kernel was developed upon general ideas from many ancestors, including

- **Unix** (and Multics): operating system layers, system calls, multitasking, processes, process priorities, virtual memory, global file system, file system permissions, device files, buffer cache
- **BSD:** paged virtual memory, demand paging, fast file system (FFS), TCP/IP network stack, sockets
- **Solaris:** VFS, NFS, page cache, unified page cache, slab allocator, and (in progress) ZFS and DTrace
- **Plan 9:** resource forks (rfork), for creating different levels of sharing between processes and threads (*tasks*)

Linux kernel features, especially those related to performance, include the following. Many of these include the Linux kernel version where they were first introduced.

- **CPU scheduling classes:** Various advanced CPU scheduling algorithms have been developed, including scheduling domains (2.6.7) to make better decisions regarding non-uniform memory access (NUMA). See Chapter 6, CPUs.
- **I/O scheduling classes:** Different block I/O scheduling algorithms have been developed, including deadline (2.5.39), anticipatory (2.5.75), and completely fair queueing (CFQ) (2.6.6). See Chapter 9, Disks.
- **TCP congestion:** Newer TCP congestion algorithms are supported by the Linux kernel, which allows them to be selected as needed. There have also been numerous TCP enhancements. See Chapter 10, Network.
- **Overcommit:** Along with the out-of-memory (OOM) killer, this is a strategy to do more with less main memory. See Chapter 7, Memory.
- **Futex** (2.5.7): Short for *fast user-space mutex*, this is used to provide high-performing user-level synchronization primitives.
- **Huge pages** (2.5.36): This provides support for preallocated large memory pages by the kernel and the memory management unit (MMU). See Chapter 7, Memory.
- **OProfile** (2.5.43): a system profiler for studying CPU usage and other events, for both the kernel and applications.
- **RCU** (2.5.43): The kernel provides a read-copy update synchronization mechanism that allows multiple reads to occur concurrently with updates, improving performance and scalability for data that is mostly read.

- **epoll** (2.5.46): a system call for efficiently waiting for I/O across many open file descriptors, which improves the performance of server applications.

- **Modular I/O scheduling** (2.6.10): Linux provides pluggable scheduling algorithms for scheduling block device I/O. See Chapter 9, Disks.

- **DebugFS** (2.6.11): a simple unstructured interface for the kernel to expose data to user level, which is used by some performance tools.

- **Cpusets** (2.6.12): exclusive CPUs grouping for processes.

- **Voluntary kernel preemption** (2.6.13): This process provides low-latency scheduling without the complexity of full preemption.

- **inotify** (2.6.13): a framework for monitoring file system events.

- **blktrace** (2.6.17): a framework and tool for the tracing of block I/O events (later migrated into tracepoints).

- **splice** (2.6.17): a system call to move data quickly between file descriptors and pipes, without a trip through user-space.

- **Delay accounting** (2.6.18): tracks per-task delay states. See Chapter 4, Observability Tools.

- **IO accounting** (2.6.20): measures various storage I/O statistics per process.

- **DynTicks** (2.6.21): Dynamic ticks allow the kernel timer interrupt (clock) to not fire unless necessary (*tickless*), saving CPU resources and power.

- **SLUB** (2.6.22): a new and simplified version of the slab memory allocator.

- **CFS** (2.6.23): completely fair scheduler. See Chapter 6, CPUs.

- **cgroups** (2.6.24): Control groups allow resource usage to be measured and limited for groups of processes.

- **latencytop** (2.6.25): instrumentation and a tool for observing sources of latency in the operating system.

- **Tracepoints** (2.6.28): static kernel tracepoints (aka *static probes*) that instrument logical execution points in the kernel, for use by tracing tools (previously *kernel markers*). Tracing tools are introduced in Chapter 4, Observability Tools.

- **perf** (2.6.31): Linux Performance Events (perf) is a set of tools for performance observability, including CPU performance counter profiling and static and dynamic tracing. See Chapter 6, CPUs, for an introduction.

- **Transparent huge pages** (2.6.38): This is a framework to allow easy use of huge (large) memory pages. See Chapter 7, Memory.

- **Uprobes** (3.5): the infrastructure for dynamic tracing of user-level software, used by other tools (perf, SystemTap, etc.).

- **KVM:** The Kernel-based Virtual Machine (KVM) technology was developed for Linux by Qumranet, which was purchased by Red Hat in 2008. KVM allows virtual operating system instances to be created, running their own kernel. See Chapter 11, Cloud Computing.

Some of these features, including epoll and KVM, have been ported or reimplemented for Solaris-based systems.

Linux has also indirectly contributed to many other operating systems by its vast support for device drivers and the push to have them open-sourced.

3.3.4 Differences

While they are both Unix descendants and share the same operating system concepts, the Linux and Solaris-based kernels do differ in many ways, both large and small. There is no neat and simple way to summarize the complexity.

The key advantages of Linux-based systems come largely not from the kernel or operating system proper, but from application package support, device driver support, the large community, and the fact that it is open source. Most Solaris-based kernels are also open source (Oracle Solaris currently is not), but they do not have the same extensive driver support (which can be a problem for laptop use).

Solaris-based systems provide ZFS for an enterprise-level file system, and DTrace for virtually unlimited observability. While these are being ported to Linux, they are already available and mature on Solaris-based systems, where they have been used in production since 2003. Linux does have a number of newer accounting and tracing frameworks that provide extended observability (described in the next chapter), but they may not yet be commonly enabled or installed by default.

Solaris-based systems also have kernel crash dumps enabled by default, so that kernel panics can be analyzed and solved from the first occurrence.

Apart from these major differences, there are many, many minor differences between the kernels, especially with performance optimizations. To understand how these may affect you, analyze the intended workload to see which will be relevant.

As an example of a minor difference, the POSIX `fadvise()` call is currently implemented on Linux but ignored by Solaris-based kernels. This can be used by applications to inform the kernel not to cache data associated with a file descriptor and therefore allow the Linux kernel to cache more efficiently, improving performance. Here is an example of its usage, from the MySQL database:

```
storage/innobase/row/row0merge.c:
        /* Each block is read exactly once.  Free up the file cache. */
        posix_fadvise(fd, ofs, sizeof *buf, POSIX_FADV_DONTNEED);
```

Minor differences like these can change quickly, and this particular issue may be fixed in Solaris-based kernels by the time you are reading this book.[2] While there are minor differences in delivered performance depending on the workload, the largest difference may be performance *observability*, particularly support for dynamic tracing. If one kernel supports you finding 10x and greater wins in your production environment, any 10% or so differences found earlier may not look as important.

Observability tools are covered in the next chapter.

3.4 Exercises

1. Answer the following questions about OS terminology:
   - What is the difference between a process, a thread, and a task?
   - What is a context switch?
   - What is the difference between paging and swapping?
   - What is the difference between I/O-bound and CPU-bound workloads?

2. Answer the following conceptual questions:
   - Describe the role of the kernel.
   - Describe the role of system calls.
   - Describe the role of VFS and its location in the I/O stack.

3. Answer the following deeper questions:
   - List the reasons why a thread would leave the CPU.
   - Describe the advantages of virtual memory and demand paging.

3.5 References

[Graham 68]   Graham, B. "Protection in an Information Processing Utility," *Communications of the ACM*, May 1968.

[Ritchie 74]   Ritchie, D. M., and K. Thompson. "The UNIX Time-Sharing System," *Communications of the ACM* 17, no. 7 (July 1974), pp. 365–75.

[Thompson 78]   Thompson, K. *UNIX Implementation*. Bell Laboratories, 1978.

---

2. A ticket has been filed for this and is assigned to me.

[Bach 86]   Bach, M. J. *The Design of the UNIX Operating System*. Prentice Hall, 1986.

[Cantrill 96]   Cantrill, B. *Runtime Performance Analysis of the M-to-N Scheduling Model* (Thesis). Brown University, 1996.

[Mauro 01]   Mauro, J., and R. McDougall. *Solaris Internals: Core Kernel Architecture*. Prentice Hall, 2001.

[Corbet 05]   Corbet, J., A. Rubini, and G. Kroah-Hartman. *Linux Device Drivers, 3rd Edition*. O'Reilly, 2005.

[McDougall 06a]   McDougall, R., and J. Mauro. *Solaris Internals: Solaris 10 and OpenSolaris Kernel Architecture*. Prentice Hall, 2006.

[RFC 1589]   *A Kernel Model for Precision Timekeeping*, 1994.

Kernel internals is a fascinating and extensive topic. This chapter summarized only the essentials. In addition to the sources mentioned in this chapter, the following are also excellent references for kernel internals:

[Goodheart 94]   Goodheart, B., and J. Cox. *The Magic Garden Explained: The Internals of UNIX System V Release 4, an Open Systems Design*. Prentice Hall, 1994.

[Vahalia 96]   Vahalia, U. *UNIX Internals: The New Frontiers*. Prentice Hall, 1996.

[Neville-Neil 04]   Neville-Neil, G. V., and M. K. McKusick. *The Design and Implementation of the FreeBSD Operating System*. Addison-Wesley, 2004.

[Bovet 05]   Bovet, D., and M. Cesati. *Understanding the Linux Kernel, 3rd Edition*. O'Reilly, 2005.

[Singh 06]   Singh, A. *Mac OS X Internals: A Systems Approach*. Addison-Wesley, 2006.

[Love 10]   Love, R. *Linux Kernel Development, 3rd Edition*. Addison-Wesley, 2010.

4

Observability Tools

Operating systems have historically provided many tools for observing system software and hardware components. To the newcomer, the wide range of available tools suggested that everything—or at least everything important—could be observed. In reality, there were many gaps, and systems performance experts became skilled in the art of inference and interpretation: figuring out activity from indirect tools and statistics.

For example, network packets could be examined individually (sniffing), but disk I/O could not (at least, not remotely easily). Conversely, disk utilization (percent busy) was easily observable from operating system tools, but network interface utilization was not.

With the addition of tracing frameworks, especially dynamic tracing, everything can now be observed, and virtually any activity can be observed directly. This has had a profound effect on systems performance, making it possible to create hundreds of new observability tools (the potential number is unlimited).

This chapter describes the types of operating system observability tools, including key examples, and the frameworks upon which they are built. The focus here is the frameworks, including /proc, kstat, /sys, DTrace, and SystemTap. Many more tools that use these frameworks are introduced in later chapters, including Linux Performance Events (LPE) in Chapter 6, CPUs.

4.1 Tool Types

Performance observability tools can be categorized as providing *system-wide* or *per-process* observability, and most are based on either *counters* or *tracing*. These attributes are shown in Figure 4.1, along with tool examples.

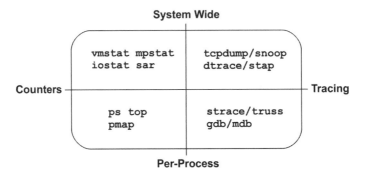

Figure 4-1 Observability tool types

Some tools fit in more than one quadrant; for example, `top(1)` also has a system-wide summary, and DTrace also has per-process capabilities.

There are also performance tools that are based on *profiling*. These observe activity by taking a series of snapshots either system-wide or per process.

The following sections summarize tools that use counters, tracing, and profiling as well as those that perform monitoring.

4.1.1 Counters

Kernels maintain various statistics, called *counters*, for counting events. They are usually implemented as unsigned integers that are incremented when events occur. For example, there are counters for the number of network packets received, disk I/O issued, and system calls performed.

Counters are considered "free" to use since they are enabled by default and maintained continually by the kernel. The only additional cost when using them is the act of reading their values from user-land (which should be negligible). The following example tools read these system-wide or per process.

System-Wide

These tools examine system-wide activity in the context of system software or hardware resources, using kernel counters. Examples are

- **vmstat:** virtual and physical memory statistics, system-wide
- **mpstat:** per-CPU usage
- **iostat:** per-disk I/O usage, reported from the block device interface
- **netstat:** network interface statistics, TCP/IP stack statistics, and some per-connection statistics
- **sar:** various statistics; can also archive them for historical reporting

These tools are typically viewable by all users on the system (non-root). Their statistics are also commonly graphed by monitoring software.

Many follow a usage convention where they accept an optional *interval* and *count*, for example, vmstat(8) with an interval of one second and an output count of three:

```
$ vmstat 1 3
procs -----------memory---------- ---swap-- -----io---- -system-- ----cpu----
 r  b   swpd   free   buff  cache   si   so    bi    bo   in   cs us sy id wa
 4  0      0 34455620 111396 13438564    0    0     0     5    1    2  0  0 100  0
 4  0      0 34458684 111396 13438588    0    0     0     0 2223 15198 13 11 76  0
 4  0      0 34456468 111396 13438588    0    0     0     0 1940 15142 15 11 74  0
```

The first line of output is the summary-since-boot, which shows averages for the entire time the system has been up. The subsequent lines are the one-second interval summaries, showing current activity. At least, this is the intent: this Linux version mixes summary-since-boot and current values for the first line.

Per-Process

These tools are process-oriented and use counters that the kernel maintains for each process. Examples are

- **ps:** process status, shows various process statistics, including memory and CPU usage.
- **top:** shows top processes, sorted by one of the statistics such as CPU usage. Solaris-based systems provide prstat(1M) for this purpose.
- **pmap:** lists process memory segments with usage statistics.

These tools typically read statistics from the /proc file system.

4.1.2 Tracing

Tracing collects per-event data for analysis. Tracing frameworks are not typically enabled by default, since tracing incurs CPU overhead to capture the data and can require significant storage to save it. These overheads can slow the target of tracing and need to be accounted for when interpreting measured times.

Logging, including the system log, can be thought of as low-frequency tracing that *is* enabled by default. Logging includes per-event data, although usually only for infrequent events such as errors and warnings.

The following are examples of system-wide and per-process tracing tools.

System-Wide

These tracing tools examine system-wide activity in the context of system software or hardware resources, using kernel tracing facilities. Examples are

- **tcpdump:** network packet tracing (uses libpcap)
- **snoop:** network packet tracing for Solaris-based systems
- **blktrace:** block I/O tracing (Linux)
- **iosnoop:** block I/O tracing (DTrace-based)
- **execsnoop:** tracing of new processes (DTrace-based)
- **dtruss:** system-wide buffered syscall tracing (DTrace-based)
- **DTrace:** tracing of kernel internals and the usage of any resource (not just network or block I/O), using static and dynamic tracing
- **SystemTap:** tracing of kernel internals and the usage of any resource, using static and dynamic tracing
- **perf:** Linux Performance Events, tracing static and dynamic probes

As DTrace and SystemTap are programming environments, system-wide tracing tools can be built upon them, including the few included in this list. More examples are provided throughout this book.

Per-Process

These tracing tools are process-oriented, as are the operating system frameworks on which they are based. Examples are

- **strace:** system call tracing for Linux-based systems
- **truss:** system call tracing for Solaris-based systems

- **gdb:** a source-level debugger, commonly used on Linux-based systems
- **mdb:** an extensible debugger for Solaris-based systems

The debuggers can examine per-event data, but they must do so by stopping and starting the execution of the target.

Tools such as DTrace, SystemTap, and perf all support a mode of execution where they can examine a single process only, although they are better described as system-wide tools.

4.1.3 Profiling

Profiling characterizes the target by collecting a set of samples or snapshots of its behavior. CPU usage is a common example, where samples are taken of the program counter or stack trace to characterize the code paths that are consuming CPU cycles. These samples are usually collected at a fixed rate, such as 100 or 1,000 Hz (cycles per second) across all CPUs. Profiling tools, or *profilers*, sometimes vary this rate slightly to avoid sampling in lockstep with target activity, which could lead to over- or undercounting.

Profiling can also be based on untimed hardware events, such as CPU hardware cache misses or bus activity. It can also show which code paths are responsible, information that can especially help developers optimize their code for the usage of system resources.

System-Wide and Per-Process

Here are some examples of profilers, all of which perform timer- and hardware-cache-based profiling:

- **oprofile:** Linux system profiling
- **perf:** a Linux performance toolkit, which includes profiling subcommands
- **DTrace:** programmatic profiling, timer-based using its `profile` provider, and hardware-event-based using its `cpc` provider
- **SystemTap:** programmatic profiling, timer-based using its `timer` tapset, and hardware-event-based using its `perf` tapset
- **cachegrind:** from the valgrind toolkit, can profile hardware cache usage and be visualized using kcachegrind
- **Intel VTune Amplifier XE:** Linux and Windows profiling, with a graphical interface including source browsing
- **Oracle Solaris Studio:** Solaris and Linux profiling with its Performance Analyzer, which has a graphical interface including source browsing

Programming languages often have their own special-purpose profilers that can inspect language context.

See Chapter 6, CPUs, for more about profiling tools.

4.1.4 Monitoring (sar)

Monitoring was introduced in Chapter 2, Methodology. The most commonly used tool for monitoring a single operating system host is the system activity reporter, sar(1), originating from AT&T Unix. sar(1) is counter-based and has an agent that executes at scheduled times (via cron) to record the state of system counters. The sar(1) tool allows these to be viewed at the command line, for example:

```
# sar
Linux 3.2.6-3.fc16.x86_64 (web100)    04/15/2013    _x86_64_    (16 CPU)
05:00:00       CPU     %user    %nice    %system    %iowait    %steal    %idle
05:10:00       all     12.61    0.00     4.58       0.00       0.00      82.80
05:20:00       all     21.62    0.00     9.59       0.93       0.00      67.86
05:30:00       all     23.65    0.00     9.61       3.58       0.00      63.17
05:40:00       all     28.95    0.00     8.96       0.04       0.00      62.05
05:50:00       all     29.54    0.00     9.32       0.19       0.00      60.95
Average:       all     23.27    0.00     8.41       0.95       0.00      67.37
```

By default, sar(1) reads its statistics archive (if enabled) to print recent historic statistics. You can specify an optional interval and count for it to examine current activity at the rate specified.

Specific uses of sar(1) are described later in this book; see Chapters 6, 7, 8, 9, and 10. Appendix C is a summary of the sar(1) options.

While sar(1) can report many statistics, it may not cover all you really need, and those it does provide have at times been misleading (especially on Solaris-based systems [McDougall 06b]). Alternatives have been developed, such as System Data Recorder and Collectl.

In Linux, sar(1) is provided via the sysstat package. Third-party monitoring products are often built on sar(1), or the same observability statistics it uses.

4.2 Observability Sources

The sections that follow describe various interfaces and frameworks that provide the statistics and data for observability tools. They are summarized in Table 4.1.

The main sources of systems performance statistics are covered next: /proc, /sys, and kstat. Delay accounting and microstate accounting are then described, and other sources are summarized. After these, the DTrace and SystemTap tools are introduced, which are built upon some of these frameworks.

Table 4.1 Observability Sources

Type	Linux	Solaris
Per-process counters	/proc	/proc, lxproc
System-wide counters	/proc, /sys	kstat
Device driver and debug info	/sys	kstat
Per-process tracing	ptrace, uprobes	procfs, dtrace
CPU performance counters	perf_event	libcpc
Network tracing	libpcap	libdlpi, libpcap
Per-thread latency metrics	delay accounting	microstate accounting
System-wide tracing	tracepoints, kprobes, ftrace	dtrace

4.2.1 /proc

This is a file system interface for kernel statistics. /proc contains a number of directories, where each directory is named after the process ID for the process it represents. These directories contain a number of files containing information and statistics about each process, mapped from kernel data structures. On Linux, there are additional files in /proc for system-wide statistics.

/proc is dynamically created by the kernel and is not backed by storage devices (it runs in-memory). It is mostly read-only, providing statistics for observability tools. Some files are writeable, for controlling process and kernel behavior.

The file system interface is convenient: it's an intuitive framework for exposing kernel statistics to user-land via the directory tree and has a well-known programming interface via the POSIX file system calls: open(), read(), close(). The file system also provides user-level security, through use of file access permissions.

The following shows how per-process statistics are read by top(1), traced using strace(1):

```
stat("/proc/14704", {st_mode=S_IFDIR|0555, st_size=0, ...}) = 0
open("/proc/14704/stat", O_RDONLY)      = 4
read(4, "14704 (sshd) S 1 14704 14704 0 -"..., 1023) = 232
close(4)
```

This has opened a file called stat in a directory named after the process ID, and then read the file contents.

top(1) repeats this for all active processes on the system. On some systems, especially those with many processes, the overhead from performing these can become noticeable, especially for versions of top(1) that repeat this sequence for every process on every screen update. This can lead to a situation where top(1) reports that top(1) itself is the highest CPU consumer!

The file system type for /proc on Linux is "proc" and for Solaris-based systems it is "procfs."

Linux

Various files are provided in /proc for per-process statistics. Here is an example of those that may be available:

```
$ ls -F /proc/28712
attr/           cpuset    io        mountinfo   oom_score    sessionid  syscall
auxv            cwd@      latency   mounts      pagemap      smaps      task/
cgroup          environ   limits    mountstats  personality  stack      wchan
clear_refs      exe@      loginuid  net/        root@        stat
cmdline         fd/       maps      numa_maps   sched        statm
coredump_filter fdinfo/   mem       oom_adj     schedstat    status
```

The exact list of files available depends on the kernel version and CONFIG options.

Those related to per-process performance observability include

- **limits:** in-effect resource limits
- **maps:** mapped memory regions
- **sched:** various CPU scheduler statistics
- **schedstat:** CPU runtime, latency, and time slices
- **smaps:** mapped memory regions with usage statistics
- **stat:** process status and statistics, including total CPU and memory usage
- **statm:** memory usage summary in units of pages
- **status:** stat and statm information, human-readable
- **task:** directory of per-task statistics

Linux has also extended /proc to include system-wide statistics, contained in these additional files and directories:

```
$ cd /proc; ls -Fd [a-z]*
acpi/       dma           kallsyms     mdstat       schedstat    timer_list
buddyinfo   driver/       kcore        meminfo      scsi/        timer_stats
bus/        execdomains   keys         misc         self@        tty/
cgroups     fb            key-users    modules      slabinfo     uptime
cmdline     filesystems   kmsg         mounts@      softirqs     version
consoles    fs/           kpagecount   mtrr         stat         vmallocinfo
cpuinfo     interrupts    kpageflags   net@         swaps        vmstat
```

```
crypto      iomem        latency_stats  pagetypeinfo  sys/           zoneinfo
devices     ioports      loadavg        partitions    sysrq-trigger
diskstats   irq/         locks          sched_debug   sysvipc/
```

System-wide files related to performance observability include

- **cpuinfo:** physical processor information, including every virtual CPU, model name, clock speed, and cache sizes.
- **diskstats:** disk I/O statistics for all disk devices
- **interrupts:** interrupt counters per CPU
- **loadavg:** load averages
- **meminfo:** system memory usage breakdowns
- **net/dev:** network interface statistics
- **net/tcp:** active TCP socket information
- **schedstat:** system-wide CPU scheduler statistics
- **self:** a symlink to the current process ID directory, for convenience
- **slabinfo:** kernel slab allocator cache statistics
- **stat:** a summary of kernel and system resource statistics: CPUs, disks, paging, swap, processes
- **zoneinfo:** memory zone information

These are read by system-wide tools. For example, here's vmstat(8) reading /proc, as traced by strace(1):

```
open("/proc/meminfo", O_RDONLY)          = 3
lseek(3, 0, SEEK_SET)                     = 0
read(3, "MemTotal:         889484 kB\nMemF"..., 2047) = 1170
open("/proc/stat", O_RDONLY)              = 4
read(4, "cpu  14901 0 18094 102149804 131"..., 65535) = 804
open("/proc/vmstat", O_RDONLY)            = 5
lseek(5, 0, SEEK_SET)                     = 0
read(5, "nr_free_pages 160568\nnr_inactive"..., 2047) = 1998
```

/proc files are usually text formatted, allowing them to be read easily from the command line and processed by shell scripting tools. For example:

```
$ cat /proc/meminfo
MemTotal:        889484 kB
MemFree:         636908 kB
Buffers:         125684 kB
Cached:           63944 kB
```

continues

```
SwapCached:               0 kB
Active:              119168 kB
[...]
$ grep Mem /proc/meminfo
MemTotal:            889484 kB
MemFree:             636908 kB
```

While this is convenient, it does add overhead for the kernel to encode the statistics as text, and for any user-land tool that then processes the text.

The contents of /proc are documented in the proc(5) man page and in the Linux kernel documentation: Documentation/filesystems/proc.txt. Some parts have extended documentation, such as diskstats in Documentation/iostats.txt and scheduler stats in Documentation/scheduler/sched-stats.txt. Apart from the documentation, you can also study the kernel source code to understand the exact origin of all items in /proc. It can also be helpful to read the source to the tools that consume them.

Some of the /proc entries depend on CONFIG options: schedstats are enabled with CONFIG_SCHEDSTATS, and sched with CONFIG_SCHED_DEBUG.

Solaris

On Solaris-based systems, /proc contains only process status statistics. System-wide observability is provided via other frameworks, mostly kstat.

Here is a list of files in a /proc process directory:

```
$ ls -F /proc/22449
as          cred  fd/    lstatus  map       path/  rmap    status  xmap
auxv        ctl   ldt    lusage   object/   priv   root@   usage
contracts/  cwd@  lpsinfo  lwp/   pagedata  psinfo  sigact  watch
```

Files related to performance observability include

- **map:** virtual address space mappings
- **psinfo:** miscellaneous process information, including CPU and memory usage
- **status:** process state information
- **usage:** extended process activity statistics, including process microstates, fault, block, context switch, and syscall counters
- **lstatus:** similar to status, but containing statistics for each thread
- **lpsinfo:** similar to psinfo, but containing statistics for each thread
- **lusage:** similar to usage, but containing statistics for each thread

- **lwpsinfo:** lightweight process (thread) statistics for the representative LWP (currently most active); there are also lwpstatus and lwpsinfo files
- **xmap:** extended memory mapping statistics (undocumented)

The following truss(1) output shows prstat(1M) reading status for a process:

```
open("/proc/4363/psinfo", O_RDONLY)            = 5
pread(5, "01\0\0\001\0\0\0\v11\0\0".., 416, 0)  = 416
```

The format of these files is binary, as seen by the pread() data above. psinfo contains

```
typedef struct psinfo {
    int pr_flag;                /* process flags (DEPRECATED: see below) */
    int pr_nlwp;                /* number of active lwps in the process */
    int pr_nzomb;               /* number of zombie lwps in the process */
    pid_t pr_pid;               /* process id */
    pid_t pr_ppid;              /* process id of parent */
    pid_t pr_pgid;              /* process id of process group leader */
    pid_t pr_sid;               /* session id */
    uid_t pr_uid;               /* real user id */
    uid_t pr_euid;              /* effective user id */
    gid_t pr_gid;               /* real group id */
    gid_t pr_egid;              /* effective group id */
    uintptr_t pr_addr;          /* address of process */
    size_t pr_size;             /* size of process image in Kbytes */
    size_t pr_rssize;           /* resident set size in Kbytes */
    dev_t pr_ttydev;            /* controlling tty device (or PRNODEV) */
    ushort_t pr_pctcpu;         /* % of recent cpu time used by all lwps */
    ushort_t pr_pctmem;         /* % of system memory used by process */
    timestruc_t pr_start;       /* process start time, from the epoch */
    timestruc_t pr_time;        /* cpu time for this process */
    timestruc_t pr_ctime;       /* cpu time for reaped children */
    char pr_fname[PRFNSZ];      /* name of exec'ed file */
    char pr_psargs[PRARGSZ];    /* initial characters of arg list */
    int pr_wstat;               /* if zombie, the wait() status */
    int pr_argc;                /* initial argument count */
    uintptr_t pr_argv;          /* address of initial argument vector */
    uintptr_t pr_envp;          /* address of initial environment vector */
    char pr_dmodel;             /* data model of the process */
    lwpsinfo_t pr_lwp;          /* information for representative lwp */
    taskid_t pr_taskid;         /* task id */
    projid_t pr_projid;         /* project id */
    poolid_t pr_poolid;         /* pool id */
    zoneid_t pr_zoneid;         /* zone id */
    ctid_t pr_contract;         /* process contract id */
} psinfo_t;
```

This can be read directly to a psinfo_t variable in user-space, where the members can then be dereferenced. This makes the Solaris /proc more suitable for processing by programs written in C, which can include the struct definitions from the system-supplied header files.

/proc is documented by the proc(4) man page, and by the sys/procfs.h header file. As with Linux, if the kernel is open source, it can be helpful to study the origin of these statistics and how tools consume them.

lxproc

There has been the occasional need for a Linux-like /proc on Solaris-based systems. One reason is for porting Linux observability tools (e.g., htop(1)), which can otherwise be difficult to port due to the /proc differences: from a text-based interface to binary.

One solution is the lxproc file system: it provides a loosely Linux-compatible /proc for Solaris-based systems and can be mounted in parallel with the standard procfs /proc. For example, lxproc can be mounted on /lxproc, and applications that require a Linux-like proc can be modified to load process information from /lxproc instead of /proc—what should be a minor change.

```
smartos# more /lxproc/meminfo
           total:      used:     free:  shared: buffers:   cached:
Mem:   1073741824 88395776 985346048        0        0        0
Swap: 2147483648 267640832 1879842816
MemTotal:    1048576 kB
MemFree:      962252 kB
[...]
```

Like Linux /proc, there are also directories for each process containing process information.

lxproc may be incomplete and require additions: it is provided only as a best-effort interface for simple Linux /proc users.

4.2.2 /sys

Linux provides a sysfs file system, mounted on /sys, which was introduced with the 2.6 kernel to provide a directory-based structure for kernel statistics. This differs from /proc, which has evolved over time and had various system statistics added to the top-level directory. sysfs was originally designed to provide device driver statistics but has been extended to include any statistic type.

For example, the following lists /sys files for CPU 0 (truncated):

```
$ find /sys/devices/system/cpu/cpu0 -type f
/sys/devices/system/cpu/cpu0/crash_notes
/sys/devices/system/cpu/cpu0/cache/index0/type
/sys/devices/system/cpu/cpu0/cache/index0/level
/sys/devices/system/cpu/cpu0/cache/index0/coherency_line_size
/sys/devices/system/cpu/cpu0/cache/index0/physical_line_partition
```

```
/sys/devices/system/cpu/cpu0/cache/index0/ways_of_associativity
/sys/devices/system/cpu/cpu0/cache/index0/number_of_sets
/sys/devices/system/cpu/cpu0/cache/index0/size
/sys/devices/system/cpu/cpu0/cache/index0/shared_cpu_map
/sys/devices/system/cpu/cpu0/cache/index0/shared_cpu_list
[...]
/sys/devices/system/cpu/cpu0/topology/physical_package_id
/sys/devices/system/cpu/cpu0/topology/core_id
/sys/devices/system/cpu/cpu0/topology/thread_siblings
/sys/devices/system/cpu/cpu0/topology/thread_siblings_list
/sys/devices/system/cpu/cpu0/topology/core_siblings
/sys/devices/system/cpu/cpu0/topology/core_siblings_list
```

Many of those listed provide information about the CPU hardware caches. The following output shows their contents (using grep(1), so that the file name is included with the output):

```
$ grep . /sys/devices/system/cpu/cpu0/cache/index*/level
/sys/devices/system/cpu/cpu0/cache/index0/level:1
/sys/devices/system/cpu/cpu0/cache/index1/level:1
/sys/devices/system/cpu/cpu0/cache/index2/level:2
/sys/devices/system/cpu/cpu0/cache/index3/level:3
$ grep . /sys/devices/system/cpu/cpu0/cache/index*/size
/sys/devices/system/cpu/cpu0/cache/index0/size:32K
/sys/devices/system/cpu/cpu0/cache/index1/size:32K
/sys/devices/system/cpu/cpu0/cache/index2/size:256K
/sys/devices/system/cpu/cpu0/cache/index3/size:8192K
```

This shows that CPU 0 has access to two Level 1 caches, each 32 Kbytes, a Level 2 cache of 256 Kbytes, and a Level 3 cache of 8 Mbytes.

The /sys file system typically has tens of thousands of statistics in read-only files, as well as many writeable files for changing kernel state. For example, CPUs can be set to online or offline by writing "1" or "0" to a file named "online." As with reading statistics, setting state can be performed by using text strings at the command line (echo 1 > filename), rather than a binary interface.

4.2.3 kstat

Solaris-based systems have a kernel statistics (kstat) framework used by system-wide observability tools. kstat includes statistics for most resources, including CPUs, disks, network interfaces, memory, and many software components in the kernel. A typical system has tens of thousands of statistics available from kstat.

Unlike /proc or /sys, there is no pseudo file system for kstat, and it is read from /dev/kstat via ioctl(). This is usually performed via the libkstat library, which provides convenience functions, or via Sun::Solaris::Kstat, a Perl library for the same purpose (although it is being phased out in some distributions in favor of libkstat). The kstat(1M) tool provides the statistics at the command line and can be used with shell scripting.

kstats are structured as a four-tuple:

```
module:instance:name:statistic
```

These are

- **module:** This usually refers to the kernel module that created the statistic, such as sd for the SCSI disk driver, or zfs for the ZFS file system.

- **instance:** Some modules exist as multiple instances, such as an sd module for each SCSI disk. The instance is an enumeration.

- **name:** This is a name for the group of statistics.

- **statistic:** This is the individual statistic name.

For example, the following reads the nproc statistic using kstat(1M) and specifying the full four-tuple:

```
$ kstat -p unix:0:system_misc:nproc
unix:0:system_misc:nproc        94
```

This statistic shows the currently running number of processes. The -p option to kstat(1M) was used to print parseable output (colon-separated). A blank field is treated as a wildcard. Trailing colons can also be dropped. These rules together allow the following to match and print all statistics from the system_misc group:

```
$ kstat -p unix:0:system_misc
unix:0:system_misc:avenrun_15min            201
unix:0:system_misc:avenrun_1min 383
unix:0:system_misc:avenrun_5min 260
unix:0:system_misc:boot_time    1335893569
unix:0:system_misc:class        misc
unix:0:system_misc:clk_intr     1560476763
unix:0:system_misc:crtime       0
unix:0:system_misc:deficit      0
unix:0:system_misc:lbolt        1560476763
unix:0:system_misc:ncpus        2
unix:0:system_misc:nproc        94
unix:0:system_misc:snaptime     15604804.5606589
unix:0:system_misc:vac   0
```

The avenrun* statistics are used to calculate the system *load averages*, as reported by tools including uptime(1) and top(1).

Many statistics in kstat are *cumulative*. Instead of providing the current value, they show the total since boot. For example:

```
$ kstat -p unix:0:vminfo:freemem
unix:0:vminfo:freemem   184882526123755
```

This freemem statistic is incremented per second with the number of free pages. This allows the average over time intervals to be calculated. The summary-since-boot, as printed by many system-wide observability tools, can also be calculated by dividing the current value by seconds since boot.

Another version of freemem provides the instantaneous value (unix:0:system_ pages:freemem). This mitigates a shortcoming in the cumulative version: it takes at least one second to know the current value, so that would be the minimum time for which a delta could be calculated.

Without any statistic name, kstat(1M) lists all statistics. For example, the following commands pipe the list of all statistics into grep(1) to search for those containing freemem, and then wc(1) to count the number of total statistics:

```
$ kstat -p | grep freemem
unix:0:system_pages:freemem     5962178
unix:0:vminfo:freemem   184893612065859
$ kstat -p | wc -l
   33195
```

The kstat statistics are not formally documented because they are considered an *unstable interface*—subject to change whenever the kernel changes. To understand what each does, the locations that increment them can be studied in the kernel source (if available). For example, the cumulative freemem statistic originates from the following kernel code:

```
usr/src/uts/common/sys/sysinfo.h:
typedef struct vminfo {        /* (update freq) update action        */
        uint64_t freemem;      /* (1 sec) += freemem in pages        */
        uint64_t swap_resv;    /* (1 sec) += reserved swap in pages  */
        uint64_t swap_alloc;   /* (1 sec) += allocated swap in pages */
        uint64_t swap_avail;   /* (1 sec) += unreserved swap in pages */
        uint64_t swap_free;    /* (1 sec) += unallocated swap in pages */
        uint64_t updates;      /* (1 sec) ++                         */
} vminfo_t;

usr/src/uts/common/os/space.c:
vminfo_t         vminfo;       /* VM stats protected by sysinfolock mutex */

usr/src/uts/common/os/clock.c:
static void
```

continues

```
clock(void)
{
[...]
        if (one_sec) {
[...]
                vminfo.freemem += freemem;
```

The freemem statistic is incremented once per second in the kernel clock() routine, by the value of a global called freemem. Locations that modify freemem can be inspected to see all the code involved.

The source code to the existing system tools (if available) can also be studied for example kstat usage.

4.2.4 Delay Accounting

Linux systems with the CONFIG_TASK_DELAY_ACCT option track time per task in the following states:

- **Scheduler latency:** waiting for a turn on-CPU
- **Block I/O:** waiting for a block I/O to complete
- **Swapping:** waiting for paging (memory pressure)
- **Memory reclaim:** waiting for the memory reclaim routine

Technically, the scheduler latency statistic is sourced from schedstats (mentioned earlier, in /proc) but is exposed with the other delay accounting states. (It is in struct sched_info, not struct task_delay_info.)

These statistics can be read by user-level tools using taskstats, which is a netlink-based interface for fetching per-task and process statistics. The kernel source Documentation/accounting directory has both the documentation, delay-accounting.txt, and an example consumer, getdelays.c:

```
$ ./getdelays -dp 17451
print delayacct stats ON
PID     17451

CPU             count    real total  virtual total  delay total  delay average
                386      3452475144    31387115236   1253300657        3.247ms
IO              count    delay total  delay average
                302      1535758266            5ms
SWAP            count    delay total  delay average
                0                 0            0ms
RECLAIM         count    delay total  delay average
                0                 0            0ms
```

Times are in nanoseconds unless specified otherwise. This example was taken from a heavily CPU-loaded system, and the process inspected was suffering scheduler latency.

4.2.5 Microstate Accounting

Solaris-based systems have per-thread and per-CPU *microstate accounting*, which records a set of high-resolution times for predefined states. These were a vast improvement of accuracy over the prior tick-based metrics and also provided additional states for performance analysis [McDougall 06b]. They are exposed to user-level tools via kstat for per-CPU metrics and /proc for per-thread metrics.

The CPU microstates are shown as the usr, sys, and idl columns of mpstat(1M) (see Chapter 6, CPUs). You can find them in the kernel code as CMS_USER, CMS_SYSTEM, and CMS_IDLE.

The thread microstates are visible as the USR, SYS, . . . columns from prstat -m and are summarized in Section 6.6.7, prstat of Chapter 6, CPUs.

4.2.6 Other Observability Sources

Various other observability sources include

- **CPU performance counters:** These are programmable hardware registers that provide low-level performance information, including CPU cycle counts, instruction counts, stall cycles, and so on. On Linux they are accessed via the perf_events interface and the perf_event_open() syscall and are consumed by tools including perf(1). On Solaris-based systems they are accessed via libcpc and consumed by tools including cpustat(1M). For more about these counters and tools, see Chapter 6, CPUs.

- **Per-process tracing:** This traces user-level software events, such as syscalls and function calls. It is usually expensive to perform, slowing the target. On Linux there is the ptrace() syscall for controlling process tracing, which is used by strace(1) for tracing syscalls. Linux also has uprobes for user-level dynamic tracing. Solaris-based systems trace syscalls using procfs and the truss(1) tool and dynamic tracing via DTrace.

- **Kernel tracing:** On Linux, tracepoints provide static kernel probes (originally *kernel makers*), and kprobes provide dynamic probes. Both of these are used by tracing tools such as ftrace, perf(1), DTrace, and SystemTap. On Solaris-based systems, static and dynamic probes are provided by the dtrace kernel module. Both DTrace and SystemTap, consumers of kernel tracing, will be covered in the following sections, which also explain the terms *static* and *dynamic* probes.

- **Network sniffing:** These interfaces provide a way to capture packets from network devices for detailed investigations into packet and protocol performance. On Linux, sniffing is provided via the libpcap library and /proc/net/dev and is consumed by the `tcpdump(8)` tool. On Solaris-based systems sniffing is provided via the libdlpi library and /dev/net and is consumed by the `snoop(1M)` tool. A port of libpcap and `tcpdump(8)` has also been developed for Solaris-based systems. There are overheads, both CPU and storage, for capturing and examining all packets. See Chapter 10, Network, for more about network sniffing.

- **Process accounting:** This dates back to mainframes and the need to bill departments and users for their computer usage, based on the execution and runtime of processes. It exists in some form for both Linux- and Solaris-based systems and can sometimes be helpful for performance analysis at the process level. For example, the `atop(1)` tool uses process accounting to catch and display information from short-lived processes that would otherwise be missed when taking snapshots of /proc [1].

- **System calls:** Some system or library calls may be available to provide some performance metrics. These include `getrusage()`, a function call for processes to get their own resource usage statistics, including user- and system-time, faults, messages, and context switches. Solaris-based systems also have `swapctl()`, a system function for swap device management and statistics (Linux has /proc/swap).

If you are interested in how each of these works, you will find that documentation is usually available, intended for the developer who is building tools upon these interfaces.

And More

Depending on your kernel version and enabled options, even more observability sources may be available. Some are mentioned in later chapters of this book.

Here are a few more:

- **Linux:** I/O accounting, blktrace, timer_stats, lockstat, debugfs
- **Solaris:** extended accounting, flow accounting, Solaris Auditing

One technique to find such sources is to read the kernel code you are interested in observing and see what statistics or tracepoints have been placed there.

In some cases there may be no kernel statistics for what you are after. Apart from dynamic tracing, covered next, you may find that debuggers can fetch kernel variables to shed some light on an investigation. These include `gdb(1)` and mdb(1) (Solaris only). A similar and even more desperate approach is used by tools that open /dev/mem or /dev/kmem to read kernel memory directly.

Multiple observability sources with different interfaces can be a burden to learn and can be inefficient when their capabilities overlap. As DTrace has been part of the Solaris kernel since 2003, there have been efforts to move some old tracing frameworks to DTrace, and to serve all new tracing needs from it. This consolidation has been working very well and has simplified tracing on Solaris-based systems. We can hope that this trend continues, and that the future for both kernels brings fewer, yet more powerful, observability frameworks.

4.3 DTrace

DTrace is an observability framework that includes a programming language and a tool. This section summarizes DTrace basics, including dynamic and static tracing, probes, providers, D, actions, variables, one-liners, and scripting. It is intended as a DTrace primer, providing you with enough background for understanding its use later in this book, where it is used to extend performance observability on both Solaris- and Linux-based systems.

DTrace can observe all user- and kernel-level code via instrumentation points called *probes*. When probes are hit, arbitrary actions may be performed in its D language. Actions can include counting events, recording timestamps, performing calculations, printing values, and summarizing data. These actions can be performed in *real time*, while tracing is still enabled.

As an example of using DTrace for dynamic tracing, the following instruments the kernel ZFS (file system) spa_sync() function, showing the completion time and duration in nanoseconds (illumos kernel):

```
# dtrace -n 'fbt:zfs:spa_sync:entry { self->start = timestamp; }
    fbt:zfs:spa_sync:return /self->start/ { printf("%Y: %d ns",
    walltimestamp, timestamp - self->start); self->start = 0; }'
dtrace: description 'fbt:zfs:spa_sync:entry ' matched 2 probes
CPU     ID                   FUNCTION:NAME
  7   65353            spa_sync:return 2012 Oct 30 00:20:27: 63849335 ns
 12   65353            spa_sync:return 2012 Oct 30 00:20:32: 39754457 ns
 18   65353            spa_sync:return 2012 Oct 30 00:20:37: 261013562 ns
  8   65353            spa_sync:return 2012 Oct 30 00:20:42: 29800786 ns
 17   65353            spa_sync:return 2012 Oct 30 00:20:47: 250368664 ns
 20   65353            spa_sync:return 2012 Oct 30 00:20:52: 37450783 ns
 11   65353            spa_sync:return 2012 Oct 30 00:20:57: 56010162 ns
[...]
```

The spa_sync() function flushes written data to the ZFS storage devices, causing bursts of disk I/O. It is of particular interest for performance analysis, as I/O can sometimes queue behind the issued disk I/O. Using DTrace, information about the rate at which `spa_sync()` fires, and the duration, can be immediately seen and studied. Thousands of other kernel functions can be studied in a similar way, by either printing per-event details or summarizing them.

A key difference of DTrace from other tracing frameworks (e.g., syscall tracing) is that DTrace is designed to be production-safe, with minimized performance overhead. One way it does this is by use of per-CPU kernel buffers, which improve memory locality, reduce cache coherency overheads, and can remove the need for synchronization locks. These buffers are also used to pass data to user-land at a gentle rate (by default, once per second), minimizing context switches. DTrace also provides a set of actions that can summarize and filter data in-kernel, which also reduces data overheads.

DTrace supports both *static* and *dynamic* tracing, each providing complementary functionality. Static probes have a documented and stable interface, and dynamic probes allow virtually unlimited observability as needed.

4.3.1 Static and Dynamic Tracing

One way to understand static and dynamic tracing is to examine the source and CPU instructions involved. Consider the following code from the kernel block device interface (illumos), usr/src/uts/common/os/bio.c:

```
/*
 * Mark I/O complete on a buffer, release it if I/O is asynchronous,
 * and wake up anyone waiting for it.
 */
void
biodone(struct buf *bp)
{
        if (bp->b_flags & B_STARTED) {
                DTRACE_IO1(done, struct buf *, bp);
                bp->b_flags &= ~B_STARTED;
        }
[...]
```

The `DTRACE_IO1` macro is an example of a *static probe*, which is added to the code before compilation. There is no visible example of dynamic probes in the source code, since these are added after compilation while the software is running.

The compiled instructions for this function are (truncated)

```
> biodone::dis
biodone:                        pushq   %rbp
biodone+1:                      movq    %rsp,%rbp
biodone+4:                      subq    $0x20,%rsp
biodone+8:                      movq    %rbx,-0x18(%rbp)
```

```
biodone+0xc:       movq    %rdi,-0x8(%rbp)
biodone+0x10:      movq    %rdi,%rbx
biodone+0x13:      movl    (%rdi),%eax
biodone+0x15:      testl   $0x2000000,%eax
[...]
```

When using *dynamic tracing* to probe the entry to the `biodone()` function, the first instruction is changed:

```
> biodone::dis
biodone:           int     $0x3
biodone+1:         movq    %rsp,%rbp
biodone+4:         subq    $0x20,%rsp
biodone+8:         movq    %rbx,-0x18(%rbp)
biodone+0xc:       movq    %rdi,-0x8(%rbp)
biodone+0x10:      movq    %rdi,%rbx
biodone+0x13:      movl    (%rdi),%eax
biodone+0x15:      testl   $0x2000000,%eax
[...]
```

The `int` instruction calls a soft interrupt, which is programmed to perform the dynamic tracing action. When dynamic tracing is disabled, the instruction is returned to its original state. This is *live patching* of the kernel address space, and the technique used can vary between processor types.

Instructions are added only when dynamic tracing is enabled. When it is not enabled, there are no additional instructions for instrumentation, and therefore no probe effect. This is described as *zero overhead when not in use*. The overhead when it is in use from the additional instructions is proportional to the rate at which the probes fire: the rate of events that are traced, and the actions they perform.

DTrace can dynamically trace the entry and return of functions, and any instruction in user-space. Since this dynamically builds probes from CPU instructions, which can vary between software releases, it is considered an *unstable interface*. Any DTrace one-liners or scripts based on dynamic tracing may need updating for newer releases of the software that they trace.

4.3.2 Probes

DTrace probes are named with a four-tuple:

```
provider:module:function:name
```

The *provider* is the collection of related probes, similar to a software library. The *module* and *function* are dynamically generated and specify the code location of the probe. The *name* is the name of the probe itself.

When specifying these, wildcards ("*") may be used. Leaving a field blank ("::") is equivalent to a wildcard (":*:"). Blank left fields may also be dropped from the probe specification (e.g., ":::BEGIN" == "BEGIN").

For example:

```
io:::start
```

is the start probe from the io provider. The module and function fields are left blank, so these will match all locations of the start probe.

4.3.3 Providers

The DTrace providers available depend on your DTrace and operating system version. They may include

- **syscall:** system call trap table
- **vminfo:** virtual memory statistics
- **sysinfo:** system statistics
- **profile:** sampling at arbitrary rates
- **sched:** kernel scheduling events
- **proc:** process-level events: create, exec, exit
- **io:** block device interface tracing (disk I/O)
- **pid:** user-level dynamic tracing
- **tcp:** TCP protocol events: connections, send and receive
- **ip:** IP protocol events: send and receive
- **fbt:** kernel-level dynamic tracing

There are many additional providers for higher-level languages: Java, JavaScript, Node.js, Perl, Python, Ruby, Tcl, and others.

Many of the providers are implemented using static tracing, so that they have a stable interface. It's preferable to use these (over dynamic tracing) where possible, so that your scripts work for different versions of the target software. The trade-off is that visibility is limited in comparison, as only the essentials are promoted to the stable interface, to minimize maintenance and the documentation burden.

4.3.4 Arguments

Probes can provide data via a set of variables called *arguments*. The use of arguments depends on the provider.

For example, the syscall provider provides entry and return probes for each system call. These set the following argument variables:

- **Entry:** arg0, ..., argN: arguments to system call
- **Return:** arg0 or arg1: return value; errno is also set

The fbt and pid providers set arguments similarly, allowing the data passed and returned to kernel- or user-level functions to be examined.

To find out what the arguments are for each provider, refer to its documentation (you can also try dtrace(1) with the −lv options, which prints a summary).

4.3.5 D Language

The D language is awk-like and can be used in one-liners or scripts (the same as awk). DTrace statements have the form

```
probe_description /predicate/ { action }
```

The *action* is a series of optional semicolon-delimited statements that are executed when the probe fires. The *predicate* is an optional filtering expression.

For example, the statement

```
proc:::exec-success /execname == "httpd"/ { trace(pid); }
```

traces the exec-success probe from the proc provider and performs the printing action trace(pid) if the process name is equal to "httpd". The exec-success probe is commonly used to trace the creation of new processes and instruments a successful exec() system call. The current process name is retrieved using the built-in variable execname, and the current process ID via pid.

4.3.6 Built-in Variables

Built-in variables can be used in calculations and predicates and can be printed using actions such as trace() and printf(). Commonly used built-ins are listed in Table 4.2.

Table 4.2 Commonly Used Built-in Variables

Variable	Description
execname	on-CPU process name (string)
uid	on-CPU user ID
pid	on-CPU process ID
timestamp	current time, nanoseconds since boot
vtimestamp	time thread was on-CPU, nanoseconds
arg0..N	probe arguments (uint64_t)
args[0]..[N]	probe arguments (typed)
curthread	pointer to current thread kernel structure
probefunc	function component of probe description (string)
probename	name component of probe description (string)
curpsinfo	current process information

4.3.7 Actions

Commonly used actions include those listed in Table 4.3.

Table 4.3 Commonly Used Actions

Action	Description
trace(arg)	print arg
printf(format, arg, ...)	print formatted string
stringof(addr)	return a string from a kernel address
copyinstr(addr)	return a string from a user-space address (this requires the kernel to perform a *copy in* from user-space to kernel-space)
stack(count)	print kernel-level stack trace, truncated if a count is provided
ustack(count)	print user-level stack trace, truncated if a count is provided
func(pc)	return a kernel function name, from the kernel program counter (pc)
ufunc(pc)	return a user function name, from the user program counter (pc)
exit(status)	exit DTrace and return status
trunc(@agg, count)	truncate the aggregation, either fully (delete all keys) or to the number of keys specified (count)
clear(@agg)	delete values from an aggregation (keep keys)
printa(format, @agg)	print aggregation, formatted

The last three actions listed are for a special variable type called an *aggregation*.

4.3.8 Variable Types

Table 4.4 summarizes the types of variables, listed in order of usage preference (aggregations are chosen first, then low to high overhead).

Table 4.4 Variable Types and Their Overhead

Type	Prefix	Scope	Overhead	Multi-CPU Safe	Example Assignment
Aggregation	@	global	low	yes	`@x = count();`
Aggregation with keys	@[]	global	low	yes	`@x[pid] = count();`
Clause-local	this->	clause instance	very low	yes	`this->x = 1;`
Thread-local	self->	thread	medium	yes	`self->x = 1;`
Scalar	none	global	low–medium	no	`x = 1;`
Associative array	none	global	medium–high	no	`x[y] = 1;`

The *thread-local* variable has a per-thread scope. This allows data, such as timestamps, to be easily associated with a thread.

The *clause-local* variable is used for intermediate calculations and is valid only during action clauses for the same probe description.

Multiple CPUs writing to the same scalar at the same time can lead to a corrupt variable state, hence the "no." It's unlikely, but has happened, and has been noticed for string scalars (leading to a corrupted string).

An *aggregation* is a special variable type that can be tallied per CPU and combined later for passing to user-land. These have the lowest overhead and are used for summarizing data in different ways.

Actions that populate aggregations are listed in Table 4.5.

Table 4.5 Aggregating Actions

Aggregating Action	Description
`count()`	count occurrences
`sum(value)`	sum value

continues

Table 4.5 Aggregating Actions (*Continued*)

Aggregating Action	Description
min(value)	record minimum of value
max(value)	record maximum of value
quantize(value)	record value as a power-of-two histogram
lquantize(value, min, max, step)	record value as a linear histogram, with minimum, maximum, and step provided
llquantize(value, factor, min_magnitude, max_magnitude, steps)	record value as a hybrid log/linear histogram

As an example of an aggregation and a histogram action, quantize(), the following shows the returned sizes for the read() syscall:

```
# dtrace -n 'syscall::read:return { @["rval (bytes)"] = quantize(arg0); }'
dtrace: description 'syscall::read:return ' matched 1 probe
^C
  rval (bytes)
           value  ------------- Distribution ------------- count
              -1 |                                         0
               0 |@@@@@@@@@@@@@@                           447
               1 |@@@                                      100
               2 |                                         5
               4 |                                         0
               8 |                                         2
              16 |                                         2
              32 |@@                                       53
              64 |                                         1
             128 |                                         0
             256 |                                         0
             512 |                                         4
            1024 |@                                        19
            2048 |                                         10
            4096 |@                                        34
            8192 |@@@@                                     130
           16384 |@@@@@@                                   170
           32768 |@@@@                                     125
           65536 |@@@@                                     114
          131072 |                                         5
          262144 |                                         5
          524288 |                                         0
```

This one-liner gathers statistics while tracing and prints a summary when dtrace ends, in this case, when Ctrl-C was typed. The first line of output, dtrace: description ..., is printed by default by dtrace, providing an indication of when tracing has begun.

The value column is the minimum size for the quantized range, and the count column is the occurrences for that range. The middle shows an ASCII representation of the distribution. In this case, the most frequently returned size was zero bytes, which occurred 447 times. Many of the returned reads were between 8,192 and 131,071 bytes, with 170 in the 16,384 to 32,767 range. This bimodal distribution would not have been noticed in a tool that reported only an average.

4.3.9 One-Liners

DTrace allows you to write concise and powerful one-liners like those I demonstrated earlier. Following are some more examples.

Trace open() system calls, printing the process name and file path name:

```
dtrace -n 'syscall::open:entry { printf("%s %s", execname, copyinstr(arg0)); }'
```

Note that Oracle Solaris 11 significantly modified the system call trap table (which is probed by DTrace to create the syscall provider), such that tracing open() on that system becomes

```
dtrace -n 'syscall::openat:entry { printf("%s %s", execname, copyinstr(arg1)); }'
```

Summarize CPU cross calls by process name:

```
dtrace -n 'sysinfo:::xcalls { @[execname] = count(); }'
```

Sample kernel-level stacks at 99 Hz:

```
dtrace -n 'profile:::profile-99 { @[stack()] = count(); }'
```

Many more DTrace one-liners are used throughout this book and are listed in Appendix D.

4.3.10 Scripting

DTrace statements can be saved to a file for execution, allowing much longer DTrace programs to be written.

For example, the bitesize.d script shows requested disk I/O sizes by process name:

```
#!/usr/sbin/dtrace -s

#pragma D option quiet

dtrace:::BEGIN
{
        printf("Tracing... Hit Ctrl-C to end.\n");
}

io:::start
{
        this->size = args[0]->b_bcount;
        @Size[pid, curpsinfo->pr_psargs] = quantize(this->size);
}

dtrace:::END
{
        printf("\n%8s  %s\n", "PID", "CMD");
        printa("%8d  %S\n%@d\n", @Size);
}
```

Since this file begins with an interpreter line (#!), it can be made executable and then run from the command line.

The #pragma line sets quiet mode, which suppresses the default DTrace output (which was seen in the earlier spa_sync() example and consists of the CPU, ID, and FUNCTION:NAME columns).

The actual enabling in this script by the io:::start probe is straightforward. The dtrace:::BEGIN probe fires at the start to print an informational message, and dtrace:::END fires at the end to format and print the summary.

Here is some example output:

```
# ./bitesize.d
Tracing... Hit Ctrl-C to end.
^C

    PID  CMD
   3424  tar cf /dev/null .\0

        value  ------------- Distribution ------------- count
          512 |                                         0
         1024 |@@@                                      39
         2048 |@@@@@@                                   71
         4096 |@@@@@@@@@                                111
         8192 |@@@@@@@@@@@@@@@@@@@@@@                    259
        16384 |                                         6
        32768 |@                                        8
        65536 |                                         0
```

While tracing, most of the disk I/O was requested by the tar command, with sizes shown above.

bitesize.d is from a collection of DTrace scripts called the DTraceToolkit, which can be found online.

4.3.11 Overheads

As has been mentioned, DTrace minimizes instrumentation overhead by use of per-CPU kernel buffers and in-kernel aggregation summaries. By default, it also passes data from kernel-space to user-space at a gentle asynchronous rate of once per second. It has various other features that reduce overhead and improve safety, including a routine whereby it will abort tracing if it detects that the system may have become unresponsive.

The overhead cost of performing tracing is relative to the frequency of traces and the actions they perform. Tracing block device I/O is typically so infrequent (1,000 I/O per second or less) that the overheads are negligible. On the other hand, tracing network I/O, when packet rates can reach millions per second, can cause significant overhead.

The action also comes at a cost. For example, I frequently sample kernel stacks at a rate of 997 Hz across all CPUs (using stack()) without a noticeable overhead. Sampling user-level stacks is more involved (using ustack()), for which I typically reduce the rate to 97 Hz.

There are also overheads when saving data into variables, especially associative arrays. While the use of DTrace typically comes without noticeable overhead, you do need to be aware that it is possible, and to use some caution.

4.3.12 Documentation and Resources

The reference for DTrace, which documents all actions, built-ins, and standard providers, is the *Dynamic Tracing Guide*, originally by Sun Microsystems and made freely available online [2]. For background on dynamic tracing, the problems it solves, and the evolution of DTrace, see [Cantrill 04] and [Cantrill 06].

Appendix D lists handy DTrace one-liners. Apart from their utility, they may be a useful reference for learning DTrace, one line at a time.

For a reference of scripts and strategy, see the text *DTrace: Dynamic Tracing in Oracle Solaris, Mac OS X and FreeBSD* [Gregg 11]. The scripts from this book are available online [3].

The DTraceToolkit contains over 200 scripts and is currently hosted on my home page [4]. Many of the scripts are wrapped in shell or Perl, to provide command-line options and behavior like other Unix tools, for example, execsnoop:

```
# execsnoop -h
USAGE: execsnoop [-a|-A|-ehjsvZ] [-c command]
       execsnoop                 # default output
                -a               # print all data
                -A               # dump all data, space delimited
                -e               # safe output, parseable
                -j               # print project ID
                -s               # print start time, us
                -v               # print start time, string
                -Z               # print zonename
                -c command       # command name to snoop
  eg,
          execsnoop -v           # human readable timestamps
          execsnoop -Z           # print zonename
          execsnoop -c ls        # snoop ls commands only
```

GUIs have also been built upon DTrace, including Oracle ZFS Appliance Analytics and Joyent Cloud Analytics.

4.4 SystemTap

SystemTap also provides static and dynamic tracing for user- and kernel-level code and was conceived for Linux by a team from Red Hat, IBM, and Intel [Eigler 05], at a time when no ports of DTrace for Linux were available. As with DTrace, instrumentation points called *probes* can be programmed to perform arbitrary actions, including counting events, recording timestamps, performing calculations, printing values, summarizing data, and so forth. These actions are performed in real time, while tracing is still enabled. SystemTap can be used from the command line as one-liners or scripts.

SystemTap sources other kernel frameworks for tracing: tracepoints for static probes, kprobes for dynamic probes, and uprobes for user-level probes. These sources are also used by other tools (perf, LTTng).

After several years of development, SystemTap has made good progress in matching the DTrace feature set and in some cases has surpassed it. However, stability has been an issue, with some versions causing kernel panics or hangs.[1] SystemTap has had other issues as well, though minor in comparison: slower start-up time, confusing error messages, undocumented implicit functionality, and a less-concise language.

---

1. The SystemTap wiki has always reported "safe use on production systems" as "yes." This is despite bug 2725, reported in 2006, which induces a kernel hang when tracing all kernel function probes. The latest comment from August 2012 for this issue reads: "Kernel bugs are believed to be responsible for the remaining occurrences of such crashes."

Meanwhile, two separate projects have been begun to port DTrace to Linux. One is by Oracle for Oracle Enterprise Linux; the other is a largely solo effort by a UK-based programmer, Paul Fox. These ports have been used to provide the DTrace Linux examples in this book. Since these are new projects and still in development, they, too, can induce kernel panics.

If you wish or need to use SystemTap instead, it should be possible to convert most of the DTrace scripts in this book. Appendix E is a short guide to this conversion.

The next section summarizes SystemTap basics—probes, tapsets, actions, and built-ins—and then provides two examples of SystemTap for comparison.

4.4.1 Probes

Probe definitions are period-delimited with optional embedded arguments in parentheses. Some examples are

- **begin:** start of program
- **end:** end of program
- **syscall.read:** start of the read() syscall
- **syscall.read.return:** end of the read() syscall
- **kernel.function("sys_read"):** start of the kernel sys_read() function
- **kernel.function("sys_read").return:** end of the sys_read() function
- **socket.send:** a socket send
- **timer.ms(100):** a probe that fires every 100 ms on one CPU
- **timer.profile:** a probe that fires on all CPUs at the kernel clock rate, used for sampling/profiling
- **process("a.out").statement("*@main.c:100"):** trace the target process, executable "a.out", line 100 of main.c

Many of the probes provide related data as built-in variables. For example, the syscall.read probe provides the requested size as $count.

4.4.2 Tapsets

Groups of related probes are called *tapsets*. Many of the probes include the tapset name at the beginning of the probe name. Examples of tapsets are

- **syscall:** system calls
- **ioblock:** block device interface and I/O scheduler

- **scheduler:** kernel CPU scheduler events
- **memory:** process and virtual memory usage
- **scsi:** SCSI target events
- **networking:** network device events, including receive and transmit
- **tcp:** TCP protocol events, including for send and receive events
- **socket:** socket events

Tapsets are also used to provide additional executable actions.

4.4.3 Actions and Built-ins

SystemTap also provides many actions and built-ins, including `execname()` for the process name, `pid()` for the current process ID, and `print_backtrace()` to print the kernel stack backtrace. More are listed in Appendix E.

4.4.4 Examples

The following one-liner traces the `read()` system call, saving a power-of-two histogram of the returned read size. This has been included both as an example of SystemTap and as a comparison to DTrace, for which the equivalent one-liner was demonstrated earlier.

```
# stap -ve 'global stats; probe syscall.read.return { stats <<< $return; }
    probe end { printf("\n\trval (bytes)\n"); print(@hist_log(stats)); }'
Pass 1: parsed user script and 77 library script(s) using 202200virt/22864res/3060shr
kb, in 100usr/10sys/125real ms.
Pass 2: analyzed script: 2 probe(s), 1 function(s), 2 embed(s), 1 global(s) using
370116virt/143020res/91712shr kb, in 350usr/110sys/711real ms.
Pass 3: translated to C into "/tmp/stapgOPjnH/stap_82838d54d78482c02d20b14d10b2eb13_
6394.c" using 370116virt/144708res/93400shr kb, in 40usr/10sys/549real ms.
Pass 4: compiled C into "stap_82838d54d78482c02d20b14d10b2eb13_6394.ko" in 560usr/
0sys/5638real ms.
Pass 5: starting run.
^C
        rval (bytes)
value |-------------------------------------------------- count
  -32 |                                                       0
  -16 |                                                       0
   -8 |@@@@@@@@@@@@@@@@@@@@@@                                 22
   -4 |                                                       0
   -2 |                                                       0
   -1 |                                                       0
    0 |@@@@@@@@@@@@@@@@@@@@@@@@@@@@@@@                        31
    1 |@@@                                                    3
    2 |@@@@                                                   4
    4 |                                                       0
    8 |@                                                      1
   16 |@@@@@                                                  5
```

```
  32 |@@@@@@                                                    6
  64 |                                                          0
 128 |                                                          0
 256 |@                                                         1
 512 |@@@@@@@@@@@@@@@@@@@@@@@@@@@@@@@@@@@@@@                    29
1024 |                                                          0
2048 |                                                          0
```

The −v option prints verbose information about the compilation stages, which informs the user when tracing has been enabled ("starting run"). Without it, SystemTap prints nothing by default, leaving you wondering when tracing has begun. In some cases the compilation stages can take over 20 seconds, and an early Ctrl-C will not only abort tracing altogether but can print confusing error messages depending on the stage of compilation that was interrupted.

The one-liner begins by declaring a global variable stats—SystemTap requires pre-declarations. The probe definition is prefixed with the keyword probe and matches the return of read() system calls. The action is to record the return value, provided as $return, in the stats variable using the statistics operator <<<. This records values in a generic fashion, allowing them to be summarized in different ways later.

The end probe is required to print this statistics variable as a histogram. Without it, SystemTap prints a basic numerical summary on exit.

One final note from the histogram: the $return value for read() is sometimes negative—set to a negative version of the error number (errno). This follows the kernel convention instead of the POSIX standard and could be confusing to users who are expecting to see the latter. It also isn't clear that this is intentional, as the purpose of $return is undocumented.

Here are the equivalent one-liners, first SystemTap, then DTrace:

```
stap -e 'global stats; probe syscall.read.return { stats <<< $return; }
    probe end { printf("\trval (bytes)\n"); print(@hist_log(stats)); }'

dtrace -n 'syscall::read:return { @["rval (bytes)"] = quantize(arg0); }'
```

Comparisons like this can provide a deeper understanding of each individual technology. Here is a different example, this time using SystemTap to highlight limitations with DTrace:

```
# stap -e 'global s; probe syscall.read.return {
    if ($return >= 0) { s[execname()] <<< $return; } }
    probe end { printf("\n%-36s %8s %8s %10s\n", "EXEC", "CALLS", "AVGSZ",
    "TOTAL"); foreach (k in s+) { printf("%-36s %8d %8d %10d\n", k,
    @count(s[k]), @avg(s[k]), @sum(s[k])); } }'
^C
```

continues

```
EXEC                             CALLS    AVGSZ      TOTAL
tty                                  1      832        832
hostname                             2      832       1664
sendmail                             2       25         50
systemd                              3       14         44
dbus-daemon                          4       16         65
tput                                 4     1272       5088
dircolors                            4     1585       6340
systemd-logind                       5      191        958
grep                                 8     1116       8930
id                                   9      703       6329
systemd-cgroups                     12      586       7036
tar                                 49      607      29769
stapio                              52        0         12
bash                                54     1793      96875
sshd                               313      995     311535
```

This one-liner saves a statistic of read return sizes by process name. It is printed using three different functions, providing the columns for the number of calls, average size (bytes), and total bytes. DTrace requires three separate aggregations to be populated for this, one for each type.

This also makes use of `if` statements and a `foreach` loop. DTrace does not provide `if`, instead providing branch functionality via predicates, which can at times be unnatural for programmers to follow. DTrace also currently has no loop capability, apart from unrolled loops, as for safety it never performs backward jumps. SystemTap solved this issue by providing an upper bound to the loop, so that an infinite loop in a SystemTap script would not hang in kernel context.

One final difference: statistic values can be accessed directly in SystemTap, such as with `s[k]`, whereas DTrace aggregations can be printed only in their entirety, or processed by aggregating functions.

4.4.5 Overheads

The overheads of using SystemTap are similar to those described earlier for DTrace, with the same cautions for use. Additionally, the compilation stages of SystemTap can consume CPU resources (for several seconds) when programs are first executed. SystemTap caches programs so that this overhead does not occur for every use. It should also be possible to compile SystemTap programs on a different system, then transfer the cached result to the target system.

Another additional overhead is the requirement for kernel debug information for kernel analysis, which is not typically included in a Linux distribution (it can be hundreds of megabytes in size).

4.4.6 Documentation and Resources

SystemTap has an extensive collection of man pages, including pages for individual probes. For example, for the `ioblock.request` probe:

```
$ man probe::ioblock.request
PROBE::IOBLOCK.REQ(3stapIO Scheduler and block IO TapPROBE::IOBLOCK.REQ(3stap)

NAME
        probe::ioblock.request - Fires whenever making a generic block I/O
        request.

SYNOPSIS
        ioblock.request

VALUES
        None

DESCRIPTION
        name - name of the probe point devname - block device name ino - i-node
        number of the mapped file sector - beginning sector for the entire bio
        flags - see below BIO_UPTODATE 0 ok after I/O completion BIO_RW_BLOCK 1
        RW_AHEAD set, and read/write would block BIO_EOF 2 out-out-bounds error
        BIO_SEG_VALID 3 nr_hw_seg valid BIO_CLONED 4 doesn't own data
        BIO_BOUNCED 5 bio is a bounce bio BIO_USER_MAPPED 6 contains user pages
        BIO_EOPNOTSUPP 7 not supported
[...]
```

The SystemTap language is documented online in the *SystemTap Language Reference* [5]. There is also a tutorial, beginner's guide, and tapset reference on the SystemTap documentation site [6].

You can also treat all the DTrace examples in this book as examples of possible SystemTap functionality. See Appendix E for their conversion.

4.5 perf

Linux Performance Events (LPE), perf for short, has been evolving to support a wide range of performance observability activities. While it doesn't currently have the real-time programmatic capabilities of DTrace or SystemTap, it can perform static and dynamic tracing (based on tracepoints, kprobes, and uprobes), as well as profiling. It can also inspect stack traces, local variables, and data types. Since it is part of the mainline kernel, it may be the easiest to use (if it is already there) and may provide enough observability to answer many of your questions.

Some of the tracing overheads from `perf(1)` should be similar to those of DTrace. In typical use, DTrace programs are written to summarize data in-kernel (aggregations), which `perf(1)` does not currently do. With `perf(1)`, data is passed to the user level for post-processing (it has a scripting framework to help), which can cause significant additional overhead when tracing frequent events.

See Section 6.6, Analysis, in Chapter 6, CPUs, for an introduction to perf(1) and a demonstration of many of its capabilities.

4.6 Observing Observability

Observability tools and the statistics upon which they are built are implemented in software, and all software has the potential for bugs. The same is true for the documentation that describes the software. Regard with a healthy skepticism any statistics that are new to you, questioning what they really mean and whether they are really correct.

Metrics may be subject to any of the following problems:

- Tools are not always right.

- Man pages are not always right.

- Available metrics may be incomplete.

- Available metrics may be poorly designed.

When multiple observability tools have overlapping coverage, you can use them to cross-check each other. Ideally, they will source different frameworks to check for bugs there, too. Dynamic tracing is especially useful for this purpose, as custom tools can be created with it.

Another verification technique is to apply *known workloads* and then to check that the observability tools agree with the results you expect. This can involve the use of micro-benchmarking tools that report their own statistics for comparison.

Sometimes it isn't the tool or statistic that is in error, but the documentation that describes it, including man pages. The software may have evolved without the documentation being updated.

Realistically, you may not have time to double-check every performance measurement you use and will do this only if unusual results are encountered or particularly important results are used. Even if you do not double-check, it can be valuable to be aware that you didn't, and that you assumed the tools were correct.

Apart from metrics being incorrect, they can also be incomplete. When faced with a large number of tools and metrics, it may be tempting to assume that they provide complete and effective coverage. This is often not the case: metrics may have been added by programmers to debug their own code and later built into observability tools without much study of real customer needs. Some programmers may not have added any at all to new subsystems.

An absence of metrics can be more difficult to identify than the presence of poor metrics. Chapter 2, Methodology, can help you find these missing metrics by studying the questions you need answered for performance analysis.

4.7 Exercises

1. Answer the following questions about observability tool terminology:
   - What is profiling?
   - What is tracing?
   - What is the difference between static and dynamic tracing?

4.8 References

[Cantrill 04]   Cantrill, B., M. Shapiro, and A. Leventhal. "Dynamic Instrumentation of Production Systems." USENIX, 2004.

[Eigler 05]   Eigler, F. Ch., et al. *Architecture of SystemTap: A Linux Trace / Probe Tool*, http://sourceware.org/systemtap/archpaper.pdf, 2005.

[Cantrill 06]   Cantrill, B. "Hidden in Plain Sight," *ACM Queue*, 2006.

[McDougall 06b]   McDougall, R., J. Mauro, and B. Gregg. *Solaris Performance and Tools: DTrace and MDB Techniques for Solaris 10 and OpenSolaris*. Prentice Hall, 2006.

[Gregg 11]   Gregg, B., and J. Mauro. *DTrace: Dynamic Tracing in Oracle Solaris, Mac OS X and FreeBSD*. Prentice Hall, 2011.

[1]   www.atoptool.nl/index.php

[2]   http://dtrace.org/guide

[3]   www.dtracebook.com

[4]   www.brendangregg.com/dtrace.html

[5]   http://sourceware.org/systemtap/langref

[6]   http://sourceware.org/systemtap/documentation.html

Applications

Performance is best tuned closest to where the work is performed: in the applications. These include databases, web servers, application servers, load balancers, file servers, and more. The chapters that follow approach applications from the perspectives of the resources they consume: CPUs, memory, file systems, disks, and the network. This chapter addresses the application level.

Applications themselves can become extremely complex, especially in distributed application environments involving many components. The study of application internals is usually the domain of the application developer and can include the use of third-party tools for introspection. For those studying systems performance, including system administrators, application performance analysis includes configuration of the application to make best use of system resources, characterization of how the application is using the system, and analysis of common pathologies.

This chapter discusses application basics, fundamentals for application performance, programming languages and compilers, and strategies for generic application performance analysis.

5.1 Application Basics

Before diving into application performance, you should familiarize yourself with the role of the application, its basic characteristics, and its ecosystem in the industry. This forms the context within which you can understand application activity. It also gives you opportunities to learn about common performance issues and tuning and provides avenues for further study. To learn this context, try answering the following questions:

- **Function:** What is the role of the application? Is it a database server, web server, load balancer, file server, object store?

- **Operation:** What requests does the application serve, or what operations does it perform? Databases serve *queries* (and *commands*), web servers serve *HTTP requests*, and so on. This can be measured as a rate, to gauge load and for capacity planning.

- **CPU mode:** Is the application implemented as user-level or kernel-level software? Most applications are user-level, executing as one or more processes, but some are implemented as kernel services (for example, NFS).

- **Configuration:** How is the application configured, and why? This information may be found in a configuration file or via administration tools. Check if any tunable parameters related to performance have been changed, including buffer sizes, cache sizes, parallelism (processes or threads), and other options.

- **Metrics:** Are application metrics provided, such as an operation rate? They may be provided by bundled tools or third-party tools, via API requests, or by processing operation logs.

- **Logs:** What operation logs does the application create? What logs can be enabled? What performance metrics, including latency, are available from the logs? For example, MySQL supports a *slow query log*, providing valuable performance details for each query slower than a certain threshold.

- **Version:** Is the application the latest version? Have performance fixes or improvements been noted in the release notes for recent versions?

- **Bugs:** Is there a bug database for the application? What are the "performance" bugs for your version of the application? If you have a current performance issue, search the bug database to see if anything like it has happened before, how it was investigated, and what else was involved.

- **Community:** Is there a community for the application where performance findings are shared? Communities may include forums, blogs, Internet Relay Chat (IRC) channels, meetups, and conferences. Meetups and conferences often post slides and videos online, which are useful resources for years afterward. They may also have a community manager who shares community updates and news.

- **Books:** Are there books about the application and/or its performance?

- **Experts:** Who are the recognized performance experts for the application? Learning their names can help you find material they have authored.

Regardless of the source, you are aiming to understand the application at a high level—what it does, how it operates, and how it performs. An immensely useful resource, if you can find one, is a *functional diagram* illustrating application internals.

The next sections cover other application basics: setting objectives, optimizing the common case, observability, and big O notation.

5.1.1 Objectives

A performance goal provides direction for your performance analysis work and helps you select which activities to perform. Without a clear goal, performance analysis risks turning into a random "fishing expedition."

For application performance, you can start with what operations the application performs (as described earlier) and what the goal for performance is. The goal may be

- **Latency:** a low application response time
- **Throughput:** a high application operation rate or data transfer rate
- **Resource utilization:** efficiency for a given application workload

It is better if these can be quantified, using metrics that may be derived from business or quality-of-service requirements. Examples are

- An average application request latency of 5 ms
- 95% of requests at a latency of 100 ms or less
- Elimination of latency outliers: zero requests beyond 1,000 ms
- A maximum throughput of at least 10,000 application requests per second per server
- Average disk utilization under 50% for 10,000 application requests per second

Once a goal has been chosen, you can work on the limiters for that goal. For latency, the limiter may be disk or network I/O; for throughput, it may be CPU usage. The strategies in this and other chapters will help you identify them.

For throughput-based goals, note that not all operations are equal in terms of performance or cost. If the goal is a certain rate of operations, it may be important to also specify what type of operations they are. This may be a distribution based on expected or measured workloads.

Section 5.2, Application Performance Techniques, describes common methods for improving application performance. Some of these may make sense for one goal but not another; for example, selecting a larger I/O size may improve throughput at the expense of latency. Remember the goal that you are pursuing to see which topics are most applicable.

5.1.2 Optimize the Common Case

Software internals can be complex, with many different possible code paths and behaviors. This may be especially evident if you browse the source code: applications are commonly tens of thousands of lines of code, while operating system kernels are upward of hundreds of thousands. Picking areas to optimize at random may involve a great deal of work for not much gain.

One way to efficiently improve application performance is to find the most common code path for the production workload and begin by improving that. If the application is CPU-bound, that may mean the code paths that are frequently on-CPU. If the application is I/O-bound, you should be looking at the code paths that frequently lead to I/O. These can be determined by analysis and profiling of the application, including studying stack traces, as covered in later chapters. A higher level of context for understanding the common case may also be provided by application observability tools.

5.1.3 Observability

As is described in many chapters of this book, the biggest performance wins in operating systems can come from *eliminating unnecessary work*. The same is true for applications.

This fact sometimes gets overlooked when an application is being chosen based on performance. If benchmarking showed application A to be 10% faster than application B, it may be tempting to choose application A. However, if application A is opaque and application B provides a rich set of observability tools, it's very likely that application B will be the better choice in the long run. Those observability tools make it possible to see and eliminate unnecessary work, and active work can be better understood and tuned. The performance wins gained through enhanced observability may dwarf the initial 10% performance difference.

5.1.4 Big O Notation

Big O notation, commonly taught as a computer science subject, is used to analyze the complexity of algorithms and to model how they will perform as the input dataset scales. This helps programmers pick more efficient and performant algorithms when developing applications ([Knuth 76], [Knuth 97]).

Common big O notations and algorithm examples are listed in Table 5.1.

Table 5-1 Example Big O Notations

Notation	Examples
O(1)	Boolean test
O(log n)	binary search of a sorted array
O(n)	linear search of a linked list
O(n log n)	quick sort (average case)
O(n^2)	bubble sort (average case)
O(2^n)	factoring numbers; exponential growth
O(n!)	brute force of traveling salesman problem

The notation allows programmers to estimate speedup of different algorithms, determining which areas of code will lead to the greatest improvements. For example, for searching a sorted array of 100 items, the difference between linear search and binary search is a factor of 21 (100/log(100)).

The performance of these algorithms is pictured in Figure 5.1, showing their trend as they scale.

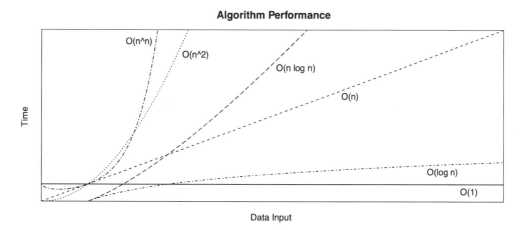

Figure 5-1 Runtime versus input size for different algorithms

This classification helps the systems performance analyst to understand that some algorithms will perform very poorly at scale. Performance problems may show up when applications are pushed to service higher numbers of users or data objects than they ever have before, at which point algorithms such as O(n^2) may begin to be pathological. The fix may be for the developer to use a more efficient algorithm, or to partition the population differently.

Big O notation does ignore some constant computation costs incurred for the selection of each algorithm. For cases where n (the input data size) is small, these costs may dominate.

5.2 Application Performance Techniques

This section describes some commonly used techniques by which application performance can be improved: selecting an I/O size, caching, buffering, polling, concurrency and parallelism, non-blocking I/O, and processor binding. Refer to the application documentation to see which of these are used, and for any additional application-specific features.

5.2.1 Selecting an I/O Size

Costs associated with performing I/O can include initializing buffers, making a system call, context switching, allocating kernel metadata, checking process privileges and limits, mapping addresses to devices, executing kernel and driver code to deliver the I/O, and, finally, freeing metadata and buffers. "Initialization tax" is paid for small and large I/O alike. For efficiency, the more data transferred by each I/O, the better.

Increasing the I/O size is a common strategy used by applications to improve throughput. It's usually much more efficient to transfer 128 Kbytes as a single I/O than as 128 x 1 Kbyte I/O, considering any fixed per-I/O costs. Disk I/O, in particular, has historically had a high per-I/O cost due to seek time.

There's a downside when the application doesn't need larger I/O sizes. A database performing 8 Kbyte random reads may run more slowly with a 128 Kbyte I/O size, as 120 Kbytes of data transfer is wasted. This introduces I/O latency, which can be lowered by selecting a smaller I/O size that more closely matches what the application is requesting. Unnecessarily larger I/O sizes can also waste cache space.

5.2.2 Caching

The operating system uses caches to improve file system read performance and memory allocation performance; applications often use caches for a similar reason.

Instead of always performing an expensive operation, the results of commonly performed operations may be stored in a local cache for future use. An example is the database buffer cache, which stores the results of commonly performed database queries.

A common task when deploying applications is to determine which caches are provided, or can be enabled, and then to configure their sizes to suit the system.

An important aspect of the cache is how it manages integrity, so that lookups do not return stale data. This is called *cache coherency* and can be expensive to perform—ideally not more so than the benefit the cache provides.

While caches improve read performance, their storage is often used as buffers to improve write performance.

5.2.3 Buffering

To improve write performance, data may be coalesced in a buffer before being sent to the next level. This increases the I/O size and efficiency of the operation. Depending on the type of writes, it may also increase write latency, as the first write to a buffer waits for subsequent writes before being sent.

A ring buffer (or *circular buffer*) is a type of fixed buffer that can be used for continuous transfer between components, which act upon the buffer asynchronously. It may be implemented using start and end pointers, which can be moved by each component as data is appended or removed.

5.2.4 Polling

Polling is a technique in which the system waits for an event to occur by checking the status of the event in a loop, with pauses between checks. There are some potential performance problems with polling:

- Costly CPU overhead of repeated checks
- High latency between the occurrence of the event and the next polled check

Where this is a performance problem, applications may be able to change their behavior to listen for the event to occur, which immediately notifies the application and executes the desired routine.

poll() System Call

There is a `poll()` syscall to check for the status of file descriptors, which serves a similar function to polling, although it is event-based so it doesn't suffer the performance cost of polling.

The poll() interface supports multiple file descriptors as an array, which requires the application to scan the array when events occur to find the related file descriptors. This scanning is O(n) (see Section 5.1.4, Big O Notation), whose overhead can become a performance problem at scale. A different interface is available: on Linux it is epoll(), which can avoid the scan and therefore be O(1). Solaris-based systems have a similar feature called *event ports*, which use port_get(3C) instead of poll().

5.2.5 Concurrency and Parallelism

Time-sharing systems (including all derived from Unix) provide program *concurrency*: the ability to load and begin executing multiple runnable programs. While their runtimes may overlap, they do not necessarily execute on-CPU at the same instant. Each of these programs may be an application process.

Apart from executing different applications concurrently, different functions within an application can also be made concurrent. This can be achieved using multiple processes (*multiprocess*) or multiple threads (*multithreaded*), each performing its own task.

Another approach is *event-based concurrency*, whereby an application services different functions and switches between them when events occur. For example, the Node.js runtime uses this approach. This provides concurrency but may do so using a single thread or process, which can eventually become a scalability bottleneck as it can utilize only one CPU.

To take advantage of a multiprocessor system, an application must execute on multiple CPUs at the same time. This is *parallelism*, which an application may accomplish by being multiprocess or multithreaded. For reasons explained in Chapter 6, CPUs, multiple threads (or the equivalent tasks) are more efficient and are therefore the preferred approach.

Apart from increased throughput of CPU work, multiple threads (or processes) allow I/O to be performed concurrently, as other threads can execute while a thread blocked on I/O waits.

Since multithreaded programming shares the same address space as the process, threads can read and write the same memory directly, without the need for more expensive interfaces (such as inter-process communication (IPC) for multiprocess programming). For integrity, synchronization primitives are used so that data does not become corrupted by multiple threads reading and writing simultaneously. These may be used in conjunction with hash tables to improve performance.

Synchronization Primitives

Synchronization primitives police access to memory, similarly to the way traffic lights regulate access to an intersection. And, like traffic lights, they halt the flow of traffic, causing wait time (latency). The three commonly used types are

- **Mutex (MUTually EXclusive) locks:** Only the holder of the lock can operate. Others block and wait off-CPU.
- **Spin locks:** Spin locks allow the holder to operate, while others requiring the lock *spin* on-CPU in a tight loop, checking for the lock to be released. While these can provide low-latency access—the blocked thread never leaves CPU and is ready to run in a matter of cycles once the lock is available—they also waste CPU resources while threads spin, waiting.
- **RW locks:** Reader/writer locks ensure integrity by allowing either multiple readers, or one writer only and no readers.

Mutex locks may be implemented by the library or kernel as *adaptive mutex locks*: a hybrid of spin and mutex locks, which spin if the holder is currently running on another CPU and block if it isn't (or if a spin threshold is reached). Adaptive mutex locks are optimized to provide low-latency access without wasting CPU resources and have been in use on Solaris-based systems for many years. They were implemented for Linux in 2009, where they are called *adaptive spinning mutexes* [1].

Investigating performance issues involving locks can be time-consuming and often requires familiarity with the application source code. This is usually an activity for the developer.

Hash Tables

A hash table of locks can be used to employ the optimum number of locks for a large number of data structures. While hash tables are summarized here, this is an advanced topic that assumes a programming background.

Picture the following two approaches:

- A single global mutex lock for all data structures. While this solution is simple, concurrent access will encounter contention for the lock and latency while waiting for it. Multiple threads that need the lock will *serialize*—execute in sequence, rather than concurrently.
- A mutex lock for every data structure. While this reduces contention to only the times it is really needed—concurrent access to the same data structure—there are storage overheads for the lock, and CPU overheads for the creation and destruction of the lock for every data structure.

A hash table of locks is an in-between solution and is suitable when lock contention is expected to be light. A fixed number of locks are created, and a hashing algorithm is used to select which lock is used for which data structure. This avoids the creation and destruction cost with the data structure and also avoids the problem of having only a single lock.

The example hash table shown in Figure 5.2 has four entries, called *buckets*, each of which contains its own lock.

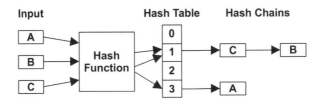

Figure 5-2 Example hash table

This example also shows one approach for solving *hash collisions*, where two or more input data structures hash to the same bucket. Here, a chain of data structures is created to store them all under the same bucket, where they will be found again by the hashing function. These hash chains can be a performance problem if they become too long and are walked serially. The hash function and table size can be selected with the goal of uniformly spreading data structures over many buckets, to keep hash chain length to a minimum.

Ideally, the number of hash table buckets should be equal to or greater than the CPU count, for the potential of maximum parallelism. The hashing algorithm may be as simple as taking low-order bits of the data structure address and using this as an index into a power-of-two-size array of locks. Such simple algorithms are also fast, allowing data structures to be located quickly.

With an array of adjacent locks in memory, a performance problem can arise when locks fall within the same cache line. Two CPUs updating different locks in the same cache line will encounter cache coherency overhead, with each CPU invalidating the cache line in the other's cache. This situation is called *false sharing* and is commonly solved by *padding* hash locks with unused bytes so that only one lock exists in each cache line in memory.

5.2.6 Non-Blocking I/O

The Unix process life cycle, pictured in Chapter 3, Operating Systems, shows processes blocking and entering the sleep state during I/O. There are a couple of performance problems with this model:

- For many concurrent I/O, each I/O consumes a thread (or process) while it is blocked. In order to support many concurrent I/O, the application must create many threads (typically one for each client), which have a cost associated with thread creation and destruction.

- For frequent short-lived I/O, the overhead of frequent context switching can consume CPU resources and add application latency.

The *non-blocking I/O* model issues I/O asynchronously, without blocking the current thread, which can then perform other work. This has been a key feature of Node.js [2], a server-side JavaScript application environment that directs code to be developed in non-blocking ways.

5.2.7 Processor Binding

For NUMA environments, it can be advantageous for a process or thread to remain running on a single CPU and to run on the same CPU as it did previously after performing I/O. This can improve the memory locality of the application, reducing the cycles for memory I/O and improving overall application performance. Operating systems are well aware of this and are designed to keep application threads on the same CPUs (*CPU affinity*). These topics are introduced in Chapter 7, Memory.

Some applications force this behavior by *binding* themselves to CPUs. This can significantly improve performance for some systems. It can also reduce performance when the bindings conflict with other CPU bindings, such as device interrupt mappings to CPUs.

Be especially careful about the risks of CPU binding when there are other tenants or applications running on the same system. This is a problem we've encountered in cloud computing for OS virtualization, where an application can see all the CPUs and then bind to some, on the assumption that it is the only application on the server. When a server is shared by other tenant applications that are also binding, there can be conflicts and scheduler latency as the bound CPUs are busy with other tenants, even though other CPUs are idle.

5.3 Programming Languages

Programming languages may be compiled or interpreted and may also be executed via a virtual machine. Many languages list "performance optimizations" as features, but, strictly speaking, these are usually features of the software that *executes* the language, not the language itself. For example, the Java HotSpot Virtual Machine software includes a just-in-time (JIT) compiler to dynamically improve performance.

Interpreters and language virtual machines also provide different levels of performance observability support via their own specific tools. For the system performance analyst, basic profiling using these tools can lead to some quick wins. For example, high CPU usage may be identified as a result of garbage collection (GC), and then fixed via some commonly used tunables. Or it may be caused by a code path that can be found as a known bug in a bug database and fixed by upgrading the software version (this happens a lot).

The following sections describe basic performance characteristics per programming language type. For more about individual language performance, look for texts about that language.

5.3.1 Compiled Languages

Compilation takes a program and emits machine instructions in advance of runtime that are stored in binary executable files called *binaries*. These can be run at any time without compiling again. Compiled languages include C and C++. Some languages may have both interpreters and compilers.

Compiled code is generally high-performing and doesn't require further translation before execution by the CPUs. The operating system kernel is written almost entirely in C, with a few critical paths written in assembly.

Performance analysis of compiled languages is usually straightforward, as the executed machine code usually maps closely to the original program (although this depends on compilation optimizations). During compilation, a symbol table can be generated which maps addresses to program functions and object names. Later profiling and tracing of CPU execution can then be mapped directly to these program names, allowing the analyst to study program execution. Stack traces, and the numerical addresses they contain, can also be mapped and translated to function names to provide code path ancestry.

Compilers can improve performance by use of *compiler optimizations*—routines that optimize the choice and placement of CPU instructions.

Compiler Optimizations

The gcc(1) compiler provides a range from 0 to 3, where 3 uses the largest number of optimizations. gcc(1) can be queried to show which optimizations it uses for different levels. For example:

```
$ gcc -Q -O3 --help=optimizers
The following options control optimizations:
  -O
  -Ofast
  -Os
```

```
 -falign-functions                   [enabled]
 -falign-jumps                       [enabled]
 -falign-labels                      [enabled]
 -falign-loops                       [enabled]
 -fasynchronous-unwind-tables        [enabled]
 -fbranch-count-reg                  [enabled]
 -fbranch-probabilities              [disabled]
 -fbranch-target-load-optimize       [disabled]
[...]
 -fomit-frame-pointer                [disabled]
[...]
```

The full list includes about 180 options, some of which are enabled, even at –O0. As an example of what one of these options does, the `-fomit-frame-pointer` option, seen in this list, is described in the `gcc(1)` man page:

> Don't keep the frame pointer in a register for functions that don't need one. This avoids the instructions to save, set up and restore frame pointers; it also makes an extra register available in many functions. **It also makes debugging impossible on some machines.**

This is an example of a trade-off: omitting the frame pointer typically breaks the operation of analyzers that profile stack traces.

Given the usefulness of stack profilers, this option may be sacrificing much in terms of later performance wins that can no longer be found easily, which may far outweigh the performance gains that this option initially offers. A solution, in this case, can be to compile with `-fno-omit-frame-pointer`, to avoid this optimization.

Should performance issues arise, it may be tempting to simply recompile the application with a reduced optimization level (from –O3 to –O2, for example), in the hope that any debugging needs could then be met. This turns out not to be simple: the changes to the compiler output can be massive and important, and they can affect the behavior of the issue you were originally trying to analyze.

5.3.2 Interpreted Languages

Interpreted languages execute a program by translating it into actions during runtime, a process that adds execution overhead. Interpreted languages are not expected to exhibit high performance and are used for situations where other factors are more important, such as ease of programming and debugging. *Shell scripting* is an example of an interpreted language.

Unless observability tools are provided, performance analysis of interpreted languages can be difficult. CPU profiling can show the operation of the interpreter—including parsing, translating, and performing actions—but it may not show the original program function names, leaving essential program context a mystery.

This interpreter analysis may not be totally fruitless, as there can be performance issues with the interpreter itself, even when the code it is executing appears to be well designed.

Depending on the interpreter, program context may be easy to fetch indirectly (e.g., dynamic tracing of the parser). Often these programs are studied by simply adding print statements and timestamps. More rigorous performance analysis is uncommon, since interpreted languages are not commonly selected for high-performance applications in the first place.

5.3.3 Virtual Machines

A *language virtual machine* (also called a *process virtual machine*) is software that simulates a computer. Some programming languages, including Java and Erlang, are commonly executed using virtual machines (VMs), which provide them with a platform-independent programming environment. The application program is compiled to the virtual machine instruction set (*bytecode*) and then executed by the virtual machine. This allows portability of the compiled objects, provided a virtual machine is available to run them on the target platform.

The bytecode is *compiled* from the original program and then *interpreted* by the language virtual machine, which translates it to machine code. The Java HotSpot Virtual Machine supports JIT compilation, which compiles bytecode to machine code ahead of time, so that during execution the native machine code can be executed. This provides the performance advantages of compiled code, together with the portability of a virtual machine.

Virtual machines are typically the most difficult of the language types to observe. By the time the program is executing on-CPU, multiple stages of compilation or interpretation may have passed, and information about the original program may not be readily available. Performance analysis usually focuses on the toolset provided with the language virtual machine, many of which provide DTrace probes, and on third-party tools.

5.3.4 Garbage Collection

Some languages use automatic memory management, where allocated memory does not need to be explicitly freed, leaving that to an asynchronous garbage collection process. While this makes programs easier to write, there can be disadvantages:

- **Memory growth**: There is less control of the application's memory usage, which may grow when objects are not identified automatically as eligible to be freed. If the application grows too large, it may either hit its own limits or encounter system paging, severely harming performance.

- **CPU cost**: GC will typically run intermittently and involves searching or scanning objects in memory. This consumes CPU resources, reducing what is available to the application for short periods. As the memory of the application grows, CPU consumption by GC may also grow. In some cases and implementations, this can reach the point where GC continually consumes an entire CPU.

- **Latency outliers**: Application execution may be paused while GC executes, causing occasional application responses with high latency. This depends on the GC type: stop-the-world, incremental, or concurrent.

GC is a common target for performance tuning, to reduce CPU cost and occurrence of latency outliers. For example, the Java VM provides many tunable parameters to set the GC type, number of GC threads, maximum heap size, target heap free ratio, and more.

If tuning is not effective, the problem may be the application creating too much garbage, or leaking references. These are issues for the application developer.

5.4 Methodology and Analysis

This section describes methodologies for application analysis and tuning. The tools used for analysis are either introduced here or are referenced from other chapters. The topics are summarized in Table 5.2.

Table 5-2 Application Performance Methodologies

Methodology	Type
Thread state analysis	observational analysis
CPU profiling	observational analysis
Syscall analysis	observational analysis
I/O profiling	observational analysis
Workload characterization	observational analysis, capacity planning
USE method	observational analysis
Drill-down analysis	observational analysis
Lock analysis	observational analysis
Static performance tuning	observational analysis, tuning

See Chapter 2, Methodology, for additional general methodologies and the introduction to some of these. Also see the chapters that follow for the analysis of system resources and virtualization.

These methodologies may be followed individually or used in combination. My suggestion is to try them in the order listed in the table.

In addition to these, look for custom analysis techniques for the specific application and the programming language in which it is developed. These may consider logical behavior of the application, including known issues, and lead to some quick performance wins.

5.4.1 Thread State Analysis

The goal is to identify at a high level where application threads are spending their time, which solves some issues immediately and directs the investigation of others. This is done by dividing each application's thread time into a number of meaningful states.

Two State

At a minimum, there are two thread states:

- **On-CPU**: executing
- **Off-CPU**: waiting for a turn on-CPU, or for I/O, locks, paging, work, and so on

If time is largely spent on-CPU, CPU profiling can usually explain this quickly (covered later). This is the case for many performance issues, so spending time measuring other states may not be necessary.

If time is found to be spent off-CPU, various other methodologies can be used, although without a better starting point this can be time-consuming.

Six State

Here is an expanded list, this time using six thread states (and a different naming scheme), which gives better starting points for the off-CPU cases:

- **Executing:** on-CPU
- **Runnable:** and waiting for a turn on-CPU
- **Anonymous paging:** runnable, but blocked waiting for anonymous page-ins
- **Sleeping:** waiting for I/O, including network, block, and data/text page-ins
- **Lock:** waiting to acquire a synchronization lock (waiting on someone else)
- **Idle:** waiting for work

These have been selected as a minimal and useful set; you may wish to add more states to your list. For example, the executing state may be split into user- and kernel-mode execution, and the sleeping state can be divided based on the target. (I had to restrain myself to keep this list to six.)

Performance is improved by reducing the time in the first five of these states, which increases the time spent in idle (headroom). Other things being equal, this would mean that application requests have lower latency, and the application can handle more load.

Once you've established in which of the first five states the threads are spending their time, you can investigate them further:

- **Executing:** Check whether this is user- or kernel-mode time and the reason for CPU consumption by using profiling. Profiling can determine which code paths are consuming CPU and for how long, which can include time spent spinning on locks. See Section 5.4.2, CPU Profiling.

- **Runnable:** Spending time in this state means the application needs more CPU resources. Examine CPU load for the entire system, and any CPU limits present for the application (e.g., resource controls).

- **Anonymous paging:** A lack of available main memory for the application can cause anonymous paging and delays. Examine memory usage for the entire system and any memory limits present for the application. See Chapter 7, Memory, for details.

- **Sleeping:** Analyze the resource on which the application is blocked. See Section 5.4.3, Syscall Analysis, and Section 5.4.4, I/O Profiling.

- **Lock:** Identify the lock, the thread holding it, and the reason why the holder held it for so long. The reason may be that the holder was blocked on another lock, which requires further unwinding. This is an advanced activity, usually performed by the software developer who has intimate knowledge of the application and its locking hierarchy.

Because of how applications typically wait for work, you will often find that time in the sleeping and lock states is actually idle time. An application worker thread may wait on a conditional variable for work (lock state), or for network I/O (sleeping state). So when you see large sleeping and lock state times, remember to drill down a little to check if this is really idle time.

The following summarizes how these thread states may be measured on Linux- and Solaris-based systems; the tools and technologies mentioned are covered more in other sections of this book. Check for developments, especially for new tools and tool options, that make finding these easier.

Linux

The time spent executing is not hard to determine: top(1) reports this as %CPU. Measuring times in the other states can require some digging, as follows.

Runnable is tracked by the kernel *schedstats* feature and is exposed via /proc/*/schedstat. The perf sched tool can also provide metrics for understanding time spent runnable and waiting.

Time waiting for anonymous paging (in Linux, *swapping*) can be measured by the kernel *delay accounting* feature, provided it is enabled. It provides separate states for swapping and for time blocked during memory reclaim (also related to memory pressure). There isn't a commonly used tool to expose these states; however, the kernel documentation contains an example program to do this: getdelays.c, which was demonstrated in Chapter 4, Observability Tools. Another approach is to use tracing tools such as DTrace or SystemTap.

Time blocked in the sleeping state can be loosely estimated using other tools, for example, pidstat -d to determine if a process is performing disk I/O, and probably sleeping. Delay and other I/O accounting features, if they are enabled, do provide time blocked on block I/O, which can also be observed using iotop(1). Other reasons for blocking can be investigated using tracing tools such as DTrace or SystemTap. The application may also have instrumentation, or instrumentation can be added, to track time performing explicit I/O (disk and network).

If the application is stuck in the sleeping state for very long intervals (seconds), you can try pstack(1) to determine why. This takes a single snapshot of the threads and their user stack traces, which should include the sleeping threads and the reason they are sleeping. Be warned, however: pstack(1) may briefly pause the target while it does this, so use with caution.

Lock time can be investigated using tracing tools.

Solaris

On Solaris-based systems, the *microstate accounting* statistics, introduced in Chapter 4, Observability Tools, provide most of the thread states directly. These can be viewed using prstat(1M):

```
$ prstat -mLcp 4937 1
Please wait...
   PID USERNAME USR SYS TRP TFL DFL LCK SLP LAT VCX ICX SCL SIG PROCESS/LWPID
  4937 root      7.4 7.9 0.0 0.0  15 0.0  69 0.2 239  31  3K    0 redis-server/1
  4937 root      0.0 0.0 0.0 0.0 0.0 100 0.0 0.0   0   0   0    0 redis-server/3
  4937 root      0.0 0.0 0.0 0.0 0.0 100 0.0 0.0   0   0   0    0 redis-server/2
Total: 1 processes, 3 lwps, load averages: 5.28, 5.36, 5.36
[...]
```

The eight columns, from USR to LAT, are all microstate accounting thread states and divide the thread time into percentages. The sum of these columns is 100%. Here is a mapping of these to the states we are interested in:

- **Executing:** USR + SYS
- **Runnable:** LAT
- **Anonymous paging:** DFL
- **Sleeping:** SLP
- **Lock:** LCK
- **Idle:** also in SLP + LCK

While this is not a perfect match, getting this far so easily has tremendous value. The separation of idle time can be performed using DTrace to examine the stack trace when a thread leaves CPU, to determine what it is waiting for. If a thread is stuck in a sleep state for a long period (seconds), try pstack(1), with the caveat that it will briefly pause the target, so use with caution.

See Chapter 6, CPUs, for more about prstat(1M) and these columns.

5.4.2 CPU Profiling

CPU profiling is described in Section 6.5.4, Profiling, in Chapter 6, CPUs, which also provides detailed examples using DTrace and perf(1). Profiling is an important activity that is summarized here from the application perspective.

The intent is to determine why an application is consuming CPU resources. An effective technique is to sample the on-CPU user-level stack trace and coalesce the results. The stack traces shows the code path taken, which can reveal both high- and low-level reasons for the application consuming CPU.

Sampling stack traces can generate many thousands of lines of output to examine, even when summarizing the output to print only unique stacks. One way to understand the profile quickly is to visualize it using flame graphs, which are shown in Chapter 6, CPUs.

Apart from sampling the stack trace, the currently running function alone can be sampled. In some cases this is sufficient to identify why the application is using the CPU and produces much less output, making it quicker to read and understand. This example, from Chapter 6, CPUs, uses DTrace:

```
# dtrace -n 'profile-997 /arg1 && execname == "beam.smp"/ {
    @[ufunc(arg1)] = count(); } tick-10s { exit(0); }'
[...]
```

continues

```
innostore_drv.so`os_aio_array_get_nth_slot            80
beam.smp`process_main                                127
libc.so.1`mutex_trylock_adaptive                     140
innostore_drv.so`os_aio_simulated_handle             158
beam.smp`sched_sys_wait                              202
libc.so.1`memcpy                                     258
innostore_drv.so`ut_fold_binary                    1800
innostore_drv.so`ut_fold_ulint_pair                4039
```

In this case, it was the `ut_fold_ulint_pair()` function that was on-CPU the most during sampling.

It can also be useful to study the caller of the currently running function, which some profiling software (including DTrace) can easily do. For example, if the previous example identified `malloc()` as on-CPU the most, that doesn't tell us a lot. The caller of `malloc()` should be much more interesting to profile and also doesn't require capturing stack traces.

The study of interpreted and virtual machine CPU usage can be difficult; there may be no easy mapping from the executing software back to the original program. How this can be solved depends on the language environment: it may support debug features that can be enabled to do this, or there may be third-party tools.

As an example, DTrace uses *ustack helpers* to look inside VMs and translate stacks back to the original program. There are ustack helpers for Java, Python, and Node.js.

For example, sampling Java on-CPU stacks with DTrace `jstack()`:

```
# dtrace -n 'profile-97 /pid == 1742/ { @[jstack(100)] = count(); }'
dtrace: description 'profile-97 ' matched 1 probe
^C
[...]
      libc.so.1`_so_send+0x7
      libjvm.so`__1cDhpiEsend6Fipcii_i_+0xac
      libjvm.so`JVM_Send+0x31
      libnet.so`Java_java_net_SocketOutputStream_socketWrite0+0x100
      java/net/SocketOutputStream.socketWrite0
      java/net/SocketOutputStream.socketWrite
      java/net/SocketOutputStream.write
      java/io/DataOutputStream.write
      TransThread.TransTCP
      TransThread.run
      StubRoutines (1)
      libjvm.so`__1cJJavaCallsLcall_helper6FpnJJavaValue_pnMmethodHandle_pnRJ...
      libjvm.so`__1cCosUos_exception_wrapper6FpFpnJJavaValue_pnMmethodHandle_...
      libjvm.so`__1cJJavaCallsEcall6FpnJJavaValue_nMmethodHandle_pnRJavaCallA...
      libjvm.so`__1cJJavaCallsMcall_virtual6FpnJJavaValue_nLKlassHandle_nMsym...
      libjvm.so`__1cJJavaCallsMcall_virtual6FpnJJavaValue_nGHandle_nLKlassHan...
      libjvm.so`__1cMthread_entry6FpnKJavaThread_pnGThread__v_+0xd0
      libjvm.so`__1cKJavaThreadRthread_main_inner6M_v_+0x51
      libjvm.so`__1cKJavaThreadDrun6M_v_+0x105
      libjvm.so`__1cG_start6Fpv_0_+0xd2
      libc.so.1`_thr_setup+0x4e
      libc.so.1`_lwp_start
       10
```

The output has been truncated, showing only the most frequent stack, which was sampled ten times. The stack shows the internals of the JVM (libjvm), with each function shown as C++ signatures. The Java stack has been translated from the JVM, highlighted here in bold, which shows the classes and methods responsible for this CPU code path. For this stack, it was java/io/DataOutputStream.write.

See the other methodologies and tools in Chapter 6, CPUs, for different ways to examine application CPU usage.

5.4.3 Syscall Analysis

The thread state analysis methodology began by describing two thread states to study: on-CPU and off-CPU. It can be useful, and sometimes more practical, to study these based on system call execution:

- **Executing:** on-CPU (user mode)
- **Syscalls:** time during a system call (kernel mode running or waiting)

The syscall time includes I/O, locks, and other syscall types. Other thread states, such as runnable (and waiting for a CPU) and anonymous paging, are left out of this simplification. If either is true (CPU saturation or memory saturation), it can be identified system-wide via the USE method.

The executing state can be studied by the CPU profiling methodology mentioned earlier.

System calls (syscalls) can be studied in a number of ways. The intent is to find out where syscall time is spent, including the type of syscall and the reason it is called.

Breakpoint Tracing

The traditional style of syscall tracing involves setting breakpoints for syscall entry and return. These are invasive, and for applications with high syscall rates their performance may be worsened by an order of magnitude.

Depending on application performance requirements, this style of tracing may be acceptable to use for short durations, to determine the syscall types being called.

strace

On **Linux**, this is performed using the `strace(1)` command. For example:

```
$ strace -ttt -T -p 1884
1356982510.395542 close(3)                    = 0 <0.000267>
1356982510.396064 close(4)                    = 0 <0.000293>
1356982510.396617 ioctl(255, TIOCGPGRP, [1975]) = 0 <0.000019>
```

continues

```
1356982510.396980 rt_sigprocmask(SIG_SETMASK, [], NULL, 8) = 0 <0.000024>
1356982510.397288 rt_sigprocmask(SIG_BLOCK, [CHLD], [], 8) = 0 <0.000014>
1356982510.397365 wait4(-1, [{WIFEXITED(s) && WEXITSTATUS(s) == 0}],
WSTOPPED|WCONTINUED, NULL) = 1975 <0.018187>
1356982510.415710 rt_sigprocmask(SIG_BLOCK, [CHLD TSTP TTIN TTOU], [CHLD], 8) = 0
<0.000018>
1356982510.416047 ioctl(255, SNDRV_TIMER_IOCTL_SELECT or TIOCSPGRP, [1884]) = 0
<0.000016>
1356982510.416118 rt_sigprocmask(SIG_SETMASK, [CHLD], NULL, 8) = 0 <0.000154>
[...]
```

The options used were (see the man page for all)

- **-ttt:** prints the first column of time-since-epoch, in units of seconds with microsecond resolution.

- **-T:** prints the last field (*<time>*), which is the duration of the system call, in units of seconds with microsecond resolution.

- **-p PID:** trace this process ID. A command can also be specified so that strace(1) launches and traces it.

A feature of strace(1) can be seen in the output—translation of syscall arguments into a human-readable form. This is especially useful for determining the use of ioctl().

This form of strace(1) prints a line of output per syscall. The –c option can be used to summarize system call activity:

```
$ strace -c -p 1884
Process 1884 attached - interrupt to quit
^CProcess 1884 detached
% time     seconds  usecs/call     calls    errors syscall
------ ----------- ----------- --------- --------- ----------------
 83.29    0.007994           9       911       455 wait4
 14.41    0.001383           3       455           clone
  0.85    0.000082           0      2275           ioctl
  0.68    0.000065           0       910           close
  0.63    0.000060           0      4551           rt_sigprocmask
  0.15    0.000014           0       455           setpgid
  0.00    0.000000           0       455           rt_sigreturn
  0.00    0.000000           0       455           pipe
------ ----------- ----------- --------- --------- ----------------
100.00    0.009598                 10467       455 total
```

The output includes

- **time:** percentage showing where system CPU time was spent

- **seconds:** total system CPU time, in seconds

- **usecs/call:** average system CPU time per call, in microseconds

- **calls:** number of system calls during strace(1)
- **syscall:** system call name

This would be of greater use if the overhead was not such a problem.

To illustrate this, the dd(1) command is used to perform 5 million 1 Kbyte transfers and is tested without and with strace(1). Without:

```
$ dd if=/dev/zero of=/dev/null bs=1k count=5000k
5120000+0 records in
5120000+0 records out
5242880000 bytes (5.2 GB) copied, 1.91247 s, 2.7 GB/s
```

The output of dd(1) includes runtime and throughput statistics. This test took around 2 s to complete.

Here is the same command while strace(1) summarizes syscall usage:

```
$ strace -c dd if=/dev/zero of=/dev/null bs=1k count=5000k
5120000+0 records in
5120000+0 records out
5242880000 bytes (5.2 GB) copied, 140.722 s, 37.3 MB/s
% time     seconds  usecs/call     calls    errors syscall
------ ----------- ----------- --------- --------- ----------------
 51.46    0.008030           0   5120005            read
 48.54    0.007574           0   5120003            write
  0.00    0.000000           0        20        13 open
  0.00    0.000000           0        10           close
  0.00    0.000000           0         5           fstat
  0.00    0.000000           0         1           lseek
  0.00    0.000000           0        14           mmap
  0.00    0.000000           0         8           mprotect
  0.00    0.000000           0         2           munmap
  0.00    0.000000           0         3           brk
  0.00    0.000000           0         6           rt_sigaction
  0.00    0.000000           0         1           rt_sigprocmask
  0.00    0.000000           0         5         5 access
  0.00    0.000000           0         2           dup2
  0.00    0.000000           0         1           execve
  0.00    0.000000           0         1           getrlimit
  0.00    0.000000           0         1           arch_prctl
  0.00    0.000000           0         2         1 futex
  0.00    0.000000           0         1           set_tid_address
  0.00    0.000000           0         1           set_robust_list
------ ----------- ----------- --------- --------- ----------------
100.00    0.015604              10240092        19 total
```

The runtime increased by a factor of 73, with an equivalent drop in throughput. This is a particularly severe case, as dd(1) performs a high rate of system calls.

truss

On **Solaris**-based systems, the `truss(1)` command serves this role. For example:

```
$ truss -dE -p 81573
Base time stamp:  1356985396.2469  [ Mon Dec 31 20:23:16 UTC 2012 ]
 0.0016  0.0000 waitid(P_ALL, 0, 0x08047A80, WEXITED|WTRAPPED|WSTOPPED|WCONTINUED) =
0
 0.0018  0.0000 lwp_sigmask(SIG_SETMASK, 0x06820000, 0x00000000, 0x00000000,
0x00000000) = 0xFFBFFEFF [0xFFFFFFFF]
 0.0019  0.0000 ioctl(255, TIOCGSID, 0x08047AEC)                  = 0
 0.0019  0.0000 getsid(0)                                         = 81573
 0.0020  0.0000 ioctl(255, TIOCSPGRP, 0x08047B24)                 = 0
 0.0021  0.0000 lwp_sigmask(SIG_SETMASK, 0x00020000, 0x00000000, 0x00000000,
0x00000000) = 0xFFBFFEFF [0xFFFFFFFF]
 0.0022  0.0000 ioctl(255, TCGETS, 0x0811D640)                    = 0
 0.0023  0.0000 ioctl(255, TIOCGWINSZ, 0x08047B48)                = 0
[...]
```

The options used were (see the man page for all)

- **-d**: prints the first column of timestamps, showing seconds since epoch.
- **-E**: prints the second column of timestamps, showing the elapsed time during the system call, in seconds.
- **-p PID**: trace this process ID. A command can also be specified so that `truss(1)` launches and traces it.

The output includes one line per system call and has useful translations of arguments into human-readable format. The timestamps have only 0.1 ms resolution, which makes them of limited use.

`truss(1)` also supports summary mode using –c:

```
$ truss -c dd if=/dev/zero of=/dev/null bs=1k count=10k
10240+0 records in
10240+0 records out

syscall               seconds   calls  errors
_exit                    .000       1
read                     .075   10252
write                    .073   10246
open                     .000       9       1
close                    .000      10
brk                      .000       6
getpid                   .000       1
fstat                    .000       6
sysi86                   .000       1
ioctl                    .000       1       1
execve                   .000       1
sigaction                .000       2
getcontext               .000       1
setustack                .000       1
mmap                     .000       8
```

```
mmapobj                    .000      1
getrlimit                  .000      1
memcntl                    .000      3
sysconfig                  .000      3
sysinfo                    .000      1
lwp_private                .000      1
llseek                     .000      3
schedctl                   .000      1
resolvepath                .000      3
stat64                     .000      2
fstat64                    .000      4
open64                     .000      2
                       --------   ------   ----
sys totals:                .150    20571      2
usr time:                  .029
elapsed:                   .880
```

The seconds column shows the system CPU time in the system calls. The calls column shows the count.

truss(1) can also perform a form of *dynamic tracing* of user-level function calls using the –u option. For example, tracing printf() calls:

```
$ truss -u 'libc:*printf*' uptime
/1:     open("/usr/lib/locale/en_US.UTF-8/LC_MESSAGES/SUNW_OST_OSCMD.mo", O_RDONLY)
Err#2 ENOENT
/1:      -> libc:printf(0x403363, 0x0, 0x0, 0x0, 0x0, 0xffffffd7fffdfeab0)
/1:      <- libc:printf() = 4
/1:      -> libc:printf(0x403368, 0x58, 0x0, 0x0, 0x0, 0x10)
/1:      <- libc:printf() = 11
[...]
```

As with strace(1), the overheads can be severe for high rates of system calls, or traced function calls, making this prohibitive for most production use cases.

Buffered Tracing

With *buffered tracing*, instrumentation data can be buffered in-kernel while the target program continues to execute. This differs from breakpoint tracing, which interrupts the target program for each tracepoint.

DTrace provides both buffered tracing and aggregations to reduce tracing overhead and allows custom programs to be written for syscall analysis. Some examples are shown in this section. In Linux 3.7, a trace subcommand was added to perf(1) to perform buffered tracing of syscalls (and more).

The following DTrace one-liners demonstrate some basic syscall analysis and are intended for both Linux- and Solaris-based systems (demonstrated on the latter). There are many more example one-liners in Appendix D.

This one-liner traces process signals (via the kill() syscall), showing source PID and process name, and destination PID and signal number:

```
# dtrace -qn 'syscall::kill:entry {
    printf("%Y: %s (PID %d) sent a SIG %d to PID %d\n",
    walltimestamp, execname, pid, arg1, arg0); }'
2013 Apr 17 00:27:37: bash (PID 2583) sent a SIG 9 to PID 2638
2013 Apr 17 00:27:51: postgres (PID 25906) sent a SIG 16 to PID 25896
2013 Apr 17 00:27:51: postgres (PID 2676) sent a SIG 17 to PID 25906
2013 Apr 17 00:27:51: postgres (PID 2676) sent a SIG 17 to PID 25906
```

While tracing, this caught a bash process sending a -9 (SIGKILL) to PID 2638, and some signals from postgres (PostgreSQL database). The inclusion of timestamps can be helpful for correlation with other activity.

This one-liner counts syscalls (using an aggregation) for processes named "postgres" (PostgreSQL database):

```
# dtrace -n 'syscall:::entry /execname == "postgres"/ { @[probefunc] = count(); }'
dtrace: description 'syscall:::entry ' matched 233 probes
^C

    setitimer                                                         4
    semsys                                                           22
    open64                                                           35
    kill                                                             79
    lwp_sigmask                                                      79
    setcontext                                                       79
    write                                                           126
    fcntl                                                           252
    pollsys                                                        2498
    read                                                           2750
    send                                                           9542
    recv                                                          12096
    llseek                                                        27925
```

During tracing, the llseek() syscall was executed the most—27,925 times.

The next one-liner measures the duration (also called *latency*) of read() syscalls by PostgreSQL:

```
# dtrace -n 'syscall::read:entry /execname == "postgres"/ {
    self->ts = timestamp; } syscall::read:return /self->ts/ { @["ns"] =
    quantize(timestamp - self->ts); self->ts = 0; }'
dtrace: description 'syscall::read:entry ' matched 2 probes
^C

  ns
           value  ------------- Distribution ------------- count
             256 |                                         0
             512 |@@                                       1124
            1024 |@@@@@@@                                  5108
            2048 |@@@@@@@@@@@@@@@@@@@@@@@                   15427
            4096 |@@@@@@                                   4391
            8192 |@                                        777
           16384 |@                                        425
           32768 |                                         114
           65536 |                                         5
```

```
131072 |                                                    4
262144 |                                                    4
524288 |                                                    0
```

While tracing, most of the `read()` syscalls were between 1 and 8 µs (1,024–8,191 ns). The `read()` syscall operates on a file descriptor which may be a file system object or a network socket. Identifying each is demonstrated in the respective chapters, by use of the `fds[]` DTrace array, to map file descriptors to their file system types.

For this one-liner, if the `timestamp` built-in is changed to `vtimestamp`, it measures CPU time during the system call only. This can be used to compare with the duration times, to see if the system call spent more time in kernel code or blocked for I/O.

More sophisticated DTrace scripts may be written to express syscall times in different ways. Examples include (from the DTraceToolkit [3])

- **dtruss:** DTrace version of `truss(1)`, operates system-wide
- **execsnoop:** trace new process execution via the `exec()` syscall
- **opensnoop:** trace `open()` syscalls with various details
- **procsystime:** summarize syscall time in various ways

These have solved numerous performance issues, often by identifying high-level process activity that can be tuned or eliminated. This is a type of workload characterization: the workload is the application system calls.

For example, the following shows running execsnoop with −v for string timestamps on a cloud-based system:

```
# execsnoop -v
STRTIME                   UID    PID    PPID ARGS
2013 Jan 12 22:10:05        0  15044  14378 /usr/bin/date +%M
2013 Jan 12 22:10:05        0  15039  15038 /opt/mon/bin/rrdtool graph /opt/mo...
2013 Jan 12 22:10:05        0  15037  15036 /opt/mon/bin/rrdtool update /opt/m...
2013 Jan 12 22:10:05        0  15041  15040 /opt/mon/bin/rrdtool graph /opt/mo...
2013 Jan 12 22:10:05        0  15043  15042 /opt/mon/bin/rrdtool graph /opt/mo...
2013 Jan 12 22:10:06        0  15046  15045 /usr/bin/echo
2013 Jan 12 22:10:06        0  15048  15045 /usr/bin/tail -200
2013 Jan 12 22:10:06        0  15049  15048 /usr/bin/cat -sv /var/adm/messages...
2013 Jan 12 22:10:06        0  15050  15049 /usr/bin/ls -trl /var/adm/messages...
2013 Jan 12 22:10:06        0  15045  14377 /usr/bin/sh /usr/bin/dmesg
[...]
```

The timestamps show that all of these processes were executed during a 2 s period. A high rate of short-lived processes can consume CPU resources and interfere with other applications due to CPU cross calls (tearing down the MMU contexts during process exit).

5.4.4 I/O Profiling

Similar to the role of CPU profiling, I/O profiling determines why and how I/O-related system calls are being performed. This can be done using DTrace, examining the user-level stack traces for system calls.

For example, this one-liner traces PostgreSQL read() syscalls, gathers the user-level stack trace, and aggregates them:

```
# dtrace -n 'syscall::read:entry /execname == "postgres"/ {
    @[ustack()] = count(); }'
dtrace: description 'syscall::read:entry ' matched 1 probe
^C
[...]
                libc.so.1`__read+0x15
                postgres`XLogRead+0xb7
                postgres`XLogSend+0x115
                postgres`WalSenderMain+0x10c6
                postgres`PostgresMain+0x1aa
                postgres`ServerLoop+0x6fe
                postgres`PostmasterMain+0x7e2
                postgres`main+0x412
                postgres`_start+0x83
                210

                libc.so.1`__read+0x15
                postgres`WaitLatchOrSocket+0xb1
                postgres`PgstatCollectorMain.isra.21+0x2ed
                postgres`pgstat_start+0x68
                postgres`reaper+0x5bd
                libc.so.1`__sighndlr+0x15
                libc.so.1`call_user_handler+0x292
                libc.so.1`sigacthandler+0x77
                libc.so.1`syscall+0x13
                libc.so.1`thr_sigsetmask+0x1c2
                libc.so.1`sigprocmask+0x52
                postgres`ServerLoop+0xb7
                postgres`PostmasterMain+0x7e2
                postgres`main+0x412
                postgres`_start+0x83
               10723
```

The output (truncated) shows user-level stacks and then a count for the number of occurrences. These stacks include application internal function names. You probably won't be able to understand these without studying the source code, but you may be able to glean enough useful meaning from their names. The first stack contains XLogRead: it may be related to a type of database log. The second stack contains PgstatCollectorMain.isra, which sounds like monitoring activity.

Stack traces show *why* the system calls are being performed. It can be useful to study the other attributes from the workload characterization methodology as well (from Chapter 2, Methodology):

- **Who:** process ID, username
- **What:** I/O syscall target (e.g., file system or socket), I/O size, IOPS, through-put (bytes per second), other attributes
- **How:** IOPS variation over time

In addition to the workload applied, the resulting performance—syscall latency—can be studied as described for the previous methodology.

5.4.5 Workload Characterization

The application applies work to system resources—CPUs, memory, file system, disk, and network—as well as to the operating system via system calls. All of these can be studied using the workload characterization methodology, introduced in Chapter 2, Methodology, and discussed in later chapters.

In addition, the workload sent to the application can be studied. This focuses on the operations that the application serves, and their attributes, and may be a key metric included in performance monitoring and used for capacity planning.

5.4.6 USE Method

As introduced in Chapter 2, Methodology, and applied in later chapters, the USE method checks the utilization, saturation, and errors of all hardware resources. Many application performance issues may be solved this way, by showing that a resource has become a bottleneck.

The USE method can also be applied to software resources, depending on the application. If you can find a functional diagram showing the internal components of an application, consider the utilization, saturation, and error metrics for each software resource and see what makes sense.

For example, the application may use a pool of worker threads to process requests, with a queue for requests waiting their turn. Treating this as a resource, the three metrics could then be defined in this way:

- **Utilization:** average number of threads busy processing requests during an interval, as a percentage of the total threads. For example, 50% would mean that, on average, half the threads were busy working on requests.
- **Saturation:** average length of the request queue during an interval. This shows how many requests have backed up waiting for a worker thread.
- **Errors:** requests denied or failed for any reason.

Your task is then to find how these metrics can be measured. They may already be provided by the application somewhere, or they may need to be added or measured using another tool, such as dynamic tracing.

Queueing systems, like this example, can also be studied using queueing theory (see Chapter 2, Methodology).

For a different example, consider file descriptors. The system may impose a limit, such that these are a finite resource. The three metrics could be as follows:

- **Utilization:** number of in-use file descriptors, as a percentage of the limit.
- **Saturation:** depends on the OS behavior: if threads block waiting for file descriptor allocation, this can be the number of blocked threads waiting for this resource.
- **Errors:** allocation error, such as EFILE, "Too many open files."

Repeat this exercise for the components of your application, and skip any metrics that don't make sense.

This process may help you develop a short checklist for checking application health before moving on to other methodologies such as drill-down analysis.

5.4.7 Drill-Down Analysis

For applications, drill-down analysis can begin with examining the operations the application serves and then drilling down into application internals to see how it is performing them. For I/O, this drill-down analysis can enter system libraries, syscalls, and the kernel.

This is an advanced activity that will quickly lead to application internals, which are ideally open source so that they can be studied. Dynamic tracing tools (DTrace, SystemTap, perf(1)) can instrument these internals, in some languages more easily than in others. Check if the language has its own toolset for analysis, which may be more appropriate to use.

There are also specific tools for investigating library calls: ltrace(1) on Linux, and apptrace(1) on Solaris-based systems (although its use has given way to DTrace).

5.4.8 Lock Analysis

For multithreaded applications, locks can become a bottleneck, inhibiting parallelism and scalability. They can be analyzed by

- Checking for contention
- Checking for excessive hold times

The first identifies whether there is a problem *now*. Excessive hold times are not necessarily a problem, but they may be in the future, with more parallel load. For each, try to identify the name of the lock (if it exists) and the code path that led to using it.

While there are special-purpose tools for lock analysis, you can sometimes solve issues from CPU profiling alone. For *spin locks*, contention shows up as CPU usage and can easily be identified using CPU profiling of stack traces. For *adaptive mutex locks*, contention often involves some spinning, which can also be identified by CPU profiling of stack traces. In that case, be aware that the CPU profile gives only a part of the story, as threads may have blocked and slept while waiting for the locks. See Section 5.4.2, CPU Profiling.

Examples of special-purpose lock analysis tools on Solaris-based systems are

- **plockstat(1M)**: analysis of user-level locks
- **lockstat(1M)**: analysis of kernel-level locks

These commands have similar behavior. They are also implemented using DTrace, which can be used directly for deeper lock analysis.

Here is an example usage of lockstat(1M):

```
# lockstat -n 1000000 -C -s5 sleep 5 > lockstat.txt
# more lockstat.txt

Adaptive mutex spin: 134438 events in 5.058 seconds (26577 events/sec)

-------------------------------------------------------------------------------
Count indv cuml rcnt     nsec Lock                       Caller
14144  11%  11% 0.00     1787 0xffffff0d71404348         zfs_range_unlock+0x2a

      nsec ------ Time Distribution ------ count    Stack
       256 |@                              902      zfs_read+0x239
       512 |@@@@                           1948     fop_read+0x8b
      1024 |@@@@@@                         3033     read+0x2a7
      2048 |@@@@@@@@@                       4286     read32+0x1e
      4096 |@@@@@@                         3143
      8192 |@                              656
     16384 |                               148
     32768 |                               24
     65536 |                               2
    131072 |                               0
    262144 |                               0
    524288 |                               0
   1048576 |                               2
-------------------------------------------------------------------------------
Count indv cuml rcnt     nsec Lock                       Caller
13701  10%  21% 0.00     1769 0xffffff0d71404348         zfs_range_lock+0x86

      nsec ------ Time Distribution ------ count    Stack
       256 |@@                             1119     zfs_read+0x101
       512 |@@@@                           1970     fop_read+0x8b
      1024 |@@@                            1492     read+0x2a7
      2048 |@@@@@@@@@                       4976     read32+0x1e
```

continues

```
     4096 |@@@@@@@                        3469
     8192 |@                             520
    16384 |                             124
    32768 |                              24
    65536 |                               7
----------------------------------------------------------------------
[...]

Adaptive mutex block: 399 events in 5.058 seconds (79 events/sec)


----------------------------------------------------------------------
Count indv cuml rcnt      nsec Lock              Caller
   21   5%   5% 0.00     21053 0xffffff0d71404348 zfs_range_unlock+0x2a

       nsec ------ Time Distribution ------ count   Stack
       8192 |@@@@@                         4        zfs_read+0x239
      16384 |@@@@                          3        fop_read+0x8b
      32768 |@@@@@@@@@@@@@@                11        read+0x2a7
      65536 |@@@@                          3        read32+0x1e
----------------------------------------------------------------------
Count indv cuml rcnt      nsec Lock              Caller
   20   5%  10% 0.00     15107 0xffffff0d71404348 zfs_range_lock+0x86

       nsec ------ Time Distribution ------ count   Stack
       8192 |@@@@                          3        zfs_read+0x101
      16384 |@@@@@@@@@@@@                  8        fop_read+0x8b
      32768 |@@@@@@@@@@@@@                 9        read+0x2a7
                                                   read32+0x1e
[...]

Spin lock spin: 2174 events in 5.058 seconds (430 events/sec)


----------------------------------------------------------------------
Count indv cuml rcnt      nsec Lock              Caller
  589  27%  27% 0.00     73972 cp_default        disp_lock_enter+0x26

       nsec ------ Time Distribution ------ count   Stack
        512 |@@@                          65        disp_getbest+0x28
       1024 |@@@@@@@@@@@@                 239       disp_getwork+0x37
       2048 |@                            23        idle+0x55
       4096 |                             6         thread_start+0x8
       8192 |@                            39
      16384 |@                            37
      32768 |@@                           53
      65536 |@@                           43
     131072 |@@                           45
     262144 |                             18
     524288 |                             3
    1048576 |                             7
    2097152 |                             4
    4194304 |                             7
[...]

R/W reader blocked by writer: 1 events in 5.058 seconds (0 events/sec)


----------------------------------------------------------------------
Count indv cuml rcnt      nsec Lock              Caller
    1 100% 100% 0.00 259688397 0xffffff0d6f0cf898 as_fault+0x2a9

       nsec ------ Time Distribution ------ count   Stack
  268435456 |@@@@@@@@@@@@@@@@@@@@@@@@@@@@@@@@ 1     pagefault+0x96
                                                   trap+0x2c7
                                                   cmntrap+0xe6

----------------------------------------------------------------------
```

Here, `lockstat(1M)` traced contention events (`-C`) with five levels of stack trace (`-s5`) and was executed with a coprocess (`sleep(1)`) for the purpose of providing a time-out of 5 s. The output was redirected to a file for easier browsing (it is over 100,000 lines long).

The output begins with adaptive spin times and distribution plots showing the time for each contention event, along with the name of the lock and the stack trace. The highest was `zfs_range_unlock`, which had 14,144 occurrences of contention, with an average spin time of 1,787 ns. The distribution plot shows that there were two occurrences where the spin time was over 1,048,576 ns (in the 1 to 2 ms bucket). The number of these that blocked can be seen in the adaptive mutex block section of the output.

Tracing of kernel- or user-level locks does add overhead. These particular tools are based on DTrace, which minimizes this overhead as much as possible. Alternatively, as described earlier, CPU profiling at a fixed rate (e.g., 97 Hz) will identify many (but not all) lock issues, without the per-event tracing overhead.

5.4.9 Static Performance Tuning

Static performance tuning focuses on issues of the configured environment. For application performance, examine the following aspects of the static configuration:

- What version of the application is running? Are there newer versions? Do their release notes mention performance improvements?
- What known performance issues are there with the application? Is there a bug database that can be searched?
- How is the application configured?
- If it was configured or tuned differently from the defaults, what was the reason? (Was it based on measurements and analysis, or guesswork?)
- Does the application employ a cache of objects? How is it sized?
- Does the application run concurrently? How is that configured (e.g., thread pool sizing)?
- Is the application running in a special mode? (For example, debug mode may have been enabled and be reducing performance.)
- What system libraries does the application use? What versions are they?
- What memory allocator does the application use?
- Is the application configured to use large pages for its heap?
- Is the application compiled? What version of the compiler? What compiler options and optimizations? 64-bit?

- Has the application encountered an error, and is it now running in a degraded mode?
- Are there system-imposed limits or resource controls for CPU, memory, file system, disk, or network usage? (These are common with cloud computing.)

Answering these questions may reveal configuration choices that have been overlooked.

5.5 Exercises

1. Answer the following questions about terminology:
   - What is a cache?
   - What is a ring buffer?
   - What is a spin lock?
   - What is an adaptive mutex lock?
   - What is the difference between concurrency and parallelism?
   - What is CPU affinity?

2. Answer the following conceptual questions:
   - What are the general pros and cons of using a large I/O size?
   - What is a hash table of locks used for?
   - Describe general performance characteristics of the runtime of compiled languages, interpreted languages, and those using virtual machines.
   - Explain the role of garbage collection and how it can affect performance.

3. Choose an application, and answer the following basic questions about it:
   - What is the role of the application?
   - What discrete operation does the application perform?
   - Does the application run in user mode or kernel mode?
   - How is the application configured? What key options are available regarding performance?
   - What performance metrics are provided by the application?
   - What logs does the application create? Do they contain performance information?
   - Has the most recent version of the application fixed performance issues?
   - Are there known performance bugs for the application?

- Does the application have a community (e.g., IRC, meetups)? A performance community?
- Are there books about the application? Performance books?
- Are there well-known performance experts for the application? Who are they?

4. Choose an application that is under load, and perform these tasks (many of which may require the use of dynamic tracing):

- Before taking any measurements, do you expect the application to be CPU-bound or I/O-bound? Explain your reasoning.
- Identify using observability tools if it is CPU-bound or I/O-bound.
- Characterize the size of I/O it performs (e.g., file system reads/writes, network sends/receives).
- Does the application have caches? Identify their size and hit rate.
- Measure the latency (response time) for the operation that the application serves. Show the average, minimum, maximum, and full distribution.
- Perform drill-down analysis of the operation, investigating the origin of the bulk of the latency.
- Characterize the workload applied to the application (especially who and what).
- Step through the static performance tuning checklist.
- Does the application run concurrently? Investigate its use of synchronization primitives.

5. (optional, advanced) Develop a tool for Linux called `tsastat(1)` that prints columns for each of the six thread state analysis states, with time spent in each. This can behave similarly to `pidstat(1)` and produce a rolling output.

5.6 References

[Knuth 76]   Knuth, D. "Big Omicron and Big Omega and Big Theta," *ACM SIGACT News,* 1976.

[Knuth 97]   Knuth, D. *The Art of Computer Programming,* Volume 1, *Fundamental Algorithms, 3rd Edition.* Addison-Wesley, 1997.

[1]   http://lwn.net/Articles/314512/

[2]   http://nodejs.org

[3]   www.brendangregg.com/dtrace.html#DTraceToolkit

6

CPUs

CPUs drive all software and are often the first target for systems performance analysis. Modern systems typically have many CPUs, which are shared among all running software by the kernel scheduler. When there is more demand for CPU resources than there are resources available, process threads (or tasks) will queue, waiting their turn. Waiting can add significant latency during the runtime of applications, degrading performance.

The usage of the CPUs can be examined in detail to look for performance improvements, including eliminating unnecessary work. At a high level, CPU usage by process, thread, or task can be examined. At a lower level, the code path within applications and the kernel can be profiled and studied. At the lowest level, CPU instruction execution and cycle behavior can be studied.

This chapter consists of five parts:

- **Background** introduces CPU-related terminology, basic models of CPUs, and key CPU performance concepts.

- **Architecture** introduces processor and kernel scheduler architecture.

- **Methodology** describes performance analysis methodologies, both observational and experimental.

- **Analysis** describes CPU performance analysis tools on Linux- and Solaris-based systems, including profiling, tracing, and visualizations.

- **Tuning** includes examples of tunable parameters.

The first three sections provide the basis for CPU analysis, and the last two show its practical application to Linux- and Solaris-based systems.

The effects of memory I/O on CPU performance are covered, including CPU cycles stalled on memory and the performance of CPU caches. Chapter 7, Memory, continues the discussion of memory I/O, including MMU, NUMA/UMA, system interconnects, and memory busses.

6.1 Terminology

For reference, CPU-related terminology used in this chapter includes the following:

- **Processor:** the physical chip that plugs into a socket on the system or processor board and contains one or more CPUs implemented as cores or hardware threads.

- **Core:** an independent CPU instance on a *multicore processor*. The use of cores is a way to scale processors, called *chip-level multiprocessing* (CMP).

- **Hardware thread:** a CPU architecture that supports executing multiple threads in parallel on a single core (including Intel's Hyper-Threading Technology), where each thread is an independent CPU instance. One name for this scaling approach is *multithreading*.

- **CPU instruction:** a single CPU operation, from its *instruction set*. There are instructions for arithmetic operations, memory I/O, and control logic.

- **Logical CPU:** also called a *virtual processor*,[1] an operating system CPU instance (a schedulable CPU entity). This may be implemented by the processor as a hardware thread (in which case it may also be called a *virtual core*), a core, or a single-core processor.

- **Scheduler:** the kernel subsystem that assigns threads to run on CPUs.

- **Run queue:** a queue of runnable threads that are waiting to be serviced by CPUs. For Solaris, it is often called a *dispatcher queue*.

Other terms are introduced throughout this chapter. The Glossary includes basic terminology for reference, including *CPU*, *CPU cycle*, and *stack*. Also see the terminology sections in Chapters 2 and 3.

---

1. It is also sometimes called a *virtual CPU*; however, that term is more commonly used to refer to virtual CPU instances provided by a virtualization technology. See Chapter 11, Cloud Computing.

6.2 Models

The following simple models illustrate some basic principles of CPUs and CPU performance. Section 6.4, Architecture, digs much deeper and includes implementation-specific details.

6.2.1 CPU Architecture

Figure 6.1 shows an example CPU architecture, for a single processor with four cores and eight hardware threads in total. The physical architecture is pictured, along with how it is seen by the operating system.

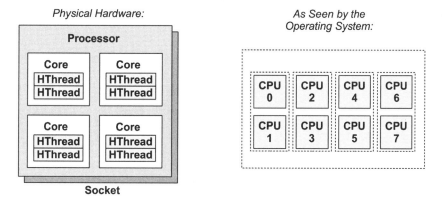

Figure 6-1 CPU architecture

Each hardware thread is addressable as a *logical CPU*, so this processor appears as eight CPUs. The operating system may have some additional knowledge of topology, such as which CPUs are on the same core, to improve its scheduling decisions.

6.2.2 CPU Memory Caches

Processors provide various hardware caches for improving memory I/O performance. Figure 6.2 shows the relationship of cache sizes, which become smaller and faster (a trade-off) the closer they are to the CPU.

The caches that are present, and whether they are on the processor (integrated) or external to the processor, depend on the processor type. Earlier processors provided fewer levels of integrated cache.

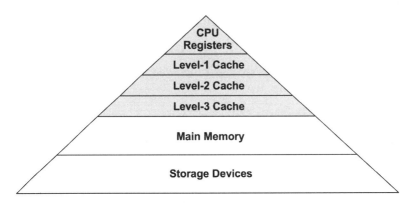

Figure 6-2 CPU cache sizes

6.2.3 CPU Run Queues

Figure 6.3 shows a CPU run queue, which is managed by the kernel scheduler.

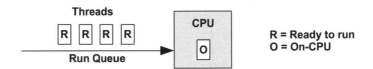

Figure 6-3 CPU run queue

The thread states shown in the figure, ready to run and on-CPU, are covered in Figure 3.7 in Chapter 3, Operating Systems.

The number of software threads that are queued and ready to run is an important performance metric indicating CPU saturation. In this figure (at this instant) there are four, with an additional thread running on-CPU. The time spent waiting on a CPU run queue is sometimes called *run-queue latency* or *dispatcher-queue latency*. In this book, the term *scheduler latency* is used instead, as it is appropriate for all dispatcher types, including those that do not use queues (see the discussion of CFS in Section 6.4.2, Software).

For multiprocessor systems, the kernel typically provides a run queue for each CPU and aims to keep threads on the same run queue. This means that threads are more likely to keep running on the same CPUs, where the CPU caches have cached their data. (These caches are described as having *cache warmth*, and the approach to favor CPUs is called *CPU affinity*.) On NUMA systems, *memory locality* may also be improved, which also improves performance (this is described in Chapter 7, Memory).

It also avoids the cost of thread synchronization (mutex locks) for queue operations, which would hurt scalability if the run queue was global and shared among all CPUs.

6.3 Concepts

The following are a selection of important concepts regarding CPU performance, beginning with a summary of processor internals: the CPU clock rate and how instructions are executed. This is background for later performance analysis, particularly for understanding the cycles-per-instruction (CPI) metric.

6.3.1 Clock Rate

The clock is a digital signal that drives all processor logic. Each CPU instruction may take one or more cycles of the clock (called *CPU cycles*) to execute. CPUs execute at a particular clock rate; for example, a 5 GHz CPU performs 5 billion clock cycles per second.

Some processors are able to vary their clock rate, increasing it to improve performance or decreasing it to reduce power consumption. The rate may be varied on request by the operating system, or dynamically by the processor itself. The kernel idle thread, for example, can request the CPU to throttle down to save power.

Clock rate is often marketed as the primary feature of the processor, but this can be a little misleading. Even if the CPU in your system appears to be fully utilized (a bottleneck), a faster clock rate may not speed up performance—it depends on what those fast CPU cycles are actually doing. If they are mostly stall cycles while waiting on memory access, executing them more quickly doesn't actually increase the CPU instruction rate or workload throughput.

6.3.2 Instruction

CPUs execute instructions chosen from their instruction set. An instruction includes the following steps, each processed by a component of the CPU called a *functional unit*:

1. Instruction fetch
2. Instruction decode
3. Execute
4. Memory access
5. Register write-back

The last two steps are optional, depending on the instruction. Many instructions operate on registers only and do not require the memory access step.

Each of these steps takes at least a single clock cycle to be executed. Memory access is often the slowest, as it may take dozens of clock cycles to read or write to main memory, during which instruction execution has *stalled* (and these cycles while stalled are called *stall cycles*). This is why CPU caching is important, as described in Section 6.4: it can dramatically reduce the number of cycles needed for memory access.

6.3.3 Instruction Pipeline

The instruction pipeline is a CPU architecture that can execute multiple instructions in parallel, by executing different components of different instructions at the same time. It is similar to a factory assembly line, where stages of production can be executed in parallel, increasing throughput.

Consider the instruction steps previously listed. If each were to take a single clock cycle, it would take five cycles to complete the instruction. At each step of this instruction, only one functional unit is active and four are idle. By use of pipelining, multiple functional units can be active at the same time, processing different instructions in the pipeline. Ideally, the processor can then complete one instruction with every clock cycle.

6.3.4 Instruction Width

But we can go faster still. Multiple functional units can be included of the same type, so that even more instructions can make forward progress with each clock cycle. This CPU architecture is called *superscalar* and is typically used with pipelining to achieve a high instruction throughput.

The instruction *width* describes the target number of instructions to process in parallel. Modern processors are *3-wide* or *4-wide*, meaning they can complete up to three or four instructions per cycle. How this works depends on the processor, as there may be different numbers of functional units for each stage.

6.3.5 CPI, IPC

Cycles per instruction (CPI) is an important high-level metric for describing where a CPU is spending its clock cycles and for understanding the nature of CPU utilization. This metric may also be expressed as *instructions per cycle* (IPC), the inverse of CPI.

A high CPI indicates that CPUs are often stalled, typically for memory access. A low CPI indicates that CPUs are often not stalled and have a high instruction throughput. These metrics suggest where performance tuning efforts may be best spent.

Memory-intensive workloads, for example, may be improved by installing faster memory (DRAM), improving memory locality (software configuration), or reducing the amount of memory I/O. Installing CPUs with a higher clock rate may not improve performance to the degree expected, as the CPUs may need to wait the same amount of time for memory I/O to complete. Put differently, a faster CPU may mean more stall cycles but the same rate of completed instructions.

The actual values for high or low CPI are dependent on the processor and processor features and can be determined experimentally by running known workloads. As an example, you may find that high-CPI workloads run with a CPI at ten or higher, and low CPI workloads run with a CPI at less than one (which is possible due to instruction pipelining and width, described earlier).

It should be noted that CPI shows the efficiency of instruction *processing*, but not of the instructions themselves. Consider a software change that added an inefficient software loop, which operates mostly on CPU registers (no stall cycles): such a change may result in a lower overall CPI, but higher CPU usage and utilization.

6.3.6 Utilization

CPU utilization is measured by the time a CPU instance is busy performing work during an interval, expressed as a percentage. It can be measured as the time a CPU is not running the kernel idle thread but is instead running user-level application threads or other kernel threads, or processing interrupts.

High CPU utilization may not necessarily be a problem, but rather a sign that the system is doing work. Some people also consider this an ROI indicator: a highly utilized system is considered to have good ROI, whereas an idle system is considered wasted. Unlike with other resource types (disks), performance does not degrade steeply under high utilization, as the kernel supports priorities, preemption, and time sharing. These together allow the kernel to understand what has higher priority, and to ensure that it runs first.

The measure of CPU utilization spans all clock cycles for eligible activities, including memory stall cycles. It may seem a little counterintuitive, but a CPU may be highly utilized because it is often stalled waiting for memory I/O, not just executing instructions, as described in the previous section.

CPU utilization is often split into separate kernel- and user-time metrics.

6.3.7 User-Time/Kernel-Time

The CPU time spent executing user-level application code is called *user-time*, and kernel-level code is *kernel-time*. Kernel-time includes time during system calls, kernel threads, and interrupts. When measured across the entire system, the user-time/kernel-time ratio indicates the type of workload performed.

Applications that are computation-intensive may spend almost all their time executing user-level code and have a user/kernel ratio approaching 99/1. Examples include image processing, genomics, and data analysis.

Applications that are I/O-intensive have a high rate of system calls, which execute kernel code to perform the I/O. For example, a web server performing network I/O may have a user/kernel ratio of around 70/30.

These numbers are dependent on many factors and are included to express the kinds of ratios expected.

6.3.8 Saturation

A CPU at 100% utilization is *saturated*, and threads will encounter *scheduler latency* as they wait to run on-CPU, decreasing overall performance. This latency is the time spent waiting on the CPU run queue or other structure used to manage threads.

Another form of CPU saturation involves CPU resource controls, as may be imposed in a multitenant cloud computing environment. While the CPU may not be 100% utilized, the imposed limit has been reached, and threads that are runnable must wait their turn. How visible this is to users of the system depends on the type of virtualization in use; see Chapter 11, Cloud Computing.

 A CPU running at saturation is less of a problem than other resource types, as higher-priority work can preempt the current thread.

6.3.9 Preemption

Preemption, introduced in Chapter 3, Operating Systems, allows a higher-priority thread to preempt the currently running thread and begin its own execution instead. This eliminates the run-queue latency for higher-priority work, improving its performance.

6.3.10 Priority Inversion

Priority inversion occurs when a lower-priority thread holds a resource and blocks a higher-priority thread from running. This reduces the performance of the higher-priority work, as it is blocked waiting.

Solaris-based kernels implement a full *priority inheritance* scheme to avoid priority inversion. Here is an example of how this can work (based on a real-world case):

1. Thread A performs monitoring and has a low priority. It acquires an address space lock for a production database, to check memory usage.

2. Thread B, a routine task to perform compression of system logs, begins running.

3. There is insufficient CPU to run both. Thread B preempts A and runs.

4. Thread C is from the production database, has a high priority, and has been sleeping waiting for I/O. This I/O now completes, putting thread C back into the runnable state.

5. Thread C preempts B, runs, but then blocks on the address space lock held by thread A. Thread C leaves CPU.

6. The scheduler picks the next-highest-priority thread to run: B.

7. With thread B running, a high-priority thread, C, is effectively blocked on a lower-priority thread, B. This is priority inversion.

8. Priority inheritance gives thread A thread C's high priority, preempting B, until it releases the lock. Thread C can now run.

Linux since 2.6.18 has provided a user-level mutex that supports priority inheritance, intended for real-time workloads [1].

6.3.11 Multiprocess, Multithreading

Most processors provide multiple CPUs of some form. For an application to make use of them, it needs separate threads of execution so that it can run in parallel. For a 64-CPU system, for example, this may mean that an application can execute up to 64 times faster if it can make use of all CPUs in parallel, or handle 64 times the load. The degree to which the application can effectively scale with an increase in CPU count is a measure of *scalability*.

The two techniques to scale applications across CPUs are *multiprocess* and *multithreading*, which are pictured in Figure 6.4.

On Linux both the multiprocess and multithread models may be used, and both are implemented by tasks.

Differences between multiprocess and multithreading are shown in Table 6.1.

With all the advantages shown in the table, multithreading is generally considered superior, although more complicated for the developer to implement.

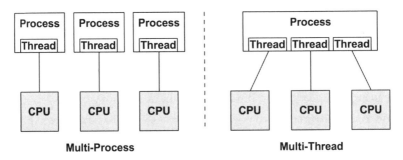

Figure 6-4 Software CPU scalability techniques

Table 6-1 Multiprocess and Multithreading Attributes

Attribute	Multiprocess	Multithreading
Development	Can be easier. Use of `fork()`.	Use of threads API.
Memory overhead	Separate address space per process consumes some memory resources.	Small. Requires only extra stack and register space.
CPU overhead	Cost of `fork()`/`exit()`, which includes MMU work to manage address spaces.	Small. API calls.
Communication	Via IPC. This incurs CPU cost including context switching for moving data between address spaces, unless shared memory regions are used.	Fastest. Direct access to share memory. Integrity via synchronization primitives (e.g., mutex locks).
Memory usage	While some memory may be duplicated, separate processes can `exit()` and return all memory back to the system.	Via system allocator. This may incur some CPU contention from multiple threads, and fragmentation before memory is reused.

Whichever technique is used, it is important that enough processes or threads be created to span the desired number of CPUs—which, for maximum performance, may be all of the CPUs available. Some applications may perform better when running on fewer CPUs, when the cost of thread synchronization and reduced memory locality outweighs the benefit of running across more CPUs.

Parallel architectures are also discussed in Chapter 5, Applications.

6.3.12 Word Size

Processors are designed around a maximum *word size*—32-bit or 64-bit—which is the integer size and register size. Word size is also commonly used, depending on the processor, for the address space size and data path width (where it is some-times called the *bit width*).

Larger sizes can mean better performance, although it's not as simple as it sounds. Larger sizes may cause memory overheads for unused bits in some data types. The data footprint also increases when the size of pointers (word size) increases, which can require more memory I/O. For the x86 64-bit architecture, these overheads are compensated by an increase in registers and a more efficient register calling convention, so 64-bit applications will more likely be faster than their 32-bit versions.

Processors and operating systems can support multiple word sizes and can run applications compiled for different word sizes simultaneously. If software has been compiled for the smaller word size, it may execute successfully but perform rela-tively poorly.

6.3.13 Compiler Optimization

The CPU runtime of applications can be significantly improved through compiler options (including setting word size) and optimizations. Compilers are also fre-quently updated to take advantage of the latest CPU instruction sets and to imple-ment other optimizations. Sometimes application performance can be significantly improved simply by using a newer compiler.

This topic is covered in more detail in Chapter 5, Applications.

6.4 Architecture

This section introduces CPU architecture and implementation, for both hardware and software. Simple CPU models were introduced in Section 6.2, Models, and generic concepts in the previous section.

These topics have been summarized as background for performance analysis. For more details, see vendor processor manuals and texts on operating system internals. Some are listed at the end of this chapter.

6.4.1 Hardware

CPU hardware includes the processor and its subsystems, and the CPU intercon-nect for multiprocessor systems.

Processor

Components of a generic two-core processor are shown in Figure 6.5.

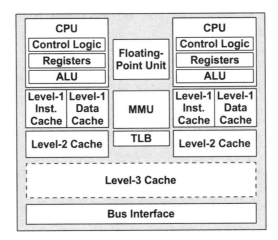

Figure 6-5 Generic two-core processor components

The *control unit* (pictured as *control logic*) is the heart of the CPU, performing instruction fetch, decoding, managing execution, and storing results.

This example processor depicts a shared floating-point unit and (optional) shared Level 3 cache. The actual components in your processor will vary depending on its type and model. Other performance-related components that may be present include the following:

- **P-cache:** prefetch cache (per CPU)
- **W-cache:** write cache (per CPU)
- **Clock:** signal generator for the CPU clock (or provided externally)
- **Timestamp counter:** for high-resolution time, incremented by the clock
- **Microcode ROM:** quickly converts instructions to circuit signals
- **Temperature sensors:** for thermal monitoring
- **Network interfaces:** if present on-chip (for high performance)

Some processor types use the temperature sensors as input for dynamic over-clocking of individual cores (including Intel Turbo Boost technology), improving performance while the core remains in its temperature envelope.

CPU Caches

Various hardware caches are usually included in the processor (referred to as *on-chip*, *on-die*, *embedded*, or *integrated*) or with the processor (*external*). These improve memory performance by using faster memory types for caching reads and

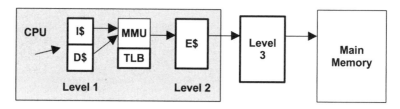

Figure 6-6 CPU cache hierarchy

buffering writes. The levels of cache access for a generic processor are shown in Figure 6.6.

They include

- **Level 1 instruction cache** (I$)
- **Level 1 data cache** (D$)
- **Translation lookaside buffer** (TLB)
- **Level 2 cache** (E$)
- **Level 3 cache** (optional)

The E in E$ originally stood for *external* cache, but with the integration of Level 2 caches it has since been cleverly referred to as *embedded* cache. The "Level" terminology is used nowadays instead of the "E$"-style notation, which avoids such confusion.

The caches available on each processor depend on its type and model. Over time, the number and sizes of these caches have been increasing. This is illustrated in Table 6.2 by the listing of Intel processors since 1978, including advances in caches [Intel 12].

Table 6-2 Example Intel Processor Cache Sizes from 1978 to 2011

Processor	Date	Max Clock	Transistors	Data Bus	Level 1	Level 2	Level 3
8086	1978	8 MHz	29 K	16-bit	—		
Intel 286	1982	12.5 MHz	134 K	16-bit	—		
Intel 386 DX	1985	20 MHz	275 K	32-bit	—	—	—
Intel 486 DX	1989	25 MHz	1.2 M	32-bit	8 KB	—	—
Pentium	1993	60 MHz	3.1 M	64-bit	16 KB	—	—
Pentium Pro	1995	200 MHz	5.5 M	64-bit	16 KB	256/512 KB	—

continues

Table 6-2 Example Intel Processor Cache Sizes from 1978 to 2011 (*Continued*)

Processor	Date	Max Clock	Transistors	Data Bus	Level 1	Level 2	Level 3
Pentium II	1997	266 MHz	7 M	64-bit	32 KB	256/512 KB	—
Pentium III	1999	500 MHz	8.2 M	64-bit	32 KB	512 KB	—
Intel Xeon	2001	1.7 GHz	42 M	64-bit	8 KB	512 KB	—
Pentium M	2003	1.6 GHz	77 M	64-bit	64 KB	1 MB	—
Intel Xeon MP	2005	3.33 GHz	675 M	64-bit	16 KB	1 MB	8 MB
Intel Xeon 7410	2006	3.4 GHz	1.3 B	64-bit	64 KB	2 x 1 MB	16 MB
Intel Xeon 7460	2008	2.67 GHz	1.9 B	64-bit	64 KB	3 x 3 MB	16 MB
Intel Xeon 7560	2010	2.26 GHz	2.3 B	64-bit	64 KB	256 KB	24 MB
Intel Xeon E7-8870	2011	2.4 GHz	2.2 B	64-bit	64 KB	256 KB	30 MB

For multicore and multithreading processors, some of these caches may be shared between cores and threads.

Apart from the increasing number and sizes of CPU caches, there is also a trend toward provide these on-chip, where access latency can be minimized, instead of providing them externally to the processor.

Latency

Multiple levels of cache are used to deliver the optimum configuration of size and latency. The access time for the Level 1 cache is typically a few CPU clock cycles, and for the larger Level 2 cache around a dozen clock cycles. Main memory can take around 60 ns (around 240 cycles, for a 4 GHz processor), and address translation by the MMU also adds latency.

The CPU cache latency characteristics for your processor can be determined experimentally using micro-benchmarking [Ruggiero 08]. Figure 6.7 shows the result of this, plotting memory access latency for an Intel Xeon E5620 2.4 GHz tested over increasing ranges of memory using LMbench [2].

Both axes are logarithmic. The steps in the graphs show when a cache level was exceeded, and access latency becomes a result of the next (slower) cache level.

Associativity

Associativity is a cache characteristic describing a constraint for locating new entries in the cache. Types are

- **Fully associative:** The cache can locate new entries anywhere. For example, an LRU algorithm could evict the least recently used entry in the entire cache.

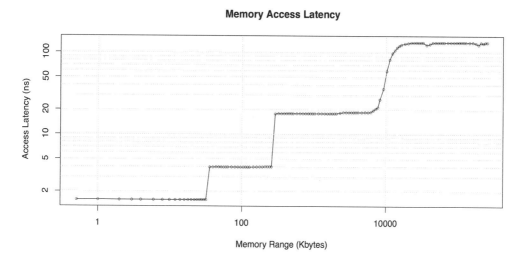

Figure 6-7 Memory access latency testing

- **Direct mapped:** Each entry has only one valid location in the cache, for example, a hash of the memory address, using a subset of the address bits to form an address in the cache.

- **Set associative:** A subset of the cache is identified by mapping (e.g., hashing), from within which another algorithm (e.g., LRU) may be performed. It is described in terms of the subset size; for example, *four-way set associative* maps an address to four possible locations, and then picks the best from those four.

CPU caches often use set associativity as a balance between fully associative (which is expensive to perform) and direct mapped (which has poor hit rates).

Cache Line

Another characteristic of CPU caches is their *cache line* size. This is a range of bytes that are stored and transferred as a unit, improving memory throughput. A typical cache line size for x86 processors is 64 bytes. Compilers take this into account when optimizing for performance. Programmers sometimes do as well; see Hash Tables in Section 5.2.5 of Chapter 5, Applications.

Cache Coherency

Memory may be cached in multiple CPU caches on different processors at the same time. When one CPU modifies memory, all caches need to be aware that their cached copy is now *stale* and should be discarded, so that any future reads will retrieve the newly modified copy. This process, called *cache coherency*, ensures that

CPUs are always accessing the correct state of memory. It is also one of the greatest challenges when designing scalable multiprocessor systems, as memory can be
modified rapidly.

MMU

The MMU is responsible for virtual-to-physical address translation. A generic
MMU is pictured in Figure 6.8, along with CPU cache types. This MMU uses an
on-chip TLB to cache address translations. Cache misses are satisfied by translation tables in main memory (DRAM), called *page tables*, which are read directly by
the MMU (hardware).

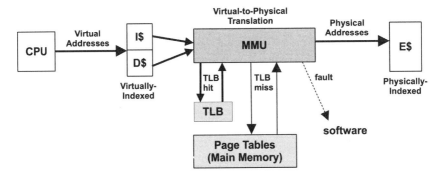

Figure 6-8 Memory management unit and CPU caches

These factors are processor-dependent. Some (older) processors handle TLB
misses using software to walk the page tables, and then populate the TLB with the
requested mappings. Such software may maintain its own, larger, in-memory cache
of translations, called the *translation storage buffer* (TSB). Newer processors can
service TLB misses in hardware, greatly reducing their cost.

Interconnects

For multiprocessor architectures, processors are connected using either a shared
system bus or a dedicated interconnect. This is related to the memory architecture
of the system, uniform memory access (UMA) or NUMA, as discussed in Chapter 7,
Memory.

A shared system bus, called the *front-side bus*, used by earlier Intel processors is
illustrated by the four-processor example in Figure 6.9.

The use of a system bus has scalability problems when the processor count is
increased, due to contention for the shared bus resource. Modern servers are typically multiprocessor, NUMA, and use a CPU interconnect instead.

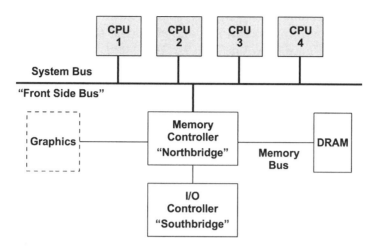

Figure 6-9 Example Intel front-side bus architecture, four-processor

Interconnects can connect components other than processors, such as I/O controllers. Example interconnects include Intel's Quick Path Interconnect (QPI) and AMD's HyperTransport (HT). An example Intel QPI architecture for a four-processor system is shown in Figure 6.10.

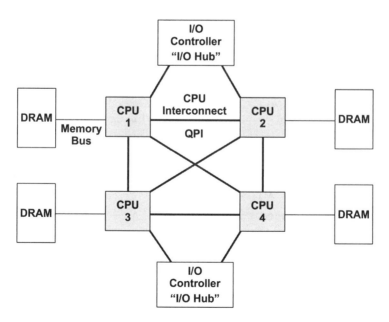

Figure 6-10 Example Intel QPI architecture, four-processor

The private connections between processors allow for noncontended access and also allow higher bandwidths than the shared system bus. Some example speeds for Intel FSB and QPI are shown in Table 6.3 [Intel 09].

Table 6-3 Intel CPU Interconnect Bandwidths

Intel	Transfer Rate	Width	Bandwidth
FSB (2007)	1.6 GT/s	8 bytes	12.8 Gbytes/s
QPI (2008)	6.4 GT/s	2 bytes	25.6 Gbytes/s

QPI is *double-pumped*, performing a data transfer on both edges of the clock, doubling the data transfer rate. This explains the bandwidth shown in the table (6.4 GT/s x 2 bytes x double = 25.6 Gbytes/s).

Apart from external interconnects, processors have internal interconnects for core communication.

Interconnects are typically designed for high bandwidth, so that they do not become a systemic bottleneck. If they do, performance will degrade as CPU instructions encounter stall cycles for operations that involve the interconnect, such as remote memory I/O. A key indicator for this is a rise in CPI. CPU instructions, cycles, CPI, stall cycles, and memory I/O can be analyzed using CPU performance counters.

CPU Performance Counters

CPU performance counters (CPCs) go by many names, including *performance instrumentation counters* (PICs), *performance monitoring unit* (PMU), *hardware events*, and *performance monitoring events*. They are processor registers that can be programmed to count low-level CPU activity. They typically include counters for the following:

- **CPU cycles:** including stall cycles and types of stall cycles
- **CPU instructions:** retired (executed)
- **Level 1, 2, 3 cache accesses:** hits, misses
- **Floating-point unit:** operations
- **Memory I/O:** reads, writes, stall cycles
- **Resource I/O:** reads, writes, stall cycles

Each CPU has a small number of registers, usually between two and eight, that can be programmed to record events like these. Those available depend on the processor type and model and are documented in the processor manual.

As a relatively simple example, the Intel P6 family of processors provide performance counters via four model-specific registers (MSRs). Two MSRs are the counters and are read-only. The other two MSRs are used to program the counters,
called *event-select* MSRs, and are read-write. The performance counters are 40-bit
registers, and the event-select MSRs are 32-bit. The format of the event-select
MSRs is shown in Figure 6.11.

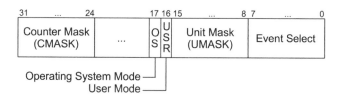

Figure 6-11 Example Intel performance event-select MSR

The counter is identified by the event select and the UMASK. The event select
identifies the type of event to count, and the UMASK identifies subtypes or groups
of subtypes. The OS and USR bits can be set so that the counter is incremented
only while in kernel mode (OS) or user mode (USR), based on the processor protection rings. The CMASK can be set to a threshold of events that must be reached
before the counter is incremented.

The Intel processor manual (volume 3B [Intel 13]) lists the dozens of events that
can be counted by their event-select and UMASK values. The selected examples in
Table 6.4 provide an *idea* of the different targets (processor functional units) that
may be observable. You will need to refer to your current processor manual to see
what you actually have.

There are many, many more counters, especially for newer processors. The Intel
Sandy Bridge family of processors provide not only more counter types, but also
more counter registers: three fixed and four programmable counters per hardware
thread, and an additional eight programmable counters per core ("general-
purpose"). These are 48-bit counters when read.

Since performance counters vary among manufacturers, a standard has been
developed to provide a consistent interface across them. This is the *Processor
Application Programmers Interface* (PAPI). Instead of the Intel names seen in
Table 6.4, PAPI assigns generic names to the counter types, for example, PAPI_
tot_cyc for total cycle counts, instead of CPU_CLK_UNHALTED.

Table 6-4 Selected Examples of Intel CPU Performance Counters

Event Select	UMASK	Unit	Name	Description
0x43	0x00	data cache	DATA_MEM_REFS	All loads from any memory type. All stores to any memory type. Each part of a split is counted separately. . . . Does not include I/O accesses or other nonmemory accesses.
0x48	0x00	data cache	DCU_MISS_OUTSTANDING	Weighted number of cycles while a DCU miss is outstanding, incremented by the number of outstanding cache misses at any particular time. Cacheable read requests only are considered. . . .
0x80	0x00	instruction fetch unit	IFU_IFETCH	Number of instruction fetches, both cacheable and noncacheable, including UC (uncacheable) fetches.
0x28	0x0F	L2 cache	L2_IFETCH	Number of L2 instruction fetches. . . .
0xC1	0x00	floating-point unit	FLOPS	Number of computational floating-point operations retired. . . .
0x7E	0x00	external bus logic	BUS_SNOOP_STALL	Number of clock cycles during which the bus is snoop stalled.
0xC0	0x00	instruction decoding and retirement	INST_RETIRED	Number of instructions retired.
0xC8	0x00	interrupts	HW_INT_RX	Number of hardware interrupts received.
0xC5	0x00	branches	BR_MISS_PRED_RETIRED	Number of mispredicted branches retired.
0xA2	0x00	stalls	RESOURCE_STALLS	Incremented by one during every cycle for which there is a resource-related stall. . . .
0x79	0x00	clocks	CPU_CLK_UNHALTED	Number of cycles during which the processor is not halted.

6.4.2 Software

Kernel software to support CPUs includes the scheduler, scheduling classes, and the idle thread.

Scheduler

Key functions of the kernel CPU scheduler are shown in Figure 6.12.

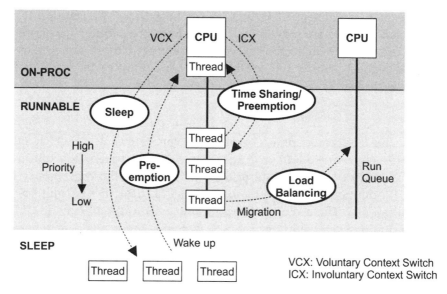

Figure 6-12 Kernel CPU scheduler functions

These are

- **Time sharing:** multitasking between runnable threads, executing those with the highest priority first.
- **Preemption:** For threads that have become runnable at a high priority, the scheduler can preempt the currently running thread, so that execution of the higher-priority thread can begin immediately.
- **Load balancing:** moving runnable threads to the run queues of idle or less busy CPUs.

The figure shows run queues per CPU. There are also run queues per priority level, so that the scheduler can easily manage which thread of the same priority should run.

A brief summary of how scheduling works for recent Linux and Solaris-based kernels follows. Function names are included, so that you can find them in the source code for further reference (although they may have changed). Also refer to internals texts, listed in the Bibliography.

Linux

On Linux, time sharing is driven by the system timer interrupt by calling `scheduler_tick()`, which calls scheduler class functions to manage priorities and the expiry of units of CPU time called *time slices*. Preemption is triggered when threads become runnable and the scheduler class `check_preempt_curr()` function is called. Switching of threads is managed by `__schedule()`, which selects the highest-priority thread via `pick_next_task()` for running. Load balancing is performed by the `load_balance()` function.

Solaris

On Solaris-based kernels, time sharing is driven by `clock()`, which calls scheduler class functions including `ts_tick()` to check for time slice expiration. If the thread has exceeded its time, its priority is reduced, allowing another thread to preempt. Preemption is handled by `preempt()` for user threads and `kpreempt()` for kernel threads. The `swtch()` function manages a thread leaving CPU for any reason, including from voluntary context switching, and calls dispatcher functions to find the best runnable thread to take its place: `disp()`, `disp_getwork()`, or `disp_getbest()`. Load balancing includes the idle thread calling similar functions to find runnable threads from another CPU's dispatcher queue (run queue).

Scheduling Classes

Scheduling classes manage the behavior of runnable threads, specifically their priorities, whether their on-CPU time is *time-sliced*, and the duration of those *time slices* (also known as *time quantum*). There are also additional controls via scheduling *policies*, which may be selected within a scheduling class and can control scheduling between threads of the same priority. Figure 6.13 depicts them along with the thread priority range.

The priority of user-level threads is affected by a user-defined *nice* value, which can be set to lower the priority of unimportant work. In Linux, the nice value sets the *static priority* of the thread, which is separate from the *dynamic priority* that the scheduler calculates.

Note that the priority ranges are inverted between Linux and Solaris-based kernels. The original Unix priority range (6th edition) used lower numbers for higher priority, the system Linux uses now.

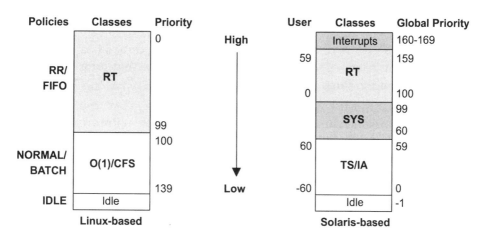

Figure 6-13 Thread scheduler priorities

Linux

For Linux kernels, the scheduling classes are

- **RT:** provides fixed and high priorities for real-time workloads. The kernel supports both user- and kernel-level preemption, allowing RT tasks to be dispatched with low latency. The priority range is 0–99 (MAX_RT_PRIO–1).

- **O(1):** The O(1) scheduler was introduced in Linux 2.6 as the default time-sharing scheduler for user processes. The name comes from the algorithm complexity of O(1) (see Chapter 5, Applications, for a summary of big O notation). The prior scheduler contained routines that iterated over all tasks, making it O(n), which became a scalability issue. The O(1) scheduler dynamically improves the priority of I/O-bound over CPU-bound workloads, to reduce latency of interactive and I/O workloads.

- **CFS:** Completely fair scheduling was added to the Linux 2.6.23 kernel as the default time-sharing scheduler for user processes. The scheduler manages tasks on a red-black tree instead of traditional run queues, which is keyed from the task CPU time. This allows low CPU consumers to be easily found and executed in preference to CPU-bound workloads, improving the performance of interactive and I/O-bound workloads.

The scheduling class behavior can be adjusted by user-level processes by calling `sched_setscheduler()` to set the scheduler policy. The RT class supports the SCHED_RR and SCHED_FIFO policies, and the CFS class supports SCHED_NORMAL and SCHED_BATCH.

Scheduler policies are as follows:

- **RR:** SCHED_RR is round-robin scheduling. Once a thread has used its time quantum, it is moved to the end of the run queue for that priority level, allowing others of the same priority to run.
- **FIFO:** SCHED_FIFO is first-in first-out scheduling, which continues running the thread at the head of the run queue until it voluntarily leaves, or until a higher-priority thread arrives. The thread continues to run, even if other threads of the same priority are on the run queue.
- **NORMAL:** SCHED_NORMAL (previously known as SCHED_OTHER) is time-sharing scheduling and is the default for user processes. The scheduler dynamically adjusts priority based on the scheduling class. For O(1), the time slice duration is set based on the static priority: longer durations for higher-priority work. For CFS, the time slice is dynamic.
- **BATCH:** SCHED_BATCH is similar to SCHED_NORMAL, but with the expectation that the thread will be CPU-bound and should not be scheduled to interrupt other I/O-bound interactive work.

Other classes and policies may be added over time. Scheduling algorithms have been researched that are *hyperthreading-aware* [Bulpin 05] and *temperature-aware* [Otto 06], which optimize performance by accounting for additional processor factors.

When there is no thread to run, a special *idle task* (also called *idle thread*) is executed as a placeholder until another thread is runnable.

Solaris

For Solaris-based kernels, the scheduling classes are as follows:

- **RT:** Real-time scheduling provides fixed and high priorities for real-time workloads. These preempt all other work (except interrupt service routines) so that application response time can be deterministic—a typical requirement for real-time workloads.
- **SYS:** System is a high-priority scheduling class for kernel threads. These threads have a fixed priority and execute for as long as needed (or until preempted by RT or interrupts).
- **TS:** Time sharing is the default for user processes; it dynamically adjusts priority and quantum based on recent CPU usage. Thread priority is demoted if it uses its quantum, and the quantum is increased. This causes CPU-bound workloads to run at a low priority with large time quantums (reducing

scheduler costs), and I/O-bound workloads—which voluntarily context switch before their quantum is used—to run at a high priority. The result is that the performance of I/O-bound workloads is not affected by the presence of long-running CPU jobs. This class also applies the nice value, if set.

- **IA:** Interactive is similar to TS, but with a slightly higher default priority. It is rarely used today (it was previously used to improve the responsiveness of graphical X sessions).

- **FX:** Fixed (not pictured in Figure 6.13) is a process scheduling class for setting fixed priorities, in the same global priority range as TS (0–59).

- **FSS:** Fair-share scheduling (not pictured in Figure 6.13) manages CPU usage between groups of processes, either *projects* or *zones*, based on share values. This allows groups of projects to use the CPUs fairly based on shares, instead of based on their number of threads or processes. Each process group can consume a fraction of CPU calculated from its share value divided by the total *busy* shares on the system at that time. This means that if that group is the only busy group, it can use all CPU resources. FSS is in popular use for cloud computing, so that tenants (zones) can be allocated shares fairly and can also consume more CPU if it is available and unused. FSS exists in the same global priority range as TS (0–59) and has a fixed time quantum.

- **SYSDC:** The system duty cycle scheduling class is for kernel threads that are large CPU consumers, such as the ZFS transaction group flush thread. It allows a target duty cycle to be specified (the ratio of CPU time to runnable time) and will deschedule the thread to match the duty cycle. This prevents long-running kernel threads, which would otherwise be in the SYS class, from starving other threads that need to use that CPU.

- **Interrupts:** For the purpose of scheduling interrupt threads, they are given a priority that is 159 + IPL (see Section 3.2.3, Interrupts and Interrupt Threads, in Chapter 3, Operating Systems).

Solaris-based systems also support scheduling policies (not pictured in Figure 6.13) that are set using sched_setscheduler(): SCHED_FIFO, SCHED_RR, and SCHED_OTHER (time sharing).

The idle thread is a special case, running with the lowest priority.

Idle Thread

The kernel "idle" thread (or *idle task*) runs on-CPU when there is no other runnable thread and has the lowest possible priority. It is usually programmed to inform the processor that CPU execution may either be halted (halt instruction) or throttled down to conserve power. The CPU will wake up on the next hardware interrupt.

NUMA Grouping

Performance on NUMA systems can be significantly improved by making the kernel *NUMA-aware*, so that it can make better scheduling and memory placement decisions. This can automatically detect and create groups of localized CPU and memory resources and organize them in a topology to reflect the NUMA architecture. This topology allows the cost of any memory access to be estimated.

On **Linux** systems, these are called *scheduling domains* [3], which are in a topology beginning with the *root domain*.

On **Solaris**-based systems, these are called *locality groups* (lgrps) and begin with the *root group*.

A manual form of grouping can be performed by the system administrator, either by binding processes to run on one or more CPUs only, or by creating an exclusive set of CPUs for processes to run on. See Section 6.5.10, CPU Binding.

Processor Resource-Aware

Other than for NUMA, the CPU resource topology can be understood by the kernel so that it can make better scheduling decisions for power management and load balancing. On Solaris-based systems, this is implemented by *processor groups*.

6.5 Methodology

This section describes various methodologies and exercises for CPU analysis and tuning. Table 6.5 summarizes the topics.

Table 6-5 CPU Performance Methodologies

Methodology	Types
Tools method	observational analysis
USE method	observational analysis
Workload characterization	observational analysis, capacity planning
Profiling	observational analysis
Cycle analysis	observational analysis
Performance monitoring	observational analysis, capacity planning
Static performance tuning	observational analysis, capacity planning
Priority tuning	tuning
Resource controls	tuning
CPU binding	tuning

Table 6-5 CPU Performance Methodologies (*Continued*)

Methodology	Types
Micro-benchmarking	experimental analysis
Scaling	capacity planning, tuning

See Chapter 2, Methodology, for more strategies and the introduction to many of these. You are not expected to use them all; treat this as a cookbook of recipes that may be followed individually or used in combination.

My suggestion is to use the following, in this order: performance monitoring, the USE method, profiling, micro-benchmarking, and static analysis.

Section 6.6, Analysis, shows operating system tools for applying these strategies.

6.5.1 Tools Method

The tools method is a process of iterating over available tools, examining key metrics they provide. While this is a simple methodology, it can overlook issues for which the tools provide poor or no visibility, and it can be time-consuming to perform.

For CPUs, the tools method can involve checking the following:

- **uptime:** Check load averages to see if CPU load is increasing or decreasing over time. A load average over the number of CPUs in the system usually indicates saturation.
- **vmstat:** Run vmstat per second, and check the idle column to see how much headroom there is. Less than 10% can be a problem.
- **mpstat:** Check for individual hot (busy) CPUs, identifying a possible thread scalability problem.
- **top/prstat:** See which processes and users are the top CPU consumers.
- **pidstat/prstat:** Break down the top CPU consumers into user- and system-time.
- **perf/dtrace/stap/oprofile:** Profile CPU usage stack traces for either user- or kernel-time, to identify why the CPUs are in use.
- **perf/cpustat:** Measure CPI.

If an issue is found, examine all fields from the available tools to learn more context. See Section 6.6, Analysis, for more about each tool.

6.5.2 USE Method

The USE method is for identifying bottlenecks and errors across all components, early in a performance investigation, before deeper and more time-consuming strategies are followed.

For each CPU, check for

- **Utilization:** the time the CPU was busy (not in the idle thread)
- **Saturation:** the degree to which runnable threads are queued waiting their turn on-CPU
- **Errors:** CPU errors, including correctable errors

Errors may be checked first since they are typically quick to check and the easiest to interpret. Some processors and operating systems will sense an increase in correctable errors (error-correcting code, ECC) and will offline a CPU as a precaution, before an uncorrectable error causes a CPU failure. Checking for these errors can be a matter of checking that all CPUs are still online.

Utilization is usually readily available from operating system tools as *percent busy*. This metric should be examined per CPU, to check for scalability issues. It can also be examined per core, for cases where a core's resources are heavily utilized, preventing idle hardware threads from executing. High CPU and core utilization can be understood by using profiling and cycle analysis.

For environments that implement CPU limits or quotas (resource controls), as occurs in some cloud computing environments, CPU utilization may need to be measured in terms of the imposed limit, in addition to the physical limit. Your system may exhaust its CPU quota well before the physical CPUs reach 100% utilization, encountering saturation earlier than expected.

Saturation metrics are commonly provided system-wide, including as part of load averages. This metric quantifies the degree to which the CPUs are overloaded, or a CPU quota, if present, is used up.

6.5.3 Workload Characterization

Characterizing the load applied is important in capacity planning, benchmarking, and simulating workloads. It can also lead to some of the largest performance gains by identifying unnecessary work that can be eliminated.

Basic attributes for characterizing CPU workload are

- Load averages (utilization + saturation)
- User-time to system-time ratio

- Syscall rate
- Voluntary context switch rate
- Interrupt rate

The intent is to characterize the applied load, not the delivered performance. The load average is suited for this, as it reflects the CPU load requested, regardless of the delivered performance as shown by the utilization/saturation breakdown. See the example and further explanation in Section 6.6.1, uptime.

The rate metrics are a little harder to interpret, as they reflect both the applied load and to some degree the delivered performance, which can throttle their rate.

The user-time to system-time ratio shows the type of load applied, as introduced earlier in Section 6.3.7, User-Time/Kernel-Time. High user-time rates are due to applications spending time performing their own compute. High system-time shows time spent in the kernel instead, which may be further understood by the syscall and interrupt rate. I/O-bound workloads have higher system-time, syscalls, and also voluntary context switches as threads block waiting for I/O.

Here is an example workload description that you might receive, designed to show how these attributes can be expressed together:

On our busiest application server, the load average varies between 2 and 8 during the day depending on the number of active clients. The user/system ratio is 60/40, as this is an I/O-intensive workload performing around 100 K syscalls/s, and a high rate of voluntary context switches.

These characteristics can vary over time as different load is encountered.

Advanced Workload Characterization/Checklist

Additional details may be included to characterize the workload. These are listed here as questions for consideration, which may also serve as a checklist when studying CPU issues thoroughly:

- What is the CPU utilization system-wide? Per CPU?
- How parallel is the CPU load? Is it single-threaded? How many threads?
- Which applications or users are using the CPUs? How much?
- Which kernel threads are using the CPUs? How much?
- What is the CPU usage of interrupts?
- What is the CPU interconnect utilization?
- Why are the CPUs being used (user- and kernel-level call paths)?
- What types of stall cycles are encountered?

See Chapter 2, Methodology, for a higher-level summary of this methodology and the characteristics to measure (who, why, what, how). The sections that follow expand upon the last two questions in this list: how call paths can be analyzed using profiling, and stall cycles using cycle analysis.

6.5.4 Profiling

Profiling builds a picture of the target for study. CPU usage can be profiled by sampling the state of the CPUs at timed intervals, following these steps:

1. **Select** the type of profile data to capture, and the rate.
2. **Begin** sampling at a timed interval.
3. **Wait** while the activity of interest occurs.
4. **End** sampling and collect sample data.
5. **Process** the data.

Some profiling tools, including DTrace, allow real-time processing of the captured data, which can be analyzed while sampling is still occurring.

Processing and navigating the data may be enhanced by a separate toolset from the one used to collect the data. One example is flame graphs (covered later), which process the output of DTrace and other profiling tools. Another is the Performance Analyzer from Oracle Solaris Studio, which automates collecting and browsing the profile data with the target source code.

The types of CPU profile data are based on the following factors:

- User level, kernel level, or both
- Function and offset (program-counter-based), function only, partial stack trace, or full stack trace

Selecting full stack traces for both user and kernel level captures the complete profile of CPU usage. However, it typically generates an excessive amount of data. Capturing only user or kernel, partial stacks (e.g., five levels deep), or even just the executing function name may prove sufficient for identifying CPU usage from much less data.

As a simple example of profiling, the following DTrace one-liner samples the user-level function name at 997 Hz for a duration of 10 s:

```
# dtrace -n 'profile-997 /arg1 && execname == "beam.smp"/ {
    @[ufunc(arg1)] = count(); } tick-10s { exit(0); }'
[...]
```

```
libc.so.1`mutex_lock_impl                             29
libc.so.1`atomic_swap_8                               33
beam.smp`make_hash                                    45
libc.so.1`__time                                      71
innostore_drv.so`os_aio_array_get_nth_slot            80
beam.smp`process_main                                127
libc.so.1`mutex_trylock_adaptive                     140
innostore_drv.so`os_aio_simulated_handle             158
beam.smp`sched_sys_wait                              202
libc.so.1`memcpy                                     258
innostore_drv.so`ut_fold_binary                     1800
innostore_drv.so`ut_fold_ulint_pair                 4039
```

DTrace has already performed step 5, processing the data by aggregating function names and printing the sorted frequency counts. This shows that the most common on-CPU user-level function while tracing was ut_fold_ulint_pair(), which was sampled 4,039 times.

A frequency of 997 Hz was used to avoid sampling in lockstep with any activity (e.g., timed tasks running at 100 or 1,000 Hz).

By sampling the full stack trace, the code path for CPU usage can be identified, which typically points to higher-level reasons for CPU usage. More examples of sampling are given in Section 6.6, Analysis. Also see Chapter 5, Applications, for more on CPU profiling, including fetching other programming language context from the stack.

For the usage of specific CPU resources, such as caches and interconnects, profiling can use CPC-based event triggers instead of timed intervals. This is described in the next section on cycle analysis.

6.5.5 Cycle Analysis

By using the CPU performance counters (CPCs), CPU utilization can be understood at the cycle level. This may reveal that cycles are spent stalled on Level 1, 2, or 3 cache misses, memory I/O, or resource I/O, or spent on floating-point operations or other activity. This information may lead to performance wins by adjusting compiler options or changing the code.

Begin cycle analysis by measuring CPI. If CPI is high, continue to investigate types of stall cycles. If CPI is low, look for ways in the code to reduce instructions performed. The values for "high" or "low" CPI depend on your processor: low could be less than one, and high could be greater than ten. You can get a sense of these values by performing known workloads that are either memory-I/O-intensive or instruction-intensive and measuring the resulting CPI for each.

Apart from measuring counter values, CPC can be configured to interrupt the kernel on the overflow of a given value. For example, at every 10,000 Level 2 cache misses, the kernel could be interrupted to gather a stack backtrace. Over time, the kernel builds a profile of the code paths that are causing Level 2 cache misses, without the prohibitive overhead of measuring every single miss. This is typically used by integrated developer environment (IDE) software, to annotate code with the locations that are causing memory I/O and stall cycles. Similar observability is possible using DTrace and the cpc provider.

Cycle analysis is an advanced activity that can take days to perform with command-line tools, as demonstrated in Section 6.6, Analysis. You should also expect to spend some quality time with your CPU vendor's processor manuals. Performance analyzers such as Oracle Solaris Studio can save time as they are programmed to find the CPCs of interest to you.

6.5.6 Performance Monitoring

Performance monitoring can identify active issues and patterns of behavior over time. Key metrics for CPUs are

- **Utilization:** percent busy
- **Saturation:** either run-queue length, inferred from load average, or as a measure of thread scheduler latency

Utilization should be monitored on a per-CPU basis to identify thread scalability issues. For environments that implement CPU limits or quotas (resource controls), such as some cloud computing environments, CPU usage compared to these limits also needs to be recorded.

A challenge when monitoring CPU usage is choosing an interval to measure and archive. Some monitoring tools use 5 minutes, which can hide the existence of shorter bursts of CPU utilization. Per-second measurements are preferable, but you should be aware that there can be bursts even within a second. These can be identified from saturation.

6.5.7 Static Performance Tuning

Static performance tuning focuses on issues of the configured environment. For CPU performance, examine the following aspects of the static configuration:

- How many CPUs are available for use? Are they cores? Hardware threads?
- Is the CPU architecture single- or multiprocessor?
- What is the size of the CPU caches? Are they shared?

- What is the CPU clock speed? Is it dynamic (e.g., Intel Turbo Boost and SpeedStep)? Are those dynamic features enabled in the BIOS?
- What other CPU-related features are enabled or disabled in the BIOS?
- Are there performance issues (bugs) with this processor model? Are they listed in the processor errata sheet?
- Are there performance issues (bugs) with this BIOS firmware version?
- Are there software-imposed CPU usage limits (resource controls) present? What are they?

The answers to these questions may reveal previously overlooked configuration choices.

The last question is especially true for cloud computing environments, where CPU usage is commonly limited.

6.5.8 Priority Tuning

Unix has always provided a `nice()` system call for adjusting process priority, which sets a nice-ness value. Positive nice values result in lower process priority (nicer), and negative values—which can be set only by the superuser (root)—result in higher priority. A `nice(1)` command became available to launch programs with nice values, and a `renice(1M)` command was later added (in BSD) to adjust the nice value of already running processes. The man page from Unix 4th edition provides this example [4]:

> The value of 16 is recommended to users who wish to execute long-running programs without flak from the administration.

The nice value is still useful today for adjusting process priority. This is most effective when there is contention for CPUs, causing scheduler latency for high-priority work. Your task is to identify low-priority work, which may include monitoring agents and scheduled backups, that can be modified to start with a nice value. Analysis may also be performed to check that the tuning is effective, and that the scheduler latency remains low for high-priority work.

Beyond nice, the operating system may provide more advanced controls for process priority such as changing the scheduler class or scheduler policy, or changing the tuning of the class. Both Linux and Solaris-based kernels include the *real-time scheduling class*, which can allow processes to preempt all other work. While this can eliminate scheduler latency (other than for other real-time processes and interrupts), make sure you understand the consequences. If the real-time application encounters a bug where multiple threads enter an infinite loop, it can cause all CPUs to become unavailable for all other work—including the administrative shell required to manually fix the problem. This particular scenario is usually solved only by rebooting the system (oops!).

6.5.9 Resource Controls

The operating system may provide fine-grained controls for allocating CPU cycles to processes or groups of processes. These may include fixed limits for CPU utilization and shares for a more flexible approach—allowing idle CPU cycles to be consumed based on a share value. How these work is implementation-specific and discussed in Section 6.8, Tuning.

6.5.10 CPU Binding

Another way to tune CPU performance involves binding processes and threads to individual CPUs, or collections of CPUs. This can increase CPU cache warmth for the process, improving its memory I/O performance. For NUMA systems it also improves memory locality, also improving performance.

There are generally two ways this is performed:

- **Process binding:** configuring a process to run only on a single CPU, or only on one CPU from a defined set.
- **Exclusive CPU sets:** partitioning a set of CPUs that can be used only by the process(es) assigned to them. This can improve CPU cache further, as when the process is idle other processes cannot use the CPUs, leaving the caches warm.

On Linux-based systems, the exclusive CPU sets approach can be implemented using *cpusets*. On Solaris-based systems, this is called *processor sets*. Configuration examples are provided in Section 6.8, Tuning.

6.5.11 Micro-Benchmarking

There are various tools for CPU micro-benchmarking, which typically measure the time taken to perform a simple operation many times. The operation may be based on the following:

- **CPU instructions:** integer arithmetic, floating-point operations, memory loads and stores, branch and other instructions

- **Memory access:** to investigate latency of different CPU caches and main memory throughput

- **Higher-level languages:** similar to CPU instruction testing, but written in a higher-level interpreted or compiled language

- **Operating system operations:** testing system library and system call functions that are CPU-bound, such as getpid() and process creation

An early example of a CPU benchmark is Whetstone by the National Physical Laboratory, written in 1972 in Algol 60 and intended to simulate a scientific workload. The Dhrystone benchmark was later developed in 1984 to simulate integer workloads of the time and became a popular means to compare CPU performance. These, and various Unix benchmarks including process creation and pipe throughput, were included in a collection called *UnixBench*, originally from Monash University and published by *BYTE* magazine [Hinnant 84]. More recent CPU benchmarks have been created to test compression speeds, prime number calculation, encryption, and encoding.

Whichever benchmark you use, when comparing results between systems it's important that you understand what is really being tested. Benchmarks like those described previously often end up testing compiler optimizations between different compiler versions, rather than the benchmark code or CPU speed. Many benchmarks also execute single-threaded, but these results lose meaning in systems with multiple CPUs. A four-CPU system may benchmark slightly faster than an eight-CPU system, but the latter is likely to deliver much greater throughput when given enough parallel runnable threads.

For more on benchmarking, see Chapter 12, Benchmarking.

6.5.12 Scaling

Here is a simple scaling method, based on capacity planning of resources:

1. Determine the target user population or application request rate.

2. Express CPU usage per user or per request. For existing systems, CPU usage can be monitored with the current user count or request rate. For future systems, load generation tools can simulate users so that CPU usage can be measured.

3. Extrapolate users or requests when the CPU resources reach 100% utilization. This provides the theoretical limit for the system.

System scalability can also be modeled to account for contention and coherency latency, for a more realistic prediction of performance. See Section 2.6, Modeling, in Chapter 2, Methodology, for more about this, and also Section 2.7, Capacity Planning, of the same chapter for more on scaling.

6.6 Analysis

This section introduces CPU performance analysis tools for Linux- and Solaris-based operating systems. See the previous section for strategies to follow when using them.

The tools in this section are listed in Table 6.6.

Table 6-6 CPU Analysis Tools

Linux	Solaris	Description
uptime	uptime	load averages
vmstat	vmstat	includes system-wide CPU averages
mpstat	mpstat	per-CPU statistics
sar	sar	historical statistics
ps	ps	process status
top	prstat	monitor per-process/thread CPU usage
pidstat	prstat	per-process/thread CPU breakdowns
time	ptime	time a command, with CPU breakdowns
DTrace, perf	DTrace	CPU profiling and tracing
perf	cpustat	CPU performance counter analysis

The list begins with tools for CPU statistics, and then drills down to tools for deeper analysis including code-path profiling and CPU cycle analysis. This is a selection of tools and capabilities to support Section 6.5, Methodology. See the documentation for each tool, including its man pages, for full references of its features.

While you may be interested in only Linux or only Solaris-based systems, consider looking at the other operating system's tools and the observability that they provide for a different perspective.

6.6.1 uptime

uptime(1) is one of several commands that print the system *load averages*:

```
$ uptime
 9:04pm  up 268 day(s), 10:16,  2 users,  load average: 7.76, 8.32, 8.60
```

The last three numbers are the 1-, 5-, and 15-minute load averages. By comparing the three numbers, you can determine if the load is increasing, decreasing, or steady during the last 15 minutes (or so).

Load Averages

The load average indicates the demand for CPU resources and is calculated by summing the number of threads running (utilization) and the number that are queued waiting to run (saturation). A newer method for calculating load averages uses utilization plus the sum of thread scheduler latency, rather than sampling the queue length, which improves accuracy. For reference, the internals of these calculations on Solaris-based kernels are documented in [McDougall 06b].

To interpret the value, if the load average is higher than the CPU count, there are not enough CPUs to service the threads, and some are waiting. If the load average is lower than the CPU count, it (probably) means that there is headroom, and the threads could run on-CPU when they wanted.

The three load average numbers are exponentially damped moving averages, which reflect load beyond the 1-, 5-, and 15-minute times (the times are actually constants used in the exponential moving sum [Myer 73]). Figure 6.14 shows the results of a simple experiment where a single CPU-bound thread was launched and the load averages plotted.

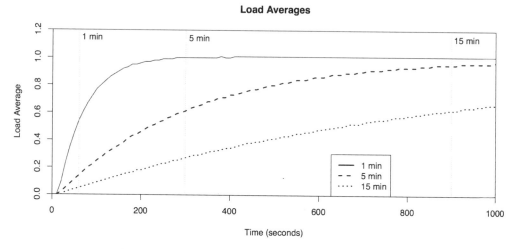

Figure 6-14 Exponentially damped load averages

By the 1-, 5-, and 15-minute marks, the load averages had reached about 61% of the known load of 1.0.

Load averages were introduced to Unix in early BSD and were based on sched-uler average queue length and load averages commonly used by earlier operating systems (CTSS, Multics [Saltzer 70], TENEX [Bobrow 72]). They were described in [RFC 546]:

[1] The TENEX load average is a measure of CPU demand. The load average is an average of the number of runable processes over a given time period. For example, an hourly load average of 10 would mean that (for a single CPU system) at any time dur-ing that hour one could expect to see 1 process running and 9 others ready to run (i.e., not blocked for I/O) waiting for the CPU.

As a modern example, a system with 64 CPUs has a load average of 128. This means that on average there is always one thread running on each CPU, and one thread waiting for each CPU. The same system with a load average of ten would indicate significant headroom, as it could run another 54 CPU-bound threads before all CPUs are busy.

Linux Load Averages

Linux currently adds tasks performing disk I/O in the uninterruptable state to the load averages. This means that the load average can no longer be interpreted to mean CPU headroom or saturation only, since it is unknown from the value alone to what degree it reflects CPU or disk load. Comparisons of the three load average numbers are also difficult, as the load may have varied among CPUs and disks over time.

A different way to incorporate other resource load is to use separate load aver-ages for each resource type. (I've prototyped examples of this for disk, memory, and network load, each providing its own set of load averages, and found it a similar and useful overview for non-CPU resources.)

It is best to use other metrics to understand CPU load on Linux, such as those provided by vmstat(1) and mpstat(1).

6.6.2 vmstat

The virtual memory statistics command, vmstat(8), prints system-wide CPU averages in the last few columns, and a count of runnable threads in the first col-umn. Here is example output from the **Linux** version:

```
$ vmstat 1
procs -----------memory---------- ---swap-- -----io---- -system-- ----cpu----
 r  b   swpd   free   buff  cache   si   so    bi    bo   in   cs us sy id wa
15  0   2852 46686812 279456 1401196    0    0     0     0    0    0  0  0 100  0
16  0   2852 46685192 279456 1401196    0    0     0     0 2136 36607 56 33 11  0
```

```
15  0   2852 46685952 279456 1401196    0    0     0    56 2150 36905 54 35 11  0
15  0   2852 46685960 279456 1401196    0    0     0     0 2173 36645 54 33 13  0
[...]
```

The first line of output is the summary-since-boot, with the exception of r on Linux—which begins by showing current values. The columns are

- **r:** run-queue length—the total number of runnable threads (see below)
- **us:** user-time
- **sy:** system-time (kernel)
- **id:** idle
- **wa:** wait I/O, which measures CPU idle when threads are blocked on disk I/O
- **st:** stolen (not shown in the output), which for virtualized environments shows CPU time spent servicing other tenants

All of these values are system-wide averages across all CPUs, with the exception of r, which is the total.

On **Linux**, the r column is the total number of tasks waiting *plus* those running. The man page currently describes it as something else—"the number of processes waiting for run time"—which suggests it counts only those waiting and not running. As insight into what this is supposed to be, the original vmstat(1) by Bill Joy and Ozalp Babaoglu for 3BSD in 1979 begins with an RQ column for the number of runnable *and* running processes, as the Linux vmstat(8) currently does. The man page needs updating.

On **Solaris**, the r column counts only the number of threads *waiting* in the dispatcher queues (run queues). The value can appear erratic, as it is sampled only once per second (from clock()), whereas the other CPU columns are based on high-resolution CPU microstates. These other columns currently do not include wait I/O or stolen. See Chapter 9, Disks, for more about wait I/O.

6.6.3 mpstat

The multiprocessor statistics tool, mpstat, can report statistics per CPU. Here is some example output from the **Linux** version:

```
$ mpstat -P ALL 1
02:47:49   CPU    %usr   %nice    %sys %iowait    %irq   %soft %steal %guest   %idle
02:47:50   all   54.37    0.00   33.12    0.00    0.00    0.00   0.00   0.00   12.50
02:47:50     0   22.00    0.00   57.00    0.00    0.00    0.00   0.00   0.00   21.00
02:47:50     1   19.00    0.00   65.00    0.00    0.00    0.00   0.00   0.00   16.00
```

continues

```
02:47:50    2    24.00    0.00   52.00    0.00    0.00    0.00    0.00    0.00   24.00
02:47:50    3   100.00    0.00    0.00    0.00    0.00    0.00    0.00    0.00    0.00
02:47:50    4   100.00    0.00    0.00    0.00    0.00    0.00    0.00    0.00    0.00
02:47:50    5   100.00    0.00    0.00    0.00    0.00    0.00    0.00    0.00    0.00
02:47:50    6   100.00    0.00    0.00    0.00    0.00    0.00    0.00    0.00    0.00
02:47:50    7    16.00    0.00   63.00    0.00    0.00    0.00    0.00    0.00   21.00
02:47:50    8   100.00    0.00    0.00    0.00    0.00    0.00    0.00    0.00    0.00
02:47:50    9    11.00    0.00   53.00    0.00    0.00    0.00    0.00    0.00   36.00
02:47:50   10   100.00    0.00    0.00    0.00    0.00    0.00    0.00    0.00    0.00
02:47:50   11    28.00    0.00   61.00    0.00    0.00    0.00    0.00    0.00   11.00
02:47:50   12    20.00    0.00   63.00    0.00    0.00    0.00    0.00    0.00   17.00
02:47:50   13    12.00    0.00   56.00    0.00    0.00    0.00    0.00    0.00   32.00
02:47:50   14    18.00    0.00   60.00    0.00    0.00    0.00    0.00    0.00   22.00
02:47:50   15   100.00    0.00    0.00    0.00    0.00    0.00    0.00    0.00    0.00
[...]
```

The -P ALL option was used to print the per-CPU report. By default, mpstat(1) prints only the system-wide summary line (all). The columns are

- **CPU:** logical CPU ID, or all for summary

- **%usr:** user-time

- **%nice:** user-time for processes with a nice'd priority

- **%sys:** system-time (kernel)

- **%iowait:** I/O wait

- **%irq:** hardware interrupt CPU usage

- **%soft:** software interrupt CPU usage

- **%steal:** time spent servicing other tenants

- **%guest:** CPU time spent in guest virtual machines

- **%idle:** idle

Key columns are %usr, %sys, and %idle. These identify CPU usage per CPU and show the user-time/kernel-time ratio (see Section 6.3.7, User-Time/Kernel-Time). This can also identify "hot" CPUs—those running at 100% utilization (%usr + %sys) while others are not—which can be caused by single-threaded application workloads or device interrupt mapping.

For **Solaris**-based systems, mpstat(1M) begins with the summary-since-boot, followed by the interval summaries. For example:

```
$ mpstat 1
CPU minf mjf xcal  intr ithr  csw icsw migr smtx  srw syscl  usr sys  wt idl
[...]
  0 8243    0  288  3211 1265 1682   40  236  262    0  8214   47  19   0  34
  1 43708   0 1480  2753 1115 1238   58  406 1967    0 26157   17  59   0  24
  2 11987   0  393  2994 1186 1761   79  281  522    0 10035   46  21   0  34
  3 3998    0  135   935   55  238   22   60   97    0  2350   88   6   0   6
```

```
 4 12649  0  414 2885 1261 3130  82 365  619  0 14866   7 26  0 67
 5 30054  0  991  745  241 1563  52 349 1108  0 17792   8 40  0 52
 6 12882  0  439  636  167 2335  73 289  747  0 12803   6 23  0 71
 7   981  0   40  793   45  870  11  81   70  0  2022  78  3  0 19
 8  3186  0  100  687   27  450  15  75  156  0  2581  66  7  0 27
 9  8433  0  259  814  315 3382  38 280  552  0  9376   4 18  0 78
10  8451  0  283  512  153 2158  20 194  339  0  9776   4 16  0 80
11  3722  0  119  800  349 2693  12 199  194  0  6447   2 10  0 88
12  4757  0  138  834  214 1387  29 142  380  0  6153  35 10  0 55
13  5107  0  147 1404  606 3856  65 268  352  0  8188   4 14  0 82
14  7158  0  229  672  205 1829  31 133  292  0  7637  19 12  0 69
15  5822  0  209  866  232 1333   9 145  180  0  5164  30 13  0 57
```

The columns include

- **CPU:** logical CPU ID
- **xcal:** CPU cross calls
- **intr:** interrupts
- **ithr:** interrupts serviced as threads (lower IPL)
- **csw:** context switches (total)
- **icsw:** involuntary context switches
- **migr:** thread migrations
- **smtx:** spins on mutex locks
- **srw:** spins on reader/writer locks
- **syscl:** system calls
- **usr:** user-time
- **sys:** system-time (kernel)
- **wt:** wait I/O (deprecated, always zero)
- **idl:** idle

Key columns to check are

- **xcal**, to see if there is an excess rate, which consumes CPU resources. For example, look for at least 1,000/s across several CPUs. Drill-down analysis can explain their cause (see the example of this in Section 6.6.10, DTrace).
- **smtx**, to see if there is an excess rate, which consumes CPU resources and may also be evidence of lock contention. Lock activity can then be explored using other tools (see Chapter 5, Applications).
- **usr**, **sys**, and **idl**, to characterize CPU usage per CPU and the user-time/kernel-time ratio.

6.6.4 sar

The system activity reporter, sar(1), can be used to observe current activity and can be configured to archive and report historical statistics. It was introduced in Chapter 4, Observability Tools, and is mentioned in other chapters as appropriate.

The **Linux** version provides the following options:

- **-P ALL:** same as mpstat -P ALL
- **-u:** same as mpstat(1)'s default output: system-wide average only
- **-q:** includes run-queue size as runq-sz (waiting plus running, the same as vmstat's r) and load averages

The **Solaris** version provides

- **-u:** system-wide averages for %usr, %sys, %wio (zero), and %idl
- **-q:** includes run-queue size as runq-sz (waiting only), and percent of time the run queue had threads waiting as %runocc, although this value is inaccurate between 0 and 1

Per-CPU statistics are not available in the Solaris version.

6.6.5 ps

The process status command, ps(1), lists details on all processes, including CPU usage statistics. For example:

```
$ ps aux
USER         PID %CPU %MEM    VSZ   RSS TTY     STAT START   TIME COMMAND
root           1  0.0  0.0  23772  1948 ?       Ss   2012    0:04 /sbin/init
root           2  0.0  0.0      0     0 ?       S    2012    0:00 [kthreadd]
root           3  0.0  0.0      0     0 ?       S    2012    0:26 [ksoftirqd/0]
root           4  0.0  0.0      0     0 ?       S    2012    0:00 [migration/0]
root           5  0.0  0.0      0     0 ?       S    2012    0:00 [watchdog/0]
[...]
web        11715 11.3  0.0 632700 11540 pts/0   Sl   01:36   0:27 node indexer.js
web        11721 96.5  0.1 638116 52108 pts/1   Rl+  01:37   3:33 node proxy.js
[...]
```

This style of operation originated from BSD and can be recognized by a lack of a dash before the aux options. These list all users (a), with extended user-oriented details (u), and include processes without a terminal (x). The terminal is shown in the teletype (TTY) column.

A different style, from SVR4, uses options preceded by a dash:

```
$ ps -ef
UID          PID  PPID  C STIME TTY       TIME CMD
root           1     0  0 Nov13 ?     00:00:04 /sbin/init
root           2     0  0 Nov13 ?     00:00:00 [kthreadd]
root           3     2  0 Nov13 ?     00:00:00 [ksoftirqd/0]
root           4     2  0 Nov13 ?     00:00:00 [migration/0]
root           5     2  0 Nov13 ?     00:00:00 [watchdog/0]
[...]
```

This lists every process (-e) with full details (-f). ps(1) on most Linux- and Solaris-based systems supports both the BSD and SVR4 arguments.

Key columns for CPU usage are TIME and %CPU.

The TIME column shows the total CPU time consumed by the process (user + system) since it was created, in hours:minutes:seconds.

On **Linux**, the %CPU column shows the CPU usage during the previous second as the sum across all CPUs. A single-threaded CPU-bound process will report 100%. A two-thread CPU-bound process will report 200%.

On **Solaris**, %CPU is normalized for the CPU count. For example, a single CPU-bound thread will be shown as 12.5% for an eight-CPU system. This metric also shows *recent* CPU usage, using similar decayed averages as with load averages.

Various other options are available for ps(1), including -o to customize the output and columns shown.

6.6.6 top

top(1) was created by William LeFebvre in 1984 for BSD. He was inspired by the VMS command MONITOR PROCESS/TOPCPU, which showed the top CPU-consuming jobs with CPU percentages and an ASCII bar chart histogram (but not columns of data).

The top(1) command monitors top running processes, updating the screen at regular intervals. For example, on **Linux**:

```
$ top
top - 01:38:11 up 63 days,  1:17,  2 users,  load average: 1.57, 1.81, 1.77
Tasks: 256 total,   2 running, 254 sleeping,   0 stopped,   0 zombie
Cpu(s):  2.0%us,  3.6%sy,  0.0%ni, 94.2%id,  0.0%wa,  0.0%hi,  0.2%si,  0.0%st
Mem:  49548744k total, 16746572k used, 32802172k free,   182900k buffers
Swap: 100663292k total,        0k used, 100663292k free, 14925240k cached

  PID USER      PR  NI  VIRT  RES  SHR S %CPU %MEM    TIME+  COMMAND
11721 web       20   0  623m  50m 4984 R   93  0.1  0:59.50 node
11715 web       20   0  619m  20m 4916 S   25  0.0  0:07.52 node
   10 root      20   0     0    0    0 S    1  0.0 248:52.56 ksoftirqd/2
   51 root      20   0     0    0    0 S    0  0.0  0:35.66 events/0
11724 admin     20   0 19412 1444  960 R    0  0.0  0:00.07 top
    1 root      20   0 23772 1948 1296 S    0  0.0  0:04.35 init
```

A system-wide summary is at the top and a process/task listing at the bottom, sorted by the top CPU consumer by default. The system-wide summary includes the load averages and CPU states: %us, %sy, %ni, %id, %wa, %hi, %si, %st. These states are equivalent to those printed by mpstat(1), as described earlier, and are averaged across all CPUs.

CPU usage is shown by the TIME and %CPU columns, which were introduced in the previous section on ps(1).

This example shows a TIME+ column, which is the same as the one shown above, but at a resolution of hundredths of a second. For example, "1:36.53" means 1 minute and 36.53 seconds of on-CPU time in total. Some versions of top(1) provide an optional "cumulative time" mode, which includes the CPU time from child processes that have exited.

On **Linux**, the %CPU column by default is not normalized by CPU count; top(1) calls this "Irix mode," after its behavior on IRIX. This can be switched to "Solaris mode," which divides the CPU usage by the CPU count. In that case, the hot two-thread process on a 16-CPU server would report percent CPU as 12.5.

Though top(1) is often a tool for beginning performance analysts, you should be aware that the CPU usage of top(1) itself can become significant and place top(1) as the top CPU-consuming process! This has been due to the available system calls—open(), read(), close()—and their cost when iterating over /proc entries for many processes. Some versions of top(1) for Solaris-based systems have reduced the overhead by leaving file descriptors open and calling pread(), which the prstat(1M) tool also does.

Since top(1) takes snapshots of /proc, it can miss short-lived processes that exit before a snapshot is taken. This commonly happens during software builds, where the CPUs can be heavily loaded by many short-lived tools from the build process. A variant of top(1) for Linux, called atop(1), uses process accounting to catch the presence of short-lived processes, which it includes in its display.

6.6.7 prstat

The prstat(1) command was introduced as "top for Solaris-based systems." For example:

```
$ prstat
   PID USERNAME  SIZE   RSS STATE  PRI NICE      TIME  CPU PROCESS/NLWP
 21722 101        23G   20G cpu0    59    0  72:23:41 2.6% beam.smp/594
 21495 root      321M  304M sleep    1    0   2:57:41 0.9% node/5
 20721 root      345M  328M sleep    1    0   2:49:53 0.8% node/5
 20861 root      348M  331M sleep    1    0   2:57:07 0.7% node/6
 15354 root      172M  156M cpu9     1    0   0:31:42 0.7% node/5
 21738 root      179M  143M sleep    1    0   2:37:48 0.7% node/4
 20385 root      196M  174M sleep    1    0   2:26:28 0.6% node/4
```

```
23186 root        172M  149M sleep    1    0    0:10:56 0.6% node/4
18513 root        174M  138M cpu13    1    0    2:36:43 0.6% node/4
21067 root        187M  162M sleep    1    0    2:28:40 0.5% node/4
19634 root        193M  170M sleep    1    0    2:29:36 0.5% node/4
10163 root        113M  109M sleep    1    0   12:31:09 0.4% node/3
12699 root        199M  177M sleep    1    0    1:56:10 0.4% node/4
37088 root       1069M 1056M sleep   59    0   38:31:19 0.3% qemu-system-x86/4
10347 root         67M   64M sleep    1    0   11:57:17 0.3% node/3
Total: 390 processes, 1758 lwps, load averages: 3.89, 3.99, 4.31
```

A one-line system summary is at the bottom. The CPU column shows recent CPU
usage and is the same metric shown by top(1) on Solaris. The TIME column
shows consumed time.

prstat(1M) consumes fewer CPU resources than top(1) by using pread() to
read /proc status with file descriptors left open, instead of the open(), read(),
close() cycle.

Thread microstate accounting statistics can be printed by prstat(1M) using
the –m option. The following example uses –L to report this per thread (per LWP)
and –c for continual output (instead of screen refreshes):

```
$ prstat -mLc 1
   PID USERNAME USR SYS TRP TFL DFL LCK SLP LAT VCX ICX SCL SIG PROCESS/LWPID
 30650 root      20 2.7 0.0 0.0 0.0 0.0  76 0.5 839  36  5K   0 node/1
 42370 root      11 2.0 0.0 0.0 0.0 0.0  87 0.1 205  23  2K   0 node/1
 42501 root      11 1.9 0.0 0.0 0.0 0.0  87 0.1 201  24  2K   0 node/1
 42232 root      11 1.9 0.0 0.0 0.0 0.0  87 0.1 205  25  2K   0 node/1
 42080 root      11 1.9 0.0 0.0 0.0 0.0  87 0.1 201  24  2K   0 node/1
 53036 root     7.0 1.4 0.0 0.0 0.0 0.0  92 0.1 158  22  1K   0 node/1
 56318 root     6.8 1.4 0.0 0.0 0.0 0.0  92 0.1 154  21  1K   0 node/1
 55302 root     6.8 1.3 0.0 0.0 0.0 0.0  92 0.1 156  23  1K   0 node/1
 54823 root     6.7 1.3 0.0 0.0 0.0 0.0  92 0.1 154  23  1K   0 node/1
 54445 root     6.7 1.3 0.0 0.0 0.0 0.0  92 0.1 156  24  1K   0 node/1
 53551 root     6.7 1.3 0.0 0.0 0.0 0.0  92 0.1 153  20  1K   0 node/1
 21722 103      6.3 1.5 0.0 0.0 3.3 0.0  88 0.0  40   0  1K   0 beam.smp/578
 21722 103      6.2 1.3 0.0 0.0 8.7 0.0  84 0.0  43   0  1K   0 beam.smp/585
 21722 103      5.1 1.2 0.0 0.0 3.2 0.0  90 0.0  38   1  1K   0 beam.smp/577
 21722 103      4.7 1.1 0.0 0.0 0.0 0.0  87 0.0  45   0 985   0 beam.smp/580
Total: 390 processes, 1758 lwps, load averages: 3.92, 3.99, 4.31
```

The eight highlighted columns show time spent in each microstate and sum to
100%. They are

- **USR:** user-time
- **SYS:** system-time (kernel)
- **TRP:** system trap
- **TFL:** text faults (page faults for executable segments)
- **DFL:** data faults

- **LCK:** time spent waiting for user-level locks
- **SLP:** time spent sleeping, including blocked on I/O
- **LAT:** scheduler latency (dispatcher queue latency)

This breakdown of thread time is extremely useful. Here are suggested paths for further investigation (also see Section 5.4.1, Thread State Analysis, in Chapter 5, Applications):

- **USR:** profiling of user-level CPU usage
- **SYS:** check system calls used and profile kernel-level CPU usage
- **SLP:** depends on the sleep event; trace syscall or code path for more details
- **LAT:** check system-wide CPU utilization and any imposed CPU limit/quota

Many of these can also be performed using DTrace.

6.6.8 pidstat

The Linux pidstat(1) tool prints CPU usage by process or thread, including user- and system-time breakdowns. By default, a rolling output is printed of only active processes. For example:

```
$ pidstat 1
Linux 2.6.35-32-server (dev7)    11/12/12      _x86_64_        (16 CPU)

22:24:42          PID    %usr %system  %guest    %CPU   CPU  Command
22:24:43         7814    0.00    1.98    0.00    1.98     3  tar
22:24:43         7815   97.03    2.97    0.00  100.00    11  gzip

22:24:43          PID    %usr %system  %guest    %CPU   CPU  Command
22:24:44          448    0.00    1.00    0.00    1.00     0  kjournald
22:24:44         7814    0.00    2.00    0.00    2.00     3  tar
22:24:44         7815   97.00    3.00    0.00  100.00    11  gzip
22:24:44         7816    0.00    2.00    0.00    2.00     2  pidstat
[...]
```

This example captured a system backup, involving a tar(1) command to read files from the file system, and the gzip(1) command to compress them. The user-time for gzip(1) is high, as expected, as it becomes CPU-bound in compression code. The tar(1) command spends more time in the kernel, reading from the file system.

The -p ALL option can be used to print all processes, including those that are idle. -t prints per-thread statistics. Other pidstat(1) options are included in other chapters of this book.

6.6.9 time, ptime

The time(1) command can be used to run programs and report CPU usage. It is provided either in the operating system under /usr/bin, or as a shell built-in.

This example runs time twice on a cksum(1) command, calculating the checksum of a large file:

```
$ time cksum Fedora-16-x86_64-Live-Desktop.iso
560560652 633339904 Fedora-16-x86_64-Live-Desktop.iso

real    0m5.105s
user    0m2.810s
sys     0m0.300s
$ time cksum Fedora-16-x86_64-Live-Desktop.iso
560560652 633339904 Fedora-16-x86_64-Live-Desktop.iso

real    0m2.474s
user    0m2.340s
sys     0m0.130s
```

The first run took 5.1 s, during which 2.8 s was in user mode—calculating the checksum—and 0.3 s was in system-time—the system calls required to read the file. There is a missing 2.0 s (5.1 - 2.8 - 0.3), which is likely time spent blocked on disk I/O reads, as this file was only partially cached. The second run completed more quickly, in 2.5 s, with almost no time blocked on I/O. This is expected, as the file may be fully cached in main memory for the second run.

On **Linux**, the /usr/bin/time version supports verbose details:

```
$ /usr/bin/time -v cp fileA fileB
        Command being timed: "cp fileA fileB"
        User time (seconds): 0.00
        System time (seconds): 0.26
        Percent of CPU this job got: 24%
        Elapsed (wall clock) time (h:mm:ss or m:ss): 0:01.08
        Average shared text size (kbytes): 0
        Average unshared data size (kbytes): 0
        Average stack size (kbytes): 0
        Average total size (kbytes): 0
        Maximum resident set size (kbytes): 3792
        Average resident set size (kbytes): 0
        Major (requiring I/O) page faults: 0
        Minor (reclaiming a frame) page faults: 294
        Voluntary context switches: 1082
        Involuntary context switches: 1
        Swaps: 0
        File system inputs: 275432
        File system outputs: 275432
        Socket messages sent: 0
        Socket messages received: 0
        Signals delivered: 0
        Page size (bytes): 4096
        Exit status: 0
```

The -v option is not typically provided in the shell built-in version.

Solaris-based systems include an additional ptime(1) version of time(1), which provides high-precision times based on thread microstate accounting. Nowadays, time(1) on Solaris-based systems ultimately uses the same source of statistics. ptime(1) is still useful, as it provides a –m option to print the full set of thread microstate times, including scheduler latency (lat):

```
$ ptime -m cp fileA fileB

real         8.334800250
user         0.016714684
sys          1.899085951
trap         0.000003874
tflt         0.000000000
dflt         0.000000000
kflt         0.000000000
lock         0.000000000
slp          6.414634340
lat          0.004249234
stop         0.000285583
```

In this case, the runtime was 8.3 s, during which 6.4 s was sleeping (disk I/O).

6.6.10 DTrace

DTrace can be used to profile CPU usage for both user- and kernel-level code, and to trace the execution of functions, CPU cross calls, interrupts, and the kernel scheduler. These abilities support workload characterization, profiling, drill-down analysis, and latency analysis.

The following sections introduce DTrace for CPU analysis on Solaris- and Linux-based systems. Unless noted, the DTrace commands are intended for both operating systems. A DTrace primer was included in Chapter 4, Observability Tools.

Kernel Profiling

Previous tools, including mpstat(1) and top(1), showed system-time—CPU time spent in the kernel. DTrace can be used to identify what the kernel is doing.

The following one-liner, demonstrated on a Solaris-based system, samples kernel stack traces at 997 Hz (to avoid lockstep, as explained in Section 6.5.4, Profiling). The predicate ensures that the CPU is in kernel mode when sampling, by checking that the kernel program counter (arg0) is nonzero:

```
# dtrace -n 'profile-997 /arg0/ { @[stack()] = count(); }'
dtrace: description 'profile-997 ' matched 1 probe
^C
```

```
[...]
                unix`do_copy_fault_nta+0x49
                genunix`uiomove+0x12e
                zfs`dmu_write_uio_dnode+0xac
                zfs`dmu_write_uio_dbuf+0x54
                zfs`zfs_write+0xc60
                genunix`fop_write+0x8b
                genunix`write+0x250
                genunix`write32+0x1e
                unix`_sys_sysenter_post_swapgs+0x149
                302

                unix`do_splx+0x65
                genunix`disp_lock_exit+0x47
                genunix`post_syscall+0x318
                genunix`syscall_exit+0x68
                unix`0xfffffffffb800ed9
                621

                unix`i86_mwait+0xd
                unix`cpu_idle_mwait+0x109
                unix`idle+0xa7
                unix`thread_start+0x8
            23083
```

The most frequent stack is printed last, which in this case is for the idle thread, which was sampled 23,083 times. For the other stacks, the top function and ancestry are shown.

Many pages were truncated from this output. The following one-liners show other ways to sample kernel CPU usage, some of which condense the output much further.

One-Liners

Sample kernel stacks at 997 Hz:

```
dtrace -n 'profile-997 /arg0/ { @[stack()] = count(); }'
```

Sample kernel stacks at 997 Hz, top ten only:

```
dtrace -n 'profile-997 /arg0/ { @[stack()] = count(); } END { trunc(@, 10); }'
```

Sample kernel stacks, five frames only, at 997 Hz:

```
dtrace -n 'profile-997 /arg0/ { @[stack(5)] = count(); }'
```

Sample kernel on-CPU functions at 997 Hz:

```
dtrace -n 'profile-997 /arg0/ { @[func(arg0)] = count(); }'
```

Sample kernel on-CPU modules at 997 Hz:

```
dtrace -n 'profile-997 /arg0/ { @[mod(arg0)] = count(); }'
```

User Profiling

CPU time spent in user mode can be profiled similarly to the kernel. The following one-liner matches on user-level code by checking on `arg1` (user PC) and also matches processes named "`mysqld`" (MySQL database):

```
# dtrace -n 'profile-97 /arg1 && execname == "mysqld"/ { @[ustack()] =
    count(); }'
dtrace: description 'profile-97 ' matched 1 probe
^C
[...]
libc.so.1`__priocntlset+0xa
libc.so.1`getparam+0x83
libc.so.1`pthread_getschedparam+0x3c
libc.so.1`pthread_setschedprio+0x1f
mysqld`_Z16dispatch_command19enum_server_commandP3THDPcj+0x9ab
mysqld`_Z10do_commandP3THD+0x198
mysqld`handle_one_connection+0x1a6
libc.so.1`_thrp_setup+0x8d
libc.so.1`_lwp_start
4884

mysqld`_Z13add_to_statusP17system_status_varS0_+0x47
mysqld`_Z22calc_sum_of_all_statusP17system_status_var+0x67
mysqld`_Z16dispatch_command19enum_server_commandP3THDPcj+0x1222
mysqld`_Z10do_commandP3THD+0x198
mysqld`handle_one_connection+0x1a6
libc.so.1`_thrp_setup+0x8d
libc.so.1`_lwp_start
5530
```

The last stack shows that MySQL was in `do_command()` and performing `calc_sum_of_all_status()`, which was frequently on-CPU. The stack frames look a little mangled as they are C++ signatures (the `c++filt(1)` tool can be used to unmangle them).

The following one-liners show other ways to sample user CPU usage, provided user-level actions are available (this feature is currently not yet ported to Linux).

One-Liners

Sample user stacks at 97 Hz, for PID 123:

```
dtrace -n 'profile-97 /arg1 && pid == 123/ { @[ustack()] = count(); }'
```

Sample user stacks at 97 Hz, for all processes named "`sshd`":

```
dtrace -n 'profile-97 /arg1 && execname == "sshd"/ { @[ustack()] = count(); }'
```

Sample user stacks at 97 Hz, for all processes on the system (include process name in output):

```
dtrace -n 'profile-97 /arg1/ { @[execname, ustack()] = count(); }'
```

Sample user stacks at 97 Hz, top ten only, for PID 123:

```
dtrace -n 'profile-97 /arg1 && pid == 123/ { @[ustack()] = count(); }
    END { trunc(@, 10); }'
```

Sample user stacks, five frames only, at 97 Hz, for PID 123:

```
dtrace -n 'profile-97 /arg1 && pid == 123/ { @[ustack(5)] = count(); }'
```

Sample user on-CPU functions at 97 Hz, for PID 123:

```
dtrace -n 'profile-97 /arg1 && pid == 123/ { @[ufunc(arg1)] = count(); }'
```

Sample user on-CPU modules at 97 Hz, for PID 123:

```
dtrace -n 'profile-97 /arg1 && pid == 123/ { @[umod(arg1)] = count(); }'
```

Sample user stacks at 97 Hz, including during system-time when the user stack is frozen (typically on a syscall), for PID 123:

```
dtrace -n 'profile-97 /pid == 123/ { @[ustack()] = count(); }'
```

Sample which CPU a process runs on, at 97 Hz, for PID 123:

```
dtrace -n 'profile-97 /pid == 123/ { @[cpu] = count(); }'
```

Function Tracing

While profiling can show the total CPU time consumed by functions, it doesn't show the runtime distribution of those function calls. This can be determined by using tracing and the vtimestamp built-in—a high-resolution timestamp that increments only when the current thread is on-CPU. A function's CPU time can be measured by tracing its entry and return and calculating the vtimestamp delta.

For example, using dynamic tracing (fbt provider) to measure the CPU time in the kernel ZFS zio_checksum_generate() function:

```
# dtrace -n 'fbt::zio_checksum_generate:entry { self->v = vtimestamp; }
    fbt::zio_checksum_generate:return /self->v/ { @["ns"] =
    quantize(vtimestamp - self->v); self->v = 0; }'
dtrace: description 'fbt::zio_checksum_generate:entry ' matched 2 probes
^C

  ns
           value  ------------- Distribution ------------- count
             128 |                                         0
             256 |                                         3
             512 |@                                        62
            1024 |@                                        79
            2048 |                                         13
            4096 |                                         21
            8192 |                                         8
           16384 |                                         2
           32768 |                                         41
           65536 |@@@@@@@@@@@@@@@@@@@@@@@@@@@@@@@@@@@@@@@@@  3740
          131072 |@                                        134
          262144 |                                         0
```

Most of the time this function took between 65 and 131 µs of CPU time. This includes the CPU time of all subfunctions.

This particular style of tracing can add overhead if the function is called frequently. It is best used in conjunction with profiling, so that results can be cross-checked.

Similar dynamic tracing may be performed for user-level code via the PID provider, if available.

Dynamic tracing via the fbt or pid providers is considered an unstable interface, as functions may change between releases. There are static tracing providers available for tracing CPU behavior, which are intended to provide a stable interface. These include probes for CPU cross calls, interrupts, and scheduler activity.

CPU Cross Calls

Excessive CPU cross calls can reduce performance due to their CPU consumption. Prior to DTrace, the origin of cross calls was difficult to determine. It's now as easy as a one-liner, tracing cross calls and showing the code path that led to them:

```
# dtrace -n 'sysinfo:::xcalls { @[stack()] = count(); }'
dtrace: description 'sysinfo:::xcalls ' matched 1 probe
^C
[...]
              unix`xc_sync+0x39
              kvm`kvm_xcall+0xa9
              kvm`vcpu_clear+0x1d
              kvm`vmx_vcpu_load+0x3f
              kvm`kvm_arch_vcpu_load+0x16
              kvm`kvm_ctx_restore+0x3d
              genunix`restorectx+0x37
              unix`_resume_from_idle+0x83
               97
```

This was demonstrated on a Solaris-based system with the sysinfo provider.

Interrupts

DTrace allows interrupts to be traced and examined. **Solaris**-based systems ship with intrstat(1M), a DTrace-based tool for summarizing interrupt CPU usage. For example:

```
# intrstat 1
[...]
      device |   cpu4 %tim    cpu5 %tim    cpu6 %tim    cpu7 %tim
-------------+------------------------------------------------------
      bnx#0  |    0   0.0       0   0.0      0   0.0       0   0.0
     ehci#0  |    0   0.0       0   0.0      0   0.0       0   0.0
     ehci#1  |    0   0.0       0   0.0      0   0.0       0   0.0
      igb#0  |    0   0.0       0   0.0      0   0.0       0   0.0
  mega_sas#0 |    0   0.0    5585   7.1      0   0.0       0   0.0
     uhci#0  |    0   0.0       0   0.0      0   0.0       0   0.0
     uhci#1  |    0   0.0       0   0.0      0   0.0       0   0.0
     uhci#2  |    0   0.0       0   0.0      0   0.0       0   0.0
     uhci#3  |    0   0.0       0   0.0      0   0.0       0   0.0
[...]
```

The output is typically pages long on multi-CPU systems and includes interrupt counts and percent CPU times for each driver, for each CPU. The preceding excerpt shows that the mega_sas driver was consuming 7.1% of CPU 5.

If intrstat(1M) is not available (as is currently the case on **Linux**), interrupt activity can be examined by use of dynamic function tracing.

Scheduler Tracing

The scheduler provider (sched) provides probes for tracing operations of the kernel CPU scheduler. Probes are listed in Table 6.7.

Table 6-7 sched Provider Probes

Probe	Description
on-cpu	The current thread begins execution on-CPU.
off-cpu	The current thread is about to end execution on-CPU.
remain-cpu	The scheduler has decided to continue running the current thread.
enqueue	A thread is being enqueued to a run queue (examine it via args[ ]).
dequeue	A thread is being dequeued from a run queue (examine it via args[ ]).
preempt	The current thread is about to be preempted by another.

Since many of these fire in thread context, the curthread built-in refers to the thread in question, and thread-local variables can be used. For example, tracing on-CPU runtime using a thread-local variable (self->ts):

```
# dtrace -n 'sched:::on-cpu /execname == "sshd"/ { self->ts = timestamp; }
    sched:::off-cpu /self->ts/ { @["ns"] = quantize(timestamp - self->ts);
    self->ts = 0; }'
dtrace: description 'sched:::on-cpu ' matched 6 probes
^C

  ns
           value  ------------- Distribution ------------- count
            2048 |                                         0
            4096 |                                         1
            8192 |@@                                       8
           16384 |@@@                                      12
           32768 |@@@@@@@@@@@@@@@@@@@@@@@@@@@@@@@@          94
           65536 |@@@                                      14
          131072 |@@@                                      12
          262144 |@@                                       7
          524288 |@                                        4
         1048576 |@                                        5
         2097152 |                                         2
         4194304 |                                         1
         8388608 |                                         1
        16777216 |                                         0
```

This traced the on-CPU runtime for processes named "sshd". Most of the time it was on-CPU only briefly, between 32 and 65 µs.

6.6.11 SystemTap

SystemTap can also be used on Linux systems for tracing of scheduler events. See Section 4.4, SystemTap, in Chapter 4, Observability Tools, and Appendix E for help with converting the previous DTrace scripts.

6.6.12 perf

Originally called Performance Counters for Linux (PCL), the perf(1) command has evolved and become a collection of tools for profiling and tracing, now called Linux Performance Events (LPE). Each tool is selected as a subcommand. For example, perf stat executes the stat command, which provides CPC-based statistics. These commands are listed in the USAGE message, and a selection is reproduced here in Table 6.8 (from version 3.2.6-3).

Table 6-8 perf Subcommands

Command	Description
annotate	Read perf.data (created by perf record) and display annotated code.
diff	Read two perf.data files and display the differential profile.
evlist	List the event names in a perf.data file.
inject	Filter to augment the events stream with additional information.
kmem	Tool to trace/measure kernel memory (slab) properties.
kvm	Tool to trace/measure kvm guest OS.
list	List all symbolic event types.
lock	Analyze lock events.
probe	Define new dynamic tracepoints.
record	Run a command and record its profile into perf.data.
report	Read perf.data (created by perf record) and display the profile.
sched	Tool to trace/measure scheduler properties (latencies).
script	Read perf.data (created by perf record) and display trace output.
stat	Run a command and gather performance counter statistics.
timechart	Tool to visualize total system behavior during a workload.
top	System profiling tool.

Key commands are demonstrated in the following sections.

System Profiling

perf(1) can be used to profile CPU call paths, summarizing where CPU time is spent in both kernel- and user-space. This is performed by the record command, which captures samples at regular intervals to a perf.data file. A report command is then used to view the file.

In the following example, all CPUs (-a) are sampled with call stacks (-g) at 997 Hz (-F 997) for 10 s (sleep 10). The --stdio option is used to print all the output, instead of operating in interactive mode.

```
# perf record -a -g -F 997 sleep 10
[ perf record: Woken up 44 times to write data ]
[ perf record: Captured and wrote 13.251 MB perf.data (~578952 samples) ]
# perf report --stdio
[...]
# Overhead    Command      Shared Object                                    Symbol
# ........   ..........   ...............   ..............   ...........................
#
    72.98%      swapper  [kernel.kallsyms]  [k] native_safe_halt
                         |
                         --- native_safe_halt
                             default_idle
                             cpu_idle
                             rest_init
                             start_kernel
                             x86_64_start_reservations
                             x86_64_start_kernel

     9.43%           dd  [kernel.kallsyms]  [k] acpi_pm_read
                         |
                         --- acpi_pm_read
                            ktime_get_ts
                            |
                            |--87.75%-- __delayacct_blkio_start
                            |           io_schedule_timeout
                            |           balance_dirty_pages_ratelimited_nr
                            |           generic_file_buffered_write
                            |           __generic_file_aio_write
                            |           generic_file_aio_write
                            |           ext4_file_write
                            |           do_sync_write
                            |           vfs_write
                            |           sys_write
                            |           system_call
                            |           __GI___libc_write
                            |
   [...]
```

The full output is many pages long, in descending sample count order. These sample counts are given as percentages, which show where the CPU time was spent. This example indicates that 72.98% of time was spent in the idle thread, and 9.43% of time in the dd process. Out of that 9.43%, 87.5% is composed of the stack shown, which is for ext4_file_write().

These kernel and process symbols are available only if their debuginfo files are available; otherwise hex addresses are shown.

perf(1) operates by programming an overflow interrupt for the CPU cycle counter. Since the cycle rate varies on modern processors, a "scaled" counter is used that remains constant.

Process Profiling

Apart from profiling across all CPUs, individual processes can be targeted. The following command executes the *command* and creates the perf.data file:

```
# perf record -g command
```

As before, debuginfo must be available for perf(1) to translate symbols when viewing the report.

Scheduler Latency

The sched command records and reports scheduler statistics. For example:

```
# perf sched record sleep 10
[ perf record: Woken up 108 times to write data ]
[ perf record: Captured and wrote 1723.874 MB perf.data (~75317184 samples) ]
# perf sched latency

  -----------------------------------------------------------------------------------------
  ------------------------------
   Task                   |   Runtime ms  | Switches | Average delay ms | Maximum delay
ms  | Maximum delay at      |
  -----------------------------------------------------------------------------------------
  ------------------------------
   kblockd/0:91           |    0.009 ms  |      1 | avg:     1.193 ms | max:      1.193
ms  | max at: 105455.615096 s
   dd:8439                |  9691.404 ms  |    763 | avg:     0.363 ms | max:     29.953
ms  | max at: 105456.540771 s
   perf_2.6.35-32:8440    |  8082.543 ms  |    818 | avg:     0.362 ms | max:     29.956
ms  | max at: 105460.734775 s
   kjournald:419          |   462.561 ms  |    457 | avg:     0.064 ms | max:     12.112
ms  | max at: 105459.815203 s
[...]
  INFO: 0.976% lost events (167317 out of 17138781, in 3 chunks)
  INFO: 0.178% state machine bugs (4766 out of 2673759) (due to lost events?)
  INFO: 0.000% context switch bugs (3 out of 2673759) (due to lost events?)
```

This shows the average and maximum scheduler latency while tracing.

Scheduler events are frequent, so this type of tracing incurs CPU and storage overhead. The perf.data file in this example was 1.7 Gbytes for 10 s of tracing. The INFO lines in the output show that some events were dropped. This points out an advantage of the DTrace model of in-kernel filtering and aggregation: it can summarize data while tracing and pass only the summary to user-space, minimizing overhead.

stat

The `stat` command provides a high-level summary of CPU cycle behavior based on CPC. In the following example it launches a `gzip(1)` command:

```
$ perf stat gzip file1

 Performance counter stats for 'gzip perf.data':

       62250.620881  task-clock-msecs        #      0.998 CPUs
                 65  context-switches        #      0.000 M/sec
                  1  CPU-migrations          #      0.000 M/sec
                211  page-faults             #      0.000 M/sec
       149282502161  cycles                  #   2398.089 M/sec
       227631116972  instructions            #      1.525 IPC
        39078733567  branches                #    627.765 M/sec
         1802924170  branch-misses           #      4.614 %
           87791362  cache-references        #      1.410 M/sec
           24187334  cache-misses            #      0.389 M/sec

       62.355529199  seconds time elapsed
```

The statistics include the cycle and instruction count, and the IPC (inverse of CPI). As described earlier, this is an extremely useful high-level metric for determining the types of cycles occurring and how many of them are stall cycles.

The following lists other counters that can be examined:

```
# perf list

List of pre-defined events (to be used in -e):

  cpu-cycles OR cycles                      [Hardware event]
  instructions                              [Hardware event]
  cache-references                          [Hardware event]
  cache-misses                              [Hardware event]
  branch-instructions OR branches           [Hardware event]
  branch-misses                             [Hardware event]
  bus-cycles                                [Hardware event]
  [...]
  L1-dcache-loads                           [Hardware cache event]
  L1-dcache-load-misses                     [Hardware cache event]
  L1-dcache-stores                          [Hardware cache event]
  L1-dcache-store-misses                    [Hardware cache event]
  [...]
```

Look for both "Hardware event" and "Hardware cache event." Those available depend on the processor architecture and are documented in the processor manuals (e.g., the Intel *Software Developer's Manual*).

These events can be specified using —e. For example (this is from an Intel Xeon):

```
$ perf stat -e instructions,cycles,L1-dcache-load-misses,LLC-load-misses,dTLB-load-
misses gzip file1

Performance counter stats for 'gzip file1':

   12278136571  instructions              #     2.199 IPC
    5582247352  cycles
      90367344  L1-dcache-load-misses
       1227085  LLC-load-misses
        685149  dTLB-load-misses

    2.332492555  seconds time elapsed
```

Apart from instructions and cycles, this example also measured the following:

- **L1-dcache-load-misses:** Level 1 data cache load misses. This gives you a measure of the memory load caused by the application, after some loads have been returned from the Level 1 cache. It can be compared with other L1 event counters to determine cache hit rate.

- **LLC-load-misses:** Last level cache load misses. After the last level, this accesses main memory, and so this is a measure of main memory load. The difference between this and L1-dcache-load-misses gives an idea (other counters are needed for completeness) of the effectiveness of the CPU caches beyond Level 1.

- **dTLB-load-misses:** Data translation lookaside buffer misses. This shows the effectiveness of the MMU to cache page mappings for the workload and can measure the size of the memory workload (working set).

Many other counters can be inspected. perf(1) supports both descriptive names (like those used for this example) and hexadecimal values. The latter may be necessary for esoteric counters you find in the processor manuals, for which a descriptive name isn't provided.

Software Tracing

perf record —e can be used with various software instrumentation points for tracing activity of the kernel scheduler. These include software events and trace-point events (static probes), as listed by perf list. For example:

```
# perf list
  context-switches OR cs                    [Software event]
  cpu-migrations OR migrations              [Software event]
  [...]
```

continues

```
sched:sched_kthread_stop                              [Tracepoint event]
sched:sched_kthread_stop_ret                          [Tracepoint event]
sched:sched_wakeup                                    [Tracepoint event]
sched:sched_wakeup_new                                [Tracepoint event]
sched:sched_switch                                    [Tracepoint event]
sched:sched_migrate_task                              [Tracepoint event]
sched:sched_process_free                              [Tracepoint event]
sched:sched_process_exit                              [Tracepoint event]
sched:sched_wait_task                                 [Tracepoint event]
sched:sched_process_wait                              [Tracepoint event]
sched:sched_process_fork                              [Tracepoint event]
sched:sched_stat_wait                                 [Tracepoint event]
sched:sched_stat_sleep                                [Tracepoint event]
sched:sched_stat_iowait                               [Tracepoint event]
sched:sched_stat_runtime                              [Tracepoint event]
sched:sched_pi_setprio                                [Tracepoint event]
[...]
```

The following example uses the context switch software event to trace when applications leave the CPU and collects call stacks for 10 s:

```
# perf record -f -g -a -e context-switches sleep 10
[ perf record: Woken up 1 times to write data ]
[ perf record: Captured and wrote 0.417 MB perf.data (~18202 samples) ]
# perf report --stdio
# ========
# captured on: Wed Apr 10 19:52:19 2013
# hostname : 9d219ce8-cf52-409f-a14a-b210850f3231
[...]
#
# Events: 2K context-switches
#
# Overhead    Command     Shared Object       Symbol
# ........    ........    ................    ..........
#
    47.60%       perl   [kernel.kallsyms]   [k] __schedule
                   |
                   --- __schedule
                       schedule
                       retint_careful
                       |
                       |--50.11%-- Perl_pp_unstack
                       |
                       |--26.40%-- Perl_pp_stub
                       |
                       --23.50%-- Perl_runops_standard

    25.66%        tar   [kernel.kallsyms]   [k] __schedule
                   |
                   --- __schedule
                       |
                       |--99.72%-- schedule
                       |           |
                       |           |--99.90%-- io_schedule
                       |           |           sleep_on_buffer
                       |           |           __wait_on_bit
                       |           |           out_of_line_wait_on_bit
                       |           |           __wait_on_buffer
                       |           |           |
                       |           |           |--99.21%-- ext4_bread
                       |           |           |
```

```
                    |          |          |          |--99.72%-- htree_dirbl...
                    |          |          |          |           ext4_htree_f...
                    |          |          |          |           ext4_readdir
                    |          |          |          |           vfs_readdir
                    |          |          |          |           sys_getdents
                    |          |          |          |           system_call
                    |          |          |          |           __getdents64
                    |          |          |          --0.28%-- [...]
                    |          |          |
                    |          |          --0.79%--  __ext4_get_inode_loc
      [...]
```

This truncated output shows two applications, perl and tar, and their call stacks when they context switched. Reading the stacks shows the tar program was sleeping on file system (ext4) reads. The perl program was involuntary context switched as it is performing heavy compute, although that isn't clear from this output alone.

More information can be found using the sched tracepoint events. Kernel scheduler functions can also be traced directly using *dynamic tracepoints* (dynamic tracing), which along with the static probes can provide similar data to what was seen earlier from DTrace, although it can require more post-processing to produce the results you are after.

Chapter 9, Disks, includes another example of static tracing with perf(1): block I/O tracepoints. Chapter 10, Network, includes an example of dynamic tracing with perf(1) for the tcp_sendmsg() kernel function.

Documentation

For more on perf(1), see its man pages, documentation in the Linux kernel source under tools/perf/Documentation, the "Perf Tutorial" [4], and "The Unofficial Linux Perf Events Web-Page" [5].

6.6.13 cpustat

On **Solaris**-based systems, the tools for examining CPC are cpustat(1M) for system-wide analysis and cputrack(1M) for process analysis. These refer to CPC using the term *performance instrumentation counters* (PICs).

For example, to measure CPI, both cycles and instructions must be counted. Using the PAPI names:

```
# cpustat -tc PAPI_tot_cyc,PAPI_tot_ins,sys 1
   time cpu event      tsc       pic0       pic1
  1.001   0  tick 2390794244 2095800691 910588497
  1.002   1  tick 2391617432 2091867238 832659178
  1.002   2  tick 2392676108 2075492108 917078382
  1.003   3  tick 2393561424 2067362862 831551337
  1.003   4  tick 2393739432 2020553426 909065542
[...]
```

cpustat(1M) produces a line of output per CPU. This output can be post-processed (e.g., with awk) so that the CPI calculation can be made.

The sys token was used so that both user- and kernel-mode cycles are counted. This sets the flag described in CPU Performance Counters in Section 6.4.1, Hardware.

Measuring the same counters using the platform-specific event names:

```
# cpustat -tc cpu_clk_unhalted.thread_p,inst_retired.any_p,sys 1
```

Run cpustat -h for the full list of supported counters for your processor. The output usually ends with a reference to the vendor processor manual; for example:

See Appendix A of the "Intel 64 and IA-32 Architectures Software Developer's Manual Volume 3B: System Programming Guide, Part 2" Order Number: 253669-026US, February 2008.

The manuals describe low-level processor behavior in detail.

Only one instance of cpustat(1M) can be running on the system at the same time, as the kernel does not support multiplexing.

6.6.14 Other Tools

Other **Linux** CPU performance tools include

- **oprofile:** the original CPU profiling tool by John Levon.
- **htop:** includes ASCII bar charts for CPU usage and has a more powerful interactive interface than the original top(1).
- **atop:** includes many more system-wide statistics and uses process accounting to catch the presence of short-lived processes.
- **/proc/cpuinfo:** This can be read to see processor details, including clock speed and feature flags.
- **getdelays.c:** This is an example of delay accounting observability and includes CPU scheduler latency per process. It was demonstrated in Chapter 4, Observability Tools.
- **valgrind:** a memory debugging and profiling toolkit [6]. It contains callgrind, a tool to trace function calls and gather a call graph, which can be visualized using kcachegrind; and cachegrind for analysis of hardware cache usage by a given program.

For **Solaris**:

- **lockstat/plockstat:** for lock analysis, including spin locks and CPU consumption from adaptive mutexes (see Chapter 5, Applications).
- **psrinfo:** processor status and information (-vp).
- **fmadm faulty:** to check if a CPU has been predictively faulted due to an increase in correctable ECC errors. Also see fmstat(1M).
- **isainfo -x:** to list processor feature flags.
- **pginfo, pgstat:** processor group statistics, showing CPU topology and how CPU resources are shared.
- **lgrpinfo:** for locality group statistics. This can be useful for checking that lgrps are in use, which requires processor and operating system support.

There are also sophisticated products for CPU performance analysis, including Oracle Solaris Studio, which is available for Solaris and Linux.

6.6.15 Visualizations

CPU usage has historically been visualized as line graphs of utilization or load average, including the original X11 load tool (xload(1)). Such line graphs are an effective way to show variation, as magnitudes can be visually compared. They can also show patterns over time, as was shown in Section 2.9, Monitoring, of Chapter 2, Methodology.

However, line graphs of per-CPU utilization don't scale with the CPU counts we see today, especially for cloud computing environments involving tens of thousands of CPUs—a graph of 10,000 lines can become paint.

Other statistics plotted as line graphs, including averages, standard deviations, maximums, and percentiles, provide some value and do scale. However, CPU utilization is often *bimodal*—composed of idle or near-idle CPUs, and then some at 100% utilization—which is not effectively conveyed with these statistics. The full distribution often needs to be studied. A utilization heat map makes this possible.

The following sections introduce CPU utilization heat maps, CPU subsecond-offset heat maps, and flame graphs. I created these visualization types to solve problems in enterprise and cloud performance analysis.

Utilization Heat Map

Utilization versus time can be presented as a heat map, with the saturation (darkness) of each pixel showing the number of CPUs at that utilization and time range. Heat maps were introduced in Chapter 2, Methodology.

Figure 6.15 shows CPU utilization for an entire data center (availability zone), running a public cloud environment. It includes over 300 physical servers and 5,312 CPUs.

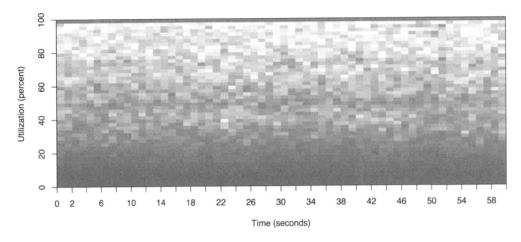

Figure 6-15 CPU utilization heat map, 5,312 CPUs

The darker shading at the bottom of this heat map shows that most CPUs are running between 0% and 30% utilization. However, the solid line at the top shows that, over time, there are also some CPUs at 100% utilization. The fact that the line is dark shows that multiple CPUs were at 100%, not just one.

This particular visualization is provided by real-time monitoring software (Joyent Cloud Analytics), which allows points to be selected with a click to reveal more details. In this case, the 100% CPU line can be clicked to reveal which servers these CPUs belonged to, and what tenants and applications are driving CPUs at that rate.

Subsecond-Offset Heat Map

This heat map type allows activity within a second to be examined. CPU activity is typically measured in microseconds or milliseconds; reporting this data as averages over an entire second can wipe out useful information. This type of heat map puts the subsecond offset on the y axis, with the number of non-idle CPUs at each offset shown by the saturation. This visualizes each second as a column, "painting" it from bottom to top.

Figure 6.16 shows a CPU subsecond-offset heat map for a cloud database (Riak).

What is interesting about this heat map isn't the times that the CPUs were busy servicing the database, but the times that they were not, indicated by the

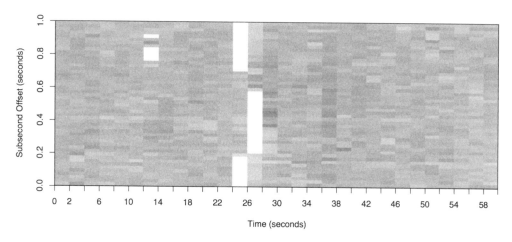

Figure 6-16 CPU subsecond-offset heat map, 5,312 CPUs

white columns. The duration of these gaps was also interesting: hundreds of milliseconds during which none of the database threads were on-CPU. This led to the discovery of a locking issue where the entire database was blocked for hundreds of milliseconds at a time.

If we had examined this data using a line graph, a dip in per-second CPU utilization might have been dismissed as variable load and not investigated further.

Flame Graphs

Profiling stack traces is an effective way to explain CPU usage, showing which kernel- or user-level code paths are responsible. It can, however, produce thousands of pages of output. Flame graphs visualize the profile stack frames, so that CPU usage can be understood more quickly and more clearly.

Flame graphs can be built upon data from DTrace, perf, or SystemTap. The example in Figure 6.17 shows the Linux kernel profiled using perf.

The flame graph has the following characteristics:

- Each box represents a function in the stack (a "stack frame").
- The *y* axis shows stack depth (number of frames on the stack). The top box shows the function that was on-CPU. Everything beneath that is ancestry. The function beneath a function is its parent, just as in the stack traces shown earlier.
- The *x* axis spans the sample population. It does not show the passing of time from left to right, as most graphs do. The left-to-right ordering has no meaning (it's sorted alphabetically).

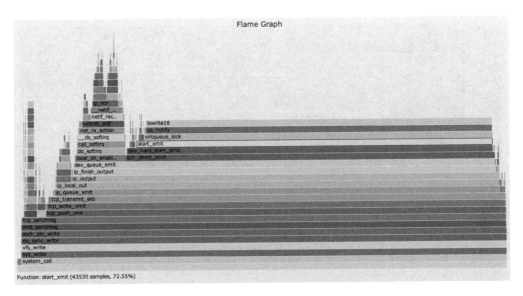

Figure 6-17 Linux kernel flame graph

- The width of the box shows the total time it was on-CPU or part of an ancestry that was on-CPU (based on sample count). Wider box functions may be slower than narrow box functions, or they may simply be called more often. The call count is not shown (nor is it known via sampling).

- The sample count can exceed elapsed time if multiple threads were running and sampled in parallel.

The colors are not significant and are picked at random to be warm colors. It's called a "flame graph" because it shows what is hot on-CPU.

It is also *interactive*. It is an SVG with an embedded JavaScript routine that when opened in a browser allows you to mouse over elements to reveal details at the bottom. In the Figure 6.17 example, `start_xmit()` was highlighted, which shows that it was present in 72.55% of the sampled stacks.

6.7 Experimentation

This section describes tools for actively testing CPU performance. See Section 6.5.11, Micro-Benchmarking, for background.

When using these tools, it's a good idea to leave `mpstat(1)` continually running to confirm CPU usage and parallelism.

6.7.1 Ad Hoc

While this is trivial and doesn't measure anything, it can be a useful known workload for confirming that observability tools show what they claim to show. This creates a single-threaded workload that is CPU-bound ("hot on one CPU"):

```
# while :; do :; done &
```

This is a Bourne shell program that performs an infinite loop in the background. It will need to be killed once you no longer need it.

6.7.2 SysBench

The SysBench system benchmark suite has a simple CPU benchmark tool that calculates prime numbers. For example:

```
# sysbench --num-threads=8 --test=cpu --cpu-max-prime=100000 run
sysbench 0.4.12:  multi-threaded system evaluation benchmark

Running the test with following options:
Number of threads: 8

Doing CPU performance benchmark

Threads started!
Done.

Maximum prime number checked in CPU test: 100000


Test execution summary:
    total time:                          30.4125s
    total number of events:              10000
    total time taken by event execution: 243.2310
    per-request statistics:
         min:                            24.31ms
         avg:                            24.32ms
         max:                            32.44ms
         approx.  95 percentile:         24.32ms

Threads fairness:
    events (avg/stddev):           1250.0000/1.22
    execution time (avg/stddev):   30.4039/0.01
```

This executed eight threads, with a maximum prime number of 100,000. The runtime was 30.4 s, which can be used for comparison with the results from other systems or configurations (assuming many things, such as that identical compiler options were used to build the software; see Chapter 12, Benchmarking).

6.8 Tuning

For CPUs, the biggest performance wins are typically those that eliminate unnecessary work, which is an effective form of tuning. Section 6.5, Methodology, and
Section 6.6, Analysis, introduced many ways to analyze and identify the work performed, helping you find any unnecessary work. Other methodologies for tuning
were also introduced: priority tuning and CPU binding. This section includes these
and other tuning examples.

The specifics of tuning—the options available and what to set them to—depend
on the processor type, the operating system version, and the intended workload.
The following, organized by type, provide examples of what options may be available and how they are tuned. The earlier methodology sections provide guidance
on when and why these tunables would be tuned.

6.8.1 Compiler Options

Compilers, and the options they provide for code optimization, can have a dramatic effect on CPU performance. Common options include compiling for 64-bit
instead of 32-bit, and selecting a level of optimizations. Compiler optimization is
discussed in Chapter 5, Applications.

6.8.2 Scheduling Priority and Class

The nice(1) command can be used to adjust process priority. Positive nice values
decrease priority, and negative nice values *increase* priority, which only the superuser can set. The range is from -20 to +19. For example:

```
$ nice -n 19 command
```

runs the command with a nice value of 19—the lowest priority that nice can set. To
change the priority of an already running process, use renice(1).

On **Linux**, the chrt(1) command can show and set the scheduling priority
directly, and the scheduling policy. The scheduling priority can also be set directly
using the setpriority() syscall, and the priority and scheduling policy can be
set using the sched_setscheduler() syscall.

On **Solaris**, you can set scheduling classes and priorities directly using the
priocntl(1) command. For example:

```
# priocntl -s -c RT -p 10 -i pid PID
```

This sets the target process ID to run in the real-time scheduling class with a priority of 10. Be careful when setting this: you can lock up your system if the real-time threads consume all CPU resources.

6.8.3 Scheduler Options

Your kernel may provide tunable parameters to control scheduler behavior, although it is unlikely that these will ever need to be tuned.

On **Linux** systems, config options can be set, including the examples in Table 6.9 from a 3.2.6 kernel, with defaults from Fedora 16.

Table 6-9 Example Linux Scheduler Config Options

Option	Default	Description
CONFIG_CGROUP_SCHED	y	allows tasks to be grouped, allocating CPU time on a group basis
CONFIG_FAIR_GROUP_SCHED	y	allows CFS tasks to be grouped
CONFIG_RT_GROUP_SCHED	y	allows real-time tasks to be grouped
CONFIG_SCHED_AUTOGROUP	y	automatically identifies and creates task groups (e.g., build jobs)
CONFIG_SCHED_SMT	y	hyperthreading support
CONFIG_SCHED_MC	y	multicore support
CONFIG_HZ	1,000	sets kernel clock rate (timer interrupt)
CONFIG_NO_HZ	y	tickless kernel behavior
CONFIG_SCHED_HRTICK	y	use high-resolution timers
CONFIG_PREEMPT	n	full kernel preemption (exception of spin lock regions and interrupts)
CONFIG_PREEMPT_NONE	n	no preemption
CONFIG_PREEMPT_VOLUNTARY	y	preemption at voluntary kernel code points

Some Linux kernels provide additional tunables (e.g., in /proc/sys/sched).

On **Solaris**-based systems, the kernel tunable parameters shown in Table 6.10 modify scheduler behavior.

For reference, find the matching documentation for your operating system version (e.g., for Solaris, the *Solaris Tunable Parameters Reference Manual*). Such documentation should list key tunable parameters, their type, when to set them, their defaults, and the valid ranges. Be careful when using these, as their ranges may not be fully tested. (Tuning them may also be prohibited by company or vendor policy.)

Table 6-10 Example Solaris Scheduler Tunables

Parameter	Default	Description
rechoose_interval	3	CPU affinity duration (clock ticks)
nosteal_nsec	100,000	avoid thread steals (idle CPU looking for work) if thread ran this recently (nanoseconds)
hires_tick	0	change to 1 for a 1,000 Hz kernel clock rate, instead of 100 Hz

Scheduler Class Tuning

Solaris-based systems also provide a means to modify the time quantum and priorities used by scheduling classes, via the dispadmin(1) command. For example, printing out the table of tunables (called the *dispatcher table*) for the time-sharing scheduling class (TS):

```
# dispadmin -c TS -g -r 1000
# Time Sharing Dispatcher Configuration
RES=1000

# ts_quantum  ts_tqexp  ts_slpret  ts_maxwait ts_lwait  PRIORITY LEVEL
      200         0        50          0          50        #     0
      200         0        50          0          50        #     1
      200         0        50          0          50        #     2
      200         0        50          0          50        #     3
      200         0        50          0          50        #     4
      200         0        50          0          50        #     5
[...]
```

This output includes

- **ts_quantum:** time quantum (in milliseconds, as set resolution using -r 1000)
- **ts_tqexp:** new priority provided when the thread expires its current time quantum (priority reduction)
- **ts_slpret:** new priority after thread sleeps (I/O) then wakes up (priority promotion)
- **ts_maxwait:** maximum seconds waiting for CPU before being promoted to the priority in ts_lwait
- **PRIORITY LEVEL:** priority value

This can be written to a file, modified, then reloaded by dispadmin(1M). You ought to have a reason for doing this, such as having first measured priority contention and scheduler latency using DTrace.

6.8.4 Process Binding

A process may be bound to one or more CPUs, which may increase its performance by improving cache warmth and memory locality.

On **Linux**, this is performed using the taskset(1) command, which can use a CPU mask or ranges to set CPU affinity. For example:

```
$ taskset -pc 7-10 10790
pid 10790's current affinity list: 0-15
pid 10790's new affinity list: 7-10
```

This sets PID 10790 to run only on CPUs 7 through 10.

On **Solaris**-based systems, this is performed using pbind(1). For example:

```
$ pbind -b 10 11901
process id 11901: was not bound, now 10
```

This sets PID 11901 to run on CPU 10. Multiple CPUs cannot be specified. For similar functionality, use exclusive CPU sets.

6.8.5 Exclusive CPU Sets

Linux provides *cpusets*, which allow CPUs to be grouped and processes assigned to them. This can improve performance similarly to process binding, but performance can be improved further by making the cpuset exclusive—preventing other processes from using it. The trade-off is a reduction in available CPU for the rest of the system.

The following commented example creates an exclusive set:

```
# mkdir /dev/cpuset
# mount -t cpuset cpuset /dev/cpuset
# cd /dev/cpuset
# mkdir prodset              # create a cpuset called "prodset"
# cd prodset
# echo 7-10 > cpus           # assign CPUs 7-10
# echo 1 > cpu_exclusive     # make prodset exclusive
# echo 1159 > tasks          # assign PID 1159 to prodset
```

For reference, see the cpuset(7) man page.

On **Solaris**, you can create exclusive CPU sets using the psrset(1M) command.

6.8.6 Resource Controls

Apart from associating processes with whole CPUs, modern operating systems provide resource controls for fine-grained allocation of CPU usage.

Solaris-based systems have resource controls (added in Solaris 9) for processes or groups of processes called *projects*. CPU usage can be controlled in a flexible way using the fair share scheduler and *shares*, which control how idle CPU can be consumed by those who need it. Limits can also be imposed, in terms of total percent CPU utilization, for cases where consistency is more desirable than the dynamic behavior of shares.

For **Linux**, there are container groups (cgroups), which can also control resource usage by processes or groups of processes. CPU usage can be controlled using shares, and the CFS scheduler allows fixed limits to be imposed (*CPU bandwidth*), in terms of allocating microseconds of CPU cycles per interval. CPU bandwidth is relatively new, added in 2012 (3.2).

Chapter 11, Cloud Computing, describes a use case of managing CPU usage of OS-virtualized tenants, including how shares and limits can be used in concert.

6.8.7 Processor Options (BIOS Tuning)

Processors typically provide settings to enable, disable, and tune processor-level features. On x86 systems, these are typically accessed via the BIOS settings menu at boot time.

The settings usually provide maximum performance by default and don't need to be adjusted. The most common reason I adjust these today is to disable Intel Turbo Boost, so that CPU benchmarks execute with a consistent clock rate (bearing in mind that, for production use, Turbo Boost should be enabled for slightly faster performance).

6.9 Exercises

1. Answer the following questions about CPU terminology:
   - What is the difference between a process and a processor?
   - What is a hardware thread?
   - What is the run queue (also called a dispatcher queue)?
   - What is the difference between user-time and kernel-time?
   - What is CPI?

2. Answer the following conceptual questions:
   - Describe CPU utilization and saturation.
   - Describe how the instruction pipeline improves CPU throughput.
   - Describe how processor instruction width improves CPU throughput.
   - Describe the advantages of multiprocess and multithreaded models.

3. Answer the following deeper questions:
   - Describe what happens when the system CPUs are overloaded with runnable work, including the effect on application performance.
   - When there is no runnable work to perform, what do the CPUs do?
   - When handed a suspected CPU performance issue, name three methodologies you would use early during the investigation, and explain why.

4. Develop the following procedures for your operating system:
   - A USE method checklist for CPU resources. Include how to fetch each metric (e.g., which command to execute) and how to interpret the result. Try to use existing OS observability tools before installing or using additional software products.
   - A workload characterization checklist for CPU resources. Include how to fetch each metric, and try to use existing OS observability tools first.

5. Perform these tasks:
   - Calculate the load average for the following system, whose load is at steady state:
     - The system has 64 CPUs.
     - The system-wide CPU utilization is 50%.
     - The system-wide CPU saturation, measured as the total number of runnable and queued threads on average, is 2.0.
   - Choose an application, and profile its user-level CPU usage. Show which code paths are consuming the most CPU.
   - Describe CPU behavior visible from this Solaris-based screen shot alone:

```
# prstat -mLc 10
   PID USERNAME USR SYS TRP TFL DFL LCK SLP LAT VCX ICX SCL SIG PROCESS/LWPID
 11076 mysql    4.3 0.7 0.0 0.0 0.0  58  31 5.7 790  48 12K   0 mysqld/15620
 11076 mysql    3.5 1.0 0.0 0.0 0.0  42  46 7.6  1K  42 18K   0 mysqld/15189
 11076 mysql    3.0 0.9 0.0 0.0 0.0  34  53 8.9  1K  20 17K   0 mysqld/14454
 11076 mysql    3.1 0.6 0.0 0.0 0.0  55  36 5.7 729  27 11K   0 mysqld/15849
 11076 mysql    2.5 1.1 0.0 0.0 0.0  28  59 8.6  1K  35 19K   0 mysqld/16094
 11076 mysql    2.4 1.1 0.0 0.0 0.0  34  54 8.3  1K  45 20K   0 mysqld/16304
                                                                    continues
```

```
11076 mysql     2.5 0.8 0.0 0.0 0.0   56   32 8.8   1K   16 15K    0 mysqld/16181
11076 mysql     2.3 1.1 0.0 0.0 0.0 8.5   79 9.0   1K   21 20K    0 mysqld/15856
11076 mysql     2.3 1.0 0.0 0.0 0.0   12   76 9.2   1K   40 16K    0 mysqld/15411
11076 mysql     2.2 1.0 0.0 0.0 0.0   29   57  11   1K   53 17K    0 mysqld/16277
11076 mysql     2.2 0.8 0.0 0.0 0.0   36   54 7.1 993   27 15K    0 mysqld/16266
11076 mysql     2.1 0.8 0.0 0.0 0.0   34   56 7.1   1K   19 16K    0 mysqld/16320
11076 mysql     2.3 0.7 0.0 0.0 0.0   44   47 5.8 831   24 12K    0 mysqld/15971
11076 mysql     2.1 0.7 0.0 0.0 0.0   54   37 5.3 862   22 13K    0 mysqld/15442
11076 mysql     1.9 0.9 0.0 0.0 0.0   45   46 6.3   1K   23 16K    0 mysqld/16201
Total: 34 processes, 333 lwps, load averages: 32.68, 35.47, 36.12
```

6. (optional, advanced) Develop `bustop(1)`—a tool that shows physical bus or interconnect utilization—with a presentation similar to `iostat(1)`: a list of busses, columns for throughput in each direction, and utilization. Include saturation and error metrics if possible. This will require using CPC.

6.10 References

[Saltzer 70]   Saltzer, J., and J. Gintell. "The Instrumentation of Multics," *Communications of the ACM*, August 1970.

[Bobrow 72]   Bobrow, D., et al. "TENEX: A Paged Time Sharing System for the PDP-10*," *Communications of the ACM*, March 1972.

[Myer 73]   Myer, T. H., J. R. Barnaby, and W. W. Plummer. *TENEX Executive Manual*. Bolt, Baranek and Newman, Inc., April 1973.

[Hinnant 84]   Hinnant, D. "Benchmarking UNIX Systems," *BYTE* magazine 9, no. 8 (August 1984).

[Bulpin 05]   Bulpin, J., and I. Pratt. "Hyper-Threading Aware Process Scheduling Heuristics," USENIX, 2005.

[McDougall 06b]   McDougall, R., J. Mauro, and B. Gregg. *Solaris Performance and Tools: DTrace and MDB Techniques for Solaris 10 and OpenSolaris*. Prentice Hall, 2006.

[Otto 06]   Otto, E. *Temperature-Aware Operating System Scheduling* (Thesis). University of Virginia, 2006.

[Ruggiero 08]   Ruggiero, J. *Measuring Cache and Memory Latency and CPU to Memory Bandwidth*. Intel (Whitepaper), 2008.

[Intel 09]   *An Introduction to the Intel QuickPath Interconnect*. Intel, 2009.

[Intel 12]   *Intel 64 and IA-32 Architectures Software Developer's Man-ual*, Combined Volumes 1, 2A, 2B, 2C, 3A, 3B, and 3C. Intel, 2012.

[Intel 13]   *Intel 64 and IA-32 Architectures Software Developer's Man-ual*, Volume 3B, *System Programming Guide, Part 2*. Intel, 2013.

[RFC 546]   *TENEX Load Averages for July 1973,* August 1973. http://tools.ietf.org/html/rfc546.

[1]   http://lwn.net/Articles/178253/

[2]   www.bitmover.com/lmbench/

[3]   http://minnie.tuhs.org/cgi-bin/utree.pl?file=V4

[4]   https://perf.wiki.kernel.org/index.php/Tutorial

[5]   www.eece.maine.edu/~vweaver/projects/perf_events

[6]   http://valgrind.org/docs/manual/

7

Memory

System main memory stores application and kernel instructions, their working data, and file system caches. In many systems, the secondary storage for this data is the primary storage devices—the disks—which operate orders of magnitude more slowly. Once main memory has filled, the system may begin switching data between main memory and the storage devices. This is a slow process that will often become a system bottleneck, dramatically decreasing performance. The system may also terminate the largest memory-consuming process.

Other performance factors to consider include the CPU expense of allocating and freeing memory, copying memory, and managing memory address space mappings. On multisocket architectures, memory locality can become a factor, as memory attached to local sockets has lower access latency than remote sockets.

This chapter has five parts, the first three providing the basis for memory analysis, and the last two showing its practical application to Linux- and Solaris-based systems. The parts are as follows:

- **Background** introduces memory-related terminology and key memory performance concepts.

- **Architecture** provides generic descriptions of hardware and software memory architecture.

- **Methodology** explains performance analysis methodology.

- **Analysis** describes performance tools for memory analysis.

- **Tuning** explains tuning and example tunable parameters.

The on-CPU memory caches (Level 1/2/3, TLB) are covered in Chapter 6, CPUs.

7.1 Terminology

For reference, memory-related terminology used in this chapter includes the following:

- **Main memory:** Also referred to as *physical memory*, this describes the fast data storage area of a computer, commonly provided as DRAM.
- **Virtual memory:** an abstraction of main memory that is (almost) infinite and noncontended. Virtual memory is not real memory.
- **Resident memory:** memory that currently resides in main memory.
- **Anonymous memory:** memory with no file system location or path name. It includes the working data of a process address space, called the *heap*.
- **Address space:** a memory context. There are virtual address spaces for each process, and for the kernel.
- **Segment:** an area of memory flagged for a particular purpose, such as for storing executable or writeable pages.
- **OOM:** out of memory, when the kernel detects low available memory.
- **Page:** a unit of memory, as used by the OS and CPUs. Historically it is either 4 or 8 Kbytes. Modern processors have *multiple page size support* for larger sizes.
- **Page fault:** an invalid memory access. These are normal occurrences when using on-demand virtual memory.
- **Paging:** the transfer of pages between main memory and the storage devices.
- **Swapping:** From Unix, this is the transfer of entire processes between main memory and the swap devices. Linux often uses *swapping* to refer to *paging* to the swap device (the transfer of *swap pages*). In this book the original definition is used: swapping is for entire processes.
- **Swap:** an on-disk area for paged anonymous data and swapped processes. It may be an area on a storage device, also called a *physical swap device*, or a file system file, called a *swap file*. Some tools use the term *swap* to refer to virtual memory (which is confusing and incorrect).

Other terms are introduced throughout this chapter. The Glossary includes basic terminology for reference if needed, including *address*, *buffer*, and *DRAM*. Also see the terminology sections in Chapters 2 and 3.

7.2 Concepts

The following are a selection of important concepts regarding memory and memory performance.

7.2.1 Virtual Memory

Virtual memory is an abstraction that provides each process and the kernel with its own large, linear, and private address space. It simplifies software development, leaving physical memory placement for the operating system to manage. It also supports multitasking, as virtual address spaces are separated by design, and also oversubscription, since in-use memory can extend beyond main memory. Virtual memory was introduced in Chapter 3, Operating Systems. For historical background, see [Denning 70].

Figure 7.1 shows the role of virtual memory for a process, on a system with a swap device (secondary storage). A page of memory is shown, as most virtual memory implementations are page-based.

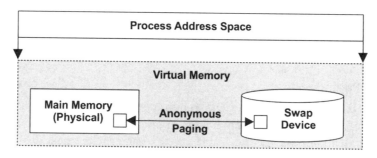

Figure 7-1 Process virtual memory

The process address space is mapped by the virtual memory subsystem to main memory and the physical swap device. Pages of memory can be moved between them by the kernel as needed, a process called *paging*. This allows the kernel to *oversubscribe* main memory.

The kernel may impose a limit to oversubscription. On Solaris-based kernels, it is the size of both main memory and the physical swap devices. The kernel will fail allocations that try to exceed this limit. Such "out of virtual memory" errors can be confusing at first, since virtual memory itself is an abstract resource.

Linux can be configured to support the same behavior, but it also allows other behaviors, including placing *no* bounds on memory allocation. This is termed *overcommit* and is described after the following sections on paging and demand paging, which are necessary for overcommit to work.

7.2.2 Paging

Paging is the movement of pages in and out of main memory, which are referred to as *page-ins* and *page-outs* respectively. It was first introduced by the Atlas Computer in 1962 [Corbató 68], allowing

- Partially loaded programs to execute
- Programs larger than main memory to execute
- Efficient movement of programs between main memory and storage devices

These abilities are still true today. Unlike swapping out entire programs, paging is a fine-grained approach to managing and freeing main memory, since the page size unit is relatively small (e.g., 4 Kbytes).

Paging with virtual memory (*paged virtual memory*) was introduced to Unix via BSD [Babaoglu 79] and became the standard.

With the later addition of the page cache for sharing file system pages (see Chapter 8, File Systems), two different types of paging became available: *file system paging* and *anonymous paging*.

File System Paging

File system paging is caused by the reading and writing of pages in memory-mapped files. This is normal behavior for applications that use file memory mappings (mmap()), and on file systems that use the page cache (most do; see Chapter 8, File Systems). It has been referred to as "good" paging [McDougall 06b].

When needed, the kernel can free memory by paging some out. This is where the terminology gets a bit tricky: if a file system page has been modified in main memory ("dirty"), the page-out will require it to be written to disk. If, instead, the file system page has not been modified ("clean"), the page-out merely frees the memory for immediate reuse, since a copy already exists on disk. Because of this, the term *page-out* means that a page was moved out of memory—this may or may not have included a write to a storage device (you may see this defined differently).

Anonymous Paging

Anonymous paging involves data that is private to processes: the process heap and stacks. It is termed *anonymous* because it has no named location in the operating system (i.e., no file system path name). Anonymous page-outs require moving the data to the physical swap devices or swap files. Linux uses the term *swapping* to refer to this type of paging.

Anonymous paging hurts performance and has therefore been referred to as "bad" paging [McDougall 06b]. When applications access memory pages that have been paged out, they block on the disk I/O required to read them back to main memory. This is an *anonymous page-in*, which introduces synchronous latency to the application. Anonymous page-outs may not affect application performance directly, as they can be performed asynchronously by the kernel.

Performance is best when there is no anonymous paging (or swapping). This can be achieved by configuring applications to remain within the main memory available and by monitoring page scanning, memory utilization, and anonymous paging, to ensure that there are no longer indicators of a memory shortage.

7.2.3 Demand Paging

Operating systems that support demand paging (most do) map pages of virtual memory to physical memory on demand, as shown in Figure 7.2. This defers the CPU overhead of creating the mappings until they are actually needed and accessed, instead of at the time a range of memory is first allocated.

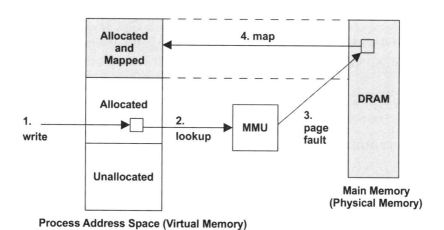

Figure 7-2 Page fault example

The sequence shown in Figure 7.2 begins with a write to a newly allocated page of virtual memory, resulting in on-demand mapping to physical memory. A *page fault* occurs as a page is accessed when there is initially no page mapping from virtual to physical.

The first step could also be a read, in the case of a mapped file, which does contain data but isn't yet mapped to this process address space.

If the mapping can be satisfied from another page in memory, it is called a *minor fault*. This may occur for mapping a new page from available memory, during memory growth of the process (as pictured). It can also occur for mapping to another existing page, such as reading a page from a mapped shared library.

Page faults that require storage device access (not shown in this figure), such as accessing an uncached memory-mapped file, are called *major faults*.

The result of the virtual memory model and demand allocation is that any page of virtual memory may be in one of the following states:

A. Unallocated

B. Allocated, but unmapped (unpopulated and not yet faulted)

C. Allocated, and mapped to main memory (RAM)

D. Allocated, and mapped to the physical swap device (disk)

State (D) is reached if the page is paged out due to system memory pressure. A transition from (B) to (C) is a page fault. If it requires disk I/O, it is a major page fault; otherwise, a minor page fault.

From these states, two memory usage terms can also be defined:

- **Resident set size** (RSS): the size of allocated main memory pages (C)
- **Virtual memory size**: the size of all allocated areas (B + C + D)

Demand paging was added to Unix via BSD, along with paged virtual memory.

7.2.4 Overcommit

Linux supports the notion of *overcommit*, which allows more memory to be allocated than the system can possibly store—more than physical memory and swap devices combined. It relies on demand paging and the tendency of applications to not use much of the memory they have allocated.

With overcommit, application requests for memory (e.g., `malloc()`) will succeed when they would otherwise have failed. Instead of allocating memory conservatively to remain within virtual memory limits, an application programmer can allocate memory generously and later use it sparsely on demand.

On Linux, the behavior of overcommit can be configured with a tunable parameter. See Section 7.6, Tuning, for details. The consequences of overcommit depend on how the kernel manages memory pressure; see the discussion of the OOM killer in Section 7.3, Architecture.

7.2.5 Swapping

Swapping is the movement of entire processes between main memory and the physical swap device or swap file. This is the original Unix technique for managing main memory and is the origin of the term *swap* [Thompson 78].

To swap out a process, all of its private data must be written to the swap device, including thread structures and the process heap (anonymous data). Data that originated from file systems and has not been modified can be dropped and read from the original locations again when needed.

Processes that are swapped out are still known by the kernel, as a small amount of process metadata is always resident in kernel memory. To swap a process back in, the kernel takes into account thread priority, the time it was waiting on disk, and the size of the process. Long-waiting and smaller processes are favored.

Swapping severely hurts performance, as a process that has been swapped out requires numerous disk I/O to run again. It made more sense on early Unix for the machines of the time, such as the PDP-11, which had a maximum process size of 64 Kbytes [Bach 86].

While Solaris-based systems can still swap, they do so only if paging cannot free sufficient memory quickly enough for application demands (since paging is bounded by the rate of page scanning; see Section 7.3, Architecture). Linux systems do not swap processes at all and rely only on paging.

When people say, "The system is swapping," they usually mean it is paging. On Linux, the term *swapping* refers to paging to the swap file or device (anonymous paging).

7.2.6 File System Cache Usage

It is normal for memory usage to grow after system boot as the operating system uses available memory to cache the file system, improving performance. The principle is: If there is spare main memory, use it for something useful. This can distress naïve users who see the available free memory shrink to near zero sometime after boot. But it does not pose a problem for applications, as the kernel should be able to quickly free memory from the file system cache when applications need it.

For more about the various file system caches that can consume main memory, see Chapter 8, File Systems.

7.2.7 Utilization and Saturation

Main memory utilization can be calculated as used memory versus total memory. Memory used by the file system cache can be treated as unused, as it is available for reuse by applications.

If demands for memory exceed the amount of main memory, main memory becomes *saturated*. The operating system may then free memory by employing paging, swapping, and, on Linux, the OOM killer (described later). Any of these activities is an indicator of main memory saturation.

Virtual memory can also be studied in terms of capacity utilization, if the system imposes a limit on the amount of virtual memory it is willing to allocate (Linux overcommit will not). If so, once virtual memory is exhausted, the kernel will fail allocations; for example, `malloc()` returns ENOMEM.

Note that the currently available virtual memory on a system is sometimes (confusingly) called *available swap*.

7.2.8 Allocators

While virtual memory handles multitasking of physical memory, the actual allocation and placement within a virtual address space are often handled by allocators. These are either user-land libraries or kernel-based routines, which provide the software programmer with an easy interface for memory usage (e.g., `malloc()`, `free()`).

Allocators can have a significant effect on performance, and a system may provide multiple user-level allocator libraries to pick from. They can improve performance by use of techniques including per-thread object caching, but they can also hurt performance if allocation becomes fragmented and wasteful. Specific examples are covered in Section 7.3, Architecture.

7.2.9 Word Size

As introduced in Chapter 6, CPUs, processors may support multiple word sizes, such as 32-bit and 64-bit, allowing software for either to run. As the address space size is bounded by the addressable range from the word size, applications requiring more than 4 Gbytes (and usually a little less) are too large for a 32-bit address space and need to be compiled for 64 bits or higher.

Memory performance may be improved by using larger bit widths depending on the CPU architecture. A small amount of memory may be wasted, in cases where a data type has unused bits at the larger bit width.

7.3 Architecture

This section introduces memory architecture, both hardware and software, including processor and operating system specifics.

These topics have been summarized as background for performance analysis and tuning. For more details, see the vendor processor manuals and texts on operating system internals listed at the end of this chapter.

7.3.1 Hardware

Memory hardware includes main memory, busses, CPU caches, and the MMU.

Main Memory

The common type of main memory in use today is *dynamic random-access memory* (DRAM). This is a type of volatile memory—its contents are lost when power is lost. DRAM provides high-density storage, as each bit is implemented using only two logical components: a capacitor and a transistor. The capacitor requires a periodic refresh to maintain charge.

Enterprise servers are configured with different amounts of DRAM depending on their purpose, typically ranging from 1 Gbyte to 1 Tbyte and larger. These can dwarf the memory of cloud computing instances, which are typically between 512 Mbytes and 64 Gbytes each. However, cloud computing is designed to spread load over a pool of instances, so they can collectively bring much more DRAM online for a distributed application, although at a much higher coherency cost.

Latency

The access time of main memory can be measured as the *column address strobe* (CAS) latency: the time between sending a memory module the desired address (column) and when the data is available to be read. This varies depending on the type of memory (for DDR3 it is around 10 ns). For memory I/O transfers, this latency may occur multiple times for a memory bus (e.g., 64 bits wide) to transfer a cache line (e.g., at 64 *bytes* wide). There are also other latencies involved with the CPU and MMU for then reading the newly available data.

Main Memory Architecture

An example main memory architecture for a generic two-processor *uniform memory access* (UMA) system is shown in Figure 7.3.

Each CPU has uniform access latency to all of memory, via a shared system bus. When managed by a single operating system kernel instance that runs uniformly across all processors, this is also a symmetric multiprocessing (SMP) architecture.

For comparison, an example two-processor *non-uniform memory access* (NUMA) system is shown in Figure 7.4, which uses a CPU interconnect that becomes part of the memory architecture. For this architecture, the access time for main memory varies based on its location relative to the CPU.

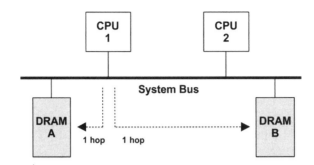

Figure 7-3 Example UMA main memory architecture, two-processor

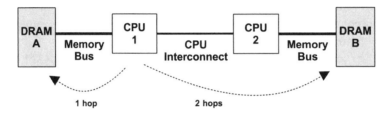

Figure 7-4 Example NUMA main memory architecture, two-processor

CPU 1 can perform I/O to DRAM A directly, via its memory bus. This is referred to as *local memory*. CPU 1 performs I/O to DRAM B via CPU 2 and the CPU interconnect (two hops). This is referred to as *remote memory* and has a higher access latency.

The banks of memory connected to each CPU are referred to as *memory nodes*, or just *nodes*. The operating system may be aware of the memory node topology based on information provided by the processor. This then allows it to assign memory and schedule threads based on *memory locality*, favoring local memory as much as possible to improve performance.

Busses

How main memory is physically connected to the system depends on the main memory architecture, as previously pictured. The actual implementation may involve additional controllers and busses between the CPUs and memory and be accessed in one of the following ways:

- **Shared system bus:** single or multiprocessor, via a shared system bus, a memory bridge controller, and finally a memory bus. This was pictured as the UMA example, Figure 7.3, and as the Intel front-side bus example, Figure 6.9 in Chapter 6, CPUs. The memory controller in that example was a Northbridge.

- **Direct:** single processor with directly attached memory via a memory bus.
- **Interconnect:** multiprocessor, each with directly attached memory via a memory bus, and processors connected via a CPU interconnect. This was pictured earlier as the NUMA example in Figure 7.4; CPU interconnects are discussed in Chapter 6, CPUs.

If you suspect your system is none of the above, find a system functional diagram and follow the data path between CPUs and memory, noting all components along the way.

DDR SDRAM

The speed of the memory bus, for any architecture, is often dictated by the memory interface standard supported by the processor and system board. A common standard in use since 1996 is *double data rate synchronous dynamic random-access memory* (DDR SDRAM). The term *double data rate* refers to the transfer of data on both the rise and fall of the clock signal (also called *double-pumped*). The term *synchronous* refers to the memory being clocked synchronously with the CPUs.

Example DDR SDRAM standards are shown in Table 7.1.

Table 7-1 Example DDR Bandwidths

Standard	Memory Clock (MHz)	Data Rate (MT/s)	Peak Bandwidth (MB/s)
DDR-200	100	200	1,600
DDR-333	167	333	2,667
DDR2-667	167	667	5,333
DDR2-800	200	800	6,400
DDR3-1333	167	1,333	10,667
DDR3-1600	200	1,600	12,800
DDR4-3200	200	3,200	25,600

The DDR4 interface standard was released in September 2012. These are also named using "PC-" followed by the data transfer rate in megabytes per second, for example, PC-1600.

Multichannel

System architectures may support the use of multiple memory busses in parallel, to improve bandwidth. Common multiples are dual-, triple-, and quad-channel. For example, the Intel Core i7 processors support up to quad-channel DDR3-1600, for a maximum memory bandwidth of 51.2 Gbytes/s.

CPU Caches

Processors typically include on-chip hardware caches to improve memory access performance. The caches may include the following levels, of decreasing speed and increasing size:

- **Level 1:** usually split into a separate instruction cache and data cache
- **Level 2:** a cache for both instructions and data
- **Level 3:** another larger level of cache

Level 1 is typically referenced by virtual memory addresses, and Level 2 onward by physical memory addresses, depending on the processor.

These caches were discussed further in Chapter 6, CPUs. An additional type of hardware cache, the TLB, is discussed in this chapter.

MMU

The memory management unit is responsible for virtual-to-physical address translations. These are performed per page, and offsets within a page are mapped directly. The MMU was introduced in Chapter 6, CPUs, in the context of nearby CPU caches.

A generic MMU is pictured in Figure 7.5, with levels of CPU caches and main memory.

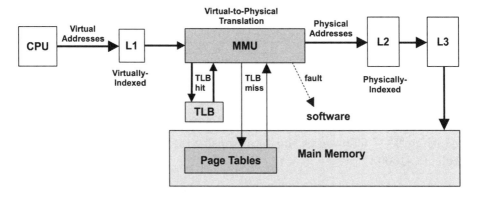

Figure 7-5 Memory management unit

Multiple Page Sizes

Modern processors support multiple page sizes, which allow different page sizes to be used by the operating system and the MMU, for example, 4 Kbytes, 2 Mbytes, 1 Gbyte. Solaris-based kernels support multiple page sizes and the dynamic creation of larger sizes, calling this feature *multiple page size support* (MPSS).

Linux has a feature called *huge pages*, which sets aside a portion of physical memory for use with a particular large page size, such as 2 Mbytes. The early reservation of huge pages is less flexible than the Solaris-based approach of dynamic allocation; however, it also avoids a problem of memory fragmentation preventing larger pages being dynamically allocated.

TLB

The MMU pictured in Figure 7.5 uses a TLB as the first level of address translation cache, followed by the page tables in main memory. The TLB may be divided into separate caches for instruction and data pages.

Since the TLB has a limited number of entries for mappings, the use of larger page sizes increases the range of memory that can be translated from its cache (its *reach*), which reduces TLB misses and improves system performance. The TLB may be further divided into separate caches for each of these page sizes, improving the probability of retaining larger mappings in cache.

As an example of TLB sizes, a typical Intel Core i7 processor provides the four TLBs shown in Table 7.2 [Intel 12].

Table 7-2 TLBs for a Typical Intel Core i7 Processor

Type	Page Size	Entries
Instruction	4 K	64 per thread, 128 per core
Instruction	large	7 per thread
Data	4 K	64
Data	large	32

This processor has one level of data TLB. The Intel Core microarchitecture supports two levels, in the same way that CPUs provide multiple levels of main memory cache.

The exact makeup of the TLB is specific to the processor type. Refer to the vendor processor manuals for details on the TLBs in your processor and further information on their operation.

7.3.2 Software

Software for memory management includes the virtual memory system, address translation, swapping, paging, and allocation. The topics most related to performance are included in this section: freeing memory, free list, page scanning, swapping, the process address space, and memory allocators.

Freeing Memory

When the available memory on the system becomes low, there are various methods that the kernel can use to free up memory, adding it to the *free list* of pages. These methods are pictured in Figure 7.6, in the *general* order in which they are used as available memory decreases.

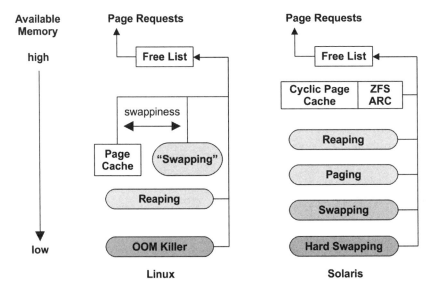

Figure 7-6 Freeing memory

These methods include

- **Free list:** a list of pages that are unused (also called *idle memory*) and available for immediate allocation. This is usually implemented as multiple *free page lists*, one for each locality group (NUMA).
- **Reaping:** When a low-memory threshold is crossed, kernel modules and the kernel slab allocator can be instructed to immediately free any memory that can easily be freed. This is also known as *shrinking*.

On **Linux**, specifically, the methods are

- **Page cache:** the file system cache. A tunable parameter called *swappiness* sets the degree to which to favor freeing memory from the page cache as opposed to swapping.
- **Swapping:** This is paging by the page-out daemon, kswapd, which finds not-recently-used pages to add to the free list, including application memory. They are paged out, which may involve writing to either a file-system-based swap file or a swap device. This is available only if a swap file or device has been configured.
- **OOM killer:** The out-of-memory killer will free memory by finding and killing a sacrificial process, found using select_bad_process() and then killed by calling oom_kill_process(). This may be logged in the system log (/var/log/messages) as an "Out of memory: Kill process" message.

On **Solaris**-based systems, specifically, the methods are

- **Cyclic page cache:** This contains a list of valid but currently unreferenced file system pages, called the *cachelist*, which can be added to the free list as needed. This avoids the overhead of page scanning.
- **ZFS ARC:** The ZFS file system will detect that the system may begin page scanning soon and will perform its own reaping to free up memory using arc_kmem_reap_now().
- **Paging:** Performed by the page-out daemon (also called the *page scanner*), this finds not-recently-used pages to add to the free list, including application memory. They are paged out, which may involve writing to either the file system or the swap device.
- **Swapping:** Still present on Solaris-based systems, this moves entire processes to the swap device and is the original Unix method for handling main memory pressure.
- **Hard swapping:** unloads kernel modules that are not active and sequentially swaps out processes to the swap device.

Comparisons between the systems are interesting. On Solaris-based systems, the file system cache should be empty by the time paging occurs. Linux provides a way to balance this behavior: swappiness, a parameter between 0 and 100 (the default value is 60), where higher values favor freeing memory by paging applications, and lower values by reclaiming it from the page cache (similar to the behavior of Solaris-based systems). This allows system throughput to be improved, by preserving warm file system cache while paging out cold application memory [1].

It is also interesting to ask what happens if no swap device or swap file is configured on either system. This limits virtual memory size, so unless overcommit is in use, memory allocations will fail sooner. On Linux, this may also mean that the OOM killer is used sooner.

Consider an application issue with endless memory growth. With swap, this is likely to first become a performance issue due to paging, which is an opportunity to debug the issue live. Without swap, there is no paging grace period, so either the application hits an "Out of memory" error, or the OOM killer terminates it. This may delay debugging the issue if it is seen only after hours of usage.

The sections that follow describe the free list, reaping, and the page-out daemon in more detail, for Linux- and Solaris-based operating systems.

Free List(s)

The original Unix memory allocator used a memory map and a first-fit scan. With the introduction of paged virtual memory in BSD, a *free list* and a *page-out daemon* were added [Babaoglu 79]. The free list, pictured in Figure 7.7, allows available memory to be located immediately.

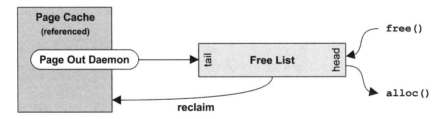

Figure 7-7 Free list operations

Memory freed is added to the head of the list, for future allocations. Memory that is freed by the page-out daemon—and that may still contain useful cached file system pages—is added to the tail. Should a future request for one of these pages occur before the useful page has been reused, it can be *reclaimed* and removed from the free list.

A form of free list is still in use by Linux- and Solaris-based systems, as pictured in Figure 7.6. Free lists are typically consumed via allocators, such as the slab allocator for the kernel, and libc malloc for user-space. These in turn consume pages and then expose them via their allocator API.

Having a single free list is also a simplification; how this is implemented depends on the kernel type and version.

Linux

Linux uses the buddy allocator for managing pages. This provides multiple free lists for different-size memory allocations, following a power-of-two scheme. The term *buddy* refers to finding neighboring pages of free memory so that they can be allocated together. For historical background, see [Peterson 77].

The buddy free lists are at the bottom of the following hierarchy, beginning with the per-memory node `pg_data_t`:

- **Nodes:** banks of memory, NUMA-aware
- **Zones:** ranges of memory for certain purposes (direct memory access (DMA), normal, highmem)
- **Migration types:** unmovable, reclaimable, movable, . . .
- **Sizes:** power-of-two number of pages

Allocating within the node free lists improves memory locality and performance.

Solaris

Solaris-based systems use multiple free lists for different memory locations (mnodes), page sizes, and page coloring. These also behave in a buddylike way, grouping pages into larger page sizes. The lists are declared in vm_dep.h:

```
/*
 * Per page size free lists. Allocated dynamically.
 * dimensions [mtype][mmu_page_sizes][colors]
 *
 * mtype specifies a physical memory range with a unique mnode.
 */

extern page_t ****page_freelists;
```

Page coloring is the mapping between virtual and physical page addresses, which may be hashed, round-robin, or use some other scheme. This is another strategy to improve access performance.

Reaping

Reaping mostly involves freeing memory from the kernel slab allocator caches. These caches contain unused memory in slab-size chunks, ready for reuse. Reaping returns this memory to the system for page allocations.

On **Linux**, kernel modules can also call `register_shrinker()` to register specific functions for reaping their own memory.

On **Solaris**-based systems, reaping is largely driven from the slab allocator with `kmem_reap()`.

Page Scanning

Freeing memory by paging is managed by the kernel page-out daemon. When available main memory in the free list drops below a threshold, the page-out daemon begins *page scanning*.

Page scanning occurs only when needed. A normally balanced system may not page scan very often and may do so only in short bursts. Solaris-based systems use other mechanisms to free memory before page scanning, as shown earlier, and page scanning for more than several seconds is typically a sign of a memory pressure issue.

Linux

The page-out daemon is called `kswapd()`, which scans LRU page lists of inactive and active memory to free pages. It is woken up based on free memory and two thresholds to provide hysteresis, as shown in Figure 7.8.

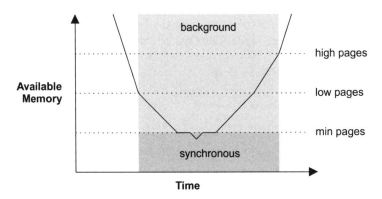

Figure 7-8 kswapd wake-ups and modes

Once free memory has reached the lowest threshold, kswapd operates in *synchronous* mode, freeing pages of memory as they are requested (the kernel is exempt from this requirement) [Gorman 04]. This lowest threshold is tunable (vm.min_free_kbytes), and the others are scaled based on it (by 2x, 3x).

The page cache has separate lists for *inactive pages* and *active pages*. These operate in an LRU fashion, allowing kswapd to find free pages quickly. They are shown in Figure 7.9.

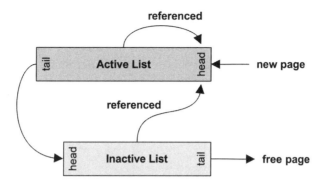

Figure 7-9 kswapd lists

kswapd scans the inactive list first, and then the active if needed. The term *scanning* refers to checking pages as the list is walked: a page may be ineligible to be freed if it is locked or dirty. This term has a different meaning with the original page-out daemon, which scans all of memory and still exists in Solaris-based systems.

Solaris

Page scanning walks all pages of memory in a continual loop, finding least-recently-used pages and then scheduling them to be moved to the physical swap device. This was originally added in BSD with paged virtual memory [Babaoglu 79] and was later enhanced to include two pointers to scan memory instead of one, as pictured in Figure 7.10 (this clocklike representation dates back to Multics [Corbató 68]).

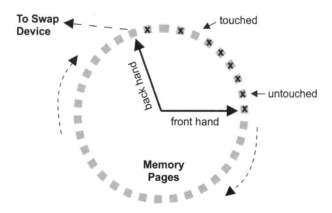

Figure 7-10 Two-handed page scanner

The first hand sets a bit on each page, indicating that it hasn't been accessed. When pages are accessed, this bit is cleared. The second hand checks if the bit is still set. If it is, the page scanner knows it is *not recently used* and can be paged out. The distance between the hands is tunable (handspreadpages).

The rate at which pages are scanned is dynamic, based on the available free memory. This is pictured in Figure 7.11 for an example 128 Gbyte system, along with the tunable names (based on [McDougall 06a]).

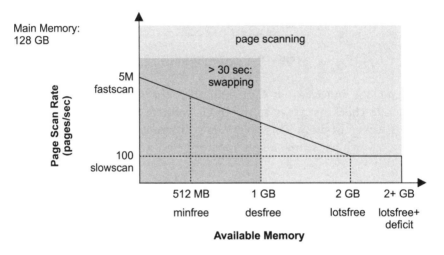

Figure 7-11 Page scan rate

When available memory drops below desfree, and then minfree, the page-out daemon is woken up more frequently to scan pages. If available memory drops below desfree for 30 s, the kernel also begins *swapping*.

These tunables are initialized in the `setupclock()` function, which sets them based on ratios of main memory. For example, lotsfree is set to 1/64. The deficit parameter is dynamic and will grow when memory consumption is rapid, so that the kernel grows the free list sooner.

Page scanning became expensive for larger systems, which led to the addition of the cyclic page cache so that pages could be found quickly. This is similar to how the Linux page-out daemon finds pages.

7.3.3 Process Address Space

Managed by both hardware and software, the process virtual address space is a range of virtual pages that are mapped to physical pages as needed. The addresses are split into areas called *segments* for storing the thread stacks, process executable, libraries, and heap. Examples for 32-bit processes are shown in Figure 7.12, for both x86 and SPARC processors.

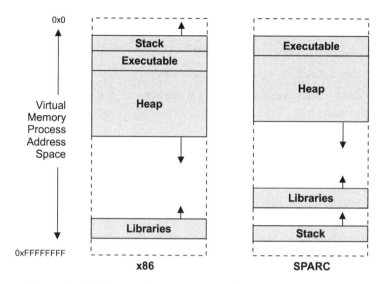

Figure 7-12 Example process virtual memory address space

The program executable segment contains separate text and data segments. Libraries are also composed of separate executable text and data segments. These different segment types are

- **Executable text:** contains the executable CPU instructions for the process. This is mapped from the text segment of the binary program on the file system. It is read-only with the execute permission.
- **Executable data:** contains initialized variables mapped from the data segment of the binary program. This has read/write permissions, so that the variables can be modified while the program is running. It also has a private flag, so that modifications are not flushed to disk.
- **Heap:** This is the working memory for the program and is anonymous memory (no file system location). It grows as needed and is allocated via `malloc()`.
- **Stack:** stacks of the running threads, mapped read/write.

The library text segments may be shared by other processes that use the same library, each of which has a private copy of the library data segment.

vth

A common source of confusion is the endless growth of heap. Is it a memory leak? For most allocators, a free() does not return memory to the operating system; rather, it keeps it ready to serve future allocations. This means the process resident memory will only ever grow, which is normal. Methods for processes to reduce memory include

- **Re-exec:** calling exec() to begin from an empty address space
- **Memory mapping:** using mmap() and munmap(), which will return memory to the system

Some allocators support mmap as a mode of operation. See Section 8.3.10, Memory-Mapped Files, in Chapter 8, File Systems.

Allocators

There are a variety of user- and kernel-level allocators for memory allocation. Figure 7.13 shows the role of allocators, including some common types.

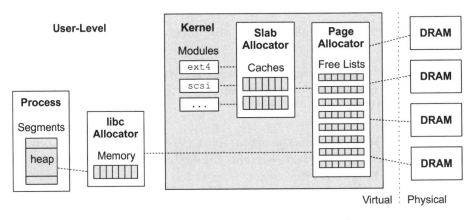

Figure 7-13 User- and kernel-level memory allocators

Page management was described earlier in Section 7.3.2 under Free List(s). Memory allocator features can include

- **Simple API:** for example, malloc(), free().
- **Efficient memory usage:** When servicing memory allocations of a variety of sizes, memory usage can become *fragmented*, where there are many unused

regions that waste memory. Allocators can strive to coalesce the unused regions, so that larger allocations can make use of them, improving efficiency.

- **Performance:** Memory allocations can be frequent, and on multithreaded environments they can perform poorly due to contention for synchronization primitives. Allocators can be designed to use locks sparingly and also make use of per-thread or per-CPU caches to improve memory locality.

- **Observability:** An allocator may provide statistics and debug modes to show how it is being used, and which code paths are responsible for allocations.

The sections that follow describe kernel-level allocators—slab and SLUB—and user-level allocators—libmalloc, libumem, and mtmalloc.

Slab

The kernel slab allocator manages caches of objects of a specific size, allowing them to be recycled quickly without the overhead of page allocation. This is especially effective for kernel allocations, which are frequently for fixed-size structs.

As an example from the kernel, the following two lines are from ZFS arc.c:

```
df = kmem_alloc(sizeof (l2arc_data_free_t), KM_SLEEP);

head = kmem_cache_alloc(hdr_cache, KM_PUSHPAGE);
```

The first, kmem_alloc(), shows a traditional-style kernel allocation whose size is passed as an argument. The kernel maps this to a slab cache (or an oversize arena) based on that size. The second, kmem_cache_alloc(), operates directly on a custom slab allocator cache, in this case (kmem_cache_t *)hdr_cache.

Developed for Solaris 2.4 [Bonwick 94], it was later enhanced with per-CPU caches called *magazines* [Bonwick 01]:

Our basic approach is to give each CPU an M-element cache of objects called a magazine, by analogy with automatic weapons. Each CPU's magazine can satisfy M allocations before the CPU needs to reload—that is, exchange its empty magazine for a full one.

Apart from high performance, Solaris provides various debug and analysis facilities for the slab allocator. These including auditing, where allocation details can be traced, including stack.

The slab allocator was introduced to Linux in version 2.2, where it was the default option for many years. Recent kernel versions provide SLUB as an option or as the default.

SLUB

The Linux kernel SLUB allocator is based on the slab allocator and is designed to address various concerns, especially regarding the complexity of the slab allocator. These include the removal of object queues, and also per-CPU caches—leaving NUMA optimization to the page allocator (see the earlier Free List(s) section).

The SLUB allocator was made the default option in Linux 2.6.23 [2].

libc

The Solaris user-level allocator provided by libc is simple and general-purpose. While typically the default allocator (depending on compiler configuration), the man page recommends against its usage (malloc(3C)):

> These default memory allocation routines are safe for use in multithreaded applications but are not scalable. Concurrent accesses by multiple threads are single-threaded through the use of a single lock. Multithreaded applications that make heavy use of dynamic memory allocation should be linked with allocation libraries designed for concurrent access, such as libumem(3LIB) or libmtmalloc(3LIB).

Apart from performance issues, the allocator is heap-based and subject to fragmentation over time.

glibc

The GNU libc allocator is based on dlmalloc by Doug Lea. The behavior depends on the allocation request size. Small allocations are served from bins of memory, containing units of a similar size, which can be coalesced using a buddylike algorithm. Larger allocations can use a tree lookup to find space efficiently. And very large allocations switch to using mmap(). The net result is a high-performing allocator that uses the benefits from multiple allocation policies.

libumem

On Solaris-based systems, libumem is a user-space version of the slab allocator. It can be used by linking or preloading the library and provides improved performance for multithreaded applications.

libumem was designed from the onset to be scalable, along with debugging and analysis capabilities that cost the minimum overhead in both time and space. Other memory analysis tools slow the target when operating in analysis mode—sometimes to the point where the problems no longer occur, and often to a degree that makes them unsuitable for production use.

mtmalloc

This is another high-performance multithreaded user-level allocator for Solaris-based systems. It uses a per-thread cache for small allocations and a single over-size area for large allocations. The per-thread caches avoid lock contention issues with the traditional allocator.

7.4 Methodology

This section describes various methodologies and exercises for memory analysis and tuning. The topics are summarized in Table 7.3.

Table 7-3 Memory Performance Methodologies

Methodology	Types
Tools method	observational analysis
USE method	observational analysis
Characterizing usage	observational analysis, capacity planning
Cycle analysis	observational analysis
Performance monitoring	observational analysis, capacity planning
Leak detection	observational analysis
Static performance tuning	observational analysis, capacity planning
Resource controls	tuning
Micro-benchmarking	experimental analysis

See Chapter 2, Methodology, for more strategies and an introduction to many of these.

These methods may be followed individually or used in combination. My suggestion is to use the following strategies to start with, in this order: performance monitoring, the USE method, and characterizing usage.

Section 7.5, Analysis, shows operating system tools for applying these methods.

7.4.1 Tools Method

The tools method is a process of iterating over available tools, examining key metrics they provide. While a simple methodology, it can overlook issues for which the tools provide poor or no visibility and can be time-consuming to perform.

For memory, the tools method can involve checking the following:

- **Page scanning:** Look for continual page scanning (more than 10 s) as a sign of memory pressure. On Linux, this can be done using `sar -B` and checking the pgscan columns. On Solaris, you can use `vmstat(1M)` and check the `sr` column.
- **Paging:** The paging of memory is a further indication that the system is low on memory. On Linux, you can use `vmstat(8)` and check the `si` and `so` columns (here, the term *swapping* means anonymous paging). On Solaris, `vmstat -p` shows paging by type; check for anonymous paging.
- **vmstat:** Run `vmstat` per second and check the `free` column for available memory.
- **OOM killer:** On Linux only, these events can be seen in the system log /var/log/messages, or from `dmesg(1)`. Search for "Out of memory."
- **Swapping:** On Solaris only, this is usually noticed after the fact, by running `vmstat` and checking the w column, which indicates swapped-out threads. To see swapping live, use `vmstat -S` and check `si` and `so`.
- **top/prstat:** See which processes and users are the top physical memory consumers (resident) and virtual memory consumers (see the man page for the names of the columns, which differ depending on version). These tools also summarize free memory.
- **dtrace/stap/perf:** Trace memory allocations with stack traces, to identify the cause of memory usage.

If an issue is found, examine all fields from the available tools to learn more context. See Section 7.5, Analysis, for more about each tool. Other methodologies may identify more types of issues.

7.4.2 USE Method

The USE method is for identifying bottlenecks and errors across all components, early in a performance investigation, before deeper and more time-consuming strategies are followed.

Check system-wide for

- **Utilization:** how much memory is in use, and how much is available. Both physical memory and virtual memory should be checked.
- **Saturation:** the degree of page scanning, paging, swapping, and Linux OOM killer sacrifices performed, as measures to relieve memory pressure.
- **Errors:** failed memory allocations.

Saturation may be checked first, as continual saturation is a sign of a memory issue. These metrics are usually readily available from operating system tools, including vmstat(1), sar(1), and dmesg(1), for OOM killer sacrifices. For systems configured with a separate disk swap device, any activity to the swap device is also a sign of memory pressure.

Utilization is typically harder to read and interpret. You know when you are out of physical memory by the saturation metrics: the system begins paging or processes are sacrificed (OOM). To determine physical utilization, you need to know how much memory is available (free). Different tools may report this differently, depending on whether they account for unreferenced file system cache pages or inactive pages. A system may report that it has only 10 Mbytes of available memory when it actually has 10 Gbytes of file system cache that can be reclaimed by applications immediately when needed. Check the tool documentation to see what is included.

Virtual memory utilization may also need to be checked, depending on whether the system performs overcommit. For those systems that do not, memory allocations will fail once virtual memory is exhausted—a type of memory error.

Historically, memory errors have been left for the applications to report, although not all applications do (and, with Linux overcommit, developers may not have felt it necessary to do so). A system error counter was recently added to SmartOS to report on per-zone failed brk() calls, as a type of memory-related error counter.

For environments that implement memory limits or quotas (resource controls), as occurs in some cloud computing environments, memory saturation may need to be measured differently. For example, OS virtualization on Solaris-based systems uses a different mechanism for enforcing memory quotas for each guest instance, which is reported differently to the page-out scanner (see Chapter 11, Cloud Computing). Your OS instance may be at its memory limit and paging, even though the system is not scanning using the traditional page-out scanner.

7.4.3 Characterizing Usage

Characterizing memory usage is an important exercise when capacity planning, benchmarking, and simulating workloads. It can also lead to some of the largest performance gains by identifying misconfigurations. For example, a database cache may be configured too small and have low hit rates, or too large and cause system paging.

For memory, this involves identifying where and how much memory is used:

- System-wide physical and virtual memory utilization
- Degree of saturation: paging, swapping, OOM killing

- Kernel and file system cache memory usage
- Per-process physical and virtual memory usage
- Usage of memory resource controls, if present

Here is an example description to show how these attributes can be expressed together:

> The system has 256 Gbytes of main memory, which is only at 1% utilization, with 30% in a file system cache. The largest process is a database, consuming 2 Gbytes of main memory (RSS), which is its configured limit from the previous system it was migrated from.

These characteristics can vary over time as more memory is used to cache working data. Kernel or application memory may also grow continually over time due to a memory leak—a software error—aside from regular cache growth.

Advanced Usage Analysis/Checklist

Additional details may be included to understand usage in more detail. These are listed here as questions for consideration, which may also serve as a checklist when studying memory issues thoroughly:

- Where is the kernel memory used? Per slab?
- How much of the file system cache (or page cache) is active as opposed to inactive?
- Where is the process memory used?
- Why are processes allocating memory (call paths)?
- Why is the kernel allocating memory (call paths)?
- What processes are actively being paged/swapped out?
- What processes have previously been paged/swapped out?
- May processes or the kernel have memory leaks?
- In a NUMA system, how well is memory distributed across memory nodes?
- What are the CPI and memory stall cycle rates?
- How balanced are the memory busses?
- How much local memory I/O is performed as opposed to remote memory I/O?

The sections that follow can help answer some of these questions. See Chapter 2, Methodology, for a higher-level summary of this methodology and the characteristics to measure (who, why, what, how).

7.4.4 Cycle Analysis

Memory bus load can be determined by inspecting the CPU performance counters (CPCs), which can be programmed to count memory stall cycles. They can also be used to measure cycles per instruction (CPI), as a measure of how memory-dependent the CPU load is. See Chapter 6, CPUs.

7.4.5 Performance Monitoring

Performance monitoring can identify active issues and patterns of behavior over time. Key metrics for memory are

- **Utilization:** percent used, which may be inferred from available memory
- **Saturation:** paging, swapping, OOM killing

For environments that implement memory limits or quotas (resource controls), statistics related to the imposed limits may also need to be collected.

Errors can also be monitored (if available), which are described with utilization and saturation in Section 7.4.2, USE Method.

Monitoring memory usage over time, especially by process, can help identify the presence and rate of memory leaks.

7.4.6 Leak Detection

This problem occurs when an application or kernel module grows endlessly, consuming memory from the free lists, from the file system cache, and eventually from other processes. This may be first noticed because the system is now paging, in response to the endless memory pressure.

This type of issue is caused by either

- **A memory leak:** a type of software bug where memory is forgotten but never freed. This is fixed by modifying the software code, or by applying patches or upgrades (which modify the code).
- **Memory growth:** The software is consuming memory normally, but at a much higher rate than is desirable for the system. This is fixed either by changing the software configuration, or by the software developer changing how the application consumes memory.

Memory growth issues are often misidentified as memory leaks. The first question to ask is: Is it supposed to do that? Check the configuration.

How memory leaks can be analyzed depends on the software and language type. Some allocators provide debug modes for recording allocation details, which can then be analyzed postmortem for identifying the call path responsible. There are also tools the developer can use for memory leak investigations.

7.4.7 Static Performance Tuning

Static performance tuning focuses on issues of the configured environment. For memory performance, examine the following aspects of the static configuration:

- How much main memory is there in total?
- How much memory are applications configured to use (their own config)?
- Which memory allocators do the applications use?
- What is the speed of main memory? Is it the fastest type available?
- What is the system architecture? NUMA, UMA?
- Is the operating system NUMA-aware?
- How many memory busses are present?
- What are the number and size of the CPU caches? TLB?
- Are large pages configured and used?
- Is overcommit available and configured?
- What other system memory tunables are in use?
- Are there software-imposed memory limits (resource controls)?

Answering these questions may reveal configuration choices that have been overlooked.

7.4.8 Resource Controls

The operating system may provide fine-grained controls for the allocation of memory to processes or groups of processes. These controls may include fixed limits for main memory and virtual memory usage. How they work is implementation-specific and is discussed in Section 7.6, Tuning.

7.4.9 Micro-Benchmarking

Micro-benchmarking may be used to determine the speed of main memory and characteristics such as CPU cache and cache line sizes. It may be helpful when analyzing differences between systems, as the speed of memory access may have a greater effect on performance than CPU clock speed, depending on the application and workload.

In Chapter 6, CPUs, the Latency section under CPU Caches (in Section 6.4.1) shows the result of micro-benchmarking memory access latency to determine characteristics of the CPU caches.

7.5 Analysis

This section introduces memory analysis tools for Linux- and Solaris-based operating systems. See the previous section for strategies to follow when using them.

The tools in this section are shown in Table 7.4.

Table 7-4 Memory Analysis Tools

Linux	Solaris	Description
vmstat	vmstat	virtual and physical memory statistics
sar	sar	historical statistics
slabtop	::kmastat	kernel slab allocator statistics
ps	ps	process status
top	prstat	monitor per-process memory usage
pmap	pmap	process address space statistics
DTrace	DTrace	allocation tracing

This is a selection of tools and capabilities to support Section 7.4, Methodology, beginning with system-wide memory usage statistics, then drilling down to per-process and allocation tracing. See the tool documentation, including man pages, for full references for their features. Also see Chapter 8, File Systems, for more tools for investigating file system memory usage.

While your interest may be in Linux- or Solaris-based systems only, consider the other operating system tools and the observability that they provide for a different perspective.

7.5.1 vmstat

The virtual memory statistics command, vmstat, provides a high-level view of system memory health, including current free memory and paging statistics. CPU statistics are also included, as described in Chapter 6, CPUs.

It was introduced by Bill Joy and Ozalp Babaoglu in 1979 for BSD. The original man page included

BUGS: So many numbers print out that it's sometimes hard to figure out what to watch.

Many of the columns remain largely unchanged since the first version, especially for Solaris. The sections that follow show the columns and options for the Linux and Solaris-based versions.

Linux

Here is example output:

```
$ vmstat 1
procs -----------memory---------- ---swap-- -----io---- -system-- ----cpu----
 r  b    swpd    free   buff  cache   si   so    bi    bo   in   cs us sy id wa
 4  0       0 34454064 111516 13438596  0    0     0     5    2    0  0  0 100  0
 4  0       0 34455208 111516 13438596  0    0     0     0 2262 15303 16 12 73  0
 5  0       0 34455588 111516 13438596  0    0     0     0 1961 15221 15 11 74  0
 4  0       0 34456300 111516 13438596  0    0     0     0 2343 15294 15 11 73  0
[...]
```

This version of vmstat(8) does not print summary-since-boot values for the memory columns on the first line of output, showing current status immediately. The columns are in kilobytes by default and are

- **swpd:** amount of swapped-out memory
- **free:** free available memory
- **buff:** memory in the buffer cache
- **cache:** memory in the page cache
- **si:** memory swapped in (paging)
- **so:** memory swapped out (paging)

The buffer and page caches are described in Chapter 8, File Systems. It is normal for the free memory in the system to drop after boot and be used by these caches to improve performance. It can be released for application use when needed.

If the si and so columns are continually nonzero, the system is under memory pressure and is paging to a swap device or file (see swapon(8)). Other tools, including memory by process, can be used to investigate what is consuming memory.

On systems with large amounts of memory, the columns can become unaligned and a little difficult to read. You can try changing the output units to megabytes using the -S option:

```
$ vmstat 1 -Sm
procs -----------memory---------- ---swap-- -----io---- -system-- ----cpu----
 r  b   swpd   free   buff  cache   si   so    bi    bo   in   cs us sy id wa
 4  0      0  35280    114  13761    0    0     0     5    2    1  0  0 100  0
 4  0      0  35281    114  13761    0    0     0     0 2027 15146 16 13 70  0
[...]
```

There is also a −a option for printing a breakdown of *inactive* and *active* memory from the page cache:

```
$ vmstat -a 1
procs -----------memory---------- ---swap-- -----io---- -system-- ----cpu----
 r  b   swpd     free   inact active   si   so    bi    bo   in   cs us sy id wa
 5  0      0 34453536 10358040 3201540  0    0     0     5    2    0  0  0 100  0
 4  0      0 34453228 10358040 3200648  0    0     0     0 2464 15261 16 12 71  0
[...]
```

These memory statistics can be printed as a list using the −s option.

Solaris

On Solaris-based systems, the vmstat(1) command more closely resembles the original from BSD. There are many fields showing activity of the page-out daemon, making it a little unfriendly for those who have yet to learn the page scanner internals.

Here is example output:

```
$ vmstat 1
 kthr     memory            page            disk          faults      cpu
 r b w   swap  free   re  mf pi po fr de sr lf rm s0 s1   in   sy   cs us sy id
 1 0 9 85726296 6870964 273 9852 124 241 261 0 1165 0 -784 -0 152 37912 60785 22501
14 7 79
 0 0 113 106216432 26827696 535 4840 24 0 0 0 0 0 29 36891 85679 29106 11 5 84
 0 0 113 106223888 26831880 128 1608 8 0 0 0 0 0 0 10 40656 74944 26552 19 5 76
 1 0 113 106224396 26827560 3 1450 40 0 0 0 0 0 0 24 35755 74409 27757 19 5 77
[...]
```

On systems with large amounts of memory, the columns become unaligned. The first line of output is the summary-since-boot. The memory-related columns are

- **w:** number of swapped-out threads
- **swap:** available virtual memory (Kbytes)
- **free:** free available memory, including page cache and free lists (Kbytes)
- **re:** pages reclaimed from the page cache (cache hits)
- **mf:** minor faults

- **pi:** memory paged in, all types (Kbytes)
- **po:** memory paged out, all types (Kbytes)
- **fr:** page cache memory freed by the page scanner or file system (Kbytes)
- **de:** deficit—the anticipated short-term memory shortfall (Kbytes) (see the Solaris section of Section 7.3.2, Software)
- **sr:** pages scanned by the page-out daemon

The example output shows a system that has had a problem in the past, with 113 threads swapped out (w). The page scanner is not currently running (sr), so the system is not currently under excessive memory pressure. There is a small rate of page-ins (pi), although they could be normal (file system) or abnormal (anonymous).

The -p option shows the breakdown of page-ins, page-outs, and frees:

```
$ vmstat -p 1
     memory              page          executable       anonymous        filesystem
   swap    free   re  mf   fr  de  sr  epi epo epf  api apo apf  fpi fpo fpf
85726500 6871164 273 9852 261 0 1165 0    0   0   0  123 240 261   1   0   1
106233644 26826364 10 1035 0 0 0     0    0   0   0   12   0   0   0   0   0
106247632 26842396 127 2092 0 0 0    0    0   0   0   48   0   0   0   0   0
106240192 26842796 5 1625 0 0  0     0    0   0   0   20   0   0   0   0   0
[...]
```

This system has a rate of anonymous page-ins (api), which is the "bad" paging. This causes synchronous disk I/O-level latency during application runtime. In this case, it would be due to a previous memory pressure event that paged out memory and the active threads are currently being paged back in.

If needed, many of these statistics can be observed per CPU from kstat. See the cpu::vm: groups of statistics. kstat was introduced in Chapter 4, Observability Tools.

It is normal for the free memory (free) to drop after system boot, as memory is used by the page cache and other kernel caches. This memory can be returned for application use when needed. It is not normal for the system to have a continual rate of page scanning (sr), which is a sign of a memory pressure issue. If this is the case, use other tools, such as memory by process, to see where the memory is used.

7.5.2 sar

The system activity reporter, sar(1), can be used to observe current activity and can be configured to archive and report historical statistics. It is mentioned in various chapters in this book for the different statistics it provides.

Linux

The Linux version provides memory statistics via the following options:

- **-B:** paging statistics
- **-H:** huge pages statistics
- **-r:** memory utilization
- **-R:** memory statistics
- **-S:** swap space statistics
- **-W:** swapping statistics

These span memory usage, activity of the page-out daemon, and huge pages usage. See Section 7.3, Architecture, for background on these topics.

Statistics provided include those in Table 7.5.

Table 7-5 Linux sar Statistics

Option	Statistic	Description	Units
-B	pgpgin/s	page-ins	Kbytes/s
-B	pgpgout/s	page-outs	Kbytes/s
-B	fault/s	both major and minor faults	count/s
-B	majflt/s	major faults	count/s
-B	pgfree/s	pages added to free list	count/s
-B	pgscank/s	pages scanned by background page-out daemon (kswapd)	count/s
-B	pgscand/s	direct page scans	count/s
-B	pgsteal/s	page and swap cache reclaims	count/s
-B	%vmeff	ratio of page steal/page scan, which shows page reclaim efficiency	percent
-H	hbhugfree	free huge pages memory (large page size)	Kbytes
-H	hbhugused	used huge pages memory	Kbytes
-r	kbmemfree	free memory	Kbytes
-r	kbmemused	used memory (excluding the kernel)	Kbytes
-r	kbbuffers	buffer cache size	Kbytes
-r	kbcached	page cache size	Kbytes
-r	kbcommit	main memory committed: an estimate of the amount needed to serve the current workload	Kbytes

continues

Table 7-5 Linux sar Statistics (*Continued*)

Option	Statistic	Description	Units
-r	%commit	main memory committed for current workload, estimate	percent
-r	kbactive	active list memory size	Kbytes
-r	kbinact	inactive list memory size	Kbytes
-R	frpg/s	memory pages freed; negative indicates allocations	pages/s
-R	bufpg/s	buffer cache page additions (growth)	pages/s
-R	campg/s	page cache page additions (growth)	pages/s
-S	kbswpfree	free swap space	Kbytes
-S	kbswpused	used swap space	Kbytes
-S	kbswpcad	cached swap space: this resides in both main memory and the swap device and so can be paged out without disk I/O	Kbytes
-W	pswpin/s	page-ins (Linux "swap-ins")	pages/s
-W	pswpout/s	page-outs (Linux "swap-outs")	pages/s

Many of the statistic names include the units measured: pg for pages, kb for kilobytes, % for a percentage, and /s for per second. See the man page for the full list, which includes some additional percentage-based statistics.

It is important to remember that this much detail is available, when needed, on the usage and operation of high-level memory subsystems. To understand these in deeper detail, you may need to browse the source code in mm, specifically mm/vmscan.c. There are also many posts to the linux-mm mailing list that provide further insight, as the developers discuss what the statistics should be.

The %vmeff metric is an interesting measure of page reclaim efficiency. High means pages are successfully stolen from the inactive list (healthy); low means the system is struggling. The man page describes near 100% as high, and less than 30% as low.

Solaris

The Solaris version provides these options:

- **-g:** paging statistics
- **-k:** kernel memory allocation statistics
- **-p:** paging activities
- **-r:** unused memory metrics
- **-w:** swapping statistics

These span memory usage, kernel allocations, paging, and swapping. See Section 7.3, Architecture, for background on these topics.

Statistics provided include those shown in Table 7.6.

Table 7-6 Solaris sar Statistics

Option	Statistic	Description	Units
-g	pgout/s	page-out requests	operations/s
-g	ppgout/s	pages paged out	pages/s
-g	pgfree/s	page added to free list by the page-out daemon	pages/s
-g	pgscan/s	page scanned by the page-out daemon	pages/s
-k	small	memory in small kmem caches (object size <= 256 bytes)	bytes
-k	large	memory in larger kmem caches (object size > 256 bytes)	bytes
-k	ovsz_alloc	memory in kmem oversize (usually > 128 Kbyte objects)	bytes
-p	atch/s	reclaims (attaches) from the page cache	pages/s
-p	pgin/s	page-in requests	operations/s
-p	ppgin/s	pages paged in	pages/s
-p	pflt/s	page faults from protection or copy-on-write (COW)	pages/s
-p	vflt/s	page faults from address translation	pages/s
-p	slock/s	page faults from software lock requests requiring disk I/O	pages/s
-r	freemem	free memory (see units)	pages
-r	freeswap	free physical swap (see units)	blocks (sectors)
-w	swpin/s	swap-ins (process swapping)	count/s
-w	swpout/s	swap-outs (process swapping)	count/s

The -k breakdown into "small" and "large" pools seems unusual today. I suspect this is a historic leftover from supporting SVR4's lazy buddy allocator, which used large and small memory pools [Vahalia 96].

More statistics for the memory subsystems can be read from kstat or constructed dynamically using DTrace.

7.5.3 slabtop

The Linux slabtop(1) command prints kernel slab cache usage from the slab allocator. Like top(1), it refreshes the screen in real time.

Here is some example output:

```
$ slabtop -sc
 Active / Total Objects (% used)   : 3590651 / 3682877 (97.5%)
 Active / Total Slabs (% used)     : 94610 / 94610 (100.0%)
 Active / Total Caches (% used)    : 58 / 83 (69.9%)
 Active / Total Size (% used)      : 432643.91K / 477592.84K (90.6%)
 Minimum / Average / Maximum Object : 0.01K / 0.13K / 12.75K

  OBJS ACTIVE  USE OBJ SIZE  SLABS OBJ/SLAB CACHE SIZE NAME
3345069 3334148  99%    0.10K  85771       39    343084K buffer_head
151728  77833  51%    0.55K   5232       29     83712K radix_tree_node
  5520   4495  81%    2.00K    345       16     11040K kmalloc-2048
 11193  11185  99%    0.82K    287       39      9184K ext3_inode_cache
  9464   9464 100%    0.61K    182       52      5824K inode_cache
 29064  28977  99%    0.19K    692       42      5536K dentry
  4896   4734  96%    0.66K    102       48      3264K proc_inode_cache
   380    344  90%    5.73K     76        5      2432K task_struct
 20094  20094 100%    0.08K    394       51      1576K sysfs_dir_cache
[...]
```

The output has a summary at the top and a list of slabs, including their object count (OBJS), how many are active (ACTIVE), percent used (USE), the size of the objects (OBJ SIZE, bytes), and the total size of the cache (CACHE SIZE, bytes).

In this example, the -sc option was used to sort by cache size, with the largest at the top.

The slab statistics are from /proc/slabinfo and can also be printed using vmstat -m.

7.5.4 ::kmastat

On Solaris-based systems, the ::kmastat debugger command (dcmd) for mdb(1) summarizes kernel memory usage. The output is in three parts: slab allocator cache usage, usage summaries, and vmem usage summaries.

Here is some example output:

```
# mdb -k
> ::kmastat
cache                          buf      buf      buf memory    alloc alloc
name                          size   in use    total in use   succeed fail
------------------------------ ----- --------- --------- ------ ---------- -----
kmem_magazine_1                  16     6547     55471   884K     550935     0
kmem_magazine_3                  32    22454     23125   740K      57447     0
kmem_magazine_7                  64    18045     29698   1.87M     98639     0
kmem_magazine_15                128     8083     41075   5.18M    5838996     0
kmem_magazine_31                256    13452     13470   3.51M      21535     0
```

```
kmem_magazine_47                   384       158     18890  7.38M      23037    0
[...]
---------------------------- ----- ---------- ---------- ------ ---------- -----
Total [hat_memload]                                    18.0M 2904783556    0
Total [kmem_msb]                                         593M  125192718    0
Total [kmem_va]                                        11.0G    2232820    0
Total [kmem_default]                                   11.1G 3156770876    0
Total [kmem_io_64G]                                    3.99M       4083    0
Total [kmem_io_4G]                                     1.99M       7156    0
Total [kmem_io_2G]                                       20K         52    0
Total [bp_map]                                          512K      33145    0
Total [umem_np]                                        2.25M       2494    0
Total [id32]                                              8K       1634    0
Total [zfs_file_data]                                  23.1G   46011272    0
Total [zfs_file_data_buf]                              23.4G   50697539    0
Total [segkp]                                          1.69M    2869123    0
[...]
vmem                         memory    memory    memory    alloc alloc
name                         in use     total    import  succeed  fail
---------------------------- ---------- ---------- ---------- ---------- -----
heap                           13.2G      971G         0 368844548    0
   vmem_metadata               617M      617M      617M    147416    0
      vmem_seg                 575M      575M      575M    147133    0
      vmem_hash               41.6M     41.6M     41.6M        79    0
      vmem_vmem                373K      416K      380K       238    0
   static                         0         0         0         0    0
      static_alloc                0         0         0         0    0
   hat_memload               18.0M     18.0M     18.0M      4620    0
   kstat                      1.60M     1.65M     1.59M     14523    0
   kmem_metadata               676M      676M      676M    152699    0
[...]
```

The output was over 500 lines long and has been truncated here. While verbose, this can be invaluable when tracking down the source of kernel memory growth.

Other useful memory-related dcmds include ::kmem_slabs, ::kmem_slabs -v, and ::memstat. For example:

```
> ::memstat
Page Summary              Pages              MB  %Tot
------------        ------------------  ------------------  ----
Kernel                   3793378              14817   30%
ZFS File Data            5924809              23143   47%
Anon                     2194335               8571   17%
Exec and libs              11649                 45    0%
Page cache                 51625                201    0%
Free (cachelist)           12733                 49    0%
Free (freelist)           589031               2300    5%

Total                   12577560              49131
Physical                12577559              49131
```

While this is a useful summary, a downside is that you must be the superuser (root) and running mdb -k to view it.

7.5.5 ps

The process status command, ps(1), lists details on all processes, including memory usage statistics. Its usage was introduced in Chapter 6, CPUs.

For example, using the BSD-style options:

```
$ ps aux
USER          PID %CPU %MEM    VSZ    RSS TTY   STAT START    TIME COMMAND
[...]
bind         1152  0.0  0.4 348916 39568 ?     Ssl  Mar27   20:17 /usr/sbin/named -u bind
root         1371  0.0  0.0  39004  2652 ?     Ss   Mar27   11:04 /usr/lib/postfix/master
root         1386  0.0  0.6 207564 50684 ?     Sl   Mar27    1:57 /usr/sbin/console-kit-
daemon --no-daemon
rabbitmq     1469  0.0  0.0  10708   172 ?     S    Mar27    0:49 /usr/lib/erlang/erts-
5.7.4/bin/epmd -daemon
rabbitmq     1486  0.1  0.0 150208  2884 ?     Ssl  Mar27 453:29 /usr/lib/erlang/erts-
5.7.4/bin/beam.smp -W w -K true -A30 ...
```

This output includes the following columns:

- **%MEM:** main memory usage (physical memory, RSS) as a percentage of the total in the system
- **RSS:** resident set size (Kbytes)
- **VSZ:** virtual memory size (Kbytes)

While RSS shows main memory usage, it includes shared segments such as system libraries, which may be mapped by dozens of processes. If you were to sum the RSS column, you may find it exceeds the memory available in the system, due to overcounting of this shared memory. See the later pmap(1) command for analysis of shared memory usage.

These columns may be selected using the SVR4-style –o option, for example:

```
# ps -eo pid,pmem,vsz,rss,comm
  PID %MEM  VSZ  RSS COMMAND
[...]
13419  0.0 5176 1796 /opt/local/sbin/nginx
13879  0.1 31060 22880 /opt/local/bin/ruby19
13418  0.0 4984 1456 /opt/local/sbin/nginx
15101  0.0 4580   32 /opt/riak/lib/os_mon-2.2.6/priv/bin/memsup
10933  0.0 3124 2212 /usr/sbin/rsyslogd
[...]
```

The **Linux** version can also print columns for major and minor faults (maj_flt, min_flt).

On **Solaris**, major and minor fault information is available in /proc but not currently exposed from ps(1). Also note that there was a bug with the aux output where the RSS and VSZ columns can be merged—a whitespace separator is missing. This was fixed in recent illumos/SmartOS.

The output of ps(1) can be post-sorted on the memory columns so that the highest consumers can be quickly identified. Or, try the top(1) and prstat(1M) tools, which provide sorting options.

7.5.6 top

The top(1) command monitors top running processes and includes memory usage statistics. It was introduced in Chapter 6, CPUs. For example, on **Linux**:

```
top - 00:53:33 up 242 days,  2:38,   7 users,  load average: 1.48, 1.64, 2.10
Tasks: 261 total,   1 running, 260 sleeping,   0 stopped,   0 zombie
Cpu(s):  0.0%us,  0.0%sy,  0.0%ni, 99.9%id,  0.0%wa,  0.0%hi,  0.0%si,  0.0%st
Mem:   8181740k total,  6658640k used,  1523100k free,   404744k buffers
Swap:  2932728k total,   120508k used,  2812220k free,  2893684k cached

  PID USER       PR  NI  VIRT  RES  SHR S %CPU %MEM   TIME+  COMMAND
29625 scott      20   0 2983m 2.2g 1232 S   45 28.7  81:11.31 node
 5121 joshw      20   0  222m 193m  804 S    0  2.4 260:13.40 tmux
 1386 root       20   0  202m  49m 1224 S    0  0.6   1:57.70 console-kit-dae
 6371 stu        20   0 65196  38m  292 S    0  0.5  23:11.13 screen
 1152 bind       20   0  340m  38m 1700 S    0  0.5  20:17.36 named
15841 joshw      20   0 67144  23m  908 S    0  0.3 201:37.91 mosh-server
18496 root       20   0 57384  16m 1972 S    3  0.2   2:59.99 python
 1258 root       20   0  125m 8684 8264 S    0  0.1  2052:01 l2tpns
16295 wesolows   20   0 95752 7396  944 S    0  0.1   4:46.07 sshd
23783 brendan    20   0 22204 5036 1676 S    0  0.1   0:00.15 bash
[...]
```

The summary at the top shows total, used, and free for both main memory (Mem) and virtual memory (Swap). The sizes of the buffer cache (buffers) and page cache (cached) are also shown.

In this example, the per-process output has been sorted on %MEM by configuring top using O and changing the sort order. The largest process in this example is node, using 2.2 Gbytes of main memory and almost 3 Gbytes of virtual memory.

The main memory percentage column (%MEM), virtual memory size (VIRT), and resident set size (RES) have the same meanings as the equivalent columns from ps(1) described earlier.

7.5.7 prstat

The prstat(1M) command was introduced as a top for Solaris-based systems and was covered in Chapter 6, CPUs. For example:

```
$ prstat -cs rss 1
Please wait...
   PID USERNAME  SIZE   RSS STATE   PRI NICE      TIME  CPU PROCESS/NLWP
  4937 root       65G   45G sleep    60    0  21:03:47 0.7% redis-server/3
    47 root      455M  330M cpu3     59    0  38:18:13 2.1% node/6
   289 root      439M  311M cpu8     59    0  38:07:13 2.1% node/6
 25433 root      310M  272M sleep    59    0   2:23:32 0.9% node/2
 26533 root      308M  263M cpu5     59    0   2:19:51 0.8% node/2
 26068 root      284M  244M cpu15    59    0   2:14:33 1.2% node/2
 26219 root      275M  243M sleep    59    0   2:27:36 1.4% node/2
 26334 root      283M  240M sleep    59    0   2:29:36 0.8% node/2
 26067 root      277M  235M cpu0     59    0   2:16:57 1.1% node/2
 25260 root      271M  233M sleep    59    0   2:13:22 0.8% node/2
 25154 root      263M  225M sleep    59    0   2:17:11 1.0% node/2
 10987 root      296M  223M sleep    59    0  14:37:14 1.8% node/6
 15247 root     2917M  195M sleep   100    -   0:07:22 0.0% node/5
  4042 root      194M  154M cpu13    59    0   4:57:23 0.9% node/6
  8891 1001      300M  126M sleep    59    0   0:26:46 0.1% splunkd/24
```

In this example, the sort order was set to RSS (-s rss) so that the largest memory consumers were listed at the top. The process named redis-server is the largest by far, consuming 45 Gbytes of main memory (RSS) and 65 Gbytes of virtual memory (SIZE).

prstat(1M) can print microstate accounting statistics, which include text- and data-fault times. For this server:

```
$ prstat -mLcp 4937 1
Please wait...
   PID USERNAME USR SYS TRP TFL DFL LCK SLP LAT VCX ICX SCL SIG PROCESS/LWPID
  4937 root     7.4 7.9 0.0 0.0  15 0.0  69 0.2 239  31  3K   0 redis-server/1
  4937 root     0.0 0.0 0.0 0.0 0.0 100 0.0 0.0   0   0   0   0 redis-server/3
  4937 root     0.0 0.0 0.0 0.0 0.0 100 0.0 0.0   0   0   0   0 redis-server/2
Total: 1 processes, 3 lwps, load averages: 5.28, 5.36, 5.36
[...]
```

This large redis-server process has a percentage of time spent waiting for data faults (DFL). This is the same server from the earlier vmstat -p example, which showed a rate of anonymous page-ins. These two things may be related: the system may have run low on memory and paged out redis-server, which is now spending time waiting (DFL) as it is paged back in.

7.5.8 pmap

The pmap(1) command lists the memory mappings of a process, showing their sizes, permissions, and mapped objects. This allows process memory usage to be examined in more detail, and shared memory to be quantified.

For example, on a Solaris-based system:

```
# pmap -x 13504
13504:  /opt/local/bin/postgres -D /var/pgsql/data90
 Address   Kbytes       RSS    Anon  Locked Mode     Mapped File
08027000      132       132       4       - rw---    [ stack ]
08050000     4204      1880       -       - r-x--    postgres
0847A000       28        28       -       - rwx--    postgres
08481000      260        48       -       - rwx--    postgres
084C2000      248       212      20       - rwx--    [ heap ]
FC400000    36112     36112       -   36112 rwxsR    [ ism shmid=0x1 ]
FE8E0000      904        68       -       - r-x--    libiconv.so.2.5.0
FE9D1000        4         4       -       - rwx--    libiconv.so.2.5.0
FE9E0000     1220      1220       -       - r-x--    libc_hwcap1.so.1
FEB21000       36        36      12       - rwx--    libc_hwcap1.so.1
FEB2A000        8         8       -       - rwx--    libc_hwcap1.so.1
FEB30000      416       416       -       - r-x--    libnsl.so.1
FEBA8000        8         8       -       - rw---    libnsl.so.1
FEBAA000       20        20       -       - rw---    libnsl.so.1
FEBD0000      304       304       -       - r-x--    libm.so.2
FEC2B000       16        16       -       - rwx--    libm.so.2
FEC81000        4         4       -       - rwxs-    [ anon ]
FEC90000       64         8       -       - rwx--    [ anon ]
FECAC000       76        32       -       - r----    LCL_DATA
[...]
```

This shows the memory mappings of a PostgreSQL database, including virtual memory (Kbytes), main memory (RSS), private anonymous memory (Anon), and permissions (Mode). For most of the mappings, very little memory is anonymous, and much of it is read-only (r-x), meaning those pages can be shared with other processes. This is especially the case for system libraries. The bulk of the memory consumed in this example is in a shared memory segment (ism).

The **Linux** version of pmap(1) is similar and is based on the Solaris version. More recent versions use the term Dirty instead of Anon.

The **Solaris** version provides a -s option to show the page size of mappings:

```
# pmap -xs 13504
13504:  /opt/local/bin/postgres -D /var/pgsql/data90
 Address   Kbytes       RSS    Anon  Locked Pgsz Mode    Mapped File
08027000      132       132       4       -   4K rw---   [ stack ]
[...]
FC400000    34816     34816       -   34816   2M rwxsR   [ ism shmid=0x1 ]
FE600000     1296      1296       -    1296   4K rwxsR   [ ism shmid=0x1 ]
[...]
```

The shared-memory segment for this PostgreSQL database was mostly using 2 Mbyte pages.

The output of pmap(1) can be long for processes with many mappings. It also pauses the process as it reports memory usage, which can hurt the performance of active work. It is useful to run when needed for diagnosis and analysis, but it shouldn't be run regularly as a monitoring tool.

7.5.9 DTrace

DTrace can be used to trace user- and kernel-level allocations, minor and major page faults, and the operation of the page-out daemon. These abilities support characterizing usage and drill-down analysis.

The following sections introduce DTrace for memory analysis on Solaris- and Linux-based systems. Unless noted, the DTrace commands are intended for both operating systems. A DTrace primer was included in Chapter 4, Observability Tools.

Allocation Tracing

User-level allocators can be traced using the pid provider, if available. This is a dynamic tracing provider, which means software can be instrumented at any moment, without restarting, and without needing to configure allocators to run in debug mode beforehand.

The following example summarizes the requested size of `malloc()` calls, for PID 15041 (a Riak database):

```
# dtrace -n 'pid$target::malloc:entry { @["requested bytes"] =
    quantize(arg0); }' -p 15041
dtrace: description 'pid$target::malloc:entry ' matched 3 probes
^C

  requested bytes
            value  ------------- Distribution ------------- count
              256 |                                         0
              512 |@@@@                                     3824
             1024 |@@@@@@@@@@@@@@@@@@                       17807
             2048 |@@@@@@@@@@@@@@                           13564
             4096 |@@@@@@                                   5907
             8192 |@                                        1040
            16384 |                                         0
```

All of the requested allocations were between 512 bytes and 16,383 bytes, and most were in the 1–2 Kbyte range.

This one-liner summarizes the requested bytes for `malloc()`, which is the first argument, by passing it (`arg0`) to the power-of-two `quantize()` aggregating function. If desired, the return value of `malloc()` can be traced as well, to check that the allocation succeeded.

The key was set to `"requested bytes"` merely to decorate the output with a description. This key can include the user-level stack trace using the `ustack()` action:

```
# dtrace -n 'pid$target::malloc:entry { @["requested bytes, for:", ustack()] =
    quantize(arg0); }' -p 15041
dtrace: description 'pid$target::malloc:entry ' matched 3 probes
[...]
  requested bytes, for:
              libumem.so.1`malloc
              libstdc++.so.6.0.13`_Znwm+0x1e
              libstdc++.so.6.0.13`_Znam+0x9

              eleveldb.so`_ZN7leveldb9ReadBlockEPNS_16RandomAccessFileERKNS_...

              eleveldb.so`_ZN7leveldb5Table11BlockReaderEPvRKNS_11ReadOption...

              eleveldb.so`_ZN7leveldb12_GLOBAL__N_116TwoLevelIterator13InitD...

              eleveldb.so`_ZN7leveldb12_GLOBAL__N_116TwoLevelIterator4SeekER...

              eleveldb.so`_ZN7leveldb12_GLOBAL__N_115MergingIterator4SeekERK...

              eleveldb.so`_ZN7leveldb12_GLOBAL__N_16DBIter4SeekERKNS_5SliceE...
              eleveldb.so`eleveldb_iterator_move+0x24b
              beam.smp`process_main+0x6939
              beam.smp`sched_thread_func+0x1cf
              beam.smp`thr_wrapper+0xbe
              0xfffffd7fe4d7b862
              0xb8c0000000000000

        value  ------------- Distribution ------------- count
          256 |                                         0
          512 |@@@@@                                    1
         1024 |@@@@@@@@@@                               2
         2048 |@@@@@@@@@@@@@@@@@@@@@@@@@@@               5
         4096 |                                         0
```

In this case, the output was many pages long and has been truncated to fit. It shows user-level stack traces that led to the allocation, along with a distribution of the requested allocation size.

Since allocations are a frequent activity, the cost of tracing—although fast per event—can start to add up and cause performance overhead while tracing.

Other internals of user-level allocators can be investigated. For example, listing the entry probes for the libumem allocator:

```
# dtrace -ln 'pid$target:libumem::entry' -p 15041
   ID    PROVIDER        MODULE                    FUNCTION NAME
73348    pid15041        libumem.so.1                malloc entry
73350    pid15041        libumem.so.1        vmem_heap_init entry
73351    pid15041        libumem.so.1        umem_type_init entry
73352    pid15041        libumem.so.1     umem_get_max_ncpus entry
73353    pid15041        libumem.so.1   __umem_agent_free_bp entry
73354    pid15041        libumem.so.1         umem_do_abort entry
73355    pid15041        libumem.so.1       print_stacktrace entry
73356    pid15041        libumem.so.1            umem_panic entry
73357    pid15041        libumem.so.1   umem_err_recoverable entry
73358    pid15041        libumem.so.1   __umem_assert_failed entry
73359    pid15041        libumem.so.1                   T.4 entry
73360    pid15041        libumem.so.1     umem_lockup_cache entry
[...]
```

The output listed 163 entry probes. These can be used to build more complex one-liners and scripts to investigate allocator internals.

Kernel-level allocators can be traced in a similar way, using the dynamic fbt provider. For example, on **Solaris**-based systems, the following one-liner traces the slab allocator:

```
# dtrace -n 'fbt::kmem_cache_alloc:entry {
    @[stringof(args[0]->cache_name), stack()] = count(); }'
dtrace: description 'fbt::kmem_cache_alloc:entry ' matched 1 probe
[...]
  zio_cache
                zfs`zio_create+0x79
                zfs`zio_null+0x77
                zfs`zio_root+0x2d
                zfs`dmu_buf_hold_array_by_dnode+0x113
                zfs`dmu_buf_hold_array+0x78
                zfs`dmu_read_uio+0x5c
                zfs`zfs_read+0x1a3
                genunix`fop_read+0x8b
                genunix`read+0x2a7
                genunix`read32+0x1e
                unix`_sys_sysenter_post_swapgs+0x149
            38686
  streams_dblk_16
                genunix`allocb+0x9e
                fifofs`fifo_write+0x1a5
                genunix`fop_write+0x8b
                genunix`write+0x250
                unix`sys_syscall+0x17a
            38978
```

The output includes the name of the cache, followed by the kernel stack trace for allocations, and then the count while tracing.

The following one-liners show different ways to trace allocations, for both user- and kernel-level allocators.

One-Liners

Summarize user-level `malloc()` request size for process PID:

```
dtrace -n 'pid$target::malloc:entry { @["request"] = quantize(arg0); }' -p PID
```

Summarize user-level `malloc()` request size with call stack for process PID:

```
dtrace -n 'pid$target::malloc:entry { @[ustack()] = quantize(arg0); }' -p PID
```

Count libumem function calls:

```
dtrace -n 'pid$target:libumem::entry { @[probefunc] = count(); }' -p PID
```

Count user-level stacks for heap growth (via brk()):

```
dtrace -n 'syscall::brk:entry { @[execname, ustack()] = count(); }'
```

Trace kernel-level slab allocations by cache name and stack (Solaris):

```
dtrace -n 'fbt::kmem_cache_alloc:entry { @[stringof(args[0]->cache_name),
    stack()] = count(); }'
```

Fault Tracing

Tracing of page faults can provide further insight into how the system is serving memory. It can be performed using either the dynamic fbt provider or the stable vminfo provider where available.

For example, on **Solaris**-based systems, the following one-liner traces minor faults for processes named "beam.smp" (this is the Erlang VM, which in this case is running the Riak database) and frequency counts the user-level stack trace, five levels deep:

```
# dtrace -n 'vminfo:::as_fault /execname == "beam.smp"/ {
    @[ustack(5)] = count(); }
dtrace: description 'vminfo:::as_fault ' matched 1 probe
[...]
              beam.smp`erts_add_monitor+0x29d
              beam.smp`monitor_2+0x293
              beam.smp`process_main+0x51db
              beam.smp`sched_thread_func+0x1cf
              beam.smp`thr_wrapper+0xbe
              723

              beam.smp`erts_sweep_monitors+0xae
              beam.smp`process_info_aux+0x154a
              beam.smp`process_info_2+0x70f
              beam.smp`process_main+0x69e8
              beam.smp`sched_thread_func+0x1cf
          43745
```

This summarizes the code paths that are consuming memory and causing minor faults. In this case, it is the Erlang garbage collect code. Major faults can also be traced using the vminfo:::maj_fault probe.

Another useful fault-related probe is `vminfo:::anonpgin`, for anonymous page-ins. For example:

```
# dtrace -n 'vminfo:::anonpgin { @[pid, execname] = count(); }'
dtrace: description 'vminfo:::anonpgin ' matched 1 probe
^C

    26533  node                                                         1
    26067  node                                                         6
     4937  redis-server                                               907
```

This traced system-wide, frequency counting the process ID and process name that led to anonymous page-ins. This is the same system shown by the earlier `vmstat(1)` example that identified anonymous page-ins, and the `prstat(1M)` example that identified that `redis-server` was spending time in data faults. This DTrace one-liner has connected the dots, confirming that the `redis-server` is spending time in *anonymous* page-ins, which are a result of low system memory and paging.

Page-Out Daemon

If needed, the internal operation of the page-out daemon can also be traced using the fbt provider. The specifics depend on the kernel version.

7.5.10 SystemTap

SystemTap can also be used on Linux systems for dynamic tracing of file system events. See Section 4.4, SystemTap, in Chapter 4, Observability Tools, and Appendix E for help with converting the previous DTrace scripts.

7.5.11 Other Tools

Other **Linux** memory performance tools include the following:

- **free:** report free memory, with buffer cache and page cache (see Chapter 8, File Systems).
- **dmesg:** check for "Out of memory" messages from the OOM killer.
- **valgrind:** a performance analysis suite, including memcheck, a wrapper for user-level allocators for memory usage analysis including leak detection. This costs significant overhead; the manual advises that it can cause the target to run 20 to 30 times slower [3].

- **swapon:** to add and observe physical swap devices or files.
- **iostat:** If the swap device is a physical disk or slice, device I/O may be observable using iostat(1), which indicates that the system is paging.
- **perf:** Introduced in Chapter 6, CPUs, this can be used to investigate CPI, MMU/TSB events, and memory bus stall cycles from the CPU performance instrumentation counters. It also provides probes for page faults and several kernel memory (kmem) events.
- **/proc/zoneinfo:** statistics for memory zones (NUMA nodes).
- **/proc/buddyinfo:** statistics for the kernel buddy allocator for pages.

Other **Solaris** memory performance tools include the following:

- **prtconf:** shows physical memory installed size (which can be filtered from the output using either | grep Mem, or –m on newer versions).
- **prtdiag:** shows physical memory layout (on systems that support it).
- **swap:** swap statistics: list swap devices (-l), and summarize usage (-s).
- **iostat:** If the swap device is a physical disk or slice, device I/O may be observable using iostat(1), which indicates that the system is paging or swapping.
- **cpustat:** Introduced in Chapter 6, CPUs, this can be used to investigate CPI, MMU/TSB events, and memory bus stall cycles from the CPU performance instrumentation counters.
- **trapstat:** print trap statistics, including TLB/TSB miss rates for different page sizes, and percent CPU consumed. Currently supported only on SPARC processors.
- **kstat:** contains more statistics for understanding kernel memory usage. For most of these, the only documentation is the source code (if available).

Applications and virtual machines (e.g., the Java VM) may also provide their own memory analysis tools. See Chapter 5, Applications.

Some allocators maintain their own statistics for observability. For example, the libumem library can be investigated using mdb(1) dcmds on **Solaris**:

```
# mdb leaky_core.11493
Loading modules: [ libumem.so.1 libc.so.1 ld.so.1 ]
> ::vmem
ADDR              NAME              INUSE       TOTAL     SUCCEED  FAIL
fffffd7ffdb6d4f0  sbrk_top          14678769664 31236771840 34038748 64125
fffffd7ffdb6e0f8   sbrk_heap        14678769664 14678769664 34038748     0
fffffd7ffdb6ed00    vmem_internal   320589824   320589824   71737       0
                                                                  continues
```

```
fffffd7ffdb6f908        vmem_seg          293679104    293679104     71699    0
fffffd7ffdb70510        vmem_hash          26870272     26873856        33    0
fffffd7ffdb71118        vmem_vmem             46200        55344        15    0
000000000067e000      umem_internal        91463936     91467776     20845    0
000000000067f000        umem_cache          113696       180224        44    0
0000000000680000        umem_hash          7455232      7458816        54    0
0000000000681000        umem_log                 0            0         0    0
0000000000682000      umem_firewall_va           0            0         0    0
0000000000683000      umem_firewall              0            0         0    0
0000000000684000      umem_oversize      5964579061   6179110912  32905555    0
0000000000686000      umem_memalign              0            0         0    0
0000000000695000      umem_default       8087601152   8087601152   1040611    0
> ::umem_malloc_info
CACHE              BUFSZ MAXMAL BUFMALLC  AVG_MAL    MALLOCED    OVERHEAD   %OVER
0000000000697028       8      0        0        0           0           0   0.0%
0000000000698028      16      8    19426        8      155400      160349 103.1%
0000000000699028      32     16    19529       16      312464      322383 103.1%
000000000069a028      48     32  1007337       24    24186306    24933364 103.0%
000000000069b028      64     48    54161       40     2166755     1354569  62.5%
[...]
00000000006b7028    4096   4080     5760     3489    20096972     3956788  19.6%
00000000006b8028    4544   4528   205210     4294   881092360    70876830   8.0%
00000000006b9028    8192   8176   544525     5560  3027503427  1476807373  48.7%
00000000006ba028    9216   9200    44217     8653   382609833    26574285   6.9%
00000000006bb028   12288  12272    76066    10578   804644858   136139430  16.9%
00000000006bc028   16384  16368    43619    13811   602419234   115723982  19.2%
```

This shows ::vmem, which prints the internal virtual memory structures used by libumem and their usage, and ::umem_malloc_info, which shows allocation statistics by cache, which can indicate the usage pattern of memory by size (compare BUFSZ with MALLOCED). While providing only basic attributes, these commands can shed light on what are typically opaque process heaps.

7.6 Tuning

The most important memory tuning is ensuring that the applications remain in main memory, and that paging and swapping do not occur frequently. Identifying this problem was covered in Section 7.4, Methodology, and Section 7.5, Analysis. This section discusses other memory tuning: kernel tunable parameters, configuring large pages, allocators, and resource controls.

The specifics of tuning—the options available and what to set them to—depend on the operating system version and the intended workload. The following sections, organized by tuning type, provide examples of what may be available, and why they may need to be tuned.

7.6.1 Tunable Parameters

This section describes tunable parameter examples for recent Linux and Solaris-based kernels.

Linux

Various memory tunable parameters are described in the kernel source documentation in Documentation/sysctl/vm.txt and can be set using `sysctl(8)`. The examples in Table 7.7 are from a 3.2.6 kernel, with defaults from Fedora 16.

Table 7-7 Example Linux Memory Tunables

Option	Default	Description
vm.dirty_background_bytes	0	amount of dirty memory to trigger pdflush background write-back
vm.dirty_background_ratio	10	percentage of dirty system memory to trigger pdflush background write-back
vm.dirty_bytes	0	amount of dirty memory that causes a writing process to start write-back
vm.dirty_ratio	20	ratio of dirty system memory to cause a writing process to begin write-back
vm.dirty_expire_centisecs	3,000	minimum time for dirty memory to be eligible for pdflush (promotes *write cancellation*)
vm.dirty_writeback_centisecs	500	pdflush wake-up interval (0 to disable)
vm.min_free_kbytes	dynamic	sets the desired free memory amount (some kernel atomic allocations can consume this)
vm.overcommit_memory	0	0 = use a heuristic to allow reasonable over-commits; 1 = always overcommit; 2 = don't overcommit
vm.swappiness	60	the degree to favor swapping (paging) for freeing memory over reclaiming it from the page cache
vm.vfs_cache_pressure	100	the degree to reclaim cached directory and inode objects; lower values retain them more; 0 means never reclaim—can easily lead to out-of-memory conditions

The tunables use a consistent naming scheme that includes the units. Note that dirty_background_bytes and dirty_background_ratio are mutually exclusive, as are dirty_bytes and dirty_ratio (only one may be set).

The size of vm.min_free_kbytes is set dynamically as a fraction of main memory. The algorithm to choose this is not linear, as the needs for free memory do not linearly scale with main memory size. (For reference, it is documented in mm/page_alloc.c.) vm.min_free_kbytes can be reduced to free up some memory for applications, but that can also cause the kernel to be overwhelmed during memory pressure and resort to using OOM sooner.

Another parameter for avoiding OOM is vm.overcommit_memory, which can be set to 2 to disable overcommit and avoid cases where this leads to OOM. If control of the OOM killer on a per-process basis is desired, check your kernel version for /proc tunables such as oom_adj or oom_score_adj. These should be described in Documentation/filesystems/proc.txt.

The vm.swappiness tunable can significantly affect performance should it begin swapping application memory earlier than desired. The value of this tunable can be between 0 and 100, with high values favoring swapping applications and therefore retaining the page cache. It may be desirable to set this to zero, so that application memory is retained as long as possible at the expense of the page cache. When there is still a memory shortage, the kernel can still use swapping.

Solaris

Table 7.8 shows key tunables for memory, which can be set in /etc/system, along with typical defaults. See the vendor documentation for the full list, instructions for setting each, descriptions, and warnings. Some of these were shown earlier in Figure 7.11.

Table 7-8 Example Solaris Memory Tunables

Option	Default	Units	Description
lotsfree	1/64 mem	pages	threshold to begin page scanning (with deficit)
desfree	1/128 mem	pages	target free memory; below this for 30 s triggers swapping
minfree	1/256 mem	pages	begin blocking memory allocations
throttlefree	1/256 mem	pages	threshold to block memory allocations (sleep)
pageout_reserve	1/512 mem	pages	reserved pages for page-out and scheduler
slowscan	100	pages/s	rate to begin scanning
fastscan	64 Mbytes	pages/s	maximum scan rate
maxpgio	40	pages	maximum queued page I/O allowed

The pagesize(1) command can be used to determine what these units mean. Note that adjusting kernel tunables is sometimes prohibited by company or vendor policy (check first). These should also be set to appropriate rates already and should not need adjusting.

On large memory systems (beyond 100 Gbytes), it can be worthwhile to tune some of these to lower values, to free up more memory for applications to use. On systems with multiple storage devices (e.g., storage arrays), maxpgio may need to be increased so that the queue length is more appropriate for the I/O capacity available.

7.6.2 Multiple Page Sizes

Large page sizes can improve memory I/O performance by improving the hit ratio of the TLB cache (increasing its reach). Most modern processors support multiple page sizes, such as a 4 Kbyte default and a 2 Mbyte large page.

On **Linux**, large pages (called *huge pages*) can be configured in a number of ways. For reference, see Documentation/vm/hugetlbpage.txt.

These usually begin with the creation of huge pages:

```
# echo 50 > /proc/sys/vm/nr_hugepages
# grep Huge /proc/meminfo
AnonHugePages:         0 kB
HugePages_Total:      50
HugePages_Free:       50
HugePages_Rsvd:        0
HugePages_Surp:        0
Hugepagesize:       2048 kB
```

One way for an application to consume huge pages is via the shared memory segments, and the SHM_HUGETLBS flag to shmget().

Another way involves creating a huge-page-based file system for applications to map memory from:

```
# mkdir /mnt/hugetlbfs
# mount -t hugetlbfs none /mnt/hugetlbfs -o pagesize=2048K
```

Other ways include the MAP_ANONYMOUS|MAP_HUGETLB flags to mmap() and use of the libhugetlbfs API [4].

More recently, support has been developed for *transparent huge pages* (THP). This uses huge pages when appropriate, without manual steps from the system administrator [5]. For reference, see Documentation/vm/transhuge.txt.

On **Solaris**-based systems, large pages can be configured by configuring the application environment to use the libmpss.so.1 library. For example:

```
$ LD_PRELOAD=$LD_PRELOAD:mpss.so.1
$ MPSSHEAP=2M
$ export LD_PRELOAD MPSSHEAP
```

These can be placed in a start script for the application. Large pages are created dynamically by the kernel, and it is successful only if enough pages are available to create them (otherwise the default is smaller pages).

Programs compiled using Oracle Solaris Studio may automatically use large pages so do not need manual preloading of mpss.

7.6.3 Allocators

Different user-level allocators may be available, offering improved performance for multithreaded applications. These may be selected at compile time, or at execution time by setting the LD_PRELOAD environment variable.

For example, on **Solaris** the libumem allocator can be selected using

```
export LD_PRELOAD=libumem.so
```

This may be placed in its start-up script.

7.6.4 Resource Controls

Basic resource controls, including setting a main memory limit and a virtual memory limit, may be available using ulimit(1).

For **Linux**, the container groups (cgroups) memory subsystem provides various additional controls. These include

- **memory.memsw.limit_in_bytes:** the maximum allowed memory and swap space, in bytes
- **memory.limit_in_bytes:** the maximum allowed user memory, including file cache usage, in bytes
- **memory.swappiness:** similar to vm.swappiness described earlier but can be set for a cgroup
- **memory.oom_control:** can be set to 0, to allow the OOM killer for this cgroup, or 1, to disable it

On **Solaris**-based systems, per-zone or per-project memory limits can be applied using resource controls and the prctl(1) command. These can enforce their limit by paging out memory, rather than failing allocations, which may be more desirable depending on the target application. These are described in Section 11.2, OS Virtualization, in Chapter 11, Cloud Computing.

7.7 Exercises

1. Answer the following questions about memory terminology:
   - What is a page of memory?
   - What is resident memory?
   - What is virtual memory?
   - Using Unix terminology, what is the difference between paging and swapping?
   - Using Linux terminology, what is the difference between paging and swapping?

2. Answer the following conceptual questions:
   - What is the purpose of demand paging?
   - Describe memory utilization and saturation.
   - What is the purpose of the MMU and the TLB?
   - What is the role of the page-out daemon?
   - What is the role of the OOM killer?

3. Answer the following deeper questions:
   - What is anonymous paging, and why is it more important to analyze than file system paging?
   - Describe the steps the kernel takes to free up more memory when free memory becomes exhausted on Linux- or Solaris-based systems (pick one).
   - Describe the performance advantages of slab-based allocation.

4. Develop the following procedures for your operating system:
   - A USE method checklist for memory resources. Include how to fetch each metric (e.g., which command to execute) and how to interpret the result. Try to use existing OS observability tools before installing or using additional software products.
   - A workload characterization checklist for memory resources. Include how to fetch each metric, and try to use existing OS observability tools first.

5. Perform these tasks:
   - Choose an application, and summarize code paths that lead to memory allocation (`malloc()`).
   - Choose an application that has some degree of memory growth (calling `brk()`), and summarize code paths that lead to this growth.

- Describe the memory activity visible in the following Linux screen shot alone:

```
# vmstat 1
procs -----------memory-------- ---swap-- -----io---- --system-- -----cpu-----
 r  b   swpd   free  buff cache  si   so   bi    bo   in   cs us sy id wa st
 2  0 413344  62284    72 6972   0    0    17    12    1    1  0  0 100  0  0
 2  0 418036  68172    68 3808   0 4692  4520  4692 1060 1939 61 38  0  1  0
 2  0 418232  71272    68 1696   0  196 23924   196 1288 2464 51 38  0 11  0
 2  0 418308  68792    76 2456   0   76  3408    96 1028 1873 58 39  0  3  0
 1  0 418308  67296    76 3936   0    0  1060     0 1020 1843 53 47  0  0  0
 1  0 418308  64948    76 3936   0    0     0     0 1005 1808 36 64  0  0  0
 1  0 418308  62724    76 6120   0    0  2208     0 1030 1870 62 38  0  0  0
 1  0 422320  62772    76 6112   0 4012     0  4016 1052 1900 49 51  0  0  0
 1  0 422320  62772    76 6144   0    0     0     0 1007 1826 62 38  0  0  0
 1  0 422320  60796    76 6144   0    0     0     0 1008 1817 53 47  0  0  0
 1  0 422320  60788    76 6144   0    0     0     0 1006 1812 49 51  0  0  0
 3  0 430792  65584    64 5216   0 8472  4912  8472 1030 1846 54 40  0  6  0
 1  0 430792  64220    72 6496   0    0  1124    16 1024 1857 62 38  0  0  0
 2  0 434252  68188    64 3704   0 3460  5112  3460 1070 1964 60 40  0  0  0
 2  0 434252  71540    64 1436   0    0 21856     0 1300 2478 55 41  0  4  0
 1  0 434252  66072    64 3912   0    0  2020     0 1022 1817 60 40  0  0  0
[...]
```

6. (optional, advanced) Find or develop metrics to show how well the kernel NUMA memory locality policies are working in practice. Develop "known" workloads that have good or poor memory locality for testing the metrics.

7. (optional, advanced) Develop a tool that measures or estimates the working set size of a process. This should be safe to use in production systems (a requirement that may make this impossible). A partial solution is to do this for file system pages only (not the heap).

7.8 References

[Corbató 68]   Corbató, F. J. *A Paging Experiment with the Multics System*. MIT Project MAC Report MAC-M-384, 1968.

[Denning 70]   Denning, P. "Virtual Memory," *ACM Computing Surveys (CSUR)* 2, no. 3 (1970).

[Peterson 77]   Peterson, J., and T. Norman. "Buddy Systems," *Communications of the ACM*, 1977.

[Thompson 78]   Thompson, K. *UNIX Implementation*. Bell Laboratories, 1978.

[Babaoglu 79]   Babaoglu, O., W. Joy, and J. Porcar. *Design and Implementation of the Berkeley Virtual Memory Extensions to the UNIX*

	Operating System. Computer Science Division, Department of Electrical Engineering and Computer Science, University of California, Berkeley, 1979.
[Bach 86]	Bach, M. J. *The Design of the UNIX Operating System*. Prentice Hall, 1986.
[Bonwick 94]	Bonwick, J. "The Slab Allocator: An Object-Caching Kernel Memory Allocator." USENIX, 1994.
[Vahalia 96]	Vahalia, U. *UNIX Internals: The New Frontiers*. Prentice Hall, 1996.
[Bonwick 01]	Bonwick, J., and J. Adams. "Magazines and Vmem: Extending the Slab Allocator to Many CPUs and Arbitrary Resources." USENIX, 2001.
[Gorman 04]	Gorman, M. *Understanding the Linux Virtual Memory Manager*. Prentice Hall, 2004.
[McDougall 06a]	McDougall, R., and J. Mauro. *Solaris Internals: Solaris 10 and OpenSolaris Kernel Architecture*. Prentice Hall, 2006.
[McDougall 06b]	McDougall, R., J. Mauro, and B. Gregg. *Solaris Performance and Tools: DTrace and MDB Techniques for Solaris 10 and OpenSolaris*. Prentice Hall, 2006.
[Intel 12]	*Intel 64 and IA-32 Architectures Software Developer's Manual,* Combined Volumes: 1, 2A, 2B, 2C, 3A, 3B and 3C. Intel, 2012.
[1]	http://lwn.net/Articles/83588/, 2004
[2]	http://lwn.net/Articles/229096/, 2007
[3]	http://valgrind.org/docs/manual/, 2012
[4]	http://lwn.net/Articles/375096/, 2010
[5]	http://lwn.net/Articles/423584/, 2011

8

File Systems

When studying application I/O performance, the performance of the file system matters more than disk performance. File systems use caching, buffering, and asynchronous I/O to avoid subjecting applications to disk-level (or remote system) latency. Nevertheless, performance analysis and the available toolsets have historically focused on the performance of the disks.

In the era of dynamic tracing, file system analysis is now easy and practical. This chapter shows how file system requests can be examined in detail, including the use of dynamic tracing to measure start to completion time from the application context. This often allows file systems, and their underlying disk devices, to be quickly ruled out as the source of poor performance, allowing investigation to move on to other areas.

This chapter consists of five parts, the first three providing the basis for file system analysis and the last two showing its practical application to Linux- and Solaris-based systems. The parts are as follows:

- **Background** introduces file-system-related terminology, basic models, illustrating file system principles, and key file system performance concepts.
- **Architecture** introduces generic and specific file system architecture.
- **Methodology** describes performance analysis methodologies, both observational and experimental.
- **Analysis** shows file system performance tools for Linux- and Solaris-based systems, including static and dynamic tracing.
- **Tuning** describes file system tunable parameters.

8.1 Terminology

For reference, file-system-related terminology used in this chapter includes the following:

- **File system:** an organization of data as files and directories, with a file-based interface for accessing them, and file permissions to control access. Additional content may include special file types for devices, sockets, and pipes, and metadata including file access timestamps.

- **File system cache:** an area of main memory (usually DRAM) used to cache file system contents, which may include different caches for various data and metadata types.

- **Operations:** File system operations are the requests of the file system, including read( ), write( ), open( ), close( ), stat( ), mkdir( ), and other operations.

- **I/O:** input/output. File system I/O can be defined in several ways; here it is used to mean only operations that directly read and write (performing I/O), including read( ), write( ), stat( ) (read statistics), and mkdir( ) (write a new directory entry). I/O does not include open( ) and close( ).

- **Logical I/O:** I/O issued by the application to the file system.

- **Physical I/O:** I/O issued directly to disks by the file system (or via raw I/O).

- **Throughput:** the current data transfer rate between applications and the file system, measured in bytes per second.

- **inode:** An index node (inode) is a data structure containing metadata for a file system object, including permissions, timestamps, and data pointers.

- **VFS:** virtual file system, a kernel interface to abstract and support different file system types. On Solaris, a VFS inode is called a *vnode*.

- **Volume manager:** software for managing physical storages devices in a flexible way, creating *virtual volumes* from them for use by the OS.

Other terms are introduced throughout this chapter. The Glossary includes basic terminology for reference, including *fsck*, *IOPS*, *operation rate*, and *POSIX*. Also see the terminology sections in Chapters 2 and 3.

8.2 Models

The following simple models illustrate some basic principles of file systems and their performance.

8.2.1 File System Interfaces

A basic model of a file system is shown in Figure 8.1, in terms of its interfaces.

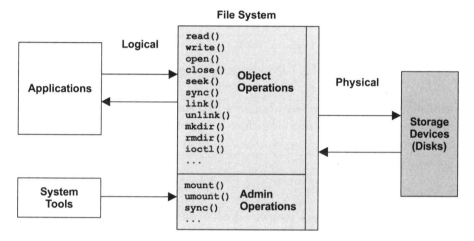

Figure 8-1 File system interfaces

The locations where *logical* and *physical* operations occur are also labeled in the figure. See Section 8.3.12, Logical versus Physical I/O, for more about these.

One approach for studying file system performance is to treat it as a black box, focusing on the latency of the object operations. This is explained in more detail in Section 8.5.2, Latency Analysis.

8.2.2 File System Cache

A generic file system cache stored in main memory is pictured in Figure 8.2, servicing a read operation.

The read returns either from cache (*cache hit*) or from disk (*cache miss*). Cache misses are stored in the cache, populating the cache (warming it up).

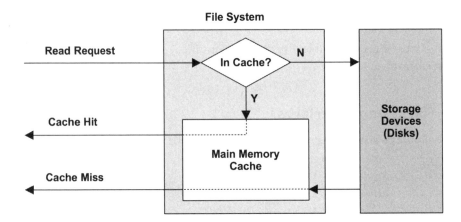

Figure 8-2 File system main memory cache

The file system cache may also buffer writes to be written (flushed) later. The mechanisms for doing this differ for different file system types and are described in Section 8.4, Architecture.

8.2.3 Second-Level Cache

Second-level cache may be any memory type; Figure 8.3 shows it as flash memory. This cache type was first developed for ZFS.

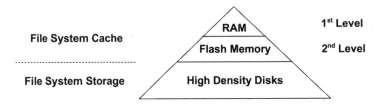

Figure 8-3 File system second-level cache

8.3 Concepts

Following is a selection of important concepts regarding file system performance.

8.3.1 File System Latency

File system latency is the primary metric of file system performance, measured as the time from a logical file system request to its completion. It is inclusive of time spent in the file system, kernel disk I/O subsystem, and waiting on disk devices—the physical I/O. Application threads often block during an application request to wait for file system requests to complete, for which file system latency *directly* and *proportionally* affects application performance.

Cases where applications may not be directly affected include the use of non-blocking I/O, or when I/O is issued from an asynchronous thread (e.g., a background flush thread). It may be possible to identify these cases from the application, if it provides detailed metrics for its file system usage. If not, a generic approach is to use a kernel tracing tool that can show the user-level stack trace that led to a logical file system I/O. This stack trace can then be studied to see which application routines issued it.

Operating systems have not historically made file system latency readily observable, instead providing disk-device-level metrics. But there are many cases where such metrics do not directly affect the application, making them confusing to interpret, if not downright irrelevant. An example of this is where file systems perform background flushing of written data, which may appear as bursts of high-latency disk I/O. From the disk-device-level metrics, this looks alarming; however, no application is waiting on these to complete. See Section 8.3.12, Logical versus Physical I/O, for more cases.

8.3.2 Caching

After booting, the file system will typically use main memory (RAM) as a cache to improve performance. For applications, this process is transparent: their logical I/O latency becomes much lower, as it can be served from main memory rather than the much slower disk devices.

Over time, the cache grows, while free memory for the operating system shrinks. This can distress new users but is perfectly normal. The principle is: If there is spare main memory, remember something useful. When applications need more memory, the kernel should quickly free it from the file system cache for use.

File systems use caching to improve read performance, and buffering (in the cache) to improve write performance. Multiple types of cache are typically used by the file system and the block device subsystem, which may include those in Table 8.1.

Specific cache types are described in Section 8.4, Architecture, and Chapter 3, Operating Systems, has the full list of caches (including application- and device-level).

Table 8-1 Example Cache Types

Cache	Example
Page cache	operating system page cache
File system primary cache	ZFS ARC
File system secondary cache	ZFS L2ARC
Directory cache	directory cache, DNLC
inode cache	inode cache
Device cache	ZFS vdev
Block device cache	buffer cache

8.3.3 Random versus Sequential I/O

A series of logical file system I/O can be described as *random* or *sequential*, based on the file offset of each I/O. With sequential I/O, the next I/O begins at the end of the previous I/O. Random I/O have no apparent relationship between them, and the offset changes randomly. A random file system workload may also refer to accessing many different files at random. Figure 8.4 illustrates these access patterns, showing an ordered series of I/O and example file offsets.

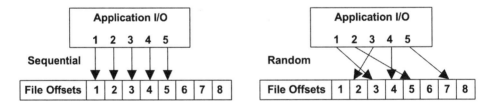

Figure 8-4 Sequential and random file I/O

Due to the performance characteristics of certain storage devices (described in Chapter 9, Disks), file systems have historically attempted to reduce random I/O by placing file data on disk sequentially and contiguously. The term *fragmentation* describes when file systems do this poorly, causing file placement to become scattered over a drive, so that sequential logical I/O yields random physical I/O.

File systems may measure logical I/O access patterns so that they can identify sequential workloads, and then improve their performance using prefetch or read-ahead. The next sections cover these topics.

8.3.4 Prefetch

A common file system workload involves reading a large amount of file data sequentially, for example, for a file system backup. This data may be too large to fit in the cache, or it may be read only once and is unlikely to be retained in the cache (depending on the cache eviction policy). Such a workload would perform relatively poorly, as it would have a low cache hit rate.

Prefetch is a common file system feature for solving this problem. It can detect a sequential read workload based on the current and previous file I/O offsets, and then predict and issue disk reads before the application has requested them. This populates the file system cache, so that if the application does perform the expected read, it results in a cache hit (the data needed was already in the cache). An example scenario is as follows, given no data cached to begin with:

1. An application issues a file read(), passing execution to the kernel.
2. The file system issues the read to disk.
3. The previous file offset pointer is compared to the current location, and if they are sequential, the file system issues additional reads.
4. The first read completes, and the kernel passes the data and execution back to the application.
5. Any additional reads complete, populating the cache for future application reads.

This scenario is also illustrated in Figure 8.5, where application reads to offsets 1 and then 2 trigger prefetch of the next three offsets.

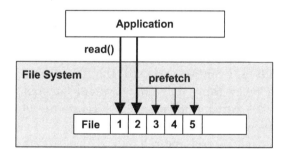

Figure 8-5 File system prefetch

When prefetch detection works well, applications show significantly improved sequential read performance; the disks keep ahead of application requests. When prefetch detection works poorly, unnecessary I/O is issued that the application does not need, polluting the cache and consuming disk and I/O transport resources. File systems typically allow prefetch to be tuned as needed.

8.3.5 Read-Ahead

Historically, prefetch has also been known as *read-ahead*. More recently, Linux has adopted the read-ahead term for a system call, `readahead(2)`, that allows applications to explicitly warm up the file system cache.

8.3.6 Write-Back Caching

Write-back caching is commonly used by file systems to improve write performance. It works by treating writes as completed after the transfer to main memory, and writing them to disk sometime later, *asynchronously*. The file system process for writing this "dirty" data to disk is called *flushing*. An example sequence is as follows:

1. An application issues a file `write()`, passing execution to the kernel.
2. Data from the application address space is copied to the kernel.
3. The kernel treats the `write()` syscall as completed, passing execution back to the application.
4. Sometime later, an asynchronous kernel task finds the written data and issues disk writes.

The trade-off is reliability. DRAM-based main memory is volatile, and dirty data can be lost in the event of a power failure, despite the application believing that the write completed. It could also be written to disk *incompletely*, leaving behind an on-disk state that is *corrupted*.

If file system metadata becomes corrupted, the file system may no longer load. Such a state may be recoverable only from system backups, causing prolonged downtime. Worse, if the corruption affects file contents, which the application reads and uses, the business may be in jeopardy.

To balance needs for both speed and reliability, file systems can offer write-back caching by default, and a *synchronous write* option to bypass this behavior and write directly to persistent storage devices.

8.3.7 Synchronous Writes

A synchronous write completes only when fully written to persistent storage (e.g., disk devices), which includes writing any file system metadata changes that are necessary. These are much slower than asynchronous writes (write-back caching), since synchronous writes incur disk device I/O latency. Synchronous writes are used by some applications such as database log writers, where the risk of data corruption from asynchronous writes is unacceptable.

There are two forms of synchronous writes: individual I/O which is written synchronously, and groups of previous writes which are synchronously committed.

Individual Synchronous Writes

Write I/O is synchronous when a file is opened using the flag O_SYNC or one of the variants, O_DSYNC and O_RSYNC (which as of Linux 2.6.31 were just mapped by glib to O_SYNC). Some file systems have mount options to force all write I/O to all files to be synchronous.

Synchronously Committing Previous Writes

Rather than synchronously writing individual I/O, an application may synchronously commit previous asynchronous writes at checkpoints in their code, using the fsync() system call. This can improve performance by grouping the synchronous writes.

There are other situations that will commit previous writes, such as closing file handles, or when there are too many uncommitted buffers on a file. The former is often noticed when unpacking an archive of many files, especially over NFS.

8.3.8 Raw and Direct I/O

These are other types of I/O that an application may use:

Raw I/O is issued directly to disk offsets, bypassing the file system altogether. It has been used by some applications, especially databases, that can manage and cache their own data better than the file system cache. A drawback is administration difficulties: the regular file system toolset can't be used for backup/restore or observability.

Direct I/O allows applications to use a file system but bypass the file system cache. This is similar to synchronous writes (but without the guarantees that O_SYNC offers), and it works for reads as well. It isn't as direct as raw device I/O, since mapping of file offsets to disk offsets must still be performed by file system code, and I/O may also be resized to match the size used by the file system for on-disk layout (its record size). Depending on the file system, this may not only disable read caching and write buffering but may also disable prefetch.

Direct I/O can be used by applications that perform file system backups, to avoid polluting the file system cache with data that will be read only once. Both raw and direct I/O can be used to avoid double caching for applications that employ their own application-level cache in the process heap.

8.3.9 Non-Blocking I/O

Normally, file system I/O will either complete immediately (e.g., from cache), or after waiting (e.g., for disk device I/O). If waiting is required, the application thread will *block* and leave CPU, allowing other threads to execute while it waits. While the blocked thread cannot perform other work, this typically isn't a problem since multithreaded applications can create additional threads to execute while some are blocked.

In some cases, non-blocking I/O is desirable, such as when avoiding the performance or resource overhead of thread creation. Non-blocking I/O may be performed by using the O_NONBLOCK or O_NDELAY flags to the open() syscall, which cause reads and writes to return an EAGAIN error instead of blocking, which tells the application to try again later. (Support for this depends on the file system, which may honor non-blocking only for advisory or mandatory file locks.)

Non-blocking I/O was also discussed in Chapter 5, Applications.

8.3.10 Memory-Mapped Files

For some applications and workloads, file system I/O performance can be improved by mapping files to the process address space and accessing memory offsets directly. This avoids the syscall execution and context switch overheads incurred when calling read() and write() syscalls to access file data. It can also avoid double copying of data, if the kernel supports direct copying of the file data buffer to the process address space.

Memory mappings are created using the mmap() syscall and removed using munmap(). Mappings can be tuned using madvise(), as summarized in Section 8.8, Tuning. Some applications provide an option to use the mmap syscalls (which may be called "mmap mode") in their configuration. For example, the Riak database can use mmap for its in-memory data store.

I've noticed a tendency to try mmap() to solve file system performance issues without first analyzing them. If the issue is high I/O latency from disk devices, avoiding the small syscall overheads with mmap() may accomplish very little, when the high disk I/O latency is still present and dominates.

A disadvantage of using mappings on multiprocessor systems can be the over-head to keep each CPU MMU in sync, specifically the CPU cross calls to remove mappings (*TLB shootdowns*). Depending on the kernel and mapping, these may be minimized by delaying TLB updates (*lazy shootdowns*) [Vahalia 96].

8.3.11 Metadata

While *data* describes the contents of files and directories, *metadata* describes information about them. Metadata may refer to information that can be read from the file system interface (POSIX) or information needed to implement the file system on-disk layout. These are called logical and physical metadata respectively.

Logical Metadata

Logical metadata is information that is read and written to the file system by consumers (applications), either

- **Explicitly:** reading file statistics (stat()), creating and deleting files (creat(), unlink()) and directories (mkdir(), rmdir())
- **Implicitly:** file system access timestamp updates, directory modification timestamp updates

A workload that is "metadata-heavy" typically refers to logical metadata, for example, web servers that stat() files to ensure they haven't changed since caching, at a much greater rate than actually reading file data contents.

Physical Metadata

Physical metadata refers to the on-disk layout metadata necessary to record all file system information. The metadata types in use depend on the file system type and may include superblocks, inodes, blocks of data pointers (primary, secondary, . . .), and free lists.

Logical and physical metadata are one reason for the difference between logical and physical I/O.

8.3.12 Logical versus Physical I/O

Although it may seem counterintuitive, I/O requested by applications to the file system (logical I/O) may not match disk I/O (physical I/O), for several reasons.

File systems do much more than present persistent storage (the disks) as a file-based interface. They cache reads, buffer writes, and create additional I/O to maintain the on-disk physical layout metadata that they need to record where everything is. This can cause disk I/O that is unrelated, indirect, inflated, or deflated as compared to application I/O. Examples follow.

Unrelated

This is disk I/O that is not related to the application and may be due to these factors:

- **Other applications:** The disk I/O is from another application.
- **Other tenants:** The disk I/O is from another tenant (visible via system tools under some virtualization technologies).
- **Other kernel tasks:** for example, when the kernel is rebuilding a software RAID volume or performing asynchronous file system checksum verification (see Section 8.4, Architecture).

Indirect

This is application I/O that does not have an immediate corresponding disk I/O. This may be due to these factors:

- **File system prefetch:** adding additional I/O that may or may not be used by the application.
- **File system buffering:** the use of write-back caching to defer and coalesce writes for later flushing to disk. Some systems may buffer writes for tens of seconds before writing, which then appear as large, infrequent bursts.

Deflated

This is where the disk I/O is smaller than the application I/O, or even nonexistent. This may be due to these factors:

- **File system caching:** satisfying reads from main memory instead of disk.
- **File system write cancellation:** The same byte offsets are modified multiple times before being flushed once to disk.
- **Compression:** reducing the data volume from logical to physical I/O.
- **Coalescing:** merging sequential I/O before issuing them to disk.
- **In-memory file system:** Content may never be written to disk (e.g., tmpfs).

Inflated

In this case the disk I/O is larger than the application I/O. This may be due to these factors:

- **File system metadata:** adding additional I/O
- **File system record size:** rounding up I/O size (inflating bytes), or fragmenting I/O (inflating count)
- **Volume manager parity:** read-modify-write cycles, adding additional I/O

Example

To show how these factors can happen in concert, the following enumerated example describes what can happen with a 1-byte application write:

1. An application performs a 1-byte write to an existing file.
2. The file system identifies the location as part of a 128 Kbyte file system record, which is not cached (but the metadata to reference it is).
3. The file system requests that the record be loaded from disk.
4. The disk device layer breaks the 128 Kbyte read into smaller reads suitable for the device.
5. The disks perform multiple smaller reads, totaling 128 Kbytes.
6. The file system now replaces the 1 byte in the record with the new byte.
7. Sometime later, the file system requests that the 128 Kbyte dirty record be written back to disk.
8. The disks write the 128 Kbyte record (broken up if needed).
9. The file system writes new metadata, for example, references (for copy-on-write) or access time.
10. The disks perform more writes.

So, while the application performed only a single 1-byte write, the disks performed multiple reads (128 Kbytes in total) and more writes (over 128 Kbytes).

8.3.13 Operations Are Not Equal

As may be clear from the previous sections, file system operations can exhibit different performance based on their type. You can't tell much about a workload of "500 operations/s" from the rate alone. Some operations may return from the file system cache at main memory speeds; others may return from disk and be orders of magnitude slower. Other determinant factors include whether operations are random or sequential, reads or writes, synchronous writes or asynchronous writes, their I/O size, whether they include other operation types, and their CPU execution cost.

It is common practice to micro-benchmark different file system operations to determine these performance characteristics. As an example, the results in Table 8.2 are from a ZFS file system, on an Intel Xeon 2.4 GHz multicore processor.

Table 8-2 Example File System Operation Latencies

Operation	Average (μs)
open()	2.2
close()	0.7
read() 4 Kbytes (cached)	3.3
read() 128 Kbytes (cached)	13.9
write() 4 Kbytes (async)	9.3
write() 128 Kbytes (async)	55.2

These tests did not involve the storage devices but are a test of the file system software and CPU speed. Some special file systems never access storage devices.

8.3.14 Special File Systems

The intent of a file system is usually to store data persistently, but there are special file system types used for other purposes, including temporary files (/tmp), kernel device paths (/dev), and system statistics (/proc).

8.3.15 Access Timestamps

Many file systems support access timestamps, which record the time that each file and directory was accessed (read). This causes file metadata to be updated whenever files are read, creating a write workload that consumes disk I/O resources. Section 8.8, Tuning, shows how to turn off these updates.

Some file systems optimize access timestamp writes by deferring and grouping them to reduce interference with the active workload.

8.3.16 Capacity

When file systems fill, performance may degrade for a couple of reasons. When writing new data, it may take more time to locate the free blocks on disk for computation, and any disk I/O needed. Areas of free space on disk are likely to be smaller and more sparsely located, degrading performance due to smaller I/O or random I/O.

How much of a problem this is depends on the file system type, its on-disk layout, and its storage devices. Various file system types are described in the next section.

8.4 Architecture

This section introduces generic and specific file system architecture, beginning with the I/O stack, VFS, file system caches and features, common file system types, volumes, and pools. Such background is useful when determining which file system components to analyze and tune. For deeper internals and other file system topics, refer to source code, if available, and external documentation. Some of these are listed at the end of this chapter.

8.4.1 File System I/O Stack

Figure 8.6 depicts a general model of the file system I/O stack. Specific components and layers depend on the operating system type, version, and file systems used. See Chapter 3, Operating Systems, for the full diagram.

This shows the path of I/O through the kernel. The path from system calls direct to the disk device subsystem is *raw I/O*. The path via VFS and the file system is file system I/O, including direct I/O which skips the file system cache.

8.4.2 VFS

VFS (the virtual file system interface) provides a common interface for different file system types. Its location is shown in Figure 8.7.

Some operating systems (including the original SunOS implementation) treat VFS as two interfaces: *VFS* and *vnode*, as was logically divided in the earlier model of a file system [McDougall 06a]. VFS includes file-system-wide operations, such as mount and umount. The vnode interface includes VFS inode (*vnode*) file operations such as open, close, read, and write.

The terminology used by the Linux VFS interface can be a little confusing, since it reuses the terms *inodes* and *superblocks* to refer to VFS objects—terms that originated from Unix file system on-disk data structures. The terms used for Linux

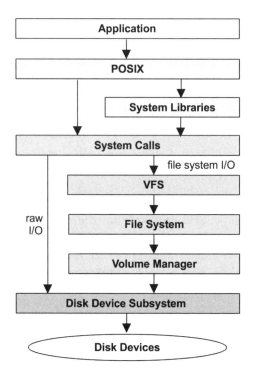

Figure 8-6 Generic file system I/O stack

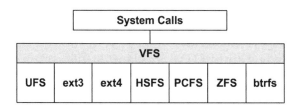

Figure 8-7 Virtual file system interface

on-disk data structures are usually prefixed with their file system type, for example, ext4_inode and ext4_super_block. These VFS inodes and VFS superblocks are in-memory only.

The VFS interface can also serve as a common location for measuring the performance of any file system. Doing this may be possible using operating-system-supplied statistics or static or dynamic tracing.

8.4.3 File System Caches

Unix originally had only the buffer cache to improve the performance of block device access. Nowadays, Linux and Solaris have multiple different cache types. This section begins with Solaris-based systems, to discuss the origins of some of these.

Solaris

An overview of file system caches on Solaris-based systems is shown in Figure 8.8, showing caches for both UFS and ZFS.

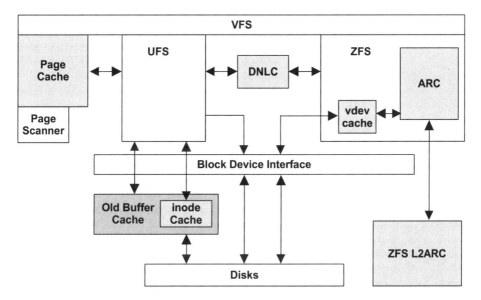

Figure 8-8 Solaris file system caches

Three of these caches are operating-system-generic: the old buffer cache, the page cache, and the DNLC. The remainder are file-system-specific and are explained later.

Old Buffer Cache

Original Unix used a buffer cache at the block device interface to cache disk device blocks. This was a separate, fixed-size cache and, with the addition of the page cache, presented tuning problems when balancing different workloads between them, as well as double caching and synchronization overhead. These problems have largely been addressed by using the page cache to store the buffer cache, an approach introduced by SunOS called the *unified buffer cache*, as shown in Figure 8.9.

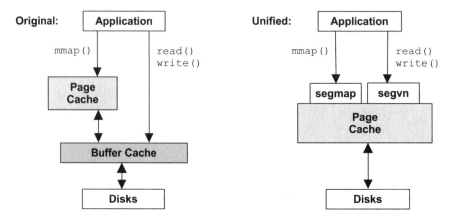

Figure 8-9 Original and unified buffer cache

In Solaris, the original ("old") buffer cache still exists, used only for UFS inode and file metadata, which are addressed by their block location and not by file. Its size is dynamic, and access counts are observable from kstat.

The inode cache also grows dynamically, holding at least all inodes for open files (referenced), and those mapped by the DNLC. A number of additional inodes are kept cached on an idle queue.

Page Cache

The page cache was introduced during a virtual memory rewrite for SunOS 4 in 1985 and added to SVR4 [Vahalia 96]. It cached virtual memory pages, including mapped file system pages. It was more efficient for file access than the buffer cache, which required translation from file offset to disk offset for each lookup.

Multiple file system types use the page cache, including the original consumers UFS and NFS (but not ZFS). The size of the page cache is dynamic, and it will grow to use available memory, freeing it again when applications need it.

Pages of memory that are dirty, and are being used for a file system, are written to disk by a kernel thread called the *file system flush daemon* (fsflush), which periodically scans the entire page cache. If there is a system memory deficit, another kernel thread, the page-out daemon (pageout, also known as the *page scanner*), may also find and schedule dirty pages to be written to disk so that it can free the memory pages for reuse (see Chapter 7, Memory). For observability, pageout and fsflush show up as PIDs 2 and 3, even though they are kernel threads, not processes.

There are two main kernel drivers for the page cache: *segvn*, to map files to process address spaces, and *segmap*, to cache file system reads and writes. See Chapter 7, Memory, for more details about these and the page scanner.

DNLC

The directory name lookup cache (DNLC) remembers directory-entry-to-vnode mappings and was developed in the early 1980s by Kevin Robert Elz. It improves the performance of path name lookups (e.g., via open()) because when a path name is traversed, each name lookup can check the DNLC for a direct vnode mapping, instead of stepping through the directory contents. The DNLC has been designed for performance and scalability, with entries stored in a hash table, which is hashed by the parent vnode and directory entry name.

Various capability and performance features have been added to the Solaris DNLC over the years. The DNLC originally used pointers for the hash chains, and additional pointers for an LRU list. Solaris 2.4 dropped the LRU pointers, which avoided LRU list lock contention. LRU behavior was then implemented by freeing from the tails of the hash chains. Solaris 8 added two new features: *negative caching*, which remembers lookups for nonexistent entries, and *directory caching*, to deliberately cache entire directories. Negative caching aids the performance of failed lookups, which commonly occur for library path lookup. Directory caching improves performance during file creation by obviating the need to scan the directory to see if the new file name is already in use.

The DNLC size is adjustable using tunables, and the current size and hit and miss counts are observable from kstat.

Linux

Figure 8.10 gives an overview of file system caches on Linux, showing generic caches available for standard file system types.

Buffer Cache

Linux originally used a buffer cache as with Unix. Since Linux 2.4, the buffer cache has been stored in the page cache (hence the dotted border in Figure 8.10) following the SunOS unified buffer approach, avoiding the double caching and synchronization overhead. The buffer cache functionality still exists, improving the performance of block device I/O.

The size of the buffer cache is dynamic and is observable from /proc.

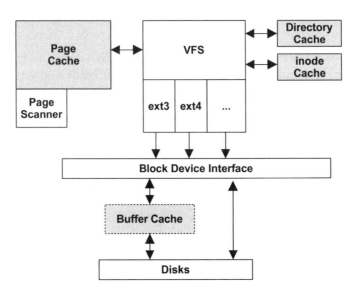

Figure 8-10 Linux file system caches

 Page Cache

The page cache caches virtual memory pages, including file system pages, improving the performance of file and directory I/O. The size of the page cache is dynamic, and it will grow to use available memory, freeing it again when applications need it (along with paging, as controlled by swappiness; see Chapter 7, Memory).

Pages of memory that are dirty (modified) and are for use by a file system are flushed to disk by kernel threads. Prior to Linux 2.6.32, there was a pool of page dirty flush (*pdflush*) threads, between two and eight as needed. These have since been replaced by the *flusher threads* (named *flush*), which are created per device to better balance the per-device workload and improve throughput. Pages are flushed to disk for the following reasons:

- After an interval (30 s)
- The sync(), fsync(), or msync() system calls
- Too many dirty pages (dirty_ratio)
- No available pages in the page cache

If there is a system memory deficit, another kernel thread, the page-out daemon (*kswapd*, also known as the *page scanner*), may also find and schedule dirty pages to be written to disk so that it can free the memory pages for reuse (see

Chapter 7, Memory). For observability, the kswapd and flush threads are visible as kernel tasks from operating system performance tools.

See Chapter 7, Memory, for more details about the page scanner.

Dentry Cache

The dentry cache (Dcache) remembers mappings from directory entry (struct dentry) to VFS inode, much like the earlier Unix DNLC. This improves the performance of path name lookups (e.g., via open()), as when a path name is traversed, each name lookup can check the Dcache for a direct inode mapping, instead of stepping through the directory contents. The Dcache entries are stored in a hash table for fast and scalable lookup (hashed by the parent dentry and directory entry name).

Performance has been further improved over the years, including with the read-copy-update-walk (RCU-walk) algorithm [1]. This attempts to walk the path name without updating dentry reference counts, which were causing scalability issues due to cache coherency with high rates on multi-CPU systems. If a dentry is encountered that isn't in the cache, RCU-walk reverts to the slower reference-count walk (ref-walk), since reference counts will be necessary during file system lookup and blocking. For busy workloads, it's expected that the dentrys will likely be cached, and so the RCU-walk approach will succeed.

The Dcache also performs *negative caching*, which remembers lookups for non-existent entries. This improves the performance of failed lookups, which commonly occur for library path lookup.

The Dcache grows dynamically, shrinking via LRU when the system needs more memory. Its size can be seen via /proc.

Inode Cache

This cache contains VFS inodes (`struct inode`), each describing properties of a file system object, many of which are returned via the `stat()` system call. These properties are frequently accessed for file system workloads, such as checking permissions when opening files, or updating timestamps during modification. These VFS inodes are stored on a hash table for fast and scalable lookup (hashed by inode number and file system superblock), although most of the lookups will be done via the dentry cache.

The inode cache grows dynamically, holding at least all inodes mapped by the Dcache. When there is system memory pressure, the inode cache will shrink, dropping inodes that do not have associated dentries. Its size can be seen via /proc.

8.4.4 File System Features

Apart from caching, other key file system features that affect performance are described here.

Block versus Extent

Block-based file systems store data in fixed-size blocks, referenced by pointers stored in metadata blocks. For large files this can require many block pointers and metadata blocks, and the placement of blocks may become scattered, leading to random I/O. Some block-based file systems attempt to place blocks contiguously to avoid this. Another approach is to use *variable block sizes*, so that larger sizes can be used as the file grows, which also reduces the metadata overhead.

Extent-based file systems preallocate contiguous space for files (extents), growing them as needed. For the cost of space overhead, this improves streaming performance and can improve random I/O performance as file data is localized.

Journaling

A file system journal (or *log*) records changes to the file system so that in the event of a system crash, changes can be replayed atomically—either succeeding in their entirety or failing. This allows file systems to recover to a consistent state quickly. Non-journaled file systems can become corrupted during a system crash, if data and metadata relating to a change were incompletely written. Recovering from such a crash requires walking all file system structures, which can take hours for large (terabytes) file systems.

The journal is written to disk synchronously, and for some file systems it can be configured to use a separate device. Some journals record both data and metadata, which consumes storage I/O resources as all I/O is written twice. Others write only metadata and maintain data integrity by employing copy-on-write.

There is a file system type that consists of only a journal: a *log-structured file system*, where all data and metadata updates are written to a continuous and circular log. This optimizes write performance, as writes are always sequential and can be merged to use larger I/O sizes.

Copy-on-Write

A copy-on-write (COW) file system does not overwrite existing blocks but instead follows these steps:

1. Write blocks to a new location (a new copy).
2. Update references to new blocks.
3. Add old blocks to the free list.

This helps file system integrity in the event of a system failure and also improves performance by turning random writes into sequential ones. [?] [image] [?]

Scrubbing

This is a file system feature that asynchronously reads all data blocks and verifies checksums, to detect failed drives as early as possible, ideally while the failure is still recoverable due to RAID. However, scrubbing read I/O can negatively affect performance, so it should be issued at a low priority.

8.4.5 File System Types

Much of this chapter describes generic *characteristics* that can be applied to all file system types. The following sections summarize specific performance features for commonly used file systems. Their analysis and tuning are covered in later sections.

FFS

Many file systems are based on FFS, which was designed to address issues with the original Unix file system.[1] Some background can help explain the state of file systems today.

The original Unix file system on-disk layout consisted of a table of inodes, 512-byte storage blocks, and a superblock of information used when allocating resources ([Ritchie 74], [Lions 77]). The inode table and storage blocks divided disk partitions into two ranges, which caused performance issues when seeking between them. Another issue was the use of the small fixed-block size, 512 bytes, which limited throughput and increased the amount of metadata (pointers) required to store large files. An experiment to double this to 1,024 bytes, and the bottleneck then encountered, was described by [McKusick 84]:

> Although the throughput had doubled, the old file system was still using only about four percent of the disk bandwidth. The main problem was that although the free list was initially ordered for optimal access, it quickly became scrambled as files were created and removed. Eventually the free list became entirely random, causing files to have their blocks allocated randomly over the disk. This forced a seek before every block access. Although old file systems provided transfer rates of up to 175 kilobytes per second when they were first created, this rate deteriorated to 30 kilobytes per second after a few weeks of moderate use because of this randomization of data block placement.

---

1. The original Unix file system is not to be confused with later file systems called UFS, which are based on FFS. There are also different versions of UFS—the term is clearly overloaded!

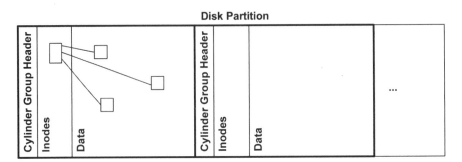

Figure 8-11 Cylinder groups

This excerpt describes free list *fragmentation*, which decreases performance over time as the file system is used.

The Berkeley Fast File System (FFS) improved performance by splitting the partition into numerous *cylinder groups*, shown in Figure 8.11, each with its own inode array and data blocks. File inodes and data were kept within one cylinder group where possible, as pictured in Figure 8.12, reducing disk seek. Other related data was also placed nearby, including the inodes for a directory and its entries. The design of an inode was similar [Bach 86] (triply indirect blocks are not shown here).

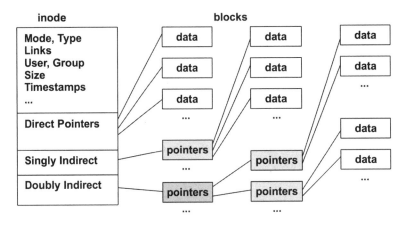

Figure 8-12 inode data structure

The block size was increased to a 4 Kbyte minimum, improving throughput. This reduced the number of data blocks necessary to store a file, and therefore the number of indirect blocks needed to refer to the data blocks. The number of required indirect pointer blocks was further reduced because they were also larger. For space efficiency with small files, each block could be split into 1 Kbyte fragments.

Another performance feature of FFS was *block interleaving*: placing sequential file blocks on disk with a spacing between them of one or more blocks [Doeppner 10]. These extra blocks gave the kernel and the processor time to issue the next sequential file read, as they were more directly involved with controlling the disk at the time. Without interleaving, the next block may pass the disk head before it is ready to issue the read, causing latency as it waits for almost a full rotation.

UFS

FFS was introduced in SunOS 1.0 in 1984 as UFS [McDougall 06a]. Various features were added to SunOS UFS during the next two decades: I/O clustering, file system growth, multiterabyte support, logging, direct I/O, snapshots, access controls lists (ACLs,) and extended attributes. Linux currently has support to read UFS, but not to write it, instead supporting another UFS-like file system (ext3).

Key UFS performance features include the following:

- **I/O clustering:** This groups data blocks on disk by delaying writes until a *cluster* is filled, allowing them to be placed sequentially. When sequential read workloads are detected, UFS performs prefetch (which it called *read-ahead*) by reading these clusters.

- **Logging** (journaling): for metadata only. This improves boot performance after a system crash, as log replay can avoid needing to run fsck (file system check). It may also improve the performance of some write workloads by coalescing metadata writes.

- **Direct I/O:** to bypass the page cache and avoid double caching for applications such as databases.

Configurable features are documented in the mkfs_ufs(1M) man page. For more about UFS and its internals, see *Solaris Internals, 2nd Edition*, Chapter 15 [McDougall 06a].

ext3

The Linux extended file system (ext) was developed in 1992 as the first file system for Linux and its VFS, based on the original Unix file system. The second version, ext2 in 1993, included multiple timestamps and cylinder groups from FFS. The third version, ext3 in 1999, includes file system growth and journaling.

Key performance features, including those added since its release, are:

- **Journaling:** either *ordered mode*, for metadata only, or *journal mode*, for metadata and data. Journaling improves boot performance after a system crash, avoiding the need to run fsck. It may also improve the performance of some write workloads by coalescing metadata writes.

- **Journal device:** An external journal device can be used, so that the journal workload doesn't contend with the read workload.
- **Orlov block allocator:** This spreads top-level directories across cylinder groups, so that the subdirectories and contents are more likely to be colocated, reducing random I/O.
- **Directory indexes:** These add hashed B-trees to the file system for faster directory lookups.

Configurable features are documented in the MKE2FS(8) man page.

ext4

The Linux ext4 file system was released in 2008, extending ext3 with various features and performance improvements: extents, large capacity, preallocation with fallocate(), delayed allocation, journal checksumming, faster fsck, multiblock allocator, nanosecond timestamps, and snapshots.

Key performance features, including those added since its release, are

- **Extents:** Extents improve contiguous placement, reducing random I/O and increasing the I/O size for sequential I/O.
- **Preallocation:** Via the fallocate() syscall, this allows applications to pre-allocate space that is likely contiguous, improving later write performance.
- **Delayed allocation:** Block allocation is delayed until it is flushed to disk, allowing writes to group (via the *multiblock allocator*), reducing fragmentation.
- **Faster fsck:** Unallocated blocks and inode entries are marked, reducing fsck time.

Configurable features are documented in the MKE2FS(8) man page. Some of the features, such as extents, can be applied to ext3 file systems.

ZFS

ZFS was developed by Sun Microsystems and released in 2005, combining the file system with the volume manager and including numerous enterprise features: pooled storage, logging, COW, ARC, large capacity, variable-size blocks, dynamic striping, multiple prefetch streams, snapshots, clones, compression, scrubbing, and 128-bit checksums. Additional features were added in updates, including (some of these will be explained more in a moment) hot spares, double-parity RAID, gzip compression, SLOG, L2ARC, user and group quotas, triple-parity RAID, data deduplication, hybrid RAID allocation, and encryption. This feature set has made ZFS an attractive choice for file servers (*filers*), which have been developed by Sun/Oracle and other companies based on the open-sourced ZFS version.

Key performance features, including those added since its release, are

- **Pooled storage:** All storage devices are placed in a pool, from which file systems are created. This allows all devices to be used in parallel for maximum throughput and IOPS. Different RAID types can be used: 0, 1, 10, Z (based on RAID-5), Z2 (double-parity), and Z3 (triple-parity).

- **COW:** groups and writes data sequentially.

- **Logging:** ZFS flushes *transaction groups* (TXGs) of changes, which succeed or fail as a whole so that the on-disk format is always consistent. These also batch writes for improved asynchronous write throughput.

- **ARC:** The Adaptive Replacement Cache achieves a high cache hit rate by using multiple cache algorithms at the same time: most recently used (MRU) and most frequently used (MFU). Main memory is balanced between these based on their performance, which is known by maintaining extra metadata (*ghost lists*) to see how each would perform if it ruled all of main memory.

- **Variable block sizes:** Each file system has a configurable maximum block size (record size) that can be picked to match the workload. Smaller sizes are used for smaller files.

- **Dynamic striping:** This stripes across all storage devices for maximum throughput and includes extra devices in the stripe as they are added.

- **Intelligent prefetch:** ZFS applies different types of prefetch as appropriate: for metadata, for znodes (file contents), and for vdevs (virtual devices).

- **Multiple prefetch streams:** Multiple streaming readers on one file can create a random I/O workload as the file system seeks between them (this was a problem in UFS). ZFS tracks individual prefetch streams, allowing new streams to join them, and issues I/O efficiently.

- **Snapshots:** Due to the COW architecture, snapshots can be created nearly instantaneously, deferring the copying of new blocks until needed.

- **ZIO pipeline:** Device I/O is processed by a pipeline of stages, each stage serviced by a pool of threads to improve performance.

- **Compression:** Multiple algorithms are supported, which usually reduce performance due to the CPU overhead. The lzjb (Lempel-Ziv Jeff Bonwick) option is lightweight and can marginally improve storage performance by reducing I/O load (as it is compressed) at the cost of some CPU.

- **SLOG:** The ZFS separate intent log allows synchronous writes to be written to separate devices, avoiding contention with the pool disks workload. Writes to the SLOG are read only in the event of system failure, for replay. These can greatly improve the performance of synchronous writes.

- **L2ARC:** The Level 2 ARC is a second level of cache after main memory, intended to cache random read workloads on flash-memory-based solid-state disks (SSDs). It does not buffer write workloads and contains only clean data that already resides on the storage pool disks. The L2ARC extends the caching reach of the system, helping avoid the performance cliff when a workload grows beyond main memory caching. It also provides hysteresis as population is slow compared to main memory, and it will contain copies of long-term data. Should a perturbation pollute the main memory cache, the L2ARC can recover the "hot" main memory cache state quickly.

- **vdev cache:** similar to the role of the original buffer cache, ZFS uses separate vdev caches per virtual device, which support LRU and read-ahead. (This may be disabled in some operating systems.)

- **Data deduplication:** a file-system-level feature that avoids recording multiple copies of the same data. This feature has significant performance implications, both good (reduced device I/O) and bad (when the hash table no longer fits in main memory, device I/O is inflated, perhaps significantly). The initial version is intended only for workloads where the hash table is expected to always fit in main memory.

The L2ARC and SLOG are part of the ZFS Hybrid Storage Pool (HSP) model, to intelligently use both read- and write-optimized SSDs in a ZFS storage pool. The read-optimized SSDs have a price/performance ratio in between main memory and disk, making them suitable for use as the extra caching tier.

Other minor performance features have been included, such as "Don't mind the gap," to issue larger reads when appropriate, even if small parts (gaps) are not needed; and hybrid RAID, to support different policies in one pool.

There is a behavior of ZFS that can reduce performance when compared to other file systems: by default, ZFS issues cache flush commands to the storage devices, to ensure that writes have completed in the case of a power outage. This is one of the ZFS integrity features; however, it comes at a cost: it can induce latency for ZFS operations that must wait for the cache flush, and some workloads can perform worse on ZFS when compared to other file systems. ZFS can be tuned to not perform the cache flush to improve performance; however, as with other file systems, this introduces the potential of partial writes and data corruption on power outage, depending on the storage devices used.

There are two projects for bringing ZFS to Linux. One is ZFS on Linux, produced at Lawrence Livermore National Laboratory [2], which is a native kernel port. The other is ZFS-FUSE, which runs ZFS in user-space, which is expected to have worse performance due to context-switching overheads.

btrfs

The B-tree file system (btrfs) is based on copy-on-write B-trees. This is a modern file system and volume manager combined architecture, similar to ZFS, and is expected to eventually offer a similar feature set. Current features include pooled storage, large capacity, extents, COW, volume growth and shrinking, subvolumes, block device addition and removal, snapshots, clones, compression, and CRC-32C checksums. Development was begun by Oracle in 2007, and it is still in heavy development and considered unstable.

Key performance features include the following:

- **Pooled storage:** Storage devices are placed in a volume, from which file systems are created. This allows all devices to be used in parallel for maximum throughput and IOPS. Different RAID types can be used: 0, 1, and 10.
- **COW:** groups and writes data sequentially.
- **Online balancing:** Objects may be moved between storage devices to balance their workload.
- **Extents:** improve sequential layout and performance.
- **Snapshots:** Due to the COW architecture, snapshots can be created nearly instantaneously, deferring the copying of new blocks until needed.
- **Compression:** supports zlib and LZO.
- **Journaling:** A per-subvolume log tree can be created to journal synchronous COW workloads.

Planned performance-related features include RAID-5 and 6, object-level RAID, incremental dumps, and data deduplication.

8.4.6 Volumes and Pools

Historically, file systems were built upon a single disk or disk partition. Volumes and pools allow file systems to be built upon multiple disks and can be configured using different RAID strategies (see Chapter 9, Disks).

Volumes present multiple disks as one virtual disk, upon which the file system is built. When built upon whole disks (and not slices or partitions), volumes isolate workloads, reducing performance issues of contention.

Volume management software includes the Logical Volume Manager (LVM) for Linux-based systems, and the Solaris Volume Manager (SVM). Volumes, or virtual disks, may also be provided by hardware RAID controllers.

Pooled storage includes multiple disks in a storage pool, from which multiple file systems can be created. This is shown in Figure 8.13 with volumes for comparison. Pooled storage is more flexible than volume storage, as file systems can grow and shrink regardless of the backing devices. This approach is used by modern file systems, including ZFS and btrfs.

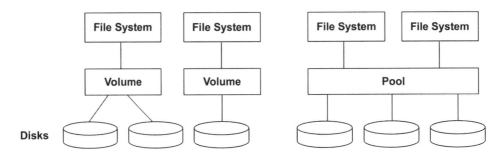

Figure 8-13 Volumes and pools

Pooled storage can use all disk devices for all file systems, improving performance. Workloads are not isolated; in some cases, multiple pools may be used to separate workloads, given the trade-off of some flexibility, as disk devices must be initially placed in one pool or another.

Additional performance considerations when using either software volume managers or pooled storage include the following:

- **Stripe width:** matching this to the workload.
- **Observability:** The virtual device utilization can be confusing; check the separate physical devices.
- **CPU overhead:** especially when performing RAID parity computation. This has become less of an issue with modern, faster CPUs.
- **Rebuilding:** Also called *resilvering*, this is when an empty disk is added to a RAID group (e.g., replacing a failed disk), and it is populated with the necessary data to join the group. This can significantly affect performance as it consumes I/O resources and may last for hours or even days.

➤ Rebuilding may become a worse problem in the future, as the capacity of storage devices increases faster than their throughput, increasing rebuild time.

8.5 Methodology

This section describes various strategies and exercises for file system analysis and tuning. The topics are summarized in Table 8.3.

Table 8-3 File System Performance Methodologies

Methodology	Types
Disk analysis	observational analysis
Latency analysis	observational analysis
Workload characterization	observational analysis, capacity planning
Performance monitoring	observational analysis, capacity planning
Event tracing	observational analysis
Static performance tuning	observational analysis, capacity planning
Cache tuning	observational analysis, tuning
Workload separation	tuning
In-memory file systems	tuning
Micro-benchmarking	experimental analysis

See Chapter 2, Methodology, for more strategies and the introduction to many of these.

These may be followed individually or used in combination. My suggestion is to use the following strategies to start with, in this order: latency analysis, performance monitoring, workload characterization, micro-benchmarking, static analysis, and event tracing. You may come up with a different combination and ordering that works best in your environment.

Section 8.6, Analysis, shows operating system tools for applying these methods.

8.5.1 Disk Analysis

A common strategy has been to ignore the file system and focus on *disk* performance instead. This assumes that the worst I/O is disk I/O, and so by analyzing only the disks you have conveniently focused on the expected source of problems.

With simpler file systems and smaller caches, this generally worked. Nowadays, this approach becomes confusing and misses entire classes of issues (see Section 8.3.12, Logical versus Physical I/O).

8.5.2 Latency Analysis

For latency analysis, begin by measuring the latency of file system operations. This should include all object operations, not just I/O (e.g., include `sync()`).

operation latency = time (operation completion) - time (operation request)

These times can be measured from one of four nearby layers, as shown in Table 8.4.

Table 8-4 Targets (Layers) for Analyzing File System Latency

Layer	Pros	Cons
Application	Closest measure of the effect of file system latency on the application; can also inspect application context and determine if latency is occurring during the application's primary function, or if it is asynchronous.	Technique varies between applications and application software versions.
Syscall interface	Well-documented interface. Commonly observable via operating system tools and static tracing.	Syscalls catch all file system types, including non-storage file systems (statistics, sockets), which may be confusing unless filtered. Adding to the confusion, there may also be multiple syscalls for the same file system function. For example, for read, there may be `read()`, `pread()`, `read64()`, etc., all of which need to be measured.
VFS	Standard interface for all file systems; one call for file system operations (e.g., `vfs_write()`)	VFS traces all file system types, including non-storage file systems, which may be confusing unless filtered.
Top of file system	Target file system type traced only; some file system internal context for extended details.	File-system-specific; tracing technique may vary between file system software versions (although the file system may have a VFS-like interface that maps to VFS, and as such doesn't change often).

Choosing the layer may depend on tool availability. Check the following:

- **Application documentation:** Some applications already provide file system latency metrics, or the capability to enable their collection.

- **Operating system tools:** Operating systems may also provide metrics, ideally as separate statistics for each file system or application.
- **Dynamic tracing:** If your system has dynamic tracing, all layers can be inspected via custom scripts, without restarting anything.

Latency may be presented as

- **Per-interval averages:** for example, average read latency per second
- **Full distributions:** as histograms or heat maps; see Section 8.6.18, Visualizations
- **Per-operation latency:** listing every operation; see Section 8.5.5, Event Tracing

For file systems that have a high cache hit rate (over 99%), per-interval averages can become dominated by cache hit latency. This may be unfortunate when there are isolated instances of high latency (outliers) that are important to identify but difficult to see from an average. Examining full distributions or per-operation latency allows such outliers to be investigated, along with the effect of different tiers of latency, including file system cache hits and misses.

Once high latency has been found, continue with drill-down analysis into the file system to determine the origin.

Transaction Cost

Another way to present file system latency is as the total time spent waiting on the file system during an application transaction (e.g., a database query):

percent time in file system = 100 * total blocking file system latency/application transaction time

This allows the cost of file system operations to be quantified in terms of application performance, and performance improvements to be predicted. The metric may be presented as the average either for all transactions during an interval, or for individual transactions.

Figure 8.14 shows the time spent on an application thread that is servicing a transaction. This transaction issues a single file system read; the application blocks and waits for its completion, transitioning to off-CPU. The total blocking time in this case is the time for the single file system read. If multiple blocking I/O were called during a transaction, the total time is their sum.

As a specific example, an application transaction takes 200 ms, during which it waits for a total of 180 ms on multiple file system I/O. The time that the application

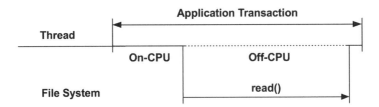

Figure 8-14 Application and file system latency

was blocked by the file system is 90% (100 * 180 ms/200 ms). Eliminating file system latency may improve performance by up to 10x.

As another example, if an application transaction takes 200 ms, during which only 2 ms was spent in the file system, the file system—and the entire disk I/O stack—is contributing only 1% to the transaction runtime. This result is incredibly useful, as it can steer the performance investigation to the real source of latency and avoid time wasted investigating where it isn't.

If the application were issuing I/O as *non-blocking*, the application can continue to execute on-CPU while the file system responds. In this case, the blocking file system latency measures only the time the application was blocked off-CPU.

8.5.3 Workload Characterization

Characterizing the load applied is an important exercise when capacity planning, benchmarking, and simulating workloads. It can also lead to some of the largest performance gains by identifying unnecessary work that can be eliminated.

Here are the basic attributes for characterizing the file system workload:

- Operation rate and operation types
- File I/O throughput
- File I/O size
- Read/write ratio
- Synchronous write ratio
- Random versus sequential file offset access

Operation rate and throughput are defined in Section 8.1, Terminology. Synchronous writes and random versus sequential were described in Section 8.3, Concepts.

These characteristics can vary from second to second, especially for timed application tasks that execute at intervals. To better characterize the workload, capture maximum values as well as averages. Better still, examine the full distribution of values over time.

Here is an example workload description, to show how these attributes can be expressed together:

> On a financial trading database, the file system has a random read workload, averaging 18,000 reads/s with an average read size of 2 Kbytes. The total operation rate is 21,000 ops/s, which includes reads, stats, opens, closes, and around 200 synchronous writes/s. The write rate is steady while the read rate varies, up to a peak of 39,000 reads/s.

These characteristics may be described in terms of a single file system instance, or all instances on a system of the same type.

Advanced Workload Characterization/Checklist

Additional details may be included to characterize the workload. These have been listed here as questions for consideration, which may also serve as a checklist when studying file system issues thoroughly:

- What is the file system cache hit ratio? Miss rate?
- What are the file system cache capacity and current usage?
- What other caches are present (directory, inode, buffer) and what are their statistics?
- Which applications or users are using the file system?
- What files and directories are being accessed? Created and deleted?
- Have any errors been encountered? Was this due to invalid requests, or issues from the file system?
- Why is file system I/O issued (user-level call path)?
- To what degree is the file system I/O application synchronous?
- What is the distribution of I/O arrival times?

Many of these questions can be posed per application or per file. Any of them may also be checked over time, to look for maximums and minimums, and time-based variations. Also see Section 2.5.10, Workload Characterization, in Chapter 2, Methodology, which provides a higher-level summary of the characteristics to measure (who, why, what, how).

Performance Characterization

The following questions (contrast with the previous workload characterization questions) characterize the resulting performance of the workload:

- What is the average file system operation latency?
- Are there any high-latency outliers?
- What is the full distribution of operation latency?
- Are system resource controls for file system or disk I/O present and active?

The first three questions may be asked for each operation type separately.

8.5.4 Performance Monitoring

Performance monitoring can identify active issues and patterns of behavior over time. Key metrics for file system performance are

- Operation rate
- Operation latency

The operation rate is the most basic characteristic of the applied workload, and the latency is the resulting performance. The value for normal or bad latency depends on your workload, environment, and latency requirements. If you aren't sure, micro-benchmarks of known-to-be-good versus bad workloads may be performed to investigate latency (e.g., workloads that usually hit from the file system cache versus those that usually miss). See Section 8.7, Experimentation.

The operation latency metric may be monitored as a per-second average and can include other values such as the maximum and standard deviation. Ideally, it would be possible to inspect the full distribution of latency, such as by using a histogram or heat map, to look for outliers and other patterns.

Both rate and latency may also be recorded for each operation type (read, write, stat, open, close, etc.). Doing this will greatly help investigations of workload and performance changes, by identifying differences in particular operation types.

For systems that impose file-system-based resource controls (e.g., ZFS I/O throttling), statistics can be included to show if and when throttling was in use.

8.5.5 Event Tracing

Event tracing captures details for every file system operation. For observational analysis, this is the last resort. It adds performance overhead due to the capturing and saving of these details, which are usually written to log files for later inspection. These log files can contain the following details for each operation:

- File system type
- File system mount point
- Operation type: read, write, stat, open, close, mkdir, . . .
- Operation size (if applicable): bytes
- Operation start timestamp: when the operation was issued to the file system
- Operation completion timestamp: when the file system completed the operation
- Operation completion status: errors
- Path name (if applicable)
- Process ID
- Application name

The start and completion timestamps allow operation latency to be calculated. Many tracing frameworks allow calculations to be performed while tracing, so the latency could be calculated and included in the log. It could also be used to filter the output, so that only operations slower than a certain threshold are logged. File system operation rates can reach the millions per second, so filtering may be a very good idea, when appropriate.

Event tracing may be performed at any of the four layers listed in Section 8.5.2, Latency Analysis. See Section 8.6, Analysis, for examples.

8.5.6 Static Performance Tuning

Static performance tuning focuses on issues of the configured environment. For file system performance, examine the following aspects of the static configuration:

- How many file systems are mounted and actively used?
- What is the file system record size?
- Are access timestamps enabled?
- What other file system options are enabled (compression, encryption, . . .)?
- How has the file system cache been configured? Maximum size?
- How have other caches (directory, inode, buffer) been configured?
- Is a second-level cache present and in use?

- How many storage devices are present and in use?
- What is the storage device configuration? RAID?
- Which file system types are used?
- What is the version of the file system (or kernel)?
- Are there file system bugs/patches that should be considered?
- Are there resource controls in use for file system I/O?

Answering these questions can reveal configuration choices that have been over-looked. Sometimes a system has been configured for one workload, and then repurposed for another. This method will revisit those choices.

8.5.7 Cache Tuning

The kernel and file system may use many different caches, including a buffer cache, directory cache, inode cache, and file system (page) cache. Various caches were described in Section 8.4, Architecture, which can be tuned as described in Section 2.5.17, Cache Tuning, in Chapter 2, Methodology. In summary, check which caches exist, check that they are working, check how well they are working, check their sizes, then tune the workload for the cache and tune the cache for the workload.

8.5.8 Workload Separation

Some types of workloads can perform better when configured to use their own file systems and disk devices. This approach has been known as using "separate spindles," since creating random I/O by seeking between two different workload locations is particularly bad for rotational disks (see Chapter 9, Disks).

For example, a database may benefit from having separate file systems and disks for its log files and its database files.

8.5.9 Memory-Based File Systems

Another configuration approach to improve performance is the use of memory-based file systems. These are kept in memory so that the file contents are served as quickly as possible. They are usually deployed only as work-arounds, as many applications have their own (configurable) application-specific cache in process memory, which is more efficient to access than going via a file and syscall interface. Memory-based file systems are also often not worth the effort on modern systems, which employ large file system caches.

/tmp

The standard /tmp file system is used to store temporary files and is commonly configured to be memory-based. For example, Solaris uses tmpfs for /tmp, which is a memory-based file system backed by swap devices. There is also a tmpfs for Linux, which is used for a few special file system types.

8.5.10 Micro-Benchmarking

Benchmark tools for file system and disk benchmarking (of which there are many) can be used to test the performance of different file system types or settings within a file system, for given workloads. Typical factors that may be tested include

- **Operation types:** the rate of reads, writes, and other file system operations
- **I/O size:** 1 byte up to 1 Mbyte and larger
- **File offset pattern:** random or sequential
- **Random-access pattern:** uniform random or Pareto distribution
- **Write type:** asynchronous or synchronous (O_SYNC)
- **Working set size:** how well it fits in the file system cache
- **Concurrency:** number of I/O in flight, or number of threads performing I/O
- **Memory mapping:** file access via mmap(), instead of read()/write()
- **Cache state:** whether the file system cache is "cold" (unpopulated) or "warm"
- **File system tunables:** may include compression, data deduplication, and so on

Common combinations include random read, sequential read, random write, and sequential write.

The most critical factor is often the *working set size*: the volume of data that is accessed during the benchmark. Depending on the benchmark, this may be the total size of the files in use. A small working set size may return entirely from the file system cache in main memory (DRAM). A large working set size may return mostly from storage devices (disks). The performance difference can be multiple orders of magnitude.

Consider the general expectations for different benchmarks, which include the total size of the files (working set size), in Table 8.5.

Some file system benchmark tools are not clear about what they are testing and may imply a *disk* benchmark but use a small total file size and return entirely from cache instead. See Section 8.3.12, Logical versus Physical I/O, to understand the difference between testing the file system (logical I/O) and testing the disks (physical I/O).

Table 8-5 File System Benchmark Expectations

System Memory	Total File Size	Benchmark	Expectation
128 Gbytes	10 Gbytes	random read	100% cache hits
128 Gbytes	1,000 Gbytes	random read	mostly disk reads, with ~12% cache hits
128 Gbytes	10 Gbytes	sequential read	100% cache hits
128 Gbytes	1,000 Gbytes	sequential read	mixture of cache hits (most due to prefetch) and disk reads
128 Gbytes	10 Gbytes	writes	mostly cache hits (buffering), with some blocking on writes depending on file system behavior
128 Gbytes	10 Gbytes	synchronous writes	100% disk writes

Some *disk* benchmark tools operate via the file system by using direct I/O to avoid caching and buffering. The file system still plays a minor role, adding code path overheads and mapping differences between file and on-disk placement. This is sometimes a deliberate strategy for testing the *file system*: analyzing worst-case performance (0% cache hit rate). This strategy is becoming increasingly unrealistic, as applications are more commonly expecting a significant cache hit rate due to larger memory systems.

See Chapter 12, Benchmarking, for more on this general topic.

8.6 Analysis

This section introduces file system performance analysis tools for Linux- and Solaris-based operating systems. See the previous section for strategies to follow when using these.

The tools in this section are listed in Table 8.6.

Table 8-6 File System Analysis Tools

Linux	Solaris	Description
—	vfsstat	file system statistics, including average latency
—	fsstat	file system statistics
strace	truss	system call debuggers
DTrace	DTrace	dynamic tracing of file system operations, latency

Table 8-6 File System Analysis Tools (*Continued*)

Linux	Solaris	Description
free	—	cache capacity statistics
top	top	includes memory usage summary
vmstat	vmstat	virtual memory statistics
sar	sar	various statistics, including historic
slabtop	mdb ::kmastat	kernel slab allocator statistics
—	fcachestat	various cache hit rates and sizes
/proc/meminfo	mdb ::memstat	kernel memory breakdowns
—	kstat	various file system and cache statistics

This is a selection of tools and capabilities to support the preceding methodology section, beginning with system-wide and per-file-system observability, then operation and latency analysis, and finishing with cache statistics. See the tool documentation, including man pages, for full references of their features.

While your interest may be in Linux- or Solaris-based systems only, consider the other operating system tools and the observability that they provide for a different perspective.

8.6.1 vfsstat

vfsstat(1) is an iostat(1M)-like tool for the VFS level, first developed by Bill Pijewski for SmartOS. It prints per-interval summaries of file system operations (logical I/O), including the average latency experienced by the user-level applications. This information is more relevant to application performance than the statistics from iostat(1), which show disk I/O (physical I/O), including asynchronous types.

```
$ vfsstat 1
   r/s   w/s   kr/s  kw/s ractv wactv read_t writ_t  %r  %w   d/s  del_t zone
   2.5   0.1    1.5   0.0   0.0   0.0    0.0    2.6   0   0   0.0    8.0 dev (5)
1540.4 0.0 95014.9   0.0   0.0   0.0    0.0    0.0   3   0   0.0    0.0 dev (5)
1991.7 0.0 74931.5   0.0   0.0   0.0    0.0    0.0   4   0   0.0    0.0 dev (5)
1989.8 0.0 84697.0   0.0   0.0   0.0    0.0    0.0   4   0   0.0    0.0 dev (5)
[...]
```

The first line of output is the summary-since-boot, followed by per-second summaries. The columns include

- **r/s, w/s:** file system reads and writes per second
- **kr/s, kw/s:** file system kilobytes read and written per second

- **ractv**, **wactv**: average number of read and write operations in service
- **read_t**, **writ_t**: average VFS read and write latency (ms)
- **%r, %w**: percent of time VFS read and write operations are pending
- **d/s, del_t**: I/O throttle delays per second, and average delay in microseconds

vfsstat(1) provides information for characterizing the workload as well as the resulting performance. It also includes information about ZFS I/O throttling, which is used in SmartOS cloud computing environments to balance tenants.

The previous example shows a read workload of between 1.5 and 2 K reads/s, and a throughput between 73 and 92 Mbytes/s. The average latency is so small that it has been rounded down to 0.0 ms. This workload, which is likely returning from the file system cache, is keeping the file system busy (active) only between 3% and 4% of the time.

8.6.2 fsstat

The Solaris fsstat tool reports various file system statistics:

```
$ fsstat /var 1
 new   name   name  attr  attr lookup rddir  read read  write write
 file  remov  chng   get   set    ops   ops   ops bytes   ops bytes
8.98K   520    177 1.61M 2.26K  3.57M 18.2K 3.78M 6.85G 2.98M 9.10G /var
    0     0      0     0     0      0     0     0     0     1   152 /var
    0     0      0     1     0      3     0     2    24     1   109 /var
    0     0      0    51     0     35     0     0     0     1    14 /var
[...]
```

These can be used for workload characterization and can be examined on a per-file-system basis. Note that fsstat does not include latency statistics.

8.6.3 strace, truss

Previous operating system tools for measuring file system latency in detail included the debuggers for the syscall interface, such as strace(1) for Linux and truss(1) for Solaris. Such debuggers can hurt performance and may be suitable for use only when the performance overhead is acceptable and other methods to analyze latency are not possible.

This example shows strace(1) timing reads on an ext4 file system:

```
$ strace -ttT -p 845
[...]
18:41:01.513110 read(9, "\334\260/\224\356k..."..., 65536) = 65536 <0.018225>
```

```
18:41:01.531646 read(9,  "\371X\265|\244\317...".., 65536) = 65536 <0.000056>
18:41:01.531984 read(9,  "\357\311\347\1\241...".., 65536) = 65536 <0.005760>
18:41:01.538151 read(9,  "*\263\264\204|\370...".., 65536) = 65536 <0.000033>
18:41:01.538549 read(9,  "\205q\327\304f\370...".., 65536) = 65536 <0.002033>
18:41:01.540923 read(9,  "\6\2738>zw\321\353...".., 65536) = 65536 <0.000032>
```

The -tt option prints the relative timestamps on the left, and -T prints the syscall times on the right. Each read() was for 64 Kbytes, the first taking 18 ms, followed by 56 µs (likely cached), then 5 ms. The reads were to file descriptor 9. To check that this is to a file system (and isn't a socket), either the open() syscall will be visible in earlier strace(1) output, or another tool such as lsof(8) can be used.

8.6.4 DTrace

DTrace can be used to examine file system behavior from the syscall interface, from the VFS interface, and from within the file system. These abilities support workload characterization and latency analysis.

The following sections introduce DTrace for file system analysis on Solaris- and Linux-based systems. Unless noted, the DTrace commands are intended for both operating systems. A DTrace primer was included in Chapter 4, Observability Tools.

Operation Counts

Summarizing file system operations by application and by type provides useful measures for workload characterization.

This **Solaris** one-liner counts file system operations by application name, using the fsinfo (file system info) provider:

```
# dtrace -n 'fsinfo::: { @[execname] = count(); }'
dtrace: description 'fsinfo::: ' matched 46 probes
^C
[...]
  fsflush                                                          970
  splunkd                                                         2147
  nginx                                                           7338
  node                                                           25340
```

The output shows that processes named node performed 25,340 file system operations while tracing. A tick-1s probe can be included to report by-second summaries, allowing rates to be observed.

The type of operation can be reported by aggregating on `probename` instead of `execname`. For example:

```
# dtrace -n 'fsinfo::: /execname == "splunkd"/ { @[probename] = count(); }'
dtrace: description 'fsinfo::: ' matched 46 probes
^C
[...]
  read                                                                    13
  write                                                                   16
  seek                                                                    22
  rwlock                                                                  29
  rwunlock                                                                29
  getattr                                                                131
  lookup                                                                 565
```

This also shows how a particular application can be examined, in this case filtering on `"splunkd"`.

On **Linux**, file system operations can be observed from the syscall and fbt providers, until fsinfo is available. For example, using fbt to trace kernel vfs functions:

```
# dtrace -n 'fbt::vfs_*:entry { @[execname] = count(); }'
dtrace: description 'fbt::vfs_*:entry ' matched 39 probes
^C
[...]
  sshd                                                                   913
  ls                                                                    1367
  bash                                                                  1462
  sysbench                                                             10295
```

The largest number of file system operations during this trace was called by applications with the name `sysbench` (a benchmarking tool [3]).

Counting the type of operation by aggregating on `probefunc`:

```
# dtrace -n 'fbt::vfs_*:entry /execname == "sysbench"/ { @[probefunc] = count(); }'
dtrace: description 'fbt::vfs_*:entry ' matched 39 probes
^C
  vfs_write                                                             4001
  vfs_read                                                              5999
```

This matched a sysbench process while it performed a random read-write benchmark, showing the ratio of operations. To strip the `vfs_` from the output, instead of `@[probefunc]`, use `@[probefunc + 4]` (pointer plus offset).

File Opens

The previous one-liners used DTrace to summarize event counts. The following demonstrates printing all event data separately, in this case, details for the open() system call, system-wide:

```
# opensnoop -ve
STRTIME                      UID    PID COMM       FD ERR PATH
2012 Sep 13 23:30:55 45821  24218 ruby        23   0 /var/run/name_service_door
2012 Sep 13 23:30:55 45821  24218 ruby        23   0 /etc/inet/ipnodes
2012 Sep 13 23:30:55    80   3505 nginx       -1   2 /public/dev-3/vendor/
2012 Sep 13 23:30:56    80  25308 php-fpm       5   0 /public/etc/config.xml
2012 Sep 13 23:30:56    80  25308 php-fpm       5   0 /public/etc/local.xml
2012 Sep 13 23:30:56    80  25308 php-fpm       5   0 /public/etc/local.xml
[...]
```

opensnoop is a DTrace-based tool from the DTraceToolkit; it is included by default in Oracle Solaris 11 and Mac OS X and is available for other OSs. It provides a certain view of the file system workload, showing processes, path names, and errors for open()s, which is useful for both performance analysis and troubleshooting. In this example, the nginx process encountered a failed open (ERR 2 == file not found).

Other popular DTraceToolkit scripts include rwsnoop and rwtop, which trace and summarize logical I/O. rwsnoop traces the read() and write() syscalls, and rwtop uses the sysinfo provider to summarize throughput (bytes).

System Call Latency

This one-liner measures file system latency at the system call interface, summarizing it as a histogram in units of nanoseconds:

```
# dtrace -n 'syscall::read:entry /fds[arg0].fi_fs == "zfs"/ {
    self->start = timestamp; }
syscall::read:return /self->start/ {
    @["ns"] = quantize(timestamp - self->start); self->start = 0; }'
dtrace: description 'syscall::read:entry ' matched 2 probes
^C
  ns
           value  ------------- Distribution ------------- count
            1024 |                                         0
            2048 |                                         2
            4096 |@@@@@@                                   103
            8192 |@@@@@@@@@@                               162
           16384 |                                         3
           32768 |                                         0
           65536 |                                         0
          131072 |                                         1
          262144 |                                         0
          524288 |                                         1
         1048576 |                                         3
         2097152 |@@@                                      48
         4194304 |@@@@@@@@@@@@@@@@@@@@@                    345
         8388608 |                                         0
```

The distribution shows two peaks, the first between 4 and 16 µs (cache hits), and the second between 2 and 8 ms (disk reads). Instead of quantize(), the avg() function could be used to show the average (mean). However, that would average the two peaks, which would be misleading.

This approach traces individual system calls, in this case read(). To capture all file system operations, all related system calls need to be traced, including variants of each type (e.g., pread(), pread64()). This can be performed by building a script to capture all types, or, for a given application, checking which system call types it uses (via DTrace) and then tracing only those.

This approach also captures all file system activity, including non-storage file systems such as sockfs. For this one-liner, the file system type was filtered by checking the value of fds[arg0].fi_fs, which translates the file descriptor (arg0 for read()) into the file system type (fds[].fi_fs). Other useful filters can be applied in this context, such as by application name or PID, mount point, or path name components.

Note that this latency may or may not directly affect application performance, as mentioned in Section 8.3.1, File System Latency. It depends on whether the latency is encountered during an application request, or if it is during an asynchronous background task. You can use DTrace to begin answering this question by capturing the user-level stack trace for syscall I/O, which may explain why it was performed (e.g., aggregate using @[ustack(), "ns"]). This can become an advanced activity depending on the complexity of the application and its source code.

VFS Latency

The VFS interface can be traced, either via a static provider (if one exists) or via dynamic tracing (the fbt provider).

On **Solaris**, VFS can be traced via the fop_*() functions, for example:

```
# dtrace -n 'fbt::fop_read:entry /stringof(args[0]->v_op->vnop_name) == "zfs"/ {
    self->start = timestamp; } fbt::fop_read:return /self->start/ {
    @["ns"] = quantize(timestamp - self->start); self->start = 0; }'
dtrace: description 'fbt::fop_read:entry ' matched 2 probes
^C
  ns
            value  ------------- Distribution ------------- count
              512 |                                         0
             1024 |                                         12
             2048 |@@@@@@@@@@@@@@@@@@@@@@@@                  2127
             4096 |@@@@@@@@@@@@@@@@@@@                       1732
             8192 |                                         10
            16384 |                                         0
```

Unlike the previous syscall example, this shows a fully cached workload. This one-liner also has broader visibility as it matches all read variants.

Other VFS operations can be similarly traced. Listing entry probes:

```
# dtrace -ln 'fbt::fop_*:entry'
   ID    PROVIDER          MODULE                         FUNCTION NAME
 15164        fbt         genunix                  fop_inactive entry
 16462        fbt         genunix                   fop_addmap entry
 16466        fbt         genunix                   fop_access entry
 16599        fbt         genunix                   fop_create entry
 16611        fbt         genunix                   fop_delmap entry
 16763        fbt         genunix                   fop_frlock entry
 16990        fbt         genunix                   fop_lookup entry
 17100        fbt         genunix                    fop_close entry
[...39 lines truncaed...]
```

Note that the fbt provider is considered an unstable interface, so any fbt-based one-liners or scripts may need updates to match the kernel as it changes (which is fairly unlikely, as the VFS implementation doesn't change often).

On **Linux**, using a DTrace prototype:

```
# dtrace -n 'fbt::vfs_read:entry /stringof(((struct file *)arg0)->
f_path.dentry->d_sb->s_type->name) == "ext4"/ { self->start = timestamp; }
    fbt::vfs_read:return /self->start/ {
    @["ns"] = quantize(timestamp - self->start); self->start = 0; }'
dtrace: description 'fbt::vfs_read:entry ' matched 2 probes
^C
  ns
          value  ------------- Distribution ------------- count
           1024 |                                         0
           2048 |@                                        13
           4096 |@@@@@@@@@@@@                             114
           8192 |@@@                                      26
          16384 |@@@                                      32
          32768 |@@@                                      29
          65536 |@@                                       23
         131072 |@                                        9
         262144 |@                                        5
         524288 |@@                                       14
        1048576 |@                                        6
        2097152 |@@@                                      31
        4194304 |@@@@@@                                   55
        8388608 |@@                                       14
       16777216 |                                         0
```

This time the predicate matches on the ext4 file system. Peaks for both cache hits and misses can be seen, with expected latency.

Listing VFS function entry probes:

```
# dtrace -ln 'fbt::vfs_*:entry'
   ID    PROVIDER          MODULE                         FUNCTION NAME
 15518        fbt          kernel                   vfs_llseek entry
 15552        fbt          kernel                    vfs_write entry
 15554        fbt          kernel                     vfs_read entry
```

continues

```
15572         fbt            kernel            vfs_writev entry
15574         fbt            kernel            vfs_readv entry
15678         fbt            kernel        vfs_kern_mount entry
15776         fbt            kernel           vfs_getattr entry
15778         fbt            kernel           vfs_fstatat entry
[...31 lines truncated...]
```

Block Device I/O Stacks

Examining kernel stack traces for block device I/O is a great way to see how file systems work internally, and the code path that leads to disk I/O. It can also help explain the cause of additional disk I/O (asynchronous, metadata) beyond the expected rate for the workload.

Exposing **ZFS** internals by frequency counting kernel stack traces when block device I/O is issued:

```
# dtrace -n 'io:::start { @[stack()] = count(); }'
dtrace: description 'io:::start ' matched 6 probes
^C
[...]
              genunix`ldi_strategy+0x53
              zfs`vdev_disk_io_start+0xcc
              zfs`zio_vdev_io_start+0xab
              zfs`zio_execute+0x88
              zfs`vdev_queue_io_done+0x70
              zfs`zio_vdev_io_done+0x80
              zfs`zio_execute+0x88
              genunix`taskq_thread+0x2d0
              unix`thread_start+0x8
              1070

              genunix`ldi_strategy+0x53
              zfs`vdev_disk_io_start+0xcc
              zfs`zio_vdev_io_start+0xab
              zfs`zio_execute+0x88
              zfs`zio_nowait+0x21
              zfs`vdev_mirror_io_start+0xcd
              zfs`zio_vdev_io_start+0x250
              zfs`zio_execute+0x88
              zfs`zio_nowait+0x21
              zfs`arc_read_nolock+0x4f9
              zfs`arc_read+0x96
              zfs`dsl_read+0x44
              zfs`dbuf_read_impl+0x166
              zfs`dbuf_read+0xab
              zfs`dmu_buf_hold_array_by_dnode+0x189
              zfs`dmu_buf_hold_array+0x78
              zfs`dmu_read_uio+0x5c
              zfs`zfs_read+0x1a3
              genunix`fop_read+0x8b
              genunix`read+0x2a7
              2690
```

The output shows stack traces followed by their occurrence counts while tracing. The top stack shows an asynchronous ZFS I/O (from a taskq thread running the ZIO pipeline) and a synchronous I/O originating from a read syscall. To gather further details, each line of these stacks may be traced individually using dynamic tracing via the DTrace fbt provider.

Exposing **ext4** using the same approach:

```
# dtrace -n 'io:::start { @[stack()] = count(); }'
dtrace: description 'io:::start ' matched 6 probes
^C
[...]
              kernel`generic_make_request+0x68
              kernel`submit_bio+0x87
              kernel`do_mpage_readpage+0x436
              kernel`mpage_readpages+0xd7
              kernel`ext4_readpages+0x1d
              kernel`__do_page_cache_readahead+0x1c7
              kernel`ra_submit+0x21
              kernel`ondemand_readahead+0x115
              kernel`page_cache_async_readahead+0x80
              kernel`generic_file_aio_read+0x48b
              kernel`do_sync_read+0xd2
              kernel`vfs_read+0xb0
              kernel`sys_read+0x4a
              kernel`system_call_fastpath+0x16
          109
```

This path shows a `read()` syscall triggering a read-ahead by the page cache.

File System Internals

When necessary, latency can be pinpointed in the file system by tracing its implementation.

Listing **ZFS** function entry probes on Solaris:

```
# dtrace -ln 'fbt:zfs::entry'
   ID   PROVIDER            MODULE                          FUNCTION NAME
47553       fbt               zfs                          buf_hash entry
47555       fbt               zfs          buf_discard_identity entry
47557       fbt               zfs                     buf_hash_find entry
47559       fbt               zfs                   buf_hash_insert entry
47561       fbt               zfs                   buf_hash_remove entry
47563       fbt               zfs                          buf_fini entry
47565       fbt               zfs                          hdr_cons entry
47567       fbt               zfs                          buf_cons entry
[...2328 lines truncated...]
```

ZFS has a straightforward mapping to VFS, making high-level tracing easy. For example, tracing ZFS read latency:

```
# dtrace -n 'fbt::zfs_read:entry { self->start = timestamp; }
    fbt::zfs_read:return /self->start/ {
    @["ns"] = quantize(timestamp - self->start); self->start = 0; }'
dtrace: description 'fbt::zfs_read:entry ' matched 2 probes
```

continues

```
^C

ns
          value  ------------- Distribution ------------- count
            512 |                                                 0
           1024 |@                                                6
           2048 |@@                                               18
           4096 |@@@@@@@                                          79
           8192 |@@@@@@@@@@@@@@@@@@                                191
          16384 |@@@@@@@@@@                                        112
          32768 |@                                                14
          65536 |                                                 1
         131072 |                                                 1
         262144 |                                                 0
         524288 |                                                 0
        1048576 |                                                 0
        2097152 |                                                 0
        4194304 |@@@                                              31
        8388608 |@                                                9
       16777216 |                                                 0
```

The output shows a peak of I/O around 8 μs (cache hits), and another around 4 ms (cache misses). This works because `zfs_read()` synchronously blocks on the syscall. Deeper into ZFS internals, functions will issue I/O but not block waiting for its completion, and so measuring I/O time becomes more involved.

ext4 file system internals on Linux can be traced in a similar way:

```
# dtrace -ln 'fbt::ext4_*:entry'
   ID    PROVIDER           MODULE                      FUNCTION NAME
20430         fbt           kernel       ext4_lock_group.clone.14 entry
20432         fbt           kernel   ext4_get_group_no_and_offset entry
20434         fbt           kernel            ext4_block_in_group entry
20436         fbt           kernel            ext4_get_group_desc entry
20438         fbt           kernel           ext4_has_free_blocks entry
20440         fbt           kernel         ext4_claim_free_blocks entry
20442         fbt           kernel         ext4_should_retry_alloc entry
20444         fbt           kernel          ext4_new_meta_blocks entry
[...347 lines truncated...]
```

Some of these functions are synchronous, for example, `ext4_readdir()`, whose latency can be measured in the same way as the earlier `zfs_read()` example. Other functions are not synchronous, including `ext4_readpage()` and `ext4_readpages()`. To measure their latency, times between I/O issue and completion will need to be associated and compared. Or trace higher in the stack, as was demonstrated in the VFS example.

Slow Event Tracing

DTrace can print details for every file system operation, just as iosnoop from Chapter 9, Disks, prints every disk I/O. Tracing at the file system level, however, can produce a much greater volume of output, since it includes file system cache hits. One way around this is to print only slow operations, which helps in analyzing a particular class of issue: latency outliers.

The zfsslower.d script [4] prints ZFS-level operations slower than a set number of milliseconds:

```
# ./zfsslower.d 10
TIME                      PROCESS       D    KB    ms FILE
2011 May 17 01:23:12 mysqld           R    16    19 /z01/opt/mysql5-64/data/xxxxx.ibd
2011 May 17 01:23:13 mysqld           W    16    10 /z01/var/mysql/xxxxx.ibd
2011 May 17 01:23:33 mysqld           W    16    11 /z01/var/mysql/xxxxx.ibd
2011 May 17 01:23:33 mysqld           W    16    10 /z01/var/mysql/xxxxx.ibd
2011 May 17 01:23:51 httpd            R    56    14 /z01/home/xxxxx/xxxxx/xxxxx
^C
```

This redacted output shows file system operations slower than 10 ms.

Advanced Tracing

Dynamic tracing can explore file systems in more detail when needed for advanced analysis. To provide an idea of the possibilities, Table 8.7 shows scripts from the (108-page) File Systems chapter of *DTrace* [Gregg 11] (these scripts are also available online [4]).

Table 8-7 Advanced File System Tracing Scripts

Script	Layer	Description
sysfs.d	syscall	shows reads and writes by process and mount point
fsrwcount.d	syscall	counts read/write syscalls by file system and type
fsrwtime.d	syscall	measures time in read/write syscalls by file system
fsrtpk.d	syscall	measures file system read time per kilobyte
rwsnoop	syscall	traces syscall read and writes, with FS details
mmap.d	syscall	traces mmap() of files with details
fserrors.d	syscall	shows file system syscall errors
fswho.d	VFS	summarizes processes and file reads/writes
readtype.d	VFS	compares logical versus physical file system reads
writetype.d	VFS	compares logical versus physical file system writes
fssnoop.d	VFS	traces file system calls using fsinfo
solvfssnoop.d	VFS	traces file system calls using fbt on Solaris
sollife.d	VFS	shows file creation and deletion on Solaris
fsflush_cpu.d	VFS	shows file system flush tracer CPU time

continues

Table 8-7 Advanced File System Tracing Scripts (*Continued*)

Script	Layer	Description
fsflush.d	VFS	shows file system flush statistics
dnlcps.d	DNLC	shows DNLC hits by process
ufssnoop.d	UFS	traces UFS calls directly using fbt
ufsreadahead.d	UFS	shows UFS read-ahead rates for sequential I/O
ufsimiss.d	UFS	traces UFS inode cache misses with details
zfssnoop.d	ZFS	traces ZFS calls directly using fbt
zfslower.d	ZFS	traces slow ZFS reads/writes
zioprint.d	ZFS	shows ZIO event dump
ziosnoop.d	ZFS	shows ZIO event tracing, detailed
ziotype.d	ZFS	shows ZIO type summary by pool
perturbation.d	ZFS	shows ZFS read/write time during given perturbation
spasync.d	ZFS	shows storage pool allocator (SPA) sync tracing with details
nfswizard.d	NFS	summarizes NFS performance client-side
nfs3sizes.d	NFS	shows NFSv3 logical versus physical read sizes
nfs3fileread.d	NFS	shows NFSv3 logical versus physical reads by file
tmpusers.d	TMP	shows users of /tmp and tmpfs by tracing open()
tmpgetpage.d	TMP	measures whether tmpfs paging is occurring, with I/O time

While this degree of observability is incredible, many of these dynamic tracing scripts are tied to specific kernel internals and will require maintenance to match changes in newer kernel versions.

As an example of advanced tracing, the following DTraceToolkit script traced events from multiple layers while a 50 Kbyte file was read from UFS:

```
# ./fsrw.d
Event            Device RW    Size Offset Path
sc-read              .  R     8192      0 /extra1/50k
  fop_read           .  R     8192      0 /extra1/50k
    disk_io      cmdk0  R     8192      0 /extra1/50k
    disk_ra      cmdk0  R     8192      8 /extra1/50k
sc-read              .  R     8192      8 /extra1/50k
  fop_read           .  R     8192      8 /extra1/50k
    disk_ra      cmdk0  R    34816     16 /extra1/50k
sc-read              .  R     8192     16 /extra1/50k
  fop_read           .  R     8192     16 /extra1/50k
sc-read              .  R     8192     24 /extra1/50k
  fop_read           .  R     8192     24 /extra1/50k
sc-read              .  R     8192     32 /extra1/50k
  fop_read           .  R     8192     32 /extra1/50k
sc-read              .  R     8192     40 /extra1/50k
  fop_read           .  R     8192     40 /extra1/50k
```

```
sc-read                 .  R     8192      48 /extra1/50k
   fop_read             .  R     8192      48 /extra1/50k
sc-read                 .  R     8192      50 /extra1/50k
   fop_read             .  R     8192      50 /extra1/50k
^C
```

The first event was a syscall read (`sc-read`) of 8 Kbytes, which was processed as a
VFS read (`fop_read`) and then a disk read (`disk_io`) followed by a read-ahead of
the next 8 Kbytes (`disk_ra`). The next syscall read at offset 8 (Kbytes) does not
trigger a disk read, since it is cached, but instead triggers a read-ahead starting at
offset 16 for the next 34 Kbytes—the rest of the 50 Kbyte file. The remaining syscalls return from cache, and only the VFS events can be seen.

8.6.5 SystemTap

SystemTap can also be used on Linux systems for dynamic tracing of file system
events. See Section 4.4, SystemTap, in Chapter 4, Observability Tools, and Appendix E for help with converting the previous DTrace scripts.

8.6.6 LatencyTOP

LatencyTOP is a tool for reporting sources of latency, aggregated system-wide and
per process [5]. It was developed for Linux and has since been ported to Solaris-
based systems.

File system latency is reported by LatencyTOP. For example:

```
Cause                                     Maximum      Percentage
Reading from file                      209.6 msec         61.9 %
synchronous write                       82.6 msec         24.0 %
Marking inode dirty                      7.9 msec          2.2 %
Waiting for a process to die             4.6 msec          1.5 %
Waiting for event (select)               3.6 msec         10.1 %
Page fault                               0.2 msec          0.2 %

Process gzip (10969)            Total: 442.4 msec
Reading from file                      209.6 msec         70.2 %
synchronous write                       82.6 msec         27.2 %
Marking inode dirty                      7.9 msec          2.5 %
```

The top section is the system-wide summary, and the bottom is for a single
`gzip(1)` process, which is compressing a file. Most of the latency for `gzip(1)` is
due to `Reading from file` at 70.2%, with 27.2% in `synchronous write` as the
new compressed file is written.

LatencyTOP requires the following kernel options: CONFIG_LATENCYTOP
and CONFIG_HAVE_LATENCYTOP_SUPPORT.

8.6.7 free

The Linux free(1) command shows memory and swap statistics:

```
$ free -m
              total       used       free     shared    buffers     cached
Mem:            868        799         68          0        130        608
-/+ buffers/cache:          60        808
Swap:             0          0          0
```

The buffers column shows the buffer cache size, and the cached column shows
the page cache size. The -m option was used to present the output in megabytes.

8.6.8 top

Some versions of the top(1) command include file system cache details. This line
from a Linux top includes the buffer cache size, which is also reported by free(1):

```
Mem:    889484k total,   819056k used,    70428k free,   134024k buffers
```

See Chapter 6, CPUs, for more about top(1).

8.6.9 vmstat

The vmstat(1) command, like top(1), also may include details on the file system cache. For more details on vmstat(1), see Chapter 7, Memory.

Linux

The following runs vmstat(1) with an interval of 1 to provide one-second
updates:

```
$ vmstat 1
procs -----------memory---------- ---swap-- -----io---- --system-- -----cpu-----
 r  b   swpd   free   buff  cache   si   so    bi    bo   in   cs us sy id wa st
 0  0      0  70296 134024 623100    0    0     1     1    7    6  0  0 100  0  0
 0  0      0  68900 134024 623100    0    0     0     0   46   96  1  2 97  0  0
[...]
```

The buff column shows the buffer cache size, and cache shows the page cache
size, both in kilobytes.

Solaris

The default output of Solaris vmstat(1) does not show cache sizes but is worth mentioning here:

```
$ vmstat 1
 kthr      memory            page            disk          faults      cpu
 r b w   swap  free  re  mf pi po fr de sr rm s0 s1 --  in   sy   cs us sy id
 0 0 36 88812996 3883956 324 3099 5 1 1 0 6 -1546 -0 92 0 28521 79147 37128 5 5 90
 1 0 317 86830644 2981520 23 137 43 2 2 0 0  0  1  0 23063 59809 31454 1 3 96
 0 0 317 86826504 2977588 1876 40670 0 0 0 0 0 0 0 0 44264 110777 32383 15 10 76
 [...]
```

The free column is in kilobytes. Since Solaris 9, the page cache is treated as free memory, and its size is included in this column.

The -p option shows page-in/page-out breakdowns by type:

```
$ vmstat -p 1 5
     memory           page          executable      anonymous      filesystem
   swap free  re  mf  fr  de  sr  epi epo epf  api apo apf  fpi fpo fpf
 8740292 1290896 75 168 0   0  12    0   0   0   11   0   0    0   0   0
 10828352 3214300 155 42 0  0   0    0   0   0    0   0   0    0 12931 0   0
 10828352 3221976 483 62 0  0   0    0   0   0    0   0   0    0 15568 0   0
 [...]
```

This allows file system paging to be differentiated from anonymous paging (low memory). Unfortunately, the file system columns do not currently include ZFS file system events.

8.6.10 sar

The system activity reporter, sar(1), provides various file system statistics and may be configured to record these historically. sar(1) is mentioned in various chapters in this book for the different statistics it provides.

Linux

Executing sar(1) with an interval for reporting current activity:

```
# sar -v 1
Linux 2.6.35.14-103.fc14.x86_64 (fedora0)      07/13/2012      _x86_64_   (1 CPU)

12:07:32 AM dentunusd   file-nr   inode-nr   pty-nr
12:07:33 AM     11498       384      14029        6
12:07:34 AM     11498       384      14029        6
 [...]
```

The −v option provides the following columns:

- **dentunusd:** directory entry cache unused count (available entries)
- **file-nr:** number of file handles in use
- **inode-nr:** number of inodes in use

There is also a −r option, which prints kbbuffers and kbcached columns for buffer cache and page cache sizes, in kilobytes.

Solaris

Executing sar(1) with an interval and count to report current activity:

```
$ sar -v 1 1
[...]
03:16:47  proc-sz   ov  inod-sz   ov  file-sz   ov   lock-sz
03:16:48   95/16346   0 7895/70485   0  882/882    0    0/0
```

The −v option provides inod-sz, showing the inode cache size and maximum. There is also a −b option to provide statistics on the old buffer cache.

8.6.11 slabtop

The Linux slabtop(1) command prints information about the kernel slab caches, some of which are used for file system caches:

```
# slabtop -o
 Active / Total Objects (% used)    : 151827 / 165106 (92.0%)
 Active / Total Slabs (% used)      : 7599 / 7599 (100.0%)
 Active / Total Caches (% used)     : 68 / 101 (67.3%)
 Active / Total Size (% used)       : 44974.72K / 47255.53K (95.2%)
 Minimum / Average / Maximum Object : 0.01K / 0.29K / 8.00K

  OBJS ACTIVE  USE OBJ SIZE  SLABS OBJ/SLAB CACHE SIZE NAME
 35802  27164  75%   0.10K    918       39     3672K buffer_head
 26607  26515  99%   0.19K   1267       21     5068K dentry
 26046  25948  99%   0.86K   2894        9    23152K ext4_inode_cache
 12240  10095  82%   0.05K    144       85      576K shared_policy_node
 11228  11228 100%   0.14K    401       28     1604K sysfs_dir_cache
  9968   9616  96%   0.07K    178       56      712K selinux_inode_security
  6846   6846 100%   0.55K    489       14     3912K inode_cache
  5632   5632 100%   0.01K     11      512       44K kmalloc-8
[...]
```

Without the −o output mode, slabtop(1) will refresh and update the screen. Slabs may include

- **dentry:** dentry cache
- **inode_cache:** inode cache
- **ext3_inode_cache:** inode cache for ext3
- **ext4_inode_cache:** inode cache for ext4

slabtop(1) uses /proc/slabinfo, which exists if CONFIG_SLAB is enabled.

8.6.12 mdb ::kmastat

Detailed kernel memory allocator statistics on Solaris can be viewed using the ::kmastat in mdb -k, which includes various caches in use by the file systems:

```
> ::kmastat
cache                         buf         buf       buf memory    alloc alloc
name                          size     in use    total in use   succeed fail
-------------------------     -----  ---------  -------- ------  --------- -----
kmem_magazine_1                 16       7438     18323  292K      90621    0
[...]
zfs_file_data_4096              4K        223      1024    4M       1011    0
zfs_file_data_8192              8K    2964824   3079872 23.5G    8487977    0
zfs_file_data_12288            12K        137       440 5.50M        435    0
zfs_file_data_16384            16K         26       176 2.75M        185    0
[...]
ufs_inode_cache                368      27061     27070 10.6M      27062    0
[...]
```

The output is many pages long, showing all of the kernel allocator caches. The memory in use column can be studied to determine which caches are storing the most data, providing an insight into kernel memory usage. In this example, 23.5 Gbytes was in use by the ZFS 8 Kbyte file data cache. Allocations to specific caches can also be dynamically traced if needed, to identify the code path and consumer.

8.6.13 fcachestat

This is an open-source tool for Solaris-based systems that uses the Perl Sun::Solaris::Kstat library and prints a summary suitable for cache activity analysis on UFS:

```
~/Dev/CacheKit/CacheKit-0.96> ./fcachestat 1 5
 --- dnlc ---    -- inode ---    -- ufsbuf --    -- segmap --    -- segvn ---
 %hit   total   %hit   total    %hit   total    %hit   total    %hit   total
99.45  476.6M  15.35  914326   99.78    7.4M   93.41   10.7M   99.89  413.7M
70.99    2754  17.52     799   98.71     696   52.51    2510   35.94    2799
72.64    1356   0.00     371   98.94     377   51.10    1779   35.32    2421
71.32    1231   0.00     353   96.49     427   47.23    2581   42.37    4406
84.90    1517   0.00     229   97.27     330   48.57    1748   47.85    3162
```

The first line is the summary-since-boot. There are five groups of columns for the various caches and drivers. ufsbuf is the old buffer cache, and segmap and segvn show the drivers to the page cache. The columns show hit/miss ratio as a percent (%hit) and total number of accesses (total).

fcachestat may need updating to work properly; it is included here to show what kinds of information can be made available from the system.[2]

8.6.14 /proc/meminfo

The Linux /proc/meminfo file provides a summary of memory breakdowns and is read by tools such as free(1):

```
$ cat /proc/meminfo
MemTotal:       49548744 kB
MemFree:        46704484 kB
Buffers:          279280 kB
Cached:          1400792 kB
[...]
```

This includes the buffer cache (Buffers) and page cache (Cached) and provides other high-level breakdowns of memory usage by the system. These are covered in Chapter 7, Memory.

8.6.15 mdb ::memstat

The Solaris ::memstat command for mdb -k provides a high-level breakdown of Solaris memory usage:

```
> ::memstat
Page Summary                Pages                    MB   %Tot
------------        -----------------    -----------------   ----
Kernel                    3745224                 14629    30%
ZFS File Data             6082651                 23760    48%
Anon                      2187140                  8543    17%
Exec and libs               13085                    51     0%
Page cache                  71065                   277     1%
Free (cachelist)            16778                    65     0%
Free (freelist)            461617                  1803     4%

Total                    12577560                 49131
Physical                 12577559                 49131
```

---

2. fcachestat is part of CacheKit, an experimental collection of cache analysis tools I wrote for Solaris.

This includes ZFS File Data as cached by the ARC, and Page cache, which includes UFS cached data.

8.6.16 kstat

The raw statistics from the previous tools are available from kstat, which can be accessed via the Perl Sun::Solaris::Kstat library, the C libkstat library, or the kstat(1) command. The commands in Table 8.8 display groups of file system statistics, along with the number available (from a recent kernel version).

Table 8-8 kstat Commands for File System Statistics

kstat Command	Description	Statistics
kstat -n segmap	page cache statistics for reads/writes	23
kstat cpu_stat	includes page cache statistics for mapped files	90 per CPU
kstat -n dnlcstats	DNLC statistics	31
kstat -n biostats	old buffer cache statistics	9
kstat -n inode_cache	inode cache statistics	20
kstat -n arcstats	ZFS ARC and L2ARC statistics	56
kstat zone_vfs	per-zone VFS counters	18 per zone

As an example of one of these:

```
$ kstat -n inode_cache
module: ufs                      instance: 0
name:   inode_cache              class:    ufs
        cache allocs             772825
        cache frees              973443
        crtime                   36.947583642
        hits                     139468
        kmem allocs              214347
        kmem frees               206439
        lookup idles             0
        maxsize                  70485
        maxsize reached          90170
        misses                   772825
        pushes at close          0
        puts at backlist         65379
        puts at frontlist        766776
        queues to free           3148
        scans                    485005142
        size                     7895
        snaptime                 5506613.86119402
        thread idles             722525
        vget idles               0
```

While kstats can provide a wealth of information, they have historically not been documented. Sometimes the statistic name is self-descriptive; sometimes it is necessary to check the kernel source code (if available) to determine what each statistic is for.

Available statistics also vary between kernel versions. On recent SmartOS/illumos kernels, the following counters were added:

```
$ kstat zone_vfs
module: zone_vfs                                instance: 3
name:   961ebd45-7fcc-4f18-8f90-ba1353  class:     zone_vfs
        100ms_ops                               5
        10ms_ops                                73
        10s_ops                                 0
        1s_ops                                  1
[...]
```

These count file system operations that have taken longer than the described periods and record them by zone. This information can be invaluable when tracking down file system latency on cloud computing environments.

8.6.17 Other Tools

Other tools and observability frameworks may exist for investigating file system performance and characterizing its usage. These include

- **df(1):** report file system usage and capacity statistics
- **mount(8):** can show file system mounted options (static performance tuning)
- **inotify:** a Linux framework for monitoring file system events

Some file system types have their own specific performance tools, in addition to those provided by the operating system, for example, ZFS.

ZFS

ZFS comes with zpool(1M), which has an iostat suboption for observing ZFS pool statistics. It reports pool operation rates (reads and writes) and throughput.

A popular add-on has been the arcstat.pl tool, which reports ARC and L2ARC size and hit and miss rates. For example:

```
$ arcstat 1
     time  read  miss  miss%  dmis  dm%  pmis  pm%  mmis  mm%  arcsz    c
 04:45:47     0     0      0     0    0     0    0     0    0    14G  14G
 04:45:49   15K    10      0    10    0     0    0     1    0    14G  14G
```

```
04:45:50   23K    81      0    81    0    0    0    1    0    14G    14G
04:45:51   65K    25      0    25    0    0    0    4    0    14G    14G
[...]
```

The statistics are per interval and are

- **read**, **miss:** total ARC accesses, misses
- **miss%**, **dm%**, **pm%**, **mm%:** ARC miss percent total, demand, prefetch, metadata
- **dmis**, **pmis**, **mmis:** misses for demand, prefetch, metadata
- **arcsz**, **c:** ARC size, ARC target size

arcstat.pl is a Perl program that reads statistics from kstat.

8.6.18 Visualizations

The load applied to file systems can be plotted over time as a line graph, to help identify time-based usage patterns. It can be useful to plot separate graphs for reads, writes, and other file system operations.

The distribution of file system latency is expected to be bimodal: one mode at low latency for file system cache hits, and another at high latency for cache misses (storage device I/O). For this reason, representing the distribution as a single value—such as a mean, mode, or median—is misleading.

One way to solve this problem is to use a visualization that shows the full distribution, such as a heat map (heat maps were introduced in Chapter 2, Methodology). One example is given in Figure 8.15, which shows the passage of time on the x axis and I/O latency on the y axis.

This heat map shows the file system as a 1 Gbyte file is randomly read. For the first half of the heat map, a cloud of latency is seen between 3 and 10 ms, which is likely to reflect disk I/O. The line at the bottom shows the file system cache hits (DRAM). A little over halfway, the file became fully cached in DRAM, and the disk I/O cloud vanishes.

This example is from Joyent Cloud Analytics, which allows the file system operation type to be selected and isolated.

8.7 Experimentation

This section describes tools for actively testing file system performance. See Section 8.5.10, Micro-Benchmarking, for a suggested strategy to follow.

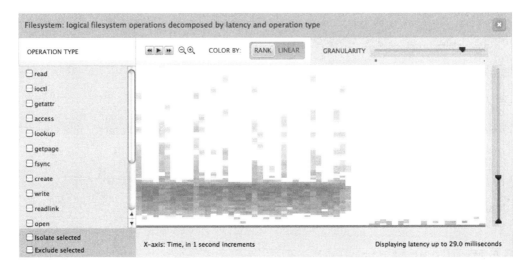

Figure 8-15 File system latency heat map

When using these tools, it's a good idea to leave `iostat(1)` continually running to confirm that the workload that reaches disk is as expected. For example, when testing a working set size that should easily fit in the file system cache, the expectation with a read workload is 100% cache hits, so `iostat(1)` should not show disk I/O. `iostat(1)` is covered in Chapter 9, Disks.

8.7.1 Ad Hoc

The `dd(1)` command (device-to-device copy) can be used to perform ad hoc tests of sequential file system performance. The following commands write, then read a 1 Gbyte file named `file1` with a 1 Mbyte I/O size:

```
write: dd if=/dev/zero of=file1 bs=1024k count=1k
read: dd if=file1 of=/dev/null bs=1024k
```

The Linux version of `dd(1)` prints statistics on completion.

8.7.2 Micro-Benchmark Tools

There are many file system benchmark tools available, including Bonnie, Bonnie++, iozone, tiobench, SysBench, fio, and FileBench. A few are discussed here, in order of increasing complexity. Also see Chapter 12, Benchmarking.

Bonnie, Bonnie++

The Bonnie tool is a simple C program to test several workloads on a single file, from a single thread. It was originally written by Tim Bray in 1989 [6]. Usage is straightforward:

```
# ./Bonnie -h
usage: Bonnie [-d scratch-dir] [-s size-in-Mb] [-html] [-m machine-label]
```

Use -s to set the size of the file to test. By default, Bonnie uses 100 Mbytes, which has entirely cached on this system:

```
$ ./Bonnie
File './Bonnie.9598', size: 104857600
Writing with putc()...done
Rewriting...done
Writing intelligently...done
Reading with getc()...done
Reading intelligently...done
Seeker 1...Seeker 3...Seeker 2...start 'em...done...done...done...
              -------Sequential Output-------- ---Sequential Input-- --Random--
              -Per Char- --Block--- -Rewrite-- -Per Char- --Block--- --Seeks---
Machine    MB K/sec %CPU K/sec %CPU K/sec %CPU K/sec %CPU K/sec %CPU  /sec %CPU
          100 123396 100.0 1258402 100.0 996583 100.0 126781 100.0 2187052 100.0
164190.1 299.0
```

The output includes the CPU time during each test, which at 100% is an indicator that Bonnie never blocked on disk I/O, instead always hitting from cache and staying on-CPU.

There is a 64-bit version called Bonnie-64, which allows larger files to be tested. There is also a rewrite in C++ called Bonnie++ by Russell Coker [7].

Unfortunately, file system benchmark tools like Bonnie can be misleading, unless you clearly understand what is being tested. The first result, a putc() test, can vary based on the system library implementation, which then becomes the target of the test rather than the file system. See the example in Section 12.3.2, Active Benchmarking, in Chapter 12, Benchmarking.

fio

The Flexible IO Tester (fio), by Jens Axboe, is a customizable file system benchmark tool with many advanced features [8]. Two that have led me to use it instead of other benchmark tools are

- **Nonuniform random distributions,** which can more accurately simulate a real-world access pattern (e.g., -random_distribution=pareto:0.9)
- **Reporting of latency percentiles,** including 99.00, 99.50, 99.90, 99.95, 99.99

Here is an example output, showing a random read workload with an 8 Kbyte I/O size, a 5 Gbyte working set size, and a nonuniform access pattern (pareto:0.9):

```
# ./fio --runtime=60 --time_based --clocksource=clock_gettime --name=randread --
numjobs=1 --rw=randread --random_distribution=pareto:0.9 --bs=8k --size=5g --
filename=fio.tmp
randread: (g=0): rw=randread, bs=8K-8K/8K-8K/8K-8K, ioengine=sync, iodepth=1
fio-2.0.13-97-gdd8d
Starting 1 process
Jobs: 1 (f=1): [r] [100.0% done] [3208K/0K/0K /s] [401 /0 /0  iops] [eta 00m:00s]
randread: (groupid=0, jobs=1): err= 0: pid=2864: Tue Feb  5 00:13:17 2013
  read : io=247408KB, bw=4122.2KB/s, iops=515 , runt= 60007msec
    clat (usec): min=3 , max=67928 , avg=1933.15, stdev=4383.30
     lat (usec): min=4 , max=67929 , avg=1934.40, stdev=4383.31
    clat percentiles (usec):
     |  1.00th=[    5],  5.00th=[    5], 10.00th=[    5], 20.00th=[    6],
     | 30.00th=[    6], 40.00th=[    6], 50.00th=[    7], 60.00th=[  620],
     | 70.00th=[  692], 80.00th=[ 1688], 90.00th=[ 7648], 95.00th=[10304],
     | 99.00th=[19584], 99.50th=[24960], 99.90th=[39680], 99.95th=[51456],
     | 99.99th=[63744]
    bw (KB/s)  : min= 1663, max=71232, per=99.87%, avg=4116.58, stdev=6504.45
    lat (usec) : 4=0.01%, 10=55.62%, 20=1.27%, 50=0.28%, 100=0.13%
    lat (usec) : 500=0.01%, 750=15.21%, 1000=4.15%
    lat (msec) : 2=3.72%, 4=2.57%, 10=11.50%, 20=4.57%, 50=0.92%
    lat (msec) : 100=0.05%
  cpu          : usr=0.18%, sys=1.39%, ctx=13260, majf=0, minf=42
  IO depths    : 1=100.0%, 2=0.0%, 4=0.0%, 8=0.0%, 16=0.0%, 32=0.0%, >=64=0.0%
     submit    : 0=0.0%, 4=100.0%, 8=0.0%, 16=0.0%, 32=0.0%, 64=0.0%, >=64=0.0%
     complete  : 0=0.0%, 4=100.0%, 8=0.0%, 16=0.0%, 32=0.0%, 64=0.0%, >=64=0.0%
     issued    : total=r=30926/w=0/d=0, short=r=0/w=0/d=0
```

The latency percentiles (`clat`) clearly show the range of cache hits, up to the 50th percentile in this case, due to their low latency. The remaining percentiles show the effect of cache misses, including the tail of the queue; in this case, the 99.99th percentile is showing a 63 ms latency.

While these percentiles lack information to really understand what is probably a multimode distribution, they do focus on the most interesting part: the tail of the slower mode (disk I/O).

For a similar but simpler tool, you can try SysBench. On the other hand, if you want even more control, try FileBench.

FileBench

FileBench is a programmable file system benchmark tool, where application workloads can be simulated by describing them in its Workload Model Language. This allows threads with different behaviors to be simulated, and for synchronous thread behavior to be specified. It ships with a variety of these configurations, called *personalities*, including one to simulate the Oracle 9i I/O model. Unfortunately, FileBench is not an easy tool to learn and use and may be of interest only to those working on file systems full-time.

8.7.3 Cache Flushing

Linux provides a way to flush (drop entries from) file system caches, which may be useful for benchmarking performance from a consistent and "cold" cache state, such as after system boot. This mechanism is described very simply in the kernel source documentation (Documentation/sysctl/vm.txt) as

```
To free pagecache:
        echo 1 > /proc/sys/vm/drop_caches
To free dentries and inodes:
        echo 2 > /proc/sys/vm/drop_caches
To free pagecache, dentries and inodes:
        echo 3 > /proc/sys/vm/drop_caches
```

There is currently no equivalent for Solaris-based systems.

8.8 Tuning

Many tuning approaches have already been covered in Section 8.5, Methodology, including cache tuning and workload characterization. The latter can lead to the highest tuning wins by identifying and eliminating unnecessary work. This section includes specific tuning parameters (tunables).

The specifics of tuning—the options available and what to set them to—depend on the operating system version, the file system type, and the intended workload. The following sections provide examples of what may be available and why they may need to be tuned. Covered are application calls and two example file system types: ext3 and ZFS. For tuning of the page cache, see Chapter 7, Memory.

8.8.1 Application Calls

Section 8.3.7, Synchronous Writes, mentioned how performance of synchronous write workloads can be improved by using `fsync()` to flush a logical group of writes, instead of individually when using the O_DSYNC/O_RSYNC `open()` flags.

Other calls that can improve performance include `posix_fadvise()` and `madvise()`, which provide hints for cache eligibility.

posix_fadvise()

This library call operates on a region of a file and has the function prototype

```
int posix_fadvise(int fd, off_t offset, off_t len, int advice);
```

The advice may be as shown in Table 8.9.

Table 8-9 posix_fadvise() Advice Flags

Advice	Description
POSIX_FADV_SEQUENTIAL	The specified data range will be accessed sequentially.
POSIX_FADV_RANDOM	The specified data range will be accessed randomly.
POSIX_FADV_NOREUSE	The data will not be reused.
POSIX_FADV_WILLNEED	The data will be used again in the near future.
POSIX_FADV_DONTNEED	The data will not be used again in the near future.

The kernel can use this information to improve performance, helping it decide when best to prefetch data, and when best to cache data. This can improve the cache hit ratio for higher-priority data, as advised by the application. See the man page on your system for the full list of advice arguments.

posix_fadvise() was used as an example in Section 3.3.4, Differences, in Chapter 3, Operating Systems, as support may vary depending on the kernel.

madvise()

This library call operates on a memory mapping and has the synopsis

```
int madvise(void *addr, size_t length, int advice);
```

The advice may be as shown in Table 8.10.

Table 8-10 madvise() Advice Flags

Advice	Description
MADV_RANDOM	Offsets will be accessed in random order.
MADV_SEQUENTIAL	Offsets will be accessed in sequential order.
MADV_WILLNEED	Data will be needed again (please cache).
MADV_DONTNEED	Data will not be needed again (don't need to cache).

As with posix_fadvise(), the kernel can use this information to improve performance, including making better caching decisions.

8.8.2 ext3

On Linux, ext2, ext3, and ext4 file systems can be tuned using the tune2fs(8) command. Various options can also be set at mount time, either manually with the mount(8) command, or at boot time in /boot/grub/menu.lst and /etc/fstab. The options available are in the man pages for tune2fs(8) and mount(8), and the current settings can be seen using tunefs -l *device* and mount (no options).

The noatime option can be used with mount(8) to disable file access timestamp updates, which—if not needed for the file system users—will reduce back-end I/O, improving overall performance.

A key option with tune2fs(8) for improving performance is

```
tune2fs -O dir_index /dev/hdX
```

This uses hashed B-trees to speed up lookups in large directories.

The e2fsck(8) command can be used to reindex directories in a file system. For example:

```
e2fsck -D -f /dev/hdX
```

The other options for e2fsck(8) are related to checking and repairing a file system.

8.8.3 ZFS

ZFS supports a large number of tunable parameters (called *properties*) per file system, with a smaller number that can be set system-wide (/etc/system).

The file system properties can be listed using the zfs(1) command. For example:

```
# zfs get all zones/var
NAME        PROPERTY       VALUE                    SOURCE
zones/var   type           filesystem               -
zones/var   creation       Sat Nov 19  0:37 2011    -
zones/var   used           60.2G                    -
zones/var   available      1.38T                    -
zones/var   referenced     60.2G                    -
zones/var   compressratio  1.00x                    -
zones/var   mounted        yes                      -
zones/var   quota          none                     default
zones/var   reservation    none                     default
zones/var   recordsize     128K                     default
```

continues

```
zones/var  mountpoint          legacy              local
zones/var  sharenfs            off                 default
zones/var  checksum            on                  default
zones/var  compression         off                 inherited from zones
zones/var  atime               off                 inherited from zones
[...]
```

The (truncated) output includes columns for the property name, current value, and source. The source shows how it was set: whether it was inherited from a higher-level ZFS dataset, the default, or set locally for that file system.

The parameters can also be set using the `zfs(1M)` command and are described in the `zfs(1M)` man page. Key parameters related to performance are listed in Table 8.11.

Table 8-11 Key ZSF Dataset Tunable Parameters

Parameter	Options	Description
recordsize	512 to 128 K	suggested block size for files
compression	on | off | lzjb | gzip | gzip-[1–9] | zle | lz4	lightweight algorithms (e.g., lzjb) can improve performance in some situations, by relieving back-end I/O congestion
atime	on | off	access timestamp updates (causes some writes after reads)
primarycache	all | none | metadata	ARC policy; cache pollution due to low-priority file systems (e.g., archives) can be reduced by using "none" or "metadata" (only)
secondarycache	all | none | metadata	L2ARC policy
logbias	latency | throughput	advice for synchronous writes: "latency" uses log devices, whereas "throughput" uses pool devices
sync	standard | always | disabled	synchronous write behavior

The most important parameter to tune is usually record size, to match the application I/O. It usually defaults to 128 Kbytes, which can be inefficient for small random I/O. Note that this does not apply to files that are smaller than the record size, which are saved using a dynamic record size equal to their file length.

Disabling atime can also improve performance (although its update behavior is already optimized), if those timestamps are not needed.

Example system-wide ZFS tunables are shown in Table 8.12. (The most relevant for performance have varied over time, depending on the ZFS version; the three in the table may well change again by the time you read this.)

Table 8-12 Example System-Wide ZFS Tunable Parameters

Parameter	Description
zfs_txg_synctime_ms	target TXG sync time, milliseconds
zfs_txg_timeout	time-out for TXGs (seconds): sets the lowest rate that they occur
metaslab_df_free_pct	percentage for metaslabs to switch behavior and optimize for space instead of time

The zfs_txg_synctime_ms and zfs_txg_timeout tunables have had their defaults reduced over the years so that TXGs were smaller and less likely to contend with other I/O due to queueing. As with other kernel tunables, check the vendor documentation for the full list, descriptions, and warnings. Setting these may also be prohibited by company or vendor policy.

For more about ZFS tuning, you may like to check the "ZFS Evil Tuning Guide" [9].

8.9 Exercises

1. Answer the following questions about file system terminology:
   - What is the difference between logical I/O and physical I/O?
   - What is the difference between random and sequential I/O?
   - What is direct I/O?
   - What is non-blocking I/O?
   - What is the working set size?

2. Answer the following conceptual questions:
   - What is the role of VFS?
   - Describe file system latency, specifically where it can be measured from.
   - What is the purpose of prefetch (read-ahead)?
   - What is the purpose of direct I/O?

3. Answer the following deeper questions:
   - Describe the advantages of using `fsync()` over O_SYNC.
   - Describe the pros and cons of `mmap()` over `read()`s/`write()`s.
   - Describe reasons why logical I/O becomes *inflated* by the time it becomes physical I/O.

- Describe reasons why logical I/O becomes *deflated* by the time it becomes physical I/O.
- Explain how file system copy-on-write can improve performance.

4. Develop the following procedures for your operating system:

- A file system cache tuning checklist. This should list the file system caches that exist, how to check their current size and usage, and hit rate.
- A workload characterization checklist for file system operations. Include how to fetch each detail, and try to use existing OS observability tools first.

5. Perform these tasks:

- Choose an application, and measure file system operations and latency. Include
  - The full distribution of file system operation latency, not just the average
  - The portion of each second that each application thread spends in file system operations
- Using a micro-benchmark tool, determine the size of the file system cache experimentally. Explain your choices when using the tool. Also show the performance degradation (using any metric) when the working set no longer caches.

6. (optional, advanced) Develop an observability tool that provides metrics for synchronous versus asynchronous file system writes. This should include their rate and latency and be able to identify the process ID that issued them, making it suitable for workload characterization.

7. (optional, advanced) Develop a tool to provide statistics for indirect and inflated file system I/O: additional bytes and I/O not issued directly by applications. This should break down this additional I/O into different types to explain their reason.

8.10 References

[Ritchie 74]   Ritchie, D., and K. Thompson. "The UNIX Time-Sharing System," *Communications of the ACM* 17, no. 7 (July 1974), pp. 365–75.

[Lions 77]   Lions, J. *A Commentary on the Sixth Edition UNIX Operating System*. University of New South Wales, 1977.

[McKusick 84]   McKusick, M., et al. "A Fast File System for UNIX." *ACM Transactions on Computer Systems (TOC)* 2, no. 3 (August 1984).

[Bach 86]   Bach, M. *The Design of the UNIX Operating System*. Prentice Hall, 1986.

[Vahalia 96]   Vahalia, U. *UNIX Internals: The New Frontiers*. Prentice Hall, 1996.

[McDougall 06a]   McDougall, R., and J. Mauro. *Solaris Internals: Solaris 10 and OpenSolaris Kernel Architecture*. Prentice Hall, 2006.

[Doeppner 10]   Doeppner, T. *Operating Systems in Depth: Design and Programming*. Wiley, 2010.

[Gregg 11]   Gregg, B., and J. Mauro. *DTrace: Dynamic Tracing in Oracle Solaris, Mac OS X and FreeBSD*. Prentice Hall, 2011.

[1]   http://lwn.net/Articles/419811, 2010

[2]   http://zfsonlinux.org

[3]   http://sysbench.sourceforge.net/docs

[4]   www.dtracebook.com

[5]   https://latencytop.org

[6]   www.textuality.com/bonnie

[7]   www.coker.com.au/bonnie++

[8]   https://github.com/axboe/fio

[9]   www.solarisinternals.com/wiki/index.php/ZFS_Evil_Tuning_Guide

9

Disks

Disk I/O can cause significant application latency and is therefore an important target of systems performance analysis. Under high load, disks become a bottleneck, leaving CPUs idle as the system waits for disk I/O to complete. Identifying and eliminating bottlenecks can improve performance and application throughput by orders of magnitude.

The term *disks* refers to the primary storage devices of the system. They include magnetic rotating disks and flash-memory-based solid-state disks (SSDs). The latter were introduced primarily to improve disk I/O performance, which they do. However, demands for capacity and I/O rates are also increasing, and flash memory devices are not immune to performance issues.

This chapter consists of five parts, the first three providing the basis for disk I/O analysis and the last two showing its practical application to Linux- and Solaris-based systems. The parts are as follows:

- **Background** introduces storage-related terminology, basic models of disk devices, and key disk performance concepts.
- **Architecture** provides generic descriptions of storage hardware and software architecture.
- **Methodology** describes performance analysis methodology, both observational and experimental.

- **Analysis** shows disk performance tools for analysis and experimentation on Linux- and Solaris-based systems, including tracing and visualizations.
- **Tuning** describes example disk tunable parameters.

The previous chapter covered the performance of file systems built upon disks.

9.1 Terminology

For reference, disk-related terminology used in this chapter includes the following:

- **Virtual disk:** an emulation of a storage device. It appears to the system as a single physical disk; however, it may be constructed from multiple disks.
- **Transport:** the physical bus used for communication, including data transfers (I/O) and other disk commands.
- **Sector:** a block of storage on disk, traditionally 512 bytes in size.
- **I/O:** Strictly speaking for disks, this is reads and writes only and would not include other disk commands. I/O consists of, at least, the direction (read or write), a disk address (location), and a size (bytes).
- **Disk commands:** Apart from reads and writes, disks may be commanded to perform other non-data-transfer commands (e.g., cache flush).
- **Throughput:** With disks, throughput commonly refers to the current data transfer rate, measured in bytes per second.
- **Bandwidth:** This is the maximum possible data transfer rate for storage transports or controllers.
- **I/O latency:** time for an I/O operation, used more broadly across the operating system stack and not just at the device level. Be aware that networking uses this term differently, with latency referring to the time to initiate an I/O, followed by data transfer time.
- **Latency outliers:** disk I/O with unusually high latency.

Other terms are introduced throughout this chapter. The Glossary includes basic terminology for reference if needed, including *disk*, *disk controller*, *storage array*, *local disks*, *remote disks*, and *IOPS*. Also see the terminology sections in Chapters 2 and 3.

9.2 Models

The following simple models illustrate some basic principles of disk I/O performance.

9.2.1 Simple Disk

Modern disks include an on-disk queue for I/O requests, as depicted in Figure 9.1.

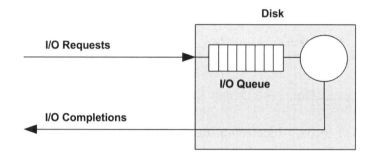

Figure 9-1 Simple disk with queue

I/O accepted by the disk may be either waiting on the queue or being serviced. This simple model is similar to a grocery store checkout, where customers queue to be serviced. It is also well suited for analysis using queueing theory.

While this may imply a first-come-first-served queue, the on-disk controller can apply other algorithms to optimize performance. These algorithms could include elevator seeking for rotational disks (see the discussion in Section 9.4.1, Disk Types), or separate queues for read and write I/O (especially for flash-memory-based disks).

9.2.2 Caching Disk

The addition of an on-disk cache allows some read requests to be satisfied from a faster memory type, as shown in Figure 9.2. This may be implemented as a small amount of memory (DRAM) that is contained within the physical disk device.

While cache hits return with very low (good) latency, cache misses are still usually present, returning with high-disk-device latency.

The on-disk cache may also be used to improve *write* performance, by using it as a *write-back* cache. This signals writes as having completed after the data transfer to cache and before the slower transfer to persistent disk storage. The counter-term is

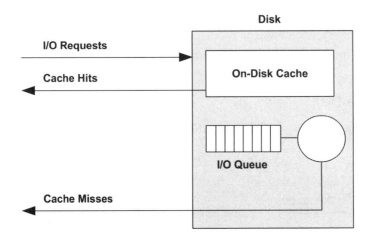

Figure 9-2 Simple disk with on-disk cache

the *write-through* cache, which completes writes only after the full transfer to the next level.

9.2.3 Controller

A simple type of disk controller is shown in Figure 9.3, bridging the CPU I/O transport with the storage transport and attached disk devices. These are also called *host bus adaptors* (HBAs).

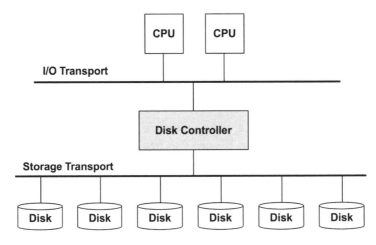

Figure 9-3 Simple disk controller and connected transports

Performance may be limited by either of these busses, the disk controller, or the disks. See Section 9.4, Architecture, for more about disk controllers.

9.3 Concepts

The following are important concepts in disk performance.

9.3.1 Measuring Time

The *response time* for storage devices (also called *disk I/O latency*) is the time from the I/O request to I/O completion. It is composed of service and wait times:

- **Service time:** the time that an I/O takes to be actively processed (serviced), excluding time waiting on a queue
- **Wait time:** the time an I/O was waiting on a queue to be serviced

These are pictured in Figure 9.4, with other terminology.

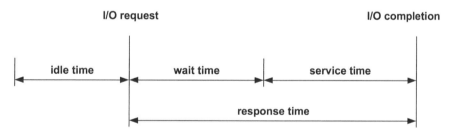

Figure 9-4 Disk I/O terminology

Response time, *service time*, and *wait time* all depend on the location from which they are measured. The following explains this by describing service time in both operating system and disk contexts (this is also a simplification):

- In the context of the operating system (the block device interface), service time may be measured as the time from when an I/O request was issued to the disk device to the time when the completion interrupt occurred. It excludes the time waiting in operating system queues and reflects only the overall performance of the disk device for the requested operation.

- In the context of disks, service time refers to the time that the disk took to actively service the I/O, excluding any time spent waiting on its own on-disk queue.

The term *service time* originates from when disks were simpler devices, managed directly by the operating system, which therefore knew when the disk was actively servicing I/O. Disks now do their own internal queueing, and the operating system service time includes time spent waiting on device queues. This operating system metric may be better described as the "disk response time."

The term *response time* can also be applied from different perspectives. For example, "disk response time" may describe the service time as observed from the operating system, while "I/O response time," from the ·perspective of the application, may refer to everything beneath the system call layer (service time, all wait times, and code path execution time).

Service time from the block device interface is generally treated as a measure of disk performance (and is what `iostat(1)` shows); however, you should be aware that this is a simplification. In Figure 9.6, a generic I/O stack is pictured, which shows three possible driver layers beneath the block device interface. Any of these may implement its own queue, or may block on mutexes, adding latency to the I/O. This latency is included in the service time as measured from the block device interface.

Calculating Time

Disk service time is typically not observable by the operating system directly; however, an average disk service time can be inferred using IOPS and utilization:

disk service time = utilization/IOPS

For example, a utilization of 60% and an IOPS of 300 gives an average service time of 2 ms (600 ms/300 IOPS). This assumes the utilization reflects a single device (or *service center*), which can process only one I/O at a time. Disks can typically process multiple I/O in parallel.

9.3.2 Time Scales

The time scale for disk I/O can vary by orders of magnitude, from tens of microseconds to thousands of milliseconds. At the slowest end of the scale, poor application response time can be caused by a single slow disk I/O; at the fastest end, disk I/O may become an issue only in great numbers (the sum of many fast I/O equaling a slow I/O).

For context, Table 9.1 provides a general idea of the possible range of disk I/O latencies. For precise and current values, consult the disk vendor documentation, and perform your own micro-benchmarking. Also see Chapter 2, Methodology, for time scales other than disk I/O.

To better illustrate the orders of magnitude involved, the Scaled column shows a comparison based on an imaginary on-disk cache hit latency of one second.

Table 9-1 Example Time Scale of Disk I/O Latencies

Event	Latency	Scaled
On-disk cache hit	< 100 µs	1 s
Flash memory read	~100 to 1,000 µs (small to large I/O)	1 to 10 s
Rotational disk sequential read	~1 ms	10 s
Rotational disk random read (7,200 rpm)	~8 ms	1.3 minutes
Rotational disk random read (slow, queueing)	> 10 ms	1.7 minutes
Rotational disk random read (dozens in queue)	> 100 ms	17 minutes
Worst-case virtual disk I/O (hardware controller, RAID-5, queueing, random I/O)	> 1,000 ms	2.8 hours

These latencies may be interpreted differently based on the environment requirements. While working in the enterprise storage industry, I considered any disk I/O taking over 10 ms to be unusually slow and a potential source of performance issues. In the cloud computing industry, there is greater tolerance for high latencies, especially in web-facing applications that already expect high latency between the network and client browser. In those environments, disk I/O may become an issue only beyond 100 ms (individually, or in total during an application request).

This table also illustrates that a disk can return two types of latency: one for on-disk cache hits (less than 100 µs) and one for misses (1–8 ms and higher, depending on the access pattern and device type). Since a disk will return a mixture of these, expressing them together as an *average* latency (as `iostat(1)` does) can be misleading, as this is really a distribution with two modes. See Figure 2.22 in Chapter 2, Methodologies, for an example disk I/O latency distribution as a histogram (measured using DTrace).

9.3.3 Caching

The best disk I/O performance is when there is none. Many layers of the software stack attempt to avoid disk I/O by caching reads and buffering writes, right down to the disk itself. The full list of these is in Table 3.2 of Chapter 3, Operating Systems, which includes application-level and file system caches. At the disk-device-driver level and below, they may include the caches listed in Table 9.2.

Table 9-2 Disk I/O Caches

Cache	Example
Device cache	ZFS vdev
Block cache	buffer cache
Disk controller cache	RAID card cache
Storage array cache	array cache
On-disk cache	disk data controller (DDC) attached DRAM

The block-based buffer cache was described in Chapter 8, File Systems. These disk I/O caches have been particularly important to improve the performance of random I/O workloads.

9.3.4 Random versus Sequential I/O

The disk I/O workload can be described using the terms *random* and *sequential*, based on the relative location of the I/O on disk (*disk offset*). These terms were discussed in Chapter 8, File Systems, regarding file access patterns.

Sequential workloads are also known as *streaming workloads*. The term *streaming* is usually used at the application level, to describe streaming reads and writes "to disk" (file system).

Random versus sequential disk I/O patterns were important to study during the era of magnetic rotational disks. For these, random I/O incurs additional latency as the disk heads seek and the platter rotates between I/O. This is shown in Figure 9.5, where both seek and rotation are necessary for the disk heads to move between sectors 1 and 2 (the actual path taken will be as direct as possible). Performance tuning involved identifying random I/O and trying to eliminate it in a number of ways, including caching, isolating random I/O to separate disks, and disk placement to reduce seek distance.

Other disk types, including flash-based SSDs, usually perform no differently between random and sequential I/O patterns. Depending on the disk, there may be a small difference due to other factors, for example, an address lookup cache that can span sequential access but not random.

Note that the disk offsets as seen from the operating system may not match the offsets on the physical disk. For example, a hardware-provided virtual disk may map

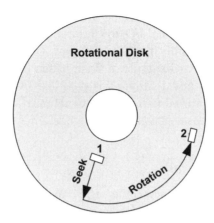

Figure 9-5 Rotational disk

a contiguous range of offsets across multiple disks. Disks may remap offsets in their own way (via the disk data controller). Sometimes random I/O isn't identified by inspecting the offsets but may be inferred by measuring increased service time.

9.3.5 Read/Write Ratio

Apart from identifying random versus sequential workloads, another characteristic measure is the ratio of reads to writes, referring to either IOPS or throughput. This can be expressed as the ratio over time, as a percentage, for example, "The system has run at 80% reads since boot."

Understanding this ratio helps when designing and configuring systems. A system with a high read rate may benefit most from adding cache. A system with a high write rate may benefit most from adding more disks to increase maximum available throughput and IOPS.

The reads and writes may themselves be different workload patterns: reads may be random I/O, while writes may be sequential (especially for copy-on-write file systems). They may also exhibit different I/O sizes.

9.3.6 I/O Size

The average I/O size (bytes), or distribution of I/O sizes, is another workload characteristic. Larger I/O sizes typically provide higher throughput, although for longer per-I/O latency.

The I/O size may be altered by the disk device subsystem (for example, quantized to 512-byte blocks). The size may also have been inflated and deflated since the I/O was issued at the application level, by kernel components such as file systems, volume managers, and device drivers. See the Inflated and Deflated sections in Section 8.3.12, Logical versus Physical I/O, in Chapter 8, File Systems.

Some disk devices, especially flash-based, perform very differently with different read and write sizes. For example, a flash-based disk drive may perform optimally with 4 Kbyte reads and 1 Mbyte writes. Ideal I/O sizes may be documented by the disk vendor or identified using micro-benchmarking. The currently used I/O size may be found using observation tools (see Section 9.6, Analysis).

9.3.7 IOPS Are Not Equal

Because of those last three characteristics, IOPS are not created equal and cannot be directly compared between different devices and workloads. An IOPS value doesn't mean a lot on its own and can't be used alone to accurately compare workloads.

For example, with rotational disks, a workload of 5,000 sequential IOPS may be much faster than one of 1,000 random IOPS. Flash-memory-based IOPS are also difficult to compare, since their I/O performance is often relative to I/O size and direction (read or write).

To make sense of IOPS, include the other details: random or sequential, I/O size, read/write. Also consider using time-based metrics, such as utilization and service time, which reflect resulting performance and can be more easily compared.

9.3.8 Non-Data-Transfer Disk Commands

Disks can be sent other commands besides I/O reads and writes. For example, disks with an on-disk cache (RAM) may be commanded to flush the cache to disk. Such a command is not a data transfer; the data was previously sent to the disk via writes. These commands can affect performance and can cause a disk to be utilized while other I/O wait.

9.3.9 Utilization

Utilization can be calculated as the time a disk was busy actively performing work during an interval.

A disk at 0% utilization is "idle," and a disk at 100% utilization is continually busy performing I/O (and other disk commands). Disks at 100% utilization are a likely source of performance issues, especially if they remain at 100% for some time. However, any rate of disk utilization can contribute to poor performance, as disk I/O is typically a slow activity.

There may also be a point between 0% and 100% (say, 60%) at which the disk's performance is no longer satisfactory due to the increased likelihood of queueing, either on disk queues or in the operating system. The exact utilization value that becomes a problem depends on the disk, workload, and latency requirements. See the M/D/1 and 60% Utilization section in Section 2.6.5, Queueing Theory, in Chapter 2, Methodology.

To confirm whether high utilization is causing application issues, study the disk response time and whether the application is blocking on this I/O. The application or operating system may be performing I/O asynchronously, such that slow I/O is not directly causing the application to wait.

Note that utilization is an interval summary. Disk I/O can occur in bursts, especially due to write flushing, which can be disguised when summarizing over longer intervals. See Section 2.3.11, Utilization, in Chapter 2, Methodology, for a further discussion about the utilization metric type.

Virtual Disk Utilization

For virtual disks supplied by hardware (e.g., disk controller), the operating system may be aware only of when the virtual disk was busy but know nothing about the performance of the underlying disks upon which it is built. This leads to scenarios where virtual disk utilization, as reported by the operating system, is significantly different from what is happening on the actual disks (and is counterintuitive):

- Virtual disks that include a write-back cache may not appear very busy during write workloads, since the disk controller returns write completions immediately, despite the underlying disks being busy sometime afterward.

- A virtual disk that is 100% busy, and is built upon multiple physical disks, may be able to accept more work. In this case, 100% may mean that some disks were busy all the time, but not all the disks all the time, and therefore some disks were idle.

For the same reasons, it can be difficult to interpret the utilization of virtual disks created by operating system software (software RAID). However, the operating system should be exposing utilization for the physical disks as well, which can be inspected.

Once a physical disk reaches 100% utilization and more I/O is requested, it becomes saturated.

9.3.10 Saturation

Saturation is a measure of queued work, beyond what the resource can deliver. For disk devices, it can be calculated as the average length of the device wait queue in the operating system (assuming it does queueing).

This provides a measure of performance beyond the 100% utilization point. A disk at 100% utilization may have no saturation (queueing), or it may have a lot, significantly affecting performance due to the queueing of I/O.

It may be assumed that disks at less than 100% utilization have no saturation. However, this depends on the utilization interval: 50% disk utilization during an interval may mean 100% utilized for half that time and idle for the rest. Any interval summary can suffer from similar issues. When it is important to know exactly what occurred, tracing can be used to examine I/O events.

9.3.11 I/O Wait

I/O wait is a per-CPU performance metric showing time spent idle, when there are threads on the CPU dispatcher queue (in sleep state) that are blocked on disk I/O. This divides CPU idle time into time spent with nothing to do, and time spent blocked on disk I/O. A high rate of I/O wait per CPU shows that the disks may be a bottleneck, leaving the CPU idle while it waits on them.

I/O wait can be a very confusing metric. If another CPU-hungry process comes along, the I/O wait value can drop: the CPUs now have something to do, instead of being idle. However, the same disk I/O is still present and blocking threads, despite the drop in the I/O wait metric. The reverse has sometimes happened when system administrators have upgraded application software and the newer version is more efficient and uses fewer CPU cycles, *revealing* I/O wait. This can make the system administrator think that the upgrade has caused a disk issue and made performance worse, when in fact disk performance is the same, and CPU performance is improved.

There are also some subtle issues with how I/O wait was being calculated on Solaris. For the Solaris 10 release, the I/O wait metric was deprecated and hardwired to zero for tools that still needed to display it (for compatibility).

A more reliable metric may be the time that application threads are blocked on disk I/O. This captures the pain endured by application threads caused by disk I/O, regardless of what other work the CPUs may be doing. This metric can be measured using static or dynamic tracing.

I/O wait is still a popular metric on Linux systems, and despite its confusing nature, it is used successfully to identify a type of disk bottleneck: disks busy, CPUs idle. One way to interpret it is to treat any wait I/O as a sign of a system bottleneck, and then tune the system to minimize it—even if the I/O is still occurring concurrently with CPU utilization. Concurrent I/O is more likely to be non-blocking I/O, and less likely to cause a direct issue. Nonconcurrent I/O, as identified by I/O wait, is more likely to be application blocking I/O, and a bottleneck.

9.3.12 Synchronous versus Asynchronous

It can be important to understand that disk I/O latency may not directly affect application performance, if the application I/O and disk I/O operate asynchronously. This commonly occurs with write-back caching, where the application I/O completes early, and the disk I/O is issued later.

Applications may use read-ahead to perform asynchronous reads, which may not block the application while the disk completes the I/O. The file system may initiate this itself to warm the cache (prefetch).

Even if an application is synchronously waiting for I/O, that application code path may be noncritical and asynchronous to client application requests.

See Sections 8.3.9, Non-Blocking I/O, 8.3.5, Read-Ahead, 8.3.4, Prefetch, and 8.3.7, Synchronous Writes, in Chapter 8, File Systems, for further explanation.

9.3.13 Disk versus Application I/O

Disk I/O is the end result of various kernel components, including file systems and device drivers. There are many reasons why the rate and volume of this disk I/O may not match the I/O issued by the application. These include

- File system inflation, deflation, and unrelated I/O. See Section 8.3.12, Logical versus Physical I/O, in Chapter 8, File Systems.
- Paging due to a system memory shortage. See Section 7.2.2, Paging, in Chapter 7, Memory.
- Device driver I/O size: rounding up I/O size, or fragmenting I/O.

This mismatch can be confusing when unexpected. It can be understood by learning the architecture and performing analysis.

9.4 Architecture

This section describes disk architecture, which is typically studied during capacity planning to determine the limits for different components and configuration choices. It should also be checked during the investigation of later performance issues, in case the problem originates from architectural choices rather than the current load and tuning.

9.4.1 Disk Types

The two most commonly used disk types at present are magnetic rotational and flash-memory-based SSDs. Both of these provide permanent storage; unlike volatile memory, their stored content is still available after a power cycle.

Magnetic Rotational

Also termed a *hard disk drive* (HDD), this type of disk consists of one or more discs, called *platters*, impregnated with iron oxide particles. A small region of these particles can be magnetized in one of two directions; this orientation is used to store a bit. The platters rotate, while a mechanical arm with circuitry to read and write data reaches across the surface. This circuitry includes the *disk heads*, and an arm may have more than one head, allowing it to read and write multiple bits simultaneously. Data is stored on the platter in circular tracks, and each track is divided into sectors.

Being mechanical devices, these perform relatively slowly. With advances in flash-memory-based technology, SSDs are displacing rotational disks, and it is conceivable that one day rotational disks will be obsolete (along with drum disks and core memory). In the meantime, rotational disks are still competitive in some scenarios, such as economical high-density storage (low cost per megabyte).

The following topics summarize factors in rotational disk performance.

Seek and Rotation

Slow I/O for magnetic rotational disks is usually caused by the seek time for the disk heads and the rotation time of the disk platter, both of which may take milliseconds. Best case is when the next requested I/O is located at the end of the currently servicing I/O, so that the disk heads don't need to seek or wait for additional rotation. As described earlier, this is known as *sequential I/O*, while I/O that requires head seeking or waiting for rotation is called *random I/O*.

There are many strategies to reduce seek and rotation wait time, including

- Caching: eliminating I/O entirely
- File system placement and behavior, including copy-on-write
- Separating different workloads to different disks, to avoid seeking between workload I/O
- Moving different workloads to different systems (some cloud computing environments can do this to reduce multitenancy effects)
- Elevator seeking, performed by the disk itself
- Higher-density disks, to tighten the workload location
- Partition (or "slice") configuration, for example, short-stroking

An additional strategy to reduce rotation wait time only is to use faster disks.

Disks are available in different rotational speeds, including 5,400, 7,200, 10,000 (10 K), and 15,000 (15 K) revolutions per minute (rpm).

Theoretical Maximum Throughput

If the maximum sectors per track of a disk is known, disk throughput can be calculated using the following formula:

max throughput = max sectors per track * sector size * rpm/60 s

This formula was more useful for older disks that exposed this information accurately. Modern disks provide a virtual image of the disk to the operating system and expose synthetic values for these attributes.

Short-Stroking

Short-stroking is where only the outer tracks of the disk are used for the workload; the remainder are either unused or used for low-throughput workloads (e.g., archives). This reduces seek time as head movement is bounded by a smaller range, and the disk may put the heads at rest at the outside edge, reducing the first seek after idle. The outer tracks usually also have better throughput due to sector zoning (see the next section). Keep an eye out for short-stroking when examining published disk benchmarks, especially those that don't include price and where many short-stroked disks may have been used.

Sector Zoning

The length of disk tracks varies, with the shortest at the center of the disk and the longest at the outside edge. Instead of the number of sectors (and bits) per track being fixed, sector zoning (also called *multiple-zone recording*) increases the sector count for the longer tracks, since more sectors can be physically written. Because the rotation speed is constant, the longer outside-edge tracks deliver higher throughput (megabytes per second) than the inner tracks.

Sector Size

The storage industry has developed a new standard for disk devices, called Advanced Format, to support larger sector sizes, particularly 4 Kbytes. This reduces I/O computational overhead, improving throughput as well as reducing overheads for the disk's per-sector stored metadata. Sectors of 512 bytes can still be provided by disk firmware via an emulation standard called Advanced Format 512e. Depending on the disk, this may increase write overheads, invoking a read-modify-write cycle to map 512 bytes to a 4 Kbyte sector. Other performance issues to be aware of include misaligned 4 Kbyte I/O, which span two sectors, inflating sector I/O to service them.

On-Disk Cache

A common component of these disks is a small amount of memory (RAM) used to cache the result of reads and to-buffer writes. This memory also allows I/O (commands) to be queued on the device and reordered in a more efficient way. With SCSI, this is Tagged Command Queueing (TCQ); with SATA, it is called Native Command Queueing (NCQ).

Elevator Seeking

The *elevator algorithm* (also known as *elevator seeking*) is one way a command queue can improve efficiency. It reorders I/O based on their on-disk location, to minimize travel of the disk heads. The result is similar to a building elevator, which does not service floors based on the order in which the floor buttons were pushed, but rather makes sweeps up and down the building, stopping at the currently requested floors.

This behavior becomes apparent when inspecting disk I/O traces and finding that sorting I/O by completion time doesn't match sorting by start time: I/O are completing out of order.

While this seems like an obvious performance win, contemplate the following scenario: A disk has been sent a batch of I/O near offset 1,000, and a single I/O at offset 2,000. The disk heads are currently at 1,000. When will the I/O at offset 2,000 be serviced? Now consider that, while servicing the I/O near 1,000, more arrive near 1,000, and more, and more—enough continual I/O to keep the disk busy near offset 1,000 for 10 s. When will the 2,000 offset I/O be serviced now, and what is its final I/O latency?

ECC

Disks store an error-correcting code at the end of each sector, so the drive can verify that the data was read correctly and possibly correct some errors. If the sector was not read correctly, the disk heads may retry the read on the next rotation (and may retry several times, varying the location of the head slightly each time). It may be important to be aware of this in the performance context as a possible explanation for unusually slow I/O. Investigate operating system and on-disk error counters to confirm.

Vibration

While disk device vendors were well aware of vibration issues, those issues weren't commonly known or taken seriously by the industry. In 2008, while investigating a mysterious performance issue, I conducted a vibration-inducing experiment by *shouting* at a disk array while it performed a write benchmark, which caused a burst of very slow I/O. My experiment was immediately videoed and put on YouTube, where it went viral, and it has been described as the first demonstration of the impact of vibration on disk performance [Turner 10]. The video has had over 800,000 views, promoting awareness of disk vibration issues [1]. Based on the e-mails I've had, I also seem to have accidentally spawned an industry in sound-proofing data centers: you can now hire professionals who will analyze data center sound levels and improve disk performance by damping vibrations.

Sloth Disks

A current performance issue with some rotational disks is the discovery of what we've named *sloth disks*. These disks sometimes return very slow I/O, over one second, without any reported errors. It might actually be better if such disks reported a failure instead of taking so long, so that the operating system or disk controllers could take corrective action, such as offlining the disk in redundant environments and reporting the failure. Sloth disks are a nuisance, especially when they are part of a virtual disk presented by a storage array, such that the operating system has no direct visibility of them, making them harder to identify.

Disk Data Controller

Mechanical disks present a simple interface to the system, implying a fixed sectors-per-track ratio and a contiguous range of addressable offsets. What actually happens on the disk is up to the disk data controller—a disk internal microprocessor, programmed by firmware. How the disk lays out the addressable offsets is up to the disk, which can implement algorithms including sector zoning. This is something to be aware of, but it's difficult to analyze—the operating system cannot see into the disk data controller.

Solid-State Drives

These are also sometimes called solid-state disks (SSDs), which refers to their use of solid-state electronics. Storage is in the form of programmable nonvolatile memory, which typically has much better performance than rotational disks. Without moving parts, these disks are also physically durable and not susceptible to performance issues caused by vibration.

The performance of this disk type is usually consistent across different offsets (no rotational or seek latency) and predictable for given I/O sizes. The random or sequential characteristic of workloads matters much less than with rotational disks. All of this makes them easier to study and do capacity planning for. However, if they do encounter performance pathologies, understanding them can be just as complex as with rotational disks, due to how they operate internally.

Some SSDs use nonvolatile DRAM (NV-DRAM). Most use flash memory.

Flash Memory

Flash-memory-based SSDs are a type of storage that offers high read performance, particularly random read performance that can beat rotational disks by orders of magnitude. Most are built using NAND flash memory, which uses electron-based trapped-charge storage media that can store electrons persistently in a no-power state [Cornwell 12]. The name "flash" relates to how data is written, which requires erasing an entire block of memory at a time (including multiple pages, usually 8 KBytes per page) and rewriting the contents. Because of these write overheads, flash memory has asymmetrical read/write performance: fast reads and slower writes.

Flash memory comes in different types. Single-level cell (SLC) stores data bits in individual cells, and multilevel cell (MLC) can store multiple bits per cell (usually two, which requires four voltage levels). There is also trilevel cell (TLC) for storing three bits (eight voltage levels). SLC tends to have higher performance when compared to MLC and is preferred for enterprise use, although it comes at a higher cost. There is also eMLC, which is MLC with advanced firmware intended for enterprise use.

Controller

The controller for an SSD has the following task [Leventhal 13]:

- **Input:** Reads and writes occur per page (usually 8 Kbytes); writes can occur only to erased pages; pages are erased in blocks of 32 to 64 (256–512 Kbytes).
- **Output:** emulates a hard drive block interface: reads or writes of arbitrary sectors (512 bytes or 4 Kbytes).

Translating between input and output is performed by the controller's flash translation layer (FTL), which must also track free blocks. It essentially uses its own file system to do this, such as a log-structured file system.

The write characteristics can be a problem for write workloads, especially when writing I/O sizes that are smaller than the flash memory block size (which may be as large as 512 Kbytes). This can cause *write amplification*, where the remainder of the block is copied elsewhere before erasure, and also latency for at least the erase-write cycle. Some flash memory drives mitigate the latency issue by providing an on-disk buffer (RAM-based) backed by a battery, so that writes can be buffered and written later, even in the event of a power failure.

The most common enterprise-grade flash memory drive I've used performs optimally with 4 Kbyte reads and 1 Mbyte writes, due to the flash memory layout. These values vary for different drives and may be found via micro-benchmarking of I/O sizes.

Given the disparity between the native operations of flash, and the exposed block interface, there has been room for improvement by the operating system and its file systems. The TRIM command is an example: it informs the SSD that a region is no longer in use, allowing the SSD to more easily assemble its pool of free blocks. (For SCSI, this can be implemented using the UNMAP or WRITE SAME commands; for ATA, the DATA SET MANAGEMENT command.)

Life Span

There are various problems with NAND flash as a storage medium, including burnout, data fade, and read disturbance [Cornwell 12]. These can be solved by the SSD controller, which can move data to avoid problems. It will typically employ wear leveling, which spreads writes across different blocks to reduce the write cycles on individual blocks, and memory overprovisioning, which reserves extra memory that can be mapped into service when needed.

While these techniques improve life span, the SSD still has a limited number of write cycles per block, depending on the type of flash memory and the mitigation features employed by the drive. Enterprise-grade drives use memory overprovisioning and the most reliable type of flash memory, SLC, to achieve write cycle rates of 1 million and higher. Consumer-grade drives based on MLC may offer as few as 1,000 cycles.

Pathologies

Here are some flash memory SSD pathologies to be aware of:

- Latency outliers due to aging, and the SSD trying harder to extract correct data (which is checked using ECC)
- Higher latency due to fragmentation (reformatting may fix this by cleaning up the FTL block maps)
- Lower throughput performance if the SSD implements internal compression

Check for more recent developments with SSD performance features and issues encountered.

9.4.2 Interfaces

The interface is the protocol supported by the drive for communication with the system, usually via a disk controller. A brief summary of the SCSI, SAS, and SATA interfaces follows. You will need to check what the current interfaces and supported bandwidths are, as they change over time as new specifications are developed and adopted.

SCSI

The Small Computer System Interface was originally a parallel transport bus, using multiple electrical connectors to transport bits in parallel. The first version, SCSI-1 in 1986, had a data bus width of 8 bits, allowing 1 byte to be transferred per clock, and delivered a bandwidth of 5 Mbytes/s. This was connected using a 50-pin Centronics C50. Later parallel SCSI versions used wider data busses and more pins for the connectors, up to 80 pins, and bandwidths in the hundreds of megabytes.

Since parallel SCSI is a shared bus, there can be performance issues due to bus contention. For example, a scheduled system backup may saturate the bus with low-priority I/O. Work-arounds included putting low-priority devices on their own SCSI bus or controller.

Clocking of parallel busses also becomes a problem at higher speeds, which along with the other issues (including limited devices and the need for SCSI terminator packs) has led to a switch to the serial version: SAS.

SAS

The Serial Attached SCSI interface is designed as a high-speed point-to-point transport, avoiding the bus contention issues from parallel SCSI. The initial SAS specification was 3 Gbits/s, with 6 Gbits/s added in 2009 and 12 Gbits/s in 2012. Link aggregations are supported, so that multiple ports can combine to deliver higher bandwidths. The actual data transfer rate is 80% of bandwidth, due to 8b/10b encoding.

Other SAS features include dual porting of drives for use with redundant connectors and architectures, I/O multipathing, SAS domains, hot swapping, and compatibility support for SATA devices. These features have often favored SAS for enterprise use, especially with redundant architectures.

SATA

For similar reasons as for SCSI and SAS, the parallel ATA (aka IDE) interface standard has evolved to become the Serial ATA interface. Created in 2003, SATA 1.0 supported 1.5 Gbits/s; later versions supported 3.0 and 6.0 Gbits/s, and additional features included native command queueing support. SATA uses 8b/10b encoding, so the data transfer rate is 80% bandwidth. SATA has been in common use for consumer desktops and laptops.

9.4.3 Storage Types

Storage can be provided to a server in a number of ways; the following sections describe four general architectures: disk devices, RAID, storage arrays, and network-attached storage (NAS).

Disk Devices

The simplest architecture is a server with internal disks, individually controlled by the operating system. The disks connect to a disk controller, which is circuitry on the main board or an expander card, and which allows the disk devices to be seen and accessed. In this architecture the disk controller merely acts as a conduit so that the system can communicate with the disks. A typical personal computer or laptop has a disk attached in this way for primary storage.

This architecture is the easiest to analyze using performance tools, as each disk is known to the operating system and can be observed separately.

Some disk controllers support this architecture, where it is called *just a bunch of disks* (JBOD).

RAID

Advanced disk controllers can provide the redundant array of independent disks (RAID) architecture for disk devices (originally the redundant array of *inexpensive* disks [Patterson 88]). RAID can present disks as a single big, fast, and reliable virtual disk. These controllers often include an on-board cache (RAM) to improve read and write performance.

Providing RAID by a disk controller card is called *hardware* RAID. RAID can also be implemented by operating system software, but hardware RAID has been preferred, as CPU-expensive checksum and parity calculations can be performed more quickly on dedicated hardware. However, advances in processors have produced CPUs with a surplus of cycles and cores, reducing the need to offload parity calculations. A number of storage solutions have moved back to software RAID (for example, using ZFS), which reduces complexity and hardware cost and improves observability from the operating system.

The following sections describe the performance characteristics of RAID.

Types

Various RAID types are available to meet varying needs for capacity, performance, and reliability. This summary focuses on the performance characteristics shown in Table 9.3.

While RAID-0 striping performs the best, it has no redundancy, making it impractical for most production use.

Table 9-3 RAID Types

Level	Description	Performance
0 (concat.)	Drives are filled one at a time.	Eventually improves random read performance when multiple drives can take part.
0 (stripe)	Drives are used in parallel, splitting (striping) I/O across multiple drives.	Best random and sequential I/O performance.
1 (mirror)	Multiple drives (usually two) are grouped, storing identical content for redundancy.	Good random and sequential read performance (can read from all drives simultaneously, depending on implementation). Writes limited by slowest disk in mirror, and throughput overheads doubled (two drives).
10	A combination of RAID-0 stripes across groups of RAID-1 drives, providing capacity and redundancy.	Similar performance characteristics to RAID-1 but allows more groups of drives to take part, like RAID-0, increasing bandwidth.
5	Data is stored as stripes across multiple disks, along with extra parity information for redundancy.	Poor write performance due to read-modify-write cycle and checksum calculations.
6	RAID-5 with two parity disks per stripe.	Similar to RAID-5 but worse.

Observability

As described in the earlier section on virtual disk utilization, the use of hardware-supplied virtual disk devices can make observability more difficult in the operating system, which does not know what the physical disks are doing. If RAID is supplied via software, individual disk devices can usually be observed, as the operating system manages them directly.

Read-Modify-Write

When data is stored as a stripe including a checksum, as with RAID-5, write I/O can incur additional read I/O and compute time. This is because writes that are smaller than the stripe size require the entire stripe to be read, the bytes modified, the checksum recalculated, and then the stripe rewritten. Writes that span the entire stripe can write over the previous contents, without needing to read them first. Performance in this environment may be improved by balancing the size of the stripe with the average I/O size of the writes, to reduce the additional read overhead.

Caches

Disk controllers that implement RAID-5 can mitigate read-write-modify performance by use of a write-back cache. These caches may be battery-backed, so that in the event of a power failure they can still complete buffered writes.

Additional Features

Be aware that advanced disk controller cards can provide advanced features that can affect performance. It's a good idea to browse the vendor documentation to be at least aware of what may be in play. For example, here are a couple of features from Dell PERC 5 cards:

- **Patrol read:** Every several days, all disk blocks are read and their checksums verified. If the disks are busy servicing requests, the resources given to the patrol read function are reduced, to avoid competing with the system workload.
- **Cache flush interval:** the time in seconds between flushing dirty data in the cache to disk. Longer times may reduce disk I/O due to write cancellation and better aggregate writes; however, they may also cause higher read latency during the larger flushes.

Both of these can have a significant effect on performance.

Storage Arrays

Storage arrays allow many disks to be connected to the system. They use advanced disk controllers so that RAID can be configured, and they usually provide a large cache (gigabytes) to improve read and write performance. These caches are also typically battery-backed, allowing them to operate in write-back mode. A common policy is to switch to write-through mode if the battery fails, which may be first noticed as a sudden drop in write performance due to waiting for the read-modify-write cycle.

An additional performance consideration is how the storage array is attached to the system—usually via an external storage controller card. The card, and the transport between it and the storage array, will both have limits for IOPS and throughput. For improvements in both performance and reliability, storage arrays are often dual-attachable, meaning they can be connected using two physical cables, to one or two different storage controller cards.

Network-Attached Storage

NAS is provided to the system over the existing network via a network protocol, such as NFS, SMB/CIFS, or iSCSI, usually from dedicated systems known as NAS appliances. These are separate systems and should be analyzed as such. Some performance analysis may be done on the client, to inspect the workload applied and I/O latencies. The performance of the network also becomes a factor, and issues can arise from network congestion and from multiple-hop latency.

9.4.4 Operating System Disk I/O Stack

The components and layers in a disk I/O stack will depend on the operating system, version, and software and hardware technologies used. Figure 9.6 depicts a general model. See Chapter 3, Operating Systems, for the full diagram.

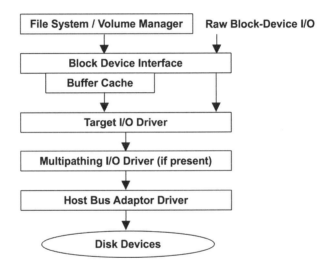

Figure 9-6 Generic disk I/O stack

Block Device Interface

The block device interface was created in early Unix for accessing storage devices in units of blocks, each 512 bytes, and to provide a buffer cache to improve performance. The interface still exists in Linux and Solaris today, although the role of the buffer cache has diminished as other file system caches have been introduced, as described in Chapter 8, File Systems.

Unix provided a path to bypass the buffer cache, called *raw block device I/O* (or just *raw I/O*), which could be used via character special device files (see Chapter 3, Operating Systems). These files are no longer commonly available by default in Linux. Raw block device I/O is different from, but in some ways similar to, the "direct I/O" file system feature, as described in Chapter 8, File Systems.

The block I/O interface can usually be observed from operating system performance tools (`iostat(1)`). It is also a common location for static tracing and more recently can be explored with dynamic tracing as well. Linux has enhanced this area of the kernel with additional features that make up a *block layer*.

Linux

The Linux block layer is pictured in Figure 9.7 ([2], [Bovet 05]).

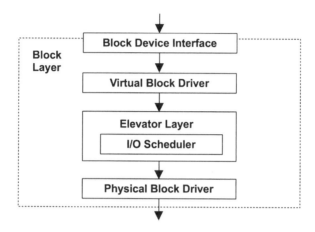

Figure 9-7 Linux block layer

The elevator layer provides generic capabilities to sort, merge, and batch requests for delivery. These include the *elevator seeking* algorithm described earlier to reduce rotation disk head travel (sorting of pending I/O based on their location), and methods to merge and coalesce I/O as shown in Figure 9.8.

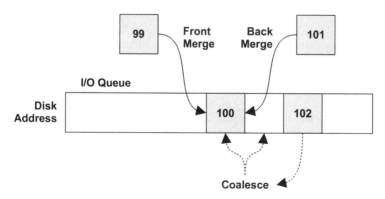

Figure 9-8 I/O merging types

These capabilities achieve higher throughput and lower I/O latency. The I/O scheduler allows I/O to be queued and reordered (or rescheduled) for optimized delivery, as determined by an additional scheduling policy. This can further improve and more fairly balance performance, especially for devices with high I/O latencies (rotational disks).

Available policies include

- **Noop:** This doesn't perform scheduling (noop is CPU-talk for no-operation) and can be used when the overhead of scheduling is deemed unnecessary (for example, in a RAMdisk).

- **Deadline:** attempts to enforce a latency deadline; for example, read and write expiry times in units of milliseconds may be selected. This can be useful for real-time systems, where determinism is desired. It can also solve problems of *starvation*: where an I/O request is starved of disk resources as newly issued I/O jump the queue, resulting in a latency outlier. Starvation can occur due to *writes starving reads*, and as a consequence of elevator seeking and heavy I/O to one area of disk starving I/O to another. The deadline scheduler solves this, in part, by using three separate queues for I/O: read FIFO, write FIFO, and sorted. For more internals, see [Love 10] and Documentation/block/deadline-iosched.txt.

- **Anticipatory:** an enhanced version of deadline, with heuristics to anticipate I/O performance, improving global throughput. These can include pausing for milliseconds after reads rather than immediately servicing writes, on the prediction that another read request may arrive during that time for a nearby disk location, thus reducing overall rotational disk head seeks.

- **CFQ:** The completely fair queueing scheduler allocates I/O time slices to processes, similar to CPU scheduling, for fair usage of disk resources. It also allows priorities and classes to be set for user processes, via the `ionice(1)` command. See Documentation/block/cfq-iosched.txt.

After I/O scheduling, the request is placed on the block device queue to be issued to the device.

Solaris

The Solaris-based kernel uses a simple block device interface, with queues in the target driver (sd). Advanced I/O scheduling is typically provided by ZFS, which can prioritize and merge I/O (including merging across caps). Unlike other file systems, ZFS is a combined volume manager and file system: it manages its own virtual disk devices and an I/O queue (pipeline).

The lower three layers shown in Figure 9.6 use drivers such as

- **Target device drivers:** sd, ssd
- **Multipathing I/O drivers:** scsi_vhci, mpxio
- **Host bus adaptor drivers:** pmcs, mpt, nv_sata, ata

The drivers in use depend on the server hardware and configuration.

9.5 Methodology

This section describes various methodologies and exercises for disk I/O analysis and tuning. The topics are summarized in Table 9.4.

Table 9-4 Disk Performance Methodologies

Methodology	Types
Tools method	observational analysis
USE method	observational analysis
Performance monitoring	observational analysis, capacity planning
Workload characterization	observational analysis, capacity planning
Latency analysis	observational analysis
Event tracing	observational analysis
Static performance tuning	observational analysis, capacity planning
Cache tuning	observational analysis, tuning
Resource controls	tuning
Micro-benchmarking	experimentation analysis
Scaling	capacity planning, tuning

See Chapter 2, Methodology, for more strategies and the introduction to many of these.

These methods may be followed individually or used in combination. When investigating disk issues, my suggestion is to use the following strategies, in this order: the USE method, performance monitoring, workload characterization, latency analysis, micro-benchmarking, static analysis, and event tracing.

Section, 9.6, Analysis, shows operating system tools for applying these methods.

9.5.1 Tools Method

The tools method is a process of iterating over available tools, examining key metrics they provide. While a simple methodology, it can overlook issues for which the tools provide poor or no visibility, and it can be time-consuming to perform.

For disks, the tools method can involve checking

- **iostat:** using extended mode to look for busy disks (over 60% utilization), high average service times (over, say, 10 ms), and high IOPS (depends)
- **iotop:** to identify which process is causing disk I/O
- **dtrace/stap/perf:** including the iosnoop(1) tool to examine disk I/O latency in detail, looking for latency outliers (over, say, 100 ms)
- **Disk-controller-specific tools** (from the vendor)

If an issue is found, examine all fields from the available tools to learn more context. See Section 9.6, Analysis, for more about each tool. Other methodologies can also be used, which can identify more types of issues.

9.5.2 USE Method

The USE method is for identifying bottlenecks and errors across all components, early in a performance investigation. The sections that follow describe how the USE method can apply to disk devices and controllers, and Section 9.6, Analysis, shows tools for measuring specific metrics.

Disk Devices

For each disk device, check for

- **Utilization:** the time the device was busy
- **Saturation:** the degree to which I/O is waiting in a queue
- **Errors:** device errors

Errors may be checked first. They can be overlooked because the system functions correctly—albeit more slowly—in spite of disk failures: disks are commonly configured in a redundant pool of disks designed to tolerate a failure. Apart from standard disk error counters from the operating system, disk devices may support a wider variety of error counters that can be retrieved by special tools (for example, SMART data).

If the disk devices are physical disks, utilization should be straightforward to find. If they are virtual disks, utilization may not reflect what the underlying physical disks are doing. See Section 9.3.9, Utilization, for more discussion about this.

Disk Controllers

For each disk controller, check for

- **Utilization:** current versus maximum throughput, and the same for operation rate
- **Saturation:** the degree to which I/O is waiting due to controller saturation
- **Errors:** controller errors

Here the utilization metric is not defined in terms of time, but rather in terms of the limitations of the disk controller card: throughput (bytes per second) and operation rate (operations per second). Operations are inclusive of read/write and other disk commands. Either throughput or operation rate may also be limited by the transport connecting the disk controller to the system, just as it may also be limited by the transport from the controller to the individual disks. Each transport should be checked the same way: errors, utilization, saturation.

You may find that the observability tools (e.g., Linux `iostat(1)`) do not present per-controller metrics but provide them only per disk. There are work-arounds for this: if the system has only one controller, you can determine the controller IOPS and throughput by summing those metrics for all disks. If the system has multiple controllers, you will need to determine which disks belong to which and sum the metrics accordingly.

Performance of disk controllers and transports is often overlooked. Fortunately, they are not common sources of system bottlenecks, as their capacity typically exceeds that of the attached disks. If total disk throughput or IOPS always levels off at a certain rate, even under different workloads, this may be a clue that the disk controllers or transports are in fact causing problems.

9.5.3 Performance Monitoring

Performance monitoring can identify active issues and patterns of behavior over time. Key metrics for disk I/O are

- Disk utilization
- Response time

Disk utilization at 100% for multiple seconds is very likely an issue. Depending on your environment, over 60% may also cause poor performance due to increased queueing.

Increased response time affects performance and can occur due to varying workloads or the addition of new competing workloads. The value for "normal" or "bad" depends on your workload, environment, and latency requirements. If you aren't sure, micro-benchmarks of known-to-be-good versus bad workloads may be performed to investigate response time (e.g., random versus sequential, small versus large I/O, one tenant versus many). See Section 9.7, Experimentation.

These metrics should be examined on a per-disk basis, to look for unbalanced workloads and individual poorly performing disks. The response time metric may be monitored as a per-second average and can include other values such as the maximum and standard deviation. Ideally, it would be possible to inspect the full distribution of response times, such as by using a histogram or heat map, to look for latency outliers and other patterns.

If the system imposes disk I/O resource controls, statistics to show if and when these were in use can also be collected. Disk I/O may be a bottleneck as a consequence of the imposed limit, not the activity of the disk itself.

Utilization and response time show the result of disk performance. More metrics may be added to characterize the workload, including IOPS and throughput, providing important data for use in capacity planning (see the next section and Section 9.5.11, Scaling).

9.5.4 Workload Characterization

Characterizing the load applied is an important exercise in capacity planning, benchmarking, and simulating workloads. It can also lead to some of the largest performance gains, by identifying unnecessary work that can be eliminated.

The following are basic attributes for characterizing disk I/O workload. Collectively, they can provide an approximation of what the disks are asked to perform:

- I/O rate
- I/O throughput
- I/O size
- Random versus sequential
- Read/write ratio

Random versus sequential, the read/write ratio, and I/O size are described in Section 9.3, Concepts. I/O rate (IOPS) and I/O throughput are defined in Section 9.1, Terminology.

These characteristics can vary from second to second, especially for applications and file systems that buffer and flush writes at intervals. To better characterize the workload, capture maximum values as well as averages. Better still, examine the full distribution of values over time.

Here is an example workload description, to show how these attributes can be expressed together:

> The system disks have a light random read workload, averaging 350 IOPS with a throughput of 3 Mbytes/s, running at 96% reads. There are occasional short bursts of sequential writes, which drive the disks to a maximum of 4,800 IOPS and 560 Mbytes/s. The reads are around 8 Kbytes in size, and the writes around 128 Kbytes.

Apart from describing these characteristics system-wide, they can also be used to describe per-disk and per-controller I/O workloads.

Advanced Workload Characterization/Checklist

Additional details may be included to characterize the workload. These have been listed here as questions for consideration, which may also serve as a checklist when studying disk issues thoroughly:

- What is the IOPS rate system-wide? Per disk? Per controller?
- What is the throughput system-wide? Per disk? Per controller?
- Which applications or users are using the disks?
- What file systems or files are being accessed?
- Have any errors been encountered? Were they due to invalid requests, or issues on the disk?
- How balanced is the I/O over available disks?
- What is the IOPS for each transport bus involved?
- What is the throughput for each transport bus involved?
- What non-data-transfer disk commands are being issued?
- Why is disk I/O issued (kernel call path)?
- To what degree is disk I/O application-synchronous?
- What is the distribution of I/O arrival times?

IOPS and throughput questions can be posed for reads and writes separately. Any of these may also be checked over time, to look for maximums, minimums, and time-based variations. Also see Section 2.5.10, Workload Characterization, in Chapter 2, Methodology, which provides a higher-level summary of the characteristics to measure (who, why, what, how).

Performance Characterization

For comparison with workload characterization, the following questions characterize the resulting performance of the workload:

- How busy is each disk (utilization)?
- How saturated is each disk with I/O (wait queueing)?
- What is the average I/O service time?
- What is the average I/O wait time?
- Are there I/O outliers with high latency?
- What is the full distribution of I/O latency?
- Are system resource controls, such as I/O throttling, present and active?
- What is the latency of non-data-transfer disk commands?

9.5.5 Latency Analysis

Latency analysis involves drilling deeper into the system to find the source of latency. With disks, this will often end at the disk interface: the time between an I/O request and the completion interrupt. If this matches the I/O latency at the application level, it's usually safe to assume that the I/O latency originates from the disks, allowing you to focus your investigation on them. If the latency differs, measuring it at different levels of the operating system stack will identify the origin.

Figure 9.9 pictures the I/O stack, with the latency shown at different levels of two I/O outliers, A and B.

The latency of I/O A is similar at each level from the application down to the disk drivers. This correlation points to the disks (or the disk driver) as the cause of the latency. This could be inferred if the layers were measured independently, based on the similar latency values between them.

The latency of B appears to originate at the file system level (locking or queueing?), with the I/O latency at lower levels contributing much less time. Be aware that different layers of the stack may inflate or deflate I/O, which means the size, count, and latency will differ from one layer to the next. The B example may be a case of only observing one I/O at the lower levels (of 10 ms), but failing to account for other related I/O that occurred to service the same file system I/O (e.g., metadata).

The latency at each level may be presented as

- **Per-interval I/O averages:** as typically reported by operating system tools
- **Full I/O distributions:** as histograms or heat maps; see Latency Heat Maps in Section 9.6.12, Visualizations
- **Per-I/O latency values:** see the next section, Event Tracing

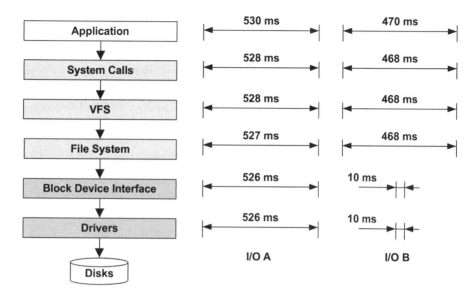

Figure 9-9 Stack latency analysis

The last two are useful for tracking the origin of outliers and can help identify cases where I/O has been split or coalesced.

9.5.6 Event Tracing

Event tracing is where information for every I/O event is captured and recorded separately. For observational analysis, it is the last resort. It adds some performance overhead due to the capturing and saving of these details, which are usually written to log files for later inspection. These log files should contain, at a minimum, the following details for each I/O:

- **Disk device ID**
- **I/O type:** read or write
- **I/O offset:** disk location
- **I/O size:** bytes
- **I/O request timestamp:** when an I/O was issued to the device (also known as an I/O *strategy*)
- **I/O completion timestamp:** when the I/O event completed (completion interrupt)
- **I/O completion status:** errors

Additional details may include, when applicable, PID, UID, application name, file name, and events for all non-data-transfer disk commands (and custom details for those commands).

The I/O request and completion timestamps allow disk I/O latency to be calculated. When reading the log, it can be helpful to sort on each separately for comparison—to see how disk I/O is reordered by the device. Arrival distributions can also be studied from the timestamps.

Because disk I/O is commonly analyzed, static tracepoints are often available for this purpose, tracing requests and completions. Dynamic tracing may also be used for advanced analysis, and similar trace logs may be captured for the following:

- Block device driver I/O

- Interface driver commands (e.g., sd)

- Disk device driver commands

Commands means both reads/writes and non-data transfers. See Section 9.6, Analysis, for examples.

9.5.7 Static Performance Tuning

Static performance tuning focuses on issues of the configured environment. For disk performance, examine the following aspects of the static configuration:

- How many disks are present? Of which types?

- What version is the disk firmware?

- How many disk controllers are present? Of which interface types?

- Are disk controller cards connected to high-speed slots?

- What version is the disk controller firmware?

- Is RAID configured? How exactly, including stripe width?

- Is multipathing available and configured?

- What version is the disk device driver?

- Are there operating system bugs/patches for any of the storage device drivers?

- Are there resource controls in use for disk I/O?

Be aware that performance bugs may exist in device drivers and firmware, which are ideally fixed by updates from the vendor.

Answering these questions can reveal configuration choices that have been overlooked. Sometimes a system has been configured for one workload, and then repurposed for another. This strategy will revisit those choices.

While working as the performance lead for Sun's ZFS storage product, the most common performance complaint I received was caused by a misconfiguration: using half a JBOD (12 disks) of RAID-Z2 (wide stripes). I learned to ask for configuration details first (usually over the phone) before spending time logging in to the system and examining I/O latency.

9.5.8 Cache Tuning

There may be many different caches present in the system, including application-level, file system, disk controller, and on the disk itself. A list of these was included in Section 9.3.3, Caching, which can be tuned as described in Section 2.5.17, Cache Tuning, in Chapter 2, Methodology. In summary, check which caches exist, check that they are working, check how well they are working, then tune the workload for the cache and tune the cache for the workload.

9.5.9 Resource Controls

The operating system may provide controls for allocating disk I/O resources to processes or groups of processes. These may include fixed limits for IOPS and throughput, or shares for a more flexible approach. How these work are implementation-specific and are discussed in Section 9.8, Tuning.

9.5.10 Micro-Benchmarking

Micro-benchmarking disk I/O was introduced in Chapter 8, File Systems, which explains the difference between testing file system I/O and testing disk I/O. Here we would like to test disk I/O, which usually means testing via the operating system's device paths, particularly the raw device path if available, to avoid all file system behavior (including caching, buffering, I/O splitting, I/O coalescing, code path overheads, and offset mapping differences).

Factors for micro-benchmarking include

- **Direction:** reads or writes
- **Disk offset pattern:** random or sequential
- **Range of offsets:** full disk or tight ranges (e.g., offset 0 only)

- **I/O size:** 512 bytes (typical minimum) up to 1 Mbyte
- **Concurrency:** number of I/O in flight, or number of threads performing I/O
- **Number of devices:** single disk tests, or multiple disks (to explore controller and bus limits)

The next two sections show how these factors can be combined to test disk and disk controller performance. See Section 9.7, Experimentation, for details of the specific tools that can be used to perform these tests.

Disks

Micro-benchmarking can be performed on a per-disk basis to determine the following, along with suggested workloads:

- **Maximum disk throughput** (megabytes per second): 128 Kbyte reads, sequential
- **Maximum disk operation rate** (IOPS): 512-byte reads, offset 0 only
- **Maximum disk random reads** (IOPS): 512-byte reads, random offsets
- **Read latency profile** (average microseconds): sequential reads, repeat for 512 bytes, 1 K, 2 K, 4 K, and so on
- **Random I/O latency profile** (average microseconds): 512-byte reads, repeat for full offset span, beginning offsets only, end offsets only

These tests can be repeated for writes. The use of "offset 0 only" is intended to cache the data in the on-disk cache, so that cache access time can be measured.

Disk Controllers

Disk controllers may be micro-benchmarked by applying a workload to multiple disks, designed to hit limits in the controller. These test may be performed using the following, along with suggested workloads for the disks:

- **Maximum controller throughput** (megabytes per second): 128 Kbytes, offset 0 only
- **Maximum controller operation rate** (IOPS): 512-byte reads, offset 0 only

Apply the workload to the disks one by one, watching for limits. It still may take over a dozen disks to find the limit in a disk controller.

9.5.11 Scaling

Disks and disk controllers have throughput and IOPS limits, which can be demonstrated via micro-benchmarking as described previously. Tuning can improve performance only up to these limits. If more disk performance is needed, and other strategies such as caching won't work, the disks will need to scale.

Here is a simple method, based on capacity planning of resources:

1. Determine the target disk workload, in terms of throughput and IOPS. If this is a new system, see Section 2.7, Capacity Planning, in Chapter 2, Methodology. If the system already has a workload, express the user population in terms of current disk throughput and IOPS, and scale these numbers to the target user population. (If cache is not scaled at the same time, the disk workload may increase, because the cache-per-user ratio becomes smaller, pushing more I/O to disk.)

2. Calculate the number of disks required to support this workload. Factor in RAID configuration. Do not use the maximum throughput and IOPS values per disk, as this would result in a plan driving disks at 100% utilization, leading to immediate performance issues due to saturation and queueing. Pick a target utilization (say, 50%) and scale values accordingly.

3. Calculate the number of disk controllers required to support this workload.

4. Check that transport limits have not been exceeded, and scale transports if necessary.

5. Calculate CPU cycles per disk I/O, and the number of CPUs required.

The maximum per-disk throughput and IOPS numbers used will depend on their type and the disk type. See Section 9.3.7, IOPS Are Not Equal. Micro-benchmarking can be used to find specific limits for a given I/O size and I/O type, and workload characterization can be used on existing workloads to see which sizes and types matter.

To deliver the disk workload requirement, it's not uncommon to find servers requiring dozens of disks, connected via storage arrays. We used to say, "Add more spindles." We may now say, "Add more flash."

9.6 Analysis

This section introduces disk I/O performance analysis tools for Linux- and Solaris-based operating systems. See the previous section for strategies to follow when using them.

The tools in this section are listed in Table 9.5.

Table 9-5 Disk Analysis Tools

Linux	Solaris	Description
iostat	iostat	various per-disk statistics
sar	sar	historical disk statistics
pidstat, iotop	iotop	disk I/O usage by process
blktrace	iosnoop	disk I/O event tracing
DTrace	DTrace	custom static and dynamic tracing
MegaCli	MegaCli	LSI controller statistics
smartctl	smartctl	disk controller statistics

This is a selection of tools to support Section 9.5, Methodology, beginning with system-wide statistics, per-process statistics, then drilling down to event tracing and controller statistics. See the tool documentation, including man pages, for full references of their features.

9.6.1 iostat

iostat(1) summarizes per-disk I/O statistics, providing metrics for workload characterization, utilization, and saturation. It can be executed by any user and is typically the first command used to investigate disk I/O issues at the command line. The statistics it sources are always maintained by the kernel, so the overhead of this tool is considered negligible.

The name "iostat" is short for "I/O statistics," although it might have been better to call it "diskiostat" to reflect the type of I/O it reports. This has led to occasional confusion when a user knows that an application is performing I/O (to the file system) but wonders why it can't be seen via iostat(1) (the disks).

iostat(1) was written in the early 1980s, and different versions are available on the different operating systems. It can be added to Linux-based systems via the sysstat package and is included by default on Solaris-based systems. While its general purpose is the same in both, the columns and options differ. Refer to the iostat man page for your operating system to see what your version supports.

The following sections describe iostat(1) for Linux- and Solaris-based systems, where the options and output differ slightly. iostat(1) can be executed with various options, followed by an optional interval and count.

Linux

Commonly used `iostat(1)` options are shown in Table 9.6.

Table 9-6 Linux iostat Options

Option	Description
-c	display CPU report
-d	display disk report
-k	use kilobytes instead of (512-byte) blocks
-m	use megabytes instead of (512-byte) blocks
-p	include per-partition statistics
-t	timestamp output
-x	extended statistics
-z	skip displaying zero-activity summaries

The default behavior is to enable both -c and -d reports; if one is specified on the command line, the other is disabled. Some older versions included an option for NFS statistics, -n. Since sysstat version 9.1.3 this was moved to the separate nfsiostat command.

Without any arguments or options, a summary-since-boot for the -c and -d reports is printed. It's covered here as an introduction to this tool; however, you are not expected to use this mode, as the extended mode covered later is generally more useful.

```
$ iostat
Linux 3.2.6-3.fc16.x86_64 (prod201)     04/14/13        _x86_64_        (16 CPU)

avg-cpu:  %user   %nice %system %iowait  %steal   %idle
           0.03    0.00    0.02    0.00    0.00   99.95

Device:            tps    kB_read/s    kB_wrtn/s    kB_read    kB_wrtn
sdb               0.01         0.75         0.87    4890780    5702856
sda               1.67         0.43        17.66    2811164  115693005
dm-0              0.22         0.75         0.87    4890245    5702856
dm-1              4.44         0.42        17.66    2783497  115669936
dm-2              0.00         0.00         0.00       5976      22748
```

By default, iostat shows a summary line for the system including the kernel version, host name, date, architecture, and CPU count, and then summary-since-boot statistics for the CPUs (`avg-cpu`) and disk devices (under `Device:`). Each disk device is shown as a row, with basic details in the columns:

- **tps:** transactions per second (IOPS)

- **kB_read/s**, **kB_wrtn/s**: kilobytes read per second, and written per second
- **kB_read**, **kB_wrtn**: total kilobytes read and written

SCSI devices, including tapes and CD-ROMs, are currently not seen by the Linux version of iostat(1). This has led to work-arounds, including SystemTap's iostat-scsi.stp script [3].[1] Also note that, while iostat(1) reports block device reads and writes, it may exclude some other types of disk device commands depending on the kernel (e.g., see the logic in blk_do_io_stat()).

As mentioned earlier, the -m option can be used to report the output as megabytes. On older versions of iostat(1) (sysstat 9.0.6 and older), the default output used blocks (512 bytes each) instead of kilobytes. The old behavior can be forced with the following environment variable:

```
$ POSIXLY_CORRECT=1 iostat
[...]
Device:            tps   Blk_read/s   Blk_wrtn/s   Blk_read   Blk_wrtn
[...]
```

Extended output can be selected by using -x and provides extra columns that are useful for many of the strategies covered earlier. These extra columns include IOPS and throughput metrics for workload characterization, utilization and queue lengths for the USE method, and disk response times for performance characterization and latency analysis.

The following output is too wide to fit on a page and is shown with left and right parts. This example includes -d for disk report only, -k for kilobytes, and -z to omit lines of all zeros (idle devices):

```
$ iostat -xkdz 1

Linux 3.2.6-3.fc16.x86_64 (prod201)     04/14/13        _x86_64_        (16 CPU)

Device:         rrqm/s   wrqm/s     r/s     w/s    rkB/s    wkB/s   \ ...
sdb               0.04     1.89    0.01    0.07     1.56     7.86   / ...
sda               0.00     0.00    0.00    0.00     0.00     0.00   \ ...
dm-0              0.00     0.00    0.05    0.10     0.19     0.39   / ...
                                                                   \ ...
Device:         rrqm/s   wrqm/s     r/s     w/s    rkB/s    wkB/s   \ ...
sdb               0.00     0.00  230.00    0.00  2292.00     0.00   \ ...
                                                                   / ...
Device:         rrqm/s   wrqm/s     r/s     w/s    rkB/s    wkB/s   \ ...
sdb               0.00     0.00  231.00    0.00  2372.00     0.00   / ...
```

---

1. Which, at the time of writing, doesn't work.

The output columns are

- **rrqm/s:** read requests placed on the driver request queue and merged per second
- **wrqm/s:** write requests placed on the driver request queue and merged per second
- **r/s:** read requests issued to the disk device per second
- **w/s:** write requests issued to the disk device per second
- **rkB/s:** kilobytes read from the disk device per second
- **wkB/s:** kilobytes written to the disk device per second

Nonzero counts in the rrqm/s and wrqm/s columns show that contiguous requests were merged before delivery to the device, to improve performance. This metric is also a sign of a sequential workload. The r/s and w/s columns show the requests actually issued to the device.

Here is the remaining output:

```
$ iostat -xkdz 1

Linux 3.2.6-3.fc16.x86_64 (prod201)     04/14/13        _x86_64_        (16 CPU)

Device:       \ ... \    avgrq-sz avgqu-sz    await r_await w_await  svctm  %util
sdb           / ... /     227.13     0.00     41.13    4.51   47.65   0.54   0.00
sda           \ ... \      11.16     0.00      1.40    1.17    2.04   1.40   0.00
dm-0          / ... /       8.00     0.00     12.83    3.61   21.05   0.04   0.00
              \ ... \
Device:       / ... /    avgrq-sz avgqu-sz    await r_await w_await  svctm  %util
sdb           \ ... \      19.93     0.99      4.30    4.30    0.00   4.30  99.00
              / ... /
Device:       \ ... \    avgrq-sz avgqu-sz    await r_await w_await  svctm  %util
sdb           / ... /      20.54     1.00      4.33    4.33    0.00   4.33 100.00
```

The output columns are

- **avgrq-sz:** average request size in sectors (512 bytes)
- **avgqu-sz:** average number of requests both waiting in the driver request queue and active on the device
- **await:** average I/O response time, including time waiting in the driver request queue and the I/O response time of the device (ms)
- **r_await:** same as await, but for reads only (ms)
- **w_await:** same as await, but for writes only (ms)
- **svctm:** average (inferred) I/O response time for the disk device (ms)
- **%util:** percent of time the device was busy processing I/O requests (utilization)

Since `avgrq-sz` is after merging, small sizes (16 sectors or less) are an indicator of a random I/O workload that was unable to be merged. Large sizes may be either large I/O or a merged sequential workload (indicated by earlier columns).

The most important metric for delivered performance is `await`. If the application and file system use a technique to mitigate write latency (e.g., write-through), `w_await` may not matter as much, and you can focus on `r_await` instead.

For resource usage and capacity planning, `%util` is important, but bear in mind it is only a measure of busyness (non-idle time) and may mean little for virtual devices backed by multiple disks. Those devices may be better understood by the load applied: IOPS (`r/s` + `w/s`) and throughput (`rkB/s` + `wkB/s`).

The `r_await` and `w_await` columns are newer additions to the `iostat(1)` tool; previous versions had just `await`. The `iostat(1)` man page warns that the `svctm` field will be removed in future versions as the metric is considered to be inaccurate. (I don't think it is inaccurate, but I do think it may have misled people, since it is an inferred value and not a measurement of device latency.)

Here is another useful combination:

```
$ iostat -xkdzt -p ALL 1
Linux 3.2.6-3.fc16.x86_64 (prod201)     04/14/13      _x86_64_        (16 CPU)

04/14/2013 10:50:20 PM
Device:          rrqm/s   wrqm/s     r/s     w/s    rkB/s    wkB/s   \ ...
sdb                0.00     0.21    0.01    0.00     0.74     0.87   / ...
sdb1               0.00     0.21    0.01    0.00     0.74     0.87   \ ...
[...]
```

The `-t` includes the timestamp, which can be useful when comparing the output to other timestamped sources. The `-p ALL` includes per-partition statistics.

Unfortunately, the current version of `iostat(1)` does not include disk errors; otherwise all USE method metrics could be checked from one tool!

Solaris

Listing options using –h (despite the "illegal option" error):

```
$ iostat -h
iostat: illegal option -- h
Usage: iostat [-cCdDeEiImMnpPrstxXYz]  [-l n] [-T d|u] [disk ...] [interval [count]]
                -c:    report percentage of time system has spent
                       in user/system/wait/idle mode
                -C:    report disk statistics by controller
                -d:    display disk Kb/sec, transfers/sec, avg.
                       service time in milliseconds
                -D:    display disk reads/sec, writes/sec,
                       percentage disk utilization
                -e:    report device error summary statistics
                -E:    report extended device error statistics
                -i:    show device IDs for -E output
```

```
        -I:     report the counts in each interval,
                instead of rates, where applicable
        -l n:   Limit the number of disks to n
        -m:     Display mount points (most useful with -p)
        -M:     Display data throughput in MB/sec instead of Kb/sec
        -n:     convert device names to cXdYtZ format
        -p:     report per-partition disk statistics
        -P:     report per-partition disk statistics only,
                no per-device disk statistics
        -r:     Display data in comma separated format
        -s:     Suppress state change messages
        -T d|u  Display a timestamp in date (d) or unix time_t (u)
        -t:     display chars read/written to terminals
        -x:     display extended disk statistics
        -X:     display I/O path statistics
        -Y:     display I/O path (I/T/L) statistics
        -z:     Suppress entries with all zero values
```

This includes -e and -E options to report error counts.

The -I option prints counts instead of the calculated interval summaries; it is typically used by monitoring software that runs iostat(1) at regular intervals, and then performs its own calculations on the output to generate summaries.

```
$ iostat
    tty       ramdisk1        sd0           sd1           cpu
 tin tout kps tps serv  kps tps serv  kps tps serv  us sy wt id
   0   10   1   0    0    0   0    0 5360 111    1   9  6  0 85
```

From left to right, the default output shows terminal (tty) input and output characters (tin, tout), then up to three groups of columns (kps, tps, serv) for disk devices, then a group for CPU statistics (cpu). On this system, the disk devices shown are ramdisk1, sd0, and sd1. More devices are not shown in this way, as iostat(1) attempts to respect 80-character-width output.

The disk device columns are

- **kps:** kilobytes per second, read and write
- **tps:** transactions per second (IOPS)
- **serv:** service time, milliseconds

This example uses -n to use the descriptive /dev names of the disk devices instead of the kernel instance names, and -z to omit lines of all zeros (idle devices):

```
$ iostat -xnz 1
                    extended device statistics
    r/s    w/s    kr/s    kw/s wait actv wsvc_t asvc_t  %w  %b device
    0.1    0.2     0.7     0.6  0.0  0.0    0.0    0.0    0   0 ramdisk1
   12.3   98.7   315.6  5007.8  0.0  0.1    0.0    0.8    0   2 c0t0d0
```

continues

```
                      extended device statistics
    r/s    w/s   kr/s   kw/s wait actv wsvc_t asvc_t  %w  %b device
 1041.7    8.0 1044.7   95.6  0.0  0.7    0.0    0.6   1  65 c0t0d0
                      extended device statistics
    r/s    w/s   kr/s   kw/s wait actv wsvc_t asvc_t  %w  %b device
 1911.9    1.0 1959.4    7.9  0.0  0.6    0.0    0.3   1  55 c0t0d0
                      extended device statistics
    r/s    w/s   kr/s   kw/s wait actv wsvc_t asvc_t  %w  %b device
  746.1    1.0 1016.6    8.0  0.0  0.8    0.0    1.0   0  75 c0t0d0
[...]
```

The output columns are

- **r/s, w/s:** reads per second, writes per second
- **kr/s, kw/s:** kilobytes read per second, kilobytes written per second
- **wait:** average number of requests waiting in the block driver queue
- **actv:** average number of requests issued and active on the device
- **wsvc_t:** average time waiting in the block driver queue (ms); wsvc_t is waiting for service time
- **asvc_t:** average time active on the device (ms); asvc_t is active service time, although this is really the average device I/O response time
- **%w:** percent of time I/O were present in a wait queue
- **%b:** percent of time I/O were busy (utilization) throughput

Average read or write I/O size is not included (it is available in the Linux version), but it can easily be calculated by dividing the by the IOPS rate, for example, average read size = (kr/s) / (r/s).

Another useful combination is

```
$ iostat -xnmpzCTd 1
April 14, 2013 08:44:58 AM UTC
                      extended device statistics
    r/s   w/s   kr/s   kw/s wait actv wsvc_t asvc_t  %w  %b device
    1.5  33.9  146.5 1062.6  0.0  0.0    0.0    1.2   0   1 c0
    0.1   0.0    0.5    0.0  0.0  0.0    0.0    0.1   0   0 c0t0d0
    0.1   0.0    0.5    0.0  0.0  0.0    0.0    0.1   0   0 c0t0d0p0
    0.0   0.0    0.0    0.0  0.0  0.0    0.0    3.6   0   0 c0t0d0p1
    1.5  33.9  146.0 1062.6  0.0  0.0    0.0    1.2   0   1 c0t1d0
    1.5  33.9  146.0 1062.6  0.0  0.0    0.0    1.2   0   1 c0t1d0s0
    0.0   0.0    0.0    0.0  0.0  0.0    0.0    6.0   0   0 c0t1d0p0
[...]
```

Per-controller statistics are shown with –C, per-partition with –p, and the output is timestamped using –Td.

Error counters can be added to the output using –e:

```
$ iostat -xnze 1
                        extended device statistics        ---- errors ---
   r/s    w/s    kr/s    kw/s wait actv wsvc_t asvc_t %w %b s/w h/w trn tot device
   0.0    0.0     0.1     0.0  0.0  0.0    0.3    0.6  0  0   0   0   0    0 lofi1
   0.0    0.0     0.2     0.1  0.0  0.0    0.0    0.0  0  0   0   0   0    0 ramdisk1
   0.1    0.0     0.5     0.0  0.0  0.0    0.0    0.1  0  0   0   0   0    0 c0t0d0
   1.5   33.9   146.0  1062.6  0.0  0.0    0.0    1.2  0  1   0   0   0    0 c0t1d0
[...]
```

Unless you have devices that are actively encountering errors, however, having the per-interval summaries may not be that helpful. To check counts since boot only, use the –E option for a different iostat output format:

```
$ iostat -En
c1t0d0          Soft Errors: 0 Hard Errors: 0 Transport Errors: 0
Vendor: iDRAC    Product: LCDRIVE            Revision: 0323 Serial No:
Size: 0.00GB <0 bytes>
Media Error: 0 Device Not Ready: 0 No Device: 0 Recoverable: 0
Illegal Request: 0 Predictive Failure Analysis: 0
c2t0d0          Soft Errors: 0 Hard Errors: 0 Transport Errors: 0
Vendor: iDRAC    Product: Virtual CD         Revision: 0323 Serial No:
Size: 0.00GB <0 bytes>
Media Error: 0 Device Not Ready: 0 No Device: 0 Recoverable: 0
Illegal Request: 0 Predictive Failure Analysis: 0
[...]
```

The Soft Errors (s/w in the -e output) are recoverable errors that may cause performance issues. Hard Errors (h/w from the -e output) are not recoverable by the disks, although they may be recoverable by the higher-level architecture (RAID), which allows the system to continue but usually also causes performance issues (e.g., I/O time-out latency followed by degraded service).

It can be easier to read the error counters using

```
$ iostat -En | grep Hard
c1t0d0          Soft Errors: 0 Hard Errors: 0 Transport Errors: 0
c2t0d0          Soft Errors: 0 Hard Errors: 0 Transport Errors: 0
c2t0d1          Soft Errors: 0 Hard Errors: 0 Transport Errors: 0
c3t0d0          Soft Errors: 0 Hard Errors: 0 Transport Errors: 0
c0t0d0          Soft Errors: 0 Hard Errors: 0 Transport Errors: 0
c0t1d0          Soft Errors: 0 Hard Errors: 0 Transport Errors: 0
```

The USE method can be derived from iostat(1M) using

- **%b:** shows disk utilization.
- **actv:** A number greater than one is an indication of saturation: queueing in the *device*. For virtual devices that front multiple physical devices, this is harder to determine (it depends on the RAID policy); an actv greater than the device count is likely to indicate device saturation.

- **wait:** A number greater than zero is an indication of saturation: queueing in the *driver*.

- **errors tot:** total error counts.

As described in the earlier Sloth Disks section of Section 9.4.1, Disk Types, there can be disk issues where the error counters are not incremented. Hopefully this is rare, and you won't encounter it. Here is an example screen shot of such an issue:

```
$ iostat -xnz 1
[...]
                    extended device statistics
    r/s    w/s    kr/s    kw/s wait actv wsvc_t asvc_t  %w  %b device
    0.0    0.0    0.0    0.0  0.0  4.0    0.0    0.0   0 100 c0t0d0
                    extended device statistics
    r/s    w/s    kr/s    kw/s wait actv wsvc_t asvc_t  %w  %b device
    0.0    0.0    0.0    0.0  0.0  4.0    0.0    0.0   0 100 c0t0d0
                    extended device statistics
    r/s    w/s    kr/s    kw/s wait actv wsvc_t asvc_t  %w  %b device
    0.0    0.0    0.0    0.0  0.0  4.0    0.0    0.0   0 100 c0t0d0
[...]
```

Note that the disk is 100% busy, yet is not performing I/O (zero counts for r/s and w/s). This particular example was from an issue with a RAID controller. If this persists for short durations, multisecond I/O latency is introduced, creating performance issues. If it goes on longer, the system can appear to have hung.

9.6.2 sar

The system activity reporter, sar(1), can be used to observe current activity and can be configured to archive and report historical statistics. It is mentioned in various chapters in this book for the different statistics it provides.

The sar(1) disk summary is printed using the –d option, demonstrated in the following examples with an interval of one second.

Linux

This disk summary output is wide and is included here in two parts:

```
$ sar -d 1
Linux 2.6.32-21-server (prod103)        04/15/2013      _x86_64_       (8 CPU)

02:39:26 AM        DEV       tps  rd_sec/s  wr_sec/s  avgrq-sz  avgqu-sz  \ ...
02:39:27 AM     dev8-16      0.00      0.00      0.00      0.00      0.00  / ...
02:39:27 AM      dev8-0    418.00      0.00  12472.00     29.84     29.35  / ...
02:39:27 AM    dev251-0      0.00      0.00      0.00      0.00      0.00  / ...
02:39:27 AM    dev251-1   1559.00      0.00  12472.00      8.00    113.87  \ ...
02:39:27 AM    dev251-2      0.00      0.00      0.00      0.00      0.00  / ...
[...]
```

Here are the remaining columns:

```
$ sar -d 1
Linux 2.6.32-21-server (prod103)        04/15/2013      _x86_64_        (8 CPU)

02:39:26 AM   \ ... \   await     svctm     %util
02:39:27 AM   / ... /    0.00      0.00      0.00
02:39:27 AM   \ ... \   70.22      0.69     29.00
02:39:27 AM   / ... /    0.00      0.00      0.00
02:39:27 AM   \ ... \   73.04      0.19     29.00
02:39:27 AM   / ... /    0.00      0.00      0.00
[...]
```

Many of the columns are similar to iostat(1) (see the earlier descriptions), with the following differences:

- **tps:** device data transfers per second
- **rd_sec/s, wr_sec/s:** read and write sectors (512 bytes) per second

Solaris

The following runs sar(1) with a 1 s interval to report current activity:

```
$ sar -d 1

SunOS prod072 5.11 joyent_20120509T003202Z i86pc     04/15/2013

02:52:30   device     %busy   avque   r+w/s   blks/s   avwait   avserv

02:52:31   sd0          0      0.0      0        0       0.0      0.0
           sd1          0      0.0      0        0       0.0      0.0
           sd2          0      0.0      0        0       0.0      0.0
           sd3          0      0.0      3       33       0.0      0.1
           sd3,a        0      0.0      0        0       0.0      0.0
           sd3,b        0      0.0      3       30       0.0      0.1
[...]
```

Output columns are similar to iostat(1M) extended mode, with different names. For example, %busy is iostat(1M)'s %b, and avwait and avserv are called wsvc_t and asvc_t in iostat(1M).

9.6.3 pidstat

The Linux pidstat(1) tool prints CPU usage by default and includes a -d option for disk I/O statistics. This is available on kernels 2.6.20 and later. For example:

```
$ pidstat -d 1
22:53:11           PID    kB_rd/s    kB_wr/s kB_ccwr/s  Command
22:53:12         10512    3366.34       0.00      0.00  tar
22:53:12         10513       0.00    6051.49  13813.86  gzip

22:53:12           PID    kB_rd/s    kB_wr/s kB_ccwr/s  Command
22:53:13         10512    5136.00       0.00      0.00  tar
22:53:13         10513       0.00    4416.00      0.00  gzip
```

Columns include

- **kB_rd/s:** kilobytes read per second
- **kB_wd/s:** kilobytes issued for write per second
- **kB_ccwr/s:** kilobytes canceled for write per second (e.g., overwritten before flush)

Only superusers (root) can access disk statistics for processes that they do not own. These are read via /proc/PID/io.

9.6.4 DTrace

DTrace can be used to examine disk I/O events from within the kernel, including block device interface I/O, I/O scheduler events, target driver I/O, and device driver I/O. These abilities support workload characterization and latency analysis.

The following sections introduce DTrace for disk I/O analysis, demonstrating capabilities that should apply to both Linux- and Solaris-based systems. The examples are taken from a Solaris-based system, unless noted as Linux. A DTrace primer was included in Chapter 4, Observability Tools.

The DTrace providers used to trace disk I/O include the ones listed in Table 9.7.

Table 9-7 DTrace Providers for I/O Analysis

Layer	Stable Providers	Unstable Providers
Application	depends on app	pid
System library	—	pid
System calls	—	syscall
VFS	fsinfo	fbt
File system	—	fbt
Block device interface	io	fbt
Target driver	—	fbt
Device driver	—	fbt

Stable providers should always be used as much as possible; however, for the disk I/O stack there really is only the io provider for serious analysis. Check whether more stable providers have been released for your operating system for the other areas. If not, the unstable-interface providers may be used, although scripts will need updates to match software changes.

io Provider

The io provider provides visibility into the block device interface and can be used to characterize disk I/O and measure latency. The probes are

- **io:::start:** An I/O request was issued to the device.
- **io:::done:** An I/O request completed on the device (completion interrupt).
- **io:::wait-start:** A thread began waiting on an I/O request.
- **io:::wait-done:** A thread completed waiting on an I/O request.

Listing these on Solaris:

```
# dtrace -ln io:::
   ID    PROVIDER          MODULE                      FUNCTION NAME
  731          io         genunix                        biodone done
  732          io         genunix                        biowait wait-done
  733          io         genunix                        biowait wait-start
  744          io         genunix                 default_physio start
  745          io         genunix                  bdev_strategy start
  746          io         genunix                        aphysio start
 2014          io             nfs                       nfs4_bio done
 2015          io             nfs                       nfs3_bio done
 2016          io             nfs                        nfs_bio done
 2017          io             nfs                       nfs4_bio start
 2018          io             nfs                       nfs3_bio start
 2019          io             nfs                        nfs_bio start
```

The MODULE and FUNCTION columns show the location of the probes (and, as an implementation detail, are not part of the stable interface). Note that on Solaris, nfs client I/O is also traced via the io provider, as seen by the nfs module probes.

The probes have stable arguments that provide details of the I/O, including

- **args[0]->b_count:** I/O size (bytes)
- **args[0]->b_blkno:** device I/O offset (blocks)
- **args[0]->b_flags:** bitwise flags, including B_READ to indicate read I/O
- **args[0]->b_error:** error status
- **args[1]->dev_statname:** device instance name + instance/minor number

- **args[1]->dev_pathname:** device path name
- **args[2]->fi_pathname:** file path name (if known)
- **args[2]->fi_fs:** file system type

Along with the standard DTrace built-ins, these allow for some powerful one-liners to be constructed.

Event Tracing

The following traces each disk I/O request, with PID, process name, and I/O size (bytes):

```
# dtrace -n 'io:::start { printf("%d %s %d", pid, execname,
    args[0]->b_bcount); }'
dtrace: description 'io:::start ' matched 6 probes
CPU     ID                    FUNCTION:NAME
  0     745              bdev_strategy:start 22747 tar 65536
  0     745              bdev_strategy:start 22747 tar 65536
  0     745              bdev_strategy:start 22747 tar 131072
  0     745              bdev_strategy:start 22747 tar 131072
  0     745              bdev_strategy:start 22747 tar 131072
[...]
```

This one-liner uses a `printf()` statement to print details for each I/O. The output shows the `tar` process with PID 22747 issued five I/O, which were either 64 or 128 Kbytes in size. In this case, the application thread was still on-CPU when the I/O request was made, allowing it to be seen via `execname`. (There are cases where this will occur asynchronously, and the kernel, `sched`, will be identified instead.)

I/O Size Summary

Summarizing disk I/O size by application name:

```
# dtrace -n 'io:::start { @[execname] = quantize(args[0]->b_bcount); }'
dtrace: description 'io:::start ' matched 6 probes
^C

  tar
           value  ------------- Distribution ------------- count
            2048 |                                         0
            4096 |                                         1
            8192 |                                         0
           16384 |                                         0
           32768 |                                         0
           65536 |@@@@                                     13
          131072 |@@@@@@@@@@@@@@@@@@@@@@@@@@@@@@@@@@@@@@@    121
          262144 |                                         0
```

```
sched
          value  ------------- Distribution ------------- count
            256 |                                              0
            512 |                                              3
           1024 |@@@@@@@                                      63
           2048 |@@@@@@@@                                     72
           4096 |@@@@@                                        46
           8192 |@@@@@                                        51
          16384 |@@@                                          31
          32768 |@                                             5
          65536 |                                              0
         131072 |@@@@@@@@@@@                                 100
         262144 |                                              0
```

Instead of using DTrace to report the average, minimum, or maximum I/O size, this one-liner produces a distribution plot to visualize the full distribution. The value column shows the ranges in bytes, and the count column shows the number of I/O that were in that range. While tracing, processes named tar performed 121 I/O with sizes between 128 and 256 Kbytes (131,072 to 262,143 bytes). The kernel (sched) has an interesting distribution (it looks bimodal), one that would not be well understood via a single average value.

Apart from summarizing by process name (execname), the I/O size can be summarized by

- **Device name:** using args[1]->dev_statname
- **I/O direction (read/write):** using args[0]->b_flags & B_READ ? "read" : "write"

The values to summarize can also be characteristics other than the size (args[0]->b_count). For example, the location on disk can be examined to measure I/O seek.

I/O Seek Summary

The I/O seek summary traces the seek distance between successive I/O to the same device and from the same application, reporting it as histograms by process. This has become too long for a one-liner and has been implemented as the following DTrace script (diskseeksize.d):

```
#!/usr/sbin/dtrace -s

self int last[dev_t];

io:::start
/self->last[args[0]->b_edev] != 0/
{
        this->last = self->last[args[0]->b_edev];
```

continues

```
        this->dist = (int)(args[0]->b_blkno - this->last) > 0 ?
            args[0]->b_blkno - this->last : this->last - args[0]->b_blkno;
        @[pid, curpsinfo->pr_psargs] = quantize(this->dist);
}

io:::start
{
        self->last[args[0]->b_edev] = args[0]->b_blkno +
            args[0]->b_bcount / 512;
}
```

This script calculates the distance in sectors between one I/O and the last sector of the previous I/O (starting offset + size). This is tracked per device, and also by each thread (using `self->`), so that workload patterns from different processes can be separated and studied.

```
# ./diskseeksize.d
dtrace: script './diskseeksize.d' matched 8 probes
^C
      3    fsflush
           value  ------------- Distribution ------------- count
               2 |                                          0
               4 |@                                         2
               8 |                                          0
              16 |@@@@@                                     15
              32 |                                          0
              64 |                                          0
             128 |                                          0
             256 |                                          0
             512 |                                          0
            1024 |                                          0
            2048 |                                          0
            4096 |                                          0
            8192 |                                          0
           16384 |@@@@@@@@@                                 24
           32768 |@@@@                                      13
           65536 |@@@@@                                     15
          131072 |@@@@@@@@@@@@                              34
          262144 |@@@                                       9
          524288 |                                          0
  [...]
```

This shows I/O from the fsflush thread, which is usually seeking further than 8,192 blocks. A distribution with a seek distance of mostly 0 would indicate a sequential workload.

I/O Latency Summary

This script (disklatency.d) traces block I/O start and completion events, summarizing the latency distribution as a histogram:

```
#!/usr/sbin/dtrace -s

io:::start
{
        start[arg0] = timestamp;
}

io:::done
/start[arg0]/
{
        @["block I/O latency (ns)"] = quantize(timestamp - start[arg0]);
        start[arg0] = 0;
}
```

A timestamp is recorded on the start probe so that the delta time can be calculated on completion. The trick to this script is associating the start with end timestamps, as many may be in flight. An associative array is used, which is keyed on a unique identifier for the I/O (which happens to be the pointer to the buffer struct).

Executing:

```
# ./disklatency.d
dtrace: script './disklatency.d' matched 10 probes
^C

  block I/O latency (ns)
           value  ------------- Distribution ------------- count
            2048 |                                         0
            4096 |                                         26
            8192 |                                         0
           16384 |                                         4
           32768 |@@@@                                     227
           65536 |@@@@@@@@@@@@@@@@@@                       1047
          131072 |@@@@@@@@@@@@@                            797
          262144 |@@@@                                     220
          524288 |@@                                       125
         1048576 |@                                        40
         2097152 |                                         18
         4194304 |                                         0
         8388608 |                                         0
        16777216 |                                         1
        33554432 |                                         0
```

While tracing, most of the I/O were in the 65,536 to 262,143 ns range (0.07 to 0.26 ms). The slowest was a single I/O in the 16 to 33 ms range. This histogram output is great for identifying such I/O latency outliers.

Here, the I/O were summarized for all devices. The script can be enhanced to produce separate histograms per device, or by process ID, or other criteria.

I/O Stacks

An I/O stack frequency counts the calling kernel stack for I/O requests, up to the block device driver (location of the `io:::start` probe). On **Solaris**-based systems:

```
# dtrace -n 'io:::start { @[stack()] = count(); }'
dtrace: description 'io:::start ' matched 6 probes
^C
[...]
                genunix`ldi_strategy+0x4e
                zfs`vdev_disk_io_start+0x170
                zfs`vdev_io_start+0x12
                zfs`zio_vdev_io_start+0x7b
                zfs`zio_next_stage_async+0xae
                zfs`zio_nowait+0x9
                zfs`vdev_queue_io_done+0x68
                zfs`vdev_disk_io_done+0x74
                zfs`vdev_io_done+0x12
                zfs`zio_vdev_io_done+0x1b
                genunix`taskq_thread+0xbc
                unix`thread_start+0x8
                751

                ufs`lufs_read_strategy+0x8a
                ufs`ufs_getpage_miss+0x2b7
                ufs`ufs_getpage+0x802
                genunix`fop_getpage+0x47
                genunix`segmap_fault+0x118
                genunix`fbread+0xc4
                ufs`ufs_readdir+0x14b
                genunix`fop_readdir+0x34
                genunix`getdents64+0xda
                unix`sys_syscall32+0x101
                3255
```

The output was many pages long and shows the exact code path taken through the kernel that led to the issuing of disk I/O, followed by the count for each stack. This is often useful when investigating unexpected additional I/O (asynchronous, metadata) beyond the expected rate for the workload. The top stack shows an asynchronous ZFS I/O (from a taskq thread running the ZIO pipeline), and the bottom shows a synchronous UFS I/O originating from a `getdents()` syscall.

Here it is on **Linux**, this time via dynamic tracing of the kernel `submit_bio()` function (the `io:::start` probe is still in development for this prototype):

```
# dtrace -n 'fbt::submit_bio:entry { @[stack()] = count(); }'
dtrace: description 'fbt::submit_bio:entry ' matched 1 probe
^C
[...]
                kernel`submit_bio+0x1
                kernel`mpage_readpages+0x105
                kernel`ext4_get_block
                kernel`ext4_get_block
                kernel`__getblk+0x2c
```

```
                    kernel`ext4_readpages+0x1d
                    kernel`__do_page_cache_readahead+0x1c7
                    kernel`ra_submit+0x21
                    kernel`ondemand_readahead+0x115
                    kernel`mutex_lock+0x1d
                    kernel`page_cache_sync_readahead+0x33
                    kernel`generic_file_aio_read+0x4f8
                    kernel`vma_merge+0x121
                    kernel`do_sync_read+0xd2
                    kernel`security_file_permission+0x93
                    kernel`rw_verify_area+0x61
                    kernel`vfs_read+0xb0
                    kernel`sys_read+0x4a
                    kernel`system_call_fastpath+0x16
                  146
```

The path shows the ancestry, starting with the syscall interface (at the bottom), VFS, page cache, and ext4.

Each line of these stacks may be traced individually using dynamic tracing via the DTrace fbt provider. See Section 9.8, Tuning, for an example of tracing the sd_start_cmds() function via fbt.

SCSI Events

This script (scsireasons.d) demonstrates tracing at the SCSI layer, reporting I/O completions with a special SCSI code that describes the reason for completion. Key excerpts are included here (see the next section for the full script reference):

```
dtrace:::BEGIN
{
        /*
         * The following was generated from the CMD_* pkt_reason definitions
         * in /usr/include/sys/scsi/scsi_pkt.h using sed.
         */
        scsi_reason[0] = "no transport errors- normal completion";
        scsi_reason[1] = "transport stopped with not normal state";
        scsi_reason[2] = "dma direction error occurred";
        scsi_reason[3] = "unspecified transport error";
        scsi_reason[4] = "Target completed hard reset sequence";
        scsi_reason[5] = "Command transport aborted on request";
        scsi_reason[6] = "Command timed out";
[...]
fbt::scsi_destroy_pkt:entry
{
        this->code = args[0]->pkt_reason;
        this->reason = scsi_reason[this->code] != NULL ?
            scsi_reason[this->code] : "";
[...]
```

The script uses an associative array to translate from SCSI reason integers to human-readable strings. This is referenced during scsi_destroy_pkt(), where the reason strings are frequency counted. No errors were found while tracing.

```
# ./scsireasons.d
Tracing... Hit Ctrl-C to end.
^C
SCSI I/O completion reason summary:

  no transport errors- normal completion                              38346

SCSI I/O reason errors by disk device and reason:

  DEVICE              ERROR REASON                                     COUNT
```

Advanced Tracing

When needed for advanced analysis, dynamic tracing can explore each layer of the kernel I/O stack in more detail. To provide an idea of the capabilities, Table 9.8 shows scripts from the (140-page) Disk I/O chapter of *DTrace* [Gregg 11] (these scripts are also available online [4]).

Table 9-8 Advanced Storage I/O Tracing Scripts

Script	Layer	Description
iopattern	block	shows disk I/O statistics including percent random
sdqueue.d	SCSI	shows I/O wait queue times as a distribution plot by device
sdretry.d	SCSI	a status tool for SCSI retries
scsicmds.d	SCSI	frequency count SCSI commands, with descriptions
scsilatency.d	SCSI	summarizes SCSI command latency by type and result
scsirw.d	SCSI	shows various SCSI read/write/sync statistics, including bytes
scsireasons.d	SCSI	shows SCSI I/O completion reasons and device names
satacmds.d	SATA	frequency count SATA commands, with descriptions
satarw.d	SATA	shows various SATA read/write/sync statistics, including bytes
satareasons.d	SATA	shows SATA I/O completion reasons and device names
satalatency.d	SATA	summarizes SATA command latency by type and result
idelatency.d	IDE	summarizes IDE command latency by type and result
iderw.d	IDE	shows IDE read/write/sync statistics, including bytes
ideerr.d	IDE	shows IDE command completion reasons with errors
mptsasscsi.d	SAS	shows SAS SCSI commands with SCSI and mpt details
mptevents.d	SAS	traces special mpt SAS events with details
mptlatency.d	SAS	shows mpt SCSI command times as a distribution plot

While this degree of observability is incredible, these dynamic tracing scripts are tied to specific kernel internals and will require maintenance to match changes in newer kernel versions.

9.6.5 SystemTap

SystemTap can also be used on Linux systems for dynamic tracing of disk I/O events, and static tracing using its ioblock provider. See Section 4.4, SystemTap, in Chapter 4, Observability Tools, and Appendix E for help with converting the previous DTrace scripts.

9.6.6 perf

The Linux perf(1) tool (introduced in Chapter 6, CPUs) provides block tracepoints, which can be traced for some basic information. Listing them:

```
# perf list | grep block:
  block:block_rq_abort                              [Tracepoint event]
  block:block_rq_requeue                            [Tracepoint event]
  block:block_rq_complete                           [Tracepoint event]
  block:block_rq_insert                             [Tracepoint event]
  block:block_rq_issue                              [Tracepoint event]
  block:block_bio_bounce                            [Tracepoint event]
  block:block_bio_complete                          [Tracepoint event]
  block:block_bio_backmerge                         [Tracepoint event]
  block:block_bio_frontmerge                        [Tracepoint event]
  block:block_bio_queue                             [Tracepoint event]
  block:block_getrq                                 [Tracepoint event]
  block:block_sleeprq                               [Tracepoint event]
  block:block_plug                                  [Tracepoint event]
  block:block_unplug                                [Tracepoint event]
  block:block_split                                 [Tracepoint event]
  block:block_bio_remap                             [Tracepoint event]
  block:block_rq_remap                              [Tracepoint event]
```

For example, the following traces block device issues with call graphs so that stack traces can be inspected. A sleep 10 command is provided as the duration of tracing.

```
# perf record -age block:block_rq_issue sleep 10
[ perf record: Woken up 4 times to write data ]
[ perf record: Captured and wrote 0.817 MB perf.data (~35717 samples) ]
# perf report | more
[...]
   100.00%           tar  [kernel.kallsyms]  [k] blk_peek_request
                     |
                     --- blk_peek_request
                         do_virtblk_request
                         blk_queue_bio
                         generic_make_request
                         submit_bio
                         submit_bh
                         |
                         |--100.00%-- bh_submit_read
                         |            ext4_ext_find_extent
                         |            ext4_ext_map_blocks
```

continues

```
                           |      ext4_map_blocks
                           |      ext4_getblk
                           |      ext4_bread
                           |      dx_probe
                           |      ext4_htree_fill_tree
                           |      ext4_readdir
                           |      vfs_readdir
                           |      sys_getdents
                           |      system_call
                           |      __getdents64
    [...]
```

The output was many pages long, showing the different code paths that led to block device I/O. The portion given here is for ext4 directory reads.

9.6.7 iotop

`iotop(1)` is a version of top that includes a disk I/O column. The first version was written in 2005 using DTrace for Solaris-based systems [McDougall 06b] as a top-style version of an earlier `psio(1)` tool (process status with I/O, which used a pre-DTrace tracing framework). `iotop(1)` and its companion, `iosnoop(1M)`, are now shipped by default on many systems with DTrace, including Mac OS X and Oracle Solaris 11. An `iotop(1)` tool is also available for Linux, based on kernel accounting statistics [5].

Linux

`iotop(1)` requires kernel version 2.6.20 (maybe a little earlier depending on back-port status) or later, and the following kernel options: CONFIG_TASK_DELAY_ACCT, CONFIG_TASK_IO_ACCOUNTING, CONFIG_TASKSTATS, and CONFIG_VM_EVENT_COUNTERS.

Usage

Various options are available to customize the output:

```
# iotop -h
Usage: /usr/bin/iotop [OPTIONS]
[...]
Options:
  --version              show program's version number and exit
  -h, --help             show this help message and exit
  -o, --only             only show processes or threads actually doing I/O
  -b, --batch            non-interactive mode
  -n NUM, --iter=NUM     number of iterations before ending [infinite]
  -d SEC, --delay=SEC    delay between iterations [1 second]
  -p PID, --pid=PID      processes/threads to monitor [all]
  -u USER, --user=USER   users to monitor [all]
  -P, --processes        only show processes, not all threads
  -a, --accumulated      show accumulated I/O instead of bandwidth
```

```
-k, --kilobytes      use kilobytes instead of a human friendly unit
-t, --time           add a timestamp on each line (implies --batch)
-q, --quiet          suppress some lines of header (implies --batch)
```

By default, iotop(1) clears the screen and prints one-second summaries.

Batch Mode

Batch mode (-b) can be used to provide a rolling output (no screen clear); it is demonstrated here with I/O processes only (-o) and an interval of 5 s (-d5):

```
# iotop -bod5
Total DISK READ:       4.78 K/s | Total DISK WRITE:       15.04 M/s
  TID  PRIO  USER     DISK READ  DISK WRITE  SWAPIN      IO    COMMAND
22400 be/4 root       4.78 K/s     0.00 B/s  0.00 % 13.76 % [flush-252:0]
  279 be/3 root       0.00 B/s 1657.27 K/s  0.00 %  9.25 % [jbd2/vda2-8]
22446 be/4 root       0.00 B/s    10.16 M/s  0.00 %  0.00 % beam.smp -K true ...
Total DISK READ:       0.00 B/s | Total DISK WRITE:       10.75 M/s
  TID  PRIO  USER     DISK READ  DISK WRITE  SWAPIN      IO    COMMAND
  279 be/3 root       0.00 B/s     9.55 M/s  0.00 %  0.01 % [jbd2/vda2-8]
22446 be/4 root.      0.00 B/s    10.37 M/s  0.00 %  0.00 % beam.smp -K true ...
  646 be/4 root       0.00 B/s   272.71 B/s  0.00 %  0.00 % rsyslogd -n -c 5
[...]
```

The output shows the beam.smp process (Riak) performing a disk write workload of around 10 Mbytes/s.

Other useful options include -a for accumulative I/O instead of interval averages, and -o to show only those processes performing disk I/O.

Solaris

iotop(1) may already be available under /opt/DTT or /usr/DTT. It's also available in the DTraceToolkit (from where it originated).

Usage

The following shows iotop(1) usage:

```
# iotop -h
USAGE: iotop [-C] [-D|-o|-P] [-j|-Z] [-d device] [-f filename]
             [-m mount_point] [-t top] [interval [count]]

           -C        # don't clear the screen
           -D        # print delta times, elapsed, us
           -j        # print project ID
           -o        # print disk delta times, us
           -P        # print %I/O (disk delta times)
           -Z        # print zone ID
           -d device     # instance name to snoop
           -f filename   # snoop this file only
```

continues

```
                    -m mount_point  # this FS only
                    -t top          # print top number only
    eg,
        iotop           # default output, 5 second samples
        iotop 1         # 1 second samples
        iotop -P        # print %I/O (time based)
        iotop -m /      # snoop events on filesystem / only
        iotop -t 20     # print top 20 lines only
        iotop -C 5 12 # print 12 x 5 second samples
```

Default

By default, the output interval is 5 s, and the usage statistic is given in bytes:

```
# iotop
2013 Mar 16 08:12:00,  load: 1.46,  disk_r: 306580 KB,  disk_w:  0 KB

  UID    PID   PPID CMD            DEVICE  MAJ MIN D          BYTES
    0  71272  33185 tar            sd5      83 320 R      314855424
```

Here, the tar(1) command read about 3 Gbytes during this 5 s interval, from the sd5 device.

Utilization

The –P option shows disk utilization, and –C prints a rolling output:

```
# iotop -CP 1
Tracing... Please wait.
2013 Mar 16 08:18:53,  load: 1.46,  disk_r:  55714 KB,  disk_w:  0 KB

  UID    PID   PPID CMD            DEVICE  MAJ MIN D     %I/O
    0  61307  33185 tar            sd5      83 320 R       82

2013 Mar 16 08:18:54,  load: 1.47,  disk_r:  55299 KB,  disk_w:  0 KB

  UID    PID   PPID CMD            DEVICE  MAJ MIN D     %I/O
    0  61307  33185 tar            sd5      83 320 R       78
[...]
```

This shows that the tar(1) command was making the sd5 disk around 80% busy.

disktop.stp

Another version of iotop(1) was written for SystemTap, called disktop.stp. The name "disktop" should be an improvement over "iotop," since "io" is ambiguous, possibly meaning application-level (VFS) or disk-level. Unfortunately, the *disk* in disktop.stp refers to "reading/writing disk from the *point of view of user-space*" and does this by tracing VFS. This means the output of disktop.stp may not match iostat(1) at all, for applications that return heavily from the file system cache.

9.6.8 iosnoop

iosnoop(1M) traces all disks simultaneously via the block device interface and prints a line of output for every disk I/O. Various command-line options are provided to output extra details, and, since iosnoop(1M) is a short DTrace script, it can easily be modified to provide more. This tool is useful for the previous tracing and latency analysis strategies.

Usage

The following shows iosnoop(1) usage:

```
# iosnoop -h
USAGE: iosnoop [-a|-A|-DeghiNostv] [-d device] [-f filename]
               [-m mount_point] [-n name] [-p PID]
          iosnoop           # default output
                   -a       # print all data (mostly)
                   -A       # dump all data, space delimited
                   -D       # print time delta, us (elapsed)
                   -e       # print device name
                   -g       # print command arguments
                   -i       # print device instance
                   -N       # print major and minor numbers
                   -o       # print disk delta time, us
                   -s       # print start time, us
                   -t       # print completion time, us
                   -v       # print completion time, string
                   -d device        # instance name to snoop
                   -f filename      # snoop this file only
                   -m mount_point   # this FS only
                   -n name          # this process name only
                   -p PID           # this PID only
      eg,
          iosnoop -v        # human readable timestamps
          iosnoop -N        # print major and minor numbers
          iosnoop -m /      # snoop events on filesystem / only
```

Tracing Disk I/O

Disk I/O when launching the (uncached) vim text editor:

```
# iosnoop
  UID   PID D    BLOCK    SIZE        COMM PATHNAME
  100  6602 R 20357048    4096        bash /usr/opt/sfw/bin/vim
  100  6602 R 20356920    4096         vim /usr/opt/sfw/bin/vim
  100  6602 R    76478    1024         vim /usr/sfw/lib/libgtk-1.2.so.0
  100  6602 R 14848848    4096         vim /usr/sfw/lib/libgtk-1.2.so.0.9.1
[...]
  100  6602 R 20357024   12288         vim /usr/opt/sfw/bin/vim
  100  6602 R  3878942    1024         vim /usr/opt/sfw/share
  100  6602 R 20356944    8192         vim /usr/opt/sfw/bin/vim
  100  6602 R  4062944    1024         vim /usr/opt/sfw/share/terminfo
  100  6602 R  4074064    6144         vim /usr/opt/sfw/share/terminfo/d
  100  6602 R  4072464    2048         vim /usr/opt/sfw/share/terminfo/d/dtterm
```

continues

```
100  6602 R 20356960   4096      vim /usr/opt/sfw/bin/vim
100  6602 R 4104304    1024      vim /usr/opt/sfw/share/vim
[...]
```

The columns identify

- **PID:** process ID
- **COMM:** process name
- **D:** direction (R = read, W = write)
- **BLOCK:** disk block address (sector)
- **SIZE:** I/O size (bytes)
- **PATHNAME:** a file system path name, if applicable and known

The preceding example traced a UFS file system, for which the path name will usually be known. Cases where it won't be known include UFS on-disk file system metadata, and currently all ZFS I/O. There is a feature request for adding ZFS path names to the DTrace io provider, which will be seen by iosnoop(1M). (In the meantime, ZFS path names may be fetched via dynamic tracing of the kernel.)

Timestamps

The following shows a Riak cloud database (using the Erlang VM, beam.smp). It is running on ZFS, which is using a virtual disk from a hardware storage controller.

```
# iosnoop -Dots
STIME(us)      TIME(us)       DELTA(us) DTIME(us) UID  PID D   BLOCK      SIZE ...
1407309985123 1407309991565 6441       3231      103  20008 R 1822533465 131072
1407309991930 1407310004498 12567      12933     103  20008 R 564575763 131072
1407310001067 1407310004955 3888       457       103  20008 R 1568995398 131072
1407309998479 1407310008407 9928       3452      103  20008 R 299165216 131072
1407309976205 1407310008875 32670      467       103  20008 R 1691114933 131072
1407310006093 1407310013903 7810       5028      103  20008 R 693606806 131072
1407310006020 1407310014495 8474       591       103  20008 R 693607318 131072
1407310009203 1407310016667 7464       2172      103  20008 R 1065600468 131072
1407310008714 1407310018792 10077      2124      103  20008 R 927976467 131072
1407310017175 1407310023456 6280       4663      103  20008 R 1155898834 131072
[...]
```

The wide output has been truncated to fit; the missing columns on the right were COMM PATHNAME, all of which contained beam.smp <none>.

The output shows a workload of 128 Kbyte reads, with a somewhat random block address. iostat(1) confirms the result of this workload:

```
# iostat -xnz 1
[...]
                     extended device statistics
    r/s    w/s    kr/s    kw/s wait actv wsvc_t asvc_t  %w  %b device
  204.9    0.0 26232.2     0.0  0.0  1.2    0.0    6.1   0  74 c0t1d0
```

What iostat(1) doesn't show is the variance for the I/O response time, shown by the iosnoop DELTA(us) column (microseconds). In this sample, I/O took between 3,888 and 32,670 µs to respond. The DTIME(us) column shows the time from that I/O completion to the previous disk event, as an estimate of the actual disk service time on that I/O.

The iosnoop(1M) output is roughly sorted on the completion time, shown by the TIME(us) column. Note that the start times, STIME(us), are not in exactly the same order. This is evidence that the disk device has reordered requests. The slowest I/O (32,670) was issued at 1407309976205, which was before a previously completed I/O issued at 1407310001067. With rotational disks, the reason for reordering can often be seen by examining the disk address (BLOCK) and considering the elevator seeking algorithm. It isn't apparent in this example, which is using a virtual disk built upon several physical disks, with an offset mapping that is known only to the disk controller.

On busy production servers, the output of iosnoop(1M) can be hundreds of lines long from just a few seconds of tracing. This is useful (you can study exactly what occurred), but it can also be time-consuming to read through. Consider visualizing the output using another tool (such as scatter plots, covered in Section 9.6.12, Visualizations), so that it can be considered more quickly.

9.6.9 blktrace

blktrace(8) is a custom tracing facility for block device I/O events on Linux, including a kernel component to trace and buffer the data (which was later moved to tracepoints), and a control and reporting mechanism for user-land tools to use. These tools include blktrace(8), blkparse(1), and btrace(8).

blktrace(8) enables kernel block driver tracing and retrieves the raw trace data, which can be processed using blkparse(1) to produce readable output. For convenience, the btrace(8) tool runs both blktrace(8) and blkparse(1), such that the following are equivalent:

```
# blktrace -d /dev/sda -o - | blkparse -i -
# btrace /dev/sda
```

Default Output

The following shows the default output of btrace(8) and captures a single disk read event by the cksum(1) command:

```
# btrace /dev/sdb
  8,16  3        1    0.429604145 20442  A   R 184773879 + 8 <- (8,17) 184773816
  8,16  3        2    0.429604569 20442  Q   R 184773879 + 8 [cksum]
  8,16  3        3    0.429606014 20442  G   R 184773879 + 8 [cksum]
  8,16  3        4    0.429607624 20442  P   N [cksum]
  8,16  3        5    0.429608804 20442  I   R 184773879 + 8 [cksum]
  8,16  3        6    0.429610501 20442  U   N [cksum] 1
  8,16  3        7    0.429611912 20442  D   R 184773879 + 8 [cksum]
  8,16  1        1    0.440227144     0  C   R 184773879 + 8 [0]
[...]
```

Eight lines of output were reported for this single disk I/O, showing each action (event) involving the block device queue and the device.

By default, there are seven columns:

1. Device major, minor number

2. CPU ID

3. Sequence number

4. Action time, in seconds

5. Process ID

6. Action identifier (see below)

7. RWBS description: may include R (read), W (write), D (block discard), B (barrier operation), S (synchronous)

These output columns may be customized using the -f option. They are followed by custom data based on the action.

The final data depends on the action. For example, 184773879 + 8 [cksum] means an I/O at block address 184773879 with size 8 (sectors), from the process named cksum.

Action Identifiers

These are described in the blkparse(1) man page:

```
         A      IO was remapped to a different device
         B      IO bounced
         C      IO completion
         D      IO issued to driver
         F      IO front merged with request on queue
         G      Get request
```

```
I        IO inserted onto request queue
M        IO back merged with request on queue
P        Plug request
Q        IO handled by request queue code
S        Sleep request
T        Unplug due to timeout
U        Unplug request
X        Split
```

This list has been included because it also shows the visibility of the blktrace framework.

Action Filtering

The blktrace(8) and btrace(8) commands can filter actions to show only the event type of interest. For example, to trace only the D actions (I/O issued), use the filter option -a issue:

```
# btrace -a issue /dev/sdb
 8,16    1        1     0.000000000   448  D  W 38978223 + 8 [kjournald]
 8,16    1        2     0.000306181   448  D  W 104685503 + 24 [kjournald]
 8,16    1        3     0.000496706   448  D  W 104685527 + 8 [kjournald]
 8,16    1        1     0.010441458 20824  D  R 184944151 + 8 [tar]
[...]
```

Other filters are described in the blktrace(8) man page, such as trace only reads (-a read), writes (-a write), or synchronous operations (-a sync).

9.6.10 MegaCli

Disk controllers (host bus adaptors) consist of hardware and firmware that are external to the system. Operating system analysis tools, even dynamic tracing, cannot directly observe their internals. Sometimes their workings can be inferred by observing the input and output carefully (including via static or dynamic kernel tracing), to see how the disk controller responds to a series of I/O.

There are some analysis tools for specific disk controllers, such as LSI's MegaCli. The following shows recent controller events:

```
# MegaCli -AdpEventLog -GetLatest 50 -f lsi.log -aALL
# more lsi.log
seqNum: 0x0000282f
Time: Sat Jun 16 05:55:05 2012
Code: 0x00000023
Class: 0
Locale: 0x20
Event Description: Patrol Read complete
```

continues

```
Event Data:
===========
None

seqNum: 0x000027ec
Time: Sat Jun 16 03:00:00 2012
Code: 0x00000027
Class: 0
Locale: 0x20
Event Description: Patrol Read started
[...]
```

The last two events show that a patrol read (which can affect performance) occurred between 3:00 and 5:55 a.m. Patrol reads were mentioned in Section 9.4.3, Storage Types; they read disk blocks and verify their checksums.

MegaCli has many other options, which can show the adaptor information, disk device information, virtual device information, enclosure information, battery status, and physical errors. These help identify issues of configuration and errors. Even with this information, some types of issues can't be analyzed easily, such as exactly why a particular I/O took hundreds of milliseconds.

Check the vendor documentation to see what, if any, interface exists for disk controller analysis.

9.6.11 smartctl

The disk has logic to control disk operation, including queueing, caching, and error handling. Similarly to disk controllers, the internal behavior of the disk is not directly observable by the operating system and instead is usually inferred by observing I/O requests and their latency.

Many modern drives provide SMART (Self-Monitoring, Analysis and Reporting Technology) data, which provides various health statistics. The following output of smartctl(8) on Linux shows the sort of data available (this is accessing the first disk in a virtual RAID device, using -d megaraid,0):

```
# smartctl --all -d megaraid,0 /dev/sdb
smartctl 5.40 2010-03-16 r3077 [x86_64-unknown-linux-gnu] (local build)
Copyright (C) 2002-10 by Bruce Allen, http://smartmontools.sourceforge.net

Device: SEAGATE  ST3600002SS        Version: ER62
Serial number: 3SS0LM01
Device type: disk
Transport protocol: SAS
Local Time is: Sun Jun 17 10:11:31 2012 UTC
Device supports SMART and is Enabled
Temperature Warning Disabled or Not Supported
SMART Health Status: OK

Current Drive Temperature:     23 C
```

```
Drive Trip Temperature:        68 C
Elements in grown defect list: 0
Vendor (Seagate) cache information
  Blocks sent to initiator = 3172800756
  Blocks received from initiator = 2618189622
  Blocks read from cache and sent to initiator = 854615302
  Number of read and write commands whose size <= segment size = 30848143
  Number of read and write commands whose size > segment size = 0
Vendor (Seagate/Hitachi) factory information
  number of hours powered up = 12377.45
  number of minutes until next internal SMART test = 56

Error counter log:
           Errors Corrected by          Total  Correction  Gigabytes   Total
                ECC          rereads/   errors  algorithm  processed uncorrected
            fast | delayed  rewrites  corrected invocations [10^9 bytes] errors
read:     7416197        0        0    7416197   7416197    1886.494         0
write:          0        0        0          0         0    1349.999         0
verify: 142475069        0        0  142475069  142475069   22222.134        0

Non-medium error count:    2661

SMART Self-test log
Num  Test               Status     segment  LifeTime  LBA_first_err [SK ASC ASQ]
     Description                    number   (hours)
# 1  Background long    Completed     16        3                 - [-    -    -]
# 2  Background short   Completed     16        0                 - [-    -    -]

Long (extended) Self Test duration: 6400 seconds [106.7 minutes]
```

While this is very useful, it does not have the resolution to answer questions about individual slow disk I/O, in a similar way to kernel tracing frameworks.

9.6.12 Visualizations

There are many types of visualizations that can help in analyzing disk I/O performance. This section demonstrates these with screen shots from various tools. See Section 2.10, Visualization, in Chapter 2, Methodology, for a discussion about visualization tools in general.

Line Graphs

Performance monitoring solutions commonly graph disk IOPS, throughput, and utilization measurements over time as line graphs. This helps illustrate time-based patterns, such as changes in load during the day, or recurring events such as file system flush intervals.

Note the metric that is being graphed. Averages across all disk devices can hide unbalanced behavior, including single device outliers. Averages across long time periods can also hide shorter-term fluctuations.

Scatter Plots

Scatter plots are useful for visualizing I/O trace data, which may include thousands of events. The example in Figure 9.10 plots 1,400 I/O events from a production MySQL database server, captured using iosnoop and plotted using R.

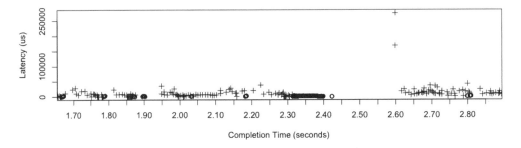

Figure 9-10 Scatter plot of disk read and write latency

The scatter plot shows reads (+) and writes (o) based on their completion time (*x* axis) and I/O response time (*y* axis). Other dimensions could be plotted, for example, disk block address on the *y* axis.

A couple of read outliers can be seen here, with latencies over 150 ms. The reason for these outliers was previously not known. This scatter plot, and others that included similar outliers, showed that they occur after a burst of writes. The writes have low latency since they returned from a RAID controller write-back cache, which will write them to the device after returning the completions. It is suspected that the reads are queueing behind the device writes.

This scatter plot showed a single server for a few seconds. Multiple servers or longer intervals can capture many more events, which merge together when plotted and become difficult to read. At that point, consider using a heat map (see the Latency Heat Maps section later in the chapter).

Offset Heat Maps

Figure 9.11 shows a heat map (more properly called a *column quantization*) to visualize the disk I/O access pattern.

Disk offset (block address) is shown on the *y* axis, and time on the *x* axis. Each pixel is colored based on the number of I/O that fell in that time and latency range, darker colors for larger numbers. The workload visualized was a file system archive, which creeps across the disk from block 0. Darker lines indicate a sequential I/O, and lighter clouds indicate random I/O.

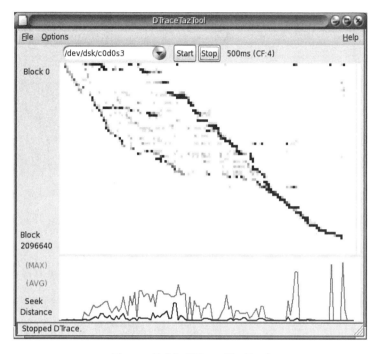

Figure 9-11 DTraceTazTool

This visualization was introduced in 1995 with taztool by Richard McDougall. This screen shot is from DTraceTazTool, a DTrace version of taztool I wrote in 2006. Disk I/O offset heat maps later appeared in other tools, including Sun ZFS Storage Appliance Analytics, Joyent Cloud Analytics, and seekwatcher (Linux).

Latency Heat Maps

Another use of heat maps is to show the full distribution of I/O latency [Gregg 10b], as in Figure 9.12.

The y axis shows I/O response time (latency), and the x axis shows the passage of time. The workload visualized was experimental, applying sequential reads to multiple disks one by one to explore bus and controller limits. The resulting heat map was unexpected (it has been described as a pterodactyl) and shows the information that would be missed when only considering averages. This particular screen shot is from Analytics on the Oracle ZFS Storage appliance.

Utilization Heat Maps

Per-device utilization may also be shown as a heat map, so that device utilization balance and individual outliers can be identified; see Figure 9.13.

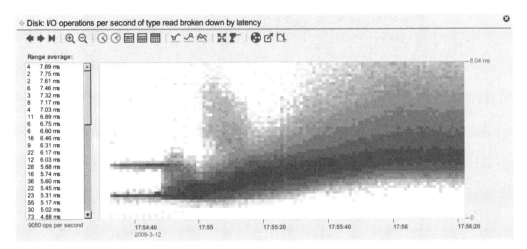

Figure 9-12 Disk latency pterodactyl

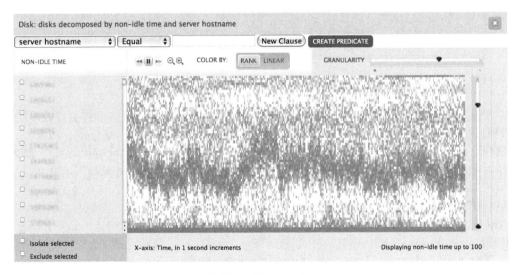

Figure 9-13 Utilization heat map

Device utilization is on the y axis, time on the x axis, and the number of devices at the utilization and time range shown by the color darkness (darker means more). This heat map shows that many devices are idle or near idle (the dark area at the bottom), and a group of devices has similar utilization that varies between about 20% and 50%. On the top right is a dark line showing that some devices have hit 100%. (This particular visualization is interactive, so those pixels can be clicked to reveal the hosts and devices responsible.)

I created this visualization type to help identify single hot disks, including sloth disks, described earlier. This screen shot is from Joyent Cloud Analytics, which is showing disk device utilization across a cloud of over 200 physical servers.

9.7 Experimentation

This section describes tools for actively testing disk I/O performance. See Section 9.5.10, Micro-Benchmarking, for a suggested methodology to follow.

When using these tools, it's a good idea to leave iostat(1) continually running so that any result can be immediately double-checked.

9.7.1 Ad Hoc

The dd(1) command (device-to-device copy) can be used to perform ad hoc tests of sequential disk performance. For example, testing sequential read with a 1 Mbyte I/O size:

```
# dd if=/dev/sda1 of=/dev/null bs=1024k count=1k
1024+0 records in
1024+0 records out
1073741824 bytes (1.1 GB) copied, 7.44024 s, 144 MB/s
```

The dd(1) version on Solaris-based systems does not currently print this summary.

Ideally, the disk device path will be *character special* so that the requested workload is applied directly. Solaris-based systems provide these by default, under /dev/rdsk. On Linux, the raw(8) command (where available) can create character special versions, under /dev/raw. If the block special file is used instead, take buffering into account.

Sequential write can be tested similarly; however, beware of destroying all data on disk, including the master boot record and partition table!

9.7.2 Custom Load Generators

To test custom workloads, you can write your own load generator and measure resulting performance using iostat(1). A custom load generator can be a short C program that opens the device path and applies the intended workload. On Linux, the block special devices files can be opened with O_DIRECT, to avoid buffering. If you use higher-level languages, try to use system-level interfaces that also avoid buffering (e.g., sysread() in Perl).

9.7.3 Micro-Benchmark Tools

Available disk benchmark tools include, for example, hdparm(8) on Linux:

```
# hdparm -Tt /dev/sdb

/dev/sdb:
 Timing cached reads:    16718 MB in  2.00 seconds = 8367.66 MB/sec
 Timing buffered disk reads:  846 MB in  3.00 seconds = 281.65 MB/sec
```

The -T option tests cached reads, and -t tests disk device reads. The results show the dramatic difference between on-disk cache hits and misses.

Do study the tool documentation to understand any caveats, and see Chapter 12, Benchmarking, for more background on micro-benchmarking. Also see Chapter 8, File Systems, for tools that test disk performance via the file system, for which many more are available.

9.7.4 Random Read Example

As an example experiment, a custom tool was written to perform a random 8 Kbyte read workload of a disk device path. From one to five instances of the tool were run concurrently, with iostat(1) running. Results for Linux- and Solaris-based systems follow.

Linux

Write columns, which were zeros, have been removed:

```
Device:      rrqm/s      r/s     rkB/s avgrq-sz avgqu-sz   await  svctm %util
sda          878.00   234.00   2224.00    19.01     1.00    4.27   4.27 100.00
[...]
Device:      rrqm/s      r/s     rkB/s avgrq-sz avgqu-sz   await  svctm %util
sda         1233.00   311.00   3088.00    19.86     2.00    6.43   3.22 100.00
[...]
Device:      rrqm/s      r/s     rkB/s avgrq-sz avgqu-sz   await  svctm %util
sda         1366.00   358.00   3448.00    19.26     3.00    8.44   2.79 100.00
[...]
Device:      rrqm/s      r/s     rkB/s avgrq-sz avgqu-sz   await  svctm %util
sda         1775.00   413.00   4376.00    21.19     4.01    9.66   2.42 100.00
[...]
Device:      rrqm/s      r/s     rkB/s avgrq-sz avgqu-sz   await  svctm %util
sda         1977.00   423.00   4800.00    22.70     5.04   12.08   2.36 100.00
```

Note the stepped increases in avgqu-sz, and the increased latency of await.

Solaris

The same experiment, from a Solaris-based system:

```
    r/s     w/s    kr/s    kw/s wait actv wsvc_t asvc_t  %w  %b device
  176.0   249.0 1407.9 3044.7  0.0  1.0    0.0    2.5   0 100 c0t1d0
[...]
    r/s     w/s    kr/s    kw/s wait actv wsvc_t asvc_t  %w  %b device
  306.0   275.0 2448.1 2819.6  0.0  2.0    0.0    3.5   0 100 c0t1d0
[...]
    r/s     w/s    kr/s    kw/s wait actv wsvc_t asvc_t  %w  %b device
  437.9   265.9 3503.2 2209.5  0.0  3.0    0.0    4.3   0 100 c0t1d0
[...]
    r/s     w/s    kr/s    kw/s wait actv wsvc_t asvc_t  %w  %b device
  531.0   267.0 4248.3 2985.7  0.0  4.0    0.0    5.1   0 100 c0t1d0
[...]
    r/s     w/s    kr/s    kw/s wait actv wsvc_t asvc_t  %w  %b device
  625.2   178.8 5001.4 1059.1  0.0  5.0    0.0    6.2   0 100 c0t1d0
```

Note the stepped increases in `actv`, and the increased latency of `asvc_t`. This is testing a virtual disk device backed by a RAID card, which allows for many concurrent I/Os (it has an sd_max_throttle of 256; see Section 9.8.1, Operating System Tunables). Physical disk devices have a lower concurrency setting and will queue the I/O in the driver sooner, ramping the `wait` column instead of the `actv` column.

9.8 Tuning

Many tuning approaches were covered in Section 9.5, Methodology, including cache tuning, scaling, and workload characterization, which can help you identify and eliminate unnecessary work. Another important area of tuning is the storage configuration, which can be studied as part of a static performance tuning methodology.

The sections that follow show different areas that can be tuned: the operating system, disk devices, and disk controller. Available tunable parameters vary between versions of an operating system, models of disks, disk controllers, and their firmware; see their respective documentation. While changing tunables can be easy to do, the default settings are usually reasonable and rarely need much adjusting.

9.8.1 Operating System Tunables

These include `ionice(1)`, resource controls, and kernel tunable parameters.

ionice

On **Linux**, the ionice(1) command can be used to set an I/O scheduling class and priority for a process. The scheduling classes are identified numerically:

- **0, none:** no class specified, so the kernel will pick a default—best effort, with a priority based on the process nice value.
- **1, real-time:** highest-priority access to the disk. If misused, this can starve other processes (just like the RT CPU scheduling class).
- **2, best effort:** default scheduling class, supporting priorities 0–7, with 0 the highest.
- **3, idle:** disk I/O allowed only after a grace period of disk idleness.

Here is example usage:

```
# ionice -c 3 -p 1623
```

This puts process ID 1623 in the idle I/O scheduling class. This may be desirable for long-running backup jobs, so that they are less likely to interfere with the production workload.

Resource Controls

Modern operating systems provide resource controls for managing disk or file system I/O usage in custom ways.

For **Linux**, the container groups (cgroups) block I/O (blkio) subsystem provides storage device resource controls for processes or process groups. This can be a proportional weight (like a share) or a fixed limit. Limits can be set for read and write independently, and for either IOPS or throughput (bytes per second).

Some **Solaris**-based systems with ZFS have ZFS I/O throttling, which throttles I/O at the file system level (not the disk level) and can be set per zone. This is described in Chapter 11, Cloud Computing.

Tunable Parameters

Example operating system tunables are

- **/sys/block/sda/queue/scheduler (Linux):** to select the I/O scheduler policy: noop, deadline, an (anticipatory), cfq. See the earlier descriptions of these in Section 9.4, Architecture.

- **sd_max_throttle (Solaris):** This regulates the maximum number of commands that can be in flight to an sd storage device. It may make sense to
  increase this for virtual devices that are backed by storage arrays of multiple
  disks, which can support more in-flight commands.

Information for tuning sd_max_throttle can be obtained by profiling the number of active commands, to see how close it is to the limit. For example (from a production cloud environment):

```
# dtrace -n 'fbt::sd_start_cmds:entry {
    @[args[0]->un_throttle] = quantize(args[0]->un_ncmds_in_transport); }'
dtrace: description 'fbt::sd_start_cmds:entry ' matched 1 probe
^C

    256
            value  ------------- Distribution ------------- count
               -1 |                                         0
                0 |@@@@@@@@@@@                              3983
                1 |@@@@@@@@@@                               3582
                2 |@@@@@@@@@                                3269
                4 |@@@@@@@                                  2553
                8 |@@@@                                     1286
               16 |                                         0
```

This shows the current active value of sd_max_throttle to be 256, and the highest
rate of I/O is only in the 8–15 range. If queueing makes more sense on the storage
devices, this does not need to be tuned.

As with other kernel tunables, check the vendor documentation for the full list,
descriptions, and warnings. Setting these may also be prohibited by company or
vendor policy.

9.8.2 Disk Device Tunables

On Linux, the hdparm(8) tool can set various disk device tunables. On Solaris,
the format(1M) command can be used.

9.8.3 Disk Controller Tunables

The available disk controller tunable parameters depend on the disk controller
model and vendor. To give you an idea of what these may include, the following
shows some of the settings from a Dell PERC 6 card, viewed using the MegaCli
command:

```
# MegaCli -AdpAllInfo -aALL
[...]
Predictive Fail Poll Interval     : 300sec
Interrupt Throttle Active Count   : 16
Interrupt Throttle Completion     : 50us
Rebuild Rate                      : 30%
PR Rate                           : 0%
BGI Rate                          : 1%
Check Consistency Rate            : 1%
Reconstruction Rate               : 30%
Cache Flush Interval              : 30s
Max Drives to Spinup at One Time  : 2
Delay Among Spinup Groups         : 12s
Physical Drive Coercion Mode      : 128MB
Cluster Mode                      : Disabled
Alarm                             : Disabled
Auto Rebuild                      : Enabled
Battery Warning                   : Enabled
Ecc Bucket Size                   : 15
Ecc Bucket Leak Rate              : 1440 Minutes
Load Balance Mode                 : Auto
[...]
```

Each setting has a reasonably descriptive name and is described in more detail in the vendor documentation.

9.9 Exercises

1. Answer the following questions about disk terminology:
   - What are IOPS?
   - What is disk I/O response time?
   - What is the difference between service time and wait time?
   - What is a latency outlier?
   - What is a non-data-transfer disk command?

2. Answer the following conceptual questions:
   - Describe disk utilization and saturation.
   - Describe the performance differences between random and sequential disk I/O.
   - Describe the role of an on-disk cache for read and write I/O.

3. Answer the following deeper questions:
   - Explain why utilization (percent busy) of virtual disks can be misleading.
   - Explain why the "I/O wait" metric can be misleading.

- Describe performance characteristics of RAID-0 (striping) and RAID-1 (mirroring).

- Describe what happens when disks are overloaded with work, including the effect on application performance.

- Describe what happens when the storage controller is overloaded with work (either throughput or IOPS), including the effect on application performance.

4. Develop the following procedures for your operating system:

- A USE method checklist for disk resources (disks and controllers). Include how to fetch each metric (e.g., which command to execute) and how to interpret the result. Try to use existing OS observability tools before installing or using additional software products.

- A workload characterization checklist for disk resources. Include how to fetch each metric, and try to use existing OS observability tools first.

5. Describe disk behavior visible in this Linux iostat output alone:

```
$ iostat -x 1
[...]
avg-cpu:  %user   %nice %system %iowait  %steal   %idle
           3.23    0.00   45.16   31.18    0.00   20.43

Device:          rrqm/s   wrqm/s     r/s     w/s    rkB/s    wkB/s avgrq-sz
avgqu-sz   await r_await w_await  svctm  %util
vda               39.78 13156.99  800.00  151.61 3466.67 41200.00    93.88
11.99    7.49    0.57   44.01    0.49   46.56
vdb                0.00     0.00    0.00    0.00    0.00     0.00     0.00
 0.00    0.00    0.00    0.00    0.00    0.00
```

6. (optional, advanced) Develop a tool to trace all disk commands *except* for reads and writes. This may require tracing at the SCSI level.

9.10 References

[Patterson 88]   Patterson, D., G. Gibson, and R. Kats. "A Case for Redundant Arrays of Inexpensive Disks." ACM SIGMOD, 1988.

[Bovet 05]   Bovet, D., and M. Cesati. *Understanding the Linux Kernel, 3rd Edition*. O'Reilly, 2005.

[McDougall 06b]   McDougall, R., J. Mauro, and B. Gregg. *Solaris Performance and Tools: DTrace and MDB Techniques for Solaris 10 and OpenSolaris*. Prentice Hall, 2006.

[Gregg 10b]   Gregg, B. "Visualizing System Latency," *Communications of the ACM*, July 2010.

[Love 10]   Love, R. *Linux Kernel Development, 3rd Edition*. Addison-Wesley, 2010.

[Turner 10]   Turner, J. "Effects of Data Center Vibration on Compute System Performance." USENIX, SustainIT'10.

[Gregg 11]   Gregg, B., and J. Mauro. *DTrace: Dynamic Tracing in Oracle Solaris, Mac OS X and FreeBSD*. Prentice Hall, 2011.

[Cornwell 12]   Cornwell, M. "Anatomy of a Solid-State Drive," *Communications of the ACM*, December 2012.

[Leventhal 13]   Leventhal, A. "A File System All Its Own," *ACM Queue*, March 2013.

[1]   www.youtube.com/watch?v=tDacjrSCeq4

[2]   http://lwn.net/Articles/332839

[3]   http://sourceware.org/systemtap/wiki/WSiostatSCSI

[4]   www.dtracebook.com

[5]   http://guichaz.free.fr/iotop

10

Network

As systems become more distributed, especially with cloud computing environments, the network plays a bigger role in performance. Apart from improving network latency and throughput, another common task is to eliminate latency outliers, which can be caused by dropped packets.

Network analysis spans hardware and software. The hardware is the physical network, which includes the network interface cards, switches, routers, and gateways (these typically have software too). The system software is the kernel protocol stack, typically TCP/IP, and the behavior of each protocol involved.

The network is often blamed for poor performance, given the potential for congestion. This chapter will show how to figure out what is really happening, which may exonerate the network so that analysis can move on.

This chapter consists of five parts, the first three providing the basis for network analysis, and the last two showing its practical application to Linux- and Solaris-based systems. The parts are as follows:

- **Background** introduces network-related terminology, basic models, and key network performance concepts.

- **Architecture** provides generic descriptions of physical network components and the network stack.

- **Methodology** describes performance analysis methodologies, both observational and experimental.

- **Analysis** shows network performance tools for analysis and experimentation on Linux- and Solaris-based systems.
- **Tuning** describes example tunable parameters.

10.1 Terminology

For reference, network-related terminology used in this chapter includes the following:

- **Interface:** The term *interface port* refers to the physical network connector. The term *interface* or *link* refers to the logical instance of a network interface port, as seen and configured by the OS.
- **Packet:** The term *packet* typically refers to an IP-level routable message.
- **Frame:** a physical network-level message, for example, an Ethernet frame.
- **Bandwidth:** the maximum rate of data transfer for the network type, usually measured in bits per second. "10 GbE" is Ethernet with a bandwidth of 10 Gbits/s.
- **Throughput:** the current data transfer rate between the network endpoints, measured in bits per second or bytes per second.
- **Latency:** Network *latency* can refer to the time it takes for a message to make a round trip between endpoints, or the time required to establish a connection (e.g., TCP handshake), excluding the data transfer time that follows.

Other terms are introduced throughout this chapter. The Glossary includes basic terminology for reference, including *client*, *Ethernet*, *host*, *RFC*, *server*, *SYN*, *ACK*. Also see the terminology sections in Chapters 2 and 3.

10.2 Models

The following simple models illustrate some basic principles of networking and network performance. Section 10.4, Architecture, digs much deeper, including implementation-specific details.

10.2.1 Network Interface

A network interface is an operating system endpoint for network connections; it is an abstraction configured and managed by the system administrators.

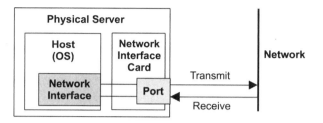

Figure 10-1 Network interface

A network interface is pictured in Figure 10.1. Network interfaces are mapped to physical network ports as part of their configuration. Ports connect to the network and typically have separate transmit and receive channels.

10.2.2 Controller

A *network interface card* (NIC) provides one or more network ports for the system and houses a *network controller*: a microprocessor for transferring packets between the ports and the system I/O transport. An example controller with four ports is pictured in Figure 10.2, showing the physical components involved.

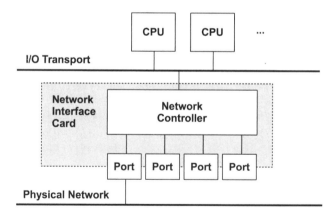

Figure 10-2 Network controller

The controller either is provided as a separate card or is built into the system board.

10.2.3 Protocol Stack

Networking is accomplished by a stack of protocols, each layer of which serves a particular purpose. Two stack models are shown in Figure 10.3, with example protocols.

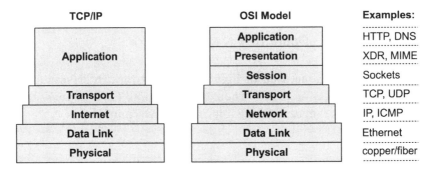

Figure 10-3

Lower layers are drawn wider to indicate protocol encapsulation. Sent messages move down the stack from the application to the physical network. Received messages move up.

Note that the Ethernet standard also describes the physical layer, and how copper or fiber is used.

While the TCP/IP stack has become standard, it can be useful to consider the OSI model as well. The OSI session layer, for example, is commonly present in TCP/IP stacks as BSD sockets. The "layer" terminology is from OSI, where *Layer 3* refers to the network protocols.

10.3 Concepts

The following are a selection of important concepts in networking and network performance.

10.3.1 Networks and Routing

A network is a group of connected hosts, related by network protocol addresses. Having multiple networks—instead of one giant worldwide network—is desirable for a number of reasons, particularly scalability. Some network messages will *broadcast* to all neighboring hosts. By creating smaller subnetworks, such broadcast messages can be isolated locally so they do not create a flooding problem at scale. This is also the basis for isolating the transmission of regular messages to only the networks between source and destination, making more efficient usage of network infrastructure.

Routing manages the delivery of messages, called *packets*, across these networks. The role of routing is pictured in Figure 10.4.

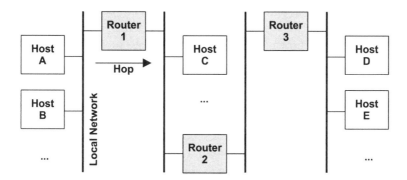

Figure 10-4 Network routing

From the perspective of host A, the *localhost* is host A itself. All other hosts pictured are *remote hosts*.

Host A can connect to host B via the local network, usually driven by a network switch (see Section 10.4, Architecture). Host A can connect to host C via router 1, and to host D via routers 1, 2, and 3. Since network components such as routers are shared, contention from other traffic (e.g., host C to host E) can hurt performance.

Connections between pairs of hosts involve *unicast* transmission. *Multicast* transmission allows a sender to transmit to multiple destinations simultaneously, which may span multiple networks. This must be supported by the router configuration to allow delivery.

The address information needed to route packets is contained in an IP header.

10.3.2 Protocols

Network protocol standards, such as those for IP, TCP, and UDP, are a necessary requirement for communication between systems and devices. Communication is performed by transferring messages called *packets*, typically by encapsulation of payload data.

Network protocols have different performance characteristics, arising from the original protocol design, extensions, or special handling by software or hardware.

For example, the different versions of the IP protocol, IPv4 and IPv6, may be processed by different kernel code paths and can exhibit different performance characteristics.

Often, there are also system tunable parameters that can affect protocol performance, by changing settings such as buffer sizes, algorithms, and various timers. These differences for specific protocols are described in later sections.

The size of the packets and their payload also affects performance, with larger sizes improving throughput and reducing packet overheads. For TCP/IP and Ethernet, packets can be between 54 and 9,054 bytes, including the 54 bytes (or more, depending on options or version) of protocol headers, which encapsulate the data.

10.3.3 Encapsulation

Encapsulation adds metadata to a payload at the start (a *header*), at the end (a *footer*), or both. This doesn't change the payload data, though it does increase the total size of the message slightly, which costs some overhead for transmission.

Figure 10.5 shows an example of encapsulation for a TCP/IP stack with Ethernet.

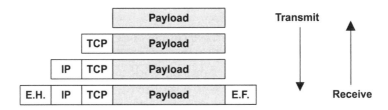

Figure 10-5 Network protocol encapsulation

E.H. is the Ethernet header, and E.F. is the optional Ethernet footer.

10.3.4 Packet Size

Packet size is usually limited by the network interface *maximum transmission unit* (MTU) size, which for many Ethernet networks is configured to be 1,500 bytes. Ethernet supports larger packets (frames) of up to approximately 9,000 bytes, termed *jumbo frames*. These can improve network throughput performance, as well as latency of data transfers, by requiring fewer packets.

The confluence of two components has interfered with the adoption of jumbo frames: older network hardware and misconfigured firewalls. Older hardware that does not support jumbo frames can either fragment the packet using the IP protocol or respond with an ICMP "can't fragment" error, letting the sender know to reduce the packet size. Now the misconfigured firewalls come into play: there have been ICMP-based attacks in the past (including the "ping of death"), to which some firewall administrators have responded by blocking all ICMP. This prevents the helpful "can't fragment" messages from reaching the sender and causes network packets to be silently dropped once their packet size increases beyond 1,500. To avoid this problem, many systems stick to the 1,500 MTU default.

The performance of 1,500 MTU frames has been improved by network interface card features, including *TCP offload* and *large segment offload*. These send larger buffers to the network card, which can then split them into smaller frames using dedicated and optimized hardware. This has, to some degree, narrowed the gap between 1,500 and 9,000 MTU network performance.

10.3.5 Latency

Latency is an important metric for network performance and can be measured in different ways, including name resolution latency, ping latency, connection latency, first-byte latency, round-trip time, and connection life span. These are described as measured by a client connecting to a server.

Name Resolution Latency

When establishing connections to remote hosts, a host name is usually resolved to an IP address, for example, by DNS resolution. The time this takes can be measured separately as name resolution latency. Worst case for this latency involves name resolution time-outs, which can take tens of seconds.

Sometimes name resolution isn't necessary for the application to function and can be disabled to avoid this latency.

Ping Latency

This is the time for an ICMP echo request to echo response, as measured by the ping(1) command. This time is used to measure network latency between hosts, including hops in between, and is measured as the time needed for a packet to make a round trip. It is in common use because it is simple and often readily available: many operating systems will respond to ping by default.

Example ping latencies are shown in Table 10.1. To better illustrate the orders of magnitude involved, the Scaled column shows a comparison based on an imaginary localhost ping latency of one second.

On the receiving side, the ICMP echo request is usually processed in interrupt context and returned immediately, minimizing the additional time spent executing kernel code. On the sending side, a little extra time may be included due to

Table 10-1 Example Ping Latencies

From	To	Via	Latency	Scaled
Localhost	localhost	kernel	0.05 ms	1 s
Host	host (same subnet)	10 GbE	0.2 ms	4 s
Host	host (same subnet)	1 GbE	0.6 ms	12 s
Host	host (same subnet)	Wi-Fi	3 ms	1 minute
San Francisco	New York	Internet	40 ms	13 minutes
San Francisco	United Kingdom	Internet	81 ms	27 minutes
San Francisco	Australia	Internet	183 ms	1 hour

timestamps being measured from user-land, such that kernel context switching and kernel code path time are included.

Connection Latency

Connection latency is the time to establish a network connection, before any data is transferred. For *TCP connection latency*, this is the TCP handshake time. Measured from the client, it is the time from sending the SYN to receiving the corresponding SYN-ACK. Connection latency might be better termed *connection establishment latency*, to clearly differentiate it from connection life span.

Connection latency is similar to ping latency, although it exercises more kernel code to establish a connection and includes time to retransmit any dropped packets. The TCP SYN packet, in particular, can be dropped by the server if its backlog is full, causing the client to retransmit the SYN. This occurs during the TCP handshake, so connection latency includes retransmission latency, adding one or more seconds.

Connection latency is followed by first-byte latency.

First-Byte Latency

Also known as *time to first byte* (TTFB), first-byte latency is the time from when the connection has been established to when the first byte of data is received. This includes the time for the remote host to accept a connection, schedule the thread that services it, and for that thread to execute and send the first byte.

While ping and connection latency measures the latency incurred by the network, first-byte latency includes the think time of the target server. This may include latency if the server is overloaded and needs time to process the request (e.g., TCP backlog) and to schedule the server (CPU run-queue latency).

Round-Trip Time

Round-trip time describes the time for a network packet to make a round trip between the endpoints.

Connection Life Span

Connection life span is the time from when a network connection is established to when it is closed. Some protocols use a *keep-alive* strategy, extending the duration of connections so that future operations can use existing connections and avoid the overheads and latency of connection establishment.

10.3.6 Buffering

Despite various network latencies that may be encountered, network throughput can be sustained at high rates by use of buffering on the sender and receiver. Larger buffers can mitigate the effects of higher round-trip times by continuing to send data before blocking and waiting for an acknowledgment.

TCP employs buffering, along with a sliding send window, to improve throughput. Network sockets also have buffers, and applications may employ their own in addition, to aggregate data before sending.

Buffering can also be performed by external network components, such as switches and routers, in an effort to improve their own throughput. Unfortunately, the use of large buffers on these components can lead to an issue called *buffer bloat*, where packets are queued for long intervals. This causes TCP congestion avoidance on the hosts, which throttles performance. Features have been added to the Linux 3.x kernels to address this problem (including byte queue limits, CoDel queue management [Nichols 12], and TCP small queues), and there is a website for discussing the issue [1].

The function of buffering (or large buffering) may be best served by the endpoints—the hosts—and not the intermediate network nodes, following a principle called *end-to-end arguments* [Saltzer 84].

10.3.7 Connection Backlog

Another type of buffering is for the initial connection requests. TCP implements a backlog, where SYN requests can queue in the kernel before being accepted by the user-land process. When there are too many TCP connection requests for the process to accept in time, the backlog reaches a limit and SYN packets are dropped, to be later retransmitted by the client. The retransmission of these packets causes latency for the client connect time.

Measuring backlog drops is one way to measure network connection *saturation.*

10.3.8 Interface Negotiation

Network interfaces may operate with different modes, autonegotiated with the other endpoint. Some examples are

- **Bandwidth:** for example, 10, 100, 1,000, 10,000 Mbits/s
- **Duplex:** half or full duplex

These examples are from Ethernet, which tends to use round base-10 numbers for bandwidth limits. Other physical-layer protocols, such as SONET, have a different set of possible bandwidths.

Network interfaces are usually described in terms of their highest bandwidth and protocol, for example, 1 Gbit/s Ethernet (1 GbE). This interface may, however, autonegotiate to lower speeds if needed. This can occur if the other endpoint cannot operate faster, or to accommodate physical problems with the connection medium (bad wiring).

Full-duplex mode allows bidirectional simultaneous transmission, with separate paths for both transmit and receive that can operate at full bandwidth. Half-duplex mode allows only one direction at a time.

10.3.9 Utilization

Network interface utilization can be calculated as the current throughput over the maximum bandwidth. Given variable bandwidth and duplex due to autonegotiation, calculating this isn't as straightforward as it sounds.

For full duplex, utilization applies to each direction and is measured as the current throughput for that direction over the current negotiated bandwidth. Usually it is just one direction that matters most, as hosts are commonly asymmetric: servers are transmit-heavy, and clients are receive-heavy.

Once a network interface direction reaches 100% utilization, it becomes a bottleneck, limiting performance.

Some operating system performance tools report activity only in terms of packets, not bytes. Since packet size can vary greatly (as mentioned earlier), it's not possible to relate packet counts to byte counts for calculating either throughput or (throughput-based) utilization.

10.3.10 Local Connections

Network connections can occur between two applications on the same system. These are *localhost* connections and use a virtual network interface: *loopback*.

Distributed application environments are often split into logical parts that communicate over the network. These can include web servers, database servers, and application servers. If they are running on the same host, their connections are to localhost.

Connecting via IP to localhost is the *IP sockets* technique of inter-process communication (IPC). Another technique is Unix domain sockets (UDS), which create a file on the file system for communication. Performance may be better with UDS, as the kernel TCP/IP stack can be bypassed, skipping kernel code and the overheads of protocol packet encapsulation.

For TCP/IP sockets, the kernel may detect the localhost connection after the handshake, and then shortcut the TCP/IP stack for data transfers, improving performance. This approach has been called *TCP fusion* on Solaris-based systems.

10.4 Architecture

This section introduces network architecture: protocols, hardware, and software. These have been summarized as background for performance analysis and tuning, with a focus on performance characteristics. For more details, including general networking topics, see networking texts ([Stevens 93], [Hassan 03]), RFCs, and vendor manuals for networking hardware. Some of these are listed at the end of the chapter.

10.4.1 Protocols

In this section, the performance characteristics of TCP and UDP are summarized.

TCP

The Transmission Control Protocol (TCP) is a commonly used Internet standard for creating reliable network connections. TCP is specified by [RFC 793] and later additions.

In terms of performance, TCP can provide a high rate of throughput even on high-latency networks, by use of buffering and a *sliding window*. TCP also employs congestion control and a *congestion window* set by the sender, so that it can maintain a high but also appropriate rate of transmission across different and varying networks. Congestion control avoids sending too many, which would cause congestion and a performance breakdown.

Following is a summary of TCP performance features, including additions since the original specification:

- **Sliding window:** This allows multiple packets up to the size of the window to be sent on the network before acknowledgments are received, providing high throughput even on high-latency networks. The size of the window is advertised by the receiver to indicate how many packets it is willing to receive at that time.

- **Congestion avoidance:** to prevent sending too much data and causing saturation, which can cause packet drops and worse performance.

- **Slow-start:** Part of TCP congestion control, this begins with a small congestion window and then increases it as acknowledgments (ACKs) are received within a certain time. When they are not, the congestion window is reduced.

- **Selective acknowledgments** (SACKs): allow TCP to acknowledge discontinuous packets, reducing the number of retransmits required.

- **Fast retransmit:** Instead of waiting on a timer, TCP can retransmit dropped packets based on the arrival of duplicate ACKs. These are a function of round-trip time and not the typically much slower timer.

- **Fast recovery:** This recovers TCP performance after detecting duplicate ACKs, by resetting the connection to perform slow-start.

In some cases these are implemented by use of extended TCP options added to the protocol header.

Important topics for TCP performance include the three-way handshake, duplicate ACK detection, congestion control algorithms, Nagle, delayed ACKs, SACK, and FACK.

Three-Way Handshake

Connections are established using a three-way handshake between the hosts. One host passively listens for connections; the other actively initiates the connection. To clarify terminology: *passive* and *active* are from [RFC 793]; however, they are commonly called *listen* and *connect* respectively, after the socket API. For the client/server model, the server performs listen and the client performs connect.

The three-way handshake is pictured in Figure 10.6.

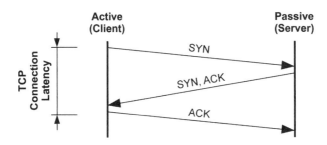

Figure 10-6 TCP three-way handshake

Connection latency from the client is indicated, which completes when the final ACK is sent. After that, data transfer may begin.

This figure shows best-case latency for a handshake. A packet may be dropped, adding latency as it is timed out and retransmitted.

Duplicate ACK Detection

Duplicate ACK detection is used by the fast retransmit and fast recovery algorithms. It is performed on the sender and works as follows:

1. The sender sends a packet with sequence number 10.
2. The receiver replies with an ACK for sequence number 11.
3. The sender sends 11, 12, and 13.
4. Packet 11 is dropped.
5. The receiver replies to both 12 and 13 by sending an ACK for 11, which it is still expecting.
6. The sender receives the duplicate 11 ACKs.

Duplicate ACK detection is also used by both the TCP Reno and Tahoe congestion avoidance algorithms.

Congestion Control: Reno and Tahoe

These algorithms for congestion control were first implemented in 4.3BSD:

- **Reno:** triple duplicate ACKs trigger: halving of the congestion window, halving of the slow-start threshold, fast retransmit, and fast recovery
- **Tahoe:** triple duplicate ACKs trigger: fast retransmit, halving the slow-start threshold, congestion window set to one maximum segment size (MSS), and slow-start state

Some operating systems (e.g., Linux and Oracle Solaris 11) allow the algorithm to be selected as part of system tuning. Newer algorithms that have been developed for TCP include Vegas, New Reno, and Hybla.

Nagle

This algorithm [RFC 896] reduces the number of small packets on the network by delaying their transmission to allow more data to arrive and coalesce. This delays packets only if there is data in the pipeline and delays are already being encountered.

The system may provide a tunable parameter to disable Nagle, which may be necessary if its operation conflicts with delayed ACKs.

Delayed ACKs

This algorithm [RFC 1122] delays the sending of ACKs up to 500 ms, so that multiple ACKs may be combined. Other TCP control messages can also be combined, reducing the number of packets on the network.

SACK and FACK

The TCP selective acknowledgment (SACK) algorithm allows the receiver to inform the sender that it received a noncontiguous block of data. Without this, a packet drop would eventually cause the entire send window to be retransmitted, to preserve a sequential acknowledgment scheme. This harms TCP performance and is avoided by most modern operating systems that support SACK.

SACK has been extended by forward acknowledgments (FACK), which are supported in Linux by default. FACKs track additional state and better regulate the amount of outstanding data in the network, improving overall performance [Mathis 96].

UDP

The User Datagram Protocol (UDP) is a commonly used Internet standard for sending messages, called *datagrams*, across a network [RFC 768]. In terms of performance, UDP provides

- **Simplicity:** Simple and small protocol headers reduce overheads of computation and size.
- **Statelessness:** lower overheads for connections and transmission.
- **No retransmits:** These add significant latencies for TCP connections.

While simple and often high-performing, UDP is not intended to be reliable, and data can be missing or sent out of order. This makes it unsuitable for many types of connections. UDP also has no congestion avoidance and can therefore contribute to congestion on the network.

Some services, including versions of NFS, can be configured to operate over TCP or UDP as desired. Others that perform broadcast or multicast data may be able to use only UDP.

10.4.2 Hardware

Networking hardware includes interfaces, controllers, switches, and routers. An understanding of their operation is useful, even if any of these components is managed by other staff (network administrators).

Interfaces

Physical network interfaces send and receive messages, called *frames*, on the attached network. They manage the electrical, optical, or wireless signaling involved, including the handling of transmission errors.

Interface types are based on Layer 2 standards, each providing a maximum bandwidth. Higher-bandwidth interfaces typically provide lower latency, although also higher cost. This is often a key choice when designing new servers, to balance the price of the server with the desired network performance.

For Ethernet, choices include wired or optical, and maximum speeds of 1 Gbit/s (1 GbE), 10 GbE, 40 GbE, or 100 GbE. Numerous vendors manufacture Ethernet interface controllers, although your operating system may not have driver support for some of them.

Interface utilization can be examined as the current negotiated bandwidth divided by the current throughput. Most interfaces have separate channels for transmit and receive, and when operating in full-duplex mode, each channel utilization must be studied separately.

Controllers

Physical network interfaces are provided to the system via controllers, either built into the system board or provided via expander cards.

Controllers are driven by microprocessors and attach to the system via an I/O transport (e.g., PCI). Either of these can become the limiter for network throughput or IOPS.

For example, a dual 10 GbE network interface card is connected to a four-channel PCI express (PCIe) Gen 2 slot. The card has a maximum bandwidth of 2 x 10 GbE = 20 Gbits/s. The slot has a maximum bandwidth of 4 x 4 Gbits/s = 16 Gbits/s. Therefore, network throughput on both ports will be limited by PCIe Gen 2 bandwidth, and it will not be possible to drive them both at line rate at the same time (I also know this from practice!).

Switches, Routers

Switches provide a dedicated communication path between any two connected hosts, allowing multiple transmissions between pairs of hosts without interference. This technology replaced hubs (and before that, shared physical busses: e.g., thick-Ethernet coaxial cable), which shared all packets with all hosts. This sharing led to contention when hosts transmitted simultaneously, which could be identified by the interface as a *collision* using a "carrier sense multiple access with collision detection" (CSMA/CD) algorithm, which would exponentially back off and retransmit until successful. Such behavior led to performance issues under load. With the use of switches this is behind us, but observability tools still have collision counters—even though these usually occur only due to errors (negotiation or bad wiring).

Routers deliver packets between networks and use network protocols and routing tables to determine efficient delivery paths. Delivering a packet between two cities may involve a dozen or more routers, plus other network hardware. The routers and routes are usually configured to update dynamically, so that the network can automatically respond to network and router outages, and to balance load. This means that at a given point in time, no one can be sure what path a packet is actually taking. With multiple paths possible, there is also the potential for packets to be delivered out of order, which can cause TCP performance problems.

This element of mystery on the network is often blamed for poor performance: perhaps heavy network traffic—from other unrelated hosts—is saturating a router between the source and destination? Network administration teams are therefore frequently required to exonerate their infrastructure. They can do so using advanced real-time monitoring tools to check all routers and other network components involved.

Both routers and switches include microprocessors, which themselves can become performance bottlenecks under load. As an extreme example, I once found that an early 10 GbE switch could drive no more than 11 Gbits/s in total across all ports, due to its limited CPU capacity.

Others

Your environment may include other physical network devices, such as hubs, bridges, repeaters, and modems. Any of these can be a source of performance bottlenecks and dropped packets.

10.4.3 Software

Networking software includes the network stack, TCP, and device drivers. Topics related to performance are discussed in this section.

Network Stack

The components and layers involved depend on the operating system type, version, protocols, and interfaces in use. Figure 10.7 depicts a general model, showing the software components.

On modern kernels the stack is multithreaded, and inbound packets can be processed by multiple CPUs. The mapping of an inbound packet to a CPU may be performed in different ways: it may be based on a hash of the source IP address, to evenly spread out load; or it may be based on the CPU where the socket was most recently processed, to benefit from CPU cache warmth and memory locality. Both

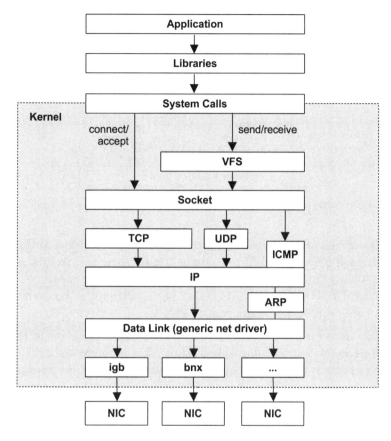

Figure 10-7 Generic network IP stack

Linux- and Solaris-based systems have different frameworks to support this behavior.

Linux

On Linux systems, the TCP, IP, and generic net driver software are core kernel components, with device drivers as additional modules. Packets are passed through these kernel components as the `struct sk_buff` data type.

Figure 10.8 shows the generic net driver in more detail, including the New API (NAPI) interface, which improves performance by coalescing interrupts.

High packet rates can be achieved by engaging multiple CPUs to process packets and the TCP/IP stack. Various methods for this have been documented for the Linux 3.7 kernel (Documentation/networking/scaling.txt), which are

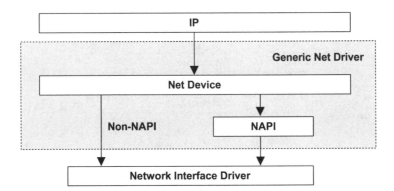

Figure 10-8 Linux lower-level network stack

- **RSS: Receive Side Scaling:** for modern NICs that support multiple queues and can hash packets to different queues, which are in turn processed by different CPUs by interrupting them directly. This hash may be based on the IP address and TCP port numbers, so that packets from the same connection end up being processed by the same CPU.

- **RPS: Receive Packet Steering:** a software implementation of RSS, for NICs that do not support multiple queues. This involves a short interrupt service routine to map the inbound packet to a CPU for processing. A similar hash can be used to map packets to CPUs, based on fields from the packet headers.

- **RFS: Receive Flow Steering:** This is similar to RPS, but with affinity for where the socket was last processed on-CPU, to improve CPU cache hit rates and memory locality.

- **Accelerated Receive Flow Steering:** This achieves RFS in hardware, for NICs that support this functionality. It involves updating the NIC with flow information so that it can determine which CPU to interrupt.

- **XPS: Transmit Packet Steering:** For NICs with multiple transmit queues, this supports transmission by multiple CPUs to the queues.

Without a CPU load-balancing strategy for network packets, an NIC may interrupt one CPU only, which can reach 100% utilization and become a bottleneck.

Mapping interrupts to CPUs based on factors such as cache coherency, as is done by RFS, can noticeably improve network performance. This can also be accomplished by the irqbalancer process, which assigns interrupt request (IRQ) lines to CPUs.

Solaris

On Solaris-based systems, the sockets layer is the `sockfs` kernel module, and the TCP, UDP, and IP protocols are combined into the `ip` module. Packets are passed through the kernel as message blocks, `mblk_t`. The lower-level stack is shown in more detail in Figure 10.9 [McDougall 06a].

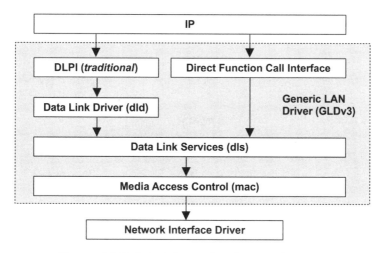

Figure 10-9 Solaris lower-level network stack

The GLDv3 software also improves performance using *vertical perimeters*: a per-CPU synchronization mechanism that is associated with a connection, avoiding the need for locks for each data structure in the network stack. This uses an abstraction called a *serialization queue* (squeue), which handles each connection.

High packet rates can be achieved by enabling *IP fanout*, which load-balances inbound packets across multiple CPUs.

Network stack internals were recently simplified by Erik Nordmark in the Solaris IP Datapath Refactoring project. This description of the state of the previous stack, including performance [2], comes from that project:

> The IP datapaths are extremely hard to follow. . . . That makes it hard to even fix bugs in that code, let alone getting it to perform. This has resulted in improving performance by creating numerous fast paths, which are subsets of the full datapaths. This further makes maintenance of the code a hazardous activity.

This project was integrated in snv_122 and reduced the IP code by 34,000 out of 140,000 lines.

TCP

The TCP protocol was described earlier. This section describes performance features of the kernel TCP implementation: backlog queues and buffers.

Bursts of connections are handled by using backlog queues. There are two such queues, one for incomplete connections while the TCP handshake completes (also known as the *SYN backlog*), and one for established sessions waiting to be accepted by the application (also known as the *listen backlog*). These are pictured in Figure 10.10.

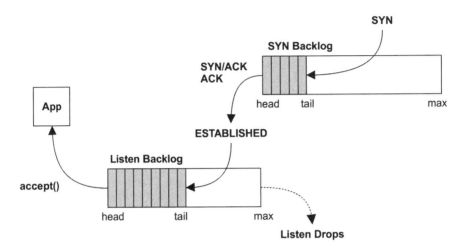

Figure 10-10 TCP backlog queues

Only one queue was used in earlier kernels, and it was vulnerable to SYN floods. A SYN flood is a type of DoS attack that involves sending numerous SYNs to the listening TCP port from bogus IP addresses. This fills the backlog queue while TCP waits to complete the handshake, preventing real clients from connecting.

With two queues, the first can act as a staging area for potentially bogus connections, which are promoted to the second queue only once the connection is established. The first queue can be made long to absorb SYN floods and optimized to store only the minimum amount of metadata necessary.

The length of these queues can be tuned independently (see Section 10.8, Tuning). The second can also be set by the application as the backlog argument to `listen()`.

Data throughput is improved by using send and receive buffers associated with the socket. These are pictured in Figure 10.11.

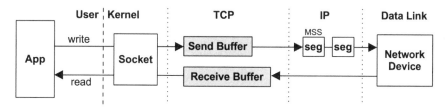

Figure 10-11 TCP send and receive buffers

For the write path, the data is buffered in the TCP send buffer, and then sent to IP for delivery. While the IP protocol has the capability to fragment packets, TCP tries to avoid this by sending data as MSS-size segments to IP. This means the unit of (re-)transmission matches the unit of fragmentation; otherwise a dropped fragment would require retransmission of the entire prefragmented packet. This approach can also improve TCP/IP stack efficiency, as it avoids fragmentation and assembly of regular packets.

The size of both the send and receive buffers is tunable. Larger sizes improve throughput performance, at the cost of more main memory spent per connection. One buffer may be set to be larger than the other if the server is expected to perform more sending or receiving. The Linux kernel will also dynamically increase the size of these buffers based on the connection activity.

Network Device Drivers

The network device driver usually has an additional buffer—a ring buffer—for sending and receiving packets between kernel memory and the NIC.

A performance feature that has become more common with the introduction of 10 GbE networking is the use of *interrupt coalescing mode*. Instead of interrupting the kernel for every arrived packet, an interrupt is sent only when either a timer (polling) or a certain number of packets is reached. This reduces the rate at which the kernel communicates with the NIC, allowing larger transfers to be buffered, resulting in greater throughput, though at some cost in latency. On Solaris-based kernels, this is called *dynamic polling*.

10.5 Methodology

This section describes various methodologies and exercises for network analysis and tuning. Table 10.2 summarizes the topics.

See Chapter 2, Methodology, for more strategies and the introduction to many of these.

Table 10-2 Network Performance Methodologies

Methodology	Types
Tools method	observational analysis
USE method	observational analysis
Workload characterization	observational analysis, capacity planning
Latency analysis	observational analysis
Performance monitoring	observational analysis, capacity planning
Packet sniffing	observational analysis
TCP analysis	observational analysis
Drill-down analysis	observational analysis
Static performance tuning	observational analysis, capacity planning
Resource controls	tuning
Micro-benchmarking	experimental analysis

These may be followed individually or used in combination. My suggestion is to use the following strategies to start with, in this order: performance monitoring, the USE method, static performance tuning, and workload characterization.

Section 10.6, Analysis, shows operating system tools for applying these methods.

10.5.1 Tools Method

The tools method is a process of iterating over available tools, examining key metrics they provide. It may overlook issues for which the tools provide poor or no visibility, and it can be time-consuming to perform.

For networking, the tools method can involve checking

- **netstat -s:** Look for a high rate of retransmits and out-of-order packets. What constitutes a "high" retransmit rate depends on the clients: an Internet-facing system with unreliable remote clients should have a higher retransmit rate than an internal system with clients in the same data center.
- **netstat -i:** Check interface error counters (specific counters depend on the OS version).
- **ifconfig** (Linux version only): Check "errors," "dropped," "overruns."
- **Throughput:** Check the rate of bytes transmitted and received—on Linux, via ip(8); on Solaris, via nicstat(1) or dladm(1M). High throughput may hit line rate for the negotiated speed and be limited. It could also cause contention and delays between network users on the system.

- **`tcpdump/snoop`:** While these can be expensive in terms of the CPU cost, using them for short periods may be enough to see who is using the network and identify unnecessary work that can be eliminated.
- **`dtrace/stap/perf`:** for selected packet inspection between the application and the wire, including examining kernel state.

If an issue is found, examine all fields from the available tools to learn more context. See Section 10.6, Analysis, for more about each tool. Other methodologies can also be used, which can identify more types of issues.

10.5.2 USE Method

The USE method is for quickly identifying bottlenecks and errors across all components. For each network interface, and in each direction—transmit (TX) and receive (RX)—check for

- **Utilization:** the time the interface was busy sending or receiving frames
- **Saturation:** the degree of extra queueing, buffering, or blocking due to a fully utilized interface
- **Errors:** for receive: bad checksum, frame too short (less than the data link header) or too long, collisions (unlikely with switched networks); for transmit: late collisions (bad wiring)

Errors may be checked first, since they are typically quick to check and the easiest to interpret.

Utilization is not commonly provided by operating system or monitoring tools directly. It can be calculated as the current throughput divided by the current negotiated speed, for each direction (RX, TX). The current throughput should be measured as bytes per second on the network, including all protocol headers.

For environments that implement network bandwidth limits (resource controls), as occurs in some cloud computing environments, network utilization may need to be measured in terms of the imposed limit, in addition to the physical limit.

Saturation of the network interface is difficult to measure. Some network buffering is normal, as applications can send data much more quickly than an interface can transmit it. It may be possible to measure as the time application threads spend blocked on network sends, which should increase as saturation increases. Also check if there are other kernel statistics more closely related to interface saturation, for example, Linux "overruns" or Solaris "nocanputs."

Retransmits at the TCP level are usually readily available as statistics and can be an indicator of network saturation. However, they are measured across the network between the server and its clients and could be occurring at any hop.

The USE method can also be applied to network controllers, and the transports between them and the processors. Since observability tools for these components are sparse, it may be easier to infer metrics based on network interface statistics and topology. For example, if network controller A houses ports A0 and A1, the network controller throughput can be calculated as the sum of the interface throughputs A0 + A1. With a known maximum throughput, utilization of the network controller can then be calculated.

10.5.3 Workload Characterization

Characterizing the load applied is an important exercise when capacity planning, benchmarking, and simulating workloads. It can also lead to some of the largest performance gains by identifying unnecessary work that can be eliminated.

The following basic attributes for characterizing network workload can, together, provide an approximation of what the network is asked to perform:

- **Network interface throughput:** RX and TX, bytes per second
- **Network interface IOPS:** RX and TX, frames per second
- **TCP connection rate:** active and passive, connections per second

The terms *active* and *passive* were described in the Three-Way Handshake section of Section 10.4.1, Protocols.

These characteristics can vary over time, as usage patterns change throughout the day. Monitoring over time is described in Section 10.5.5, Performance Monitoring.

Here is an example workload description, to show how these attributes can be expressed together:

The network throughput varies based on users and performs more writes (TX) than reads (RX). The peak write rate is 200 Mbytes/s and 210,000 packets/s, and the peak read rate is 10 Mbytes/s with 70,000 packets/s. The inbound (passive) TCP connection rate reaches 3,000 connections/s.

Apart from describing these characteristics system-wide, they can also be expressed per interface. This allows interface bottlenecks to be determined, if the throughput can be observed to have reached line rate. If network bandwidth limits (resource controls) are present, they may throttle network throughput before line rate is reached.

Advanced Workload Characterization/Checklist

Additional details may be included to characterize the workload. These have been listed here as questions for consideration, which may also serve as a checklist when studying CPU issues thoroughly:

- What is the average packet size? RX, TX?
- What is the protocol breakdown? TCP versus UDP?
- What TCP/UDP ports are active? Bytes per second, connections per second?
- Which processes are actively using the network?

The sections that follow answer some of these questions. See Chapter 2, Methodology, for a higher-level summary of this methodology and the characteristics to measure (who, why, what, how).

10.5.4 Latency Analysis

There are various times (latencies) that can be studied to help understand and express network performance. They include *network latency*—a slightly ambiguous term that is usually used to refer to connection initialization time. The various network latencies are summarized in Table 10.3.

Table 10-3 Network Latencies

Latency	Description
System call send/receive latency	time for the socket read/write calls
System call connect latency	for connection establishment; note that some applications perform this as a non-blocking syscall
TCP connection initialization time	time for the three-way handshake
TCP first-byte latency	time between the connection establishment and receiving the first data byte
TCP connection duration	time from established to closed
TCP retransmits	if present, can add thousands of milliseconds of latency to network I/O
Network round-trip time	time for a packet to travel from client to server and back
Interrupt latency	time from a network controller interrupt for a received packet to when it is serviced by the kernel
Inter-stack latency	time for a packet to move through the kernel TCP/IP stack

Some of these latencies were described in detail in Section 10.3, Concepts. Latency may be presented as

- **Per-interval averages:** best performed per client/server pair, to isolate differences in the intermediate network
- **Full distributions:** as histograms or heat maps
- **Per-operation latency:** listing details for each event, including source and destination IP addresses

A common source of issues is the presence of latency outliers caused by TCP retransmits. These can be identified using full distributions or per-operation latency tracing, including by filtering for a minimum latency threshold.

10.5.5 Performance Monitoring

Performance monitoring can identify active issues and patterns of behavior over time. It will capture variations in the number of active end users, the timed activity including distributed system monitoring, and application activities including backups over the network.

Key metrics for network monitoring are

- **Throughput:** network interface bytes per second for both receive and transmit, ideally for each interface
- **Connections:** TCP connections per second, as another indication of network load
- **Errors:** including dropped packet counters
- **TCP retransmits:** also useful to record for correlation with network issues
- **TCP out-of-order packets:** can also cause performance problems

For environments that implement network bandwidth limits (resource controls), as occurs in some cloud computing environments, statistics related to the imposed limits may also be collected.

10.5.6 Packet Sniffing

Packet sniffing (aka *packet capture*) involves capturing the packets from the network, so that their protocol headers and data can be inspected on a packet-by-packet basis. For observational analysis this may be the last resort, as it can be expensive to perform in terms of CPU and storage overhead. Network kernel code paths are typically cycle-optimized, since they need to handle up to millions of packets per second and are sensitive to any extra overhead. To attempt to reduce this overhead, ring buffers may be used by the kernel to pass packet data to the user-level trace tool via a shared memory map—for example, the Linux PF_RING option instead of the per-packet PF_PACKET [Deri 04].

A packet capture log can be created on the server, and then analyzed using other tools. Some tools print only the contents; others perform higher-level analysis of the packet data. While reading through a packet capture log can be time-consuming, it can also be very illuminating—showing exactly what is occurring on the network, and the latency between pairs of packets. This makes it possible to apply both the workload characterization and latency analysis methodologies.

Packet capture logs can contain the following for each packet:

- Timestamp
- Entire packet, including
  - All protocol headers (e.g., Ethernet, IP, TCP)
  - Partial or full payload data
- Metadata: number of packets, number of drops

As an example of packet capture, the following shows the default output of the tcpdump tool:

```
# tcpdump -ni eth4
tcpdump: verbose output suppressed, use -v or -vv for full protocol decode
listening on eth4, link-type EN10MB (Ethernet), capture size 65535 bytes
01:20:46.769073 IP 10.2.203.2.22 > 10.2.0.2.33771: Flags [P.], seq
4235343542:4235343734, ack 4053030377, win 132, options [nop,nop,TS val 328647671 ecr
2313764364], length 192
01:20:46.769470 IP 10.2.0.2.33771 > 10.2.203.2.22: Flags [.], ack 192, win 501,
options [nop,nop,TS val 2313764392 ecr 328647671], length 0
01:20:46.787673 IP 10.2.203.2.22 > 10.2.0.2.33771: Flags [P.], seq 192:560, ack 1,
win 132, options [nop,nop,TS val 328647672 ecr 2313764392], length 368
01:20:46.788050 IP 10.2.0.2.33771 > 10.2.203.2.22: Flags [.], ack 560, win 501,
options [nop,nop,TS val 2313764394 ecr 328647672], length 0
01:20:46.808491 IP 10.2.203.2.22 > 10.2.0.2.33771: Flags [P.], seq 560:896, ack 1,
win 132, options [nop,nop,TS val 328647674 ecr 2313764394], length 336
[...]
```

This output has a line summarizing each packet, including details of the IP addresses, TCP ports, and other TCP header details.

Because packet capture can be a CPU-expensive activity, most implementations include the ability to drop events instead of capturing them when overloaded. The count of dropped packets may be included in the log.

Apart from the use of ring buffers, packet capture implementations commonly allow a filtering expression to be supplied by the user and perform this filtering in the kernel. This reduces overhead by not transferring unwanted packets to user level.

10.5.7 TCP Analysis

Apart from what was covered in Section 10.5.4, Latency Analysis, other specific TCP behavior can be investigated, including

- Usage of TCP send/receive buffers
- Usage of TCP backlog queues
- Kernel drops due to the backlog queue being full
- Congestion window size, including zero-size advertisements
- SYNs received during a TCP TIME-WAIT[1] interval

The last behavior can become a scalability problem when a server is connecting frequently to another on the same destination port, using the same source and destination IP addresses. The only distinguishing factor for each connection is the client source port—the *ephemeral port*—which for TCP is a 16-bit value and may be further constrained by operating system parameters (minimum and maximum). Combined with the TCP TIME-WAIT interval, which may be 60 s, a high rate of connections (more than 65,536 during 60 s) can encounter a clash for new connections. In this scenario, a SYN is sent while that ephemeral port is still associated with a previous TCP session that is in TIME-WAIT, and the new SYN may be rejected if it is misidentified as part of the old connection (a collision). To avoid this issue, the Linux kernel attempts to reuse or recycle connections quickly (which usually works well).

10.5.8 Drill-Down Analysis

The internals of the kernel networking stack can be investigated as needed, drilling down through the layers that process the packets to the network interface driver. The internals are complex, and this is a time-consuming activity.

Reasons to perform it include

- Checking if network tunable parameters need adjusting (instead of modifying them experimentally)

---

1. While [RFC 793] uses TIME-WAIT, it is often written (and programmed) as TIME_WAIT.

- Confirming that kernel network performance features are taking effect, including, for example, CPU fanout and interrupt coalescing
- Explaining kernel-dropped packets

This typically involves using dynamic tracing to inspect the execution of the kernel network stack functions.

10.5.9 Static Performance Tuning

Static performance tuning focuses on issues of the configured environment. For network performance, examine the following aspects of the static configuration:

- How many network interfaces are available for use? Are currently in use?
- What is the maximum speed of the network interfaces?
- What is the current negotiated speed of the network interfaces?
- Are network interfaces negotiated as half or full duplex?
- What MTU is configured for the network interfaces?
- Are network interfaces trunked?
- What tunable parameters exist for the device driver? IP layer? TCP layer?
- Have any tunable parameters been changed from the defaults?
- How is routing configured? What is the default gateway?
- What is the maximum throughput of network components in the data path (all components, including switch and router backplanes)?
- Is forwarding enabled? Is the system acting as a router?
- How is DNS configured? How far away is the server?
- Are there known performance issues (bugs) with the version of the network interface firmware?
- Are there known performance issues (bugs) with the network device driver? Kernel TCP/IP stack?
- Are there software-imposed network throughput limits present (resource controls)? What are they?

The answers to these questions may reveal configuration choices that have been overlooked.

The last question is especially relevant for cloud computing environments, where network throughput may be limited.

10.5.10 Resource Controls

The operating system may provide controls to limit network resources for types of connections, processes, or groups of processes. These may include the following types of controls:

- **Network bandwidth limits:** a permitted bandwidth (maximum through-put) for different protocols or applications, applied by the kernel.
- **IP quality of service (QoS):** the prioritization of network traffic, performed by network components (e.g., routers). This can be implemented in different ways: the IP header includes type-of-service (ToS) bits, including a priority; those bits have since been redefined for newer QoS schemes, including Differentiated Services [RFC 2474]. There may be other priorities implemented by other protocol layers, for the same purpose.

Your network may have a mix of traffic that can be classified as low- or high-priority. Low-priority may include the transfer of backups and performance-monitoring traffic. High-priority may be the traffic between the production server and clients. Either resource control scheme can be used to throttle the low-priority traffic, producing more favorable performance for the high-priority traffic.

How these work is implementation-specific and is discussed in Section 10.8, Tuning.

10.5.11 Micro-Benchmarking

There are many benchmark tools for networking. They are especially useful when investigating throughput issues for a distributed application environment, to confirm that the network can at least achieve the expected network throughput. If it cannot, network performance can be investigated for the network micro-benchmark tool, which is typically much less complex and faster to debug than the application. After the network has been tuned to the desired speed, attention can return to the application.

Typical factors that may be tested include

- **Direction:** send or receive
- **Protocol:** TCP or UDP, and port
- **Number of threads**
- **Buffer size**
- **Interface MTU size**

Faster network interfaces, such as 10 Gbits/s, may require multiple client threads to be driven to maximum bandwidth.

An example network micro-benchmark tool, iperf, is introduced in Section 10.7.1, iperf.

10.6 Analysis

This section introduces network performance analysis tools for Linux- and Solaris-based operating systems. See the previous section for strategies to follow when using them.

The tools in this section are listed in Table 10.4.

Table 10-4 Network Analysis Tools

Linux	Solaris	Description
netstat	netstat	various network stack and interface statistics
sar	—	historical statistics
ifconfig	ifconfig	interface configuration
ip	dladm	network interface statistics
nicstat	nicstat	network interface throughput and utilization
ping	ping	test network connectivity
traceroute	traceroute	test network routes
pathchar	pathchar	determine network path characteristics
tcpdump	snoop/tcpdump	network packet sniffer
Wireshark	Wireshark	graphical network packet inspection
DTrace, perf	DTrace	TCP/IP stack tracing: connections, packets, drops, latency

This is a selection of tools and capabilities to support Section 10.5, Methodology, beginning with system-wide statistics, then drilling down to packet sniffing and event tracing. See the tool documentation, including man pages, for full references for their features.

10.6.1 netstat

The netstat(8) command reports various types of network statistics, based on the options used. It is like a *multi-tool* with several different functions. These include the following:

- **(default):** lists connected sockets
- **-a:** lists information for all sockets
- **-s:** network stack statistics
- **-i:** network interface statistics
- **-r:** lists the route table

Other options can modify the output, including –n to not resolve IP addresses to host names, and –v for verbose details where available.

The output of netstat(8) varies slightly between operating systems.

Linux

Here is an example of netstat(8) interface statistics:

```
$ netstat -i
Kernel Interface table
Iface MTU Met  RX-OK RX-ERR RX-DRP RX-OVR  TX-OK TX-ERR TX-DRP TX-OVR Flg
eth0   1500 0  933760207      0    0 0   1090211545      0      0      0 BMRU
eth3   1500 0  718900017      0    0 0    587534567      0      0      0 BMRU
lo    16436 0   21126497      0    0 0     21126497      0      0      0 LRU
ppp5   1496 0       4225      0    0 0         3736      0      0      0 MOPRU
ppp6   1496 0       1183      0    0 0         1143      0      0      0 MOPRU
tun0   1500 0     695581      0    0 0       692378      0      0      0 MOPRU
tun1   1462 0          0      0    0 0            4      0      0      0 PRU
```

The columns include the network interface (Iface), MTU, and a series of metrics for receive (RX-) and transmit (TX-):

- **OK:** packets transferred successfully
- **ERR:** packet errors
- **DRP:** packet drops
- **OVR:** packet overruns

The packet drops and overruns are indications of network interface *saturation* and can be examined along with errors as part of the USE method.

The –c continuous mode can be used with –i, which prints these cumulative counters every second. This provides the data for calculating the rate of packets.

Here is an example of netstat(8) network stack statistics (truncated):

```
$ netstat -s
Ip:
    2195174600 total packets received
    1896 with invalid headers
    996084485 forwarded
```

```
    4315 with unknown protocol
    0 incoming packets discarded
    1199785508 incoming packets delivered
    1786035083 requests sent out
    11 outgoing packets dropped
    589 fragments dropped after timeout
    465974 reassemblies required
    232690 packets reassembled ok
[...]
Tcp:
    102171 active connections openings
    126729 passive connection openings
    11932 failed connection attempts
    19492 connection resets received
    27 connections established
    627019277 segments received
    325718869 segments send out
    346436 segments retransmited
    5 bad segments received.
    24172 resets sent
Udp:
    12331498 packets received
    35713 packets to unknown port received.
    0 packet receive errors
    67417483 packets sent
TcpExt:
    1749 invalid SYN cookies received
    2665 resets received for embryonic SYN_RECV sockets
    7304 packets pruned from receive queue because of socket buffer overrun
    2565 ICMP packets dropped because they were out-of-window
    78204 TCP sockets finished time wait in fast timer
    67 time wait sockets recycled by time stamp
    901 packets rejects in established connections because of timestamp
    2667251 delayed acks sent
    2897 delayed acks further delayed because of locked socket
    Quick ack mode was activated 255240 times
    1051749 packets directly queued to recvmsg prequeue.
    4533681 bytes directly in process context from backlog
    953003585 bytes directly received in process context from prequeue
    372483184 packet headers predicted
    695654 packets header predicted and directly queued to user
    14056833 acknowledgments not containing data payload received
    235440239 predicted acknowledgments
    64430 times recovered from packet loss by selective acknowledgements
    167 bad SACK blocks received
    Detected reordering 60 times using FACK
    Detected reordering 132 times using SACK
    Detected reordering 36 times using time stamp
    40 congestion windows fully recovered without slow start
    366 congestion windows partially recovered using Hoe heuristic
    10 congestion windows recovered without slow start by DSACK
    60182 congestion windows recovered without slow start after partial ack
    252507 TCP data loss events
    TCPLostRetransmit: 1088
    1 timeouts after reno fast retransmit
    9781 timeouts after SACK recovery
    337 timeouts in loss state
    125688 fast retransmits
    2191 forward retransmits
    8423 retransmits in slow start
    122301 other TCP timeouts
    598 SACK retransmits failed
    1 times receiver scheduled too late for direct processing
    5543656 packets collapsed in receive queue due to low socket buffer
[...]
```

The output lists various network statistics, mostly from TCP, that are grouped by their protocol. Fortunately, many of these have long descriptive names, so their meaning may be obvious. Unfortunately, the output is inconsistent and includes spelling errors, which is a nuisance when processing this text programmatically.

A number of performance-related metrics have been highlighted in bold, to show the kind of information that is available. Many of these require an advanced understanding of TCP behavior, including the newer features and algorithms that have been introduced in recent years. Here are some example metrics to look for:

- A high rate of forwarded versus total packets received: check that the server is supposed to be forwarding (routing) packets.
- Passive connection openings: this can be monitored to show load in terms of client connections.
- A high rate of segments retransmitted versus segments sent out: can show an unreliable network. This may be expected (Internet clients).
- Packets pruned from the receive queue because of socket buffer overrun: This is a sign of network saturation and may be fixable by increasing socket buffers—provided there are sufficient system resources for the application to keep up.

Some of the statistic names include typos. These can be problematic to simply fix, if other monitoring tools have been built upon the same output. Such tools should be better served by reading the /proc sources for these statistics, which are /proc/net/snmp and /proc/net/netstat. For example:

```
$ grep ^Tcp /proc/net/snmp
Tcp: RtoAlgorithm RtoMin RtoMax MaxConn ActiveOpens PassiveOpens AttemptFails
EstabResets CurrEstab InSegs OutSegs RetransSegs InErrs OutRsts
Tcp: 1 200 120000 -1 102378 126946 11940 19495 24 627115849 325815063 346455 5 24183
```

These /proc/net/snmp statistics are also for the SNMP management information bases (MIBs), which provide further documentation for what each statistic is supposed to be. Extended statistics are in /proc/net/netstat.

An interval, in seconds, can be used with netstat(8) so that it continually prints the cumulative counters every interval. This output could then be post-processed to calculate the rate of each counter.

Solaris

Here is an example of `netstat(1M)` interface statistics:

```
$ netstat -i
Name   Mtu  Net/Dest      Address        Ipkts    Ierrs Opkts  Oerrs Collis Queue
lo0    8232 loopback      localhost      40       0     40     0     0
ixgbe0 1500 headnode      headnode       4122107616 0   4102310328 0  0      0
external0 1500 10.225.140.0 10.225.140.4 7101105  0     4574375 0    0      0
devnet0 1500 10.3.32.0    10.3.32.4      6566405  0     3895822357 0  0      0

Name   Mtu  Net/Dest      Address        Ipkts    Ierrs Opkts  Oerrs Collis
lo0    8252 localhost     localhost      40       0     40     0     0
```

The columns include the network interface (`Name`), MTU, network (`Net/Dest`), interface address (`Address`), and a series of metrics:

- **`Ipkts:`** input packets (received)
- **`Ierrs:`** input packet errors
- **`Opkts:`** output packets (transmitted)
- **`Oerrs:`** output packet errors (for example, a late collision)
- **`Collis:`** packet collisions (unlikely to happen nowadays, with buffered switches)
- **`Queue:`** always zero (hard-coded, historic)

If an interval is provided (in seconds) as an argument, the output summarizes a single interface over time. A `-I` option can be used to specify which interface is shown.

Here is an example of `netstat(1M)` network stack statistics (truncated):

```
$ netstat -s

RAWIP   rawipInDatagrams    =    184    rawipInErrors       =     0
        rawipInCksumErrs    =      0    rawipOutDatagrams   =   937
        rawipOutErrors      =      0

UDP     udpInDatagrams      =664557    udpInErrors         =     0
        udpOutDatagrams     =677322    udpOutErrors        =     0

TCP     tcpRtoAlgorithm     =      4    tcpRtoMin           =   400
        tcpRtoMax           =  60000    tcpMaxConn          =    -1
        tcpActiveOpens      =967141    tcpPassiveOpens     =  3134
        tcpAttemptFails     =110230    tcpEstabResets      =   183
        tcpCurrEstab        =      7    tcpOutSegs          =78452503
        tcpOutDataSegs      =69720123  tcpOutDataBytes     =3753060671
        tcpRetransSegs      =  12265    tcpRetransBytes     =10767035
        tcpOutAck           =19678899  tcpOutAckDelayed    =10664701
```

continues

```
            tcpOutUrg            =       0   tcpOutWinUpdate   =    3679
            tcpOutWinProbe       =       0   tcpOutControl     =1833674
            tcpOutRsts           =    1935   tcpOutFastRetrans =      23
            tcpInSegs            =50303684
            tcpInAckSegs         =       0   tcpInAckBytes     =3753841314
            tcpInDupAck          =  974778   tcpInAckUnsent    =       0
            tcpInInorderSegs     =57165053   tcpInInorderBytes =813978589
            tcpInUnorderSegs     =    1789   tcpInUnorderBytes =106836
            tcpInDupSegs         =    1880   tcpInDupBytes     =121354
            tcpInPartDupSegs     =       0   tcpInPartDupBytes =       0
            tcpInPastWinSegs     =       0   tcpInPastWinBytes =       0
            tcpInWinProbe        =       1   tcpInWinUpdate    =       0
            tcpInClosed          =      40   tcpRttNoUpdate    =       0
            tcpRttUpdate         =32655394   tcpTimRetrans     = 16559
            tcpTimRetransDrop    =     218   tcpTimKeepalive   = 25489
            tcpTimKeepaliveProbe=    2512   tcpTimKeepaliveDrop =   150
            tcpListenDrop        =       0   tcpListenDropQ0   =       0
            tcpHalfOpenDrop      =       0   tcpOutSackRetrans =    7262


    IPv4    ipForwarding         =       1   ipDefaultTTL      =     255
            ipInReceives         =3970771620 ipInHdrErrors     =       0
            ipInAddrErrors       =       0   ipInCksumErrs     =       2
            ipForwDatagrams      =3896325662 ipForwProhibits   =       0
            ipInUnknownProtos    =       4   ipInDiscards      =     188
            ipInDelivers         =74383918   ipOutRequests     =91980660
            ipOutDiscards        =    1122   ipOutNoRoutes     =       2
    [...]
```

The output lists various network statistics, grouped by protocol. Many of the names of these statistics are based on SNMP networking MIBs, which explain what they are for.

A number of performance-related metrics have been highlighted in bold, to show the kind of information that is available. Many of these require an advanced understanding of modern TCP behavior. Metrics to look for are those similar to the Linux metrics mentioned earlier, as well as

- **tcpListenDrop and tcpListenDropQ0:** These show the number of dropped packets for the socket listen backlog and the SYN backlog, respectively. A growing number of tcpListenDrops indicates more connection requests than the application can accept. This may be fixable in one of two ways: by increasing the backlog length (tcp_conn_req_max_q), allowing larger bursts of connections to queue; and/or by configuring greater system resources for the application.

The metrics reported are read from kstat, which can be accessed using the libkstat interface.

An interval can also be provided, which prints the summary-since-boot followed by interval summaries. Each summary shows the statistics for that interval (unlike the Linux version), so that rates are apparent. For example:

```
# netstat -s 1 | grep tcpActiveOpens
        tcpActiveOpens         =11460494    tcpPassiveOpens    =    783
        tcpActiveOpens         =     224    tcpPassiveOpens    =      0
        tcpActiveOpens         =     193    tcpPassiveOpens    =      0
        tcpActiveOpens         =      53    tcpPassiveOpens    =      1
        tcpActiveOpens         =     216    tcpPassiveOpens    =      0
[...]
```

This shows the rate of TCP connections, active and passive, per second.

10.6.2 sar

The system activity reporter, sar(1), can be used to observe current activity and can be configured to archive and report historical statistics. It is introduced in Chapter 4, Observability Tools, and mentioned in other chapters as appropriate.

The **Linux** version provides network statistics via the following options:

- **-n DEV:** network interface statistics
- **-n EDEV:** network interface errors
- **-n IP:** IP datagram statistics
- **-n EIP:** IP error statistics
- **-n TCP:** TCP statistics
- **-n ETCP:** TCP error statistics
- **-n SOCK:** socket usage

Statistics provided include those shown in Table 10.5.

Table 10-5 Linux sar Network Statistics

Option	Statistic	Description	Units
-n DEV	rxpkt/s	received packets	packets/s
-n DEV	txpkt/s	transmitted packets	packets/s
-n DEV	rxkB/s	received kilobytes	Kbytes/s
-n DEV	txkB/s	transmitted kilobytes	Kbytes/s
-n EDEV	rxerr/s	received packet errors	packets/s
-n EDEV	txerr/s	transmitted packet errors	packets/s
-n EDEV	coll/s	collisions	packets/s
-n EDEV	rxdrop/s	received packets dropped (buffer full)	packets/s

continues

Table 10-5 Linux sar Network Statistics (*Continued*)

Option	Statistic	Description	Units
-n EDEV	txdrop/s	transmitted packets dropped (buffer full)	packets/s
-n EDEV	rxfifo/s	received packets FIFO overrun errors	packets/s
-n EDEV	txfifo/s	transmitted packets FIFO overrun errors	packets/s
-n IP	irec/s	input datagrams (received)	datagrams/s
-n IP	fwddgm/s	forwarded datagrams	datagrams/s
-n IP	orq/s	output datagram requests (transmit)	datagrams/s
-n EIP	idisc/s	input discards (e.g., buffer full)	datagrams/s
-n EIP	odisc/s	output discards (e.g., buffer full)	datagrams/s
-n TCP	active/s	new active TCP connections (connect())	connections/s
-n TCP	passive/s	new passive TCP connections (listen())	connections/s
-n TCP	iseg/s	input segments (received)	segments/s
-n TCP	oseg/s	output segments (received)	segments/s
-n ETCP	atmptf/s	active TCP connection fails	connections/s
-n ETCP	retrans/s	TCP segments retransmitted	segments/s
-n SOCK	totsck	total sockets in use	sockets
-n SOCK	ip-frag	IP fragments currently queued	fragments
-n SOCK	tcp-tw	TCP sockets in TIME-WAIT	sockets

Many of the statistic names include the direction and units measured: rx for "received," i for "input," seg for "segments," and so on. See the man page for the full list, which includes statistics for ICMP, UDP, NFS, and IPv6 and also notes some equivalent SNMP names (e.g., ipInReceives for irec/s).

This example prints TCP statistics every second:

```
$ sar -n TCP 1
Linux 3.5.4joyent-centos-6-opt (dev99)        04/22/2013     _x86_64_ (4 CPU)

09:36:26 PM  active/s passive/s    iseg/s    oseg/s
09:36:27 PM      0.00     35.64   4084.16   4090.10
09:36:28 PM      0.00     34.00   3652.00   3671.00
09:36:29 PM      0.00     30.00   3229.00   3309.00
09:36:30 PM      0.00     33.33   3291.92   3310.10
 [...]
```

The output shows a passive connection rate (inbound) of around 30/s.

The network interface statistics column (NET) lists all interfaces; however, often just one is of interest. The following example uses a little awk(1) to filter the output:

```
$ sar -n DEV 1 | awk 'NR == 3 || $3 == "eth0"'
09:36:06 PM  IFACE  rxpck/s  txpck/s   rxkB/s   txkB/s rxcmp/s txcmp/s  rxmcst/s
09:36:07 PM   eth0  4131.68  4148.51  2628.52  2512.07    0.00    0.00      0.00
09:36:08 PM   eth0  4251.52  4266.67  2696.05  2576.82    0.00    0.00      0.00
09:36:09 PM   eth0  4249.00  4248.00  2695.03  2574.10    0.00    0.00      0.00
09:36:10 PM   eth0  3384.16  3443.56  2149.98  2060.31    0.00    0.00      0.00
[...]
```

This shows network throughput for transmit and receive. In this case, both directions have a rate of over 2 Mbytes/s.

The **Solaris** version of sar(1) does not currently provide network statistics (use netstat(1M), nicstat(1), and dladm(1M) instead).

10.6.3 ifconfig

The ifconfig(8) command allows network interfaces to be manually configured. It can also list the current configuration of all interfaces, which can be useful during static performance tuning, to check how the system, network, and routes are configured.

The **Linux** version includes statistics with the output:

```
$ ifconfig
eth0       Link encap:Ethernet  HWaddr 00:21:9b:97:a9:bf
           inet addr:10.2.0.2  Bcast:10.2.0.255  Mask:255.255.255.0
           inet6 addr: fe80::221:9bff:fe97:a9bf/64 Scope:Link
           UP BROADCAST RUNNING MULTICAST  MTU:1500  Metric:1
           RX packets:933874764 errors:0 dropped:0 overruns:0 frame:0
           TX packets:1090431029 errors:0 dropped:0 overruns:0 carrier:0
           collisions:0 txqueuelen:1000
           RX bytes:584622361619 (584.6 GB)  TX bytes:537745836640 (537.7 GB)
           Interrupt:36 Memory:d6000000-d6012800

eth3       Link encap:Ethernet  HWaddr 00:21:9b:97:a9:c5
[...]
```

The counters are the same as those described by the earlier netstat -i command.

txqueuelen is the length of the transmit queue for the interfaces. Tuning this value is described in the man page:

It is useful to set this to small values for slower devices with a high latency (modem links, ISDN) to prevent fast bulk transfers from disturbing interactive traffic like telnet too much.

On Linux, ifconfig(8) is now considered obsolete, replaced by the ip(8) command. On Solaris, various functionality of ifconfig(1M) has also become obsolete, replaced by the ipadm(1M) and dladm(1M) commands.

10.6.4 ip

The Linux ip(8) command can be used to configure network interfaces and routes, and to observe their state and statistics. For example, showing link statistics:

```
$ ip -s link
1: lo:  mtu 16436 qdisc noqueue state UNKNOWN
    link/loopback 00:00:00:00:00:00 brd 00:00:00:00:00:00
    RX: bytes  packets  errors  dropped overrun mcast
    1200720212 21176087 0        0       0       0
    TX: bytes  packets  errors  dropped carrier collsns
    1200720212 21176087 0        0       0       0
2: eth0:  mtu 1500 qdisc mq state UP qlen 1000
    link/ether 00:21:9b:97:a9:bf brd ff:ff:ff:ff:ff:ff
    RX: bytes  packets  errors  dropped overrun mcast
    507221711  933878009 0        0       0      46648551
    TX: bytes  packets  errors  dropped carrier collsns
    876109419  1090437447 0       0       0       0
3: eth1:  mtu 1500 qdisc noop state DOWN qlen 1000
[...]
```

The counters are the same as those described by the earlier netstat -i command, with the addition of receive (RX) and transmit (TX) bytes. This would allow throughput to be easily observed; however, ip(8) currently does not provide a way to print per-interval reports (use sar(1)).

10.6.5 nicstat

Originally written for Solaris-based systems, the open-source nicstat(1) utility prints network interface statistics, including throughput and utilization. nicstat(1) follows the style of the traditional resource statistic tools, iostat(1M) and mpstat(1M). Versions have been written in both C and Perl, and for both Solaris-based systems and Linux [3].

For example, here is output for version 1.92 on Linux:

```
# nicstat -z 1
    Time     Int    rKB/s    wKB/s    rPk/s    wPk/s    rAvs    wAvs  %Util    Sat
01:20:58    eth0     0.07     0.00     0.95     0.02   79.43   64.81   0.00   0.00
01:20:58    eth4     0.28     0.01     0.20     0.10   1451.3   80.11   0.00   0.00
01:20:58  vlan123    0.00     0.00     0.00     0.02   42.00   64.81   0.00   0.00
01:20:58     br0     0.00     0.00     0.00     0.00   42.00   42.07   0.00   0.00
    Time     Int    rKB/s    wKB/s    rPk/s    wPk/s    rAvs    wAvs  %Util    Sat
01:20:59    eth4  42376.0    974.5  28589.4  14002.1   1517.8   71.27   35.5   0.00
    Time     Int    rKB/s    wKB/s    rPk/s    wPk/s    rAvs    wAvs  %Util    Sat
01:21:00    eth0     0.05     0.00     1.00     0.00   56.00    0.00   0.00   0.00
01:21:00    eth4  41834.7    977.9  28221.5  14058.3   1517.9   71.23   35.1   0.00
    Time     Int    rKB/s    wKB/s    rPk/s    wPk/s    rAvs    wAvs  %Util    Sat
01:21:01    eth4  42017.9    979.0  28345.0  14073.0   1517.9   71.24   35.2   0.00
```

The first output is the summary-since-boot, followed by interval summaries. The interval summaries show that the eth4 interface is running at 35% utilization (this is reporting the highest current utilization from either the RX or TX directions) and is reading at 42 Mbytes/s.

The fields include the interface name (Int), the maximum utilization (%Util), a value reflecting interface saturation statistics (Sat), and a series of statistics prefixed with r for "read" (receive), and w for "write" (transmit):

- **KB/s:** kilobytes per second
- **Pk/s:** packets per second
- **Avs/s:** average packet size, bytes

Various options are supported in this version, including −z to skip lines of zeros (idle interfaces) and −t for TCP statistics.

nicstat(1) is particularly useful for the USE method, as it provides utilization and saturation values.

10.6.6 dladm

On Solaris-based systems, the dladm(1M) command can provide interface statistics including packet and byte rates, error rates, and utilization, and it can also show the state of physical interfaces.

Showing network traffic on the ixgbe0 interface each second:

```
$ dladm show-link -s -i 1 ixgbe0
LINK            IPACKETS    RBYTES    IERRORS   OPACKETS    OBYTES         OERRORS
ixgbe0          8442628297 5393508338540 0      8422583725  6767471933614  0
ixgbe0          1548        501475    0         1538        476283         0
ixgbe0          1581        515611    0         1592        517697         0
ixgbe0          1491        478794    0         1495        479232         0
ixgbe0          1590        566174    0         1567        477956         0
[...]
```

The first line of output is the total-since-boot, followed by the per-second summaries (−i 1). The output shows this interface is currently receiving and transmitting at about 500 Kbytes/s. dladm show-link −S provides an alternate output showing kilobyte rates, packet rates, and a %Util column.

Listing the state of physical interfaces:

```
$ dladm show-phys
LINK          MEDIA            STATE      SPEED  DUPLEX   DEVICE
ixgbe0        Ethernet         up         10000  full     ixgbe0
ixgbe1        Ethernet         up         10000  full     ixgbe1
igb0          Ethernet         unknown    0      half     igb0
igb1          Ethernet         unknown    0      half     igb1
igb2          Ethernet         unknown    0      half     igb2
igb3          Ethernet         unknown    0      half     igb3
```

This is useful for static performance tuning, to check that the interfaces have negotiated to their fastest speed.

Prior to dladm(1M), these attributes were checked using ndd(1M).

10.6.7 ping

The ping(8) command tests network connectivity by sending ICMP echo request
packets. For example:

```
# ping www.joyent.com
PING www.joyent.com (165.225.132.33) 56(84) bytes of data.
64 bytes from 165.225.132.33: icmp_req=1 ttl=239 time=67.9 ms
64 bytes from 165.225.132.33: icmp_req=2 ttl=239 time=68.3 ms
64 bytes from 165.225.132.33: icmp_req=3 ttl=239 time=69.6 ms
64 bytes from 165.225.132.33: icmp_req=4 ttl=239 time=68.1 ms
64 bytes from 165.225.132.33: icmp_req=5 ttl=239 time=68.1 ms
^C
--- www.joyent.com ping statistics ---
5 packets transmitted, 5 received, 0% packet loss, time 4005ms
rtt min/avg/max/mdev = 67.935/68.443/69.679/0.629 ms
```

The output includes the round-trip time (rtt) for each packet and has a summary
showing various statistics. Since the timestamps are measured by the ping(8)
command itself, they are inclusive of some CPU code path execution time between
fetching the timestamp and performing network I/O.

The Solaris version requires a -s option to send continuous packets in this way.

The ICMP packets used may be treated by routers at a lower priority than
application protocols, and latency may show higher variance than usual.

10.6.8 traceroute

The traceroute(8) command sends a series of test packets to experimentally
determine the current route to a host. This is performed by increasing the IP protocol time to live (TTL) by one for each packet, causing the sequence of gateways to

the host to reveal themselves by sending ICMP time exceeded response messages
(provided a firewall doesn't block them).

For example, testing the current route between a host in California and a target in Virginia:

```
# traceroute www.joyent.com
 1  165.225.148.2 (165.225.148.2)  0.333 ms  13.569 ms  0.279 ms
 2  te-3-2.car2.Oakland1.Level3.net (4.71.202.33)  0.361 ms  0.309 ms  0.295 ms
 3  ae-11-11.car1.Oakland1.Level3.net (4.69.134.41)  2.040 ms  2.019 ms  1.964 ms
 4  ae-5-5.ebr2.SanJose1.Level3.net (4.69.134.38)  1.245 ms  1.230 ms  1.241 ms
 5  ae-72-72.csw2.SanJose1.Level3.net (4.69.153.22)  1.269 ms  1.307 ms  1.240 ms
 6  ae-2-70.edge1.SanJose3.Level3.net (4.69.152.80)  1.810 ms ae-1-
60.edge1.SanJose3.Level3.net (4.69.152.16)  1.903 ms  1.735 ms
 7  Savvis-Level3.Dallas3.Level3.net (4.68.62.106)  1.829 ms  1.813 ms  1.900 ms
 8  cr2-tengig0-7-3-0.sanfrancisco.savvis.net (204.70.206.57)  3.889 ms  3.839 ms  3.805 ms
 9  cr2-ten-0-15-3-0.dck.nyr.savvis.net (204.70.224.209)  77.315 ms  92.287 ms  77.684 ms
10  er2-tengig-1-0-1.VirginiaEquinix.savvis.net (204.70.197.245)  77.144 ms  77.114 ms
77.193 ms
11  internap.VirginiaEquinix.savvis.net (208.173.159.2)  77.373 ms  77.363 ms  77.445 ms
12  border10.pc1-bbnet1.wdc002.pnap.net (216.52.127.9)  77.114 ms  77.093 ms  77.116 ms
13  joyent-3.border10.wdc002.pnap.net (64.94.31.202)  77.203 ms  85.554 ms  90.106 ms
14  165.225.132.33 (165.225.132.33)  77.089 ms  77.097 ms  77.076 ms
```

Each hop shows a series of three RTTs, which can be used as a coarse source of
network latency statistics. As with ping(8), the packets used are low-priority and
may show higher latency than for other application protocols.

The path taken can also be studied as part of static performance tuning. Networks are designed to be dynamic and responsive to outages. Performance may
have degraded as the path has changed.

traceroute(8) was first written by Van Jacobson. He later created an amazing tool called pathchar.

10.6.9 pathchar

pathchar is similar to traceroute(8) but includes the bandwidth between hops
[4]. This is determined by sending a series of network packet sizes many times and
performing statistical analysis. Here is example output:

```
# pathchar 192.168.1.10
pathchar to 192.168.1.1 (192.168.1.1)
 doing 32 probes at each of 64 to 1500 by 32
 0 localhost
 |     30 Mb/s,   79 us (562 us)
 1 neptune.test.com (192.168.2.1)
 |     44 Mb/s,  195 us (1.23 ms)
 2 mars.test.com (192.168.1.1)
 2 hops, rtt 547 us (1.23 ms), bottleneck  30 Mb/s, pipe 7555 bytes
```

Unfortunately, `pathchar` somehow missed becoming popular (perhaps because the source code was not released, as far as I know), and it is difficult to find a working version for modern operating systems. It was also very time-consuming to run, taking tens of minutes depending on the number of hops, although methods have been proposed to reduce this time [Downey 99].

10.6.10 tcpdump

Network packets can be captured and inspected using the `tcpdump(8)` utility. This can either print packet summaries on STDOUT, or write packet data to a file for later analysis. The latter is usually more practical: packet rates can be too high to follow their summaries in real time.

Dumping packets from the eth4 interface to a file in /tmp:

```
# tcpdump -i eth4 -w /tmp/out.tcpdump
tcpdump: listening on eth4, link-type EN10MB (Ethernet), capture size 65535 bytes
^C273893 packets captured
275752 packets received by filter
1859 packets dropped by kernel
```

The output notes how many packets were dropped by the kernel instead of being passed to `tcpdump(8)`, as occurs when the rate of packets is too high.

Inspecting packets from a dump file:

```
# tcpdump -nr /tmp/out.tcpdump
reading from file /tmp/out.tcpdump, link-type EN10MB (Ethernet)
02:24:46.160754 IP 10.2.124.2.32863 > 10.2.203.2.5001: Flags [.], seq
3612664461:3612667357, ack 180214943, win 64436, options [nop,nop,TS val 692339741
ecr 346311608], length 2896
02:24:46.160765 IP 10.2.203.2.5001 > 10.2.124.2.32863: Flags [.], ack 2896, win
18184, options [nop,nop,TS val 346311610 ecr 692339740], length 0
02:24:46.160778 IP 10.2.124.2.32863 > 10.2.203.2.5001: Flags [.], seq 2896:4344, ack
1, win 64436, options [nop,nop,TS val 692339741 ecr 346311608], length 1448
02:24:46.160807 IP 10.2.124.2.32863 > 10.2.203.2.5001: Flags [.], seq 4344:5792, ack
1, win 64436, options [nop,nop,TS val 692339741 ecr 346311608], length 1448
02:24:46.160817 IP 10.2.203.2.5001 > 10.2.124.2.32863: Flags [.], ack 5792, win
18184, options [nop,nop,TS val 346311610 ecr 692339741], length 0
[...]
```

Each line of output shows the time of the packet (with microsecond resolution), its source and destination IP addresses, and TCP header values. By studying these, the operation of TCP can be understood in detail, including how advanced features are working for your workload.

The –n option was used to not resolve IP addresses as host names. Various other options are available, including printing verbose details where available (–v), link-layer headers (–e), and hex-address dumps (–x or –X). For example:

```
# tcpdump -enr /tmp/out.tcpdump -vvv -X
reading from file /tmp/out.tcpdump, link-type EN10MB (Ethernet)
02:24:46.160754 80:71:1f:ad:50:48 > 84:2b:2b:61:b6:ed, ethertype IPv4 (0x0800),
length 2962: (tos 0x0, ttl 63, id 46508, offset 0, flags [DF], proto TCP (6), length
2948)
    10.2.124.2.32863 > 10.2.203.2.5001: Flags [.], cksum 0x667f (incorrect ->
0xc4da), seq 3612664461:3612667357, ack 180214943, win 64436, options [nop,nop,TS val
692339741 ecr 346311608], length 289
6
        0x0000:  4500 0b84 b5ac 4000 3f06 1fbf 0a02 7c02  E.....@.?.....|.
        0x0010:  0a02 cb02 805f 1389 d754 e28d 0abd dc9f  ....._...T......
        0x0020:  8010 fbb4 667f 0000 0101 080a 2944 441d  ....f.......)DD.
        0x0030:  14a4 4bb8 3233 3435 3637 3839 3031 3233  ..K.234567890123
        0x0040:  3435 3637 3839 3031 3233 3435 3637 3839  4567890123456789
[...]
```

During performance analysis, it can be useful to change the timestamp column to show delta times between packets (–ttt), or elapsed time since the first packet (–ttttt).

An expression can also be provided to describe how to filter packets (see pcap-filter(7)), to focus on the packets of interest. This is performed in-kernel for efficiency (except on Linux 2.0 and older).

Packet capture is expensive to perform, in terms of both CPU cost and storage. If possible, use tcpdump(8) only for short periods to limit the performance cost.

tcpdump(8) can be added to Solaris-based systems, should there be a reason not to use the snoop(1M) utility.

10.6.11 snoop

While tcpdump(8) has been ported to Solaris-based systems, the default tool for packet capture and inspection is snoop(1M). It behaves similarly to tcpdump(8) and can also create packet capture files for later inspection. With snoop(1M), the packet capture files follow the [RFC 1761] standard.

For example, capturing packets on the ixgbe0 interface to a file in /tmp:

```
# snoop -d ixgbe0 -o /tmp/out.snoop
Using device ixgbe0 (promiscuous mode)
46907 ^C
```

The output includes the packets received so far. It can be useful to suppress this using quiet mode (-q), so that the output doesn't cause additional network packets when executed over a network session.

Inspecting packets from a dump file:

```
# snoop -ri /tmp/out.snoop
   1   0.00000       10.2.0.2 -> 10.2.204.2   TCP D=5001 S=33896 Ack=2831460534
Seq=3864122818 Len=1448 Win=46 Options=<nop,nop,tstamp 2333449053 694358367>
   2   0.00000       10.2.0.2 -> 10.2.204.2   TCP D=5001 S=33896 Ack=2831460534
Seq=3864124266 Len=1448 Win=46 Options=<nop,nop,tstamp 2333449053 694358367>
   3   0.00002       10.2.0.2 -> 10.2.204.2   TCP D=5001 S=33896 Ack=2831460534
Seq=3864125714 Len=1448 Win=46 Options=<nop,nop,tstamp 2333449053 694358367>
[...]
```

The output contains a single line per packet, beginning with a packet ID number, a timestamp (in seconds, with microsecond resolution), source and destination IP addresses, and other protocol details. Resolution of IP addresses to host names was disabled using -r.

For performance investigations, the timestamps can be modified as needed. By default, they are delta timestamps, showing the time between packets. The -ta option prints absolute time: wall clock. The -tr option prints relative times: the delta to the first packet.

The -V option prints semiverbose output, including a line per protocol stack layer:

```
# snoop -ri /tmp/out.snoop -V
   1   0.00000       10.2.0.2 -> 10.2.204.2   ETHER Type=0800 (IP), size=1514 bytes
   1   0.00000       10.2.0.2 -> 10.2.204.2   IP  D=10.2.204.2 S=10.2.0.2 LEN=1500,
ID=35573, TOS=0x0, TTL=63
   1   0.00000       10.2.0.2 -> 10.2.204.2   TCP D=5001 S=33896 Ack=2831460534
Seq=3864122818 Len=1448 Win=46 Options=<nop,nop,tstamp 2333449053 694358367>

   2   0.00000       10.2.0.2 -> 10.2.204.2   ETHER Type=0800 (IP), size=1514 bytes
   2   0.00000       10.2.0.2 -> 10.2.204.2   IP  D=10.2.204.2 S=10.2.0.2 LEN=1500,
ID=35574, TOS=0x0, TTL=63
   2   0.00000       10.2.0.2 -> 10.2.204.2   TCP D=5001 S=33896 Ack=2831460534
Seq=3864124266 Len=1448 Win=46 Options=<nop,nop,tstamp 2333449053 694358367>

[...]
```

The -v (lowercase) option prints full-verbose output, often producing a page of output for each packet:

```
# snoop -ri /tmp/out.snoop -v
ETHER:  ----- Ether Header -----
ETHER:
ETHER:  Packet 1 arrived at 8:07:54.31917
ETHER:  Packet size = 1514 bytes
ETHER:  Destination = 84:2b:2b:61:b7:62,
```

```
ETHER:  Source      = 80:71:1f:ad:50:48,
ETHER:  Ethertype = 0800 (IP)
ETHER:
IP:     ----- IP Header -----
IP:
IP:     Version = 4
IP:     Header length = 20 bytes
IP:     Type of service = 0x00
IP:           xxx. .... = 0 (precedence)
IP:           ...0 .... = normal delay
IP:           .... 0... = normal throughput
IP:           .... .0.. = normal reliability
IP:           .... ..0. = not ECN capable transport
IP:           .... ...0 = no ECN congestion experienced
IP:     Total length = 1500 bytes
IP:     Identification = 35573
IP:     Flags = 0x4
IP:           .1.. .... = do not fragment
IP:           ..0. .... = last fragment
IP:     Fragment offset = 0 bytes
IP:     Time to live = 63 seconds/hops
IP:     Protocol = 6 (TCP)
IP:     Header checksum = cb1e
IP:     Source address = 10.2.0.2, 10.2.0.2
IP:     Destination address = 10.2.204.2, 10.2.204.2
IP:     No options
IP:
TCP:    ----- TCP Header -----
TCP:
TCP:    Source port = 33896
TCP:    Destination port = 5001
TCP:    Sequence number = 3864122818
TCP:    Acknowledgement number = 2831460534
TCP:    Data offset = 32 bytes
TCP:    Flags = 0x10
TCP:          0... .... = No ECN congestion window reduced
TCP:          .0.. .... = No ECN echo
TCP:          ..0. .... = No urgent pointer
TCP:          ...1 .... = Acknowledgement
TCP:          .... 0... = No push
TCP:          .... .0.. = No reset
TCP:          .... ..0. = No Syn
TCP:          .... ...0 = No Fin
TCP:    Window = 46
TCP:    Checksum = 0xe7b4
TCP:    Urgent pointer = 0
TCP:    Options: (12 bytes)
TCP:     - No operation
TCP:     - No operation
TCP:     - TS Val = 2333449053, TS Echo = 694358367
TCP:
[...]
```

Only the first packet was included in this example. snoop(1M) has been programmed to understand how to parse many protocols, allowing for quick command-line investigations for a variety of network traffic.

An expression can also be provided to describe how to filter packets (see the snoop(1M) man page) to focus on the packets of interest. As much as possible, the filtering is performed in-kernel for efficiency.

Note that by default snoop(1M) captures the entire packet, including all the payload data. This can be truncated on capture using -s to set the snap length. Many versions of tcpdump(8) will truncate by default.

10.6.12 Wireshark

While tcpdump(8) and snoop(1M) work fine for casual investigations, for deeper analysis they can be time-consuming to use at the command line. The Wireshark tool (formerly Ethereal) provides a graphical interface for packet capture and inspection and can also import packet dump files from either tcpdump(8) or snoop(1M) [5]. Useful features include identifying network connections and their related packets, so that they can be studied separately, and also translation of hundreds of protocol headers.

10.6.13 DTrace

DTrace can be used to examine network events from *within* the kernel and applications, including socket connections, socket I/O, TCP events, packet transmission, backlog drops, TCP retransmits, and other details. These abilities support workload characterization and latency analysis.

The following sections introduce DTrace for network analysis, demonstrating capabilities that should apply to both Linux- and Solaris-based systems. Many of the examples are from a Solaris-based system, with some from Linux. A DTrace primer was included in Chapter 4, Observability Tools.

The DTrace providers used to trace the network stack include those in Table 10.6.

Table 10-6 DTrace Providers for Network Analysis

Layer	Stable Providers	Unstable Providers
Application	depends on app	pid
System library	—	pid
System calls	—	syscall
Socket	—	fbt
TCP	tcp, mib	fbt
UDP	udp, mib	fbt
IP	ip, mib	fbt
Link layer	—	fbt
Device driver	—	fbt

It is desirable to use the stable providers, but they may not yet be available on your operating system and DTrace version. If not, the unstable-interface providers may be used, although scripts will require updates to match software changes.

Socket Connections

Socket activity can be traced via application functions that perform networking, the system socket libraries, the syscall layer, or in the kernel. The syscall layer is usually preferable, as it well documented, low-overhead (kernel-based), and system-wide.

Counting *outbound* connections via connect():

```
# dtrace -n 'syscall::connect:entry { @[execname] = count(); }'
dtrace: description 'syscall::connect:entry ' matched 1 probe
^C

  ssh                                                             1
  node                                                           16
  haproxy                                                        22
```

This one-liner frequency counts the number of connect() syscalls. The most in this case was by processes named haproxy, which called connect() 22 times. If desired, other details can be included in the output, including the PID, process arguments, and connect() arguments.

Counting *inbound* connections via accept():

```
# dtrace -n 'syscall::accept:return { @[execname] = count(); }'
dtrace: description 'syscall::accept:return ' matched 1 probe
^C

  sshd                                                            2
  unicorn                                                         5
  beam.smp                                                       12
  node                                                           24
```

In this case, processes named node accepted the most connections, with 24 in total.

Both kernel- and user-level stacks can be inspected during socket events to show why they were performed, as part of workload characterization. For example, the following traces connect() user-level stacks for processes named ssh:

```
# dtrace -n 'syscall::connect:entry /execname == "ssh"/ { ustack(); }'
dtrace: description 'syscall::connect:entry ' matched 1 probe
CPU     ID                    FUNCTION:NAME
  1   1011                    connect:entry
              libc.so.1`__so_connect+0x15
              libsocket.so.1`connect+0x23
              ssh`timeout_connect+0x20
```

continues

```
             ssh`ssh_connect+0x1b7
             ssh`main+0xc83
             ssh`_start+0x83
^C
```

The arguments to these syscalls can also be inspected. This requires a little more effort than usual from DTrace, because the interesting information is in a struct that must be copied from user- to kernel-space and then dereferenced. This is performed by the soconnect.d script (from [Gregg 11]):

```
#!/usr/sbin/dtrace -s

#pragma D option quiet
#pragma D option switchrate=10hz

/* If AF_INET and AF_INET6 are "Unknown" to DTrace, replace with numbers: */
inline int af_inet = AF_INET;
inline int af_inet6 = AF_INET6;

dtrace:::BEGIN
{
        /* Add translations as desired from /usr/include/sys/errno.h */
        err[0]            = "Success";
        err[EINTR]        = "Interrupted syscall";
        err[EIO]          = "I/O error";
        err[EACCES]       = "Permission denied";
        err[ENETDOWN]     = "Network is down";
        err[ENETUNREACH]  = "Network unreachable";
        err[ECONNRESET]   = "Connection reset";
        err[EISCONN]      = "Already connected";
        err[ECONNREFUSED] = "Connection refused";
        err[ETIMEDOUT]    = "Timed out";
        err[EHOSTDOWN]    = "Host down";
        err[EHOSTUNREACH] = "No route to host";
        err[EINPROGRESS]  = "In progress";

        printf("%-6s %-16s %-3s %-16s %-5s %8s %s\n", "PID", "PROCESS", "FAM",
            "ADDRESS", "PORT", "LAT(us)", "RESULT");
}

syscall::connect*:entry
{
        /* assume this is sockaddr_in until we can examine family */
        this->s = (struct sockaddr_in *)copyin(arg1, sizeof (struct sockaddr));
        this->f = this->s->sin_family;
}

syscall::connect*:entry
/this->f == af_inet/
{
        self->family = this->f;
        self->port = ntohs(this->s->sin_port);
        self->address = inet_ntop(self->family, (void *)&this->s->sin_addr);
        self->start = timestamp;
}

syscall::connect*:entry
/this->f == af_inet6/
{
        /* refetch for sockaddr_in6 */
```

```
        this->s6 = (struct sockaddr_in6 *)copyin(arg1,
            sizeof (struct sockaddr_in6));
        self->family = this->f;
        self->port = ntohs(this->s6->sin6_port);
        self->address = inet_ntoa6((in6_addr_t *)&this->s6->sin6_addr);
        self->start = timestamp;
}

syscall::connect*:return
/self->start/
{
        this->delta = (timestamp - self->start) / 1000;
        this->errstr = err[errno] != NULL ? err[errno] : lltostr(errno);
        printf("%-6d %-16s %-3d %-16s %-5d %8d %s\n", pid, execname,
            self->family, self->address, self->port, this->delta, this->errstr);
        self->family = 0;
        self->address = 0;
        self->port = 0;
        self->start = 0;
}
```

Here is example output:

```
# ./soconnect.d
PID     PROCESS         FAM ADDRESS         PORT  LAT(us)  RESULT
13489   haproxy          2  10.2.204.18     8098       32  In progress
13489   haproxy          2  10.2.204.18     8098        2  Already connected
65585   ssh              2  10.2.203.2        22      701  Success
3319    node             2  10.2.204.26       80       35  In progress
12585   haproxy          2  10.2.204.24      636       24  In progress
13674   haproxy          2  10.2.204.24      636       62  In progress
13489   haproxy          2  10.2.204.18     8098       33  In progress
[...]
```

This traces connect() syscalls, printing a line of output to summarize them. The latency of the syscall is included, and the error code (errno) returned by the syscall (RESULT) translated as a string. The error code is often "In progress," which occurs for non-blocking connect().

Apart from connect() and accept(), the socket() and close() syscalls can also be traced. This allows the file descriptor (FD) to be seen on creation, and the duration of the socket to be measured by the time difference.

Socket I/O

After establishing a socket, subsequent read and write events can be traced at the system call layer based on the file descriptor. This can be performed in one of two ways:

- Associative array of socket FDs: This involves tracing syscall::socket:return and building an associative array, for example, is_socket[pid, arg1] = 1;. The array can be checked in the predicate for future I/O syscalls to identify which FDs are sockets. Remember to clear the values on syscall::close:entry.

- The state of `fds[].fi_fs`, if available on your version of DTrace. This is a text string description of the file system type. Since sockets map to VFS, their I/O is associated with a virtual *socket file system*.

The following one-liners use the latter approach.

Counting socket reads by `execname`, via either `read()` or `recv()`:

```
# dtrace -n 'syscall::read:entry,syscall::recv:entry
    /fds[arg0].fi_fs == "sockfs"/ { @[probefunc] = count(); }'
dtrace: description 'syscall::read:entry,syscall::recv:entry ' matched 2 probes
^C

    master                                                      2
    sshd                                                       16
    beam.smp                                                   82
    haproxy                                                   208
    node                                                     1218
```

This output shows that, while tracing, processes named `node` read from sockets 1,218 times using either of those syscalls.

Counting socket writes by `execname`, via either `write()` or `send()`, is the following one-liner:

```
dtrace -n 'syscall::write:entry,syscall::send:entry
    /fds[arg0].fi_fs == "sockfs"/ { @[probefunc] = count(); }'
```

Note that your operating system may use variants of these system calls (e.g., `readv()`), which should also be traced.

The size of the I/O can also be examined, by tracing the return probes for each syscall.

Socket Latency

Given the ability to trace socket events at the syscall layer, the following measurements can be performed as part of latency analysis:

- **Connect latency:** for synchronous syscalls, the time in `connect()`. For nonblocking I/O, the time from issuing `connect()` to when either `poll()` or `select()` (or other syscall) reports that the socket is ready.

- **First-byte latency:** the time from issuing `connect()` or the return from `accept()`, and when the first data byte is received via any of the I/O syscalls for that socket.

- **Socket duration:** the time from `socket()` to `close()` for the same file descriptor. To focus more on the connection duration, it can be timed from `connect()` or `accept()`.

These can be performed either as long one-liners or as scripts. They can also be performed from other network stack layers, including TCP.

Socket Internals

The kernel internals for sockets can be traced using the fbt provider. For example, on **Linux**, listing functions that begin with `sock_`:

```
# dtrace -ln 'fbt::sock*:entry'
    ID   PROVIDER        MODULE                          FUNCTION NAME
 21690        fbt        kernel              sock_has_perm entry
 36306        fbt        kernel             socket_suspend entry
 36312        fbt        kernel               socket_reset entry
 36314        fbt        kernel               socket_setup entry
 36316        fbt        kernel        socket_early_resume entry
 36328        fbt        kernel            socket_shutdown entry
 36330        fbt        kernel              socket_insert entry
[...]
```

The output has been truncated—it listed over 100 probes. Each of these can be traced individually, along with its arguments and a timestamp, to answer arbitrary questions about socket behavior.

TCP Events

As with sockets, the kernel internals for TCP can be traced using the fbt provider. However, a stable tcp provider has been developed (originally by me) and may be available on your system. The probes are as shown in Table 10.7.

Table 10-7 DTrace tcp Provider Probes

TCP Probe	Description
`accept-established`	An inbound connection was accepted (a *passive open*).
`connect-request`	An outbound connection was initiated (an *active open*).
`connect-established`	An outbound connection has been established (three-way handshake completed).
`accept-refused`	A connection request was denied (closed local port).
`connect-refused`	A connection request was denied (closed remote port).

continues

Table 10-7 DTrace tcp Provider Probes (*Continued*)

TCP Probe	Description
send	A segment was sent (IP may map segments directly to packets).
receive	A segment was received (IP may map segments directly to packets).
state-change	A session encountered a state change (details in the probe arguments).

Most of these provide arguments showing protocol header details and internal kernel state, including the "cached" process ID. The process name, usually traced using the DTrace execname built-in, may not be valid, as kernel TCP events may occur asynchronously to the process.

Frequency counting accepted TCP connections (*passive*) with remote IP address and local port:

```
# dtrace -n 'tcp:::accept-established {
    @[args[3]->tcps_raddr, args[3]->tcps_lport] = count(); }'
dtrace: description 'tcp:::accept-established ' matched 1 probe
^C

  10.2.0.2                                              22            1
  10.2.204.24                                         8098            4
  10.2.204.28                                          636            5
  10.2.204.30                                          636            5
```

While tracing, host 10.2.204.30 connected to TCP local port 636 five times.

Similar latencies can be traced using the TCP probes, as described in the earlier Socket Latency section, using combinations of the TCP probes.

Listing the TCP probes:

```
# dtrace -ln 'tcp:::'
   ID     PROVIDER        MODULE                        FUNCTION NAME
 1810          tcp            ip              tcp_input_data accept-established
 1813          tcp            ip              tcp_input_data connect-refused
 1814          tcp            ip              tcp_input_data connect-established
 1827          tcp            ip         tcp_xmit_early_reset accept-refused
 1870          tcp            ip              tcp_input_data receive
 1871          tcp            ip          tcp_input_listener receive
[...]
```

The MODULE and FUNCTION fields show the (unstable) location of the probe in the kernel code, which can be traced using the fbt provider for further details.

Packet Transmission

To investigate kernel internals beyond the tcp provider, and also when the tcp provider is not available, the fbt provider can be used. This is one of those cases where dynamic tracing makes something possible—which is better than impossible—but not necessarily easy! The internals of the network stack are complicated, and it can take a beginner many days to become familiar with the code paths.

A quick way to navigate through the stack is to trace a deep event and then examine its stack backtrace. For example, on **Linux**, tracing ip_output() with stack:

```
# dtrace -n 'fbt::ip_output:entry { @[stack(100)] = count(); }'
dtrace: description 'fbt::ip_output:entry ' matched 1 probe
^C
[...]

              kernel`ip_output+0x1
              kernel`ip_local_out+0x29
              kernel`ip_queue_xmit+0x14f
              kernel`tcp_transmit_skb+0x3e4
              kernel`__kmalloc_node_track_caller+0x185
              kernel`sk_stream_alloc_skb+0x41
              kernel`tcp_write_xmit+0xf7
              kernel`__alloc_skb+0x8c
              kernel`__tcp_push_pending_frames+0x26
              kernel`tcp_sendmsg+0x895
              kernel`inet_sendmsg+0x64
              kernel`sock_aio_write+0x13a
              kernel`do_sync_write+0xd2
              kernel`security_file_permission+0x2c
              kernel`rw_verify_area+0x61
              kernel`vfs_write+0x16d
              kernel`sys_write+0x4a
              kernel`sys_rt_sigprocmask+0x84
              kernel`system_call_fastpath+0x16
              639
```

Each line identifies a kernel function that can be traced separately. This requires examining the source code to determine the role of each function and its arguments.

For example, given that the fourth argument to tcp_sendmsg() is the size in bytes, it can be traced using

```
# dtrace -n 'fbt::tcp_sendmsg:entry { @["TCP send bytes"] = quantize(arg3); }'
dtrace: description 'fbt::tcp_sendmsg:entry ' matched 1 probe
^C

  TCP send bytes
           value  ------------- Distribution ------------- count
              16 |                                         0
              32 |@@@@@@@@                                 154
              64 |@@@                                      54
```

continues

```
 128 |@@@@@@@@@@@@@@@@@@@@                            375
 256 |@@@@@@@@@                                       184
 512 |                                                  2
1024 |                                                  1
2048 |                                                  3
4096 |                                                  4
8192 |                                                  0
```

This one-liner used the `quantize()` action to summarize the TCP send segment size as a power-of-two distribution plot. Most of the segments were between 128 and 511 bytes.

Longer one-liners and sophisticated scripts can be written, such as for investigating TCP retransmits and backlog drops.

Retransmit Tracing

Studying TCP retransmits can be a useful activity for investigating network health. While this has historically been performed by using sniffing tools to dump all packets to a file for post-inspection, DTrace can examine retransmits in real time, and with low overhead. The following script for the **Linux** 3.2.6 kernel traces the `tcp_retransmit_skb()` function and prints useful details:

```
#!/usr/sbin/dtrace -s

#pragma D option quiet

dtrace:::BEGIN { trace("Tracing TCP retransmits... Ctrl-C to end.\n"); }

fbt::tcp_retransmit_skb:entry {
        this->so = (struct sock *)arg0;
        this->d = (unsigned char *)&this->so->__sk_common.skc_daddr;
        printf("%Y: retransmit to %d.%d.%d.%d, by:", walltimestamp,
            this->d[0], this->d[1], this->d[2], this->d[3]);
        stack(99);
}
```

Here is example output:

```
# ./tcpretransmit.d
Tracing TCP retransmits... Ctrl-C to end.
2013 Feb 23 18:24:11: retransmit to 10.2.124.2, by:
                kernel`tcp_retransmit_timer+0x1bd
                kernel`tcp_write_timer+0x188
                kernel`run_timer_softirq+0x12b
                kernel`tcp_write_timer
                kernel`__do_softirq+0xb8
                kernel`read_tsc+0x9
                kernel`sched_clock+0x9
                kernel`sched_clock_local+0x25
                kernel`call_softirq+0x1c
                kernel`do_softirq+0x65
                kernel`irq_exit+0x9e
```

```
                kernel`smp_apic_timer_interrupt+0x6e
                kernel`apic_timer_interrupt+0x6e
    [...]
```

This includes the time, the destination IP address, and the kernel stack trace—which helps explain why the retransmit occurred. For more detail, each of the functions in the kernel stack can be traced separately.

Similar scripts have been developed for **SmartOS**, as part of a toolkit for operators of the cloud [6]. These include tcpretranssnoop.d, which has the following output:

```
# ./tcpretranssnoop.d
TIME                      TCP_STATE          SRC              DST              PORT
2012 Sep  8 03:12:12 TCPS_ESTABLISHED  10.225.152.20    10.225.152.189   40900
2012 Sep  8 03:12:12 TCPS_ESTABLISHED  10.225.152.20    10.225.152.161   62450
2012 Sep  8 03:12:12 TCPS_FIN_WAIT_1   10.225.152.20    10.88.122.66     54049
2012 Sep  8 03:12:12 TCPS_ESTABLISHED  10.225.152.24    10.40.254.88     34620
2012 Sep  8 03:12:12 TCPS_ESTABLISHED  10.225.152.30    10.249.197.234   3234
2012 Sep  8 03:12:12 TCPS_ESTABLISHED  10.225.152.37    10.117.114.41    49700
[...]
```

This shows the destination IP addresses for TCP retransmits (redacted in this output) and includes the kernel TCP state.

Backlog Drops

This final example script is also from the **SmartOS** toolkit of TCP scripts and is used to estimate whether backlog tuning is necessary and will be effective. This is a longer script and is provided as an example of advanced analysis.

```
#!/usr/sbin/dtrace -s

#pragma D option quiet
#pragma D option switchrate=4hz

dtrace:::BEGIN
{
        printf("Tracing... Hit Ctrl-C to end.\n");
}

fbt::tcp_input_listener:entry
{
        this->connp = (conn_t *)arg0;
        this->tcp = (tcp_t *)this->connp->conn_proto_priv.cp_tcp;
        self->max = strjoin("max_q:", lltostr(this->tcp->tcp_conn_req_max));
        self->pid = strjoin("cpid:", lltostr(this->connp->conn_cpid));
        @[self->pid, self->max] = quantize(this->tcp->tcp_conn_req_cnt_q);
}

mib:::tcpListenDrop
{
        this->max = self->max;
```

continues

```
            this->pid = self->pid;
            this->max != NULL ? this->max : "";
            this->pid != NULL ? this->pid : "";
            @drops[this->pid, this->max] = count();
    }

    fbt::tcp_input_listener:return
    {
            self->max = 0;
            self->pid = 0;
    }

    dtrace:::END
    {
            printf("tcp_conn_req_cnt_q distributions:\n");
            printa(@);
            printf("tcpListenDrops:\n");
            printa("   %-32s %-32s %@8d\n", @drops);
    }
```

The script uses both the unstable fbt provider to fetch TCP state, and the mib provider to count when drops have occurred.

Here is example output:

```
# ./tcpconnreqmaxq-pid.d
Tracing... Hit Ctrl-C to end.
^C
tcp_conn_req_cnt_q distributions:

  cpid:11504                                          max_q:128
             value  ------------- Distribution ------------- count
                -1 |                                          0
                 0 |@@@@@@@@@@@@@@@@@@@@@@@@@@@@@@@@@@@@@@@@@@ 7279
                 1 |@@                                        405
                 2 |@                                         255
                 4 |@                                         138
                 8 |                                          81
                16 |                                          83
                32 |                                          62
                64 |                                          67
               128 |                                          34
               256 |                                          0

tcpListenDrops:
    cpid:11504                      max_q:128                         34
```

When Ctrl-C is hit, a summary is printed showing cached process IDs (cpid), the
current maximum length of the socket backlog (max_q), and a distribution plot
showing the length of the backlog, measured when new connections were added.

The output shows that PID 11504 has had 34 backlog drops, and the maximum
backlog length is 128. The distribution shows that most of the time the backlog
length was 0, with only a fraction pushing the queue to its maximum. This is a
candidate for increasing the queue length.

This backlog queue is typically tuned only when drops occur, which is visible via the tcpListenDrops counter from `netstat -s`. This DTrace script allows drops to be predicted and the tuning to be applied before the drops become a problem.

Here is another example output:

```
cpid:16480                                        max_q:128
        value ------------- Distribution ------------- count
         -1 |                                          0
          0 |@@@@@@@                                   1666
          1 |@@                                        457
          2 |@                                         262
          4 |@                                         332
          8 |@@                                        395
         16 |@@@                                       637
         32 |@@@                                       578
         64 |@@@@                                      939
        128 |@@@@@@@@@@@@@@@@@@                        3947
        256 |                                          0
```

In this case, the backlog is usually at its limit of 128. This suggests that the application is overloaded and doesn't have sufficient resources (CPU, usually) to keep up.

More Tracing

Dynamic tracing can explore networking in other ways and in more detail when needed. To provide an idea of the capabilities, Table 10.8 shows scripts from the (158-page) Network Lower-Level Protocols chapter of *DTrace* [Gregg 11]. These scripts are also online [7].

Table 10-8 Advanced Network Tracing Scripts

Script	Layer	Description
soconnect.d	socket	traces client socket connect()s showing process and host
soaccept.d	socket	traces server socket accept()s showing process and host
soclose.d	socket	traces socket connection duration: connect() to close()
socketio.d	socket	shows socket I/O by process and type
socketiosort.d	socket	shows socket I/O by process and type, sorted by process
so1stbyte.d	socket	traces connection and first-byte latency at the socket layer
sotop.d	socket	status tool to list the busiest sockets
soerror.d	socket	identifies socket errors
ipstat.d	IP	IP statistics every second

continues

Table 10-8 Advanced Network Tracing Scripts (*Continued*)

Script	Layer	Description
ipio.d	IP	IP send/receive snoop
ipproto.d	IP	IP encapsulated prototype summary
ipfbtsnoop.d	IP	trace IP packets: demonstration of fbt tracing
tcpstat.d	TCP	TCP statistics every second
tcpaccept.d	TCP	summarizes inbound TCP connections
tcpacceptx.d	TCP	summarizes inbound TCP connections, resolving host names
tcpconnect.d	TCP	summarizes outbound TCP connections
tcpioshort.d	TCP	traces TCP sends/receives live with basic details
tcpio.d	TCP	traces TCP sends/receives live with flag translation
tcpbytes.d	TCP	sums TCP payload bytes by client and local port
tcpsize.d	TCP	shows TCP send/receive I/O size distribution
tcpnmap.d	TCP	detects possible TCP port scan activity
tcpconnlat.d	TCP	measures TCP connection latency by remote host
tcp1stbyte.d	TCP	measures TCP first-byte latency by remote host
tcp_rwndclosed.d	TCP	identifies TCP receive window zero events, with latency
tcpfbtwatch.d	TCP	watches inbound TCP connections
tcpsnoop.d	TCP	traces TCP I/O with process details
udpstat.d	UDP	UDP statistics every second
udpio.d	UDP	traces UDP sends/receives live with basic details
icmpstat.d	ICMP	ICMP statistics every second
icmpsnoop.d	ICMP	traces ICMP packets with details
superping.d	ICMP	improves accuracy of ping's round-trip times
xdrshow.d	XDR	shows external data representation (XDR) calls and calling functions
macops.d	MAC	counts media access control (MAC) layer operations by interface and type
ngesnoop.d	driver	traces nge driver Ethernet events live
ngelink.d	driver	traces changes to nge link status

Also in the *DTrace* book is a chapter on Application Level Protocols, which provides many more scripts for tracing NFS, CIFS, HTTP, DNS, FTP, iSCSI, FC, SSH, NIS, and LDAP.

While this degree of observability is incredible, some of these dynamic tracing scripts are tied to specific kernel internals and will require maintenance to match changes in newer kernel versions. Others are based on specific DTrace providers, which may not yet be available on your operating system.

10.6.14 SystemTap

SystemTap can also be used on Linux systems for dynamic tracing of file system events. See Section 4.4, SystemTap, in Chapter 4, Observability Tools, and Appendix E for help with converting the previous DTrace scripts.

10.6.15 perf

The LPE toolset, introduced in Chapter 6, CPUs, can also provide some static and dynamic tracing of network events. It can be useful for identifying the stack trace that led to network activity in the kernel, as was previously demonstrated using DTrace for packet transmission and retransmit tracing. More advanced tools can also be developed using post-processing.

As an example, the following uses perf(1) to create a dynamic tracepoint for the tcp_sendmsg() kernel function, and then traces it for 5 s along with call graphs (stack traces):

```
# perf probe --add='tcp_sendmsg'
Add new event:
  probe:tcp_sendmsg    (on tcp_sendmsg)
[...]
# perf record -e probe:tcp_sendmsg -aR -g sleep 5
[ perf record: Woken up 1 times to write data ]
[ perf record: Captured and wrote 0.091 MB perf.data (~3972 samples) ]
# perf report --stdio
[...]
# Overhead  Command      Shared Object          Symbol
# ........  .......      ..................     ...........
#
   100.00%      sshd  [kernel.kallsyms]  [k] tcp_sendmsg
               |
               --- tcp_sendmsg
                   sock_aio_write
                   do_sync_write
                   vfs_write
                   sys_write
                   system_call
                   __GI___libc_write
```

The output showed the stack trace for sshd which led to the kernel calling tcp_sendmsg(), to send data over a TCP connection.

There are also some tracepoint events that are predefined for networking:

```
# perf list
[...]
  skb:kfree_skb                                    [Tracepoint event]
  skb:consume_skb                                  [Tracepoint event]
  skb:skb_copy_datagram_iovec                      [Tracepoint event]
  net:net_dev_xmit                                 [Tracepoint event]
  net:net_dev_queue                                [Tracepoint event]
  net:netif_receive_skb                            [Tracepoint event]
  net:netif_rx                                     [Tracepoint event]
```

The skb tracepoints are for socket buffer events, and net is for network devices. These can also be useful for network investigations.

10.6.16 Other Tools

Other **Linux** network performance tools include

- **strace(1):** to trace socket-related syscalls and examine the options used (note that strace(1) has high overhead)
- **lsof(8):** list open files by process ID, including socket details
- **ss(8):** socket statistics
- **nfsstat(8):** NFS server and client statistics
- **iftop(8):** summarize network interface throughput by host (sniffer)
- **/proc/net:** contains many network statistics files

For **Solaris**:

- **truss(1):** to trace socket-related syscalls and examine the options used (note that truss(1) has high overhead)
- **pfiles(1):** to examine the sockets in use by a process, including options and socket buffer sizes
- **routeadm(1M):** to check the state of routing and IP forwarding
- **nfsstat(1M):** NFS server and client statistics
- **kstat:** provides more statistics from the network stack and network device drivers (many of them undocumented outside the source code)

There are also many network monitoring solutions, either based on SNMP or running their own custom agents.

10.7 Experimentation

Beyond ping(8), traceroute(8), and pathchar (covered earlier), other experimental tools for network performance analysis include micro-benchmarks. These can be used to determine the maximum throughput between hosts, which can be used to help identify if end-to-end network throughput is a problem when debugging application performance issues.

There are many network micro-benchmarks to pick from. This section demonstrates iperf, which is popular and easy to use. Another one worth mentioning is netperf, which can also test request/response performance [8].

10.7.1 iperf

iperf is an open-source tool for testing maximum TCP and UDP throughput. It supports a variety of options, including parallel mode: where multiple client threads will be used, which can be necessary to drive a network to its limit. iperf must be executed on both the server and the client.

For example, executing iperf on the server:

```
$ iperf -s -l 128k
-------------------------------------------------------------
Server listening on TCP port 5001
TCP window size: 85.3 KByte (default)
-------------------------------------------------------------
```

This increased the socket buffer size to 128 Kbytes (-l 128k), from the default of 8 Kbytes.

The following was executed on the client:

```
# iperf -c 10.2.203.2 -l 128k -P 2 -i 1 -t 60
-------------------------------------------------------------
Client connecting to 10.2.203.2, TCP port 5001
TCP window size: 48.0 KByte (default)
-------------------------------------------------------------
[  4] local 10.2.124.2 port 41407 connected with 10.2.203.2 port 5001
[  3] local 10.2.124.2 port 35830 connected with 10.2.203.2 port 5001
[ ID] Interval       Transfer     Bandwidth
[  4]  0.0- 1.0 sec  6.00 MBytes   50.3 Mbits/sec
[  3]  0.0- 1.0 sec  22.5 MBytes   189 Mbits/sec
[SUM]  0.0- 1.0 sec  28.5 MBytes   239 Mbits/sec
[  3]  1.0- 2.0 sec  16.1 MBytes   135 Mbits/sec
[  4]  1.0- 2.0 sec  12.6 MBytes   106 Mbits/sec
[SUM]  1.0- 2.0 sec  28.8 MBytes   241 Mbits/sec
[...]
[  4]  0.0-60.0 sec   748 MBytes   105 Mbits/sec
[  3]  0.0-60.0 sec   996 MBytes   139 Mbits/sec
[SUM]  0.0-60.0 sec  1.70 GBytes   244 Mbits/sec
```

This used the following options:

- **-c host:** connect to the host name or IP address
- **-l 128k:** use a 128 Kbyte socket buffer
- **-P 2:** run in parallel mode with two client threads
- **-i 1:** print interval summaries every second
- **-t 60:** total duration of the test: 60 s

The final line shows the average throughput during the test, summed across all parallel threads: 244 Mbits/s.

The per-interval summaries can be inspected to see the variance over time. The `--reportstyle C` option can be used to output CSV, so that it can then be imported by other tools, such as graphing software.

10.8 Tuning

Network tunable parameters are usually already tuned to provide high performance. The network stack is also usually designed to respond dynamically to different workloads, providing optimum performance.

Before trying tunable parameters, it can be worthwhile to first understand network usage. This may also identify unnecessary work that can be eliminated, leading to much greater performance wins. Try the workload characterization and static performance tuning methodologies, using the tools in the previous section.

Available tunables vary between versions of an operating system. See their documentation. The sections that follow provide an idea of what may be available and how they are tuned; they should be treated as a starting point to revise based on your workload and environment.

10.8.1 Linux

Tunable parameters can be viewed and set using the `sysctl(8)` command and written to /etc/sysctl.conf. They can also be read and written from the /proc file system, under /proc/sys/net.

For example, to see what is currently available for TCP, the parameters can be searched for the text `tcp` from `sysctl(8)`:

```
# sysctl -a | grep tcp
[...]
net.ipv4.tcp_timestamps = 1
net.ipv4.tcp_window_scaling = 1
```

```
net.ipv4.tcp_sack = 1
net.ipv4.tcp_retrans_collapse = 1
net.ipv4.tcp_syn_retries = 5
net.ipv4.tcp_synack_retries = 5
net.ipv4.tcp_max_orphans = 65536
net.ipv4.tcp_max_tw_buckets = 65536
net.ipv4.tcp_keepalive_time = 7200
[...]
```

On this kernel (3.2.6-3) there are 63 containing `tcp` and many more under `net.`, including parameters for IP, Ethernet, routing, and network interfaces.

Examples of specific tuning are in the following sections.

Socket and TCP Buffers

The maximum socket buffer size for all protocol types, for both reads (`rmem_max`) and writes (`wmem_max`), can be set using

```
net.core.rmem_max = 16777216
net.core.wmem_max = 16777216
```

The value is in bytes. This may need to be set to 16 Mbytes or higher to support full-speed 10 GbE connections.

Enabling autotuning of the TCP receive buffer:

```
tcp_moderate_rcvbuf = 1
```

Setting the auto-tuning parameters for the TCP read and write buffers:

```
net.ipv4.tcp_rmem = 4096 87380 16777216
net.ipv4.tcp_wmem = 4096 65536 16777216
```

Each has three values: the minimum, default, and maximum number of bytes to use. The size used is autotuned from the default. To improve TCP throughput, try increasing the maximum value. Increasing minimum and default will consume more memory per connection, which may not be necessary.

TCP Backlog

First backlog queue, for half-open connections:

```
tcp_max_syn_backlog = 4096
```

Second backlog queue, the listen backlog, for passing connections to accept():

```
net.core.somaxconn = 1024
```

Both of these may need to be increased from their defaults, for example, to 4,096 and 1,024, or higher, to better handle bursts of load.

Device Backlog

Increasing the length of the network device backlog queue, per CPU:

```
net.core.netdev_max_backlog = 10000
```

This may need to be increased, such as to 10,000, for 10 GbE NICs.

TCP Congestion Control

Linux supports pluggable congestion-control algorithms. Listing those currently available:

```
# sysctl net.ipv4.tcp_available_congestion_control
net.ipv4.tcp_available_congestion_control = cubic reno
```

Some may be available but not currently loaded. For example, adding htcp:

```
# modprobe tcp_htcp
# sysctl net.ipv4.tcp_available_congestion_control
net.ipv4.tcp_available_congestion_control = cubic reno htcp
```

The current algorithm may be selected using

```
net.ipv4.tcp_congestion_control = cubic
```

TCP Options

Other TCP parameters that may be set include

```
net.ipv4.tcp_sack = 1
net.ipv4.tcp_fack = 1
net.ipv4.tcp_tw_reuse = 1
net.ipv4.tcp_tw_recycle = 0
```

SACK and the FACK extensions may improve throughput performance over high-latency networks, at the cost of some CPU.

The `tcp_tw_reuse` tunable allows a TIME-WAIT session to be reused when it appears safe to do so. This can allow higher rates of connections between two hosts, such as between a web server and a database, without hitting the 16-bit ephemeral port limit with sessions in TIME-WAIT.

`tcp_tw_recycle` is another way to reuse TIME-WAIT sessions, although not as safe as `tcp_tw_reuse`.

Network Interface

The TX queue length may be increased using `ifconfig(8)`, for example:

```
ifconfig eth0 txqueuelen 10000
```

This may be necessary for 10 GbE NICs. The setting can be added to /etc/rc.local so that it is applied during boot.

Resource Controls

The container groups (cgroups) network priority (net_prio) subsystem can be used to apply a priority to outgoing network traffic, for processes or groups of processes. This can be used to favor high-priority network traffic, such as production load, over low-priority traffic, such as backups or monitoring. The configured priority value is translated to an IP ToS level (or updated scheme that uses the same bits) and included in the packets.

10.8.2 Solaris

Historically, tunable parameters were either set and viewed using the `ndd(1M)` command, or set via /etc/system and viewed using `mdb(1)`. These are now being migrated to the `ipadm(1M)` command, which is a unified and flexible utility for managing IP stack properties.

For example, listing properties using `ipadm(1M)`:

```
# ipadm show-prop
PROTO PROPERTY          PERM CURRENT   PERSISTENT DEFAULT  POSSIBLE
ipv4  forwarding        rw   on        on         off      on,off
ipv4  ttl               rw   255       --         255      1-255
ipv6  forwarding        rw   off       --         off      on,off
ipv6  hoplimit          rw   255       --         255      1-255
ipv6  hostmodel         rw   weak      --         weak     strong,
                                                           src-priority,
                                                           weak
```

continues

ipv4	hostmodel	rw	src-priority	--	weak	strong, src-priority, weak
icmp	recv_maxbuf	rw	8192	--	8192	4096-65536
icmp	send_maxbuf	rw	8192	--	8192	4096-65536
tcp	ecn	rw	passive	--	passive	never,passive, active
tcp	extra_priv_ports	rw	2049,4045	--	2049,4045	1-65535
tcp	largest_anon_port	rw	65535	--	65535	1024-65535
tcp	recv_maxbuf	rw	128000	--	128000	2048-1073741824
tcp	sack	rw	active	--	active	never,passive, active
tcp	send_maxbuf	rw	49152	--	49152	4096-1073741824
tcp	smallest_anon_port	rw	32768	--	32768	1024-65535
tcp	smallest_nonpriv_port	rw	1024	--	1024	1024-32768
udp	extra_priv_ports	rw	2049,4045	--	2049,4045	1-65535
udp	largest_anon_port	rw	65535	--	65535	1024-65535
udp	recv_maxbuf	rw	57344	--	57344	128-1073741824
udp	send_maxbuf	rw	57344	--	57344	1024-1073741824
udp	smallest_anon_port	rw	32768	--	32768	1024-65535
udp	smallest_nonpriv_port	rw	1024	--	1024	1024-32768
[...]						

You would usually begin by finding the correct version of the *Solaris Tunable Parameters Reference Manual* for your Solaris version (for example, [9]). This manual provides instructions for key tunable parameters, including what type they are, when to set them, the defaults, and the valid ranges.

Examples of common tuning follow. For those that show the ndd(1M) versions, map them to ipadm(1M) as they become available. Also check first if tuning is prohibited by company or vendor policy before making changes.

Buffers

Setting various tunables for buffer sizes:

```
ndd -set /dev/tcp tcp_max_buf 16777216
ndd -set /dev/tcp tcp_cwnd_max 8388608
ndd -set /dev/tcp tcp_xmit_hiwat 1048576
ndd -set /dev/tcp tcp_recv_hiwat 1048576
```

tcp_max_buf sets the maximum socket buffer size that can be set using setsockopt(). tcp_cwnd_max is the maximum TCP congestion window. Increasing both of these can help improve network throughput performance.

The tcp_xmit_hiwat and tcp_recv_hiwat parameters set the default send and receive TCP window sizes. These are now also available in ipadm(1M) as send_maxbuf and recv_maxbuf.

TCP Backlog

Tuning the backlog queues:

```
ndd -set /dev/tcp tcp_conn_req_max_q0 4096
ndd -set /dev/tcp tcp_conn_req_max_q 1024
```

The _q0 parameter is for the half-open queue, and the _q parameter is for the listen backlog. Both of these may need to be increased from their defaults, such as to 4,096 and 1,024, to better handle bursts of load.

TCP Options

There are a few ways to tune around the issue of frequent connections between the same hosts, and a clash of reused ephemeral ports while the sessions are still in TIME-WAIT:

- `tcp_smallest_anon_port` can be reduced to 10,000 and lower on the client, to increase the ephemeral port range used. This usually helps only a little.
- `tcp_time_wait_interval` could be reduced from the default 60,000 (units are milliseconds), so that TIME-WAIT sessions are recycled more quickly. However, this is generally regarded as forbidden by the RFCs (see [RFC 1122] in particular).
- `tcp_iss_incr` can be reduced, which helps the kernel detect new sessions and automatically recycle TIME-WAIT sessions. (This was added to the illumos kernel.)

Other TCP options to tune include `tcp_slow_start_initial`—often set to the highest permissible value, so that TCP sessions more quickly reach high throughput.

Network Device

Enabling IP squeue fanout can improve performance by spreading network load across all CPUs:

```
set ip:ip_squeue_fanout=1
```

The default behavior is to associate connections with the CPU that handled their creation, which may result in an uneven distribution of connections to CPUs, with some CPUs hitting 100% utilization, and therefore becoming a bottleneck.

Resource Controls

The dladm(1M) tool can set various properties on the network interfaces, including maxbw to set its maximum bandwidth. This can be applied to virtual interfaces, as is commonly used by guest tenants for cloud computing, making this property a mechanism to throttle them.

The flowadm(1M) tool (added by the Crossbow project) has finer controls. It can be used to define *flows*, which may match on transports (TCP) and ports, and include properties such as maxbw and priority. Priority can be set to "low," "normal," "high," or "rt" (real time). These can be used to favor high-priority network traffic, such as production load, over low-priority traffic, such as backups or monitoring.

Solaris-based systems also have IP QoS (IPQoS) support for applying priorities to network packets, configured using ipqosconf(1M).

10.8.3 Configuration

Apart from tunable parameters, the following configuration options may also be available for tuning network performance:

- **Ethernet jumbo frames:** Increasing the default MTU from 1,500 to ~9,000 can improve network throughput performance, if the network infrastructure supports jumbo frames.
- **Link aggregation:** Multiple network interfaces can be grouped together so that they act as one with the combined bandwidth. This requires switch support and configuration to work properly.
- **Socket options:** The buffer size can be tuned by the application using setsockopt(), increasing it (up to the system limits described earlier) for improved throughput performance.

These are common to both operating system types.

10.9 Exercises

1. Answer the following questions about network terminology:
   - What is the difference between bandwidth and throughput?
   - What is TCP connection latency?
   - What is first-byte latency?
   - What is round-trip time?

2. Answer the following conceptual questions:

   - Describe network interface utilization and saturation.
   - What is the TCP listen backlog, and how is it used?
   - Describe the pros and cons of interrupt coalescing.

3. Answer the following deeper questions:

   - For a TCP connection, explain how a network frame (or packet) error could hurt performance.
   - Describe what happens when a network interface is overloaded with work, including the effect on application performance.

4. Develop the following procedures for your operating system:

   - A USE method checklist for network resources (network interfaces and controllers). Include how to fetch each metric (e.g., which command to execute) and how to interpret the result. Try to use existing OS observability tools before installing or using additional software products.
   - A workload characterization checklist for network resources. Include how to fetch each metric, and try to use existing OS observability tools first.

5. Perform these tasks (may require use of dynamic tracing):

   - Measure first-byte latency for outbound (active) TCP connections.
   - Measure TCP connect latency. The script should handle non-blocking `connect()` calls.

6. (optional, advanced) Measure TCP/IP inter-stack latency for RX and TX. For RX, this measures time from interrupt to socket read; for TX, the time from socket write to device transmit. Test under load. Can additional information be included to explain the cause of any latency outliers?

10.10 References

[Saltzer 84]   Saltzer, J., D. Reed, and D. Clark. "End-to-End Arguments in System Design," *ACM TOCS*, November 1984.

[Stevens 93]   Stevens, W. R. *TCP/IP Illustrated,* Volume 1. Addison-Wesley, 1993.

[Mathis 96]   Mathis, M., and J. Mahdavi. "Forward Acknowledgement: Refining TCP Congestion Control." ACM SIGCOMM, 1996.

[Downey 99]   Downey, A. "Using pathchar to Estimate Internet Link Char-
                     acteristics." ACM SIGCOMM, October 1999.

[Hassan 03]   Hassan, M., and R. Jain. *High Performance TCP/IP Network-
                     ing*. Prentice Hall, 2003.

[Deri 04]   Deri, L. "Improving Passive Packet Capture: Beyond Device
                     Polling," *Proceedings of SANE*, 2004.

[McDougall 06a]   McDougall, R., and J. Mauro. *Solaris Internals: Solaris 10
                     and OpenSolaris Kernel Architecture*. Prentice Hall, 2006.

[Gregg 11]   Gregg, B., and J. Mauro. *DTrace: Dynamic Tracing in Oracle
                     Solaris, Mac OS X and FreeBSD*. Prentice Hall, 2011.

[Nichols 12]   Nichols, K., and V. Jacobson. "Controlling Queue Delay," *Com-
                     munications of the ACM*, July 2012.

[RFC 768]   *User Datagram Protocol*, 1980.

[RFC 793]   *Transmission Control Protocol*, 1981.

[RFC 896]   *Congestion Control in IP/TCP Internetworks*, 1984.

[RFC 1122]   *Requirements for Internet Hosts—Communication Layers*,
                     1989.

[RFC 1761]   *Snoop Version 2 Packet Capture File Format*, 1995.

[RFC 2474]   *Definition of the Differentiated Services Field (DS Field) in the
                     IPv4 and IPv6 Headers*, 1998.

[1]   www.bufferbloat.net

[2]   http://hub.opensolaris.org/bin/view/Project+ip-refactor/

[3]   https://blogs.oracle.com/timc/entry/nicstat_the_solaris_and_
                     linux

[4]   ftp://ftp.ee.lbl.gov/pathchar

[5]   www.wireshark.org

[6]   https://github.com/brendangregg/dtrace-cloud-tools

[7]   www.dtracebook.com

[8]   www.netperf.org/netperf

[9]   http://docs.oracle.com/cd/E23824_01/html/821-1450/index.html

11

Cloud Computing

The rise of cloud computing solves some problems in the field of performance while posing others. Clouds are commonly built upon virtualization technologies, allowing multiple operating system instances, or tenants, to share one physical server. This means that there can be resource contention: not just from other processes, as has been the norm in Unix, but also from other entire operating systems. Isolating the performance effects of each tenant is critical, as is identifying when poor performance is caused by other tenants.

This chapter discusses the performance of cloud computing environments and consists of three parts:

- **Background** presents general cloud computing architecture and the performance implications thereof.
- **OS virtualization** is where a single kernel manages the system, creating virtual OS instances that are isolated from each other. This section uses SmartOS Zones as an example implementation.
- **Hardware virtualization** is where a hypervisor manages multiple guest operating systems, each running its own kernel with virtualized devices. This section uses Xen and KVM as examples.

Example technologies are included to discuss performance characteristics of the different types of virtualization. For full documentation of their usage, and that of other virtualization technologies, see their respective online documentation.

Cloud environments that do not use virtualization (bare-metal systems only) can be treated as distributed systems and analyzed using techniques described in the previous chapters. For virtualized systems, this chapter supplements the material that was covered earlier.

11.1 Background

Cloud computing allows computing resources to be delivered as a service, scaling from small fractions of a server to multiserver systems. There are various types, depending on how much of the software stack is installed and configured. This chapter focuses on the most basic: *infrastructure as a service* (IaaS), which provides operating systems as *server instances*. Example IaaS providers include Amazon Web Services (AWS), Rackspace, and Joyent.

Server instances are typically virtualized systems that can be created and destroyed in minutes (or fractions of a minute) and immediately put into production use. A *cloud API* is commonly provided so that this provisioning can be automated by another program.

To summarize cloud terminology, *cloud computing* describes a dynamic provisioning framework for server instances. Multiple server instances run as *guests* of a physical *host* system. The guests are also called *tenants*, and the term *multitenancy* is used to describe their effects on their neighbors. The host is managed by the cloud operators. The guests (tenants) are managed by the customers who purchased them.

Cloud computing has implications for a number of performance topics: price/performance ratio, architecture, capacity planning, storage, and multitenancy. These are summarized in the following sections.

11.1.1 Price/Performance Ratio

There are numerous *public cloud* providers who sell cloud server instances, typically by the hour and priced based on the memory (DRAM) size of the instance, with an 8 Gbyte instance costing roughly eight times as much as a 1 Gbyte instance. Other resources, such as CPUs, are scaled and priced according to the memory size. The result can be a consistent price/performance ratio, with some discounts to encourage the use of larger systems.

Some providers allow you to pay a premium for a larger allotment of CPU resources (a "high-CPU instance"). Other resource usage may also be monetized, such as network throughput and storage.

11.1.2 Scalable Architecture

Enterprise environments have traditionally used a *vertical scalability* approach for handling load: building larger single systems (mainframes). This approach has its limitations. There is a practical limit to the physical size to which a computer can be built (which may be bounded by the size of elevator doors or shipping containers), and there are increasing difficulties with CPU cache coherency as the CPU count scales. The solution to these limitations has been to scale load across many (perhaps small) systems; this is called *horizontal scalability*. In enterprise, it has been used for computer farms and clusters, especially with high-performance computing (HPC).

Cloud computing is also based on horizontal scalability. An example environment is shown in Figure 11.1, which includes load balancers, web servers, application servers, and databases.

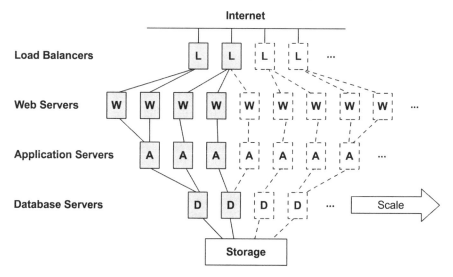

Figure 11-1 Cloud architecture: horizontal scaling

Each environment layer is composed of one or more server instances running in parallel, with more added to handle load. Instances may be added individually, or the architecture may be divided into vertical partitions, where a group composed of database servers, application servers, and web servers is added as a single unit.

The most difficult layer to execute in parallel is the database layer, due to the traditional database model where one database instance must be primary. Data for these databases, such as MySQL, can be split logically into groups called *shards*, each of which is managed by its own database (or primary/secondary pair). More recent database architectures, such as Riak, handle parallel execution dynamically, spreading load over available instances.

With the per-server instance size typically being small, say, 1 Gbyte (on physical hosts with 128 Gbytes and more of DRAM), fine-grained scaling can be used to attain optimum price/performance, rather than investing up front in huge systems that may remain mostly idle.

11.1.3 Capacity Planning

In enterprise environments, servers can be a significant infrastructure cost, both for the hardware and for service contract fees that may last for years. It can also take months for new servers to be put into production: time spent in approvals, waiting for part availability, shipping, racking, installing, and testing. Capacity planning is critically important, so that appropriately sized systems can be purchased: too small means failure, too large is costly (and, with service contracts, may be costly for years to come). Capacity planning can also help predict increases in demand well in advance, so that lengthy purchasing procedures can be completed in time.

Cloud computing is very different. Server instances are inexpensive and can be created and destroyed almost instantly. Instead of spending time planning what may be needed, companies can increase server instances *as* needed, in reaction to real load. This can also be done automatically via the cloud API, based on metrics from performance monitoring software. A small business or start-up can grow from a single small instance to thousands, without a detailed capacity planning study as would be expected in enterprise environments.

For growing start-ups, another factor to consider is the pace of code changes. Sites commonly update their production code weekly, or even daily. A capacity planning study taking weeks and, because it is based on a snapshot of performance metrics, may be out of date by the time it is completed. This differs from enterprise environments running commercial software, which may change no more than a few times per year.

Activities performed in the cloud for capacity planning include

- **Dynamic sizing:** automatically adding and removing server instances
- **Scalability testing:** purchasing a large cloud environment for a short duration, in order to test scalability versus synthetic load (this is a *benchmarking* activity)

Bearing in mind the time constraints, there is also the potential for modeling scalability (similar to enterprise studies) to estimate how actual scalability falls short of where it theoretically should be.

Dynamic Sizing

Automatically adding server instances can solve the need to quickly respond to load, but it also risks *overprovisioning*, as pictured in Figure 11.2. For example, a DoS attack may appear as an increase in load, triggering an expensive increase in server instances. There is a similar risk with application changes that regress performance, requiring more instances to handle the same load. Monitoring is important to verify that these increases make sense.

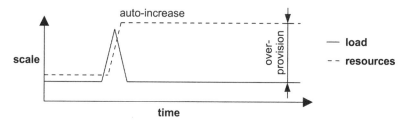

Figure 11-2 Dynamic sizing

Some clouds can also *reduce* their size when load drops. For example, in December 2012, Pinterest reported cutting costs from $54/hour to $20/hour by automatically shutting down its cloud systems after hours [1]. Similar immediate savings can also be a result of performance tuning, where the number of instances required to handle load has been reduced.

Some cloud architectures (see Section 11.2, OS Virtualization) can dynamically allocate more CPU resources instantly, if they are available, using a strategy called *bursting*. This can be provided at no extra cost and is intended to help prevent overprovisioning by providing a buffer during which the increased load can be checked to determine if it is real and likely to continue. If so, more instances can be provisioned so that resources are guaranteed going forward.

Any of these techniques should be considerably more efficient than enterprise environments—especially those with a fixed size chosen to handle expected peak load for the lifetime of the server; such servers may run mostly idle.

11.1.4 Storage

A cloud server instance typically has some local storage, served from local disks, for temporary files. This local storage is volatile and is destroyed when the server instance is destroyed. For persistent storage, an independent service is typically used, which provides storage to instances as either a

- **File store:** for example, files over NFS
- **Block store:** such as blocks over iSCSI
- **Object store:** over an API, commonly HTTP-based

These are network-attached, and both the network infrastructure and storage devices are shared with other tenants. For these reasons, performance can be much less reliable than with local disks. Both of these setups are pictured in Figure 11.3.

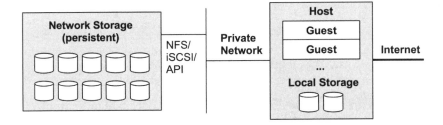

Figure 11-3 Cloud storage

The increased latency for network storage access is typically mitigated by using in-memory caches for frequently accessed data.

Some storage services allow an IOPS rate to be purchased when reliable performance is desired (e.g., AWS EBS Provisioned IOPS volume).

11.1.5 Multitenancy

Unix is a multitasking operating system, designed to deal with multiple users and processes accessing the same resources. Later additions by BSD, Solaris, and Linux have provided resource limits and controls to share these resources more fairly, and observability to identify and quantify when there are performance issues involving resource contention.

Cloud computing differs in that entire operating system instances coexist on the same physical system. Each guest is its own isolated operating system: guests cannot observe users and processes from other guests on the same host—that would be an information leak—even though they share the same physical resources.

Since resources are shared among tenants, performance issues may be caused by *noisy neighbors*. For example, another guest on the same host might perform a full database dump during your peak load, interfering with your disk and network I/O. Worse, a neighbor could be evaluating the cloud provider by executing micro-benchmarks that deliberately saturate resources in order to find their limit.

There are some solutions to this problem. Multitenancy effects can be controlled by *resource management*: setting operating system *resource controls* that provide *performance isolation* (also called *resource isolation*). This is where per-tenant limits or priorities are imposed for the usage of system resources: CPU, memory, disk or file system I/O, and network throughput. Not all cloud technologies have provided all of these, especially disk I/O limits. ZFS I/O throttling was developed for the Joyent public cloud, specifically for the noisy-disk-neighbor problem.

Apart from limiting resource usage, being able to observe multitenancy contention can help cloud operators tune the limits and better balance tenants on available hosts. The degree of observability depends on the virtualization type: OS virtualization or hardware virtualization.

11.2 OS Virtualization

OS virtualization partitions the operating system into instances that act like separate guest servers and can be administrated and rebooted independently of the host. These provide high-performance server instances for cloud customers, and high-density servers for cloud operators. OS-virtualized guests are pictured in Figure 11.4, using terminology from Solaris Zones.

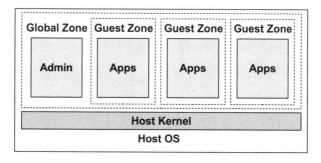

Figure 11-4 Operating system virtualization

The *global zone* is pictured in this figure; this refers to the host OS, which can see all the guest zones (which are also called *non-global zones*).

This approach has origins in the Unix `chroot(8)` command, which isolates a process to a subtree of the Unix global file system (changes the top level, "/"). In 1998, FreeBSD developed this further as *FreeBSD jails*, providing secure compartments that act as their own servers. In 2005, Solaris 10 included a version called *Solaris Zones*, with various resource controls. Via OpenSolaris and later SmartOS, zones have been put into production for the Joyent public cloud. More recently, there have been OS virtualization projects for Linux, including *lxc Linux Containers* [2] and *Open Virtuozzo* (OpenVZ) [3]. OpenVZ is supported by Parallels, Inc., and requires a modified Linux kernel [4].

A key difference from hardware virtualization technologies is that only one kernel is running. This has the following advantages:

- There is little or no performance overhead for guest application I/O, as guest applications can perform syscalls directly to the host kernel.
- Memory allocated to the guest can be used entirely for guest applications—there is no extra kernel tax, from either an OS hypervisor or other guest kernels.
- There is a unified file system cache—no double caching by both host and guest.
- All guest processes are observable from the host, allowing performance issues involving their interaction (including resource contention) to be debugged.
- CPUs are real CPUs; assumptions by adaptive mutex locks remain valid.

And there are disadvantages:

- Any kernel panic affects all guests.
- Guests cannot run different kernel versions.

To run different kernel versions and different operating systems, you need hardware virtualization (covered in Section 11.3, Hardware Virtualization). Operating system virtualization can fulfill this need to some degree, by providing alternate system call interfaces. An example of this was Solaris *lx Branded Zones*, which provided a Linux syscall interface and application environment under a Solaris kernel.

The following sections describe OS virtualization specifics: overhead, resource controls, and observability. This content is based on a public cloud that has seen many years of production use (and is also likely the largest OS virtualized cloud worldwide): the Joyent SmartOS implementation of Zones. This information should be generally applicable to all implementations of OS virtualization, with most differences relating to how resource controls are configured. Linux lxc Containers can use cgroups, for example, for uses similar to those described here.

11.2.1 Overhead

Understanding when and when not to expect performance overhead from virtualization is important in investigating cloud performance issues. This performance overhead can be summarized by describing the overhead for CPU execution, the overhead for performing I/O, and effects from other tenants.

CPU

The CPU execution overhead while a thread is running in user mode is zero. No synchronous emulation or simulation is required—threads run on-CPU directly, until they either yield or are preempted.

While not frequently called—and therefore not performance-sensitive—activities such as listing system state from the kernel may incur some extra CPU overhead as other tenant statistics are filtered. This includes the reading of /proc by status tools (e.g., `prstat(1M)`, `top(1)`) that step over all process entries, including other tenants, but return only the filtered list. The kernel code for this, from `pr_readdir_procdir()`, is

```
    /*
     * Loop until user's request is satisfied or until all processes
     * have been examined.
     */
    while ((error = gfs_readdir_pred(&gstate, uiop, &n)) == 0) {
            uint_t pid;
            int pslot;
            proc_t *p;

            /*
             * Find next entry.  Skip processes not visible where
             * this /proc was mounted.
             */
            mutex_enter(?dlock);
            while (n < v.v_proc &&
                ((p = pid_entry(n)) == NULL || p->p_stat == SIDL ||
                (zoneid != GLOBAL_ZONEID && p->p_zone->zone_id != zoneid) ||
                secpolicy_basic_procinfo(CRED(), p, curproc) != 0))
                    n++;
```

This was measured on current systems and was found to cost an extra 40 μs per 1,000 process entries. For an infrequent activity, this cost is negligible. (If it were to cost more, the kernel code would be changed.)

I/O

The I/O overhead is zero, unless extra features have been configured. For the basics of virtualization to work, no extra layer in the software stack is necessary. This is shown in Figure 11.5, which compares the I/O path of Unix processes to that of Zones.

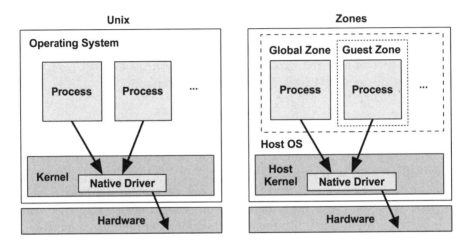

Figure 11-5 Unix process and Zones I/O path

The following shows two kernel stack traces (obtained using DTrace) for transmitting network packets, for both the host (bare-metal) and a guest:

```
Host:                                    Guest:
mac`mac_tx+0xda                          mac`mac_tx+0xda
dld`str_mdata_fastpath_put+0x53          dld`str_mdata_fastpath_put+0x53
ip`ip_xmit+0x82d                         ip`ip_xmit+0x82d
ip`ire_send_wire_v4+0x3e9                ip`ire_send_wire_v4+0x3e9
ip`conn_ip_output+0x190                  ip`conn_ip_output+0x190
ip`tcp_send_data+0x59                    ip`tcp_send_data+0x59
ip`tcp_output+0x58c                      ip`tcp_output+0x58c
ip`squeue_enter+0x426                    ip`squeue_enter+0x426
ip`tcp_sendmsg+0x14f                     ip`tcp_sendmsg+0x14f
sockfs`so_sendmsg+0x26b                  sockfs`so_sendmsg+0x26b
sockfs`socket_sendmsg+0x48               sockfs`socket_sendmsg+0x48
sockfs`socket_vop_write+0x6c             sockfs`socket_vop_write+0x6c
genunix`fop_write+0x8b                   genunix`fop_write+0x8b
genunix`write+0x250                      genunix`write+0x250
genunix`write32+0x1e                     genunix`write32+0x1e
unix`_sys_sysenter_post_swapgs+0x14      unix`_sys_sysenter_post_swapgs+0x14
```

These are identical. An extra layer would usually appear as extra frames in the stack.

For file system access, the zones may be configured to be mounted on loopback file systems, which themselves are mounted upon the host file systems. This strategy is used for the *sparse-root zones* model: a way to share read-only files (e.g., /usr/bin) between zones. If loopback file systems are used, a small amount of CPU overhead is incurred for file system I/O.

Other Tenants

The presence of other running tenants is likely to have a number of effects that hinder performance, unrelated to the virtualization technology:

- CPU caches may have a lower hit ratio, as other tenants are consuming and evicting entries.
- CPU execution may be interrupted for short periods for other tenant devices (e.g., network I/O) performing interrupt service routines.
- There may be contention for system resources (e.g., disks, network interfaces) from other tenants who are using them.

The last factor is managed by resource controls. While some of these factors exist in a traditional multiuser environment, they are much more prevalent in cloud computing.

11.2.2 Resource Controls

While the OS virtualization infrastructure manages security between neighbors, resource controls manage performance. Table 11.1 describes the areas of resource control and uses the Joyent public cloud configuration of SmartOS Zones as examples. These have been categorized into *limits* and *priorities*, which are set per guest by the cloud operator or software.

Limits are a ceiling value of resource consumption. Priorities steer resource consumption, to balance usage between neighbors based on an importance value. Either is used as appropriate—for some resources, that means both.

Table 11-1 OS Virtualization Example Resource Controls

Resource	Priority	Limit
CPU	FSS	caps
Memory capacity	rcapd/zoneadmd	VM limit
File system I/O	ZFS I/O throttling	—
File system capacity	—	ZFS quotas, file system limits
Disk I/O	see file system I/O	—
Network I/O	flow priority	bandwidth limits

CPU

Because an OS-virtualized guest can "see" all physical CPUs on the system directly, it can sometimes be allowed to consume 100% of CPU resources. For systems that run with mostly idle CPUs, this allows other guests to make use of that CPU, particularly for servicing short spikes in demand. Joyent calls this ability *bursting*; it helps cloud customers deal with short-term heavy demand without costly overprovisioning.

CPU Caps

Caps can put a limit on guest CPU usage, preventing bursting, and are expressed in terms of total CPU percentage. Some customers prefer this, as it provides a consistent performance expectation that can simplify capacity planning.

For other customers, per Joyent's default settings, the CPU cap is automatically increased to a multiple of the customer's expected share (for example, eight times). This allows the guest to burst if CPU resources are available. Should the guest keep bursting for hours or days (as identified by monitoring), the customer can be encouraged to upgrade the guest size so that the consumed CPU can be allocated reliably, instead of depending on bursting.

This can cause a problem when customers are unaware that they are bursting and may do so for weeks. At some point, another CPU-hungry tenant arrives who also consumes spare idle CPU, leaving less available for the first tenant, who experiences a drop in performance and may be unhappy about it. The situation is similar to flying economy for a month, but having been lucky enough to always have an entire row to yourself. Then you board a full flight.

Expectations can be kept in check by disabling bursting as described earlier—like putting sacks of potatoes in the spare seats, so that no passenger gets used to having the extra room. Your customers may prefer that you manage expectations by letting them know that they are bursting, rather than disabling the ability.

CPU Shares

Shares can be used via the fair-share scheduler (FSS) to divide CPU resources appropriately among guests. Shares can be allocated arbitrarily and are used to calculate the amount of CPU a busy guest will get at a given time, using the formula

guest CPU = all CPUs x guest shares/total busy shares on system

Consider a system with 100 shares, allocated to several guests. At one moment, only guests A and B want CPU resources. Guest A has 10 shares, and guest B has 30 shares. Guest A can therefore use 25% of the total CPU resources on the system: all CPUs x 10/(10 + 30).

For Joyent, each guest is given a number of shares equal to its memory size in megabytes (and, therefore, relative to price paid). Systems twice the size cost twice as much and therefore get twice as many CPU shares. This ensures that CPU resources are divided fairly among those who need them and have paid for them. CPU caps are also used to put a limit on bursting, so that expectations do not get too out of hand.

Memory Capacity

There are two types of memory resources, each with its own strategy for resource control: main memory (RSS) and virtual memory (VM). These also use the *resource controls facility*, described by the resource_controls(5) man page [5], which provides a set of tunable parameters for resource controls.

Main Memory

Limiting main memory is trickier than it sounds—imposing a hard limit is against expectations. Once a Unix system uses more main memory than is available, it begins paging (see Chapter 7, Memory).

This behavior is replicated for the guest in SmartOS by a thread in the per-zone administration daemon, *zoneadmd*. It pages out a guest early based on its memory resource control, zone.max-physical-memory. It will also maintain the target memory size by throttling page-ins using delays, to allow page-out to catch up.

This function was previously performed by the resource capping daemon, *rcapd*, which was a single process for all zones (and did not scale when there were many zones).

Virtual Memory

The resource control property for virtual memory is zone.max-swap, which is checked synchronously during allocation (malloc()). For Joyent, this is set to twice the main memory size. Once the limit is reached, allocations fail ("Out of memory" errors).

File System I/O

To address the issue of disk I/O from noisy neighbors, I/O is controlled at the file system level in a ZFS feature called *I/O throttling*, developed by Joyent's Bill Pijewski. This allocates shares to zones, similarly to FSS for CPUs, balancing I/O resources more fairly among tenants.

It works by proportionally throttling tenants who are performing the most disk I/O, to reduce their contention with other tenants. The actual throttle mechanism is to inject delays on the completion of the I/O, before returning to user-space. At this time, threads have usually blocked waiting for the I/O to complete, and the injection of extra latency is experienced as slightly slower I/O.

File System Capacity

Local file systems have a hard capacity limit: the total available space provided by the mapped storage devices. It is usually desirable to subdivide this capacity for the guests on the system, which can be done using

- Virtual volumes of a limited size
- File systems that support quotas (e.g., ZFS)

Network file systems and storage can also provide limits for file system capacity, which for cloud providers is usually tied to pricing.

Disk I/O

Current SmartOS Zones control disk I/O via access to the file system. See the earlier File System I/O section.

Network I/O

Since each zone is configured with its own virtual network interface, throughput can be limited using the maxbw (maximum bandwidth) link property from dladm(1M). Finer control of network I/O is possible using flowadm(1M), which can set both maxbw and priority values and can match traffic based on transport type and port. Joyent currently does not limit network I/O (all infrastructure is 10 GbE, and there is usually an abundance of bandwidth available) and so only sets these resource controls manually, if there is an abuser on the network.

11.2.3 Observability

With OS virtualization, the underlying technology by default allows everyone to see everything; limits must be imposed to prevent inadvertent security leaks. These limits are, at least:

- As a guest, /proc shows only processes in the guest.
- As a guest, netstat lists session information only for guest-owned sessions.
- As a guest, file system tools show only guest-owned file systems.
- As a guest, other zones cannot be listed via zone administration tools.
- As a guest, kernel internals cannot be inspected (no DTrace fbt provider or mdb -k).

The host operator can see everything: processes, TCP sessions, and file systems in both the host OS and all guests. And from the host, guest activity can be observed *directly*—without logging in to each.

The following sections demonstrate observability tools available for the host and those available for the guests and describe a strategy for analyzing performance. SmartOS and its observability tools are used to demonstrate the kinds of information that should be available from OS virtualization.

Host

When logged in to the host, all system resources (CPUs, memory, file system, disk, network) can be inspected using the tools covered in previous chapters. There are two additional factors to examine when using zones:

- Statistics per zone
- Effect of resource controls

Examining statistics per zone is sometimes provided by a -Z option. For example:

```
global# ps -efZ
    ZONE       UID    PID  PPID   C    STIME TTY     TIME CMD
   global     root      0     0   0   Oct 03 ?       0:01 sched
   global     root      4     0   0   Oct 03 ?       0:16 kcfpoold
   global     root      1     0   0   Oct 03 ?       0:07 /sbin/init
   global     root      2     0   0   Oct 03 ?       0:00 pageout
   global     root      3     0   0   Oct 03 ?     952:42 fsflush
[...]
72188ca0 0000101 16010 12735   0 00:43:07 ?       0:00 pickup -l -t fifo -u
b8b2464c    root 57428 57427   0   Oct 21 ?       0:01 /usr/lib/saf/ttymon
2e8ba1ab websrvd 13419 13418   0   Oct 03 ?       0:00 /opt/local/sbin/nginx ...
2e8ba1ab 0001003 13879 12905   0   Oct 03 ?     121:25 /opt/local/bin/ruby19 ...
2e8ba1ab    root 13418     1   0   Oct 03 ?       0:00 /opt/local/sbin/nginx ...
d305ee44 0000103 15101 15041   0   Oct 03 ?       6:07 /opt/riak/lib/os_mon-2...
8bbc4000    root 10933     1   0   Oct 03 ?       0:00 /usr/sbin/rsyslogd -c5 -n
[...]
```

The first column shows the zone name (truncated to fit).

The prstat(1M) command also supports the -Z option:

```
global# prstat -Zc 1
   PID USERNAME  SIZE   RSS STATE  PRI NICE      TIME  CPU PROCESS/NLWP
 22941 root       40M   23M wait     1    0  38:01:38 4.0% node/4
 22947 root       44M   25M wait     1    0  23:20:56 3.9% node/4
 15041 103      2263M 2089M sleep   59    0 168:09:53 0.9% beam.smp/86
[...]
ZONEID    NPROC  SWAP   RSS MEMORY      TIME  CPU ZONE
    21       23  342M  194M   0.4%   0:28:48 7.9% b8b2464c-55ed-455e-abef-bd...
     6       21 2342M 2109M   4.3% 180:29:09 0.9% d305ee44-ffaf-47ca-a558-89...
    16        2 1069M 1057M   2.1% 107:03:45 0.3% 361f610e-605a-4fd3-afa4-94...
```

continues

```
    15          2 1066M 1054M   2.1% 104:16:33 0.3% 25bedede-e3fc-4476-96a6-c4...
    19          2 1069M 1055M   2.1% 105:23:21 0.3% 9f68c2c8-75f8-4f51-8a6b-a8...
Total: 391 processes, 1755 lwps, load averages: 2.39, 2.31, 2.24
```

The top section (truncated) shows a process list as usual, with the highest CPU consumer at the top. The bottom section is a per-zone summary, showing

- **SWAP:** total zone virtual memory size
- **RSS:** total zone resident set size (main memory usage)
- **MEMORY:** main memory consumed, as a percentage of system-wide resources
- **CPU:** CPU consumed, as a percentage of system-wide resources
- **ZONE:** zone name

This is a system used for cloud computing (called a *compute node*), which hosts over a dozen dynamically created zones. Each zone has an automatically generated UUID as its zone name (the b8b2464c . . .).

The zonememstat(1M) tool shows per-zone memory usage:

```
global# zonememstat
                                     ZONE  RSS(MB)  CAP(MB)    NOVER  POUT(MB)
                                   global      156        -        -         -
      8bbc4000-5abd-4373-b599-b9fdc9155bbf      242     2048        0         0
      d305ee44-ffaf-47ca-a558-890c0bbef508     2082     2048   369976   9833581
      361f610e-605a-4fd3-afa4-94869aeb55c0     1057     2048        0         0
      476afc21-2751-4dcb-ae06-38d91a70b386     1055     2048        0         0
      9f68c2c8-75f8-4f51-8a6b-a894725df5d8     1056     2048        0         0
      9d219ce8-cf52-409f-a14a-b210850f3231     1151     2048        0         0
      b8b2464c-55ed-455e-abef-bd1ea7c42020       48     1024        0         0
[...]
```

This includes

- **CAP(MB):** the configured resource control limit
- **NOVER:** the number of times a zone has exceeded the limit
- **POUT(MB):** total data that has been paged out to keep a zone to its limit

An increasing value in POUT(MB) is usually a sign that a guest's applications have been misconfigured and are trying to use more memory than the guest has available, so the applications are being paged out by rcapd or zoneadmd.

Information for the other resource controls (CPU, ZFS I/O throttling, and network caps) can be retrieved from kstat(1M) and prctl(1).

If need be, further analysis can be performed from the host, including examining guest application call stacks and internals. The host administrator can identify the root cause of any performance issue, without logging in to the guest.

Guest

The guest should see only specific details of its processes and activity. Observability tools modified to do this are described as *zone-aware*. The /proc file system, as used by ps(1) and prstat(1M), contains processes only for that zone, making those tools zone-aware.

Shared system resources may be observable from the guests, so long as private details are not leaked. For example, guests can observe all physical CPUs and disks directly (mpstat(1M), iostat(1M)) and system-wide memory usage (vmstat(1M)).

For example, checking disk I/O on an idle zone:

```
zone# iostat -xnz 1
                    extended device statistics
    r/s    w/s    kr/s    kw/s wait actv wsvc_t asvc_t  %w  %b device
  526.4    3.0 65714.8    27.7  0.0  0.9    0.0    1.7   1  88 sd5
                    extended device statistics
    r/s    w/s    kr/s    kw/s wait actv wsvc_t asvc_t  %w  %b device
  963.0    1.0 75528.5     8.1  0.0  1.1    0.0    1.1   1  89 sd5
[...]
```

This can be confusing for people new to OS virtualization—why are the disks busy? This is because iostat(1) is showing the physical disks, including activity from other tenants. Such commands are called *system-wide* (i.e., not *zone-aware*).

To check the disk usage caused by this zone alone, statistics from the VFS level can be examined:

```
zone# vfsstat 1
  r/s    w/s  kr/s  kw/s ractv wactv read_t writ_t  %r  %w  d/s del_t zone
  1.2    1.4   6.8  17.7   0.0   0.0    0.0    0.1   0   0  0.8 81.6 b8b2464c (21)
 45.3    0.0   4.5   0.0   0.0   0.0    0.0    0.0   0   0  0.0  0.0 b8b2464c (21)
 45.3    0.0   4.5   0.0   0.0   0.0    0.0    0.0   0   0  0.0  0.0 b8b2464c (21)
[...]
```

This confirms that the zone is (almost) idle—reading 4.5 Kbytes/s (which is probably cached by the file system and not causing any disk I/O).

The mpstat(1M) is also system-wide:

```
zone# mpstat 1
CPU minf mjf xcal  intr ithr  csw icsw migr smtx  srw syscl  usr sys  wt idl
  0    1   0    0   456  177  564   10   32 17777    0 99347   53  20   0  27
  1    0   0    4  1025  437 4252  155  185 28337    0 62321   42  19   0  40
  2    0   0    1  5169 2547 3457   34   74 7037     0 28110   14   8   0  78
  3    1   0    1   400  161  798  102  127 47442    0 82525   63  23   0  14
  4    1   0    0   308  138  712   23   52 31552    0 49330   38  15   0  48
[...]
```

This shows all the physical CPUs, including activity from other tenants.

The `prstat -Z` summary is one way to show only the guest's CPU usage (other guests are not listed when run from a non-global zone):

```
zone# prstat -Zc 1
[...]
ZONEID    NPROC  SWAP    RSS MEMORY      TIME  CPU ZONE
    21       22  147M    72M   0.1%   0:26:16 0.0% b8b2464c-55ed-455e-abef-bd...
```

There are also counters from kstat that show CPU usage, along with the limits.

Ultimately, this physical resource observability provides the guests with useful statistics for performance analysis, which may help them rule out some types of issues (including noisy neighbors). This is an important difference from hardware virtualization, which hides physical resources from the guests.

Strategy

Previous chapters have covered analysis techniques for the physical system resources and included various methodologies. These can be followed for host operators, and to some extent by the guests, bearing in mind the limitations mentioned previously. For guests, high-level resource usage is typically observable, but drilling down into the kernel is not possible.

Apart from the physical resources, cloud limits imposed by resource controls should also be checked, by both the host operators and guest tenants. Since these limits, where present, are encountered long before the physical limits, they are more likely to be in effect and can be checked first.

Since many traditional observability tools were created before resource controls existed (e.g., `top(1)` and `prstat(1M)`), they do not include resource control information by default, and users may forget to check them with the other tools that do.

Here are some comments and strategies for checking each resource control:

- **CPU:** For caps, current CPU usage can be compared to the cap value. Encountering the cap causes threads to wait while in the runnable state, which can be observed as scheduler latency. This can be confusing at first, as the physical system may have substantial idle CPU.

- **Memory:** For main memory, check current usage against the limit. Once the limit has been reached, page-out will occur from zoneadmd. This may be noticed as anonymous paging and thread time spent in data faults. This can also be confusing at first, since the system pager may not be active (no `sr` seen by `vmstat`), and the physical system may have plenty of free memory.

- **File system I/O:** A high rate of I/O may be throttled, causing small increases in average latency. This can be observed by using the `vfsstat(1M)` tool.

- **File system capacity:** This should be observable as for any other file system (including using df(1M)).

- **Disk I/O:** See file system I/O.

- **Network I/O:** Check current network throughput against the bandwidth limit, if configured. Encountering the limit causes network I/O latency to increase, as tenants are throttled to their cap.

For SmartOS Zones, a USE method checklist has been developed, analyzing the resource controls first, and then the physical resources [6].

Monitoring Software

It should be noted that many monitoring tools written for stand-alone systems have yet to develop support for OS virtualization. Customers attempting to use these in the guests may find that they appear to work but are in fact showing physical system resources, based on the same counters on which these tools have always been based. Without support to observe the cloud resource controls, these tools may falsely report that systems have headroom, when in fact they have hit resource limits. They may also show high resource usage that is in fact due to other tenants.

11.3 Hardware Virtualization

Hardware virtualization creates *system virtual machine* instances, which can run entire operating systems, including their kernels. Types of hardware virtualization include the following:

- **Full virtualization—binary translations:** provides a complete virtual system composed of virtualized hardware components onto which an unmodified operating system can be installed. Pioneered by VMware for the x86 platform in 1998, this uses a mixture of direct processor execution and binary translations of instructions when needed [7]. The performance overhead for this was often acceptable for the savings provided by server consolidation.

- **Full virtualization—hardware-assisted:** provides a complete virtual system composed of virtualized hardware components onto which an unmodified operating system can be installed. This uses processor support to execute virtual machines more efficiently, specifically the AMD-V and Intel VT-x extensions introduced in 2005–2006.

- **Paravirtualization:** provides a virtual system that includes an interface for guest operating systems to efficiently use host resources (via *hypercalls*), without needing full virtualization of all components. For example, arming a timer usually involves multiple privileged instructions that must be emulated by the hypervisor. This can be simplified into a single hypercall for a paravirtualized guest. Paravirtualization may include the use of a paravirtual network device driver by the guest for passing packets more efficiently to the physical network interfaces in the host. While performance is improved, this relies on guest OS support for paravirtualization (which Windows has historically not provided).

Another type, *hybrid virtualization*, uses both hardware-assisted virtualization with some paravirtualization calls when those are more efficient, with the aim of delivering the best performance. The most common targets for paravirtualization are virtual devices such as networking cards and storage controllers.

Virtual machines are created and executed by a *hypervisor*, which may be implemented in software, firmware, or hardware.

Hardware-virtualized guests are pictured in Figure 11.6.

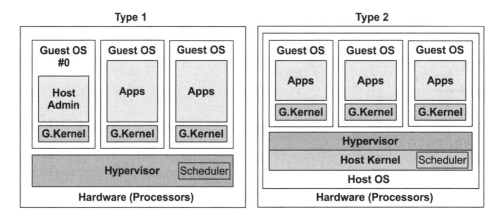

Figure 11-6 Hardware virtualization

This shows two types of hypervisors [Goldberg 73]:

- **Type 1** executes directly on the processors, and not as kernel- or user-level software of another host. Hypervisor administration may be performed by a privileged guest (pictured here as the first on the system: number 0), which can create and launch new guests. Type 1 is also called *native hypervisor* or *bare-metal hypervisor*. This hypervisor includes its own CPU scheduler for guest VMs.

- **Type 2** is executed by the host OS kernel and may be composed of kernel-level modules and user-level processes. The host OS has privileges to administer the hypervisor and launch new guests. This hypervisor is scheduled by the host kernel scheduler.

There are many different implementations of hardware virtualizations. Key examples are:

- **VMware ESX:** First released in 2001, VMware ESX is an enterprise product for server consolidation and is a key component of the VMware vSphere cloud computing product. Its hypervisor is a microkernel that runs on the bare metal, and the first virtual machine is called the *service console*, which can administer the hypervisor and new virtual machines.
- **Xen:** First released in 2003, Xen began as a research project at the University of Cambridge and was later acquired by Citrix. Xen is a type 1 hypervisor that runs paravirtualized guests for high performance; support was later added for hardware-assisted guests for unmodified OS support (Windows). Virtual machines are called *domains*, with the most privileged being *dom0,* from which the hypervisor is administered and new domains launched. Xen is open source and can be launched from Linux. (Versions have existed for Solaris; however, Oracle is now favoring Oracle VM Server instead.) The Amazon Elastic Compute Cloud (EC2) and Rackspace Cloud are based on Xen.
- **KVM:** This was developed by Qumranet, a start-up that was bought by Red Hat in 2008. KVM is a type 2 hypervisor, executing as a kernel module. It supports hardware-assisted extensions and, for high performance, uses paravirtualization for certain devices where supported by the guest OS. To create a complete hardware-assisted virtual machine instance, it is paired with a user process called QEMU (Quick Emulator). QEMU was originally a high-quality open-source type 2 hypervisor via binary translation, written by Fabrice Bellard. KVM is open source and has been ported to illumos and FreeBSD. The Linux and Windows instances of the Joyent public cloud use KVM (the SmartOS instances use OS virtualization). Google also uses KVM to drive the Google Compute Engine [8].

The following sections describe hardware virtualization topics: overhead, resource controls, and observability. These differ based on the implementation, of which there are more than the three listed previously. Check your implementation for specifics.

11.3.1 Overhead

Hardware virtualization is accomplished in various ways by the hypervisor. These hardware virtualization techniques add overhead for the guest OS whenever it tries to access hardware: commands must be translated from virtual to physical devices. These translations must be understood when studying performance; they can differ depending on the type and implementation of hardware virtualization. The differences can be summarized by describing the overheads for CPU execution, memory mapping, performing I/O, and effects from other tenants.

CPU

In general, the guest applications execute directly on the processors, with CPU-bound applications approaching the performance of a bare-metal system. Overheads may be encountered when making privileged processor calls, accessing hardware, and mapping main memory.

Following are the different hardware virtualization types:

- **Binary translation:** Guest kernel instructions that operate on physical resources are identified and translated. Binary translation was used before hardware-assisted virtualization was available. Without hardware support for virtualization, the scheme used by VMware involved running a virtual machine monitor (VMM) in processor ring 0 and moving the guest kernel to ring 1, which had previously been unused (applications run in ring 3, and most processors provide four rings). Because some guest kernel instructions assume they are running in ring 0, in order to execute from ring 1 they need to be translated, calling into the VMM so that virtualization can be applied. This translation is performed during runtime.

- **Paravirtualization:** Instructions in the guest OS that must be virtualized are replaced with hypercalls to the hypervisor. Performance can be improved if the guest OS is modified to optimize the hypercalls, making it aware that it is running on virtualized hardware.

- **Hardware-assisted:** Unmodified guest kernel instructions that operate on hardware are handled by the hypervisor, which runs a VMM at a ring level below 0. Instead of translating binary instructions, the guest kernel privileged instructions are forced to trap to the higher-privileged VMM, which can then emulate the privilege to support virtualization [Adams 06].

Hardware-assisted virtualization is generally preferred, depending on the implementation and workload, while paravirtualization is used to improve the performance of some workloads (especially I/O) if the guest OS supports it.

As an example of implementation differences, VMware's binary translation model has been heavily optimized over the years, and as they wrote in 2007 [7]:

> Due to high hypervisor to guest transition overhead and a rigid programming model, VMware's binary translation approach currently outperforms first generation hardware assist implementations in most circumstances. The rigid programming model in the first generation implementation leaves little room for software flexibility in managing either the frequency or the cost of hypervisor to guest transitions.

The rate of transitions between the guest and hypervisor, as well as the time spent in the hypervisor, can be studied as a metric of CPU overhead. These events are commonly referred to as *guest exits*, as the virtual CPU must stop executing inside the guest when this happens. Figure 11.7 shows CPU overhead related to guest exits inside KVM.

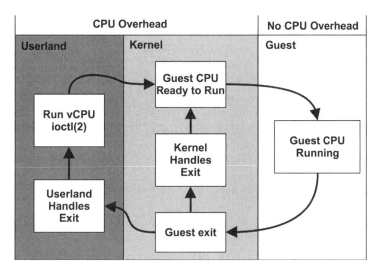

Figure 11-7 Hardware virtualization CPU overhead

The figure shows the flow of guest exits between the user process, the host kernel, and the guest. The time spent outside of the guest-handling exits is the CPU overhead of hardware virtualization; the more time spent handling exits, the greater the overhead. When the guest exits, a subset of the events can be handled directly in the kernel. Those that cannot must leave the kernel and return to the user process; this induces even greater overhead compared to exits that can be handled by the kernel.

For example, with the KVM implementation used by Joyent, these overheads can be studied via their guest exits, which are mapped in the source code to the following functions (from kvm_vmx.c):

```
static int (*kvm_vmx_exit_handlers[])(struct kvm_vcpu *vcpu) = {
        [EXIT_REASON_EXCEPTION_NMI]            = handle_exception,
        [EXIT_REASON_EXTERNAL_INTERRUPT]       = handle_external_interrupt,
        [EXIT_REASON_TRIPLE_FAULT]             = handle_triple_fault,
        [EXIT_REASON_NMI_WINDOW]               = handle_nmi_window,
        [EXIT_REASON_IO_INSTRUCTION]           = handle_io,
        [EXIT_REASON_CR_ACCESS]                = handle_cr,
        [EXIT_REASON_DR_ACCESS]                = handle_dr,
        [EXIT_REASON_CPUID]                    = handle_cpuid,
        [EXIT_REASON_MSR_READ]                 = handle_rdmsr,
        [EXIT_REASON_MSR_WRITE]                = handle_wrmsr,
        [EXIT_REASON_PENDING_INTERRUPT]        = handle_interrupt_window,
        [EXIT_REASON_HLT]                      = handle_halt,
        [EXIT_REASON_INVLPG]                   = handle_invlpg,
        [EXIT_REASON_VMCALL]                   = handle_vmcall,
        [EXIT_REASON_VMCLEAR]                  = handle_vmx_insn,
        [EXIT_REASON_VMLAUNCH]                 = handle_vmx_insn,
        [EXIT_REASON_VMPTRLD]                  = handle_vmx_insn,
        [EXIT_REASON_VMPTRST]                  = handle_vmx_insn,
        [EXIT_REASON_VMREAD]                   = handle_vmx_insn,
        [EXIT_REASON_VMRESUME]                 = handle_vmx_insn,
        [EXIT_REASON_VMWRITE]                  = handle_vmx_insn,
        [EXIT_REASON_VMOFF]                    = handle_vmx_insn,
        [EXIT_REASON_VMON]                     = handle_vmx_insn,
        [EXIT_REASON_TPR_BELOW_THRESHOLD]      = handle_tpr_below_threshold,
        [EXIT_REASON_APIC_ACCESS]              = handle_apic_access,
        [EXIT_REASON_WBINVD]                   = handle_wbinvd,
        [EXIT_REASON_TASK_SWITCH]              = handle_task_switch,
        [EXIT_REASON_MCE_DURING_VMENTRY]       = handle_machine_check,
        [EXIT_REASON_EPT_VIOLATION]            = handle_ept_violation,
        [EXIT_REASON_EPT_MISCONFIG]            = handle_ept_misconfig,
        [EXIT_REASON_PAUSE_INSTRUCTION]        = handle_pause,
        [EXIT_REASON_MWAIT_INSTRUCTION]        = handle_invalid_op,
        [EXIT_REASON_MONITOR_INSTRUCTION]      = handle_invalid_op,
};
```

While the names are terse, they may provide an idea of the reasons a guest may call into a hypervisor, incurring CPU overhead.

One common guest exit is the `halt` instruction, usually called by the idle thread when the kernel can find no more work to perform (which allows the processor to operate in low-power modes until interrupted). It is handled by `handle_halt()` (kvm_vmx.c), included here to provide an idea of the code involved:

```
static int
handle_halt(struct kvm_vcpu *vcpu)
{
        skip_emulated_instruction(vcpu);
        return (kvm_emulate_halt(vcpu));
}
```

which calls kvm_emulate_halt() (kvm_x86.c):

```
int
kvm_emulate_halt(struct kvm_vcpu *vcpu)
{
        KVM_VCPU_KSTAT_INC(vcpu, kvmvs_halt_exits);

        if (irqchip_in_kernel(vcpu->kvm)) {
                vcpu->arch.mp_state = KVM_MP_STATE_HALTED;
                return (1);
        } else {
                vcpu->run->exit_reason = KVM_EXIT_HLT;
                return (0);
        }
}
```

As with many guest exit types, the code is kept small to minimize CPU overhead. This example begins with the KVM_VCPU_KSTAT_INC() macro, which sets a kstat counter so that the rate of halts can be observed. (This is a port from the Linux version, which sets a built-in counter for the same purpose.) The remaining code performs the hardware emulation required for this privileged instruction. These functions can be studied using DTrace on the hypervisor, to track their type and the duration of their exits.

Virtualizing hardware devices such as the interrupt controller and high-resolution timers also incur some CPU (and a small amount of DRAM) overhead.

Memory Mapping

As described in Chapter 7, Memory, the operating system works with the MMU to create page mappings from virtual to physical memory, caching them in the TLB to improve performance. For virtualization, mapping a new page of memory (page fault) from the guest to the hardware involves two steps:

1. Virtual-to-guest physical translation, as performed by the guest kernel
2. Guest-physical-to-host-physical (actual) translation, as performed by the hypervisor VMM

The mapping, from guest virtual to host physical, can then be cached in the TLB, so that subsequent accesses can operate at normal speed—not requiring additional translation. Modern processors support MMU virtualization, so that mappings that have left the TLB can be recalled more quickly in hardware alone (page walk), without calling into the hypervisor. The feature that supports this is called *extended page tables* (EPT) on Intel and *nested page tables* (NPT) on AMD [9].

Without EPT/NPT, another approach to improve performance is to maintain *shadow page tables* of guest-virtual-to-host-physical mappings, which are managed by the hypervisor and then accessed during guest execution by overwriting the guest's CR3 register. With this strategy, the guest kernel maintains its own page tables, which map from guest virtual to guest physical, as normal. The hypervisor intercepts changes to these page tables and creates equivalent mappings to the host physical pages in the shadow pages. Then, during guest execution, the hypervisor overwrites the CR3 register to point to the shadow pages.

Memory Size

Unlike OS virtualization, there are some additional consumers of memory when using hardware virtualization. Each guest runs its own kernel, which consumes a small amount of memory. The storage architecture may also lead to double caching, where both the guest and host cache the same data.

I/O

A key cost of virtualization is the overhead for performing device I/O. Unlike CPU and memory I/O, where the common path can be set up to execute in a bare-metal fashion, every device I/O must be translated by the hypervisor. For high-frequency I/O, such as 10 Gbit/s networking, a small degree of overhead per I/O (packet) can cause a significant overall reduction in performance.

I/O overhead may be mitigated to some extent by using *paravirtualization*, where guest kernel drivers have been modified to operate efficiently in the virtualized environment, coalescing I/O and performing fewer device interrupts to reduce the hypervisor overhead.

Another technique is *PCI pass-through*, which assigns a PCI device directly to the guest, so it can be used as it would on a bare-metal system. PCI pass-through can provide the best performance of the available options, but it reduces flexibility when configuring the system with multiple tenants, as some devices are now owned by guests and cannot be shared. This may also complicate live migration [10].

There are some technologies to improve the flexibility of using PCI devices with virtualization, including Single Root I/O Virtualization (SR-IOV) and Multi Root I/O Virtualization (MR-IOV). These terms refer to the number of root complex PCI topologies that are exposed, providing hardware virtualization in different ways. Their usage depends on hardware and hypervisor support.

As examples of device I/O, Xen (type 1 hypervisor) and KVM (type 2 hypervisor) are pictured in Figure 11.8.

GK is "guest kernel," and domU on Xen runs the guest OS. Some of these arrows indicate the *control path*, where components inform each other, either synchronously or asynchronously, that more data is ready to transfer. The *data path* may

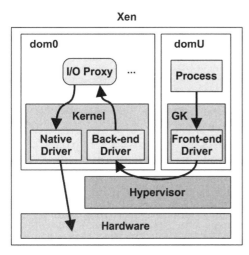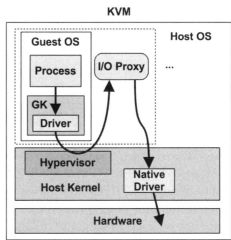

Figure 11-8 Xen and KVM I/O path

be implemented in some cases by shared memory and ring buffers. There are variations of these technologies. In this figure, both are pictured using I/O proxy processes (typically the QEMU software), which are created per guest VM.

The number of steps in the I/O path, both control and data, is critical for performance: the fewer, the better. In 2006 the KVM developers compared a privileged-guest system like Xen with KVM and found that KVM could perform I/O using half as many steps (five versus ten, although the test was performed without paravirtualization so does not reflect most modern configurations) [11].

Xen improves its I/O performance using a *device channel*—an asynchronous shared memory transport between dom0 and the guest domains (domU). This avoids the CPU and bus overhead of performing an extra copy of I/O data as it is passed between the doms. It may also use separate doms for performing I/O, as described in Section 11.3.2, Resource Controls.

A paravirtualized guest driver may be used in either case to improve I/O performance, which can apply optimum buffering and I/O coalescing for the virtualized I/O path.

Other Tenants

As with OS virtualization, the presence of other tenants can cause the CPU caches to be less warm, and guest runtime interruptions may occur while other tenants are scheduled and serviced, including device interrupts. Contention for resources can be managed by resource controls.

11.3.2 Resource Controls

As part of the guest configuration, CPU and main memory are typically config-ured with resource limits. The hypervisor software may also provide resource con-trols for network and disk I/O.

For type 2 hypervisors, the host OS ultimately controls the physical resources, and resource controls (if any) available from the OS may also be applied to the guests, in addition to the controls the hypervisor provides.

For example, Joyent configures KVM guests to run inside SmartOS Zones, allowing the resource controls listed in Section 11.2, OS Virtualization, to be applied, including ZFS I/O throttling. This is in addition to the KVM limits, provid-ing more options and flexibility for controlling resource usage. It also encapsulates each KVM instance in its own highly secure zone, providing multiple boundaries of security protection—a technique called *double-hull virtualization*.

What's available depends on the hypervisor software, type, and, for type 2 hypervisors, the host OS. See Section 11.2, OS Virtualization, for the kinds of resource controls that may be available from the host OS. The following sections describe resource controls from the Xen and KVM hypervisors, as examples.

CPU

CPU resources are usually allocated to guests as virtual CPUs (vCPUs). These are then scheduled by the hypervisor. The number of vCPUs assigned coarsely limits CPU resource usage.

For Xen, a fine-grained CPU quota for guests can be applied by a hypervisor CPU scheduler. Schedulers include ([Cherkasova 07], [Matthews 08])

- **Borrowed virtual time (BVT):** a fair-share scheduler based on the alloca-tion of virtual time, which can be borrowed in advance to provide low-latency execution for real-time and interactive applications
- **Simple earliest deadline first (SEDF):** a real-time scheduler that allows runtime guarantees to be configured, with the scheduler giving priority to the earliest deadline
- **Credit-based:** supports priorities (*weights*) and caps for CPU usage, and load balancing across multiple CPUs

For KVM, fine-grained CPU quotas can be applied by the host OS, for example, when using the host kernel *fair-share scheduler* described earlier. On Linux, this could be applied using the cgroup CPU bandwidth controls.

There are limitations on how either technology can respect guest *priorities*. A guest's CPU usage is typically opaque to the hypervisor, and guest kernel thread prior-ities cannot typically be seen or respected. For example, a Solaris kernel periodically scanning memory using the background fsflush daemon may have the same hypervisor priority as a critical application server in another guest.

For Xen, CPU resource usage can be further complicated by high-I/O workloads that consume extra CPU resources in dom0. The back-end driver and I/O proxy in the guest domain alone may consume more than their CPU allocation but are not accounted for [Cherkasova 05]. A solution has been to create isolated driver domains (IDDs), which separate out I/O servicing for security, performance isolation, and accounting. This is pictured in Figure 11.9.

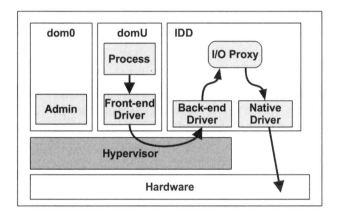

Figure 11-9 Xen with isolated driver domains

The CPU usage by IDDs can be monitored, and the guests can be charged for this usage. From [Gupta 06]:

> Our modified scheduler, SEDF-DC for SEDF-Debt Collector, periodically receives feedback from XenMon about the CPU consumed by IDDs for I/O processing on behalf of guest domains. Using this information, SEDF-DC constrains the CPU allocation to guest domains to meet the specified combined CPU usage limit.

A more recent technique used in Xen is *stub domains*, which run a mini OS.

Memory Capacity

Memory limits are imposed as part of the guest configuration, with the guest seeing only the set amount of memory. The guest kernel then performs its own operations (paging, swapping) to remain within its limit.

In an effort to increase flexibility from the static configuration, VMware developed what is referred to as a *balloon driver* [Waldspurger 02]. It is able to reduce the memory consumed by the running guest by "inflating" a balloon module inside it, which consumes guest memory. This memory is then reclaimed by the hypervisor for use by other guests. The balloon can also be deflated, returning memory to the guest kernel for use. During this process, the guest kernel executes its normal memory management routines to free memory (e.g., paging). VMware, Xen, and KVM all have support for balloon drivers.

File System Capacity

Guests are provided with virtual disk volumes from the host, which are created during guest configuration from a pool of storage disks (using ZFS) to be the size desired. From these disk volumes, the guest creates file systems and manages its own space, limited by the configured volume size. The exact details for doing this depend on the virtualization software and storage configuration.

Device I/O

Resource controls by hardware virtualization software have historically focused on controlling CPU usage, which can indirectly control I/O usage.

Network throughput may be throttled by external dedicated devices or, in the case of type 2 hypervisors, by host kernel features. For example, the illumos kernel supports network bandwidth resource controls, which could in theory be applied to guest virtual network interfaces. Linux has network bandwidth controls from cgroups, which could be used in a similar way.

Network performance isolation for Xen has been studied, with the following conclusion [Adamczyk 12]:

> . . . when the network virtualization is considered, the weak point of Xen is its lack of proper performance isolation.

The authors of [Adamczyk 12] also propose a solution for Xen network I/O scheduling, which adds tunable parameters for network I/O priority and rate. If you are using Xen, check whether this or a similar technology has been made available.

Disk and file system I/O techniques are also in development for hardware virtualization. Check your software version for what is available, and, for type 2 hypervisors, also check what resource controls are made available by the host operating system. For example, Joyent's KVM guests are disk I/O throttled using the ZFS I/O throttling technology described earlier.

11.3.3 Observability

What is observable depends on the type of hypervisor and the location from which the observability tools are launched. In general:

- **From the privileged guest (type 1) or host (type 2):** All physical resources should be observable using standard OS tools, and I/O from the I/O proxies. Per-guest resource usage statistics should be made available from the OS or virtualization software. Guest internals, including their processes, cannot be observed directly.
- **From the guests:** Physical resources and their usage are not generally observable. Virtualized resources and their usage by the guest can be seen.

From the privileged guest or host, physical resource usage can be observed at a high level: utilization, saturation, errors, IOPS, throughput, I/O type. These factors can usually be expressed per guest, so that heavy users can be quickly identified. Details of which guest processes are performing I/O and their application call stacks cannot be observed directly. These can be observed by logging in to the guest (provided a means to do so is authorized and configured, e.g., SSH) and using the observability tools that the guest OS provides.

To identify the root cause of a guest performance issue, the cloud operator may need to log in to both the privileged guest or host and the guest and execute observability tools from both. Tracing the path of I/O becomes complex due to the steps involved and may also include analysis of the hypervisor and the I/O proxy.

From the guest, physical resource usage may not be observable at all. This may tempt the guest customers to blame mysterious performance issues on physical resources being used by invisible noisy neighbors. To give cloud customers peace of mind (and reduce support tickets), information about physical resource usage (redacted) may be provided via other means, including SNMP or a cloud API.

The following sections demonstrate observability tools that can be used from different locations and describe a strategy for analyzing performance. Xen and KVM are used to demonstrate the kind of information that virtualization software may provide.

Privileged Guest/Host

All system resources (CPUs, memory, file system, disk, network) should be observable using the tools covered in previous chapters.

KVM

For type 2 hypervisors, the guest instances are visible within the host OS. For example, with KVM on SmartOS:

```
global# prstat -c 1
   PID USERNAME  SIZE   RSS STATE  PRI NICE      TIME  CPU PROCESS/NLWP
 46478 root     1163M 1150M cpu6     1    0   9:40:15 5.2% qemu-system-x86/5
  4440 root     9432K 4968K sleep   50    0 136:10:38 1.1% zoneadmd/5
```

continues

```
 15041 103       2279M 2091M sleep   60     0 168:40:09 0.4% beam.smp/87
 37494 root      1069M 1055M sleep   59     0 105:35:52 0.3% qemu-system-x86/4
 37088 root      1069M 1057M sleep    1     0 107:16:27 0.3% qemu-system-x86/4
 37223 root      1067M 1055M sleep   59     0  94:19:31 0.3% qemu-system-x86/7
 36954 root      1066M 1054M cpu7    59     0 104:28:53 0.3% qemu-system-x86/4
 [...]
```

The QEMU processes are the KVM guests, which include threads for each vCPU and threads for I/O proxies. Their CPU usage can be seen in the prstat(1M) output above, and per-vCPU usage can be examined using other prstat(1M) options (-mL). Mapping QEMU processes to their guest instance names is usually a matter of examining their process arguments (pargs(1)) to read the –name option.

Another important area for analysis is guest vCPU exits. The types of exits that occur can show what a guest is doing: whether a given vCPU is idle, performing I/O, or performing compute. On Linux, this information is collected and can be accessed through the debugfs file system, and by using tools such as perf(1). On SmartOS, this information is collected in kstats and can be summarized with the kvmstat(1) tool.

```
host# kvmstat 1
     pid vcpu |   exits :  haltx   irqx  irqwx    iox  mmiox |   irqs   emul   eptv
   12484    0 |   8955 :    551   2579    316   1114      0 |   1764   3510      0
   12484    1 |   2328 :    253    738     17    248      0 |    348    876      0
   12484    2 |   2591 :    262    579     14    638      0 |    358    837      0
   12484    3 |   3226 :    244   1551     19    239      0 |    343    960      0
   28275    0 |    196 :     12     75      1      0     82 |     14    107      0
   [...]
```

The first two fields identify the vCPU inside a specific virtual machine. The remaining columns describe the total number of exits, breaking them down into general categories. The last few columns describe other activity on the vCPU. kvmstat(1) describes the columns in its help message:

- **pid:** identifier of the process controlling the virtual CPU
- **vcpu:** virtual CPU identifier relative to its virtual machine
- **exits:** virtual machine exits for the virtual CPU
- **haltx:** virtual machine exits due to the HLT instruction
- **irqx:** virtual machine exits due to a pending external interrupt
- **irqwx:** virtual machine exits due to an open interrupt window
- **iox:** virtual machine exits due to an I/O instruction
- **mmiox:** virtual machine exits due to memory-mapped I/O
- **irqs:** interrupts injected into the virtual CPU

- **emul:** instructions emulated in the kernel
- **eptv:** extended page table violations

While it may not be easy for an operator to directly see inside a guest virtual machine, examining the exits lets you characterize how the overhead of hardware virtualization may or may not be affecting a tenant. If you see a low number of exits and a high percentage of those are haltx, you know that the guest CPU is fairly idle. On the other hand, if you have a high number of I/O operations, interrupts being both generated and injected into the guest, it is very likely that the guest is doing I/O over its virtual NICs and disks.

Xen

For type 1 hypervisors, the guest vCPUs exist in the hypervisor and are not visible from the privileged guest (dom0) using standard OS tools. For Xen, the xentop(1) tool can be used instead:

```
# xentop
xentop - 02:01:05   Xen 3.3.2-rc1-xvm
2 domains: 1 running, 1 blocked, 0 paused, 0 crashed, 0 dying, 0 shutdown
Mem: 50321636k total, 12498976k used, 37822660k free    CPUs: 16 @ 2394MHz
      NAME   STATE   CPU(sec) CPU(%)     MEM(k) MEM(%)  MAXMEM(k) MAXMEM(%) VCPUS NETS
NETTX(k) NETRX(k) VBDS    VBD_OO   VBD_RD   VBD_WR SSID
  Domain-0 -----r   6087972    2.6   9692160   19.3  no limit        n/a   16   0
0       0      0        0        0        0   0
Doogle_Win --b---    172137    2.0   2105212    4.2  2105344         4.2    1   2
0       0      2        0        0        0   0
[...]
```

The fields include

- **CPU(%):** CPU usage percentage (sum for multiple CPUs)
- **MEM(k):** main memory usage (Kbytes)
- **MEM(%):** main memory percentage of system memory
- **MAXMEM(k):** main memory limit size (Kbytes)
- **MAXMEM(%):** main memory limit as a percentage of system memory
- **VCPUS:** count of assigned vCPUs
- **NETS:** count of virtualized network interfaces
- **NETTX(k):** network transmit (Kbytes)
- **NETRX(k):** network receive (Kbytes)
- **VBDS:** count of virtual block devices

- **VBD_OO:** virtual block device requests blocked and queued (saturation)

- **VBD_RD:** virtual block device read requests

- **VBD_WR:** virtual block device write requests

The xentop output is updated every 3 s by default and is selectable using –d *delay_secs*.

Advanced Observability

For extended hypervisor analysis, there are a number of options. On Linux, perf(1) provides tracepoints for both KVM and Xen, which can be used to investigate various events. Listing example Xen tracepoints:

```
# perf list
[...]
  xen:xen_mc_batch                         [Tracepoint event]
  xen:xen_mc_issue                         [Tracepoint event]
  xen:xen_mc_entry                         [Tracepoint event]
  xen:xen_mc_entry_alloc                   [Tracepoint event]
  xen:xen_mc_callback                      [Tracepoint event]
  xen:xen_mc_flush_reason                  [Tracepoint event]
  xen:xen_mc_flush                         [Tracepoint event]
  xen:xen_mc_extend_args                   [Tracepoint event]
  xen:xen_mmu_set_pte                      [Tracepoint event]
[...]
```

There is also the xentrace(8) tool, which can retrieve a log of fixed event types from the hypervisor, which can then be viewed using xenanalyze. The log can be used to investigate scheduling issues with the hypervisor and CPU scheduler used.

For KVM, DTrace can be used to inspect internals of the hypervisor in custom ways, including the kvm kernel host driver and the QEMU process, the host kernel scheduler, the host device drivers, and interactions with other tenants.

For example, the following output of a DTrace script (kvmexitlatency.d [12]) traces KVM guest exit latency and prints a distribution plot for each type:

```
# ./kvmexitlatency.d
Tracing KVM exits (ns)... Hit Ctrl-C to stop
^C

  EXIT_REASON_CPUID
           value  ------------- Distribution ------------- count
            1024 |                                         0
            2048 |@@@@@@@@@@@@@@@@@@@@@@@@@@@@@@@@@@@@@@@@@@ 31
            4096 |@                                        1
            8192 |                                         0
[...]
```

```
EXIT_REASON_APIC_ACCESS
          value  ------------- Distribution ------------- count
           2048 |                                          0
           4096 |                                          125
           8192 |@@@@@@@@@@@@@@@@@@@@@@@@@@@@@@@@@@@@@@@@@@  11416
          16384 |@@                                        687
          32768 |                                          3
          65536 |                                          0

EXIT_REASON_IO_INSTRUCTION
          value  ------------- Distribution ------------- count
           2048 |                                          0
           4096 |@@@@@@@@@@@@@@@@@@@@@@@@@@@@@@@@@@@@@@@@@@  32623
           8192 |@                                         987
          16384 |                                          7
          32768 |                                          0
```

All of the exits in this example were 64 µs and faster, with most between 2 µs and 16 µs.

Advancing hypervisor observability is an ongoing process, with tools such as perf(1) and DTrace expanding the limits of what can be seen. An example of this is CR3 profiling.

CR3 Profiling

Thanks to Intel's VT-x instruction set for hardware-assisted virtualization, every vCPU has a virtual machine control structure (VMCS). The VMCS contains copies of the vCPU's register state, which DTrace can query. Every process on the system has its own address space and set of page tables describing the virtual-to-physical memory translations. The root of this page table is stored in the register CR3.

Using the DTrace profile provider, you can sample the CR3 register from a guest virtual machine. If a particular CR3 value is frequently seen, you know that a specific process is very active on the CPU in the guest. Although this CR3 value cannot currently be mapped to something human-readable (such as the process name), its numeric value does uniquely identify a process in the guest, which can be used to understand general system trends.

Figure 11.10, from Joyent's Cloud Analytics, is an example of visualizing CR3 samples and shows the guest kernel scheduling activity of two CPU-bound processes.

This visualization is a subsecond-offset heat map, which paints vertical columns each second with sampled data. On the right is a distorted checkerboard pattern, showing that two different CR3s were alternating on-CPU, which is due to the two different guest processes.

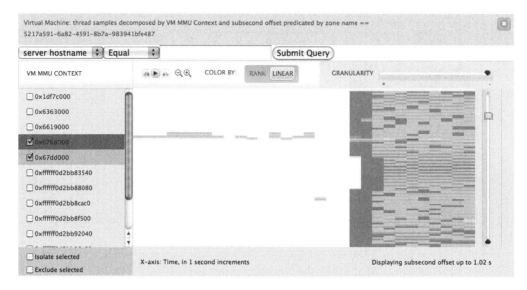

Figure 11-10 Visualizing guest vCPU CR3 register values

Guest

From the guest, only the virtual devices can be seen. The most interesting metric is *latency*, showing how the device is responding given virtualization, limits, and other tenants. Metrics such as percent busy are difficult to interpret without knowing what the underlying device is.

The vmstat(8) command on Linux includes a column for CPU percent stolen (st), which is a rare example of a virtualization-aware statistic:

```
$ vmstat 1
procs -----------memory---------- ---swap-- -----io---- --system-- -----cpu-----
 r  b   swpd   free   buff  cache   si   so    bi    bo   in   cs us sy id wa st
 1  0      0 107500 141348 301680    0    0     0     0 1006    9 99  0  0  0  1
 1  0      0 107500 141348 301680    0    0     0     0 1006   11 97  0  0  0  3
 1  0      0 107500 141348 301680    0    0     0     0  978    9 95  0  0  0  5
 3  0      0 107500 141348 301680    0    0     0     4  912   15 99  0  0  0  1
 2  0      0 107500 141348 301680    0    0     0     0   33    7  3  0  0  0 97
 3  0      0 107500 141348 301680    0    0     0     0   34    6 100  0  0  0  0
 5  0      0 107500 141348 301680    0    0     0     0   35    7  1  0  0  0 99
 2  0      0 107500 141348 301680    0    0     0    48   38   16  2  0  0  0 98
[...]
```

In this example, a Xen guest with an aggressive CPU limiting policy was tested. For the first 4 s, over 90% of CPU time was in user mode of the guest, with a few percent stolen by other tenants. This behavior then begins to change aggressively, with most of the CPU time stolen by other tenants.

Strategy

Previous chapters have covered analysis techniques for the physical system resources, which can be followed by the administrators of the physical systems, to look for bottlenecks and errors. Resource controls imposed on the guests can also be checked, to see if guests are consistently at their limit and should be informed and encouraged to upgrade. Not much more can be identified by the administrators without logging in to the guests, which may be necessary for any serious performance investigation.

For the guests, the tools and strategies for analyzing resources covered in previous chapters can be applied, bearing in mind that the resources in this case are virtual. Some resources may not be driven to their limits, due to unseen resource controls by the hypervisor or contention from other tenants. Ideally, the cloud software or vendor provides a means for customers to check redacted physical resource usage, so that they can investigate performance issues further on their own. If not, contention and limits may have to be deduced from increases in I/O and CPU scheduling latency. Such latency can be measured either at the syscall layer or in the guest kernel.

11.4 Comparisons

Comparing technologies can help you better understand them, even if you are not in a position to change the technology used by your company. The three technologies discussed in this chapter are compared in Table 11.2.

Table 11-2 Comparing Virtualization Technology Performance Attributes

Attribute	OS Virtualization	Hardware Virtualization, Type 1	Hardware Virtualization, Type 2
CPU performance	high	high (with CPU support)	high (with CPU support)
CPU allocation	flexible (FSS + "bursting")	fixed to vCPU limit	fixed to vCPU limit
I/O throughput	high (no intrinsic overhead)	low or medium (with paravirtualization)	low or medium (with paravirtualization)
I/O latency	low (no intrinsic overhead)	usually some (I/O proxy overhead)	usually some (I/O proxy overhead)
Memory access overhead	none	some (EPT/NPT or shadow page tables)	some (EPT/NPT or shadow page tables)

continues

Table 11-2 Comparing Virtualization Technology Performance Attributes (*Continued*)

Attribute	OS Virtualization	Hardware Virtualization, Type 1	Hardware Virtualization, Type 2
Memory loss	none	some (extra kernels, page tables)	some (extra kernels, page tables)
Memory allocation	flexible (unused guest memory used for file system cache)	fixed (and possible double caching)	fixed (and possible double caching)
Resource controls	many (depends on OS)	some (depends on hypervisor)	most (OS + hypervisor)
Observability: from the host	highest (see everything)	low (resource usage, hypervisor statistics)	medium (resource usage, hypervisor statistics, OS inspection of hypervisor)
Observability: from the guest	medium (see everything permitted, including some physical resource stats)	low (guest only)	low (guest only)
Hypervisor complexity	low (OS partitions)	high (complex hypervisor)	medium
Different OS guests	usually no (sometimes possible with syscall translation)	yes	yes

While this table will become out-of-date as more features are developed for these virtualization technologies, it will still serve to show the kinds of things to look for, even as entirely new virtualization technologies are developed that fit none of these categories.

Virtualization technologies are often compared using micro-benchmarking, to see which performs the best. Unfortunately, doing this overlooks observability capabilities, which can lead to the largest performance gains of all (by making it possible to identify and eliminate unnecessary work). Consider the following common scenario: A new cloud customer misconfigures an application such that it consumes too much main memory and is paged or swapped out. With OS virtualization, this can easily be pinpointed by the cloud administrators (see the earlier `zonememstat(1M)` command), who can also see the processes responsible, the application stack traces, and often the configuration files as well—identifying the root cause without logging in to the guest. For hardware virtualization, the cloud administrators see disk I/O from a guest, which may appear like any other disk I/O and be mistaken for normal activity. That the guest has run out of memory and is paging or swapping is not identifiable without logging in to the guest, which requires authentication.

Another factor to consider is maintenance complexity. This is lowest in OS virtualization, where there is only one kernel to maintain. For paravirtualization, maintentance is high, as the guest OS must provide paravirtualization support, requiring kernel changes.

For the Joyent public cloud, we prefer OS virtualization (Zones) for the high performance and observability it delivers, as long as our customers' applications can run on SmartOS. We use KVM with paravirtualization when other guest operating systems are needed (Linux, Windows), knowing that performance is likely to be much poorer for I/O-bound workloads. We tried Xen but have replaced it with the Joyent KVM port.

11.5 Exercises

1. Answer the following questions about virtualization terminology:

   - What is the difference between the host and the guest?

   - What is a tenant?

   - What is a hypervisor?

2. Answer the following conceptual questions:

   - Describe the role of performance isolation.

   - Describe the performance overheads with hardware virtualization (either type).

   - Describe the performance overheads with OS virtualization.

   - Describe physical system observability from a hardware-virtualized guest (either type).

   - Describe physical system observability from an OS-virtualized guest.

3. Choose a virtualization technology and answer the following for the guests:

   - Describe how a memory limit is applied, and how it is visible from the guest. (What does the system administrator see when guest memory is exhausted?)

   - If there is an imposed CPU limit, describe how it is applied and how it is visible from the guest.

   - If there is an imposed disk I/O limit, describe how it is applied and how it is visible from the guest.

- If there is an imposed network I/O limit, describe how it is applied and how it is visible from the guest.

4. Develop a USE method checklist for resource controls. Include how to fetch each metric (e.g., which command to execute) and how to interpret the result. Try to use existing OS observability tools before installing or using additional software products.

11.6 References

[Goldberg 73]   Goldberg, R. P. *Architectural Principles for Virtual Computer Systems* (Thesis). Harvard University, 1972.

[Waldspurger 02]   Waldspurger, C. "Memory Resource Management in VMware ESX Server," *Proceedings of the 5th Symposium on Operating Systems Design and Implementation*, 2002.

[Cherkasova 05]   Cherkasova, L., and R. Gardner. "Measuring CPU Overhead for I/O Processing in the Xen Virtual Machine Monitor." USENIX ATEC'05.

[Adams 06]   Adams, K., and O. Agesen. "A Comparison of Software and Hardware Techniques for x86 Virtualization." ASPLOS'06.

[Gupta 06]   Gupta, D., L. Cherkasova, R. Gardner, and A. Vahdat. "Enforcing Performance Isolation across Virtual Machines in Xen." ACM/IFIP/USENIX Middleware'06.

[Cherkasova 07]   Cherkasova, L., D. Gupta, and A. Vahdat. "Comparison of the Three CPU Schedulers in Xen." ACM SIGMETRICS, 2007.

[Matthews 08]   Matthews, J., et al. *Running Xen: A Hands-On Guide to the Art of Virtualization*. Prentice Hall, 2008.

[Adamczyk 12]   Adamczyk, B., and A. Chydzinski. "Performance Isolation Issues in Network Virtualization in Xen," *International Journal on Advances in Networks and Services*, 2012.

[1]   http://highscalability.com/blog/2012/12/12/pinterest-cut-costs-from-54-to-20-per-hour-by-automatically.html

[2]   http://lxc.sourceforge.net

[3]   http://openvz.org

[4]   http://lwn.net/Articles/524952/

[5]   http://illumos.org/man/5/resource_controls

[6]   http://dtrace.org/blogs/brendan/2012/12/19/the-use-method-
            smartos-performance-checklist/

[7]   www.vmware.com/files/pdf/VMware_paravirtualization.pdf

[8]   https://developers.google.com/compute/docs/faq#whatis

[9]   http://corensic.wordpress.com/2011/12/05/virtual-machines-
            virtualizing-virtual-memory/

[10]   http://wiki.xen.org/wiki/Xen_PCI_Passthrough

[11]   *KVM: Kernel-based Virtualization Driver.* Qumranet
            Whitepaper, 2006

[12]   https://github.com/brendangregg/dtrace-cloud-tools

12

Benchmarking

There are lies, damn lies and then there are performance measures.
—Anon et al., "A Measure of Transaction Processing Power" [Anon 85]

Benchmarking tests performance in a controlled manner, allowing choices to be compared and performance limits to be understood—before they are encountered in production. These limits may be system resources, software limits in a virtualized environment (cloud computing), or limits in the target application. Previous chapters have explored these components, describing the types of limits present and the tools used to analyze them.

Previous chapters have also introduced tools for micro-benchmarking, which investigate limits using simple artificial workloads. Other types of benchmarking include client workload simulations, which attempt to replicate a client usage pattern, and trace replays. Whichever type you use, it's important to analyze the benchmark so that you can confirm what is being measured. Benchmarks tell you only how fast the system can run the benchmark; it's up to you to understand the result and determine how it applies to your environment.

This chapter discusses benchmarking in general, providing advice and methodologies to help you avoid common mistakes and accurately test your systems. This is also useful background when you need to interpret the results from others, including vendor and industry benchmarks.

12.1 Background

This section describes benchmarking activities and effective benchmarking and summarizes common mistakes as the "sins of benchmarking."

12.1.1 Activities

Benchmarking may be performed for the following reasons:

- **System design:** comparing different systems, system components, or applications. For commercial products, benchmarking may provide data to aid a purchase decision, specifically the *price/performance* ratio of the available options. In some cases, results from published *industry benchmarks* can be used, which avoids the need for customers to execute the benchmarks themselves.

- **Tuning:** testing tunable parameters and configuration options, to identify those that are worth further investigation with the production workload.

- **Development:** for both *non-regression testing* and *limit investigations* during product development. Non-regression testing may be an automated battery of performance tests that run regularly, so that any performance regression can be discovered early and quickly matched to the product change. For limit investigations, benchmarking can be used to drive products to their limit during development, in order to identify where engineering effort is best spent to improve product performance.

- **Capacity planning:** determining system and application limits for capacity planning, either to provide data for modeling performance, or to find capacity limits directly.

- **Troubleshooting:** to verify that components can still operate at maximum performance, for example, testing maximum network throughput between hosts to check whether there may be a network issue.

- **Marketing:** determining maximum product performance for use by marketing (also called *benchmarketing*).

In enterprise environments, benchmarking during *proof of concepts* can be an important exercise before investing in expensive hardware and may be a process that lasts several weeks. This includes the time to ship, rack, and cable systems, and then to install operating systems before testing.

In cloud computing environments, resources are available on demand, without an expensive initial investment in hardware. These environments still, however, require some investment when choosing which application programming language to use, and which database, web server, and load balancer to run. Some of these choices can be difficult to change down the road. Benchmarking can be performed to investigate how well these choices can scale when required. The cloud computing model also makes benchmarking easy: a large-scale environment can be created in minutes, used for a benchmark run, and then destroyed, all at very little cost.

12.1.2 Effective Benchmarking

Benchmarking is surprisingly difficult to do well, with many opportunities for mistakes and oversights. As summarized by the paper "A Nine Year Study of File System and Storage Benchmarking" [Traeger 08]:

> In this article we survey 415 file system and storage benchmarks from 106 recent papers. We found that most popular benchmarks are flawed and many research papers do not provide a clear indication of true performance.

The paper also makes recommendations for what should be done; in particular, benchmark evaluations should explain *what* was tested and *why*, and they should perform some analysis of the system's expected behavior.

The essence of a good benchmark has also been summarized as [Smaalders 06]

- **Repeatable:** to facilitate comparisons
- **Observable:** so that performance can be analyzed and understood
- **Portable:** to allow benchmarking on competitors and across different product releases
- **Easily presented:** so that everyone can understand the results
- **Realistic:** so that measurements reflect customer-experienced realities
- **Runnable:** so that developers can quickly test changes

Another characteristic must be added when comparing different systems with the intent to purchase: the *price/performance* ratio. The price can be quantified as the five-year capital cost of the equipment [Anon 85].

Effective benchmarking is also about how you apply the benchmark: the analysis and the conclusions drawn.

Benchmark Analysis

When using benchmarks, you need to understand

- What is being tested
- What the limiting factor or factors are

- Any perturbations that might affect the results
- What conclusions may be drawn from the results

These needs require a deep understanding of what the benchmark software is doing, how the system is responding, and how the results relate to the destination environment.

Given a benchmark tool and access to the system that runs it, these needs are best served by performance analysis of the system while the benchmark is running. A common mistake is to have junior staff execute the benchmarks, then to bring in performance experts to explain the results after the benchmark has completed. It is best to engage the performance experts during the benchmark so they can analyze the system while it is still running. This may include drill-down analysis to explain and quantify the limiting factor.

The following is an interesting example of analysis:

> As an experiment to investigate the performance of the resulting TCP/IP implementation, we transmitted 4 Megabytes of data between two user processes on different machines. The transfer was partitioned into 1024 byte records and encapsulated in 1068 byte Ethernet packets. Sending the data from our 11/750 to our 11/780 through TCP/IP takes 28 seconds. This includes all the time needed to set up and tear down the connections, for an user-user throughput of 1.2 Megabaud. During this time the 11/750 is CPU saturated, but the 11/780 has about 30% idle time. The time spent in the system processing the data is spread out among handling for the Ethernet (20%), IP packet processing (10%), TCP processing (30%), checksumming (25%), and user system call handling (15%), with no single part of the handling dominating the time in the system.

This describes checking the limiting factors ("the 11/750 is CPU saturated"[1]), then explains details of the kernel components causing them. As an aside, being able to perform this analysis and summarize kernel time so neatly is an unusual skill today, even with advanced tools such as DTrace. This quote is from Bill Joy while he was developing the original BSD TCP/IP stack in 1981! [1]

Apart from using a given benchmark tool, you may find it more effective to develop your own custom benchmark software, or at least custom load generators. These can be kept short, focusing on only what is needed for your test, making them quick to analyze and debug.

In some cases you don't have access to the benchmark tool or the system, as when reading benchmark results from others. Consider the previous items based on the materials available, and, in addition, ask, What is the system environment? How is it configured? You may be permitted to ask the vendor to answer these questions as well. See Section 12.4, Benchmark Questions, for more vendor questions.

---

1. 11/750 is short for VAX-11/750, a minicomputer manufactured by DEC in 1980.

12.1.3 Benchmarking Sins

The following sections provide a quick checklist of specific issues to avoid, and how to avoid them. Section 12.3, Methodology, describes how to perform benchmarking.

Casual Benchmarking

To do benchmarking well is not a fire-and-forget activity. Benchmark tools provide numbers, but those numbers may not reflect what you think, and your conclusions about them may therefore be bogus.

> Casual benchmarking: you benchmark A, but actually measure B, and conclude you've measured C.

Benchmarking well requires rigor to check what is actually measured and an understanding of what was tested to form valid conclusions.

For example, many tools claim or imply that they measure disk performance but actually test file system performance. The difference between these two can be orders of magnitude, as file systems employ caching and buffering to substitute disk I/O with memory I/O. Even though the benchmark tool may be functioning correctly and testing the file system, your conclusions about the disks will be wildly incorrect.

Understanding benchmarks is particularly difficult for the beginner, who has no instinct for whether numbers are suspicious or not. If you bought a thermometer that showed the temperature of the room you're in as 1,000 degrees Fahrenheit, you'd immediately know that something was amiss. The same isn't true of benchmarks, which produce numbers that are probably unfamiliar to you.

Benchmark Faith

It may be tempting to believe that a popular benchmarking tool is trustworthy, especially if it is open source and has been around for a long time. The misconception that popularity equals validity is known as *argumentum ad populum* logic (Latin for "appeal to the people").

Analyzing the benchmarks you're using is time-consuming and requires expertise to perform properly. And, for a popular benchmark, it may seem wasteful to analyze what *surely* must be valid.

The problem isn't even necessarily with the benchmark software—although bugs do happen—but with the interpretation of the benchmark's results.

Numbers without Analysis

Bare benchmark results, provided with no analytical details, can be a sign that the author is inexperienced and has assumed that the benchmark results are trustworthy and final. Often, this is just the beginning of an investigation, and one that finds the results were wrong or confusing.

Every benchmark number should be accompanied by a description of the limit encountered and the analysis performed. I've summarized the risk this way:

> If you've spent less than a week studying a benchmark result, it's probably wrong.

Much of this book focuses on analyzing performance, which should be carried out during benchmarking. In cases where you don't have time for careful analysis, it is a good idea to list the assumptions that you haven't had time to check and include them with the results, for example:

- Assuming the benchmark tool isn't buggy
- Assuming the disk I/O test actually measures disk I/O
- Assuming the benchmark tool drove disk I/O to its limit, as intended
- Assuming this type of disk I/O is relevant for this application

This can become a to-do list, if the benchmark result is later deemed important enough to spend more effort on.

Complex Benchmark Tools

It is important that the benchmark tool not hinder benchmark analysis by its own complexity. Ideally, the program is open source so that it can be studied, and short enough that it can be read and understood quickly.

For micro-benchmarks, it is recommended to pick those written in the C programming language. For client simulation benchmarks, it is recommended to use the same programming language as the client, to minimize differences.

A common problem is one of *benchmarking the benchmark*—where the result reported is limited by the benchmark software itself. Complex benchmarks suites can make this difficult to identify, due to the sheer volume of code to comprehend and analyze.

Testing the Wrong Thing

While there are numerous benchmark tools available to test a variety of workloads, many of them may not be relevant for the target application.

For example, a common mistake is to test disk performance—based on the availability of disk benchmark tools—even though the target environment workload is expected to run entirely out of file system cache and not be related to disk I/O.

Similarly, an engineering team developing a product may standardize on a particular benchmark and spend all its performance efforts improving performance as measured by that benchmark. If it doesn't actually resemble customer workloads, however, the engineering effort will optimize for the wrong behavior [Smaalders 06].

A benchmark may have tested an appropriate workload once upon a time but hasn't been updated for years and so is now testing the wrong thing. The article "Eulogy for a Benchmark" describes how a version of the SPEC SFS industry benchmark, commonly cited during the 2000s, was based on a customer usage study from 1986 [2].

Ignoring Errors

Just because a benchmark tool produces a result doesn't mean the result reflects a *successful* test. Some—or even all—of the requests may have resulted in an error. While this issue is covered by the previous sins, this one in particular is so common that it's worth singling out.

I was reminded of this during a recent benchmark of web server performance. Those running the test reported that the average latency of the web server was too high for their needs: over one second, *on average*. Some quick analysis determined what went wrong: the web server did nothing at all during the test, as all requests were blocked by a firewall. *All* requests. The latency shown was the time it took for the benchmark client to time-out and error.

Ignoring Variance

Benchmark tools, especially micro-benchmarks, often apply a steady and consistent workload, based on the *average* of a series of measurements of real-world characteristics, such as at different times of day or during an interval. For example, a disk workload may be found to have average rates of 500 reads/s and 50 writes/s. A benchmark tool may then either simulate this rate, or simulate the ratio of 10:1 reads/writes, so that higher rates can be tested.

This approach ignores *variance*: the rate of operations may be variable. The types of operations may also vary, and some types may occur orthogonally. For example, writes may be applied in bursts every 10 s (asynchronous write-back data flushing), whereas synchronous reads are steady. Bursts of writes may cause real issues in production, such as by queueing the reads, but are not simulated if the benchmark applies steady average rates.

Ignoring Perturbations

Consider what external perturbations may be affecting results. Will a timed system activity, such as a system backup, execute during the benchmark run? For the cloud, a perturbation may be caused by unseen tenants on the same system.

A common strategy for ironing out perturbations is to make the benchmark runs longer—minutes instead of seconds. As a rule, the duration of a benchmark should not be shorter than one second. Short tests might be unusually perturbed by device interrupts (pinning the thread while performing interrupt service routines), kernel CPU scheduling decisions (waiting before migrating queued threads to preserve CPU affinity), and CPU cache warmth effects. Try running the benchmark test several times and examining the standard deviation. This should be as small as possible, to ensure repeatability.

Also collect data so that perturbations, if present, can be studied. This might include collecting the distribution of operation latency—not just the total runtime for the benchmark—so that outliers can be seen and their details recorded.

Changing Multiple Factors

When comparing benchmark results from two tests, be careful to understand all the factors that are different between the two.

For example, if two hosts are benchmarked over the network, is the network between them identical? What if one host was more hops away, over a slower network, or over a more congested network? Any such extra factors could make the benchmark result bogus.

In the cloud, benchmarks are sometimes performed by creating instances, testing them, and then destroying them. This creates the potential for many unseen factors: instances may be created on faster or slower systems, or on systems with higher load and contention from other tenants. It is recommended to test multiple instances and take the average (or better, record the distribution) to avoid outliers caused by testing one unusually fast or slow system.

Benchmarking the Competition

Your marketing department would like benchmark results showing how your product beats the competition. This is usually a bad idea, for reasons I'm about to explain.

When customers pick a product, they don't use it for 5 minutes; they use it for months. During that time, they analyze and tune the product for performance, perhaps shaking out the worst issues in the first few weeks.

You don't have a few weeks to spend analyzing and tuning your *competitor*. In the time available, you can only gather untuned—and therefore unrealistic—results. The customers of your competitor—the target of this marketing activity—may well see that you've posted untuned results, so your company loses credibility with the very people it was trying to impress.

If you must benchmark the competition, you'll want to spend serious time tuning their product. Analyze performance using the techniques described in earlier chapters. Also search for best practices, customer forums, and bug databases. You may even want to bring in outside expertise to tune the system. Then make the same effort for your own company before you finally perform head-to-head benchmarks.

Friendly Fire

When benchmarking your own products, make every effort to ensure that the top-performing system and configuration have been tested, and that the system has been driven to its true limit. Share the results with the engineering team before publication; they may spot configuration items that you have missed. And if you are on the engineering team, be on the lookout for benchmark efforts—either from your company or from contracted third parties—and help them out.

Consider this hypothetical situation: An engineering team has worked hard to develop a high-performing product. Key to its performance is a new technology that they have developed that has yet to be documented. For the product launch, a benchmark team has been asked to provide the numbers. They don't understand the new technology (it isn't documented), they misconfigure it, and then they publish numbers that undersell the product.

Sometimes the system may be configured correctly but simply hasn't been pushed to its limit. Ask the question, What is the bottleneck for this benchmark? This may be a physical resource, such as CPUs, disks, or an interconnect, that has been driven to 100% and can be identified using analysis. See Section 12.3.2, Active Benchmarking.

Another friendly fire issue is when benchmarking older versions of the software that has performance issues that were fixed in later versions, or on limited equipment that happens to be available, producing a result that is not the best possible (as may be expected by a company benchmark).

Misleading Benchmarks

Misleading benchmark results are common in the industry. Often they are a result of either unintentionally limited information about what the benchmark actually measures or deliberately omitted information. Often the benchmark result is technically correct but is then misrepresented to the customer.

Consider this hypothetical situation: A vendor achieves a fantastic result by building a custom product that is prohibitively expensive and would never be sold to an actual customer. The price is not disclosed with the benchmark result, which focuses on non–price/performance metrics. The marketing department liberally shares an ambiguous summary of the result ("We are 2x faster!"), associating it in customers' minds with either the company in general or a product line. This is a case of omitting details in order to favorably misrepresent products. While it may not be cheating—the numbers are not fake—it is *lying by omission*.

Such vendor benchmarks may still be useful for you as upper bounds for performance. They are values that you should not expect to exceed (with an exception for cases of friendly fire).

Consider this different hypothetical situation: A marketing department has a budget to spend on a campaign and wants a good benchmark result to use. They engage several third parties to benchmark their product and pick the best result from the group. These third parties are not picked for their expertise; they are picked to deliver a fast and inexpensive result. In fact, non-expertise might be considered advantageous: the greater the results deviate from reality, the better. Ideally one of them deviates greatly in a positive direction!

When using vendor results, be careful to check the fine print for what system was tested, what disk types were used and how many, what network interfaces were used and in which configuration, and other factors. For specifics to be wary of, see Section 12.4, Benchmark Questions.

Benchmark Specials

A type of sneaky activity—which in the eyes of some is considered a sin and thus prohibited—is the development of *benchmark specials*. This is when the vendor studies a popular or industry benchmark, and then engineers the product so that it scores well, while disregarding actual customer performance. This is also called *optimizing for the benchmark*.

The notion of benchmark specials became known in 1993 with the TPC-A benchmark, as described on the Transaction Processing Performance Council (TPC) history page [3]:

> The Standish Group, a Massachusetts-based consulting firm, charged that Oracle had added a special option (discrete transactions) to its database software, with the sole purpose of inflating Oracle's TPC-A results. The Standish Group claimed that Oracle had "violated the spirit of the TPC" because the discrete transaction option was something a typical customer wouldn't use and was, therefore, a benchmark special. Oracle vehemently rejected the accusation, stating, with some justification, that they had followed the letter of the law in the benchmark specifications. Oracle argued that since benchmark specials, much less the spirit of the TPC, were not addressed in the TPC benchmark specifications, it was unfair to accuse them of violating anything.

TPC added an anti-benchmark special clause:

> All "benchmark special" implementations that improve benchmark results but not real-world performance or pricing, are prohibited.

As TPC is focused on price/performance, another strategy to inflate numbers can be to base them on *special pricing*—deep discounts that no customer would actually get. Like special software changes, the result doesn't match reality when a real customer purchases the system. TPC has addressed this in its price requirements [4]:

> TPC specifications require that the total price must be within 2% of the price a customer would pay for the configuration.

While these examples may help explain the notion of benchmark specials, TPC addressed them in its specifications many years ago, and you shouldn't necessarily expect them today.

Cheating

The last sin of benchmarking is cheating: sharing fake results. Fortunately, this is either rare or nonexistent; I've not seen a case of purely made-up numbers being shared, even in the most bloodthirsty of benchmarking battles.

12.2 Benchmarking Types

A spectrum of benchmark types is pictured in Figure 12.1, based on the workload they test. The production workload is also included in the spectrum.

Figure 12-1 Benchmark types

The following sections describe the three benchmarking types: micro-benchmarks, simulations, and trace/replay. Industry-standard benchmarks are also discussed.

12.2.1 Micro-Benchmarking

Micro-benchmarking uses artificial workloads that test a particular type of operation, for example, performing a single type of file system I/O, database query, CPU instruction, or system call. The advantage is the simplicity: narrowing the number of components and code paths involved results in an easier target to study and allows performance differences to be root-caused quickly. Tests are also usually repeatable, because variation from other components is factored out as much as possible. Micro-benchmarks are also usually quick to test on different systems. And because they are deliberately artificial, micro-benchmarks are not easily confused with real workload simulations.

For micro-benchmark results to be consumed, they need to be mapped to the target workload. A micro-benchmark may test several dimensions, but only one or two may be relevant. Performance analysis or modeling of the target system can help determine which micro-benchmark results are appropriate, and to what degree.

Example micro-benchmark tools mentioned in previous chapters include, by resource type,

- **CPU:** UnixBench, SysBench
- **Memory I/O:** lmbench (in Chapter 6, CPUs)
- **File system:** Bonnie, Bonnie++, SysBench, fio
- **Disk:** hdparm
- **Network:** iperf

There are many, many more benchmark tools available. However, remember the warning from [Traeger 08]: "Most popular benchmarks are flawed."

You can also develop your own. Aim to keep them as simple as possible, identifying attributes of the workload that can be tested individually. (See Section 12.3.6, Custom Benchmarks, for more about this.)

Design Example

Consider designing a file system micro-benchmark to test the following attributes: sequential or random I/O, I/O size, and direction (read or write). Table 12.1 shows five sample tests to investigate these dimensions, along with the reason for each test.

Table 12-1 Sample File System Micro-Benchmark Tests

#	Test	Intent
1	sequential 512-byte reads	to test maximum (realistic) IOPS
2	sequential 128-Kbyte reads	to test maximum read throughput
3	sequential 128-Kbyte writes	to test maximum write throughput
4	random 512-byte reads	to test the effect of random I/O
5	random 512-byte writes	to test the effect of rewrites

More tests can be added as desired. All of these tests are multiplied by two additional factors:

- **Working set size:** the size of the data being accessed (e.g., total file size):
  - Much smaller than main memory: so that the data caches entirely in the file system cache, and the performance of the file system software can be investigated
  - Much larger than main memory: to minimize the effect of the file system cache and drive the benchmark toward testing disk I/O
- **Thread count:** assuming a small working set size:
  - Single-threaded to test file system performance based on the current CPU clock speed
  - Multithreaded—sufficient to saturate all CPUs—to test the maximum performance of the system: file system and CPUs

These can quickly multiply to form a large matrix of tests. There are statistical analysis techniques to reduce the required set to test.

Creating benchmarks that focus on top speeds has been called *sunny day* performance testing. So that issues are not overlooked, you also want to consider *cloudy day* performance testing, which involves testing nonideal situations, including contention, perturbations, and workload variance.

12.2.2 Simulation

Many benchmarks simulate customer application workloads (and are sometimes called *macro-benchmarks*). These may be based on workload characterization of the production environment (see Chapter 2, Methodology) to determine the characteristics to simulate. For example, it may be found that a production NFS workload is composed of the following operation types and probabilities: reads, 40%; writes, 7%; getattr, 19%; readdir, 1%; and so on. Other characteristics can also be measured and simulated.

Simulations can produce results that resemble how clients will perform with the real-world workload, if not closely, at least close enough to be useful. They can encompass many factors that would be time-consuming to investigate using micro-benchmarking. Simulations can also include the effects of complex system interactions that may be missed altogether when using micro-benchmarks.

The CPU benchmarks Whetstone and Dhrystone, introduced in Chapter 6, CPUs, are examples of simulations. Whetstone was developed in 1972 to simulate scientific workloads of the time. Dhrystone, from 1984, simulates integer-based workloads of the time. The SPEC SFS benchmark, mentioned earlier, is another workload simulation.

A workload simulation may be *stateless*, where each server request is unrelated to the previous request. For example, the NFS server workload described previously may be simulated by requesting a series of operations, with each operation type chosen randomly based on the measured probability.

A simulation may also be *stateful*, where each request is dependent on client state, at minimum the previous request. It may be found that NFS reads and writes tend to arrive in groups, such that the probability of a write when the previous operation was a write is much higher than if it were a read. Such a workload can be better simulated using a *Markov model*, by representing requests as states and measuring the probability of state transitions [Jain 91].

A problem with simulations is that they can ignore variance, as described in Section 12.1.3, Benchmarking Sins. Customer usage patterns can also change over time, requiring these simulations to be updated and adjusted to stay relevant. There may be resistance to this, however, if there are already published results based on the older benchmark version, which would no longer be usable for comparisons with the new version.

12.2.3 Replay

A third type of benchmarking involves attempting to replay a trace log to the target, testing its performance with the actual captured client operations. This sounds ideal—as good as testing in production, right? It is, however, problematic: when characteristics and delivered latency change on the server, the captured client workload is unlikely to respond naturally to these differences, which may prove no better than a simulated customer workload. When too much faith is placed in it, it can be worse.

Consider this hypothetical situation: A customer is considering upgrading storage infrastructure. The current production workload is traced and replayed on the new hardware. Unfortunately, performance is worse, and the sale is lost. The problem: the trace/replay operated at the disk I/O level. The old system housed 10 K rpm disks, and the new system houses slower 7,200 rpm disks. However, the new system provides 16 times the amount of file system cache and faster processors. The actual production workload would have improved, as it would have returned largely from cache—which was not simulated by replaying disk events.

While this is a case of testing the wrong thing, other subtle timing effects can mess things up, even with the correct level of trace/replay. As with all benchmarks, it is crucial to analyze and understand what's going on.

12.2.4 Industry Standards

Industry-standard benchmarks are available from independent organizations, which aim to create fair and relevant benchmarks. These are usually a collection of different micro-benchmarks and workload simulations that are well defined and documented and must be executed under certain guidelines so that the results are as intended. Vendors may participate (usually for a fee), which provides the vendor with the software to execute the benchmark. Their result usually requires full disclosure of the configured environment, which may be audited.

For the customer, these benchmarks can save a lot of time, as benchmark results may already be available for a variety of vendors and products. The task for you, then, is to find the benchmark that most closely resembles your future or current production workload. For current workloads, this may be determined by workload characterization.

The need for industry-standard benchmarks was made clear by a 1985 paper titled "A Measure of Transaction Processing Power" by Jim Gray and others [Anon 85]. It described the need to measure price/performance ratio and detailed three benchmarks that vendors could execute, called Sort, Scan, and DebitCredit. It also suggested an industry-standard measure of transactions per second (TPS), based on DebitCredit, which could be used much like miles per gallon for cars. Jim Gray and his work later encouraged the creation of the TPC [DeWitt 08].

Apart from the TPS measure, others that have been used for the same role include

- **MIPS:** millions of instructions per second. While this is *a* measure of performance, the work that is performed depends on the type of instruction, which may be difficult to compare between different processor architectures.

- **FLOPS:** floating-point operations per second—a similar role to MIPS, but for workloads that make heavy use of floating-point calculations.

Industry benchmarks typically measure a custom metric based on the benchmark, which serves only for comparisons with itself.

TPC

The TPC creates and administers various industry benchmarks, with a focus on database performance. These include

- **TPC-C:** a simulation of a complete computing environment where a population of users executes transactions against a database.

- **TPC-DS:** a simulation of a decision support system, including queries and data maintenance.
- **TPC-E:** an online transaction processing (OLTP) workload, modeling a brokerage firm database with customers who generate transactions related to trades, account inquiries, and market research.
- **TPC-H:** a decision support benchmark, simulating ad hoc queries and concurrent data modifications.
- **TPC-VMS:** The TPC Virtual Measurement Single System allows other benchmarks to be gathered for virtualized databases.

TPC results are shared online [5] and include price/performance.

SPEC

The Standard Performance Evaluation Corporation (SPEC) develops and publishes a standardized set of industry benchmarks, including

- **SPEC CPU2006:** a measure of compute-intensive workloads. This includes CINT2006 for integer performance, and CFP2006 for floating-point performance.
- **SPECjEnterprise2010:** a measure of full-system performance for Java Enterprise Edition (Java EE) 5 or later application servers, databases, and supporting infrastructure.
- **SPECsfs2008:** a simulation of a client file access workload for NFS and common Internet file system (CIFS) servers (see [2]).
- **SPECvirt_sc2010:** For virtualized environments, this measures the performance of the virtualized hardware, the platform, and the guest operating system and application software.

SPEC's results are shared online [6] and include details of how systems were tuned and a list of components, but not usually price.

12.3 Methodology

This section describes methodologies and exercises for performing benchmarking, whether micro-benchmarking, simulations, or replays. The topics are summarized in Table 12.2.

Table 12-2 Benchmark Analysis Methodologies

Methodology	Types
Passive benchmarking	experimental analysis
Active benchmarking	observational analysis
CPU profiling	observational analysis
USE method	observational analysis
Workload characterization	observational analysis
Custom benchmarks	software development
Ramping load	experimental analysis
Sanity check	observational analysis
Statistical analysis	statistical analysis

12.3.1 Passive Benchmarking

This is the fire-and-forget strategy of benchmarking—where the benchmark is executed and then ignored until it has completed. The main objective is the collection of benchmark data. This is how benchmarks are commonly executed and is described as its own methodology for comparison with active benchmarking.

These are some example passive benchmarking steps:

1. Pick a benchmark tool.
2. Run it with a variety of options.
3. Make a slide deck of the results.
4. Hand the slides to management.

Problems with this approach have been discussed previously. In summary, the results may be

- Invalid due to benchmark software bugs
- Limited by the benchmark software (e.g., single-threaded)
- Limited by a component that is unrelated to the benchmark target (e.g., a congested network)
- Limited by configuration (performance features not enabled, not a maximum configuration)
- Subject to perturbations (and not repeatable)
- Benchmarking the wrong thing entirely

Passive benchmarking is easy to perform but prone to errors. When performed by the vendor, it can create false alarms that waste engineering resources or cause lost sales. When performed by the customer, it can result in poor product choices that haunt the company later on.

12.3.2 Active Benchmarking

With active benchmarking, you analyze performance while the benchmark is running—not just after it's done—using other tools. You can confirm that the benchmark tests what it says it tests, and that you understand what that is. Active benchmarking can also identify the true limiters of the system under test, or of the benchmark itself. It can be very helpful to include specific details of the limit encountered when sharing the benchmark results.

As a bonus, this can be a good time to develop your skills with performance observability tools. In theory, you are examining a *known load* and can see how it appears from these tools.

Ideally, the benchmark can be configured and left running in steady state, so that analysis can be performed over a period of hours or days.

Example

As an example, let's look at the first test of the Bonnie++ micro-benchmark tool. It is described on its home page [7]:

Bonnie++ is a benchmark suite that is aimed at performing a number of simple tests of hard drive and file system performance.

The first test is "Sequential Output" and "Per Chr" and was executed on two different operating systems for comparison.
Fedora/Linux (under KVM virtualization):

```
# bonnie++
[...]
Version 1.03e       ------Sequential Output------ --Sequential Input- --Random-
                    -Per Chr- --Block-- -Rewrite- -Per Chr- --Block-- --Seeks--
Machine        Size K/sec %CP K/sec %CP K/sec %CP K/sec %CP K/sec %CP  /sec %CP
9d219ce8-cf52-40 2G 52384  23 47334   3 31938   3 74866  67 1009669  61 +++++ +++
[...]
```

SmartOS/illumos (under OS virtualization):

```
# bonnie++
Version 1.03e       ------Sequential Output------ --Sequential Input- --Random-
                    -Per Chr- --Block-- -Rewrite- -Per Chr- --Block-- --Seeks--
```

```
Machine        Size K/sec %CP K/sec %CP K/sec %CP K/sec %CP K/sec %CP  /sec %CP
smartos1.local  2G 162464  99 72027  86 65222  99 251249  99 2426619  99 +++++ +++
[...]
```

So SmartOS is 3.1x faster. If we were to stop right here, that would be *passive benchmarking*.

Given that Bonnie++ is a "hard drive and file system performance" benchmark, we can begin by checking the workload that was performed.

Running `iostat(1M)` on SmartOS to check disk I/O:

```
$ iostat -xnz 1
[...]
    r/s    w/s   kr/s   kw/s wait actv wsvc_t asvc_t   %w  %b device
                      extended device statistics
    r/s    w/s   kr/s   kw/s wait actv wsvc_t asvc_t   %w  %b device
                      extended device statistics
    r/s    w/s   kr/s   kw/s wait actv wsvc_t asvc_t   %w  %b device
    0.0  668.9    0.0 82964.3  0.0  6.0    0.0    8.9    1  60 c0t1d0
                      extended device statistics
    r/s    w/s   kr/s   kw/s wait actv wsvc_t asvc_t   %w  %b device
    0.0  419.0    0.0 53514.5  0.0 10.0    0.0   23.8    0 100 c0t1d0
[...]
```

The disks begin idle, then show variable write throughput during the benchmark (`kw/s`), at a rate much lower than what Bonnie++ reported as its `K/sec` result.

Running `vfsstat(1M)` on SmartOS to check file system I/O (VFS-level):

```
$ vfsstat 1
  r/s    w/s  kr/s  kw/s ractv wactv read_t writ_t  %r %w    d/s del_t zone
[...]
 45.3 1514.7   4.5 193877.3  0.0  0.1    0.0    0.0   0  6  412.4   5.5 b8b2464c
 45.3 1343.6   4.5 171979.4  0.0  0.1    0.0    0.1   0  7 1343.6  14.0 b8b2464c
 45.3 1224.8   4.5 156776.9  0.0  0.1    0.0    0.1   0  6 1157.9  12.2 b8b2464c
 45.3 1224.8   4.5 156776.9  0.0  0.1    0.0    0.1   0  6 1157.9  12.2 b8b2464c
```

Now the throughput is consistent with the Bonnie++ result. The IOPS, however, are not: `vfsstat(1M)` shows the writes are about 128 Kbytes each (`kw/s` / `w/s`), and not "Per Chr."

Using `truss(1)` on SmartOS to investigate the writes to the file system (ignoring the overhead of `truss(1)` for the moment):

```
write(4, "\001020304050607\b\t\n\v".., 131072) = 131072
write(4, "\001020304050607\b\t\n\v".., 131072) = 131072
write(4, "\001020304050607\b\t\n\v".., 131072) = 131072
```

This confirms that Bonnie++ is performing 128 Kbyte file system writes.

Using `strace(1)` on Fedora for comparison:

```
write(3, "\0\1\2\3\4\5\6\7\10\t\n\v\f\r\16\17\20\21\22\23\24"..., 4096) = 4096
write(3, "\0\1\2\3\4\5\6\7\10\t\n\v\f\r\16\17\20\21\22\23\24"..., 4096) = 4096
write(3, "\0\1\2\3\4\5\6\7\10\t\n\v\f\r\16\17\20\21\22\23\24"..., 4096) = 4096
```

This shows that Fedora is performing 4 Kbyte file system writes, whereas SmartOS was performing 128 Kbyte writes.

With more analysis (using DTrace), this was seen to be buffering of `putc()` in the system library, with each operating system defaulting to a different buffering size. As an experiment, Bonnie++ on Fedora was adjusted to use a 128 Kbyte buffer (using `setbuffer()`), which improved its performance by 18%.

Active performance analysis determined various other characteristics of how this test was performed, providing a better understanding of the result [8]. The conclusion was that it was ultimately limited by single-threaded CPU speed and spent 85% of its CPU time in user mode.

Bonnie++ is not an unusually bad benchmark tool; it has served people well on many occasions. I picked it for this example (and also chose the most suspicious of its tests to study) because it's well known, I've studied it before, and findings like this are not uncommon. But it is just one example.

It should be noted that a newer experimental version of Bonnie++ has changed the "Per Chr" test to actually perform 1-byte file system I/O. Comparing results between different Bonnie++ versions, for this test, will show significant differences. For more about Bonnie++ performance analysis, see the article by Roch Bourbonnais on "Decoding Bonnie++" [9].

12.3.3 CPU Profiling

CPU profiling of both the benchmark target and the benchmark software is worth singling out as a methodology, because it can result in some quick discoveries. It is often performed as part of an active benchmarking investigation.

The intent is to quickly check what all the software is doing, to see if anything interesting shows up. This can also narrow your study to the software components that matter the most: those in play for the benchmark.

Both user- and kernel-level stacks can be profiled. User-level CPU profiling was introduced in Chapter 5, Applications. Both were covered in Chapter 6, CPUs, with examples in Section 6.6, Analysis, including flame graphs.

Example

A disk micro-benchmark was performed on a proposed new system with some disappointing results: disk throughput was worse than on the old system. I was asked to find out what was wrong, with the expectation that either the disks or the disk controller was inferior and should be upgraded.

I began with the USE method (Chapter 2, Methodology) and found that the disks were not very busy, despite that being the point of the benchmark test. There was some CPU usage, in system-time (the kernel).

For a disk benchmark, you might not expect the CPUs to be an interesting target for analysis. Given some CPU usage in the kernel, I thought it was worth a quick check to see if anything interesting showed up, even though I didn't expect it to. I profiled and generated the flame graph shown in Figure 12.2.

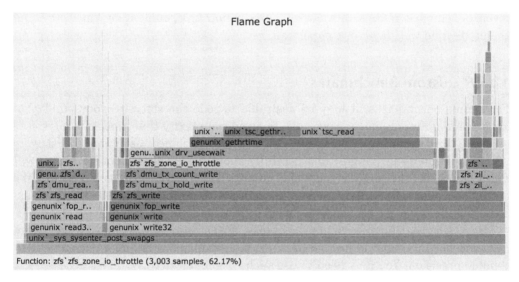

Figure 12-2 Flame graph profiling of kernel-time

Browsing the stack frames showed that 62.17% of CPU samples included a function called `zfs_zone_io_throttle()`. I didn't need to read the code for this function, as its name was enough of a clue: a resource control, ZFS I/O throttling, was active and *artificially* throttling the benchmark! This was a default setting on the new system (but not the older system) and had been overlooked when the benchmark was performed.

12.3.4 USE Method

The USE method was introduced in Chapter 2, Methodology, and is described in chapters for the resources it studies. Applying the USE method during benchmarking can ensure that a limit is found. Either some component, hardware or software, has reached 100% utilization, or you are not driving the system to its limit.

An example of using the USE method was described in Section 12.3.2, Active Benchmarking, where it helped discover that a disk benchmark was not working as intended.

12.3.5 Workload Characterization

Workload characterization was also introduced in Chapter 2, Methodology, and discussed in later chapters. This methodology can be used to determine how well a given benchmark relates to a current production environment by characterizing the production workload for comparison.

12.3.6 Custom Benchmarks

For simple benchmarks, it may be desirable to code the software yourself. Try to keep the program as short as possible, to avoid complexity that hinders analysis.

The C programming language is usually a good choice, as it maps closely to what is executed—although think carefully about how compiler optimizations will affect your code: the compiler may elide simple benchmark routines if it thinks the output is unused and therefore unnecessary to calculate. It may be worth disassembling the compiled binary to see what will actually be executed.

Languages that involve virtual machines, asynchronous garbage collection, and dynamic runtime compilation can be much more difficult to debug and control with reliable precision. You may need to use such languages anyway, if it is necessary to simulate client software written in them.

Writing custom benchmarks can also reveal subtle details about the target that can prove useful later on. For example, when developing a database benchmark, you may discover that the API supports various options for improving performance that are not currently in use in the production environment, which was developed before the options existed.

Your software may simply generate load (a *load generator*) and leave the measurements for other tools. One way to perform this is to *ramp load*.

12.3.7 Ramping Load

This is a simple method for determining the maximum throughput a system can handle. In involves adding load in small increments and measuring the delivered throughput until a limit is reached. The results can be graphed, showing a scalability profile.

This profile can be studied visually or by using scalability models (see Chapter 2, Methodology).

As an example, Figure 12.3 shows how a file system and system scale with threads. Each thread performs 8 Kbyte random reads on a cached file, and these were added one by one.

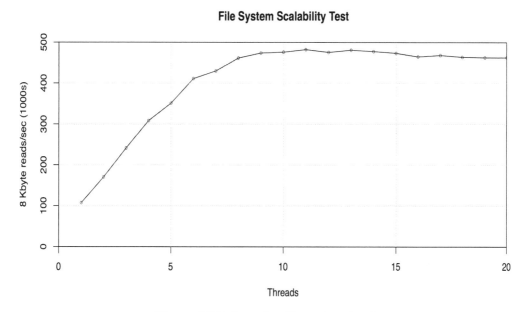

Figure 12-3 Ramping file system load

This system peaked at almost half a million reads per second. The results were checked using VFS-level statistics, which confirmed that the I/O size was 8 Kbytes, and that at peak over 3.5 Gbytes/s was transferred.

The load generator for this test was written in Perl and is short enough to include entirely as an example:

```perl
#!/usr/bin/perl -w
#
# randread.pl - randomly read over specified file.

use strict;

my $IOSIZE = 8192;                      # size of I/O, bytes
my $QUANTA = $IOSIZE;                    # seek granularity, bytes

die "USAGE: randread.pl filename\n" if @ARGV != 1 or not -e $ARGV[0];
```

continues

```
my $file = $ARGV[0];
my $span = -s $file;                    # span to randomly read, bytes
my $junk;

open FILE, "$file" or die "ERROR: reading $file: $!\n";

while (1) {
        seek(FILE, int(rand($span / $QUANTA)) * $QUANTA, 0);
        sysread(FILE, $junk, $IOSIZE);
}

close FILE;
```

This uses sysread() to call the read() syscall directly and avoid buffering.

This was written to micro-benchmark an NFS server and was executed in parallel from a farm of clients, each performing random reads on an NFS-mounted file. The results of the micro-benchmark (reads per second) were measured on the NFS server, using nfsstat(1M) and other tools.

The number of files used and their combined size were controlled (this forms the *working set size*), so that some tests could return entirely from cache, and others from disk. (See Design Example in Section 12.2.1, Micro-Benchmarking.)

The number of instances executing on the client farm was incremented one by one, to ramp up the load until a limit was reached. This was also graphed to study the scalability profile, along with resource utilization (USE method), confirming that a resource had been exhausted. In this case it was CPU resources, which initiated another investigation to improve performance further.

I used this program and this approach to find the limits in the Oracle ZFS Storage Appliance (formally the Sun ZFS Storage Appliance [10]). These limits were used as the official results—which to the best of our knowledge set world records. I also had a similar set of software written in C, but it wasn't needed in this case: I had an abundance of client CPUs, and while the switch to C reduced their utilization, it didn't make a difference for the result as the same bottleneck was reached on the target. Other, more sophisticated benchmarks were also tried, as well as other languages, but they could not improve upon these results.

When following this approach, measure latency as well as the throughput, especially the latency distribution. Once the system approaches its limit, queueing delays may become significant, causing latency to increase. If you push load too high, latency may become so high that it is no longer reasonable to consider the result as valid. Ask yourself if the delivered latency would be acceptable to a customer.

For example: You use a large array of clients to drive a target system to 990,000 IOPS, which responds with an average I/O latency of 5 ms. You'd really like it to break 1 million IOPS, but the system is already reaching saturation. By adding more and more clients, you manage to scrape past 1 million IOPS; however, all operations are now heavily queued, with average latency of over 50 ms (which is not acceptable)! Which result do you give marketing? (Answer: 990,000 IOPS.)

12.3.8 Sanity Check

This is an exercise for checking a benchmark result by investigating whether any characteristic doesn't make sense. It includes checking whether the result would have required some component to exceed its known limits, such as network bandwidth, controller bandwidth, interconnect bandwidth, or disk IOPS. If any limit has been exceeded, it is worth investigating in more detail. In most cases, this exercise ultimately discovers that the benchmark result is bogus.

Here's an example: An NFS server is benchmarked with 8 Kbyte reads and is reported to deliver 50,000 IOPS. It is connected to the network using a single 1 Gbit/s Ethernet port. The network throughput required to drive 50,000 IOPS x 8 Kbytes = 400,000 Kbytes/s, plus protocol headers. This is over 3.2 Gbits/s—well in excess of the 1 Gbit/s known limit. Something is wrong!

Results like this usually mean the benchmark has tested *client caching* and not driven the entire workload to the NFS server.

I've used this calculation to identify numerous bogus benchmarks, which have included the following throughputs over a 1 Gbit/s interface [11]:

- 120 Mbytes/s
- 200 Mbytes/s
- 350 Mbytes/s
- 800 Mbytes/s
- 1.15 Gbytes/s

These are all throughputs in a single direction. The 120 Mbyte/s result may be fine—a 1 Gbit/s interface should reach around 119 Mbytes/s. The 200 Mbyte/s result is possible only if there was heavy traffic in both directions and this was summed; however, these are single-direction results. The 350 Mbyte/s and beyond results are bogus.

When you're given a benchmark result to check, look for what simple sums you can perform on the provided numbers to discover such limits.

If you have access to the system, it may be possible to further test results by constructing new observations or experiments. This can follow the scientific method: the question you're testing now is whether the benchmark result is valid. From this, hypotheses and predictions may be drawn and then tested for verification.

12.3.9 Statistical Analysis

Statistical analysis is a process for the collection and study of benchmark data. It follows three phases:

1. **Selection** of the benchmark tool, its configuration, and system performance metrics to capture
2. **Execution** of the benchmark, collecting a large dataset of results and metrics
3. **Interpretation** of the data with statistical analysis, producing a report

Unlike active benchmarking, which focuses on analysis of the system while the benchmark is running, statistical analysis focuses on analyzing the results. It is also different from passive benchmarking, in which no analysis is performed at all.

This approach is used in environments where access to a large-scale system may be both time-limited and expensive. For example, there may be only one "max config" system available, but many teams want access to run tests at the same time, including

- **Sales:** during proof of concepts, to run a simulated customer load to show what the max config system can deliver
- **Marketing:** to get the best numbers for a marketing campaign
- **Support:** to investigate pathologies that arise only on the max config system, under serious load
- **Engineering:** to test the performance of new features and code changes
- **Quality:** to perform non-regression testing and certifications

Each team may have only a limited time to run its benchmarks on the system, but much more time to analyze the results afterward.

As the collection of metrics is expensive, make an extra effort to ensure that they are reliable and trustworthy, to avoid having to redo them later if a problem is found. Apart from checking how they are generated technically, you can also collect more statistical properties so that problems can be found sooner. These may include statistics for variation, full distributions, error margins, and others (see Section 2.8, Statistics, in Chapter 2, Methodology). When benchmarking for code changes or non-regression testing, it is crucial to understand the variation and error margins, in order to make sense of a pair of results.

Also collect as much performance data as possible from the running system (without harming the result due to the collection overhead), so that forensic analysis can be performed afterward on this data. Data collection may include the use of

tools such as `sar(1)`, third-party products, and custom tools that
tics available.

For example, on **Linux**, a custom shell script may copy the cor
statistic files before and after the run. Everything possible can be included, in case
it is needed. Such a script may also be executed at intervals during the benchmark, provided the performance overhead is acceptable. Other statistical tools may
also be used to create logs.

On **Solaris**-based systems, `kstat -p` can be used to dump all kernel statistics,
which can be recorded before and after the run and also at intervals. This output is
easy to parse and can be imported into a database for advanced analysis.

Statistical analysis of results and metrics can include *scalability analysis* and
queueing theory to model the system as a network of queues. These topics were
introduced in Chapter 2, Methodology, and are the subject of separate texts ([Jain
91], [Gunther 97], [Gunther 07]).

12.4 Benchmark Questions

If a vendor gives you a benchmark result, there are a number of questions you can
ask to better understand and apply it to your environment. The goal is to determine what is really being measured and how realistic or repeatable the result is.

The hardest question may be: Can I reproduce the result myself?

The benchmark result may be from an extreme hardware configuration (e.g.,
DRAM disks), special-case tuning (e.g., striped disks), a stroke of luck (not repeatable), or a measurement error. Any of these can be determined if you are able to
run it in your own data center and perform your own analysis: active benchmarking. This does, however, consume a lot of your time.

Here are some other questions that may be asked:

- In **general:**
  - What was the configuration of the system under test?
  - Was a single system tested, or is this the result of a cluster of systems?
  - What is the cost of the system under test?
  - What was the configuration of the benchmark clients?
  - What was the duration of the test?
  - Is the result an average or a peak? What is the average?
  - What are other distribution details (standard deviation, percentiles, or full
    distribution details)?
  - What was the limiting factor of the benchmark?

- What was the operation success/fail ratio?
- What were the operation attributes?
- Were the operation attributes chosen to simulate a workload? How were they selected?
- Does the benchmark simulate variance, or an average workload?
- Was the benchmark result confirmed using other analysis tools? (Provide screen shots.)
- Can an error margin be expressed with the benchmark result?
- Is the benchmark result reproducible?

▪ For **CPU/memory**-related benchmarks:

- What processors were used?
- Were any CPUs disabled?
- How much main memory was installed? Of what type?
- Were any custom BIOS settings used?

▪ For **storage**-related benchmarks:

- What is the storage device configuration (how many were used, their type, RAID configuration)?
- What is the file system configuration (how many were used, and their tuning)?
- What is the working set size?
- To what degree did the working set cache? Where did it cache?
- How many files were accessed?

▪ For **network**-related benchmarks:

- What was the network configuration (how many interfaces were used, their type and configuration) ?
- What TCP settings were tuned?

When studying industry benchmarks, many of these questions may be answered from the disclosure details.

12.5 Exercises

1. Answer the following conceptual questions:
   - What is a micro-benchmark?

- What is working set size, and how might it affect the results of storage benchmarks?
- What is the reason for studying the price/performance ratio?

2. Choose a micro-benchmark and perform the following tasks:

- Scale a dimension (threads, I/O size, . . .) and measure performance.
- Graph the results (scalability).
- Use the micro-benchmark to drive the target to peak performance, and analyze the limiting factor.

12.6 References

[Anon 85]   Anon et al. "A Measure of Transaction Processing Power," *Datamation*, April 1, 1985.

[Jain 91]   Jain, R. *The Art of Computer Systems Performance Analysis: Techniques for Experimental Design, Measurement, Simulation, and Modeling*. Wiley, 1991.

[Gunther 97]   Gunther, N. *The Practical Performance Analyst*. McGraw-Hill, 1997.

[Smaalders 06]   Smaalders, B. "Performance Anti-Patterns," *ACM Queue* 4, no. 1 (February 2006).

[Gunther 07]   Gunther, N. *Guerrilla Capacity Planning*. Springer, 2007.

[DeWitt 08]   DeWitt, D., and C. Levine. "Not Just Correct, but Correct and Fast," *SIGMOD Record*, 2008.

[Traeger 08]   Traeger, A., E. Zadok, N. Joukov, and C. Wright. "A Nine Year Study of File System and Storage Benchmarking," *ACM Transactions on Storage*, 2008.

[1]   http://www.rfc-editor.org/rfc/museum/tcp-ip-digest/tcp-ip-digest.v1n6.1

[2]   http://dtrace.org/blogs/bmc/2009/02/02/eulogy-for-a-benchmark/

[3]   www.tpc.org/information/about/history.asp

[4]   www.tpc.org/information/other/pricing_guidelines.asp

[5]   www.tpc.org

[6]   www.spec.org

[7]   www.coker.com.au/bonnie++/

[8]   http://dtrace.org/blogs/brendan/2012/10/23/active-benchmarking/

[9]   https://blogs.oracle.com/roch/entry/decoding_bonnie

[10]   http://dtrace.org/blogs/brendan/2009/05/26/performance-testing-
             the-7000-series-part-3-of-3/

[11]   www.beginningwithi.com/comments/2009/11/11/brendan-gregg-
             at-frosug-oct-2009/

13

Case Study

This chapter is a systems performance case study: the story of a real-world performance issue, from initial report to final resolution. This particular issue occurred in a production cloud computing environment; I chose it as a routine example of systems performance analysis.

My intent in this chapter is not to introduce new technical content but to use storytelling to show how tools and methodologies may be applied in practice, in a real work environment. This should be especially useful for beginners who have yet to work on real-world systems performance issues, providing an over-the-shoulder view of how an expert approaches them, a commentary on what that expert might be thinking during the analysis, and why. This isn't necessarily documenting the best approach possible, but rather why one approach was taken.

All names have been changed to protect the innocent. Any resemblance to real servers, online or offline, is purely coincidental.

13.1 Case Study: The Red Whale

You've got mail!

> Hey, Brendan, I know we keep context switching here, but if you get the chance tomorrow, could you take a look at this NiftyFy server? It may be consistent with some of your existing findings on performance. Nathan took a look but couldn't determine the cause.

So began an e-mail from James, a sales rep, who copy-and-pasted the help desk ticket into the e-mail. I was a little irritated; I was trying to solve two other cases at the same time and didn't want the distraction.

I work at Joyent, a cloud computing provider. While I work in engineering, I'm also the final point of escalation for performance issues from our support and operations teams. Customer problems can arise with just about any application or database running on SmartOS Zones, or KVM instances of Linux or Windows.

I decided to hop on this new issue immediately and look at it for 15 minutes or so, hoping to find some quick answer. If it looked like it might take longer, I'd need to compare its priority with that of the other cases I was working on.

The first step was to read the help desk ticket for the problem statement.

13.1.1 Problem Statement

The problem statement described software versions and configuration and commented on CPU usage variability. The customer had only recently moved onto Joyent SmartMachines (SmartOS Zones) and was surprised to find that they could use system tools to observe the physical CPUs, including the utilization rate caused by all tenants in combination.

I scanned their description to find out the following:

- What made them think there was a performance problem?
- Could their problem (if any) be expressed in terms of latency or runtime?

The answer to the first question would tell me how real the issue might be, and I could use the second to double-check the issue myself. Many tickets turn out to be just confusion about a system metric, rather than a real application issue, so verifying this early on can save time. However, the answers to these two questions are not always available to begin with.

From the customer description I learned that they were using some application called Redis, and

- The `traceroute(1M)` command was used to test the network route and latency to the server, and it was reporting packet drops.
- Sometimes Redis returned with latency over one second.

The customer suspected that these two findings were related. However, that first detail suggested to me that the issue was not, in fact, real: on these systems, `traceroute(1M)` defaults to the UDP protocol, which is permitted by design to be unreliable, and so network infrastructure may drop those packets to favor more important TCP packets. If they had been using a TCP-based test, packet drops should not occur or would be negligible.

The second point was useful—something I could measure.

Based on previous cases with similar details, I could guess that my final conclusion would be one of the following, and I could even predict the likelihood of each:

- **60%:** `traceroute(1M)` dropped packets are a red herring, and the one-second Redis latency turns out to be normal for some application-level reason.

- **30%:** `traceroute(1M)` dropped packets are a red herring. There is an entirely different issue causing the one-second Redis latency.

- **10%:** `traceroute(1M)` dropped packets are related to the issue—the network actually is dropping packets.

That first, most likely (60%) outcome is the sort that ends with "Oh, yeah, it's supposed to do that." It may be new to the customer, as they were just learning Redis, but it would be obvious to a Redis expert.

13.1.2 Support

The ticket history included details of how Joyent support had analyzed the issue. When they learned that the customer was using a third-party monitoring tool to analyze Redis performance, they asked for access to it and confirmed that the latency sometimes spiked as high as reported. They also tried to reproduce packet drops using `traceroute(1M)` but were unable to. They noted that the source location might be relevant if `traceroute(1M)` takes different network paths, some less reliable than others (which is a good guess). They tried it from different locations but were still unable to reproduce the packet drops.

Nathan on the operations team then took a look. He set up `curl(1)` to measure latency, using a nearby host as a client to minimize the network components involved. By calling `curl(1)` in a loop, he was eventually able to catch an instance of over 200 ms latency—not the one second expected, but still much greater than the normal, which he had found to be less than 1 ms while testing. In other words: an *outlier*.

He also used his own ad hoc checklist to quickly run through the system. He found that the CPUs were fine, with plenty of idle headroom, and that network I/O was moderate but not causing a problem. For a couple of reasons, it was looking less and less as if the problem might be caused by network packet drops:

- Nathan tested using a nearby client in the same data center. For the 200 ms outlier to be caused by packet drops on faulty or saturated network equipment, there would have to be problems with the switches and routers within our data center—which, given their reliability, seemed unlikely.

- 200 ms of latency is too short for a TCP retransmit on these systems.

As an aside, there are two specific latencies that shout "TCP retransmit!": 1.125 s, and 3.375 s. These odd numbers are due to a weird piece of kernel TCP code (in `tcp_init_values()` in the illumos kernel) that inflates the values of 1 s and 3 s slightly. We probably should fix that code—it has confused customers in the past, and that's not a good thing. On the other hand, those odd numbers have often been useful, their weird values quickly suggesting TCP retransmits: "I have these 3.4 s outliers . . ." In this case, however, TCP retransmits were clearly not the culprit— 200 ms is way too short.

While this probably ruled out TCP retransmits (unless, for me, there was an unknown-unknown with the way they operate), it didn't rule out the network. Nathan's data center test meant that network problems were less likely, but I was aware that they were still a possibility.

13.1.3 Getting Started

I sent a chat message to James to say I'd look at the issue right away. James told me what he'd like me to do: at this point, the suspicion was that Redis itself was to blame, and that our server was fine. James was ready to push the issue back to the customer but wanted me to double-check that the system was OK, perhaps by using some of the newer DTrace scripts I had recently developed and used successfully. As I've done before, I'd hand my findings to James, and he'd handle communication with the customer and support, letting me focus on the issue.

I hadn't finished reading the support history, but I logged in to the target system (SmartOS) to try a couple of commands, just in case it happened to be a dead-obvious issue. My first command was `tail /var/adm/messages`, a useful habit I've had since I was a sysadmin, as it can find certain issues immediately. It didn't show anything alarming.

I then picked a statistics command to run based on the mentioned dropped network packets: `netstat -s 1 | grep tcp`. This begins with a screenful of statistics showing the summary-since-boot values, and then prints another screenful every second. The summary-since-boot was

```
TCP     tcpRtoAlgorithm     =      4    tcpRtoMin          =     400
        tcpRtoMax           =  60000    tcpMaxConn         =      -1
        tcpActiveOpens      =  31326    tcpPassiveOpens    =1886858
        tcpAttemptFails     =     36    tcpEstabResets     =    6999
        tcpCurrEstab        =    474    tcpOutSegs         =4822435795
```

```
         tcpOutDataSegs       =1502467280  tcpOutDataBytes      =320023296
         tcpRetransSegs       =   10573    tcpRetransBytes      =3223066
         tcpOutAck            =89303926    tcpOutAckDelayed     =43086430
         tcpOutUrg            =        0   tcpOutWinUpdate      =   1677
         tcpOutWinProbe       =        0   tcpOutControl        =3842327
         tcpOutRsts           =     9543   tcpOutFastRetrans    =      0
         tcpInSegs            =6142268941
         tcpInAckSegs         =        0   tcpInAckBytes        =300546783
         tcpInDupAck          =1916922     tcpInAckUnsent       =      0
         tcpInInorderSegs     =904589648   tcpInInorderBytes    =3680776830
         tcpInUnorderSegs     =        0   tcpInUnorderBytes    =      0
         tcpInDupSegs         =     3916   tcpInDupBytes        =175475
         tcpInPartDupSegs     =        0   tcpInPartDupBytes    =      0
         tcpInPastWinSegs     =        0   tcpInPastWinBytes    =      0
         tcpInWinProbe        =        0   tcpInWinUpdate       =      0
         tcpInClosed          =     3201   tcpRttNoUpdate       =      0
         tcpRttUpdate         =909252730   tcpTimRetrans        =  10513
         tcpTimRetransDrop    =      351   tcpTimKeepalive      =107692
         tcpTimKeepaliveProbe=     3300    tcpTimKeepaliveDrop  =      0
         tcpListenDrop        =      127   tcpListenDropQ0      =      0
         tcpHalfOpenDrop      =        0   tcpOutSackRetrans    =     15
         tcpInErrs            =        0   udpNoPorts           =    579
```

I looked at this for several seconds, particularly tcpListenDrop, tcpListenDropQ0, and tcpRetransSegs. Those rates did not look unusual. I left the command running in the window, showing the per-interval summaries, while I finished reading the support ticket in the help desk system (it was several pages long). It struck me that I didn't know if I should be seeing the issue right away or not.

I asked James how often the high-latency Redis requests were happening. He said, "All the time." Not the answer I was after! I wanted this to be quantified a little better, to help make sense of the rolling netstat(1M) output. Should I expect to see them every second, minute, or hour? James didn't know but said he'd get back to me.

I finished reading the support ticket and brought up a couple more terminal windows to log in to the system in parallel, while a few thoughts ran through my mind:

- "This might not be a good use of my time. Nathan is a veteran performance analyst, and the others in support appear to have conducted a reasonable investigation. This feels a bit like fishing—hoping one of my special DTrace tools can catch another issue. I'll spend, say, 15 minutes taking a serious look at the system, and if I find nothing, I'll hand it back to James."

- "On the other hand, I'll get to use these DTrace tools on another real issue and develop them further. There is much more I want to do with TCP observability, and this is an opportunity to do that. However, tool development isn't a higher priority than the other customer issues I need to work on, so this should probably wait."

- "Uh, what is Redis anyway?"

I was drawing a blank on what Redis actually was. I'd heard of it before but couldn't remember what it did. Was it an application server, database, load balancer? I felt like an idiot. I wanted to know what it did, at a high level, as context for the various statistics I was about to examine.

I first took a look on the system using ps(1), to see if some detail of the Redis process or its arguments would be a reminder. I found a process called "redis-server" but that didn't ring a bell. A quick Internet search for Redis (Google) was more fruitful, giving me the answer in less than a minute (from Wikipedia): Redis is a key-value store, designed to run fast out of main memory only [1].

Now the problem statement sounded more serious: if this was in-memory, what kind of performance issue would sometimes cause it to take over one second?

This brought back memories of unusual kernel scheduler bugs, where threads could be blocked in the runnable state for that long. I could DTrace the kernel scheduler again and figure this out, but that's time-consuming. I should check that the system has a kernel version that includes those fixes.

13.1.4 Choose Your Own Adventure

There were several different directions I could take at this point:

- Study the netstat statistics, most of which I had yet to read. By now, netstat had been running for a few minutes and had printed around 10,000 individual statistics. It was printing numbers faster than I could read them. I could spend 10 minutes or so trying to read as much as possible, in the hope of finding something to investigate further.

- Use my DTrace network tools and develop them further. I could pick out events of interest from the kernel, including retransmits and packet drops, and just print the relevant details. This could be quicker than reading netstat and might expose areas not covered by the netstat statistics. I also wanted to develop these tools further, for use with other customers, and to share them publicly.

- Browse the bug database for the previous kernel scheduler issues, find out the kernel versions they were fixed in, and then check that the system was running a kernel version with those fixes. I could also investigate possible new kernel scheduler issues using DTrace. This type of issue had caused one-second database queries in the past.

- Take a step back and check overall system health, to rule out any bottlenecks to begin with. This could be done using the USE method and should take only a few minutes for the key combinations.

- Create a theoretical model of Redis using queueing theory and use it to model latency versus load: to determine when one-second latencies can occur naturally due to the tail of the wait queue. This might be interesting, but it could be very time-consuming.

- Look for an online Redis bug database and search for known performance issues, especially one-second latencies. Perhaps there was a community forum or IRC channel I could ask on too.

- Use DTrace to dive into Redis internals, starting with the read latency and then drilling down. I could take my zfsslower.d-style script and have it trace Redis reads instead, using the DTrace pid provider. That way, I could provide a latency argument and only trace reads slower than, say, 500 ms. That would be a good starting point for drilling down.

One path I wasn't contemplating was to characterize the load to Redis, in case the one-second reads were simply big reads and should be expected to take that long. For example, unknown to the customer, a user of their database might have begun to do occasional 1 Gbyte reads, which would show up as latency spikes in the customer's monitoring software. I had ruled this out because Nathan had tested with curl(1), and he had found that latency could increase with normal-size reads.

I picked the USE method. It had proven useful in the past as a starting point for performance issues. It would also help James explain to the customer that we took the issue seriously and had completed our own systems health check.

13.1.5 The USE Method

As introduced in Chapter 2, Methodology, the USE method is a way to check system health, identifying bottlenecks and errors. For each resource, I'd check three metrics: utilization, saturation, and errors. For the key resources (CPU, memory, disks, network) there would be only a dozen metrics to check, which beat the 10,000 that I had from netstat(1M) so far.

CPU

I ran fmdump(1M) to see if there were any CPU errors, to take those off the table immediately. There were not.

I then checked system-wide CPU utilization and saturation using columns from vmstat(1M), and then per CPU using mpstat(1M). They looked fine: plenty of idle headroom, and no single hot CPUs.

In case the customer had hit the cloud-imposed CPU limit, I checked their usage and limit using kstat(1M). They were well under it.

Memory

Physical error types should have already shown up in the previous fmdump(1M), so I moved to utilization and saturation.

I had also previously run vmstat 1 while investigating the system-wide CPU usage and had noticed that there was plenty of free main memory and virtual memory system-wide, and that the page scanner was not running (a measure of saturation).

I ran vmstat -p 1 to check anonymous paging, which can occur due to cloud-imposed limits even when the system has memory headroom. The anonymous page-ins column, api, was nonzero!

```
$ vmstat -p 1
        memory            page              executable      anonymous         filesystem
   swap    free   re   mf    fr   de   sr epi epo epf   api  apo  apf  fpi  fpo  fpf
60222344 10272672 331  756  2728 688  27  0   0    0     2    5    5    4 2723 2723
48966364 1023432 208  1133 2047 608   0  0   0    0   168    0    0     0 2047 2047
48959268 1016308 335  1386 3981 528   0  0   0    0   100    0    0     0 3981 3981
[...]
```

Anonymous page-ins occur when an application has grown too large for main memory (or a limit) and has been paged out to the physical swap device (or, as Linux calls it, *swapped out*). A page of memory must then be read back in as the application needs it. This adds significant disk I/O latency, instead of just main memory I/O latency, and can seriously injure application performance. One-second reads, and worse, could easily be due to anonymous page-ins.

Single metrics alone don't usually confirm performance issues (with the exception of many error types). Anonymous page-ins, however, are a very good single indicator of a real issue, almost confirming the issue immediately. I still wanted to double-check and used prstat -mLc to check per-thread microstates (from the thread state analysis methodology):

```
$ prstat -mLcp `pgrep redis-server` 1
   PID USERNAME USR SYS TRP TFL DFL LCK SLP LAT VCX ICX SCL SIG PROCESS/LWPID
 28168 103      0.2 0.7 0.0 0.0 0.0 0.0  99 0.0  41   0 434   0 redis-server/1
 28168 103      0.0 0.0 0.0 0.0 0.0 0.0 100 0.0   0   0   0   0 redis-server/3
 28168 103      0.0 0.0 0.0 0.0 0.0 0.0 100 0.0   0   0   0   0 redis-server/2
Total: 1 processes, 3 lwps, load averages: 5.01, 4.59, 4.39
   PID USERNAME USR SYS TRP TFL DFL LCK SLP LAT VCX ICX SCL SIG PROCESS/LWPID
 28168 103      0.0 0.0 0.0 0.0 0.0  98 0.0 1.8 0.0  15   0 183   0 redis-server/1
 28168 103      0.0 0.0 0.0 0.0 0.0 0.0 100 0.0   0   0   0   0 redis-server/3
 28168 103      0.0 0.0 0.0 0.0 0.0 0.0 100 0.0   1   0   0   0 redis-server/2
Total: 1 processes, 3 lwps, load averages: 5.17, 4.66, 4.41
   PID USERNAME USR SYS TRP TFL DFL LCK SLP LAT VCX ICX SCL SIG PROCESS/LWPID
 28168 103      0.2 0.3 0.0 0.0  75 0.0  24 0.0  24   0 551   0 redis-server/1
 28168 103      0.0 0.0 0.0 0.0 0.0 0.0 100 0.0   0   0   0   0 redis-server/3
 28168 103      0.0 0.0 0.0 0.0 0.0 0.0 100 0.0   0   0   0   0 redis-server/2
[...]
```

The high percentage in DFL, data fault time, showed that for some seconds a Redis server thread was spending most of its time waiting for these page-ins from disk—I/O that would normally be served from main memory.

Checking memory limits:

```
$ zonememstat -z 1a8ba189ba
                       ZONE      RSS      CAP  NOVER        POUT
                 1a8ba189ba   5794MB   8192MB  45091   974165MB
```

While the current memory usage (RSS) was below the limit (CAP), the other columns showed evidence that they had exceeded the limit frequently: 45,091 times (NOVER), resulting in 974,165 Mbytes of total data paged out (POUT).

This looked like a routine case of a misconfigured server, especially since the customer had just moved Redis to this cloud. Perhaps they didn't update the config file to keep its size within the new limit. I sent a message to James.

While the memory issue was severe, I had yet to prove that it was *the* issue causing the one-second latency. Ideally, I'd measure Redis read time and express time synchronously blocked on DFL as a ratio of that. If a one-second read is spending 99% of its time blocked on DFL, we've confirmed *why* the read is slow and can then examine Redis memory configuration to put our finger on the root cause.

Before that, I wanted to finish running through the USE method checklist. Performance issues often come in multiples.

Disks

An iostat -En showed there were no errors. An iostat -xnz 1 showed that utilization was low (%b), and there was no saturation (wait).

I left iostat(1M) running for a while to look for variation and saw a burst of writes:

```
$ iostat -xnz 1
[...]
                    extended device statistics
    r/s    w/s   kr/s    kw/s wait actv wsvc_t asvc_t  %w  %b device
   42.6    3.0   27.4    28.4  0.0  0.0    0.0    0.5   0   2 sd1
                    extended device statistics
    r/s    w/s   kr/s    kw/s wait actv wsvc_t asvc_t  %w  %b device
   62.2 2128.1   60.7 253717.1  0.0  7.7    0.0    3.5   3  87 sd1
                    extended device statistics
    r/s    w/s   kr/s    kw/s wait actv wsvc_t asvc_t  %w  %b device
    3.0 2170.6    2.5 277839.5  0.0  9.9    0.0    4.6   2 100 sd1
                    extended device statistics
    r/s    w/s   kr/s    kw/s wait actv wsvc_t asvc_t  %w  %b device
    8.0 2596.4   10.0 295813.9  0.0  9.0    0.0    3.4   3 100 sd1
                    extended device statistics
    r/s    w/s   kr/s    kw/s wait actv wsvc_t asvc_t  %w  %b device
  251.1    1.0  217.0     8.0  0.0  0.7    0.0    2.9   0  66 sd1
```

For ZFS, which batches writes into transaction groups (TXGs), this behavior is normal. The application file system I/O operates asynchronously and isn't affected by the busy disk—at least, not usually. There are some cases when the application I/O could become blocked on the TXG.

The disk I/O seen here might not be caused by Redis anyway; it might be coming from another tenant on the system, especially since Redis is an in-memory database.

Network

Network interfaces looked fine; I checked them using `netstat -i` and `nicstat`: no errors, low utilization, no saturation.

13.1.6 Are We Done?

Having a very strong lead with memory usage, and needing to return to other work, I handed the matter back to James: "It looks like a memory configuration issue—they're getting blocked on anonymous page-ins." I included the screen shots. It looked as if this was a quickly resolved issue after all.

A little later James relayed messages from the customer:

- "Are you sure it's related to memory? The memory config seems fine."
- "The one-second reads are still happening."
- "They happen every 5 minutes or so" (answering my earlier question).

Am I sure?! If the customer had been in the room with me, I'd have struggled not to sound indignant. It was very obvious that there was a serious memory issue. You have `apis` and up to 98% `DFL`—the system is in memory hell. Yes, I'm sure!

Well, come to think of it . . . I was sure there was a serious memory issue. But I hadn't actually proved that it was *the* issue causing the read latency. Finding multiple issues isn't uncommon in this line of work. Was it possible that there was *another* issue that was actually causing the read latency, and this memory paging issue was a red herring? More like a red whale!

The customer's comment about it happening every 5 minutes was also inconsistent with the memory issue. When I looked earlier, the `DFL` time was happening almost every second. This suggested that there might indeed be a second issue.

13.1.7 Take 2

Ideally, I wanted a tool that showed

- Redis read latency
- A breakdown of synchronous time components, showing where most of the time was spent during the read

I'd run that, find the slow one-second reads, and then see what the largest component of those reads was. If it was the memory issue, this tool would show that most of the time was spent waiting on an anonymous page-in.

I could start browsing the Redis online documentation to see if such a tool existed. If it did, it might take a bit of time to learn it, and to get permission from the customer to run it. It's usually quicker to take a read-only peek using DTrace from the global zone.

DTrace would need to measure Redis read latency. This was before the Redis DTrace provider existed, so I'd have to roll my own technique, based on how Redis works internally. Problem was, I had no idea how Redis works internally—not too long ago I'd forgotten what it even was. This type of internals knowledge is something you'd expect only a Redis developer or expert to have at the ready.

How to figure out Redis quickly? Three approaches sprang to mind:

- Examine syscalls using the DTrace syscall provider, and try to figure out Redis read latency from there. There are often clever ways to find such information, such as tracing accept() to close() latency on a socket, or examining send() and recv() data. It would depend on the syscalls used.
- Examine Redis internals using the DTrace pid provider. This would require tracing Redis internals, which I knew nothing about. I could read the source code, but that would be time-consuming. A quicker way is usually to go *stack fishing*: start with the syscalls servicing client I/O, and print the user-level stacks (DTrace ustack() action) to see the code path ancestry. Instead of thousands of lines of source code, this gives me a glimpse of the *actual* in-use functions that are performing work, and I can then study only those.
- Examine Redis internals using the DTrace pid provider, but go stack fishing by profiling user-level stacks at 97 Hz (e.g., with the DTrace profile provider), instead of I/O-based. I could take this data and generate a flame graph, to quickly get a sense of commonly taken code paths.

13.1.8 The Basics

I decided to start by seeing what syscalls were available:

```
# dtrace -n 'syscall:::entry /execname == "redis-server"/ {
    @[probefunc] = count(); }'
dtrace: description 'syscall:::entry ' matched 238 probes
CPU     ID                      FUNCTION:NAME
^C

  brk                                                                 1
  fdsync                                                              1
  forksys                                                             1
  lwp_self                                                            1
  rename                                                              1
  rexit                                                               1
  times                                                               1
  waitsys                                                             1
  accept                                                              2
  setsockopt                                                          2
  llseek                                                              2
  lwp_sigmask                                                         2
  fcntl                                                               3
  ioctl                                                               3
  open64                                                              3
  getpid                                                              8
  close                                                              11
  fstat64                                                            12
  read                                                             2465
  write                                                            3504
  pollsys                                                         15854
  gtime                                                          183171
```

There were a lot of `gtime()`s, `pollsys()`s, and `write()`s. The `pollsys()` shows that Redis is not using event ports, because if it were, it would be using `portfs()`. This rang a bell. Another engineer had encountered it before, and the Redis developers had rolled the fix, improving performance. I told James about this, although I recalled that event ports provided roughly a 20% performance improvement, whereas I was currently chasing down a one-second outlier.

A single `forksys()` looked odd, but something that infrequent could be monitoring (forking a process to then execute system stat commands). The `fdstat()` and `fdsync()` calls from this output were even more suspicious. These are usually file system calls; I thought Redis was in-memory only. If the file system is on the scene, so are disks, which could certainly be causing high latency.

13.1.9 Ignoring the Red Whale

To confirm that the disks were in play, and ignoring the memory issue for the moment, I decided to check the file system type of the syscalls. These calls may be to a pseudo file system, such as sockfs, and not a disk-based file system like ZFS.

To confirm that they might be contributing enough latency to add up to one second, I would also measure their latency.

I quickly wrote a number of DTrace one-liners. These included the following:

Counting the file system type of, say, the `write()` syscalls, for processes named "`redis-server`" (there is only one on this system):

```
syscall::write:entry /execname == "redis-server"/ { @[fds[arg0].fi_fs] =
count(); }
```

Measuring the latency of all the syscalls, as a sum (nanoseconds):

```
syscall:::entry /execname == "redis-server"/ { self->ts = timestamp; }
syscall:::return /self->ts/ { @[probefunc] = sum(timestamp - self->ts);
    self->ts = 0; }
```

The first piece showed me that most of the time the writes were to "`sockfs`", the network. Sometimes they were indeed to "`zfs`".

The second one-liner showed that there were sometimes hundreds of milliseconds of latency in syscalls such as `write()`, `fdsync()`, and `poll()`. The `poll()` latency might be normal (waiting for work—I'd have to check file descriptors and user-level stacks), but the others, especially `fdsync()` were suspicious.

13.1.10 Interrogating the Kernel

At this point, I ran a series of quick custom DTrace one-liners, to answer various questions about the kernel. This included moving from the syscall layer to the VFS layer, traced using the fbt provider, where I could examine other kernel internals via the probe arguments.

This quickly grew to the following one-liner, which was starting to be long enough to be made into a script:

```
# dtrace -n 'fbt::fop_*:entry /execname == "redis-server"/ {
    self->ts = timestamp; }
fbt::fop_*:return /self->ts/ { @[probefunc] = sum(timestamp - self->ts);
    self->ts = 0; }
fbt::fop_write:entry /execname == "redis-server"/ {
    @w[stringof(args[0]->v_op->vnop_name)] = count(); }
tick-15s { printa(@); trunc(@); printa(@w); trunc(@w); }'
[...]
  7   69700                          :tick-15s
  fop_addmap                                                      4932
  fop_open                                                        8870
```

continues

```
        fop_rwlock                                            1444580
        fop_rwunlock                                          1447226
        fop_read                                              2557201
        fop_write                                             9157132
        fop_poll                                             42784819

        sockfs                                                    323
    [...]
```

It prints a couple of summaries every 15 s. The first shows the VFS-level calls used by Redis, with the sum of their latency in nanoseconds. In the 15 s summary, only 42 ms was spent in fop_poll(), and 9 ms in fop_write(). The second summary shows the file system type of the writes—for this interval they were all "sockfs", the network.

About every 5 minutes, the following happened:

```
    7  69700                    :tick-15s
        fop_ioctl                                               1980
        fop_open                                                2230
        fop_close                                               2825
        fop_getsecattr                                          2850
        fop_getattr                                             7198
        fop_lookup                                             24663
        fop_addmap                                             32611
        fop_create                                             80478
        fop_read                                             2677245
        fop_rwunlock                                         6707275
        fop_rwlock                                          12485682
        fop_getpage                                         16603402
        fop_poll                                            44540898
        fop_write                                          317532328

        sockfs                                                    320
        zfs                                                     2981

    7  69700                    :tick-15s
        fop_delmap                                              4886
        fop_lookup                                              7879
        fop_realvp                                              8806
        fop_dispose                                            30618
        fop_close                                              95575
        fop_read                                              289778
        fop_getpage                                          2939712
        fop_poll                                             4729929
        fop_rwunlock                                         6996488
        fop_rwlock                                          14266786
        fop_inactive                                        15197222
        fop_write                                          493655969
        fop_fsync                                          625164797

        sockfs                                                     35
        zfs                                                     3868
```

The first interval output shows an increase in fop_write() time, reaching 317 ms during the 15 s interval, and also 2,981 zfs writes. The second interval shows 493 ms in write(), and 625 ms in fsync().

Determining the ZFS file that is being written and synced is trivial, and I'd already discovered it using one of my favorite DTrace scripts:

```
# zfsslower.d 1
TIME                       PROCESS         D   KB    ms FILE
2012 Jul 21 04:01:12 redis-server         W   128    1 /zones/1a8ba189ba/root/var/db/
redis/temp-10718.rdb
```

The output showed many 128 Kbyte writes to a `temp-10718.rdb` file. I managed to run `ls(1)` on it before it was deleted, to see its size:

```
# ls -lh /zones/1a8ba189ba/root/var/db/redis/
total 3473666
-rw-r--r--   1 103        104         856M Jul 21 04:01 dump.rdb
-rw-r--r--   1 103        104            6 Jul 18 01:28 redis.pid
-rw-r--r--   1 103        104         856M Jul 21 04:07 temp-12126.rdb
```

If it was too short-lived for `ls(1)`, I could have used DTrace to trace the file information. (I've already written a script to do that, sollife.d; see Chapter 5 of the *DTrace* book [Gregg 11].)

The file names contain `dump` and `temp-`. And they were over 800 Mbytes, which was `fsync()`ed. This sounded like a bad idea.

13.1.11 Why?

Writing an 800+ Mbyte temporary file, then `fsync()`ing it, with the combined latency taking well over one second, sounded like it could certainly be a source of Redis latency. The frequency—every 5 minutes—matched the customer's description.

An Internet search found the following explanation for the temporary files, written by Didier Spezia [2]:

RDB is like a snapshot of the memory, written to disk. During a BGSAVE operation, Redis writes a temporary file. Once the file is complete and fsync'd, it is renamed as the real dump file. So in case of crash during the dump, the existing file is never altered. All the recent changes are lost, but the file itself is always safe and can never be corrupted.

I also learned that Redis can `fork()` this BGSAVE operation, so that it can run in the background. I had seen a `forksys()` earlier but hadn't checked it.

The Redis Wikipedia page shed a bit more light [3]:

Persistence is reached in two different ways: One is called snapshotting, and is a semi-persistent durability mode where the dataset is asynchronously transferred from memory to disk from time to time. Since version 1.1 the safer alternative is an append-only file (a journal) that is written as operations modifying the dataset in memory are processed. Redis is able to rewrite the append-only file in the background in order to avoid an indefinite growth of the journal.

This suggested that the behavior could be changed dramatically, from a dump to a journal. Checking the Redis configuration file:

```
############################## SNAPSHOTTING ###############################
#
# Save the DB on disk:
#
#    save
#
#    Will save the DB if both the given number of seconds and the given
#    number of write operations against the DB occurred.
#
#    In the example below the behaviour will be to save:
#    after 900 sec (15 min) if at least 1 key changed
#    after 300 sec (5 min) if at least 10 keys changed
#    after 60 sec if at least 10000 keys changed
#
#    Note: you can disable saving at all commenting all the "save" lines.

save 900 1
save 300 10
save 60 10000
[...]
```

Oh, so there's the origin of the 5-minute interval.
    And there's more:

```
############################## APPEND ONLY MODE ###############################
[...]
# The fsync() call tells the Operating System to actually write data on disk
# instead to wait for more data in the output buffer. Some OS will really flush
# data on disk, some other OS will just try to do it ASAP.
#
# Redis supports three different modes:
#
# no: don't fsync, just let the OS flush the data when it wants. Faster.
# always: fsync after every write to the append only log . Slow, Safest.
# everysec: fsync only if one second passed since the last fsync. Compromise.
#
# The default is "everysec" that's usually the right compromise between
# speed and data safety. It's up to you to understand if you can relax this to
# "no" that will will let the operating system flush the output buffer when
# it wants, for better performances (but if you can live with the idea of
# some data loss consider the default persistence mode that's snapshotting),
# or on the contrary, use "always" that's very slow but a bit safer than
# everysec.
#
# If unsure, use "everysec".

# appendfsync always
appendfsync everysec
# appendfsync no
```

I sent this to the customer via James and didn't hear back regarding this issue again.

13.1.12 Epilogue

So, while dealing with this problem, I found three performance issues and was able to send actionable suggestions back to the customer:

- **Memory paging:** Reconfigure the application to stay within the memory limit (it may then be discovered that the memory issue was caused by the `fork()` and BGSAVE operation).

- **`pollsys()`:** Upgrade the Redis software to the version that uses event ports, for a performance improvement.

- **BGSAVE configuration:** Redis calls `fsync()` on an 800+ Mbyte file every 5 minutes for persistence, which is the likely cause of the outliers and can be tuned to behave very differently.

I'm still amazed that there was an even worse issue than the memory paging. Usually, once I find that much DFL time, the customer finds and fixes the config and I don't hear back.

I also chatted with the other engineers at Joyent about it, so we stay current with performance issues. One of them already had experience with Redis and said, "That's just a bad config. Redis is supposed to be serving small object stores—like a name service—not 800 Mbyte databases."

My 60% hunch earlier was right: "Oh, yeah, it's supposed to do that." I now know more details for the next time I encounter Redis, and perhaps then I'll get to act on some of my earlier ideas, including writing a script to trace Redis read time and express synchronous latency breakdowns.

(Update: Yes, Redis and I met again, and I wrote those scripts: redislat.d to summarize Redis latency, and redisslower.d trace outliers [4].)

13.2 Comments

This case study showed my thought process during a performance investigation, how I might typically apply the tools and methodologies that I described in previous chapters, and the order in which I used them. It also described some additional characteristics of the practice of performance analysis, including these:

- It's normal to know little about the target application to begin with, but you can quickly find out more and develop expertise.

- Making mistakes and taking wrong turns, and then getting back on track, is routine during performance analysis.
- Finding multiple issues before you hit on *the* issue is also normal.
- And all of this happens under time pressure!

For a beginner, feeling lost when you're studying a performance issue can be discouraging. This feeling, too, is normal: you will feel lost, you will make mistakes, and you will often be wrong. Quoting Niels Bohr, a Danish physicist:

> An expert is a person who has made all the mistakes that can be made in a very narrow field.

By telling you stories like this one, I hope to reassure you that mistakes and wrong turns are normal (even for the best of us) and to show you some techniques and methodologies to help you find your way.

13.3 Additional Information

For more case studies in systems performance analysis, check the bug database (or ticketing system) at your company for previous performance-related issues, and the public bug databases for the applications and operating system you use. These issues often begin with a problem statement and finish with the final fix. Many bug database systems also include a timestamped comments history, which can be studied to see the progression of analysis, including hypotheses explored and wrong turns taken.

Some systems performance case studies are published from time to time, for example, as on my blog [5]. Technical journals with a focus on practice, such as *ACM Queue* [6], also often use case studies as context when describing new technical solutions to problems.

13.4 References

[Gregg 11]   Gregg, B., and J. Mauro. *DTrace: Dynamic Tracing in Oracle Solaris, Mac OS X and FreeBSD*. Prentice Hall, 2011.

[1]   http://redis.io

[2]   https://groups.google.com/forum/?fromgroups=#!searchin/redis-db/temporary$20file/redis-db/pE1PloNh20U/4P5Y2WyU9w8J

[3]   http://en.wikipedia.org/wiki/Redis

[4]   https://github.com/brendangregg/dtrace-cloud-tools

[5]   http://dtrace.org/blogs/brendan

[6]   http://queue.acm.org

Appena

USE Method: Linux

This appendix [1] contains a checklist for Linux derived from the USE method. This is a method for checking system health, identifying common resource bottlenecks and errors, introduced in Chapter 2, Methodology. Later chapters (5, 6, 7, 9, 10) described it in specific contexts and introduced tools to support its use.

Performance tools are often enhanced and new ones are developed, so you should treat this as a starting point that will need updates. New observability frameworks and tools can also be developed to specifically make following the USE method easier.

Physical Resources

Component	Type	Metric
CPU	utilization	per CPU: `mpstat -P ALL 1`, (inverse of) `%idle`; `sar -P ALL`, `%idle`
		system-wide: `vmstat 1`, id; `sar -u`, `%idle`; `dstat -c`, idl
		per process: top, `%CPU`; htop, CPU%; `ps -o pcpu`; `pidstat 1`, `%CPU`
		per kernel thread: `top`/`htop` (K to toggle), where VIRT == 0 (heuristic)

continues

Component	Type	Metric
CPU	saturation	system-wide: `vmstat 1`, `r` > CPU count[1]; `sar -q`, `runq-sz` > CPU count; `dstat -p`, `run` > CPU count
		per process: /proc/PID/schedstat 2nd field (sched_info.run_delay); getdelays.c, `CPU`[2]; `perf sched latency` (shows average and maximum delay per schedule); dynamic tracing, e.g., SystemTap schedtimes.stp `queued(us)`[3]
CPU	errors	`perf` (LPE) if processor-specific error events (CPC) are available; e.g., AMD64's "04Ah Single-bit ECC Errors Recorded by Scrubber"[4]
Memory capacity	utilization	system-wide: `free -m`, `Mem:` (main memory), `Swap:` (virtual memory); `vmstat 1`, `free` (main memory), `swap` (virtual memory); `sar -r`, `%memused`; `dstat -m`, `free`; `slabtop -s c` for kmem slab usage
		per process: `top/htop`, `RES` (resident main memory), `VIRT` (virtual memory), `Mem` for system-wide summary
Memory capacity	saturation	system-wide: `vmstat 1`, `si/so` (swapping); `sar -B`, `pgscank + pgscand` (scanning); `sar -W`
		per process: getdelays.c, `SWAP`[2]; 10th field (min_flt) from /proc/PID/stat for minor fault rate, or dynamic tracing[5]; `dmesg	grep killed` (OOM killer)
Memory capacity	errors	`dmesg` for physical failures; dynamic tracing, e.g., uprobes for failed `malloc()`s (DTrace/SystemTap)
Network interfaces	utilization	`ip -s link`, RX/TX tput / max bandwidth; `sar -n DEV`, rx/tx kB/s / max bandwidth; /proc/net/dev, `bytes RX/TX` tput/max
Network interfaces	saturation	`ifconfig`, overruns, dropped[6]; `netstat -s`, `segments retransmited`; `sar -n EDEV`, *drop/s, *fifo/s; /proc/net/dev, RX/TX drop; dynamic tracing of other TCP/IP stack queueing
Network interfaces	errors	`ifconfig`, errors, dropped[6]; `netstat -i`, RX-ERR/TX-ERR; `ip -s link`, errors; `sar -n EDEV` all; /proc/net/dev, errs, drop; extra counters may be under /sys/class/net/ . . . ; dynamic tracing of driver function returns
Storage device I/O	utilization	system-wide: `iostat -xz 1`, `%util`; `sar -d`, `%util`; per process: iotop; /proc/PID/sched `se.statistics.iowait_sum`
Storage device I/O	saturation	`iostat -xnz 1`, `avgqu-sz` > 1, or high `await`; `sar -d` same; LPE block probes for queue length/latency; dynamic/static tracing of I/O subsystem (including LPE block probes)
Storage device I/O	errors	/sys/devices/ . . . /ioerr_cnt; `smartctl`; dynamic/static tracing of I/O subsystem response codes[7]

Component	Type	Metric
Storage capacity	utilization	swap: `swapon -s`; `free`; `/proc/meminfo SwapFree/SwapTotal`; file systems: `df -h`
Storage capacity	saturation	not sure this one makes sense—once it's full, ENOSPC
Storage capacity	file systems: errors	`strace` for ENOSPC; dynamic tracing for ENOSPC; /var/log/messages errs, depending on FS; application log errors
Storage controller	utilization	`iostat -xz 1`, sum devices and compare to known IOPS/tput limits per card
Storage controller	saturation	see storage device I/O saturation, . . .
Storage controller	errors	see storage device I/O errors, . . .
Network controller	utilization	infer from `ip -s link` (or sar, or /proc/net/dev) and known controller max tput for its interfaces
Network controller	saturation	see network interfaces, saturation, . . .
Network controller	errors	see network interfaces, errors, . . .
CPU interconnect	utilization	LPE (CPC) for CPU interconnect ports, tput/max
CPU interconnect	saturation	LPE (CPC) for stall cycles
CPU interconnect	errors	LPE (CPC) for whatever is available
Memory interconnect	utilization	LPE (CPC) for memory busses, tput/max; or CPI greater than, say, 10; CPC may also have local versus remote counters
Memory interconnect	saturation	LPE (CPC) for stall cycles
Memory interconnect	errors	LPE (CPC) for whatever is available
I/O interconnect	utilization	LPE (CPC) for tput/max if available; inference via known tput from iostat/ip/ . . .
I/O interconnect	saturation	LPE (CPC) for stall cycles
I/O interconnect	errors	LPE (CPC) for whatever is available

1. The r column reports those threads that are waiting *and* threads that are running on-CPU. See the `vmstat(1)` description in Chapter 6, CPUs.

2. Uses delay accounting; see Chapter 4, Observability Tools.

3. There is also the sched:sched_process_wait tracepoint for `perf(1)`; be careful about overheads when tracing, as scheduler events are frequent.

4. There aren't many error-related events in the recent Intel and AMD processor manuals.

5. This can be used to show who is consuming memory and leading to saturation, by seeing who is causing minor faults. This should be available in `htop(1)` as MINFLT.

6. Dropped packets are included as both saturation and error indicators, since they can occur due to both types of events.

7. This includes tracing functions from different layers of the I/O subsystem: block device, SCSI, SATA, IDE, . . . Some static probes are available (LPE `scsi` and `block` tracepoint events); otherwise use dynamic tracing.

General notes: `uptime` "load average" (or /proc/loadavg) wasn't included for CPU metrics since Linux load averages include tasks in the uninterruptable I/O state.

LPE: Linux Performance Events is a powerful observability toolkit that reads CPC and can also use dynamic and static tracing. Its interface is the `perf(1)` command. It was introduced in Chapter 6, CPUs.

CPC: CPU performance counters. See Chapter 6, CPUs, and their usage with `perf(1)`.

I/O interconnect: This includes the CPU-to-I/O controller busses, the I/O controller(s), and device busses (e.g., PCIe).

Dynamic tracing: allows custom metrics to be developed. See Chapter 4, Observability Tools, and the examples in later chapters. Dynamic tracing tools for Linux include LPE, DTrace, SystemTap, and LTTng.

For any environment that imposes resource controls (e.g., cloud computing), check USE for each resource control. These may be encountered—and limit usage—before the hardware resource is fully utilized.

Software Resources

Component	Type	Metric
Kernel mutex	utilization	with CONFIG_LOCK_STATS=y, /proc/lock_stat `holdtime-total` / `acquisitions` (also see `holdtime-min`, `holdtime-max`)[1]; dynamic tracing of lock functions or instructions (maybe)
Kernel mutex	saturation	with CONFIG_LOCK_STATS=y, /proc/lock_stat `waittime-total` / `contentions` (also see `waittime-min`, `waittime-max`); dynamic tracing of lock functions or instructions (maybe); spinning shows up with profiling (`perf record -a -g -F 997 ...`, oprofile, DTrace, SystemTap)
Kernel mutex	errors	dynamic tracing (e.g., recursive mutex enter); other errors can cause kernel lockup/panic, debug with kdump/`crash`
User mutex	utilization	`valgrind --tool=drd --exclusive-threshold=...` (held time); dynamic tracing of lock-to-unlock function time

Component	Type	Metric
User mutex	saturation	`valgrind --tool=drd` to infer contention from held time; dynamic tracing of synchronization functions for wait time; profiling (oprofile, PEL, . . .) user stacks for spins
User mutex	errors	`valgrind --tool=drd` various errors; dynamic tracing of `pthread_mutex_lock()` for EAGAIN, EINVAL, EPERM, EDEADLK, ENOMEM, EOWNERDEAD, . . .
Task capacity	utilization	top/htop, Tasks (current); `sysctl kernel.threads-max`, /proc/sys/kernel/threads-max (max)
Task capacity	saturation	threads blocking on memory allocation; at this point the page scanner should be running (`sar -B`, `pgscan*`), else examine using dynamic tracing
Task capacity	errors	"can't `fork()`" errors; user-level threads: `pthread_create()` failures with EAGAIN, EINVAL, . . . ; kernel: dynamic tracing of `kernel_thread()` ENOMEM
File descriptors	utilization	system-wide: `sar -v`, `file-nr` versus /proc/sys/fs/file-max; `dstat --fs, files`; or just /proc/sys/fs/file-nr
		per process: `ls /proc/PID/fd	wc -l` vs `ulimit -n`
File descriptors	saturation	this one may not make sense
File descriptors	errors	`strace` errno == EMFILE on syscalls returning file descriptors (e.g., `open()`, `accept()`, . . .)

1. Kernel lock analysis used to be via lockmeter, which had an interface called lockstat.

Reference

[1] http://dtrace.org/blogs/brendan/2012/03/07/the-use-method-linux-performance-checklist

Appendix B

USE Method: Solaris

This appendix [1] contains a checklist for Solaris-based systems derived from the USE method, for the same reason, and with the same caveats, as Appendix A.

Physical Resources

Component	Type	Metric
CPU	utilization	per CPU: `mpstat 1`, `idl`
		system-wide: `vmstat 1`, `id`
		per process: `prstat -c 1` (CPU == recent), `prstat -mLc 1` (USR + SYS)
		per kernel thread: `lockstat -Ii rate`, DTrace profile `stack()`
CPU	saturation	system-wide: `uptime`, load averages; `vmstat 1`, `r`; DTrace dispqlen.d (DTT) for a better `vmstat r`
		per process: `prstat -mLc 1`, LAT
CPU	errors	`fmadm faulty`; `cpustat` (CPC) for whatever error counters are supported (e.g., thermal throttling)

continues

Component	Type	Metric
Memory capacity	utilization	system-wide: `vmstat 1`, `free` (main memory), `swap` (virtual memory)
		per process: `prstat -c`, `RSS` (main memory), `SIZE` (virtual memory)
Memory capacity	saturation	system-wide: `vmstat 1`, `sr` (scanning: bad now), `w` (has swapped: was very bad); `vmstat -p 1`, `api` (anonymous page-ins == pain), `apo`
		per process: `prstat -mLc 1`, `DFL`; DTrace anonpgpid.d (DTT), vminfo:::anonpgin on execname
Memory capacity	errors	`fmadm faulty` and `prtdiag` for physical failures; `fmstat -s -m cpumem-retire` (ECC events); DTrace failed `malloc()`s
Network interfaces	utilization	`nicstat`[1]; `kstat`; `dladm show-link -s -i 1 interface`
Network interfaces	saturation	`nicstat`; `kstat` for whatever custom statistics are available (e.g., "nocanputs," "defer," "norcvbuf," "noxmtbuf"); `netstat -s`, retransmits
Network interfaces	errors	`netstat -I`, error counters; `dladm show-phys`; `kstat` for extended errors, look in the interface and "link" statistics (there are often custom counters for the card); DTrace for driver internals
Storage device I/O	utilization	system-wide: `iostat -xnz 1`, `%b`
		per process: iotop (DTT)
Storage device I/O	saturation	`iostat -xnz 1`, `wait`; DTrace iopending (DTT), sdqueue.d (DTB)
Storage device I/O	errors	`iostat -En`; DTrace I/O subsystem, e.g., ideerr.d (DTB), satareasons.d (DTB), scsireasons.d (DTB), sdretry.d (DTB)
Storage capacity	utilization	swap: `swap -s`; file systems: `df -h`; plus other commands depending on file system type
Storage capacity	saturation	not sure this one makes sense—once it's full, ENOSPC
Storage capacity	errors	DTrace; /var/adm/messages file system full messages
Storage controller	utilization	`iostat -Cxnz 1`, compare to known IOPS/tput limits per card
Storage controller	saturation	look for kernel queueing: sd (iostat `wait` again), ZFS zio pipeline
Storage controller	errors	DTrace the driver, e.g., mptevents.d (DTB); /var/adm/messages

Component	Type	Metric
Network controller	utilization	infer from `nicstat` and known controller max tput
Network controller	saturation	see network interfaces, saturation
Network controller	errors	`kstat` for whatever is there/DTrace
CPU interconnect	utilization	`cpustat` (CPC) for CPU interconnect ports, tput/max (e.g., see the amd64htcpu script [2])
CPU interconnect	saturation	`cpustat` (CPC) for stall cycles
CPU interconnect	errors	`cpustat` (CPC) for whatever is available
Memory interconnect	utilization	`cpustat` (CPC) for memory busses, tput/max; or CPI greater than, say, 10; CPC may also have local versus remote counters
Memory interconnect	saturation	`cpustat` (CPC) for stall cycles
Memory interconnect	errors	`cpustat` (CPC) for whatever is available
I/O interconnect	utilization	`busstat` (SPARC only); `cpustat` for tput/max if available; inference via known tput from iostat/nicstat/. . .
I/O interconnect	saturation	`cpustat` (CPC) for stall cycles
I/O interconnect	errors	`cpustat` (CPC) for whatever is available

1. https://blogs.oracle.com/timc/entry/nicstat_the_solaris_and_linux

2. http://dtrace.org/blogs/brendan/2009/09/22/7410-hardware-update-and-analyzing-the-hypertransport/

General notes:

`lockstat(1M)` and `plockstat(1M)` are DTrace-based since Solaris 10 FCS. See Chapter 5, Applications.

vmstat r: This is coarse as it is updated only once per second.

CPC: CPU performance counters. See Chapter 6, CPUs, and their usage with `cpustat(1M)`.

Memory capacity utilization: interpreting vmstat's `free` has been tricky across different Solaris versions due to different ways it was calculated [McDougall 06b]. It will also typically shrink as the kernel uses unused memory for caching (ZFS ARC). See Chapter 7, Memory.

DTT: DTraceToolkit scripts [2].

DTB: DTrace book scripts [3].

I/O interconnect: This includes the CPU-to-I/O controller busses, the I/O controller(s), and device busses (e.g., PCIe).

Dynamic tracing (DTrace) allows custom metrics to be developed, live and in production. See Chapter 4, Observability Tools, and the examples in later chapters.

For any environment that imposes resource controls (e.g., cloud computing), check USE for each resource control. These may be encountered—and limit usage—before the hardware resource is fully utilized.

Software Resources

Component	Type	Metric
Kernel mutex	utilization	`lockstat -H` (held time); DTrace lockstat provider
Kernel mutex	saturation	`lockstat -C` (contention); DTrace lockstat provider; spinning shows up with `dtrace -n 'profile-997 { @[stack()] = count(); }'`
Kernel mutex	errors	`lockstat -E`, e.g., recursive mutex enter (other errors can cause kernel lockup/panic, debug with `mdb -k`)
User mutex	utilization	`plockstat -H` (held time); DTrace plockstat provider
User mutex	saturation	`plockstat -C` (contention); `prstat -mLc 1`, LCK; DTrace plockstat provider
User mutex	errors	DTrace plockstat and pid providers, for EAGAIN, EINVAL, EPERM, EDEADLK, ENOMEM, EOWNERDEAD . . . ; see pthread_mutex_lock(3C)
Process capacity	utilization	`sar -v`, proc-sz; kstat, `unix:0:var:v_proc` for max, `unix:0:system_misc:nproc` for current; DTrace (`nproc vs `max_nprocs)
Process capacity	saturation	not sure this makes sense; you might get queueing on pidlinklock in `pid_allocate()`, as it scans for available slots once the table gets full
Process capacity	errors	"can't `fork()`" messages
Thread capacity	utilization	user level: kstat, `unix:0:lwp_cache:buf_inuse` for current, `prctl -n zone.max-lwps -i zone` *ZONE* for max
		kernel: `mdb -k` or DTrace, `nthread` for current, limited by memory
Thread capacity	saturation	threads blocking on memory allocation; at this point the page scanner should be running (vmstat `sr`), else examine using DTrace/mdb
Thread capacity	errors	user level: `pthread_create()` failures with EAGAIN, EINVAL, . . .
		kernel: `thread_create()` blocks for memory but won't fail
File descriptors	utilization	system-wide: no limit other than main memory
		per process: `pfiles` versus `ulimit` or `prctl -t basic -n process.max-file-descriptor` PID; a quicker check than pfiles is `ls /proc/PID/fd	wc -l`

Component	Type	Metric
File descriptors	saturation	this one may not make sense
File descriptors	errors	`truss` or DTrace (better) to look for errno == EMFILE on syscalls returning file descriptors (e.g., `open()`, `accept()`, . . .)

General notes:

lockstat/plockstat can drop events due to load; try using a limited set of probes with DTrace directly.

File descriptor utilization: While other OSs have a system-wide limit, Solaris does not.

References

[McDougall 06b]   McDougall, R., J. Mauro, and B. Gregg. *Solaris Performance and Tools: DTrace and MDB Techniques for Solaris 10 and OpenSolaris.* Prentice Hall, 2006.

[1]   http://dtrace.org/blogs/brendan/2012/03/07/the-use-method-linux-performance-checklist

[2]   www.brendangregg.com/dtrace.html#DTraceToolkit

[3]   www.dtracebook.com

Appendix C

sar Summary

This is a summary of key options and metrics from the system activity reporter, sar(1). You can use this to jog your memory of which metrics are under which options. See the man page for the full list.

sar(1) is introduced in Chapter 4, Observability Tools, and selected options are summarized in later chapters (6, 7, 8, 9, 10).

Linux

Option	Metrics	Description
-P ALL	%user %nice %system %iowait %steal %idle	per-CPU utilization
-u	%user %nice %system %iowait %steal %idle	CPU utilization
-q	runq-sz	CPU run-queue size
-B	pgpgin/s pgpgout/s fault/s majflt/s pgfree/s pgscank/s pgscand/s pgsteal/s %vmeff	paging statistics
-H	hbhugfree hbhugused	huge pages
-r	kbmemfree kbmemused kbbuffers kbcached kbcommit %commit kbactive kbinact	memory utilization
-R	frpg/s bufpg/s campg/s	memory statistics

continues

Option	Metrics	Description
-S	kbswpfree kbswpused kbswpcad	swap utilization
-W	pswpin/s pswpout/s	swapping statistics
-v	dentused file-nr inode-nr	kernel tables
-d	tps rd_sec/s wr_sec/s avgrq-sz avgqu-sz await svctm %util	disk statistics
-n DEV	rxpck/s txpck/s rxkB/s txkB/s	network interface statistics
-n EDEV	rxerr/s txerr/s coll/s rxdrop/s txdrop/s rxfifo/s txfifo/s	network interface errors
-n IP	irec/s fwddgm/s orq/s	IP statistics
-n EIP	idisc/s odisc/s	IP errors
-n TCP	active/s passive/s iseg/s oseg/s	TCP statistics
-n ETCP	atmptf/s retrans/s	TCP errors
-n SOCK	totsck ip-frag tcp-tw	socket statistics

Some sar(1) options may require kernel features enabled (e.g., huge pages), and some metrics were added in later versions of sar(1) (version 10.0.2 is shown here).

Solaris

Option	Metrics	Description
-u	%usr %sys %idl	CPU utilization
-q	runq-sz %runocc	run-queue statistics
-g	pgout/s pgpgout/s pgfree/s pgscan/s	paging statistics 1
-p	atch/s pgin/s pgpgin/s pflt/s vflt/s slock/s	paging statistics 2
-k	sml_mem lg_mem ovsz_alloc	kernel memory
-r	freemem freeswap	unused memory
-w	swpin/s swpout/s	swapping statistics
-v	inod-sz	inode size
-d	%busy avque r+w/s blks/s avwait avserv	disk statistics

The version for Solaris-based systems is long overdue for an update; I hope it has been done by the time you read this.

Appendix D

DTrace One-Liners

This appendix contains some handy DTrace one-liners. Apart from being useful in themselves, they can help you learn DTrace, one line at a time. Some of these were demonstrated in previous chapters. Many may not work right away; they may depend on the presence of certain providers, or on a specific kernel version.

See Chapter 4, Observability Tools, for an introduction to DTrace.

syscall Provider

List syscall provider entry probes:

```
dtrace -ln syscall:::entry
```

Count syscalls by process name:

```
dtrace -n 'syscall:::entry { @[execname] = count(); }'
```

Count syscalls by syscall name:

```
dtrace -n 'syscall:::entry { @[probefunc] = count(); }'
```

Count syscalls by syscall name, for process ID 123:

```
dtrace -n 'syscall:::entry /pid == 123/ { @[probefunc] = count(); }'
```

Count syscalls by syscall name, for all processes named "httpd":

```
dtrace -n 'syscall:::entry /execname == "httpd"/ { @[probefunc] = count(); }'
```

Trace exec() return by time and process name:

```
dtrace -n 'syscall::exec*:return { printf("%Y %s", walltimestamp, execname); }'
```

Trace file open()s with process name and path name:

```
dtrace -n 'syscall::open:entry { printf("%s %s", execname, copyinstr(arg0)); }'
```

Trace file open()s with process name and path name (Oracle Solaris 11):

```
dtrace -n 'syscall::openat:entry { printf("%s %s", execname, copyinstr(arg1)); }'
```

Count read syscall variants in use:

```
dtrace -n 'syscall::*read*:entry { @[probefunc] = count(); }'
```

Count read() syscalls by file system type:

```
dtrace -n 'syscall::read:entry { @[fds[arg0].fi_fs] = count(); }'
```

Count write() syscalls by file system type:

```
dtrace -n 'syscall::write:entry { @[fds[arg0].fi_fs] = count(); }'
```

Count `read()` syscalls by file descriptor path name:

```
dtrace -n 'syscall::read:entry { @[fds[arg0].fi_pathname] = count(); }'
```

Summarize `read()` requested size as a power-of-two distribution, by process name:

```
dtrace -n 'syscall::read:entry { @[execname, "req (bytes)"] = quantize(arg2); }'
```

Summarize `read()` returned size as a power-of-two distribution, by process name:

```
dtrace -n 'syscall::read:return { @[execname, "rval (bytes)"] = quantize(arg1); }'
```

Summarize total `read()` returned bytes, by process name:

```
dtrace -n 'syscall::read:return { @[execname] = sum(arg1); }'
```

Summarize `read()` latency as a power-of-two distribution, for `"mysqld"` processes:

```
dtrace -n 'syscall::read:entry /execname == "mysqld"/ { self->ts = timestamp; }
    syscall::read:return /self->ts/ { @["ns"] =
    quantize(timestamp - self->ts); self->ts = 0; }'
```

Summarize `read()` CPU time, for `"mysqld"` processes:

```
dtrace -n 'syscall::read:entry /execname == "mysqld"/ { self->v = vtimestamp; }
    syscall::read:return /self->v/ { @["on-CPU (ns)"] =
    quantize(vtimestamp - self->v); self->v = 0; }'
```

Summarize `read()` latency as a linear distribution from 0 to 10 ms with a step of 1, for `"mysqld"` processes:

```
dtrace -n 'syscall::read:entry /execname == "mysqld"/ { self->ts = timestamp; }
    syscall::read:return /self->ts/ { @["ms"] =
    lquantize((timestamp - self->ts) / 1000000, 0, 10, 1); self->ts = 0; }'
```

Summarize `read()` latency as a power-of-two distribution, for reads to ZFS files:

```
dtrace -n 'syscall::read:entry /fds[arg0].fi_fs == "zfs"/ { self->ts = timestamp; }
    syscall::read:return /self->ts/ { @["ns"] =
    quantize(timestamp - self->ts); self->ts = 0; }'
```

Count socket `accept()` by process name:

```
dtrace -n 'syscall::accept:return { @[execname] = count(); }'
```

Count socket `connect()` by process name:

```
dtrace -n 'syscall::connect:entry { @[execname] = count(); }'
```

Trace socket `connect()` with process name and user-level stack trace:

```
dtrace -n 'syscall::connect:entry { trace(execname); ustack(); }'
```

Count socket reads, via `read()` or `recv()`, by process name:

```
dtrace -n 'syscall::read:entry,syscall::recv:entry
    /fds[arg0].fi_fs == "sockfs"/ { @[execname] = count(); }'
```

Count socket writes, via `write()` or `send()`, by process name:

```
dtrace -n 'syscall::write:entry,syscall::send:entry
    /fds[arg0].fi_fs == "sockfs"/ { @[execname] = count(); }'
```

Count `brk()`s (heap extensions) with user-level stacks, for "`mysqld`":

```
dtrace -n 'syscall::brk:entry /execname == "mysqld"/ { @[ustack()] = count(); }'
```

proc Provider

Trace new processes with process name and arguments:

```
dtrace -n 'proc:::exec-success { trace(curpsinfo->pr_psargs); }'
```

Count process-level events:

```
dtrace -n 'proc::: { @[probename] = count(); }'
```

Trace process signals:

```
dtrace -n 'proc:::signal-send /pid/ { printf("%s -%d %d", execname,
    args[2], args[1]->pr_pid); }'
```

profile Provider

Sample kernel stacks at 997 Hz:

```
dtrace -n 'profile-997 /arg0/ { @[stack()] = count(); }'
```

Sample kernel stacks at 997 Hz, top ten only:

```
dtrace -n 'profile-997 /arg0/ { @[stack()] = count(); } END { trunc(@, 10); }'
```

Sample kernel stacks, five frames only, at 997 Hz:

```
dtrace -n 'profile-997 /arg0/ { @[stack(5)] = count(); }'
```

Sample kernel on-CPU functions at 997 Hz:

```
dtrace -n 'profile-997 /arg0/ { @[func(arg0)] = count(); }'
```

Sample kernel on-CPU modules at 997 Hz:

```
dtrace -n 'profile-997 /arg0/ { @[mod(arg0)] = count(); }'
```

Sample user stacks at 97 Hz, for PID 123:

```
dtrace -n 'profile-97 /arg1 && pid == 123/ { @[ustack()] = count(); }'
```

Sample user stacks at 97 Hz, for all processes named "sshd":

```
dtrace -n 'profile-97 /arg1 && execname == "sshd"/ { @[ustack()] = count(); }'
```

Sample user stacks at 97 Hz, for all processes on the system (include process name in output):

```
dtrace -n 'profile-97 /arg1/ { @[execname, ustack()] = count(); }'
```

Sample user stacks at 97 Hz, top ten only, for PID 123:

```
dtrace -n 'profile-97 /arg1 && pid == 123/ { @[ustack()] = count(); }
   END { trunc(@, 10); }'
```

Sample user stacks, five frames only, at 97 Hz, for PID 123:

```
dtrace -n 'profile-97 /arg1 && pid == 123/ { @[ustack(5)] = count(); }'
```

Sample user on-CPU functions at 97 Hz, for PID 123:

```
dtrace -n 'profile-97 /arg1 && pid == 123/ { @[ufunc(arg1)] = count(); }'
```

Sample user on-CPU modules at 97 Hz, for PID 123:

```
dtrace -n 'profile-97 /arg1 && pid == 123/ { @[umod(arg1)] = count(); }'
```

Sample user stacks at 97 Hz, including during system time when the user stack is frozen (typically on a syscall), for PID 123:

```
dtrace -n 'profile-97 /pid == 123/ { @[ustack()] = count(); }'
```

Sample which CPU a process runs on, at 97 Hz, for PID 123:

```
dtrace -n 'profile-97 /pid == 123/ { @[cpu] = count(); }'
```

sched Provider

Summarize on-CPU time as a power-of-two distribution, for "sshd":

```
dtrace -n 'sched:::on-cpu /execname == "sshd"/ { self->ts = timestamp; }
    sched:::off-cpu /self->ts/ { @["ns"] = quantize(timestamp - self->ts);
    self->ts = 0; }'
```

Summarize off-CPU time (blocked) as a power-of-two distribution, for "sshd":

```
dtrace -n 'sched:::off-cpu /execname == "sshd"/ { self->ts = timestamp; }
    sched:::on-cpu /self->ts/ { @["ns"] = quantize(timestamp - self->ts);
    self->ts = 0; }'
```

Count off-CPU events showing kernel stack trace, for "sshd":

```
dtrace -n 'sched:::off-cpu /execname == "sshd"/ { @[stack()] = count(); }'
```

Count off-CPU events showing user stack trace, for "sshd":

```
dtrace -n 'sched:::off-cpu /execname == "sshd"/ { @[ustack()] = count(); }'
```

fbt Provider

Count VFS calls (Linux):

```
dtrace -n 'fbt::vfs_*:entry'
```

Count VFS calls (Linux) for processes named "`mysqld`":

```
dtrace -n 'fbt::vfs_*:entry /execname == "mysqld"/ { @[probefunc] = count(); }'
```

Count VFS calls (Solaris-based systems; use the fsinfo provider for stability):

```
dtrace -n 'fbt::fop_*:entry { @[probefunc] = count(); }'
```

List `ext4_*()` function calls:

```
dtrace -ln 'fbt::ext4_*:entry'
```

Count `ext4_*()` function calls:

```
dtrace -n 'fbt::ext4_*:entry { @[probefunc] = count(); }'
```

Count ZFS function calls (matching on the `zfs` kernel module):

```
dtrace -n 'fbt:zfs::entry { @[probefunc] = count(); }'
```

Summarize `zio_checksum_generate()` latency as a power-of-two distribution:

```
dtrace -n 'fbt::zio_checksum_generate:entry { self->ts = timestamp; }
    fbt::zio_checksum_generate:return /self->ts/ { @["ns"] =
    quantize(timestamp - self->ts); self->ts = 0; }'
```

Summarize `zio_checksum_generate()` CPU time:

```
dtrace -n 'fbt::zio_checksum_generate:entry { self->v = vtimestamp; }
    fbt::zio_checksum_generate:return /self->v/ { @["on-CPU (ns)"] =
    quantize(vtimestamp - self->v); self->v = 0; }'
```

Summarize VFS call latency (Solaris) for processes named "`mysqld`":

```
dtrace -n 'fbt::fop_*:entry /execname == "mysqld"/ { self->ts = timestamp; }
    fbt::fop_*:return /self->ts/ { @["ns"] =
    quantize(timestamp - self->ts); self->ts = 0; }'
```

Summarize kernel stack traces leading to `tcp_sendmesg()`:

```
dtrace -n 'fbt::tcp_sendmsg:entry { @[stack()] = count(); }'
```

Summarize kernel slab allocations by cache name and kernel stack (Solaris-based systems):

```
dtrace -n 'fbt::kmem_cache_alloc:entry {
    @[stringof(args[0]->cache_name), stack()] = count(); }'
```

pid Provider

List all functions from the loaded libsocket library, for PID 123:

```
dtrace -ln 'pid$target:libsocket::entry' -p 123
```

Count libsocket function calls, for PID 123:

```
dtrace -n 'pid$target:libsocket::entry { @[probefunc] = count(); }' -p 123
```

Summarize `malloc()` request size, as a power-of-two distribution, for PID 123:

```
dtrace -n 'pid$target::malloc:entry { @["req bytes"] = quantize(arg0); }' -p 123
```

Summarize `malloc()` request size, as a power-of-two distribution, with user-level stack trace, for PID 123:

```
dtrace -n 'pid$target::malloc:entry {
    @["req bytes, for:", ustack()] = count(); }' -p 123
```

io Provider

Summarize block I/O sizes, as a power-of-two distribution:

```
dtrace -n 'io:::start { @["bytes"] = quantize(args[0]->b_bcount); }'
```

Summarize block I/O sizes, as a power-of-two distribution, with process name (valid only for some synchronous code paths):

```
dtrace -n 'io:::start { @[execname] = quantize(args[0]->b_bcount); }'
```

Count block I/O by kernel stack trace (reason):

```
dtrace -n 'io:::start { @[stack()] = count(); }'
```

Summarize block I/O latency, as a power-of-two distribution:

```
dtrace -n 'io:::start { ts[arg0] = timestamp; }
    io:::done /this->ts = ts[arg0]/ { @["ns"] =
    quantize(timestamp - this->ts); ts[arg0] = 0; }'
```

sysinfo Provider

Count CPU cross calls by process name:

```
dtrace -n 'sysinfo:::xcalls { @[execname] = count(); }'
```

Count CPU cross calls by kernel stack trace:

```
dtrace -n 'sysinfo:::xcalls { @[stack()] = count(); }'
```

Summarize syscall read sizes, as a power-of-two distribution, by process name:

```
dtrace -n 'sysinfo:::readch { @dist[execname] = quantize(arg0); }'
```

Summarize syscall write sizes, as a power-of-two distribution, by process name:

```
dtrace -n 'sysinfo:::writech { @dist[execname] = quantize(arg0); }'
```

vminfo Provider

Count minor faults by process name:

```
dtrace -n 'vminfo:::as_fault { @[execname] = sum(arg0); }'
```

Count minor faults by user stack trace for processes named "mysqld":

```
dtrace -n 'vminfo:::as_fault /execname == "mysqld"/ { @[ustack()] = count(); }'
```

Count anonymous page-ins by PID and process name:

```
dtrace -n 'vminfo:::anonpgin { @[pid, execname] = count(); }'
```

ip Provider

Count received IP packets by host address:

```
dtrace -n 'ip:::receive { @[args[2]->ip_saddr] = count(); }'
```

Summarize IP send payload size, as a power-of-two distribution, by destination

```
dtrace -n 'ip:::send { @[args[2]->ip_daddr] = quantize(args[2]->ip_plength); }'
```

tcp provider

Trace inbound TCP connections by remote address:

```
dtrace -n 'tcp:::accept-established { trace(args[3]->tcps_raddr); }'
```

Count inbound connections with remote address and local port:

```
dtrace -n 'tcp:::accept-established {
    @[args[3]->tcps_raddr, args[3]->tcps_lport] = count(); }'
```

Count refused inbound connections with remote address and local port:

```
dtrace -n 'tcp:::accept-refused {
    @[args[2]->ip_daddr, args[4]->tcp_sport] = count(); }'
```

Count outbound connections by remote address and remote port:

```
dtrace -n 'tcp:::connect-established {
    @[args[3]->tcps_raddr , args[3]->tcps_rport] = count(); }'
```

Count TCP received packets by remote address:

```
dtrace -n 'tcp:::receive { @[args[2]->ip_saddr] = count(); }'
```

Count TCP sent packets by remote address:

```
dtrace -n 'tcp:::send { @[args[2]->ip_daddr] = count(); }'
```

Summarize sent IP payload size, as a power-of-two distribution:

```
dtrace -n 'tcp:::send { @[args[2]->ip_daddr] = quantize(args[2]->ip_plength); }'
```

Count TCP events by type:

```
dtrace -n 'tcp::: { @[probename] = count(); }'
```

udp provider

Count UDP received packets by remote address:

```
dtrace -n 'udp:::receive { @[args[2]->ip_saddr] = count(); }'
```

Count UDP sent packets by remote port:

```
dtrace -n 'udp:::send { @[args[4]->udp_dport] = count(); }'
```

Appendix E

DTrace to SystemTap

This appendix is a brief guide to converting DTrace one-liners and scripts to SystemTap. Both DTrace and SystemTap were introduced in Chapter 4, Observability Tools, which you should study as background.

Selected differences in functionality, terminology, probes, built-in variables, and functions are listed here. Several one-liners are then converted as examples.

For an additional reference, see "Translating Exiting [sic] DTrace Scripts into SystemTap Scripts" on the SystemTap wiki [1]. This wiki page also shows conversions of one-liners (some of my own) as examples.

Functionality

SystemTap has very similar functionality to DTrace (by design). Here are some key differences you'll encounter when porting scripts:

DTrace	SystemTap	Description
probename	probe *probename*	Probes require a `probe` keyword.
probe { var[a] =	global *var*; *probe { var[a]* =	Some variable types, such as associative arrays, need to be predeclared as "global."

continues

DTrace	SystemTap	Description
`self->var`	`var[tid()]`	SystemTap does not have thread-local variables (`self->`). The same functionality is accomplished using an associative array, keyed on the thread ID.
`/predicate/ { …`	`{ if (test) { … }`	Instead of predicates, SystemTap can use conditionals in the probe action.

`@a = count(x);`
 	
`...`
 	
`printa(@a);`
	`a <<< x;`
	
	`...`
	
	`print(count(a));`
		Instead of aggregations tied to a function (e.g., count), SystemTap uses statistic aggregations (`<<<`) that are later processed as desired.

`arg0 … argN` `args[0] … args[N]`	*depends on tapset*	DTrace probes have a standard set of argument variables and a typed array; SystemTap provides custom typed variables depending on the tapset and probe (see [2]).

These changes are demonstrated in the later examples.

Terminology

DTrace	SystemTap
provider	tapset
aggregation	statistic aggregation (although it does more)

Probes

DTrace	SystemTap
`BEGIN`	`begin`
`END`	`end`
`syscall:::entry`	`syscall.*`
`syscall:::return`	`syscall.*.return`
`syscall::read:entry`	`syscall.read`

DTrace	SystemTap
`syscall::read:return`	`syscall.read.return`
`proc:::exec-success`	`process.begin`
`sched:::on-cpu`	`scheduler.cpu_on`
`sched:::off-cpu`	`scheduler.cpu_off`
`profile:::profile-100`	`timer.profile`
`profile:::tick-10s`	`timer.s(10)`
`fbt::foo:entry`	`kernel.function("foo")`
`fbt::foo:return`	`kernel.function("foo").return`
`io:::start`	`ioblock.request`
`io:::done`	`ioblock.end`

Built-in Variables

DTrace	SystemTap
`execname`	`execname()`
`uid`	`uid()`
`pid`	`pid()`
`cpu`	`cpu()`
`timestamp`	`gettimeofday_ns()`
`vtimestamp`	*N/A*
`walltimestamp`	`gettimeofday_s()`
`arg0..N`	*custom variable (see tapset docs [2])*
`args[0]..[N]`	*custom variable (see tapset docs [2])*
`curthread`	`task_current()`
`probename`	*N/A*
`probefunc`	`probefunc()`
`probemod`	`probemod()`
`curpsinfo->pr_psargs`	`cmdline_str()`
`$target`	`target()`

Functions

DTrace	SystemTap
copyinstr()	user_string()
stack()	print_backtrace()
ustack()	print_ubacktrace()
quantize()	@hist_log()
lquantize()	@hist_linear()
exit(*status*)	exit()

Example 1: Listing syscall Entry Probes

DTrace:

```
# dtrace -ln syscall:::entry
ID    PROVIDER          MODULE                          FUNCTION NAME
   24    syscall                                        nosys entry
   26    syscall                                        rexit entry
   28    syscall                                         read entry
   30    syscall                                        write entry
[...]
```

SystemTap:

```
# stap -l 'syscall.*'
syscall.accept
syscall.access
syscall.acct
syscall.add_key
[...]
```

Example 2: Summarize read() Returned Size

DTrace:

```
# dtrace -n 'syscall::read:return { @bytes = quantize(arg1); }'
dtrace: description 'syscall::read:return ' matched 1 probe
^C
```

```
value ------------- Distribution ------------- count
   -2 |                                            0
   -1 |                                            1
    0 |                                            0
    1 |@@@@@@@@@@@@@@@@@@@@@                       94
    2 |@@@@                                        22
    4 |                                            0
    8 |                                            0
   16 |@                                           5
   32 |@@@@@@@@@@@@                                56
   64 |                                            1
  128 |                                            1
  256 |@                                           4
  512 |@@@                                        15
 1024 |                                            0
```

DTrace summarizes `arg1`, the return of the `read()` syscall. For SystemTap, this is a custom variable from the `syscall.read.return` probe, which should be documented in the *SystemTap Tapset Reference Manual* [2]. Another way to find probes is to list them with the `-L` option, which shows the probes and their types:

```
# stap -L syscall.read.return
syscall.read.return name:string retstr:string $return:long int $fd:unsigned int
$buf:char* $count:size_t
```

The output includes `$return:long` and `$count:size_t`, both of which sound promising. Currently, `$count` is not documented in the tapset reference, tapset source [3], or *SystemTap Language Reference* [4]. It is mentioned in the *System-Tap Beginners Guide* [5]: it is the requested size. `$return` is the returned value: the actual bytes read in this case, which is what we'll use here.

SystemTap, default output:

```
# stap -e 'global bytes; probe syscall.read.return { bytes <<< $return; }'
^Cbytes @count=125 @min=-11 @max=1027 @sum=10935 @avg=87
```

The default output is a terse description of the statistic aggregation. This might include the details you want (`count`, `min`, `max`, `sum`, `avg`). Since we'd like the power-of-two distribution, we will need to print it using the `@histlog()` function.

SystemTap, power-of-two distribution:

```
# stap -e 'global bytes; probe syscall.read.return { bytes <<< $return; }
    probe end { print(@hist_log(bytes)); }'
^Cvalue |---------------------------------------------------- count
  -32 |                                            0
  -16 |                                            0
   -8 |@@@@@@@@@@@@@@@@@@@@                        19
```

continues

```
  -4 |                                                                      0
  -2 |                                                                      0
  -1 |                                                                      0
   0 |@@@@@@@@@@@@@@@@@@@@@@@@@@@@@@@@@@@@@@@@@@@                           32
   1 |@@@@@@@@@@@@@@@@@@@@@@@@@@@@@@@@                                     25
   2 |@@@@@@@@@@@@@@@@                                                    13
   4 |@                                                                   1
   8 |                                                                    0
  16 |@                                                                   1
  32 |@@@@@@@@@@@@@@@@@@@@@@@@@@@@@@@@@@                                   27
  64 |@                                                                   1
 128 |@                                                                   1
 256 |@@@@@@@@@                                                           8
 512 |@@@@@@@@@@@@@@@@@@@@@@@@@@@@@@@@@@@@@@@@@@@@@@@                      36
1024 |@@@                                                                 3
2048 |                                                                    0
4096 |                                                                    0
```

This is now equivalent to the DTrace version. The SystemTap ASCII histogram makes greater use of the horizontal range, showing more detail.

Example 3: Count syscalls by Process Name

DTrace:

```
# dtrace -n 'syscall:::entry { @[execname] = count(); }'
dtrace: description 'syscall:::entry ' matched 233 probes
^C

  svc.configd                                                      1
  mysqld                                                          10
  sshd                                                            59
  dtrace                                                        1108
  gzip                                                         12105
  tar                                                          33833
```

SystemTap, default output:

```
# stap -e 'global ops; probe syscall.* { ops[execname()] <<< 1; }'
^Cops["date"] @count=18686 @min=1 @max=1 @sum=18686 @avg=1
ops["tar"] @count=16652 @min=1 @max=1 @sum=16652 @avg=1
ops["gzip"] @count=1323 @min=1 @max=1 @sum=1323 @avg=1
ops["stapio"] @count=370 @min=1 @max=1 @sum=370 @avg=1
ops["stap"] @count=4 @min=1 @max=1 @sum=4 @avg=1
ops["rsyslogd"] @count=4 @min=1 @max=1 @sum=4 @avg=1
ops["rs:main Q:Reg"] @count=4 @min=1 @max=1 @sum=4 @avg=1
ops["rpcbind"] @count=2 @min=1 @max=1 @sum=2 @avg=1
```

In this case, the variable is an associative array of statistic aggregations. The default output of SystemTap does show what we are after—the syscall name and the count—but is a little hard to read. It can be formatted using `printf()` in a loop, stepping over each key from the associative array.

SystemTap, formatted output:

```
# stap -e 'global agg; probe syscall.* { agg[execname()] <<< 1; }
    probe end { foreach (k in agg+) {
    printf("%-36s %8d\n", k, @count(agg[k])); } }'
^Cstap                                      4
rsyslogd                                    4
rs:main Q:Reg                               4
sshd                                       74
stapio                                    148
gzip                                    70091
tar                                     83697
```

This is now equivalent, and the `printf()` can be customized further if desired. Note the use of "+" in `foreach (k in agg+)`: this iterates over the statistic aggregation in ascending value order. Use "-" for descending, and nothing if the order is unimportant.

The examples that follow use the default output of statistic aggregations and also show the commands only. Add code, like that shown in Example 2 and Example 3 to produce readable output when desired.

Example 4: Count syscalls by syscall Name, for Process ID 123

DTrace:

```
dtrace -n 'syscall:::entry /pid == 123/ { @[probefunc] = count(); }'
```

SystemTap:

```
stap -e 'global ops; probe syscall.* { if (pid() == 123) {
    ops[probefunc()] <<< 1; } }'
```

This uses `probefunc()`, which prints the kernel function name where the probe is located (e.g., "sys_write" for `write()`). You can change `probefunc()` to name, which produces just the syscall names (e.g., "write" for `write()`, although the *Language Reference* suggests this might work only most of the time).

Example 5: Count syscalls by syscall Name, for "httpd" Processes

DTrace:

```
dtrace -n 'syscall:::entry /execname == "httpd"/ { @[probefunc] = count(); }'
```

SystemTap:

```
stap -e 'global ops; probe syscall.* { if (execname() == "httpd") {
    ops[probefunc()] <<< 1; } }'
```

Example 6: Trace File open()s with Process Name and Path Name

DTrace:

```
dtrace -n 'syscall::open:entry { printf("%s %s", execname, copyinstr(arg0)); }'
```

SystemTap:

```
stap -e 'syscall.open { printf("%s %s", execname(), user_string($filename)); }'
```

Note

I've never actually seen this work.

Example 7: Summarize read() Latency for "mysqld" Processes

DTrace:

```
dtrace -n 'syscall::read:entry /execname == "mysqld"/ { self->ts = timestamp; }
    syscall::read:return /self->ts/ { @["ns"] =
    quantize(timestamp - self->ts); self->ts = 0; }'
```

SystemTap:

```
stap -ve 'global t, s; probe syscall.read { if (execname() == "mysqld") {
    t[tid()] = gettimeofday_ns(); } }
    probe syscall.read.return { if (t[tid()]) {
    s <<< gettimeofday_ns() - t[tid()]; delete t[tid()]; } }
    probe end { printf("ns\n"); print(@hist_log(s)); }'
```

SystemTap, using @entry:

```
stap -e 'global s; probe syscall.read.return { if (execname() == "mysqld") {
    s <<< gettimeofday_ns() - @entry(gettimeofday_ns()); } }
    probe end { printf("ns\n"); print(@hist_log(s)); }'
```

@entry is not currently documented in the *SystemTap Language Reference*, but it does appear in some examples. It is used here to fetch the result of gettimeofday_ns() from the entry to this system call, so that the latency can be calculated.

It is important to be aware of which probes are traced, and which variables are used, when estimating the overhead of a script. For @entry to work, I *assume* that it auto-instantiates a syscall.read entry probe which calls gettimeofday_ns(), stores the result in a thread-associated variable, and frees it after use.

Example 8: Trace New Processes with Process Name and Arguments

DTrace:

```
dtrace -n 'proc:::exec-success { trace(curpsinfo->pr_psargs); }'
```

SystemTap:

```
stap -e 'probe process.begin { printf("%s\n", cmdline_str()); }'
```

The probe locations may not be at exactly the same point during new process execution, but this should be close enough.

Example 9: Sample Kernel Stacks at 100 Hz

DTrace:

```
dtrace -n 'profile-100 { @[stack()] = count(); }'
```

SystemTap:

```
stap -e 'global s; probe timer.profile { s[backtrace()] <<< 1; }
    probe end { foreach (i in s+) { print_stack(i);
    printf("\t%d\n", @count(s[i])); } }'
```

References

[1]   http://sourceware.org/systemtap/wiki/PortingDTracetoSystemTap

[2]   http://sourceware.org/systemtap/tapsets

[3]   /usr/share/systemtap/tapset

[4]   http://sourceware.org/systemtap/langref/langref.html

[5]   https://access.redhat.com/site/documentation/en-US/Red_Hat_Enterprise_
       Linux/5/html-single/SystemTap_Beginners_Guide

Appendix F

Solutions to Selected Exercises

The following are suggested solutions to selected exercises.

Chapter 2—Methodology

Q. What is latency?

A. A measure of time, usually time waiting for something to be done. In the IT industry, it is used differently depending on context.

Chapter 3—Operating Systems

Q. List the reasons why a thread would leave the CPU.

A. Blocked on I/O, blocked on a lock, call to yield, expired time slice, preempted by another thread, device interrupt, exiting.

Chapter 6—CPUs

Q. Calculate the load average . . .

A. 34

Q. Describe CPU behavior visible from this Solaris-based screen shot alone.

A. There are many `mysqld` threads from the same process (multithreaded) on-CPU, which are spending most of their time sleeping or blocked on locks—which might be normal (it depends on how `mysqld` waits for work). The most interesting detail is the CPU run-queue latency time (`LAT`) of between 5% and 11% per thread, which is evidence of CPU saturation. The load averages of 32 and beyond should be compared to the CPU count and CPU quota available to `mysqld` (if resource controls are present), as the fix is either more CPUs, more CPU quota, or tuning `mysqld` to consume less CPU—which may involve moving some work to a different system. The `USR`/`SYS` breakdown is around 2.5/1%, which for over 10 K syscalls/s (SCL) seems reasonable.

Chapter 7—Memory

Q. Using Unix terminology, what is the difference between paging and swapping?

A. Paging is the movement of small pages; swapping is the movement of entire processes.

Q. Describe memory utilization and saturation.

A. For memory capacity, utilization is the amount that is in use and not available, measured against the total usable memory. This can be presented as a percentage, similar to file system capacity. Saturation is a measure of the demand for available memory beyond the size of memory, which usually invokes a kernel routine to free memory to satisfy this demand.

Chapter 8—File Systems

Q. What is the difference between logical I/O and physical I/O?

A. Logical I/O is to the file system interface; physical I/O is to the storage devices (disks).

Q. Explain how file system copy-on-write can improve performance.

A. Since random writes can be written to a new location, they can be grouped (by increasing I/O size) and written out sequentially. Both of these factors usually improve performance, depending on the storage device type.

Chapter 9—Disks

Q. Describe what happens when disks are overloaded with work, including the effect on application performance.

A. The disks run at a continual high utilization rate (up to 100%) and a degree of saturation (queueing). Their I/O latency is increased due to the likelihood of queueing (which can be modeled). If the application is performing file system or disk I/O, the increased latency *may* hurt application performance, provided it is a synchronous I/O type: reads, or synchronous writes. It must also occur during a critical application code path, such as while a request is serviced, and not an asynchronous background task (which may only *indirectly* cause poor application performance). Usually back pressure from the increased I/O latency will keep the rate of I/O requests in check and not cause an unbounded increase in latency.

Chapter 11—Cloud Computing

Q. Describe physical system observability from an OS-virtualized guest.

A. Depending on the host kernel implementation, the guest can see high-level metrics of all physical resources, including CPUs and disks, and notice when they are utilized by other tenants. Any metric that would be considered an information leak is blocked by the kernel. For example, utilization for a CPU may be observable (say, 50%), but not the process IDs and names from other tenants that are causing it.

Appendix G

Systems Performance Who's Who

It can be useful at times to know who created the technologies that we use. This is a list of who's who in the field of systems performance, based on the Linux- and Solaris-related technologies in this book. Identifying everyone properly is a difficult task, and this is the first attempt do so, inspired by the Unix who's who list in [Libes 89]. Apologies to those who are missing or misappropriated. For those wishing to dig further into the people and history, see the references in the Bibliography, the names listed in the Linux source code, and the authors in the illumos repository.

John Allspaw: capacity planning [Allspaw 08].

Jens Axboe: CFQ I/O Scheduler, fio, blktrace, per backing device write-back.

Jeff Bonwick: invented kernel slab allocation, co-invented user-level slab allocation, co-invented ZFS, kstat, first developed `mpstat`.

Tim Bray: authored the Bonnie disk I/O micro-benchmark, known for XML.

Bryan Cantrill: father of DTrace; Solaris kernel hi-res cyclics; debunked Solaris n:m implementation; authored Oracle ZFS Storage Appliance Analytics.

Rémy Card: primary developer for the ext2 and ext3 file systems.

Nadia Yvette Chambers: Linux hugetlbfs.

Guillaume Chazarain: `iotop(1)` for Linux.

Adrian Cockcroft: performance books ([Cockcroft 95], [Cockcroft 98]), Virtual Adrian (SE Toolkit).

Tim Cook: nicstat(1) for Linux, and enhancements.

Alan Cox: Linux network stack performance.

Mathieu Desnoyers: Linux Trace Toolkit (LTTng), Linux Trace Toolkit Viewer (LTTV), kernel tracepoints, main author of userspace RCU.

Srikar Dronamraju: Linux uprobes.

Frank Ch. Eigler: lead developer for SystemTap.

Kevin Robert Elz: DNLC.

Roger Faulkner: wrote /proc for UNIX System V, thread implementation for Solaris, and the truss(1) system call tracer.

Thomas Gleixner: Various Linux kernel performance work including hrtimers.

Sebastien Godard: sysstat package for Linux, which contains numerous performance tools including iostat(1), mpstat(1), pidstat(1), nfsiostat(1), cifsiostat(1), and an enhanced version of sar(1), sadc(8), sadf(1) (see the metrics in Appendix C).

Brendan Gregg: nicstat(1), psio, DTraceToolkit (original iosnoop, iotop, rwtop, tcptop, dtruss, execsnoop, etc.), original DTrace ip, tcp, udp, javascript providers, ZFS L2ARC; USE method, TSA method, etc.; latency, utilization, and subsecond-offset heat maps, flame graphs; books: [McDougall 06b], [Gregg 11], this one.

Dr. Neil Gunther: Universal Scalability Law, ternary plots for CPU utilization, performance books [Gunther 97].

Van Jacobson: traceroute(8), pathchar, TCP/IP performance.

Raj Jain: systems performance theory [Jain 91].

Jerry Jelinek: Solaris Zones.

Bill Joy: vmstat(1), BSD virtual memory work, TCP/IP performance, FFS.

Vamsi Krishna S: kprobes.

Christoph Lameter: SLUB allocator.

William LeFebvre: wrote the first version of top(1), inspiring many other tools.

John Levon: OProfile, DTrace ustack helper for Python.

Mike Loukides: first book on Unix systems performance [Loukides 90], which either began or encouraged the tradition of resource-based analysis: CPU, memory, disk, network.

Robert Love: Linux kernel performance work, including for preemption.

Marshall Kirk McKusick: FFS, work on BSD.

David S. Miller: Linux network stack improvements.

Cary Millsap: Method R.

Ingo Molnar: O(1) scheduler, completely fair scheduler, voluntary kernel preemption, ftrace, perf, and work on real-time preemption, mutexes, futexes, scheduler profiling, work queues.

Andrew Morton: fadvise, read-ahead.

Mike Muuss: ping(8).

Shailabh Nagar: Delay accounting, taskstats.

Dave Pacheco: DTrace ustack helper for V8/Node.js.

Rich Pettit: SE Toolkit.

Nick Piggin: Linux scheduler domains.

Bill Pijewski: vfsstat(1M), ZFS I/O throttling.

Dennis Ritchie: Unix, and its original performance features: process priorities, swapping, buffer cache, etc.

Tom Rodriguez: DTrace ustack helper for Java.

Steven Rostedt: adaptive spinning mutexes, ftrace, KernelShark.

Rusty Russell: original futexes, various Linux kernel work.

Eric Saxe: Solaris kernel performance improvements.

Michael Shapiro: co-created DTrace, Solaris /proc enhancements.

Balbir Singh: Linux memory resource controller, delay accounting, taskstats, cgroupstats, CPU accounting.

Ken Thompson: Unix, and its original performance features: process priorities, swapping, buffer cache, etc.

Linus Torvalds: the Linux kernel and numerous core components necessary for systems performance, Linux I/O scheduler.

Arjan van de Ven: latencytop, PowerTOP, irqbalance, work on Linux scheduler profiling.

Dag Wieers: dstat.

Peter Zijlstra: adaptive spinning mutex implementation, hardirq callbacks framework, other Linux performance work.

Glossary

ACK TCP acknowledgment.

adaptive mutex A mutex (mutual exclusion) synchronization lock type. See Chapter 5, Applications.

address A memory location.

address space A virtual memory context. See Chapter 7, Memory.

aggregation A grouping of data. The term is usually used in the DTrace/SystemTap context, referring to a grouping of data into buckets.

API Application programming interface.

application A program, typically user-level.

array A set of values. This is a data type for programming languages.

associative array A data type for programming languages where values are referenced by an arbitrary key, which may be a text string.

AT&T The American Telephone and Telegraph Company, which included Bell Laboratories, where Unix was developed.

balanced system A system without a bottleneck.

BSD Berkeley Software Distribution, a derivative of Unix.

buffer A region of memory used for temporary data.

C The C programming language.

cache hit A request for data that can be returned from the contents of the cache.

cache miss A request for data that was not found in the cache.

cache warmth See Hot, Cold, and Warm Caches in Section 2.3.14, Caching, in Chapter 2, Methodology.

client A consumer of a network service, referring to either the client host or the client application.

command A program executed at the shell.

concurrency See Section 5.2.5, Concurrency and Parallelism, in Chapter 5, Applications.

CPI Cycles per instruction. See Chapter 6, CPUs.

CPU Central processing unit. This term refers to the set of functional units that execute instructions, including the registers and arithmetic logic unit (ALU). It is now often used to refer to either the processor or a virtual CPU.

CPU cross call A call by a CPU to request work from others on a multi-CPU system. Cross calls can be for system-wide events such as CPU cache coherency. See Chapter 6, CPUs.

CPU cycle A unit of time based on the clock rate of the processor: for 2 GHz, each cycle is 0.5 ns. A cycle itself is an electrical signal, the rising or falling of voltage, used to trigger digital logic.

cross call See CPU cross call.

CTSS Compatible Time-Sharing System, one of the first time-sharing systems.

D The programming language supported by DTrace and processed by `dtrace(1M)` and `libdtrace(3LIB)`. It was inspired by the C and awk programming languages.

debuginfo file A Linux kernel symbol and debug information file, used by debuggers and profilers.

DEC Digital Equipment Corporation.

disk A physical storage device. Also see HDD and SSD.

disk controller A component that manages directly attached disks, making them accessible to the system, either directly or mapped as virtual disks. Disk controllers may be built into the system main board, included as expansion cards, or built into storage arrays. They support one or more storage interface types (e.g., SCSI, SATA, SAS) and are also commonly called *host bus adaptors* (HBAs), along with the interface type, for example, *SAS HBA*.

DRAM Dynamic random-access memory, a type of volatile memory in common use as main memory.

dynamic tracing Instrumentation of live software by dynamically changing the loaded instructions. See Chapter 4, Observability Tools.

ECC Error-correcting code. An algorithm for detecting errors and fixing some error types (usually single-bit errors).

Ethernet A set of standards for networking at the physical and data link layers.

expander card A physical device (card) connected to the system, usually to provide an additional I/O controller.

file descriptor An identifier for a program to use in referencing an open file.

fsck The file system check command is used to repair file systems after system failure, such as due to a power outage or kernel panic, and is a process that can take a long time (hours).

HDD Hard disk drive, a rotational magnetic storage device. See Chapter 9, Disks.

Hertz (Hz) Cycles per second.

host A system connected to the network.

I/O Input/output.

illumos An active fork of the OpenSolaris kernel. It is used by (among others) Joyent SmartOS and OmniTI OmniOS.

IOPS I/O operations per second, a measure of the rate of I/O.

IPC Inter-process communication, a means for processes to exchange data. Sockets are an IPC mechanism.

IRIX A Unix-derived operating system by Silicon Graphics, Inc. (SGI).

IRQ Interrupt request, a hardware signal to the processor to request work. See Chapter 3, Operating Systems.

kernel level The context of the kernel, in the kernel address space, and with the kernel (or privileged) CPU mode.

local disks Disks that are connected directly to the server and are managed by the server. These include disks that are internal to the server case and those attached directly via a storage transport.

logical processor Another name for a *virtual CPU*. See Chapter 6, CPUs.

LRU Least recently used. See Section 2.3.14, Caching, in Chapter 2, Methodology.

main board The circuit board that houses the processors and system interconnect; also called the *system board*.

major fault A memory access fault that was serviced from storage devices (disks). See Chapter 3, Operating Systems.

minor fault A memory access fault that was serviced from main memory. See Chapter 3, Operating Systems.

mysqld The daemon for the MySQL database.

operation rate Operations per interval (e.g., operations per second), which may include non-I/O operations.

parallel See Section 5.2.5, Concurrency and Parallelism, in Chapter 5, Applications.

PC Program counter, a CPU register that points to the currently executing instruction.

PDP Programmed Data Processor, a minicomputer series made by Digital Equipment Corporation (DEC).

POSIX Portable Operating System Interface, a family of related standards by the IEEE to define a Unix API. This includes a file system interface as used by applications, provided via system calls or system libraries built upon system calls.

process An operating system abstraction of a running program.

processor ring A protection mode for the CPU.

real-time workload One that has fixed latency requirements, usually low latency.

registers Small storage locations on a CPU, used directly from CPU instructions for data processing.

remote disks Disks (including virtual disks) that are used by a server but are connected to a remote system.

RFC Request for Comments, a document created by the network community to share networking standards and best practices.

ROI Return on investment, a business metric.

RX Receive (used in networking).

sector A data unit size for storage devices, commonly 512 bytes or 4 Kbytes. See Chapter 9, Disks.

server In networking, a network host that provides a service for network clients, such as an HTTP or database server. The term *server* can also refer to a physical system.

SmartOS An illumos kernel-based operating system, engineered for cloud computing use, that includes DTrace, ZFS, Zones, and KVM. See Chapter 11, Cloud Computing.

Solaris A Unix-derived operating system originally developed by Sun Microsystems. It is popular for enterprise use and is known for scalability, for reliability, and for introducing innovative features such as DTrace, ZFS, and Zones. Since the acquisition of Sun by Oracle Corporation, it has been renamed Oracle Solaris.

SONET Synchronous optical networking, a physical layer protocol for optical fibers.

SPARC A processor architecture (from *s*calable *p*rocessor *ar*chitecture).

SSD Solid-state drive, a storage device typically based on flash memory. See Chapter 9, Disks.

stack A group (stack) of functions and registers maintained by the CPU for tracking program state. These are often inspected as part of performance analysis, particularly CPU profiling.

static tracing Instrumentation of software with precompiled probe points. See Chapter 4, Observability Tools.

storage array A collection of disks housed in an enclosure, which can then be attached to a system. Storage arrays typically provide various features to improve disk reliability and performance.

SUT System under test.

SYN TCP synchronize.

syscall System call. See Chapter 3, Operating Systems.

task A Linux runnable entity, which may be a process, a thread from a multi-threaded process, or a kernel thread. See Chapter 3, Operating Systems.

TENEX TEN-EXtended operating system, based on TOPS-10 for the PDP-10.

thread An executable context that can be scheduled to run on a CPU. The kernel has multiple threads, and a process contains one or more. See Chapter 3, Operating Systems.

throughput For network communication devices, throughput commonly refers to the data transfer rate in either bits per second or bytes per second. Throughput may also refer to I/O completions per second (IOPS) when used with statistical analysis, especially for targets of study.

tunable Short for tunable parameter.

TX Transmit (used in networking).

user level The context of processes, in user-space with user mode.

VMS Virtual Memory System, an operating system by DEC.

x86 A processor architecture based on the Intel 8086.

Bibliography

[Amdahl 67]   Amdahl, G. "Validity of the Single Processor Approach to Achieving Large Scale Computing Capabilities." AFIPS, 1967.

[Corbató 68]   Corbató, F. J. *A Paging Experiment with the Multics System.* MIT Project MAC Report MAC-M-384, 1968.

[Graham 68]   Graham, B. "Protection in an Information Processing Utility," *Communications of the ACM*, May 1968.

[Denning 70]   Denning, P. "Virtual Memory," *ACM Computing Surveys (CSUR)* 2, no. 3 (1970).

[Saltzer 70]   Saltzer, J., and J. Gintell. "The Instrumentation of Multics," *Communications of the ACM*, August 1970.

[Bobrow 72]   Bobrow, D., et al. "TENEX: A Paged Time Sharing System for the PDP-10*," *Communications of the ACM*, March 1972.

[Goldberg 73]   Goldberg, R. P. *Architectural Principles for Virtual Computer Systems* (Thesis). Harvard University, 1973.

[Myer 73]   Myer, T. H., J. R. Barnaby, and W. W. Plummer. *TENEX Executive Manual.* Bolt, Baranek and Newman, Inc., April 1973.

[Ritchie 74]   Ritchie, D., and K. Thompson. "The UNIX Time-Sharing System," *Communications of the ACM* 17, no. 7 (July 1974), pp. 365–75.

[Knuth 76]   Knuth, D. "Big Omicron and Big Omega and Big Theta," *ACM SIGACT News*, 1976.

[Lions 77]   Lions, J. *A Commentary on the Sixth Edition UNIX Operating System*. University of New South Wales, 1977.

[Peterson 77]   Peterson, J., and T. Norman. "Buddy Systems," *Communications of the ACM*, 1977.

[Thompson 78]   Thompson, K. *UNIX Implementation*. Bell Laboratories, 1978.

[Babaoglu 79]   Babaoglu, O., W. Joy, and J. Porcar. *Design and Implementation of the Berkeley Virtual Memory Extensions to the UNIX Operating System*. Computer Science Division, Department of Electrical Engineering and Computer Science, University of California, Berkeley, 1979.

[Hinnant 84]   Hinnant, D. "Benchmarking UNIX Systems," *BYTE* magazine 9, no. 8 (August 1984).

[McKusick 84]   McKusick, M., et al. "A Fast File System for UNIX," *ACM Transactions on Computer Systems (TOC)* 2, no. 3 (August 1984).

[Saltzer 84]   Saltzer, J., D. Reed, and D. Clark. "End-to-End Arguments in System Design. *ACM TOCS*, November 1984.

[Anon 85]   Anon et al. "A Measure of Transaction Processing Power," *Datamation*, April 1, 1985.

[Bach 86]   Bach, M. J. *The Design of the UNIX Operating System*. Prentice Hall, 1986.

[Patterson 88]   Patterson, D., G. Gibson, and R. Kats. "A Case for Redundant Arrays of Inexpensive Disks." ACM SIGMOD, 1988.

[Libes 89]   Libes, D., and S. Ressler. *Life with UNIX: A Guide for Everyone*. Prentice Hall, 1989.

[Loukides 90]   Loukides, M. *System Performance Tuning*. O'Reilly, 1990.

[Jain 91]   Jain, R. *The Art of Computer Systems Performance Analysis: Techniques for Experimental Design, Measurement, Simulation, and Modeling*. Wiley, 1991.

[Stevens 93]   Stevens, W. R. *TCP/IP Illustrated,* Volume 1. Addison-Wesley, 1993.

[Bonwick 94]   Bonwick, J. "The Slab Allocator: An Object-Caching Kernel
                    Memory Allocator." USENIX, 1994.

[Goodheart 94]   Goodheart, B., and J. Cox. *The Magic Garden Explained:
                    The Internals of UNIX System V Release 4, an Open Systems
                    Design*. Prentice Hall, 1994.

[Cockcroft 95]   Cockcroft, A. *Sun Performance and Tuning*. Prentice Hall,
                    1995.

[Cantrill 96]   Cantrill, B. *Runtime Performance Analysis of the M-to-N
                    Scheduling Model* (Thesis). Brown University, 1996.

[Mathis 96]   Mathis, M., and J. Mahdavi. "Forward Acknowledgement:
                    Refining TCP Congestion Control." ACM SIGCOMM, 1996.

[Vahalia 96]   Vahalia, U. *UNIX Internals: The New Frontiers*. Prentice Hall,
                    1996.

[Gunther 97]   Gunther, N. *The Practical Performance Analyst*. McGraw-Hill,
                    1997.

[Knuth 97]   Knuth, D. *The Art of Computer Programming,* Volume 1,
                    Fundamental Algorithms, 3rd Edition. Addison-Wesley, 1997.

[Wong 97]   Wong, B. *Configuration and Capacity Planning for Solaris
                    Servers*. Prentice Hall, 1997.

[Cockcroft 98]   Cockcroft, A., and R. Pettit. *Sun Performance and Tuning:
                    Java and the Internet*. Prentice Hall, 1998.

[Downey 99]   Downey, A. "Using pathchar to Estimate Internet Link Char-
                    acteristics." ACM SIGCOMM, October 1999.

[Elling 00]   Elling, R. *Static Performance Tuning*. Sun Blueprints, 2000.

[Bonwick 01]   Bonwick, J., and J. Adams. "Magazines and Vmem: Extend-
                    ing the Slab Allocator to Many CPUs and Arbitrary
                    Resources." USENIX, 2001.

[Mauro 01]   Mauro, J., and R. McDougall. *Solaris Internals: Core Kernel
                    Architecture*. Prentice Hall, 2001.

[Musumeci 02]   Musumeci, G. D., and M. Loukides. *System Performance Tun-
                    ing, 2nd Edition*. O'Reilly, 2002.

[Waldspurger 02]   Waldspurger, C. "Memory Resource Management in VMware ESX Server," *Proceedings of the 5th Symposium on Operating Systems Design and Implementation*, 2002.

[Hassan 03]   Hassan, M., and R. Jain. *High Performance TCP/IP Networking*. Prentice Hall, 2003.

[Millsap 03]   Millsap, C., and J. Holt. *Optimizing Oracle Performance*. O'Reilly, 2003.

[Cantrill 04]   Cantrill, B., M. Shapiro, and A. Leventhal. "Dynamic Instrumentation of Production Systems." USENIX, 2004.

[Deri 04]   Deri, L. "Improving Passive Packet Capture: Beyond Device Polling," *Proceedings of SANE*, 2004.

[Gorman 04]   Gorman, M. *Understanding the Linux Virtual Memory Manager*. Prentice Hall, 2004.

[Neville-Neil 04]   Neville-Neil, G. V., and M. K. McKusick. *The Design and Implementation of the FreeBSD Operating System*. Addison-Wesley, 2004.

[Bovet 05]   Bovet, D., and M. Cesati. *Understanding the Linux Kernel, 3rd Edition*. O'Reilly, 2005.

[Bulpin 05]   Bulpin, J., and I. Pratt. "Hyper-Threading Aware Process Scheduling Heuristics." USENIX, 2005.

[Cherkasova 05]   Cherkasova, L., and R. Gardner. "Measuring CPU Overhead for I/O Processing in the Xen Virtual Machine Monitor." USENIX ATEC'05.

[Corbet 05]   Corbet, J., A. Rubini, and G. Kroah-Hartman. *Linux Device Drivers, 3rd Edition*. O'Reilly, 2005.

[Eigler 05]   Eigler, F. Ch., et al. *Architecture of systemtap: A Linux Trace/Probe Tool*, 2005. http://sourceware.org/systemtap/archpaper.pdf.

[Adams 06]   Adams, K., and O. Agesen. "A Comparison of Software and Hardware Techniques for x86 Virtualization." ASPLOS'06.

[Cantrill 06]   Cantrill, B. "Hidden in Plain Sight," *ACM Queue*, 2006.

[Gupta 06]   Gupta, D., L. Cherkasova, R. Gardner, and A. Vahdat. "Enforcing Performance Isolation across Virtual Machines in Xen." ACM/IFIP/USENIX Middleware'06.

[McDougall 06a]   McDougall, R., and J. Mauro. *Solaris Internals: Solaris 10 and OpenSolaris Kernel Architecture*. Prentice Hall, 2006.

[McDougall 06b]   McDougall, R., J. Mauro, and B. Gregg. *Solaris Performance and Tools: DTrace and MDB Techniques for Solaris 10 and OpenSolaris*. Prentice Hall, 2006.

[Otto 06]   Otto, E. *Temperature-Aware Operating System Scheduling* (Thesis). University of Virginia, 2006.

[Schlossnagle 06]   Schlossnagle, T. *Scalable Internet Architectures*. Sams Publishing, 2006.

[Singh 06]   Singh, A. *Mac OS X Internals: A Systems Approach*. Addison-Wesley, 2006.

[Smaalders 06]   Smaalders, B. "Performance Anti-Patterns," *ACM Queue* 4, no. 1 (February 2006).

[Cherkasova 07]   Cherkasova, L., D. Gupta, and A. Vahdat. "Comparison of the Three CPU Schedulers in Xen." ACM SIGMETRICS, 2007.

[Gove 07]   Gove, D. *Solaris Application Programming*. Prentice Hall, 2007.

[Gunther 07]   Gunther, N. *Guerrilla Capacity Planning*. Springer, 2007.

[Allspaw 08]   Allspaw, J. *The Art of Capacity Planning*. O'Reilly, 2008.

[DeWitt 08]   DeWitt, D., and C. Levine. "Not Just Correct, but Correct and Fast," *SIGMOD Record*, 2008.

[Matthews 08]   Matthews, J., et al. *Running Xen: A Hands-On Guide to the Art of Virtualization*. Prentice Hall, 2008.

[Ruggiero 08]   Ruggiero, J. *Measuring Cache and Memory Latency and CPU to Memory Bandwidth*. Intel (Whitepaper), 2008.

[Traeger 08]   Traeger, A., E. Zadok, N. Joukov, and C. Wright. "A Nine Year Study of File System and Storage Benchmarking," *ACM Transactions on Storage*, 2008.

[Intel 09]   *An Introduction to the Intel QuickPath Interconnect*. Intel, 2009.

[Doeppner 10]   Doeppner, T. *Operating Systems in Depth: Design and Programming*. Wiley, 2010.

[Gregg 10a]   Gregg, B. "Performance Visualizations." USENIX LISA
                   invited talk, 2010.

[Gregg 10b]   Gregg, B. "Visualizing System Latency," *Communications of
                   the ACM*, July 2010.

[Love 10]   Love, R. *Linux Kernel Development, 3rd Edition*. Addison-
                   Wesley, 2010.

[Turner 10]   Turner, J. "Effects of Data Center Vibration on Compute
                   System Performance." USENIX, SustainIT'10.

[Gregg 11]   Gregg, B., and J. Mauro. *DTrace: Dynamic Tracing in Oracle
                   Solaris, Mac OS X and FreeBSD*. Prentice Hall, 2011.

[Adamczyk 12]   Adamczyk, B., and A. Chydzinski. "Performance Isolation
                   Issues in Network Virtualization in Xen," *International Jour-
                   nal on Advances in Networks and Services*, 2012.

[Cornwell 12]   Cornwell, M. "Anatomy of a Solid-State Drive," *Communica-
                   tions of the ACM*, December 2012.

[Intel 12]   *Intel 64 and IA-32 Architectures Software Developer's Man-
                   ual,* Combined Volumes 1, 2A, 2B, 2C, 3A, 3B, and 3C. Intel,
                   2012.

[Nichols 12]   Nichols, K., and V. Jacobson. "Controlling Queue Delay,"
                   Communications of the ACM, July 2012.

[Gregg 13]   Gregg, B. "Thinking Methodically about Performance,"
                   Communications of the ACM, February 2013.

[Intel 13]   *Intel 64 and IA-32 Architectures Software Developer's Man-
                   ual,* Volume 3B, *System Programming Guide, Part 2*. Intel,
                   2013.

[Leventhal 13]   Leventhal, A. "A File System All Its Own," *ACM Queue*,
                   March 2013.

[RFC 546]   *TENEX Load Averages for July 1973*, August 1973.
                   http://tools.ietf.org/html/rfc546.

[RFC 768]   *User Datagram Protocol*, 1980.

[RFC 793]   *Transmission Control Protocol*, 1981.

[RFC 896]   *Congestion Control in IP/TCP Internetworks*, 1984.

[RFC 1122]   *Requirements for Internet Hosts—Communication Layers,* 1989.

[RFC 1589]   *A Kernel Model for Precision Timekeeping,* 1994.

[RFC 1761]   *Snoop Version 2 Packet Capture File Format,* 1995.

[RFC 2474]   *Definition of the Differentiated Services Field (DS Field) in the IPv4 and IPv6 Headers,* 1998.

Index

J

K

PRENTICE HALL

REGISTER

THIS PRODUCT

informit.com/register

Register the Addison-Wesley, Exam Cram, Prentice Hall, Que, and Sams products you own to unlock great benefits.

To begin the registration process, simply go to **informit.com/register** to sign in or create an account. You will then be prompted to enter the 10- or 13-digit ISBN that appears on the back cover of your product.

Registering your products can unlock the following benefits:

- Access to supplemental content, including bonus chapters, source code, or project files.
- A coupon to be used on your next purchase.

Registration benefits vary by product. Benefits will be listed on your Account page under Registered Products.

About InformIT — THE TRUSTED TECHNOLOGY LEARNING SOURCE

INFORMIT IS HOME TO THE LEADING TECHNOLOGY PUBLISHING IMPRINTS Addison-Wesley Professional, Cisco Press, Exam Cram, IBM Press, Prentice Hall Professional, Que, and Sams. Here you will gain access to quality and trusted content and resources from the authors, creators, innovators, and leaders of technology. Whether you're looking for a book on a new technology, a helpful article, timely newsletters, or access to the Safari Books Online digital library, InformIT has a solution for you.

informIT.com

THE TRUSTED TECHNOLOGY LEARNING SOURCE

Addison-Wesley | Cisco Press | Exam Cram
IBM Press | Que | Prentice Hall | Sams

SAFARI BOOKS ONLINE